MY MUSICAL LIFE

TRANSLATED FROM THE FIFTH REVISED
RUSSIAN EDITION BY JUDAH A. JOFFE
EDITED WITH AN INTRODUCTION BY
CARL VAN VECHTEN

EULENBURG BOOKS · LONDON

Nikolay Andreyevich
RIMSKY-KORSAKOV

musical Life

Originally published by Alfred A. Knopf, Inc.

This edition first published in 1974 by
Ernst Eulenburg Ltd
48 Great Marlborough Street, London WIV 2BN

© Alfred A. Knopf, Inc. 1923, 1942

ISBN 0 903873 00 1 paperback
0 903873 13 3 hardback

Printed and bound in Great Britain by
the Scolar Press, Ilkley, Yorkshire

$\mathcal{P}$REFACE

TO THE THIRD AMERICAN EDITION

THE PRESENT edition of *My Musical Life* follows faithfully the final form given to the text by the composer's son in the two latest (fourth and fifth) Russian editions, issued before the reviser's death. A. Rimsky-Korsakov painstakingly collated the Russian text with the autograph manuscript in the Manuscript Division of the State Public Library at Leningrad, restoring passages deleted, in accordance with the author's wishes, in the first Russian edition (see the Preface to that edition, page xxi of this volume), correcting errors, and adding an Introduction of his own (pages xxv–xliv of this volume). Furthermore he added over four hundred and fifty extremely valuable and illuminating footnotes. In this present edition footnotes ascribed to no one else are those of the Russian editor. All other deviations from the Russian text are enclosed in brackets.

JUDAH A. JOFFE

CONTENTS

1901–05

1905–06

Chronicle of N. A. Rimsky-Korsakov's Life

APPENDICES

ℐLLUSTRATIONS

AN INTRODUCTION

OBVIOUSLY, this book is artlessly, even badly, written in the original, a fact which has made its translation bristle with almost insurmountable difficulties. Like most other musicians, Rimsky-Korsakov was no writer of prose. An adept at arranging instruments in subtle juxtaposition, a skilled workman at setting folk-jewels in operatic platinum, an artist without a peer in spreading nervous shots of colour through his orchestration, when he had to deal with words, this composer limped and sweated. The ensuing pages are frequently filled with redundancies; the style is halting; the contents are often dry. There are long passages occupied with apparently unessential details, and other passages in which expansion or clearer thinking on the part of the writer would have improved the first impression made on a casual reader. Rimsky-Korsakov was not unaware of his lack of verbal felicity, and he refers to it rather touchingly in the last lines of his manuscript. On the other hand, he was by no means blind to the great virtue that his work indubitably possesses, a virtue which sets it in a class apart from the highly-spiced mendacities of most other musical autobiographies. *My Musical Life* is stamped with the *truth*. Stumbling, halting, perspiring, Rimsky-Korsakov put down the truth as he saw it, and this truth emerges on every page, and by cumulative effect ultimately gives his book a life and a substance which many a volume written with more regard for style entirely lacks. It is only necessary to compare this autobiography with the similar performances of Berlioz and Wagner to perceive its superiority from this point of view. If all signs of Berlioz's literary prowess or Wagner's sense of dramatic form are missing, as compensation, the reader of *My Musical Life* will search in vain for the pages of romantic fiction with which these two books are encumbered. Reading Berlioz and Wagner is doubtless an easier and more amusing pastime, but to differentiate the true from the false in their books, it is necessary to refer to a dozen commentaries. Rimsky-Korsakov's errors are errors of memory or taste, rather than of imagination. He may make a mistake in a date or he may express an opinion with which critical readers will not agree, but there can be no doubt that it is *his own* opinion that he expresses. He is brutally frank, not only in regard to the work of others, but also in regard to his own work. Note, for example, his disregard for the opinion of those who assign a high value to his *Capriccio Espagnol*. He sees it as it is, an instrumental show-piece, a brilliant, but superficial, display of musical fireworks, offering opportunities to the individual instruments for all sorts of virtuosity. Note how he acknowledges his indebtedness to other composers in the composition of *Sadko*. And note especially how, when he is planning to write a book on the philosophy of music, after endless explorations in the literature of the subject, suddenly awakening to the discovery that his mentality is entirely inadequate to cope with the project, he abandons it.

Out of these plodding pages, then, rises a portrait of an honest, industrious, sensitive, kindly giant, concerned only with his work, and giving all his powers, mental and physical, to it. If he writes as badly as Theodore Dreiser, he also has Dreiser's knack of sudden and acute observation, his power of sounding a deep note of truth, a power which a more fluent writer often lacks. His capacity for penetration and portraiture is frequently very great. His description of the home-life of the Borodins, for example, is a little masterpiece. Turgenev could have done no better.

Aside from this quality of honesty, this musical autobiography boasts two other outstanding virtues. Covering, as it does, the period between 1844 and 1906, it embraces practically the whole history of Russian art-music, at least until the days of Scriabin, Stravinsky, Rachmaninoff, Prokofiev, Shostakovich, and Markevich. Glinka and Dargomyzhsky were the only important Russian composers before the " Five " and Tchaikovsky and Rubinstein came on the scene, and the spirit of Glinka hovers incessantly over the shoulder of Rimsky-Korsakov as he writes, while Dargomyzhsky, who did not die until 1869, actually appears in the flesh. Neither are Tchaikovsky and Rubinstein slighted; they were out of the movement, the movement to Russianize Russian music, but they have their importance, an importance which Rimsky-Korsakov recognizes.[1] Towards the end of the book, the pupils of the master, Lyadov, Arensky, Ippolitov-Ivanov, Grechaninov, Cherepnin, Glazunov, Wihtol, Taneiev, and Akimenko begin to emerge. There is an appreciation for Chaliapin in his early days. And if the most famous of Rimsky-Korsakov's pupils, Igor Stravinsky, is not mentioned, he is amply provided for. His work, in fact, begins at exactly the point where Rimsky-Korsakov left off with the composition of *Le Coq d'Or*. He assumes the official robes and sceptre of the master and carries the nationalistic tradition into the twentieth century.

But the peculiar value of the book, from the point of view which at present concerns us, lies in its descriptions of the lives and methods of work of the great Five, Balakirev, Cui, Borodin, Moussorgsky, and Rimsky-Korsakov himself. These men, who laboured with clear convictions, uninfluenced by the hope of pecuniary gain and with small prospect of popular appreciation, may be studied at close range, and their various ideals and inconsistencies may be weighed and examined.

The other outstanding virtue of *My Musical Life* is more subtle, and yet I believe that it is just the quality which will give this book, primarily concerned with music and addressed to musicians, its interest and value for lay readers. I do not assign much importance to that definition which has it that genius is an infinite capacity for taking pains. My personal prejudice is rather in favour of facility. Samuel Butler has gone so far as to assert that only what is done fairly easily is done well. Nevertheless, in the case of Rimsky-

---

[1] In a letter, giving his views on Tchaikovsky, Stravinsky says, in part: " Tchaikovsky possessed a great *melodic* power, the centre of gravity in every symphony or ballet or opera that he composed. I am absolutely indifferent to the fact that the quality of his melody is very unequal in value. The point is that he was a creator of *melody,* an extremely rare and precious gift."

Korsakov, it must be admitted that the old definition fits like a Callot model. He was fundamentally an amateur. His profession was that of naval officer. In this he differs in no wise from his colleagues: Cui was an officer of engineers in the School of Artillery; Moussorgsky was a lieutenant in the Preobrazhensky Guards, and, after his retirement, worked for the government in an administrative position; Borodin was a professor of chemistry; and, late in life, Balakirev accepted a position in the St. Petersburg freight-station of the Warsaw Railroad. Like the others, Rimsky-Korsakov had had little musical training when he began to compose. He was ignorant of musical theory; unversed in harmony and orchestration; he played the piano badly and was entirely unacquainted with the other instruments; he could not even name the common chords! Under these adverse circumstances, he composed his first works and even assumed a prominence which lifted him into the chair of a professorship at the St. Petersburg Conservatory! He admits frankly enough that he learned more than his first pupils. In teaching them, he taught himself.

The sapient Antoine de la Salle once remarked: " *Celui qui commence un livre n'est que l'écolier de celui qui l'achève.*" This was certainly Rimsky-Korsakov's experience. He, who had begun by composing instinctively, now had to learn something in order to teach others. He learned still more when he became supervisor of the Imperial Naval Bands (he once asserted " Composers and musicians of the academies do not know as much as an ordinary bandmaster "). He studied vocal counterpoint while teaching choruses at the Free Music School. He wrote a quartet to become familiar with the principles that govern chamber music. He conducted a public concert without any previous training in wielding the bâton. Finally, he wrote a treatise on harmony, studying the subject himself while he worked on it! Gradually, he acquired technique, complete mastery of his medium, and gradually he learned to know not only *how* he was doing a thing, but also *what* he was doing.

This struggle towards perfection, the need for which was realized almost from the beginning of his career, was infinitely tedious and painful. As his pen gained power, Rimsky-Korsakov not only wrote new works, but he also frequently looked back over his past, with a view to the improvement, in the light of his later experience and education, of the works he had already given to the world. So, after long intervals, he made two new versions of his first opera, *Pskovityanka*, and the forms of the tone-poems, *Sadko* and *Antar*, which we hear today in the concert halls, are very different from those in which they were originally cast.

He was not content with improving his own music. He felt it both an obligation and a pleasure to use his superior skill in the revision and completion of the music of his dead colleagues. His first important work of this nature was the revision and editing of Glinka's operas, *Ruslan and Lyudmila* and *A Life for the Tsar*. He confessed later that his zeal in this direction had been misapplied. He helped Cui orchestrate *William Ratcliff*. After Dargomyzhsky's death, in 1869, he put *The Stone Guest* into shape. The lazy Borodin, distracted by his duties at the Medical Academy and his adventures into society, living, besides, a disordered and unsystematized life, in which meals were served and eaten at all hours, died, leaving his opera, *Prince Igor*, in a state of chaos. Whole scenes were yet unwritten; others, unorchestrated. That the opera can be performed at all is due to the energy of Rimsky-Korsakov. As for the music of Moussorgsky, Rimsky-Korsakov revised and edited it from beginning to end, even to the extent of completing and orchestrating fragmentary sketches. He has been much criticized in certain quarters for his temerity in attempting the revision of *Boris Godunov*. It has been claimed, not unreasonably, by certain critics that Moussorgsky was a daring and original genius, born a hundred years before his time, and that Rimsky-Korsakov's emendations of this score are a desecration. Well, perhaps they are right, but it must be remembered that Rimsky-Korsakov meant it all for the best, that he did no more for his dead friend than he was constantly doing for himself, and that he made it possible for Moussorgsky's music drama to be performed not only in Russia but also out of it. And the logic of his answer to his critics is unassailable. If, he hypothesizes, the future may decide his work on the Moussorgsky manuscripts to be an impiety, then all the future has to do is to return to the original scores, none of which he destroyed. In 1928 the original orchestral score of *Boris,* edited by Professor Paul Lamm, was published by the Russian State Publishing Company at Moscow. There have been several performances of this score, but it is yet too early to determine which version, this or that of Rimsky-Korsakov, will hold the stage.

Thus, Rimsky-Korsakov laboured, creating and rewriting his own music, and the music of his friends as well. When he began to compose, he was a naval officer; later, he became supervisor of the Naval Bands, taught in the Conservatory and the Imperial Chapel, conducted the Russian Symphony and other concerts, compiled volumes of folksongs, and attempted the writing of books. He also married and his wife bore him seven children. His life is built up of a million minutiæ. It is this manifold activity, this consistent industry, which make his career interesting. Many pages of this autobiography, therefore, which appear to be a simple catalogue of unimportant events, chronicled without colour or particulars, are immensely important in the bearing they have on this consistent occupational zeal.

II

WESTERN enthusiasm for Russian music was first directed towards Rubinstein, and more especially towards Tchaikovsky. This was but natural, as both these men have certain affiliations with Occidental style. Our knowledge of the Five came much later; now, contemporary Russian music is made known to us practically as soon as it is composed. One contemporary Russian composer, Rachmaninoff, is, indeed, to all intents and purposes, a resident of America. Of the Five, Moussorgsky stands out, perhaps, as the most important figure that Russian music has yet produced, but he is not, in one sense, so typical a figure (certainly he is by no means as lovable a figure) as Rimsky-Korsakov. Now that we know him better, the composer of *Le Coq d'Or* appears to have all the popular graces of Tchaikovsky without the latter's cloying sentimentality and tearful melancholy. The one is objective; the other subjective. Rimsky-

Korsakov's operas are lyric rather than dramatic, as befits work which is based on the folksong. The folksong, the Orient, and the sea were the three influences or inspirations which pursued Rimsky-Korsakov throughout his career, and he never got very far away from any of them, although there are indications that liturgical music had some occasional effect on his work. He turned everything in his life to artistic account: his early life at sea (reflected in *Sadko* and *Scheherazade*), his trips to the Crimea, his summer vacations, when he noted down folk- and bird-songs. He was always seduced by the picturesque and the exotic. He might be called, indeed, a musical Eurasian.

Little weight has been put, in critical estimates of Rimsky-Korsakov, on his melodic gifts. These seem to me unusually pronounced, far above those possessed by most of his Occidental contemporaries. *Le Coq d'Or* in itself is a mine of melody, melody which has its own special, original line, every bar of which is signed with the master's name. If it be objected that his melodies are founded on folksongs, I have only to suggest that they be compared with melodies which have a folksong basis, in the operas of other Russian composers. It will be found that the folk-airs have all been distilled into Rimsky-Korsakov's own particular brew. He was, of course, an adept at harmonization and orchestral colour. This was, perhaps, his greatest legacy to his successors. Under the spell of the liturgical chants of the Greek Church, he was using the Phrygian and Mixolydian modes long before they were revived in France. The influence of Rimsky-Korsakov and Moussorgsky on Debussy has been fully acknowledged.

All of Rimsky-Korsakov's operas may be traced back to Glinka, the Russian historical dramas to *A Life for the Tsar*, and the legendary dramas to *Ruslan and Lyudmila*. The legacy of Dargomyzhsky, the principles governing the composition of *The Stone Guest*, became the source of an artistic doubt that troubled the composer of *Scheherazade* almost to the end of his life. Cheshikhin, in his survey of Russian opera, compares the Russian operatic composer to Columbus, who sailed away to find India, and discovered America, a result with which he was dissatisfied, but which left his followers more or less content. In the fifteen operas of the master, there is a great variety of style — for a time he fell somewhat under the spell of Wagner — but all of them, at heart, are Russian works, and all but three have Russian subjects, and those three are based on Russian plays by Russian poets. They are only heard at their best when performed by Russian singers. Such a work as *Snyegoorochka,* for example, a simple folk-opera, full of charm but without a breath of drama, very nearly expires in alien hands. The more brilliant *Le Coq d'Or* more successfully survives the ordeal, but even this work is immeasurably more effective when sung in Russian by Russians.

CARL VAN VECHTEN

New York
June 27, 1941

PREFACE

TO THE FIRST RUSSIAN EDITION

My Musical Life justifies its name. Indeed, as an autobiography in the true sense of the word, it cannot give complete satisfaction; Nikolay Andreyevich speaks in it principally, even almost exclusively (save for the chapter on his cruise abroad), of events of his *musical* life. But even his musical life is described, in certain passages, with insufficient detail; this is especially noticeable at the end. In fact, beginning with the last half-decade of the nineteenth century, the narrative grows ever more and more succinct — as if Nikolay Andreyevich had hurried to complete his work by a set date. Nevertheless the chronicle contains very valuable biographical material, and this induced me to hasten its publication.

In preparing *My Musical Life* for the press, I was guided by what Nikolay Andreyevich had stated more than once during his lifetime, namely: when after his death the chronicle was published, first, certain abridgments were to be made as for the present necessary; secondly, to polish the style, here and there; thirdly, certain dates were to be checked as not having been quite accurately established. Thanks to V. V. Yastrebtsev's kind co-operation I have checked the dates as far as possible. Besides, for the reader's convenience, I have introduced a division into chapters. The original manuscript contains no such subdivision, but here and there marginal headings occur which I utilized for the chapter headings. Wherever no such marginal headings existed, I had to make the chapter headings myself.

The frank and severe judgments to be found in the chronicle regarding some dead persons and some still living cannot, it seems to me, offend anyone, because Nikolay Andreyevich passes judgments equally severe and frank, if not more so, on his own acts and musical compositions.

My Musical Life was written during various years, often at long intervals; thus, the story of the end of the summer of 1893 was written ten years after the description of the beginning and middle of the same period. All dates found in the manuscript I have set down as footnotes in the order in which they occur in the manuscript. It must be mentioned that frequently no record of year and month occurs for a long time.

The chronicle has been brought down to August 1906. In its last lines, so filled with secret sadness, there is mentioned a diary which Nikolay Andreyevich had intended to begin. But this intention was left unfulfilled after all. In a thick, bound blankbook were found six entries: four under the year 1904 and two under the year 1907. The first entry, quoted in its entirety, reads as follows: " In the last fifteen years I made up my mind, on several occasions, to begin my diary, but I always put it off and put it off. This time I had intended to begin it on January 1 of this year, but never did so after all. Finally I took a firm resolution to begin writing it on March 6 [19], when I turned sixty. Today, on the eve of that event, I shall narrate in brief all that has happened in my musical life since the beginning of this year; and beginning with tomorrow I shall carry on my chronicle in the form of a diary." After this note comes the narrative of events of his musical life (beginning with January 1904) which are described in the chronicle as well, and a few pages further occurs the caption *" Diary,"* after which follow two notes of March 6 [19] and 9 [22] of the same year. Entered in the back of the same blankbook were found two more brief notes of November 28 and 29 [December 11 and 12], 1907, but nothing else.

Thus Nikolay Andreyevich has not touched at all upon the last year and a half of his life. The work of composing *Zolotoy Pyetooshok (The Golden Cockerel)*, the production of *Kityezh* at the Mariinsky Theatre, and his trip to Paris in the spring of 1907 have been mentioned nowhere. Why he never described these interesting events of his musical life is unknown. I think it may be explained by the fact that while composing *The Golden Cockerel* Nikolay Andreyevich was, as always, absorbed in the composition, gave himself up to it completely, and, as a result, could not occupy himself with anything else. The whole chronicle was written in the interims between musical compositions. But when his work on *Zolotoy Pyetooshok* was over, his final illness had begun to steal over him. With it, his former healthy and buoyant frame of mind gradually faded, and he showed no further desire to continue the chronicle. After December 1907 his illness became very marked; shortness of breath precluded any brisk walking; a feeling of fatigue hindered all work; and at last all this led to paroxysms of asthma in April and to death, June 8 [21], 1908.

N. RIMSKAYA-KORSAKOVA

St. Petersburg
January 12 [25], 1908

INTRODUCTION

FROM THE MOMENT of its appearance in print, *My Musical Life* was recognized as an important source of Russian musical historiography — important in two respects: both as a record encompassing multifarious events of Russian musical life in the latter half of the nineteenth century, and as a psychological document wherein light is shed on the evolution and many features of the artistic personality of one of the most distinguished representatives of musical creative art of his epoch. It is impossible to enumerate all the instances of references made to *My Musical Life*, quotations therefrom, and proofs based on facts attested in its pages.

And even though *My Musical Life* has won such general recognition as a source of great substance and credibility, to this day we still have no serious attempt at a critical analysis of it as a historical and psychological document, for it is impossible to consider as an example of such an attempt any of the newspaper reviews by Russian music-critics with which the appearance of *My Musical Life* in 1909 was greeted — with or without quotations, depending upon the camp of the reviewer. All this literature, numerically rather voluminous, amounts, at best, to a cursory general appraisal and more or less circumstantial annotations — within the limits of articles in periodicals — to the most interesting pages of *My Musical Life*.

Though, for various reasons, in no way taking upon myself the responsible task of making a complete historico-critical, psychological, and literary analysis of *My Musical Life*, I nevertheless do not deem it out of place to lay before the reader some observations and reflections which may facilitate the proper approach to the book and be of assistance in achieving an objective appraisal of its contents and its author's personality.

The footnotes which accompany the text of the present edition can in general serve as an indirect proof of the high degree of the factual authenticity of *My Musical Life*'s contents, in addition to their immediate purpose, which is to correct minor errors of chronology and inaccuracies in the description of events, and point out slips of memory, both specified and unspecified by the author. Taken by and large, Rimsky-Korsakov's memory functioned with extraordinary exactness. However, from his letters to various persons, one can see that he did not himself always trust that source and occasionally had recourse to auxiliary means in the form of some one or another of the documents in his archives (letters, programs, newspaper clippings, etc.).

In the study of any literary work the question of its authorship arises first of all. But where the authorship is unquestioned, an analogous question comes up — namely, to what moment, to what stage and epoch in the evolution of the author's personality belongs the work studied? Thus develops the question of the history of a given work or document.

To a considerable degree *My Musical Life* is personal in material and treatment. It includes well-nigh the entire life of its author. Usually such memoirs with an autobiographical tendency are written at the end of a life, revealing the final total of the collective labour of the memory. In such cases the reel of reminiscences is unwound when life's cargo is laden full.

The circumstances were very different in the case of *My Musical Life*. It was written neither all at one stretch nor in the order of sequence of the life's events, but *in several instalments in which the periods treated did not follow their chronological sequence*. The chronology of the origin of its individual parts is approximately the following (approximately since the date of writing does not appear on every part of it). The description of the periods of childhood and youth was begun earliest of all. These pages, now constituting the first and second chapters, had been committed to writing as early as 1876 (*see* " 1844–56 ") and 1887–8 (*see* " 1856–61 ").

Why did Rimsky-Korsakov conceive a desire for delving into his childhood days precisely in the summer of 1876?

As may be seen from *My Musical Life*, the summer of 1876 was devoted, along with other works (sextet, choruses *a capella*), to a study of collections of Russian folksongs. The thought occurs that precisely this interest in folksong gave Rimsky-Korsakov the impulse to lay the first stone for the future autobiography. In the process of recalling the folksongs which he had heard in his childhood, and while resorting to the aid of his mother's musical memory for the same purpose, Rimsky-Korsakov was involuntarily drawn once more into the world of Tikhvin and its life; incidentally, in writing down these pages he probably did not miss the opportunity of utilizing a living witness of the era of his childhood — the same Sofya Vasilyevna [his mother].

The brief flash of interest in autobiographical recording in 1887–8 is hard to explain. It is possible that indirectly there manifests itself here the influence of a circumstance which is not so much positive as negative: the beginning of a decisive dying away of association with Balakirev — that is, a *sui generis* beginning of the conclusion of a whole epoch in Rimsky-Korsakov's life. On this occasion, however, he merely touched upon the account of his former relations with Mili Alekseyevich (*see* " 1856–61 "), but had not yet managed to work himself into the subsequent events, or perhaps still felt insufficiently matured for it.

The next brief period, during which nearly *one third* of *My Musical Life* came into being, is the spring and summer of 1893. Within this time " 1861–62 " to " 1866–67," " 1871–73 " to " 1876–77," and " 1892–93 " were committed to paper. The subject-matter of these chapters embraces the following events: acquaintance with Balakirev, growing intimacy, first attempts in the field of composing, life of " the circle " in the early period, the overseas voyage, return to composing and life of Balakirev's circle in the middle sixties; next, the period between the summer of 1872 and 1877 — that is, the epoch of studying the technical resources of contempo-

rary music and of Rimsky-Korsakov's own technical rearmament —
and, finally, the season of 1892–3, the closest in point of date of
recording.

Apparently the pages devoted to the period between 1878 and
1881, written in 1895, may be considered as a reflex of the same
impulse towards autobiographical recording, the inner character of
which I shall endeavour to disclose later on.

After an interruption of almost a decade Nikolay Andreyevich
takes up his reminiscences afresh. The preponderant quantity of
what he wrote during this last period falls in the years 1905 and
1906 (in the year 1906, to be more exact).

These chapters are "1867–68" and "1868–70," "1881–82,"
"1883–86" to "1888–92," and "1895–97" to "1905–06." Only a
small part — the end of "1892–93" and "1893–95" — is dated 1904.

As may be seen from the above figures, the interval which sepa-
rates the *record* of individual events from the *events themselves*
varies greatly. Now it shrinks so much that the chronicler comes
quite abreast of the events described (1893), and then again it ex-
pands greatly (the recording in 1906 of the period of 1866–7). This
explains *in part* the difference both in the minuteness of the account
of sundry portions (especially circumstantial is the record of musical events of the season 1892–3, the production of *Mlada*, etc.;
cf. "1892–93"), and in the distinctness and clearness of the reminiscences (the greatest number of chronological errors occurs in the
sixties).

Yet other conditions, too, which determine the functioning of
memory are no less essential — namely, those circumstances of the
inner life, amid which the events had been lived through in their
own time and later came to life again in the process of recording.
If in individual chapters one feels a certain enthusiasm about the
matters described, a definite will to encompass concrete live tableaux and images (Balakirev, Borodin, Moussorgsky, Lyadov,
Byelayev), elsewhere the record approaches almost a synopsis, thus
giving the impression that the author had to force himself to write
it, from the sheer sense of necessity of bringing the account to
an end.

Introduction

On the other hand, a comparison of the basic dates of the work on *My Musical Life* (1893, 1905–6) with the corresponding epochs of the inner life justifies us in making the following essential deduction: *The greater part of* My Musical Life *originated in periods of temporary creative ebb, fatigue, general depression, and even more profound inner crises with Rimsky-Korsakov.* Amidst the long series of his art works *My Musical Life* occupies the position of a sort of stepson and not of his own child.

Rimsky-Korsakov would plunge into work head over heels and knew neither how to apportion nor how to spare his strength. During periods of creative upsweep his expenditure of nervous energy was undoubtedly very great. Outward calm — the result of intense training and inner discipline — did not permit an outsider to judge the hidden agitations and a straining of forces that was merciless and knew no rest. The excessive expenditure of energy, inevitable during such periods, manifested itself later on in the feeling of fatigue and general depression. Enthusiasm would give way to dejection, imagination was hushed for the time, and stern, dry reason raised its head against a background of devastation caused by the storm and tempest. Even without these low ebbs, which were conditioned by counter-currents in creative work, Rimsky-Korsakov was predisposed in a measure, both by nature and by education, to bare the rationalistic bottom of his soul — in the form either of eminently sceptical self-inspection, self-criticism severe to the point of cavilling, or of a rather dry and straightforward review of artistic phenomena and his own relation to people.

All these traits, characteristic of the *regular* periods of temporary creative idleness, loom before us in enhanced form during the more critical and morbid epochs. Exactly among these latter belongs the rather lengthy period between 1890 and 1893. " The new tendencies " in the Byelayev circle to which Nikolay Andreyevich refers in " 1888–92 " of *My Musical Life* (p. 309) and devotes the franker lines of his letters to S. N. Krooglikov, his disappointment in many artistic phenomena around him which had long seemed indisputable, weariness from preceding years of creative activity, the dying out of his relations with Balakirev, the unbearable conditions of service in the Chapel, and a series of family misfortunes — all these causes contributed their share to the physically and psychically morbid experiences of 1890–3.

On his return from abroad in 1891 (Rimsky-Korsakov was obliged to leave his family and a sick child in Switzerland owing to Balakirev's whim as his superior: after timing Rimsky-Korsakov's return for his own departure early in August, in reality Balakirev, without any apparent reason, did not avail himself of his leave for a rather long time) Rimsky-Korsakov wrote Nadezhda Nikolayevna: " While I was abroad it seemed to me that what I was missing was music; and now, it turns out, I have no need of it at all " (letter of August 15 [27], 1891). In another letter, which related his impressions of the new works of Russian composers that he had heard at Byelayev's house, Rimsky-Korsakov characterized them with the term " boring," in another " petty and insignificant," in a third " dry and lifeless," even though the names under discussion were very close to him. He added: " In a word — beautiful harmonies, interlacings, melodic phrases, leave me absolutely unmoved, everything seems to me dry and cold. *Mlada* is decidedly cold as ice. But a quartet or symphony of Beethoven's — that's another story. There the technique and handling of the material is merely form, and everything is suffused with life and soul. . . . I think that the greater part of the Russian school — is not music, but cold and cerebral music-making. . . . Perhaps with such ideas even composing ought to be given up, but if the idea and the feelings are true, one ought to keep on. . . . Do not regret . . . that I have torn up my notebook in a fit of fool's spite, and that now I cannot recall what it contained. Upon my faith, all that was recorded in it — is not worth even a farthing . . ." (letter of August 21 [September 2], 1891).

This is not the place for probing what were the ultimate causes of so painful a disappointment in what so very recently had been intimately near and dear. For our purpose the very fact is sufficient.

I shall call to mind that the ideas here quoted began to gain upon Rimsky-Korsakov in the summer (to him unproductive) of 1891, bound up with the burdensome and ill-fated trip *en famille* (of eight persons) to Switzerland, a trip necessitated by the illness of Rimsky-Korsakov's youngest daughter. The same thoughts did not leave Nikolay Andreyevich also during the season of 1891–2, memorable to him for the unrealized production of *Mlada,* owing to the dilatoriness of Imperial theatres. Towards the summer of 1892 sceptical deliberation began to assume the stubborn form of attempts to reduce his turbulent ideas about art in general, about the Russian school and himself, to a state of complete clarity, philosophically founded (cf. " 1892–93 "). In the wake of the intensive strain caused by this work, by the autumn of 1892 there began to crop out signs of an over-fatigued brain (rushes of blood to the head, confusion of thoughts, *idées fixes,* loss of appetite, etc.).

Parallel with this inner discordancy and morbid symptoms during the period of 1890–3 there went on the protracted process of a break-up in his relations with Balakirev, a process the more painful because it went on amid surroundings of a continuing co-service and, consequently, of the necessity, for the time being, of cooking the service mess in the Chapel, which had grown unbearable, with a man who had become unbearable.

The spring and summer of 1893 — the time of writing a considerable portion of the reminiscences — is that hapless period when their youngest daughter was dying under the very eyes of Nikolay Andreyevich and Nadezhda Nikolayevna. Day after day the joyless months dragged on in Yalta, so inhospitable on this occasion, as if for spite. He continued to ponder over his own creative work; recuperation in the form of a new, absorbing work had not arrived as yet, and the will to create was dormant. Although the matter of the Chapel was inwardly settled, still official duties there hung like an oppressive burden over his soul. Here are some quotations from letters belonging to the period under consideration:

" I have resumed writing my reminiscences," Rimsky-Korsakov writes from Yalta to his oldest son, " but have met with difficulties in the matter of dates, and I must have some references, about which I want to write to Trifonov " (Yalta, June 26 [July 8]). " I am writing my reminiscences, and since I have not at hand the various materials needed in order to recall the years of old (e.g., the programs of concerts, etc.), I have described the season of 1892–3. But even this work brings misgivings upon me: is it worth while continuing? " (Yalta, July 14 [26]). " Occasionally I take up the reminiscences, but all of it somehow goes flaggingly and lazily. . . . Such lack of energy I have never experienced. . . . And, in very truth, what energy can there be when you feel over you something weighty suspended but not falling as yet? " (Yalta, July 20 [August 1]). " In the evenings I walk in the garden and gaze at the stars " (Yalta, August 3 [15]). " We here have fallen into a sort of torpor both mentally and spiritually, we are living from day to day and try not to talk of the future " (Yalta, August 5 [17]). " I can do absolutely nothing these days; most of the time I walk from one corner to another or sit and smoke without ceasing " (Yalta, August 9 [21]).

From these brief fragments one can form on the whole a sufficiently clear idea of Rimsky-Korsakov's spiritual state during the summer of 1893.

Within certain limitations, the data quoted regarding the critical years 1890–3 are applicable as well to the subsequent period when also a considerable part of *My Musical Life* originated — the years 1905–6. Here we are once more face to face with a wave of weariness and abatement of creative energy — true, not so complexly conditioned and, consequently, less disorganizing to the personality of Nikolay Andreyevich. When referring in *My Musical Life* to the summer of 1905, spent at Vyechasha, Rimsky-Korsakov characterizes his state of mind in these words: " Quite upset by the incident at the Conservatory, I could not turn to anything for a long time " (*see* " 1905–06 ").

Having somewhat regained his composure and rested from the turbulent and sorely nerve-racking experiences of 1905, Rimsky-Korsakov set himself to literary labours (analysis of *Snyegoorochka; My Musical Life;* and the *Textbook of Instrumentation*). In a letter of June 30 [July 12], 1905, to Nadezhda Nikolayevna to justify this turn in his work, " It seems to me," he says, " that the time has arrived for me to begin to occupy myself with musico-literary work instead of composing music, in which I greatly fear, and do not want, any weakening and decline. At any rate, after ten years of mental creative work (since 1894) one ought to stop or wait for a considerable time. Here in former years I had intervals, while during the last ten years there has been none. Besides, music is beginning to enter upon some new and incomprehensible phase of development (Strauss, d'Indy, Debussy, and others) whereas I, and many of us, are active workers of a different, earlier period. Is it not time to look back and compute the sum total and not to strain oneself to become identified with something alien?"

For us, who know the subsequent period of Rimsky-Korsakov's activity (*Le Coq d'Or*), the quoted words assume a symptomatic significance, bearing witness to a certain violation of inner equilibrium, to a state of fatigue and depression.

Also in other letters of the same period there frequently occur references to *My Musical Life*. "I have taken up writing my reminiscences, because, for some reason or other, music can't get into my head. I shall make an effort to push my reminiscences. When I make the clean copy, it looks as if, on the whole, they will not be without some interest" (Vyechasha, June 8 [20], from a letter to his son). "I am occupied exclusively with writing my reminiscences, which will be called *The Chronicle of My Musical Life*. Up here I have managed to record the years 1880–1–2. I should dearly like to bring them up to the year 1892, after which I have a record again; in addition to that, I have gaps between 1865 and 1872. To fill up all that is a big job" (Vyechasha, June 14 [26], 1905, from a letter to Nadezhda Nikolayevna). A letter of July 30 [August 11] of the same year, to A. K. Lyadov, is of special interest, since Rimsky-Korsakov expresses therein his views on the future of *My Musical Life*. We read there: "I am writing my reminiscences, which I began long ago and which will be published with some cuts after my death, and in full — after the death of many persons. . . ."

The same moods, the same feeling of fatigue, and the same line of thought on musico-literary work recur in the following year, 1906. We read in *My Musical Life:* " My own musical life ran somehow barrenly, owing to my feeling out of sorts and fatigued. . . . The thought whether it was not high time to write *finis* to my career as a composer (a thought that had haunted me since I finished *The*

Tale of Kityezh) did not leave me here either. The news from Russia kept up my restless frame of mind " (*see* " 1905–06 ").

In what way, it may then be asked, has the influence of these inwardly and outwardly unfortunate periods manifested itself in the contents of *My Musical Life*.

By nature Rimsky-Korsakov did not belong to the class of people who tend to soften and brim over with kindly and meek feelings under the influence of reverses and sufferings. The importunate ideas on religion and submissive reconciliation with Balakirev which at one time swayed Rimsky-Korsakov (1892; cf. *My Musical Life*, " 1892–93 ") were merely one of the symptoms of his sickly condition during that epoch. Misfortune and failures were apt rather to *irritate, to add a measure of sternness and a certain hardness* to Rimsky-Korsakov's attitude towards himself and others. As with great bodily emaciation comes the *sharpening* of the features of a person, exactly so in like critical moments did spiritual traits, peculiar to him, sharpen in Rimsky-Korsakov. *His self-consciousness as a person creatively active by nature defined itself first and foremost in his creative work,* in his being absorbed in it, in his being conscious of his own moving forward. On the other hand, whatever paralysed and destroyed his capacity to work by forcing him to sit with hands folded stimulated an instinctive resistance on his part.

Of course, as a man thoroughly honest and with a highly developed sense of fairness, Rimsky-Korsakov strove in every possible way to curb himself as far as he was aware of his own unsettled psyche, his nervous irritation and accesses of sceptical rationalism. Exactly so in his reminiscences, too, he desires to be as restrained and objective as possible. Nevertheless, against his will, occasionally there becomes evident the psychology of a man languishing from creative idleness and vainly trying to divine the nature of his own creative activity by means of philosophy such as is taught at school — the psychology of a creative artist at the time of ebb and denudation of the sandy bottom of his soul. Had *My Musical Life* been the offspring of Rimsky-Korsakov's better days and not of a state temporarily on the wane, had it been engendered by periods of the waxing new moon of his creative work and not by moonless nights, one is tempted to think that he would have taken a somewhat different attitude towards the years of his youth and his love for Balakirev. No doubt the pages devoted to that epoch and in particular to Balakirev are some of the most interesting and even brilliant in *My Musical Life*. Yet there is in them that drop of bitterness and exasperation, those words – not many, but weighty – which make one clearly recognize the strata of later experiences and thoughts – that is, a certain preconceived state of disinclination or, more correctly, an incapacity for recapturing the original mood of the described events – words which permit speaking of a not entirely fair approach towards the historic events of that period.

At the point when he wrote his reminiscences Rimsky-Korsakov had departed a long way from Balakirev's method of education. For Balakirev's chief concern was not with directing the well-spring of youthful talents into durable and permanent channels (*that* he could not do, not possessing sufficient knowledge and pedagogical experience himself), but with clearing and widening their very sources or estuaries and making them gush in a strong and unhindered stream.

Rimsky-Korsakov's attitude towards Balakirev in *My Musical Life* is, as it were, an echo of the perennial discord and difference of opinion between fathers and sons. Though differing from Balakirev in age by but a few years, Rimsky-Korsakov, thanks to his subsequent evolution, entered, as it were, the ranks of the new generation, and the Balakirev method grew strange to him, based as it was on the conviction that a gifted person can and must be taught *to fly* before he has learned *to walk*. Rimsky-Korsakov tries to put the curb of objectivity on himself, and says: "Balakirev did what he could to the best of his knowledge and ability . . ." (p. 33). But along with this he interrupts his narrative with the query: "Was Balakirev's attitude towards his pupil-friends right?" and answers: "In my opinion, absolutely wrong . . ." (p. 33). A bit further on, while speaking of his piano technique and Balakirev's disdainful treatment of it, Rimsky-Korsakov exclaims: "Oh, those were wretched times!" (p. 67).

It is in questions and exclamations of this sort and in certain deliberate stressing of the weak points of Balakirev's pedagogy that one feels all the time a cold criticizing, an inner dissent, disapproval, that there is discernible a certain impersonal watching eye, an unkind, unfeeling attitude, that there is sensed injustice springing from the desire to be just in the highest sense.

While describing his work of 1876, and particularly his work on *The Maid of Pskov*, Nikolay Andreyevich mentions that Balakirev insisted on inserting the wandering pilgrims' chorus in the guise of a song about " Aleksey, the godly man." " The fact that the action takes place near the monastery was the only reason advanced for this insertion; still, I yielded to the urgent admonitions of Balakirev; once an idea had got into his head, he usually fought stubbornly to gain his point by hook or crook, especially if it concerned somebody else's business. With my characteristic easy-going nature, I yielded to his influence, as I had been accustomed to do in the old days. But after admitting this interpolation, I was bent on further developing it " (*My Musical Life*, pp. 175 f.). These and similar lines, it seems to me, give grounds for speaking of Rimsky-Korsakov's attitude towards Balakirev in *My Musical Life* as not above reproach.

But it would, of course, be both highly unjust and uncalled for to interpret these remarks of mine in the sense that, to be sure, Rimsky-Korsakov's attitude towards his teacher could not be wholly unprejudiced, since at the time of recording his reminiscences of Balakirev their personal relations had almost ceased. The crux of the matter here is not the personal estrangement with Balakirev of the eighties and the nineties, but in Rimsky-Korsakov's changed attitude to the period of Balakirev's dictatorship in the circle. In order to convince oneself of this, it is enough to glance over the pages in which Rimsky-Korsakov speaks of himself and his compositions of that period. Hardly another example can be found of such objectivity as in Nikolay Andreyevich's analyses of his works of the Balakirev period (the First Symphony, *Sadko*, *Antar*). It is the restraint of the research scholar, the same stern tone, the same harshness, turning into captiousness. Let us also recall the mercilessness in relation to himself which Rimsky-Korsakov displays in relating the incident of the professorship at the Conservatory (*My Musical Life,* " 1870–71 "). To those who know where this step ultimately landed him, such mercilessness appears positively prejudiced and pedantic.

It is a curious fact that on resuming *My Musical Life* in 1905–6, Rimsky-Korsakov, apparently, seizes the former tone of writing of 1893 without any effort and keeps it up approximately in the same channel. The kinship of moods connecting these two periods enables him, without any forcing and straining, to avoid that noticeable seam which would appear unavoidable after a ten-year break in the recording (cf. " 1866–67 ").

The determination to give his reminiscences the title *Chronicle of My Musical Life* took definite form with Rimsky-Korsakov in 1905; it is highly indicative of the author's view of his own task. Only in manifest partisanship can one find an explanation of that " inability to understand " this view which certain contemporary reviewers have revealed. Is it possible to reprove Rimsky-Korsakov for *the absence of an all-inclusive historical fullness* in his *My Musical Life?* For it never entered his mind to call his autobiography or reminiscences *a chronicle of Russian musical life* — it is merely *a chronicle of his musical life.* Why wonder, then, that " prominent figures, even such as A. N. Serov, Anton Rubinstein, Nikolay Rubinstein, Tchaikovsky, appear on the background of the canvas filled with Rimsky-Korsakov's activities " as episodes " which were of significance only in so far as they had a bearing on Rimsky-Korsakov's compositions or activity." [1]

The title *Chronicle of My Musical Life,* then, manifestly underscores Rimsky-Korsakov's desire, in describing his musical life, on the one hand to be as much as possible *factual and, through the facts, objective,* and on the other hand *to be sincere and truthful to the limit.*

The *chronicle form* of Rimsky-Korsakov's reminiscences — as regards the factual side of their contents — is one of the most striking

---

[1] V. Valter, *Ryech',* No. 93, 1909.

characteristics of this book. As to its truthfulness, about that, in the subjective sense — in other words, about the *will for truth* — there cannot, apparently, be two opinions. " If this truth is not always the truth of verity and even not always the truth of justice, it is *always* the truth of sincerity — and that is the one thing one can demand of such a book as *My Musical Life.*" [2]

In one case only, the paths for realizing this will for the truth happened to lie in the sphere of the hampering influence of another of Rimsky-Korsakov's characteristic traits — his great restraint in everything that concerned his personal and intimate life.

In this case Rimsky-Korsakov could say, with much greater reason than Glinka, that in respect to unreserved frankness, and particularly in respect to laying his heart open before the reader, he had no desire whatever of " imitating the Geneva philosopher." Childish bashfulness and reticence in his own utterances concerning his personal life, aversion to the trait of holding one's soul " unbuttoned," the shyness of the Rimsky-Korsakovs — all these interrelated peculiarities form in their interweaving a certain *sui generis* system of " barbed-wire barriers " against attempts to peep into Nikolay Andreyevich's inner world. In one of his letters to Mme N. I. Zabyela-Vrubel (of December 1898) Rimsky-Korsakov writes: " These last years I have been striving to live so that everybody could know all my thoughts and actions and that I might have no secrets from anyone. . . ." *In this wise* Rimsky-Korsakov could speak only in his declining years, when his personal and his musical lives began to coincide almost completely in their confines. But of course it had not always been that way. And yet, by what may be called its systematic exclusion of personal and intimate life from the reader's view and by its one-sided emphasis upon his musical life, *My Musical Life* creates a far from accurate psychological perspective in depicting its author's personality.

More specifically, this tendency of Rimsky-Korsakov's has proved a manifest drawback in depicting his relations with Nadezhda Nikolayevna, by preventing him from disclosing all the profound

---

[2] Y. Engel: " Rimsky-Korsakov about Himself " (*Russkiya Vyedomosti*, No. 135, 1909).

Introduction

live value and beauty of their thirty-seven years of married life. In *My Musical Life* this theme has been left not only without a "working out," but even without "statement" of the theme. And yet Nadezhda Nikolayevna's rôle was not only determinative with regard to the outward circumstances of Rimsky-Korsakov's private and social life, but also very prominent in his purely artistic life. This Introduction is not the place for filling in the mentioned gap with facts about Mme Rimskaya-Korsakova [3] and her importance in Rimsky-Korsakov's artistic and personal life. That would be the task of a comprehensive biography of Rimsky-Korsakov or of a special study devoted to Nadezhda Nikolayevna herself.[4] But one may assume *a priori* as incontestable that so gifted an artistic nature, so musically impressionable and bright a woman, could not help playing a significant role at least in the final shaping of his creative ideas, if not in the main and fundamental line of Rimsky-Korsakov's creative work. But that bashfully restrained attitude which I have mentioned above came to the fore with full force in just this field, where artistic interests and manifestations interwove so closely with intimate personal relations.[5]

However, in addition to the unintentional inclination to put his

[3] Nadezhda Nikolayevna's friendship with Dargomyzhsky, Moussorgsky, Borodin, Lyadov, and others is well known to whoever is familiar with the facts of the history of the young Russian school. It has been attested by letters to her and by the dedications of numerous musical works to her.

[4] A special sketch has been devoted to Nadezhda Nikolayevna in A. N. Rimsky-Korsakov's book: *N. A. Rimsky-Korsakov, Life and Creative Work,* Part II, Chapter iv (Moscow, 1935).

[5] Fate destined Nadezhda Nikolayevna to survive Rimsky-Korsakov by a considerable length of time. She died of smallpox in 1919 after reaching the age of seventy. After Rimsky-Korsakov's death Nadezhda Nikolayevna became his executrix. Her efforts were responsible for the painstaking editing and publication of the posthumous musical and literary works of her husband, *My Musical Life* among them; the collecting of articles and notes on music, and of a part of Rimsky-Korsakov's correspondence with his friends. In general, till her death Nadezhda Nikolayevna invariably stood guard over Rimsky-Korsakov's artistic interests and carried on single-handed the entire business correspondence with numerous representatives of the publishing and theatrical worlds. One of Nadezhda Nikolayevna's undoubted services is the work of collecting Rimsky-Korsakov's archives and all sorts of relics connected with him personally. At the present time these two collections have been transferred: the one (archives), nationalized in 1918, to the State Public Library in Leningrad; the other, in the form of a gift from the Rimsky-Korsakov family, to the museum of the Leningrad State Conservatory, whence, in accordance with a resolution of the Lyeniskusstvo, it was transferred in turn to the Philharmonic Museum in 1930.

personal life constantly in the background, another, more objective cause leaves its mark on the contents of *My Musical Life* in the form of gaps of various sorts. This cause is the difficulty in drawing up a balance and forming an objective attitude towards what is as yet unconcluded and continues to figure as an inalienable and living part of the current life and personal relations. To my mind, here is where one must seek the cause of many omissions in *My Musical Life* — simple omissions, that is, not intentional passing over in silence, but wholly innocuous half-telling for psychological reasons. Many persons who had been in constant, close intercourse with Rimsky-Korsakov, one may say even his most intimate friends, have been favoured in *My Musical Life* with comparatively scanty lines. They give but an approximate general idea of Rimsky-Korsakov's attitude toward these friends; they are far from revealing clearly the picture of his enduring intercourse with them (for example, the lines devoted to Lyadov, Glazunov); and, again, such lines reflect only the exterior, empirical side of their subject (thus the passages mentioning Stassov were manifestly dictated by Rimsky-Korsakov's desire to resurrect in memory Stassov's peculiar personality, his characteristic manner of reacting to impressions: " Stassov went into raptures, he mumbled and he grumbled . . ."[6]). If, over and above all this, we take into consideration all the gaps which have resulted from the author's disinclination to speak of things generally known, and from the leakage of material through the large meshes of the summary exposition of the separate portions of *My Musical Life*, all these causes, taken together, abundantly explain the incompleteness of many declarations, characterizations, and descriptions.

Among other themes touched upon but by no means exhausted in *My Musical Life* there are two at which have been aimed ready reproaches for an unjust and partial attitude on the part of its author towards sundry events of the musical world of his time. These themes are Napravnik and Laroche.

In *My Musical Life* there is no general appraisal of Napravnik

[6] See G. N. Timofeyev: " N. A. Rimsky-Korsakov as a Chronicler of His Musical Life," *Russian Thought*, Vol. VIII, August 1909.

as a personality that had exerted great influence upon Russian musical life and culture. As a matter of fact, this is one of the conspicuous gaps, which, however, can be easily explained by the reasons which I have just enumerated. If this gap strikes the eye so particularly, it is because in this book space has at the same time been devoted to an estimate of Napravnik *as an artist*. The lines devoted to this subject are the fruit of Rimsky-Korsakov's long observations of Napravnik's activity in the theatre. In substance, the characterization of Napravnik's qualities as a conductor which Rimsky-Korsakov gives is not particularly individual. The collective opinion representative of the young Russian school is distinctly recognizable in it. Not without reason does Rimsky-Korsakov refer here to V. V. Stassov. At the time, some people (for instance, A. I. Ziloti) thought rather odious the conjecture made by Rimsky-Korsakov in *My Musical Life* that he had spoiled for life his relations with Napravnik by his article in 1868 on *Nizhegozodtsy*. It would be unjust to consider the general premise of the possible importance of this fact for Napravnik's peculiar psychology as the only basis for this hypothesis. Without doubt, these reasons are more weighty. They have been gathered from wholly real facts, which characterize the treatment that Rimsky-Korsakov the artist had encountered during his entire life at the hands of Napravnik.

One need but scan the history of the productions of Rimsky-Korsakov's operas at the Mariinsky Theatre and the performances of his symphonic compositions at the Imperial Russian Musical Society, and trace in it Napravnik's rôle as the person in authority on whom their acceptance and musical interpretation depended — and then one can truly marvel at the deadening coldness and official apathy which this administrator-artist had almost invariably displayed with regard to Rimsky-Korsakov's compositions. And yet it might seem that Napravnik's long years of activity in surroundings of Russian musical culture should have moved him to assume a more friendly attitude towards the creative work of one of his eminent contemporaries. Here even a casual reader will have no difficulty in sensing the influence of some deep trauma. Is there any wonder that it was felt also by Rimsky-Korsakov himself and that in his mind it involuntarily linked itself with his hostile criticism of Napravnik in a youthful article?

The other theme is Laroche. In the well-known lines, brief, but exceptional in their harshness, Rimsky-Korsakov expressed his opinion of this worker in the field of music. To argue that an essential correction in this verdict is necessary from the point of view of historical fairness is to try to force oneself through an open door. But, on the other hand, in order to avoid falling into error, and to comprehend the psychological source of Rimsky-Korsakov's view of Laroche, it is necessary to trace back the whole history of Laroche's attitude toward the young Russian school, a story of which the details have been thoroughly forgotten by us at present. Only a person who had been so intimate with the young Russian school as Rimsky-Korsakov and had so taken to heart its destinies as he had could so keenly feel Laroche as a hostile and evil force. Here again we stand face to face with a deduction from the experience of a whole life, of the life, it is true, of one creative artist and of what was near and consanguineous to him.[7]

Of course, the point here is not merely that, according to his own confession, Laroche had " overlooked " Rimsky-Korsakov.[8] A much greater sin is charged against him — he overlooked the whole young Russian school as well. That Rimsky-Korsakov could not forgive him. On this point Rimsky-Korsakov was irreconcilable.

In order to make clear Rimsky-Korsakov's standpoint in this matter I quote an excerpt from his letter of 1895 to S. N. Krooglikov. While giving to his friend in Moscow information about St. Petersburg musicians, Rimsky-Korsakov wrote: " I have just said that he [Lyadov] is chiding the young Russian school. That is quite in

---

[7] In addition, in this case there also manifests itself undoubtedly some sort of personal aversion of Rimsky-Korsakov's whole nature to a man who, in many of his traits, constituted his total opposite.

[8] In his preface to *The Musical Feuilletons and Notes of P. I. Tchaikovsky* (Moscow, 1898), Laroche wrote: " As to the school [the young Russian school is under discussion], I have maintained my stand; but as regards its spokesman (N. A. Rimsky-Korsakov), I did not divine and for a long time could not grasp that exactly he constituted one of the mainsprings of that significant current which with irresistible force had been and still is carrying away Russian music to the left towards extreme radicalism. I shall say frankly that, also in this sense, I *overlooked* Rimsky-Korsakov " (p. xxx).

fashion with us nowadays. Others do likewise. All are spitting into the well from which they had been drinking. There you have the influence of Laroche. But it particularly disturbs me when Borodin and Moussorgsky get a merciless drubbing. . . . All their lifetime Laroche hounded them and now he has brought it about that the best people have turned away from them. Read his article in *The Theatre Yearbook*. What a concoction of lies! Don't admit him to the pages of the *Artist*.[9] . . . At present he apparently ' got a bit off ' and among the symptoms of his abnormal state of mind must be counted his being enamoured of my person and *May Night*. But I keep him at a respectful distance . . ." (St. Petersburg, January 3 [15], 1895).

Is there any need of saying, after all this, how far afield M. Tchaikovsky was in his interpretation of Rimsky-Korsakov's psychology [10] when, contrary to logic and facts, he tried to affirm that there existed a certain " innerly reverential " attitude in Rimsky-Korsakov towards the fundamental tenets of Laroche's " creed," and classed among the adherents to this " creed " not only the whole of Byelayev's circle, but also its head — Rimsky-Korsakov.

If at sundry stages of his evolution Rimsky-Korsakov happened to come close to the views of Laroche in certain details of his own tastes and deductions, that was due to the pristine peculiarities of his musical nature and not to impulses from without. The activating impulses for his movement forward he gathered from *his own creative art experiences* — his successes and failures — and from such sterling *art* phenomena as the creative work of Glinka, Liszt, and Wagner.

Precisely from this side of it *My Musical Life* must in truth be recognized as a highly instructive book. Indeed, is it not something to be marvelled at — this spectacle of incessant inner work upon oneself, this instance of tireless polishing of one's own talent? For it is hardly believable that so fresh and original an opera as *Le Coq*

---

[9] The finest and most serious magazine, profusely illustrated, devoted to the interests of the stage, music, and arts, edited in Moscow by F. A. Koomanin, during the years 1889–95. J. A. J.

[10] Cf. his introduction to H. A. Laroche's *Collected Musico-critical Articles,* Vol. I (Moscow, 1913).

d'Or was written in the sixty-fourth year of its composer's life —
that is, almost on the eve of his death, and as his fifteenth work for
the stage, at that. With the prophetic vision characteristic of him,
V. V. Stassov had written Rimsky-Korsakov as early as the dawn
of his creative years: " Nobody is devoted to his task more than
you; nobody sits for ever on his student bench more than you. From
whatever angle I look at it, you never cease going to school, never
divert yourself with anything; every minute you return to your immediate task . . . you constantly observe and analyse everything,
weigh and appraise everything. A constant state of mind like this
cannot go without vestiges and results . . ." (V. V. Stassov's letter
of April 19 [May 1], 1870 to Rimsky-Korsakov; cf. *Russian Thought*,
Vol. VI, June 1910).

These qualities of *a profound searching spirit, of a seriousness
that knew no exceptions in matters of artistic conscience, and of a
merciless truthfulness towards oneself* will without doubt strike the
eye of anybody who even merely glances into this book.

In conclusion, a brief sum total of the ideas expressed in this
Introduction:

In spite of the enormous value of *My Musical Life* as a historical
monument and psychological document, it would be incautious to
form a final judgment of the human *personality* of its author on the
basis of its contents and nothing else. The story of writing it, the
tasks the author had set himself, his psychological peculiarities as a
witness of himself, and a series of minor causes give the character
of a profile or silhouette likeness to the self-portrait which unfolds
in its pages. To be more exact, it is, as it were, *a series of silhouettes
or drawings in outline, very accurate, but without shading,* and
hence they give no exhaustive conception of their author's living
personality. Only a study of the entire combination of the biographical materials can fill in and make this picture alive.

A. RIMSKY-KORSAKOV

Leningrad
March 1926

MY MUSICAL LIFE

Childhood years in Tikhvin. First manifestations of musical abilities. Studying music. Reading. Inclination towards the sea and maritime service. First attempts at composition. Leaving for St. Petersburg.

I WAS BORN in the town of Tikhvin on March 6 [18], 1844.[1] For a long time before that, my father had been on the retired list and had lived in his own house, with my mother and my uncle Pyotr Petrovich Rimsky-Korsakov, my father's brother. Our house stood almost at the end of the town, on the bank of the Tikhvinka River, on the other bank of which, opposite us, was situated the Tikhvin Monastery.

During the first year of my existence my parents[2] went to St. Petersburg for a short stay with my father's brother, Nikolay Petro-

---

[1] In Russia, the Julian Calendar, established by Julius Cæsar in 46 B.C. and adopted by the Council of Nicæa A.D. 325, remained in force until 1923. This reckoning is twelve (in the nineteenth century; thirteen in the twentieth) days behind that of the rest of Europe and America, which long ago adopted the Gregorian Calendar. Old Style dates in this work are followed by the corresponding New Style dates in brackets. C. V. V.

[2] Regarding Rimsky-Korsakov's parents, cf. A. Rimsky-Korsakov's " The Recluse of Tikhvin, His Ancestors and Family. The Childhood and Youthful Days of N. A. Rimsky-Korsakov " (*Musical Annals*, No. 1, pp. 5–60, Petrograd, 1922). This article, based on materials from the family archives, and constituting an essential supplement to the first two chapters of the present book, has been incorporated, almost unchanged, into A. N. Rimsky-Korsakov's book *N. A. Rimsky-Korsakov, Life and Creative Work,* Part I (State Musical Publishing Bureau, Moscow, 1933).

vich Rimsky-Korsakov, and took me along. After their return I lived in Tikhvin without a break until 1856.

From early childhood I manifested musical abilities. We had an old piano; my father played by ear rather decently, though with no particular fluency. His repertory included a number of melodies from the operas of his time; thus I recall the well-known romanza from Méhul's *Joseph*, the aria " *Di tanti palpiti* " from Rossini's *Tancredi*, the funeral march from Spontini's *La Vestale*, Papagena's aria from *The Magic Flute*. My father sang frequently, playing his own accompaniments. For the greater part, his vocal numbers were moralizing verses. I recall, for instance, the following:

> Remember all of ye who fain
> By reading would enlight your mind:
> Read not too many books in vain,
> Lest ye still greater darkness find!

Verses of this nature were sung by him to the tunes of various old operas. According to the accounts of my father and my mother, Pavel Petrovich, my uncle on the paternal side, was possessed of enormous musical talent and played entire overtures and other pieces very well and fluently, by ear, though unfamiliar with music. My father, it would seem, did not possess such brilliant abilities, but, at all events, had a fine ear and a passable memory and played neatly. My mother, too, had a very fine ear. The following fact is interesting: Whatever she remembered, she was in the habit of singing more slowly than was proper; thus the melody " *Kak mat' oobili* (When they killed Mother)," from Glinka's *A Life for the Tsar*, she always sang adagio. I mention this because it seems to me that this peculiarity of hers was passed on to me. In her youth my mother had taken piano lessons, but gave them up afterwards and never played at all within my recollection.

The first indications of musical talent appeared in me at a very early age. I was not fully two years old when I clearly distinguished all the tunes that my mother sang to me. Later, when three or four years of age, I beat a toy drum in perfect time while my father played the piano. Often my father would suddenly change the

4

tempo and rhythm on purpose, and I at once followed suit. Soon afterwards I began to sing quite correctly whatever my father played, and often I sang along with them. Later on I myself began to pick out on the piano the pieces and accompaniments I had heard him perform and, having learned the names of the notes, I could, from an adjoining room, recognize and name any note on the piano. When I was six or thereabouts, they began to give me piano lessons. This task was undertaken by an aged dame, a certain Yekaterina Nikolayevna Unkovskaya, a neighbour of ours. At this moment I am utterly unable to judge either how musical she was or how well she could play, or how good her method of instruction was. Probably it was all extremely mediocre, in the usual small-town fashion. Nevertheless, under her tuition I did play scales, easy exercises, and some pieces. I remember also that I played all of them badly, carelessly, and was poor at keeping time.

My abilities were not confined to music; they were excellent in other respects as well. Reading was child's play to me; I learned to read without being taught. My memory was splendid: whole pages of what my mother read to me I remembered word for word. Arithmetic I began to grasp very quickly. It cannot be said that I was fond of music at that time; I endured it and took barely sufficient pains with my studies. Occasionally, to amuse myself, I sang and played the piano, of my own accord; but I do not recall that music made a strong impression on me at that time. Perhaps it was because I was not very impressionable and possibly because at that time I had as yet heard nothing that could really produce a strong impression on a child.

Some eighteen months or two years after I had begun to study under Yekaterina Nikolayevna, she refused to give me further lessons, finding that I needed a better teacher than herself. Then I began to study with Olga Nikitishna (I don't remember her family name), a governess in the house of the Fel family, who were very good friends of ours. I do not know, but it seemed to me that she played splendidly. Under her direction I made some progress. Among the pieces which she gave me to play, there were some Beyer transcriptions of Italian operas, a piece based on a theme from a

5

ballet of Burgmüller's, and also a Beethoven sonata (D major) for four hands, which I liked. I remember that among other things I played as duets with her Marx's potpourri on melodies from *Le Prophète* and *Les Diamants de la Couronne*. Olga Nikitishna taught me for a year or a year and a half; then I was taken in hand by her pupil Olga Fyeliksovna Fel, who also played sufficiently well. Of the pieces of that period I recall the *Otello* (Rossini's) Overture for two hands (played in a tempo much slower than was proper), the A-major Scherzo of Beethoven's A-major Sonata, op. 2; a potpourri from *Les Huguenots* for two hands; a fantasy on melodies from *Rigoletto* (I do not recall whose, but it was easy); a fantasy on melodies from Lortzing's *Zar und Zimmermann*, and the Overture to *La Vestale* for four hands. I was taught by Olga Fyeliksovna for some three years — that is, until the age of twelve (1856). It seemed to me that she played rather well; but one day I was struck by the playing of a lady (I do not recall her name), a chance visitor in Tikhvin, whom I saw at Olga Fyeliksovna's; she played Henselt's *Si oiseau j'étais*. At the age of eleven or twelve I often had occasion to play four- and eight-hand pieces at the house of our friends the Kalinskys. I remember that they were visited then by Colonel of Engineers Vorobyov, who was considered a fine pianist in Tikhvin. We played the *Otello* Overture for eight hands. Of other instrumental music I heard nothing else in Tikhvin; the town boasted neither violinists nor amateur cellists. For a long time the Tikhvin ballroom orchestra consisted of a violin, on which a certain Nikolay used to scrape out polkas and quadrilles, and of a tambourine, which was artistically played by Koozma, a house-painter by trade and a heavy drinker. A few years before I had left town several Jews made their appearance (violin, cymbalon, and tambourine), who put Nikolay and Koozma in the shade and became the fashionable musicians.

As to vocal music, I heard only one Tikhvin girl, Baranova, who sang the song *Chto ty spish, muzhichok?* (Why slumberest thou, dear muzhik?). Then, besides my father's singing, there remains the church music — that is, the singing in the convent and the monastery. At the nunnery the singing was of no great account, but at the friary, as far as I recall, they sang tolerably well. I was fond

6

of some of the Cherubim choruses and other compositions by
Bortnyansky; [3] also of his concertos *Gloria in Excelsis*, and of the
plain chant *Benedice, anima mea; Cruci tuæ; Lux silens* — after
vespers. Church singing, amid the beautiful surroundings of the
archimandrite's divine service, produced a deeper impression on me
than did secular music, although, generally speaking, I was not an
impressionable boy. Of all the compositions I was acquainted with
I derived the keenest pleasure from the orphan's song and the duet
from Glinka's *A Life for the Tsar*. The music of these we had at the
house, and once I took it into my head to play them both through.
My mother told me then that they were the finest numbers in the
opera. She remembered *A Life for the Tsar* poorly, and I do not
even know whether she had ever seen it on the stage.

My uncle Pyotr Petrovich sang several fine Russian songs: *Sharlatarla from Partarla; Nye son moyu golovushku klonit* (It is not
sleep that bows my dear head down); *Kak po travkye po muravkye*
(How on the grass, the greensward), and others. He remembered
these songs from childhood days when he lived in the village Nikol-
skoye (Tikhvin district), which belonged at that time to my grandfather. My mother, too, sang some Russian songs. I loved these
songs, but heard them comparatively seldom from the people, as we
lived in town, where I none the less had the opportunity, year in,
year out, to witness the " seeing out " of Butter-week [4] with the procession and effigy. As for country life, I had three glimpses of it in
my childhood when visiting Bochevo and Pechnyevo (estates of
the Timirevs) and the Brovtsyns (I do not recall the name of the
village).

I was a reserved boy, although I skylarked and ran about,
climbed roofs and trees, and flew into tantrums for my mother,
rolling on the floor and bawling whenever I was punished. I was

---

[3] Dmitri Stepanovich Bortnyansky, according to Mrs. Newmarch (*The Russian
Opera*), was born in 1751. He began his career as a chorister in the Court Choir,
where he attracted the attention of Galuppi. In 1769, Bortnyansky joined the Italian
composer in Venice and remained there until 1779, when he was recalled to Russia.
He is now best known as a composer of sacred music, some of his compositions being
still in use in the services of the Orthodox Church, but he also wrote four operas, two
to Italian and two to French texts. C. V. V.

[4] Butter-week is the week before Lent. C. V. V.

very inventive at games, and would play all alone for hours at a stretch. Harnessing up chairs for horses and playing driver, I held long conversations with myself, in a make-believe dialogue between coachman and master. Like many children I was fond of imitating what I had seen, putting on spectacles made of paper, or taking apart and assembling a watch, because I had seen a watchmaker doing that. Aping my elder brother Voyin Andreyevich, who was at that time a naval lieutenant and used to send us letters from abroad, I fell in love with the sea, conceived a passion for it, without ever having seen it. I read Dumont d'Urville's voyage round the world, rigged up a brig, played sea-voyager, and once, after reading the book *The Wrecking of the Frigate Ingermanland*,[5] I retained in my memory a multitude of technical sea terms. While reading Zelyony's lectures on astronomy [6] (I was ten or eleven) I sought out in the sky, with the aid of a star-map, most of the northern-hemisphere constellations, which I know perfectly to this day. Among books, in addition to those mentioned, I liked Gabriel Ferry's novel *The Forest Vagabond* and a great deal in Chistyakov and Razin's *Children's Magazine*, especially the story " Svyatopolk, Prince of Lipetsk." While playing in the garden, I often acted whole scenes from *The Forest Vagabond.*

I have already said that I was not particularly fond of music, or even if I was, it scarcely ever made a strong impression on me, certainly not compared with my beloved books. But for the sake of play, for the sake of aping in the same way as I used to take apart and assemble the watch, I tried at times to compose music and write notes. With my musical and good general abilities for study, I soon succeeded by my own efforts in passably jotting down on paper what I had played on the piano and in observing the proper division into bars. After a while, without first playing it over on the piano, I began to form a mental image of what was written in notes. I was eleven years old when I conceived the idea of composing a duet for voices with piano accompaniment (probably under the

[5] A. I. Govorov: *Description of the Wrecking of the Russian 74-Cannon Ship Ingermanland* (St. Petersburg, 1844).

[6] Zelyony: *Lectures on Popular Astronomy*, delivered publicly (St. Petersburg, 1844).

influence of Glinka's duet). I took the words from a children's book; the poem, I think, was called " Butterfly." I succeeded in writing this duet. I recall that it was sufficiently coherent. Of my other compositions of that time I remember only that I began to write some sort of overture for the piano for two hands. It began adagio, then passed to andante, then to moderato, then to allegretto, allegro, and was to end presto. I did not finish writing this composition, but took keen pleasure at that time in the form I had invented.

Of course, my teachers took no part in my essays in composition, nor did they even know of them. I felt abashed to speak of my composing, and my parents looked upon it all as a mere prank, a sport — and, for the time being, such it really was. Of becoming a musician I never dreamed; I was not studying music with any particular diligence, and was fascinated by the thought of becoming a seaman. My parents wanted to send me off to the Marine Corps, as my uncle Nikolay Petrovich and my brother were in the Navy.

At the end of July [early August] 1856, for the first time in my life I took leave of my mother and my uncle; my father took me to St. Petersburg, to the Marine Corps.[7]

---

[7] Written in 1876.

The Golovins. The Marine Corps. Getting acquainted with operatic and symphonic music. Ulikh's and Kanille's lessons.

ON ARRIVING in St. Petersburg, we went to stay with P. N. Golovin, a schoolmate and friend of my brother's.

Having placed me in the Marine Corps, my father went back to Tikhvin. Every Saturday I used to go to P. N. Golovin's, who lived with his mother, and there I stayed till Sunday evening. In the corps I gained a good footing among my classmates by a show of resistance to those who tormented me as a freshman, and I was left in peace. However, I had no quarrels with anybody, and my classmates liked me. Aleksey Koozmich Davydov was the director of the Marine Corps. Flogging was in full sway: every Saturday before leave was granted, all the pupils were assembled in the vast dining-hall, where the diligent students were rewarded with apples according to the number of the marks of 10 they had received in the various subjects during the week, while the lazy ones — that is, those who had received 1 or 0 in any subject — were flogged. The so-called *starikashestvo* (grand-dad system) was in vogue among the students. *The old man*, a pupil repeatedly left back in the class, held the foremost place, was the head of the class, with the title of *grand-dad.* He bullied weaker pupils and occasionally compelled even his equals in physical strength to perform services for him, and so on. In my time, in our second company, there was one such, a

10

certain Balk, of eighteen, who went to the length of revolting acts; he forced his classmates to shine his boots, took their money and bread-rolls, spat in their faces, and so forth. He did not annoy me, however, and all went well. I was good in conduct and my studies went well, too. Somehow music was forgotten by me at the time, it did not interest me, although I began to take piano lessons with one Ulikh, on Sundays. Ulikh was a cellist at the Aleksandrinsky Theatre, but a poor pianist. The lessons went on in the most ordinary fashion. In the summer of 1857 I went on furlough to see my parents, and I remember with what regret and even grief I left Tikhvin to return to the corps late in August.

During the school year of 1857–8 I fell down in my studies, my conduct was poorer, and once I was under arrest in the school lock-up. My music lessons continued; I was more or less indifferent, but a love for music did manifest itself in me. I went to the opera twice with the Golovins: at the Russian Opera I saw Flotow's *Indra;* at the Italian Opera, *Lucia di Lammermoor.* The latter made a deep impression on me. I carried away something in my memory, tried to play it on the piano, even listened to street-organs playing snatches of that opera, attempted to write some notes; truly to " write notes," but not compose.

My elder brother returned from a long sea-voyage and was appointed commander of the target-practice ship *Prokhor.* He took me with him on a summer voyage. We were stationed all summer long at Revel, practising target-shooting. My brother was trying to accustom me to sea service; he taught me to handle a boat under sail and assigned me to duty. I lived in his cabin, away from the other pupils. Standing on the ratline under the mizzen-top, while the shrouds were being made taut, I fell into the sea — fortunately into the sea and not on the deck. I swam out, was pulled into a boat, and got off with a scare and a slight bruise (probably when I struck the water), but I had created a big rumpus and naturally had frightened my brother. At the end of the summer I went to Tikhvin on leave.

During the school year 1858–9 my studies were altogether inconsequential, my conduct tolerable. At the opera I heard *Robert le*

11

Diable, Der Freischütz, Marta, I Lombardi, La Traviata. I grew extremely fond of *Robert le Diable.* The Golovins had a piano score of this opera and I used to play it. Orchestration (although that word was unknown to me) appeared to me something mysterious and alluring. To this day I remember the impression of the sounds of the French horns at the beginning of Alice's romanza (E major). I imagine I saw *Lucia di Lammermoor* then a second time and worked at adapting the finale of that opera from four hands to two, so as to make it easier to play. I also made other arrangements of the same kind, but which, exactly, I do not recall. During the same year I heard *A Life for the Tsar* (Bulakhova, Leonova, Bulakhov, Petrov; conductor, Lyadov). This opera threw me into a veritable ecstasy, though I carried away with me very little. But I know that in addition to the purely melodious numbers: " *Nye tomi rodimy* (Do not tax me, Father!)," " *Ty priydyosh, moya zarya* (Thou wilt come, my dawn)," etc., my attention was attracted by the overture and the orchestral introduction to the chorus " *My na rabotoo v lyes* (We're off to the woods to work)." The Italian opera of that time was in full bloom; the singers were: Tamberlik, Calzolari, Bosio, La Grua, etc. I heard Rossini's *Otello, Il Barbiere di Siviglia, Don Giovanni.*

The Golovins and their circle were lovers of Italian opera. They considered Rossini an especially serious and great composer. Listening to their conversations, I thought it my duty to take it all on faith, but secretly I felt a greater attraction for *Robert le Diable* and *A Life for the Tsar.* They used to say in the Golovins' circle that *Robert le Diable* and *Les Huguenots* were beautiful and "learned" music. *A Life for the Tsar* they also approved, but of *Ruslan and Lyudmila* they said that even though very "learned," the opera was slighter than Glinka's *A Life for the Tsar* and inferior to it and that, generally speaking, it was a bore. Ulikh said that *A Life for the Tsar* was "vairy koot." These discussions of *Ruslan and Lyudmila* were occasioned by questions from me. Of *Ruslan and Lyudmila* the Golovins had the music — " *Choodny son* (Wonderful dream)," " *Lyubvi roskoshnaya zvyezda* (Resplendent star of love)," and " *O polye!* (Oh, field!)," which I found and played through. These excerpts from the unfamiliar opera struck my fancy deeply and roused my interest to a high degree. It seems to me that in them I felt for the first time in my life the immediate beauty of *harmony*. I questioned P. N. Golovin regarding *Ruslan and Lyudmila* and obtained the opinion mentioned above.

With Ulikh I played four-hands the March from *Le Prophète* and the *Hebrides* Overture; I liked both of them. Of any other symphonic music I had no idea. During this year I endeavoured to compose some things, partly in my head, partly at the piano, but nothing would come of it; they all ended in nothing but fragments and vague chimeras. Still the work of transcription from two to four hands continued (I was transcribing something from *Ruslan and Lyudmila*). With Ulikh I learned two Beethoven sonatas — one with the French horn (F major), the other with violin (also in F major). Ulikh brought to the house a horn-player (Gerner, I think, still a young man at the time) and the violinist Mich. I played those sonatas with them. I played piano duets with Golovin's sister, P. N. Novikova.

The summer of 1859 I spent again with my brother on the ship *Prokhor*. In the school years of 1859–60, 1860–1, I was a mediocre student, and went sailing in the summer on the ship *Vola* under the command of Tobshchin. My passion for music was developing. In the season 1859–60 I attended the symphony concerts given by the Director of the Imperial Theatres at the Grand Theatre, under the leadership of Karl Schubert. I also heard one of the university concerts. At the Grand Theatre I heard the Pastoral Symphony, the *Midsummer Night's Dream*, Glinka's *Jota Aragonesa*, the entr'acte from *Lohengrin*, Liszt's *Prometheus;* the rest I don't remember. At the university I heard Beethoven's Second Symphony, Schubert's *Erlkönig* (sung by La Grua). At the opera I heard Rossini's *Mosè in Egitto; Les Huguenots;* somebody's *Dmitri Donskoy;* [1] *Marta; Der Freischütz;* once more *A Life for the Tsar;* and, finally, *Ruslan and Lyudmila*. With P. N. Novikova I played four-hands Beethoven's symphonies, overtures of Mendelssohn, Mozart, etc. In this way I developed a passion for symphonic music. I took delight in

---

[1] Rubinstein's (St. Petersburg, 1852)? J. A. J.

Beethoven's Second Symphony, especially the end of its Larghetto (with the flute), when I heard it at the university; the Pastoral Symphony enraptured me; the *Jota Aragonesa* simply dazzled me. I was in love with Glinka. The *Midsummer Night's Dream*, too, I adored. Wagner and Liszt I did not understand — *Prometheus* left on me the impression of something vague and queer. With the pocket-money I possessed I began to buy piecemeal single numbers of *Ruslan and Lyudmila*. The list of single numbers printed on the cover of Stellovsky's edition lured me on with a sort of mysterious power. The Persian chorus and the dances at Nayina's I liked beyond words. I remember that I arranged the melody of the Persian chorus for the cello and gave it to O. P. Denisyev (a relative of the Golovins) to play, while I played the rest on the piano. Denisyev played out of tune, and we got nowhere. For some reason, I arranged the *Kamarinskaya* [2] for violin and piano and played it with Mich. That very year, as already mentioned, I heard *Ruslan and Lyudmila* at the Mariinsky Theatre and was thrown into indescribable rapture. My brother made me a present of the complete opera *Ruslan and Lyudmila*, for piano alone, which had just been published in that form. While staying at the corps one Sunday (as a punishment for some misdemeanour we were not allowed to go home), I grew impatient and, giving the watchman ten rubles that I had in my possession, I sent him out to buy me the complete piano score of *A Life for the Tsar*. I eagerly scanned its pages, recalling my impressions of the stage performance. As will be seen from the above, I had already become acquainted with a considerable quantity of good music; but my greatest liking was reserved for Glinka. However, I found no support in the opinions of the people who surrounded me at the time.

As a musician I was then a young dilettante — in the full sense of the word. I studied somewhat lazily under Ulikh, improving but little as a pianist; but I was extremely fond of playing four-hands. I had heard no singing (except opera), quartet-playing, or good piano-playing. I had no idea of the theory of music, had not heard

---

[2] *Kamarinskaya* is a fantasia for orchestra by Glinka, founded on a nuptial song and traditional dance he had heard in his native village. C. V. V.

the name of a single chord, was unfamiliar with the names of the intervals. I had no thorough knowledge of scales and their structure, though I could figure them out. And yet I attempted to *orchestrate* the entr'actes of *A Life for the Tsar* from the instruments mentioned in the piano arrangement. Naturally, it was a deuce of a result! Seeing that I was getting nowhere, I went twice to Stellovsky's store and asked them to show me the orchestral score of *A Life for the Tsar*, which they had. Half of it I could not make out at all, but the Italian names of the instruments, the superscriptions *col* and *come sopra*, the different clefs, and the transposition of the French horns and other instruments had some mysterious charm for me. In brief, I was a sixteen-year-old *child*, who passionately loved music and *played with it*. Between my dilettante studies and the real work of a young musician, say even of a conservatory pupil, there was almost as much of a gap as that between a child's playing at soldiers and wars, and actual military science. At that time nobody had taught me anything, nobody had guided my steps. And it would have been so simple if only there had been the person to do it! Still, Ulikh realized my musical talent and, of his own accord, refused to give me lessons, saying that I ought to go to a real pianist. F. A. Kanille was engaged as my teacher, I don't know at whose recommendation. In the fall of 1860 [3] I began to take piano lessons from him.

Kanille opened my eyes to many things. With what rapture I learned from him that *Ruslan and Lyudmila* really was *the best opera in the world*, that Glinka was a supreme genius! Until then I had felt it intuitively; now I heard it from a *real* musician. He acquainted me with Glinka's *Prince Kholmsky*,[4] *A Night in Madrid*, some of Bach's fugues, Beethoven's Quartet in E-flat major (op. 127), Schumann's compositions, and many other things. He was a good pianist; I heard from him the first really good piano-playing. When I played duets with him, we got good results, although I was

---

[3] This date is not correct. The first of the lessons taken from F. A. Kanille falls in the autumn of 1859. Cf. *Musical Annals*, No. 1, p. 58.

[4] A tragedy by Kookolnik, for which Glinka had composed incidental music. Tchaikovsky, by no means an indulgent critic of Glinka, says of this work: " Glinka here shows himself to be one of the greatest symphonic composers of his day. Many touches in *Prince Kholmsky* recall the brush of Beethoven." C. V. V.

a rather indifferent player, because he played the *primo* part. Having learned of my passion for music, he gave me the idea of devoting myself to composition. The task he set me was to write an Allegro for a sonata after the pattern of Beethoven's First Sonata (F minor). I composed something in D minor:

He set me to writing variations on a certain theme, with Glinka's variations on "*Sryedi doliny rovniya* (In the midst of a smooth valley)" as a model. He gave me choral melodies to harmonize, but did not explain the simplest methods of procedure; I got into snarls, and the results were poor. Nor did he give me sufficiently clear explanations as to the form of composition. Through him I came to know something about orchestral scores, and the transposition of French horns was explained to me by him. I tried to arrange the *Jota Aragonesa* for four hands from the orchestral score; I was getting on fairly well, but did not finish it for some reason or other. He did not give sufficient time to teaching me piano-playing; though I made some progress, it was nothing to boast of. He acquainted me with Balakirev's Overture to *King Lear,* too, and I conceived the highest respect and awe for Balakirev's name, which I had not heard of before.

In September 1861 [5] my brother, finding that I played well enough, decided I no longer needed lessons. He did not attach any importance to my passion for music, and thought I should join the Navy. This caused me grief. But Kanille told me to come to him every Sunday and that he would keep on teaching me. I went to his house on Sunday with the keenest delight. Piano lessons, in the proper sense of the word, ceased, somehow, but the composition lessons were continued and, in spite of the lack of system, I made some progress. In the Nocturne (B-flat minor) I even invented some beautiful harmonic successions. I also composed a funeral

---

[5] This date, too, must be corrected, to 1860. Cf. ibid., p. 59. For the part played by his brother Voyin Andreyevich in Rimsky-Korsakov's musical education, cf. ibid.

march in D minor, a scherzo in C minor for four hands, and something like the beginning of a symphony in E-flat minor. But all of
this was most elementary: I had no idea of counterpoint; in harmony I did not know even the fundamental rule of leading the
seventh downward nor did I know the names of the chords. Picking
up a few crumbs from Glinka's, Beethoven's, and Schumann's compositions which I played, I fell to cooking up, with considerable
labour, something thin and elementary. Kanille did not develop in
me a taste for writing melodies, and yet it would have been more
normal had I composed "cruel" songs instead of labouring with
symphonic travail.

In 1860–1 I began to manifest musical activity even within the
walls of our school. Among my schoolmates there proved to be
some lovers of music and choral singing. I led the chorus formed by
them. We rehearsed the first male chorus from *A Life for the Tsar*,
together with the finale of the opera, which, I think, I had arranged
or at least somewhat adapted for performance by a male chorus
alone. We also sang " *Hoy ty Dnyepr* (Hoy, thou Dnieper)," from
Vyerstovsky's *Askold's Tomb*,[6] etc. For some unknown reason,
choral singing was tabooed by the school authorities, and we used
to meet secretly in unoccupied classrooms; we once paid dearly for
that too. We took no part in the church choir. By that time a deep
love for *A Life for the Tsar* and partly also for *Ruslan and Lyudmila*
had developed among my schoolmates. I contributed a great deal
to the growth of this affection, by frequently playing, in the evening, excerpts from these operas on the harmoniflute [7] belonging to
one of my schoolmates — Prince A. D. Myshetsky, an ardent music-
lover. Very often the bellows were blown by K. A. Iryetsky, brother
of Natalya Aleksandrovna Iryetskaya, at present professor of the
St. Petersburg Conservatory. One of my schoolmates, N. I. Skrydlov, the hero of the Russo-Turkish War, used to sing tenor. I made
the acquaintance of his family. His mother was an excellent singer;

---

[6] An opera by Aleksey Nikolayevich Vyerstovsky (1799–1862), which attained
such popularity that it reached six hundred performances in St. Petersburg and Moscow alone, during the first twenty-five years of its existence. C. V. V.

[7] *Harmoniflute, einer der vielen Namen der ersten Harmoniums.* Riemann (1919).
Cf. Mendel V. 54. J. A. J.

I visited them frequently and accompanied her on the piano. At that time I came to know many of Glinka's songs, partly through the Skrydlovs, partly by myself. Besides Glinka's songs, I also became acquainted with some songs of Dargomyzhsky, Varlamov,[8] and others. I recollect having composed then the song beginning with the words "*Vykhodi ko mnye sinyora* (Come out to me, signora)," something like a barcarole, rather tuneful, even in the pseudo-Italian style.[9] Once, in November 1861, Kanille came to the corps, on a Monday, and announced that the following Sunday he would take me to Balakirev's house. How pleased I was! [10]

---

[8] Aleksandr Yegorovich Varlamov (1801–48) wrote 223 songs (published in twelve books by Stellovsky), of which one, *The Red Sarafan,* has become world-renowned, and has frequently been mistaken for a Russian folksong. C. V. V.

[9] In a letter to V. V. Yastryebtsev, of August 17 [30], 1906, Rimsky-Korsakov communicates a record of this piece: "The song deals with Venice. Finding myself in that place now (after 45–6 years), I conceived a desire to refresh that nonsense in my memory and to write to you." Cf. *Russian Musical Gazette,* No. 1, 1909.

[10] Written in 1887–8.

Acquaintance with Balakirev and his circle. The symphony. My father's death. Reminiscences of him. Graduation as a midshipman. Detailed to sail in foreign waters.

FROM THE very first, Balakirev produced an enormous impression upon me. A magnificent pianist, playing everything from memory; endowed with bold opinions, new ideas, and, last but not least, a gift of composition, which I already revered! At our first meeting, my Scherzo in C minor was shown to him; he approved it, except for a few critical observations. He was likewise shown my Nocturne and other things, as well as fragmentary materials for the symphony (E-flat minor). He insisted that I set to composing the symphony. I was enraptured. At his house I met Cui and Moussorgsky, of whom I had known by hearsay from Kanille. Balakirev was then orchestrating the Overture of Cui's *The Prisoner of the Caucasus*. With what delight I listened to *real business* discussions of instrumentation, part-writing, etc.! They also played Moussorgsky's Allegro in C major for four hands:

which I liked. I do not remember what Balakirev played of his own music; I think it was the last entr'acte from *King Lear*. And be-

19

sides, how much talking there was about current musical matters! All at once I had been plunged into a new world, unknown to me, where I found myself among real, talented musicians, whom I had formerly only heard of in the society of my dilettante friends. That was truly a strong impression.

During November and December I visited Balakirev every Saturday evening, often meeting there Moussorgsky and Cui. There also I made the acquaintance of V. V. Stassov. I remember V. V. Stassov [1] reading aloud to us passages from the *Odyssey* one Saturday — for the purpose of enlightening my own poor self. [2] Moussorgsky once read Kookolnik's *Prince Kholmsky,* and the painter Myasoyedov read Gogol's *Viy.* Balakirev, alone, or four-hands with Moussorgsky, would play Schumann's symphonies and Beethoven's quartets. Moussorgsky would sing something from *Ruslan and Lyudmila* (for instance, the scene between Farlaf and Nayina) with A. P. Arsenyev, who impersonated Nayina. As far as I recall, Balakirev was then composing a piano concerto, excerpts from which he would play for us. Often he explained to me instrumentation and forms of composition. From him I heard opinions that were entirely new to me. The tastes of the circle leaned towards Glinka, Schumann, and Beethoven's last quartets. Eight symphonies of Beethoven found comparatively little favour with the circle. Except for the *A Midsummer Night's Dream* Overture, the *Hebrides* Overture and the finale of the Octet, they had little respect for Mendelssohn (whom Moussorgsky often called " Mendel"); Mozart and Haydn were considered out of date and naïve; J. S. Bach was held to be petrified, yes, even a mere musico-mathematical, feelingless, and deadly nature, composing like a very machine. Handel was considered a strong nature, but he was mentioned very rarely. Chopin was likened by Balakirev to a nervous society lady. The beginning of his Funeral March (B-flat minor) roused them to rapture, but the rest was deemed utterly worthless. Some of his mazurkas found favour, but the greater part of his compositions

---

[1] Vladimir Vasiliyevich Stassov, a famous writer on art and music (1824–1906). C. V. V.

[2] Cf. " Correspondence between M. A. Balakirev and N. A. Rimsky-Korsakov " (*Musical Contemporary,* 1915–16 and 1916–17).

were looked upon as pretty lacework and no more. Berlioz, whose works they were just beginning to know, was highly esteemed. Liszt was comparatively unknown and was adjudged crippled and perverted from a musical point of view and often even a caricature. Little was said of Wagner. The attitude towards the contemporary Russian composers was as follows: They respected Dargomyzhsky for the recitative portions of *Rusalka;* his three orchestral fantasies were considered a mere curiosity (*The Stone Guest* did not exist as yet); his songs *The Paladin* and *Oriental Melody* were highly thought of; but, on the whole, he was not credited with any considerable talent and was treated with a shade of derision. This manifested itself (among other things) in Dargomyzhsky's countless nicknames in circulation at that time among the members of the Balakirev circle (Dargoman, Dargophgus, Dargopyekh, etc.). Lvov [3] was deemed a nonentity. Rubinstein had a reputation as a pianist, but was thought to have neither talent nor taste as a composer.[4] Serov had not put hand to his *Judith* at that time, and so was passed over in silence.

I listened to these opinions with avidity and absorbed the tastes of Balakirev, Cui, and Moussorgsky without reasoning or examination. Many of the opinions were in reality without proof, for often other people's compositions under discussion were played before me only in fragments, and I had no idea of the whole work; occasionally they remained altogether unknown to me. Nevertheless I conned with admiration the opinions mentioned and repeated them in the circle of my own former schoolmates who were interested in music, as if I were thoroughly convinced of their truth.

Balakirev grew very fond of me and used to say that I, as it were, had taken the place of Gusakovsky,[5] who had gone abroad and of whom they all had great expectations. If Balakirev loved me as

---

[3] The composer of what was, before the revolution, the Russian national anthem, *God Save the Tsar.* For Lvov's own account of how it came to be written see Montagu-Nathan's *History of Russian Music* (Charles Scribner's Sons), p. 57. C. V. V.

[4] Cf. an opinion of him in a letter from Balakirev to Rimsky-Korsakov, *Musical Contemporary*, 1915–16, No. 2, pp. 102 ff.

[5] For a characterization of this stage of the relations between M. A. Balakirev and Rimsky-Korsakov cf. their correspondence (*Musical Contemporary*, 1915–16, No. 2).

a son and pupil,[6] I, for my part, was literally in love with him. In my eyes his talent surpassed all bounds of possibility, and every word and opinion of his were absolute truth to me. My relations with Cui and Moussorgsky were doubtless not so warm, but, at any rate, the delight I took in them and my attachment to them were very considerable. On Balakirev's advice, I turned to composing the first movement of the E-flat minor Symphony from the beginnings in my possession. The introduction and the exposition of the subjects (up to the development) were subjected to considerable criticism by Balakirev; I kept zealously making changes. For the Christmas holidays I went to visit my parents in Tikhvin and there I finished writing the entire first movement; Balakirev approved of it and had almost no corrections to suggest. My first attempt to orchestrate this movement embarrassed me, and Balakirev orchestrated for me the first page of the Introduction, whereupon the work went better. According to the opinion of Balakirev and others, I proved to have a gift for instrumentation.

During the winter and spring of 1862 I composed the Scherzo (without the trio) for my symphony, and the Finale, which latter Balakirev and Cui praised particularly. As far as I recollect, this Finale was composed under the influence of Cui's Symphonic Allegro, at that time often played at Balakirev's; the subsidiary subject of this Cui subsequently utilized for MacGregor's narrative in his *William Ratcliff*. The principal subject of this Finale was composed by me on a train, when late in March I was returning from Tikhvin to St. Petersburg with my uncle Pyotr Petrovich.

My trip to Tikhvin was made necessary by my father's grave illness. I went there with my brother Voyin Andreyevich and, arriving on March 18 [30], found my father no longer among the living. My father died at seventy-eight. During the last years of his life he had several strokes and began to age perceptibly, though still retaining considerable vigour of memory and intellect. Until 1859–60, approximately, he enjoyed good health, walked a great deal, and daily wrote in his diary. Having renounced the Masonic order to

---

[6] Somewhat later Balakirev wrote to Rimsky-Korsakov: "From you I expect a great deal and pin my faith on you as an old aunt does on a young jurist nephew" ("Correspondence between Balakirev and Rimsky-Korsakov," Letter V).

which he had belonged in the time of Alexander I, he remained exceedingly religious, daily reading the Gospel and various spiritual and moral books, from which he constantly copied numerous extracts. His piety was pure in the extreme, without the slightest taint of hypocrisy. He went to church (at the Greater Monastery) only on holidays, but prayed long at home every morning and evening. He was an exceedingly meek and upright man. Having inherited some wealth from my grandfather and subsequently, upon the death of his first wife (Princess Myeshcherskaya by birth), having received a fine estate near Moscow, he finally found himself propertyless, thanks to his swindling friends who traded estates with him to their advantage, borrowed money from him, and the like. His last post in the government service was that of civil Governor of the Volhynian Government, where he was greatly beloved. He went into retirement in the late thirties, evidently because his kindly disposition was not in consonance with the demands made upon him by the higher authorities and the tendency to oppress the Poles. Upon retiring from service, he settled in Tikhvin with my mother and my uncle Pyotr Petrovich, drawing a small pension. Being opposed on principle to the system of serfdom, he was dismissing, within my memory, one by one, the domestics who still belonged to him; finally he set them all free. I recall our former menials, numerous enough in the years of my childhood: my nurse, her husband, the ever drunken tailor Yakov, their son, Vanya, the *dvornik* (house porter) Vasili, the other *dvornik* Konstantin, his wife, the cook Afimya, a Varvara, an Annushka, a Dunyasha, and others. Having liberated them, we were left with hired servants from among those same former serfs of ours. While living in retreat at Tikhvin, my father was highly regarded by Tikhvin society, often gave advice to many, and settled disputes and misunderstandings. On great holidays there was no end of visitors at our house.[7]

My father was buried at the Greater Monastery of Tikhvin. The following day my mother and brother went to St. Petersburg, and my uncle and I left the day after.

---

[7] The autobiographical note of Andrey Petrovich Rimsky-Korsakov, extracted from his letter to A. D. Komovsky, was published in A. Rimsky-Korsakov's article "The Recluse of Tikhvin . . ." (*Musical Annals*, No. 1, Petrograd, 1922), and in Chapter i of his book *N. A. Rimsky-Korsakov*, Part I.

Since January 1862 Voyin Andreyevich had been director of the Marine Corps. After moving to St. Petersburg, Mother and Uncle Pyotr Petrovich went to live with him, and I came there to spend Sundays. Until then, since the death of P. N. Golovin, I had been spending my holidays at the house of Golovin's sister — Praskovya Nikolayevna Novikova, with whom I often played duets.

My graduation as a midshipman took place on April 8 [20], 1862. In those days the title of midshipman was granted upon completing the course of studies. The midshipmen had no set duties to perform; the officer's commission was conferred after two years of service as a midshipman. A midshipman was something midway between pupil and officer, and he was made an officer after a certain practical examination. Usually a midshipman was sent on a two years' practice cruise. A similar assignment awaited me, too. My cruise was to be made on the clipper *Almaz*, under the command of P. A. Zelyony. The clipper was detailed to a voyage abroad. I was face to face with a voyage of two or three years, a separation from Balakirev and other musical friends, and a complete isolation from music. I had no desire to go abroad. Having become intimate with the Balakirev circle, I began to dream of a musical career; the circle had encouraged and directed me on that road. By that time I really did love music passionately.

Balakirev was deeply distressed by my impending departure and wanted to do some wire-pulling, so as to have my sailing orders cancelled. But that was unthinkable. On the other hand, Cui insisted that I should not forgo my first steps in the service, considering my youth. He said it was far more practical to go on the trip and get my commission, and that two or three years later I would have a clearer idea of what was to be done. Voyin Andreyevich was insistent upon my service and sailing. The beginnings of composition in my possession at that time did not seem to him sufficient for me to risk giving up a naval career at the very outset. My piano-playing disclosed so little of the virtuoso that even on that score I did not appear to him to be possessed of a bent for art such as promised even a moderately brilliant future. He was right, a thousand times right, in looking upon me as a dilettante: I was one.

My career in my parents' eyes. My musical preceptors. Balakirev as a teacher of composition and leader of the circle. The other members of Balakirev's circle in the early sixties and the teacher-leader's attitude towards them. Gusakovsky, Cui, Moussorgsky, and I. The tendencies and spirit at the Naval School and in the fleet in my time. Sailing abroad.

MY PARENTS, belonging to a family of old nobility, being people of the 1820–30 decade, and rarely coming in touch with prominent literary and artistic people, naturally were far from the thought of making me a musician. My father was a Governor emeritus in retirement; my mother, who had grown up in the Government of Oryol in a family of wealthy landowners, the Skaryatins, had spent all her youth in the society of aristocrats and retired men of that time. My uncle Nikolay Petrovich was a well-known admiral, director of the Marine Corps in the forties, and a favourite of Emperor Nicholas I. As if to imitate him my brother was entered in the Navy and really became a splendid seaman. Naturally, I, too, was intended for sea service, the more so as, carried away by the letters sent by my brother on his voyage abroad and the reading of books of travel, I, too, did not avoid the path laid out for me. In out-of-the-way Tikhvin there was absolutely no real music, nor did anybody come there even to give concerts. But still, when my talent and inclination for music had perceptibly manifested themselves, my parents placed me under the best piano teachers then obtainable in Tikhvin. Indeed, Olga Nikitishna and Olga Fyeliksovna Fel, already mentioned by me, were the best pianists in our town; the best because there were no others. Accordingly, my parents had done all they could do at the time. But as my instructresses had not been able to develop any genuine talent for piano-playing in me (I did not play badly, but my playing was far from serious or impressive), it is the more evident that my parents could not picture to themselves their son's future as that of a musician. Later, while at the Naval School and studying with Ulikh, I could practise piano only on Saturdays and Sundays. Of course, even then my progress was inconsiderable. Not being a real pianist, Ulikh could not teach me the proper position of the hands. And as for developing even an irregular technique, he had neither sufficient time or desire, nor proper coercive or stimulating methods. Naturally, I could acquire a genuine love for music only after I reached St. Petersburg, where I first heard *genuine* music, *genuinely* performed, even if it was an *Indra* or *Lucia di Lammermoor* on the operatic stage. But I truly began to love the art of music when I came to know *Ruslan and Lyudmila,* as I have already said in the foregoing pages of my reminiscences.

The first real musician and virtuoso I met was Kanille. I am deeply grateful to him for guiding my taste and the original general development of my gifts of composition. But I shall always find fault with him for having paid scant attention to my piano technique and not giving me sufficient instruction in harmony and counterpoint. The work of harmonizing chorales which he had suggested to me was soon given up; for, while making but few corrections in my writings, he did not show me the elementary methods of harmonization, and, groping about my tasks and running into snags, as I did, I conceived only aversion for them. While studying with Kanille I did not know even the names of the principal chords, and yet I strained to compose nocturnes, variations, and what not, which I carefully concealed from my brother and the Golovins and used to show only to Kanille. Though my love for music was growing, I was but a dilettante pupil, playing the piano after a fashion and scribbling things on music paper, when I finally got to Balakirev. And now, after attempts amateurish in their technique, but musicianly and earnest as to style and taste, I was straightway put to the task of composing a symphony.

Balakirev, who had never had any systematic course in harmony and counterpoint and had not even superficially applied himself to them, evidently thought such studies quite unnecessary. Thanks to his original talent and pianistic gifts, thanks also to the musical environment which he had found at Ulybyshev's [1] (who had a private orchestra which played Beethoven's symphonies under Balakirev's leadership), he somehow became at a bound a genuine, practical musician. An excellent pianist, a superior sight reader of music, a splendid improviser, endowed by nature with the sense of correct harmony and part-writing, he possessed a technique partly native and partly acquired through a vast musical erudition, with the help of an extraordinary memory, keen and retentive, which means so much in steering a critical course in musical literature. Then, too, he was a marvellous critic, especially a *technical* critic. He instantly felt every technical imperfection or error, he grasped a defect in form at once. Whenever I or other young men, later on, played him our essays at composition, he instantly caught all the defects of form, modulation, and so on, and forthwith seating himself at the piano, he would improvise and show how the composition in question should be changed exactly as he indicated, and frequently entire passages in other people's compositions became his and not their putative authors' at all. He was obeyed absolutely, for the spell of his personality was tremendous. Young, with marvellously alert fiery eyes, with a handsome beard; unhesitating, authoritative, and straightforward in speech; ready at any moment for beautiful piano improvisation, remembering every music bar familiar to him, instantly learning by heart the compositions played for him, he was bound to exercise that spell as none else could. Though valuing the

---

[1] A music-critic, the author of a famous work on Mozart. Balakirev was brought up in Ulybyshev's household. C. V. V.

slightest proof of talent in another, he still could not help feeling
his own superiority; nor could that other, too, help feeling it. His
influence over those around him was boundless, and resembled
some magnetic or mesmeric force. But with all his native mentality
and brilliant abilities, there was one thing he failed to understand:
that what was good for him in the matter of musical education was
of no use whatever for others, as these others not only had grown
up amid entirely different surroundings, but possessed utterly different natures; that the development of their talents was bound to
take place at different intervals and in a different manner. Moreover, he despotically demanded that the tastes of his pupils should
exactly coincide with his own. The slightest deviation from his taste
was severely censured by him. By means of raillery, a parody or
caricature played by him, whatever did not suit him at the moment
was belittled — and the pupil blushed with shame for his expressed
opinion and recanted for ever or for a long time to come.

I have already mentioned the general tendency of the taste of
Balakirev and his friends, who were manifestly under his boundless
influence. I shall add to it that, under the influence of Schumann's
compositions, melodic creative gifts were then looked upon with
disfavour. The majority of melodies and themes were regarded as
the weaker part of music; the exceptions quoted were few — for
example, the melody of Bayan's first song.[2] Nearly all the fundamental ideas of Beethoven's symphonies were thought weak; Chopin's melodies were considered sweet and womanish; Mendelssohn's, sour and bourgeois. However, the themes of Bach's fugues
were undoubtedly held in respect. The greatest amount of attention
and respect was showered on the musical elements called additions,
introductions, brief but characteristic phrases, ostinato dissonant
progressions (but not of the enharmonic variety), sequence-like
progressions, organ-points, abrupt conclusions, etc. In the majority
of cases a piece was critically judged in accordance with the separate elements: the first four bars were said to be excellent, the next

---

[2] Bayan was a famous minstrel. Rimsky-Korsakov here refers to a tenor air in
Glinka's opera, *Ruslan and Lyudmila,* sung by a character named after the celebrated
old bard. C. V. V.

28

M. A. BALAKIREV

from the drawing by Léon Bakst

eight weak, the melody immediately following good for nothing, the transition from it to the next phrase fine, and so forth. A composition was never considered as a whole in its æsthetic significance. Accordingly, the new compositions which Balakirev introduced to his circle were invariably played in fragments, in bars, and even piecemeal: first the end, then the beginning, which usually produced a queer impression on an outsider who happened to come to the circle. A pupil like myself had to submit to Balakirev a proposed composition in its embryo, say, even the first four or eight bars. Balakirev would immediately make corrections, indicating how to recast such an embryo; he would criticize it, would praise and extol the first two bars, but would censure the next two, ridicule them, and try hard to make the author disgusted with them. Vivacity of composition and fertility were not at all in favour, frequent recasting was demanded, and the composition was extended over a long space of time under the cold control of self-criticism. Having taken two or three chords and having invented a short phrase, the author endeavoured to account to himself whether he had acted properly and whether there was nothing shameful in these beginnings! At first glance such an attitude towards art seems incompatible with Balakirev's brilliant gift of improvisation. And really there is a puzzling contradiction here. Balakirev at any moment ready to play a fantasy on any theme of his own or somebody else's with the greatest gusto; Balakirev instantly detecting the flaws in the works of others and ready to show concretely how this or that was to be corrected, how to continue a certain approach or how to avoid a commonplace turn of phrase, how to improve the harmonization of a phrase, the arrangement of a chord, and so on; Balakirev, whose talent as a composer shone dazzlingly for all who came in contact with him — this very Balakirev composed with exceeding slowness and deliberation. At that time (he was twenty-four or twenty-five years of age) he had written several magnificent songs, a Spanish Overture and a Russian one, and the music to *King Lear*. Not much, but still it was his most productive period. His fertility decreased with the years. Of this, however, I will speak later.

Obviously, at the time I could not make the observations which

29

resulted in the above lines. What has been said in these lines grew
clear to me only subsequently. And, moreover, in those days Balakirev's self-criticism and manner of treating his pupils and companions in art had not as yet assumed that clear, tangible form
which could be observed beginning with 1865, when other musical
fledgelings appeared on the scene besides myself. Thus in charac-
terizing Balakirev I have run ahead, but my characterization is
nevertheless far from being complete and I shall endeavour to supplement it in the course of my reminiscences, returning again and
again to this enigmatic, contradictory, and fascinating personality.

On joining Balakirev's circle I proved to have taken, as it were,
the place of the absent Gusakovsky. Gusakovsky was a young man,
just graduated from the University as a chemist, who had gone
abroad for a long stay. He possessed a vigorous talent for composition, was Balakirev's favourite, but, according to Balakirev's and
Cui's accounts, a queer, extravagant, and sickly character. His compositions — piano pieces — were mostly unfinished: a number of
scherzos without the trios, a sonata allegro, fragments of music for
Faust, and a completed Symphonic Allegro in E-flat major, with
Balakirev's instrumentation — all beautiful music in the Beethoven-
Schumann style. Balakirev guided him in composition, but nothing
finished would result. Gusakovsky jumped from one composition to
another, and the gifted sketches sometimes remained even unrecorded, save for those retained in Balakirev's memory.

Balakirev had no difficulty in getting along with me. At his suggestion I most readily rewrote the symphonic movements composed
by me and brought them to completion with the help of his advice
and improvisations. Balakirev considered me a symphony specialist.
On the other hand, crediting Cui, as he did, with a bent for opera,
he allowed a certain degree of liberty to Cui's creative genius, treating with indulgence many an element that did not meet his own
tastes. The Auber vein in Cui's music was justified by his half-
French origin and was kindly winked at. Cui displayed no promise
of becoming a good orchestrator, and Balakirev willingly orchestrated for him some of his works — for instance, the Overture of *The
Prisoner of the Caucasus.* At that time this opera had been finished,

and *The Mandarin's Son* (a one-act opera, to Krylov's text) was being written or possibly had already been finished. Cui's Symphonic Allegro in E-flat major was apparently written under Balakirev's strict supervision, but was left unfinished after all, for not everybody could submissively endure and zealously carry out his demands as I did. Cui's instrumental compositions finished by that time were a Scherzo for orchestra in F major (Bamberg),[3] and two other scherzos in C major and G-sharp minor for the piano. Apparently Moussorgsky's symphonic attempts also came to nothing under the pressure of Balakirev's suggestions and demands. At that period the only work of Moussorgsky's recognized by the circle was the chorus from *Œdipus.* Cui's Scherzo, the dances from *The Prisoner of the Caucasus,* Balakirev's Overture to *King Lear,* Moussorgsky's above-mentioned chorus, and Gusakovsky's Allegro (with Balakirev's instrumentation) were performed partly at the concerts of the Russian Musical Society under Rubinstein's direction, partly at a theatre concert under K. N. Lyadov's direction, prior to my acquaintance with Balakirev's circle, but for some reason I did not happen to hear them.

Accordingly, during the winter of 1861-2, Balakirev's circle consisted of Cui, Moussorgsky, and myself. There is no doubt that for both Cui and Moussorgsky Balakirev was indispensable as adviser and censor, as editor and teacher. Without him they would have been unable to take a step. Who else could have given advice and shown them how to correct their compositions as regards form? Who could have put their part-writing in order? Who would have been able to give advice as to orchestration and, in case of need, do the orchestration for them? Who would have been able to correct their slips of the pen — to read the proof of their compositions, so to speak?

Cui, who had had a few lessons from Moniuszko,[4] was far from being able to manage clear and natural part-writing, and for orchestration he had neither inclination nor ability. Moussorgsky, who

---

[3] This, too, possibly, with Balakirev's instrumentation.
[4] The Polish composer (1820-72), whose principal work was the opera, *Halka.*
C. V. V.

was an excellent pianist, had not the slightest technical training as
a composer. Neither of them was a musician by profession. Cui was
an engineering officer, and Moussorgsky a retired officer of the
Preobrazhensky Regiment of the Imperial Guards. Balakirev alone
was a real musician. Since his youth he had grown accustomed to
seeing himself in the midst of Ulybyshev's orchestra; being a good
pianist, he had already appeared in public, at University concerts,
at soirées in the homes of Lvov, Odoyevsky, Vyelgorsky, and others.
He had played every variety of chamber music with the greatest
artists of the time; had accompanied Vieuxtemps and many women
singers. M. I. Glinka himself had blessed him for his activity as composer, giving him the theme of a Spanish march for his overture.
He needed Cui and Moussorgsky as friends, adherents, followers,
and comrade pupils; but he could have gone on without them. Musical experience and life gave Balakirev's brilliant talent an opportunity for rapid development. The development of the others began
later, went more slowly, and required a guide. This guide was
Balakirev, who had acquired everything by his astounding many-
sided talent and experience quite without labour and without system, and therefore had no idea of any systems. I might say even
more: having himself gone through no preparatory school, Balakirev thought it unnecessary for others as well. There was no need
of training: one must begin to compose outright, to create and learn
through one's own work of creation. Whatever would be unfinished
or unskilful in this early creative work of his comrade pupils he
himself would finish; he would set everything to rights, complete in
case of need, and the composition would be ready to be issued for
performance or publication. And it was necessary to hurry with
publication — the talents were indubitable. And yet Cui was already
twenty-five to twenty-six, Moussorgsky twenty-one to twenty-two.
Too late to go to school, high time to live and work and make themselves known. There is no doubt that this guidance and guardian-
ship over composers who failed to stand on their own legs placed a
certain general stamp on them, the stamp of Balakirev's taste and
methods, much more pronouncedly than does the simple and indifferent guidance of some professor of counterpoint. In the latter

case there come into play the common methods of counterpoint and harmony, the general deductions from current musical forms; in the former case, certain melodic turns were used, certain methods of modulation, certain instrumental colouring, etc., which had originated in the tendencies of Balakirev's taste, in his own technique, by no means faultless or varied, and in his own one-sided erudition in the field of orchestration, as became clear to me subsequently. Nevertheless, at the time, Balakirev's technique and his learning, which he had gained through practice, thanks to his own talent, taste, and innate powers of observation, infinitely surpassed the technique and knowledge of Gusakovsky, Cui, and Moussorgsky. He, at all events, was a musician by nature and profession, while they were gifted amateurs.

Was Balakirev's attitude towards his pupil-friends right? In my opinion, absolutely wrong. A truly talented pupil needs so little. It is so easy to show all that is necessary in harmony and counterpoint in order to put him on his own feet in this respect, it is easy to direct him in understanding the forms of composition, if only the thing is properly undertaken. A year or two of systematic study in the development of technique, a few exercises in free composition and orchestration, and the teaching is over, provided he has a good piano technique. The pupil is no longer a pupil, a schoolboy, but a budding composer striking out for himself. But that was not the case with all of us.

Balakirev did what he could to the best of his knowledge and ability. And if he did not understand how to manage, the cause lay in those years of darkness for the music of Russia and in his half-Russian, half-Tatar nature, nervous, impatient, easily excited, and quickly tiring, in his native talent, brilliant and aboriginal, which met nowhere any obstacle in the way of its development, and his purely Russian self-delusion and laziness. Besides the mentioned peculiarities of his nature, Balakirev was a man capable of growing warmly and deeply attached to people who struck a sympathetic chord in him, and, on the other hand, he was ready, at first sight, to conceive an eternal hatred or contempt for people who had not won his goodwill. All these complex elements had made of him a mass of contradictions, enigmatic and fascinating, but afterwards brought him to many a pass entirely unforeseen and improbable at the time.

Of all his pupil-friends I was the youngest, being only seventeen years old. What did I need? A piano technique, the technique of harmony and counterpoint, and an idea of musical forms. Balakirev should have made me sit down at the piano and learn to play well. That was so easy for him, as I worshipped him and obeyed his advice in everything. But he did not do it; declaring from the outset that I was no pianist, he gave up the whole thing as altogether unnecessary. He should have given me a few lessons in harmony and counterpoint, should have made me write a few fugues and explained the grammar of musical forms to me. He could not do it, as he had not studied systematically himself and considered it unnecessary; hence also he did not tell me to study under someone else. Having made me write a symphony after our first meeting, he cut me off from preparatory work and the acquisition of a technique. And I, who did not know the names of all intervals and chords, to whom harmony meant but the far-famed prohibition of parallel octaves and fifths, who had no idea as to what double counterpoint was, or the meaning of cadence, thesis and antithesis, and period, I set out to compose a symphony. Schumann's *Manfred* Overture and Third Symphony, Glinka's *Prince Kholmsky* and *Jota Aragonesa,* and Balakirev's *King Lear* — these were the models I followed in writing the symphony; copied, thanks to my powers of observation and imitation. As for orchestration, the perusal of Berlioz's *Traité d'Instrumentation* and of some Glinka scores gave me a little fragmentary information. I had no idea of trumpets and French horns and would get confused between writing for natural-scale and chromatic-scale instruments. But Balakirev himself had not known these instruments and became acquainted with them only through Berlioz. The bow instruments, too, were an absolute muddle to me: the movements of the bow, the strokes, were completely unknown to me — I indicated interminable legatos, impossible of execution. I had a very vague notion of the execution of double notes and chords, blindly following Berlioz's table, in case of emergency. But

Balakirev himself did not know this chapter, having the most confused notion of violin-playing and positions. I felt that I was ignorant of many things, but was convinced that Balakirev knew everything in the world, and he cleverly concealed from me and the others the insufficiency of his information. But in orchestral colouring and combination of instruments he was a good practical hand, and his counsels were invaluable to me.

In one way or another, towards May 1862, the first movement, the Scherzo, and the Finale of the symphony had been composed and somehow orchestrated by me. The Finale in particular won general approval at the time. My attempts to write an Adagio met with no success, and it was useless to hope for any: in those days one was somehow ashamed to write a cantabile melody; the fear of dropping into the commonplace precluded any kind of sincerity.

In the spring I visited Balakirev every Saturday and looked forward to those evenings as to a holiday. I also used to go to Cui's. He was living at the Voskresyensky Prospect and kept a boarding-house to prepare boys for entrance to military schools. Cui had two grand pianos, and whenever I came, there was always some eight-hand playing. The players were: Balakirev, Moussorgsky's brother, Filaret Petrovich (who went for some reason under the name of Yevgyeni Petrovich [5], Cui, and occasionally Dmitri Vasilyevich Stassov. V. V. Stassov was usually present also. They played Berlioz's *Queen Mab* scherzo and *Ball at the Capulets'*, in M. P. Moussorgsky's transcription for eight hands, as well as the procession from Balakirev's *King Lear,* in his own arrangement. They played four-hands the overtures to *The Prisoner of the Caucasus* and *The Mandarin's Son* and played also the movements of my symphony as they were completed. Moussorgsky used to sing with Cui excerpts from the latter's operas. Moussorgsky had a fair baritone voice and sang magnificently; Cui sang in a composer's voice. Cui's wife, Malvina Rafayilovna, then singing no longer, had been an amateur singer prior to my acquaintance with them.

[5] For an explanation of this curious fact, cf. V. G. Karatygin in his article " M. P. Moussorgsky's Genealogy, on the Male and the Female Sides " (*Musical Contemporary*, 1917, Nos. 5–6).

In May, Balakirev went to the Caucasus for the mineral-water cure; Moussorgsky went to the country, and Cui to his summer home. My brother left on a practice cruise; his family, my mother, and my uncle left for the island Sonion-Sari, near Viborg, in Finland, to spend the summer. Everybody had gone. I was ordered to make a sailing trip abroad on the clipper *Almaz* and was to spend the summer at Kronstadt with a ship then being fitted out. At Kronstadt I stayed at the house of K. E. Zambrzhitsky, a close acquaintance of my brother's. I don't quite remember how I spent that summer. I remember only that I did very little with my music and composed nothing; but why, I don't know. I was killing time in the company of my fellow graduates. Once Kanille paid me a visit and stayed with me for two days. I received several letters from Balakirev. I went on a few days' leave to see my folks on Sonion-Sari Island. Thus the entire summer went by — tedious and devoid of interest. My circle of schoolmates could not be called intellectual. In general, I cannot boast of the spiritual tendencies of the students of the Naval School during my whole six-year stay there. Theirs was completely the cadet spirit inherited from the days of Nicholas I and not yet affected by the new times. Horseplay that was not always decent, rough protests against the authorities, rude intercourse with fellow students, prosy obscenity in conversation, a cynical attitude towards the fair sex, a disinclination for reading, contempt for the foreign languages and subjects outside our special studies, and in the summer, during practice cruises, even drunkenness — these were characteristic of the school spirit of those days. How little this environment accorded with artistic aspirations and how deadly it proved to even the slenderest of artistic natures, seldom as these appeared there! They vegetated there, quite fouled by the military humdrum of the school. And in this atmosphere I, too, vegetated, languid and emaciated, as regards general artistic, poetic, and intellectual development. Of literary artists I had read all of Pushkin, Lermontov, and Gogol while at school, but had not gone beyond that. Though I was promoted from class to class, my writing was full of disgraceful grammatical mistakes; I knew nothing of history, and just as little of physics and chemistry. Only in mathematics and its application to navigation I got along passably. In the summer, on practice cruises, my studies in naval art — rowing, sailing, rigging — went rather slowly. I was fond of the course in making sail and was rather fearless in climbing masts and yards. I liked sea bathing and, with Skrydlov and other classmates, used to swim five ship-lengths around the vessel without pause or rest. I never was seasick and never was afraid of the sea and its perils. But, at bottom, I did not like sea service and had no aptitude for it. I possessed no presence of mind and had no executive ability at all. Subsequently, during the sail abroad, I proved to be utterly unable to give orders in military style, to scold, to swear at people, to speak reprovingly, to punish, to speak to a subordinate in the tone of a superior, and so forth. All these gifts, indispensable in naval and military service, I utterly lacked. Those were the years of rope-ends and brutal blows on the mouth. On several occasions, willy-nilly, I had to witness the punishment of sailors with two hundred to three hundred ratline blows on the bare back, in the presence of the whole crew, and to listen to the chastised man exclaiming in an imploring voice: " Your Honour, have mercy! " On the artillery ship *Prokhor*, when the drunken crew were brought in from shore leave on Sunday, Lieutenant Dek, standing at the companionway, used to greet each drunken sailor with fist-blows on the mouth. Which of the two — the drunken sailor or the lieutenant who hit him on the mouth for the love of it — had more of the beast in him is not hard to decide, in the lieutenant's favour. Commanders and officers, supervising the tasks, swore with the technique of virtuosi; the choicest billingsgate filled the air with a heavy stench. Some of the officers had a reputation for their fiery imagination and inventive genius in abusive language, others for their efficiency in knocking out teeth. For this latter exploit great was the fame of first-class Captain Boobnov, who, they said, used to stage a veritable Mamay Massacre [6] aboard his ship while tacking under sail.

I have said already that, on entering the school, I had gained a good footing by giving at once a setback to the classmates who

---

[6] The famous débâcle of the Tatars under Mamay, on the Kulikovo Field (1380). J. A. J.

annoyed me. But in my second or third year my temper somehow became flabby and timid to excess. Once I did not even pay in kind my classmate M., who hit me in the face without rhyme or reason, out of sheer malice. However, I was pretty generally liked; I kept out of quarrels and followed our school code in every detail. I was never afraid of the authorities, but my conduct was generally correct. During my last school year, after my brother had been appointed director, I did better in my studies and ranked sixth among our sixty-odd graduates.

On making Balakirev's acquaintance, I heard from him, for the first time in my life, that one must read, must look after one's own education, must become acquainted with history, polite literature, and criticism. Many thanks to him for it! Balakirev, who had only graduated from a *Gymnasium* and had but a short term at the University of Kazan, had done a great deal of reading in Russian literature and history and seemed to me highly educated. At that time we had no talks about religion, but it seems he was a perfect sceptic even then. As for me, I was nothing at that time, neither believer nor sceptic; religious questions simply did not interest me. Though brought up in a profoundly religious family, I had been rather indifferent to prayer since childhood, I don't know why. I prayed daily, in the morning, on retiring, and at church, but did so only because my parents demanded it. A strange thing! When a boy, standing at prayer, I occasionally ventured to utter blasphemies, as if to test whether the Lord God would punish me for it. He did not punish me, of course, and doubt crept into my soul; sometimes I would be seized with repentance and self-reproaches for my stupid behaviour; but, as far as I recall, these were neither deep nor strong. I suppose such pranks must be classed in psychiatry among the so-called *fixed ideas*. While at school I went to church on Sundays and was bored to death. But at Tikhvin I always had liked the archimandrite's divine service and the church singing for their beauty and solemnity. Annually during Lent I went to communion as is usual. There was one year in which I treated this ceremonial with reverence, for no obvious reason; but in the years following I was rather careless. During the last two years of my stay at school, I heard from my schoolmates S. and K.-K. that "there is no God and it's all just invention." K.-K. affirmed that he had read Voltaire's (?!) philosophy. I took rather readily to the view that "there is no God and it's all just invention." However, this thought troubled me little, and in reality I gave no thought to these weighty matters. But my piety, weak even before then, had completely evaporated, and I felt no spiritual hunger. I now recall that when a boy of but twelve or so, I was not averse to free-thinking, and once pestered my mother with questions about the freedom of the will. I told her that even though everything in the world is done according to God's will, and all phenomena of life depend on Him, man must still be free in the choice of his own acts, and consequently God's will must be powerless in this regard; otherwise how can He permit evil acts on the part of man and then inflict punishment for them? Naturally, I had not put it exactly that way, but this was the thought; and my mother was at a loss how to make answer to it.

I have already spoken of the comparative coarseness and low level of intellectual life among my schoolmates. This was so at least during my first four years at school. In the two highest classes a certain improvement could be felt, however. I have already mentioned the propensity towards music and choral singing among certain of my schoolmates in the upper classes; I have also mentioned the circle which had formed around me owing to my playing the harmonium and rehearsing choral works with them. Since I had begun seriously to study with Kanille and Balakirev, I held animated talks on music with my classmates I. A. Bronyetsky and Prince A. D. Myshetsky. With Prince Myshetsky I grew very intimate and friendly. Mention must also be made of my shortlived youthful attachment in the summer of 1859 for the pretty Miss L. P. D., whose acquaintance I had made at Revel while stationed in the local roadstead. To be sure, she was my senior by seven or eight years and considered me a mere boy, but my attentions obviously amused her. I was also a visitor at Miss D.'s home in St. Petersburg during the autumn; but my liking for her was soon over; I ceased meeting her, and my life ran along again in the usual prosaic school groove.[7] Like the majority of young men in their teens, I was somewhat shy in society and avoided ladies.

In reviewing my spiritual and intellectual life during these years at school, I have digressed from the consecutive narrative. I turn again to the interrupted story. I have already said that I spent the summer of 1862 in Kronstadt, a tedious and spiritless summer. Of these three or four summer months I have preserved no vivid recollections whatever. In September the clipper *Almaz* came into the roadstead ready to sail abroad. My brother's family, my mother, and my uncle returned to St. Petersburg. Balakirev, Cui, and the others also came back. In vain Balakirev offered to solicit a rescission of the order for my trip abroad. I had to set out at my brother's insistence, and thus at the end of October we started on the cruise. I saw Balakirev, Cui, and Kanille for the last time at the steamer-landing in St. Petersburg, where they came to see me off when I was bidding a final farewell to the capital. Some two days later, on October 21, we weighed anchor and bade farewell to Russia and Kronstadt.

[Written in February 1893.]

---

[7] This episode has been delineated in detail in A. Rimsky-Korsakov's above-mentioned article (cf. *Musical Annals*, No. 1). Voyin Andreyevich Rimsky-Korsakov, too, was not indifferent to L. P. D. Nevertheless he encouraged his brother's liking in every way, considering that " this . . . is a genuine, first youthful passion, such as there should be " (p. 58).

The cruise abroad. Sailing to England and the Libau coast. Rear-Admiral Lesovsky. The voyage to America. Our stay in the United States. Ordered to the Pacific. Captain Zelyony. From New York to Rio de Janeiro and back to Europe.

WE STARTED for Kiel, where we stayed some three days, and thence for England, to Gravesend. On putting to sea, the clipper's masts proved too short, and therefore it was proposed to order new masts and refit in England; this was done soon after our arrival. The work kept us in England (Gravesend and Greenhithe) nearly four months. My classmates and I visited London two or three times, to see the sights: Westminster Abbey, the Tower, the Crystal Palace, and so on. I also went to the opera, at Covent Garden Theatre, but do not remember the bill.[1]

On board the clipper there were four of us midshipmen, fellow graduates, together with several engineer's mates and mechanical engineers. All of us were quartered in one small cabin and were not admitted to the officers' wardroom. We midshipmen were not given any responsible duties. We stood watch in turn, assisting the officer of the watch. Nevertheless we had plenty of free time. The clipper

---

[1] Cf. " Correspondence between Balakirev and Rimsky-Korsakov " (*Musical Contemporary,* 1915–16, No. 2, p. 105).

possessed a fair library, and we read quite a bit. Every now and then we had lively discussions and debates. The new ideas of the sixties brushed us, too. There were progressives and conservatives in our midst. Among the former, P. A. Mordovin was most prominent; among the latter, A. E. Bakhtyarov. We read Buckle, whose works were in great vogue in the sixties, Macaulay, John Stuart Mill, Belinsky, Dobrolyubov,[2] and others. We read fiction, too. In England, Mordovin kept buying piles of English and French books, among them all sorts of histories of revolutions and civilizations. There was enough to argue about. That was the time of Herzen[3] and Ogaryov with their *Kolokol* (*The Bell*). We even used to get the *Kolokol*. In the meanwhile the Polish uprising began. Now there were frequent quarrels between Mordovin and Bakhtyarov over the former's sympathy for the Poles. All my sympathies lay with Mordovin; Bakhtyarov, who admired Katkov, was unsympathetic; and his convictions were not after my own heart: he was a violent partisan of serfdom, as well as a nobleman with the haughtiness of his class.[4]

Besides corresponding with my mother and my brother, I kept up a correspondence with Balakirev; he urged me to write, if possible, the Andante of my symphony. I buckled down to work, taking as a basis the Russian theme *Pro Tatarski Polon* (On the Tatar Captivity), given me by Balakirev and made known to the latter by Yakushkin.[5] I succeeded in composing the Andante while we lay at anchor in England, and sent the score to Balakirev by mail. I wrote it without a piano (we had none); perhaps once or twice I managed to play the entire composition at a restaurant on shore. Upon receiving the Andante, Balakirev wrote me that his whole circle had been taken with this composition and considered it the best movement of the symphony. Still, he suggested by letter certain changes, which I made.[6]

---

[2] Two of the most famous Russian critics. J. A. J.

[3] Aleksandr Herzen. J. A. J.

[4] For the character of the company on the clipper, cf. " Correspondence of Balakirev and Rimsky-Korsakov " (*Musical Contemporary*, 1915–16, No. 2, p. 106, Letters XXIV, XXVIII).

[5] The great Russian folklore collector. J. A. J.

[6] Cf. " Correspondence of Balakirev and Rimsky-Korsakov," Letters V–XXVI.

In London we bought a small harmoniflute.[7] On it I often played whatever came along, for my own and my comrades' amusement.

Late in February 1863, when our refitting had been completed, new and unexpected orders were forwarded to the clipper *Almaz*. The Polish uprising had burst into flame; rumours were rife that arms were being smuggled for the Poles from abroad to the coast of Libau. Our clipper was to return to the Baltic Sea to cruise within sight of the Libau shore and to see that no arms were brought into Poland. In spite of the secret sympathy within the young hearts of some of us (the members of the midshipmen's cabin) for a cause that seemed righteous to us, the cause of a distant and kindred nationality oppressed by her sister Russia, we were forced to set forth willy-nilly, at the authorities' order, to serve the oppressor faithfully. We bade farewell to foggy England, and our clipper left for Libau. I recall that in passing through the North Sea we were caught in a stiff gale. The rolling of the sea was awful; for two days no hot food could be cooked. But I was not seasick at all.

We hugged the Libau coast for nearly four months, occasionally entering Libau or Polangen for coal and provisions. Perhaps our cruise was useful in that it frightened those who had intended to ship arms and munitions to the rebellious Poles, but we never saw a single suspicious sail anywhere in our vicinity. Once the smoke of a steamer appeared in the distance; we made a dash for it, but the steamer soon vanished; we could not positively say whether it had been an enemy vessel or just a chance bottom. The cruise off Libau was tiresome. Foul weather and strong winds followed us almost constantly. Libau offered nothing of interest; Polangen even less. At rare intervals, in Polangen or ashore, we rode horseback for amusement. I remember that during those times I grew used to going without music, and that reading absorbed me completely.

In June or July our clipper was ordered back to Kronstadt. The purpose of our return was unknown to us. When we arrived in Kronstadt and had lain in the roadstead three or four days, we were ordered out again to sail in Admiral Lesovsky's squadron. We had the following ships with us: the frigate *Aleksandr Nevsky*, the cor-

---

[7] See note on p. 17.

vettes *Vityaz* and *Varyag,* and the clipper *Zhemchoog.* The admiral
was on the *Aleksandr Nevsky.* While stationed in Kronstadt, I managed to run down to St. Petersburg and Pavlovsk, where the Golovins and the Novikovs had summer homes. My mother and my
brother's family, as well as Balakirev, Cui, and the other friends,
were not in St. Petersburg then, because of the summer season.
Johann Strauss (1825–99) was then conducting in Pavlovsk and I
managed to hear Glinka's *A Night in Madrid.* I remember it gave
me the greatest pleasure.

On putting to sea, our fleet separated, and each vessel went on
her own. When we were on the high seas, we learned we were
bound for New York to join the other ships of the squadron, that
the object of our expedition was purely military. War with England was expected over the Polish uprising, and in the event of
war our squadron was to threaten English ships in the Atlantic.
We were to reach America unobserved by the English; hence our
course lay to the north, for we avoided the usual route from England to New York by making this detour, steering a course where
not a single ship could be met. On our way we put in at Kiel two
days, to coal, keeping the object of our cruise a close secret. From
Kiel we were to proceed to New York without a stop. The greater
part of this voyage was to be made under sail, for we should not
have had coal enough for so long a cruise. By doubling the north
of England we no longer met any ships whatever. On entering the
Atlantic our clipper encountered stubborn head winds which often
attained the force of gales. Though under full sail, we often literally
made no headway for days at a time, owing to the strong contrary
winds. The weather was quite cold and damp. Frequently no cooking was done, since the clipper rolled horribly under the huge
waves. While crossing the route of hurricanes, which at this season
of the year issue from the Antillean waters along the coast of North
America and turn across the ocean towards the English coast, we
noticed one fine day that we were entering the area of one of these
hurricanes. A sharp fall in the barometer and a closeness in the air
announced its approach. The wind grew stronger and stronger and
constantly changed its direction from left to right. Enormous waves

N. A. RIMSKY-KORSAKOV

were raised. We kept under one small sail. Night came and the
lightning flashed. The rolling of the sea was terrific. Towards morning the rise in the barometer denoted the passing of the hurricane.
We had cut across its right wing not far from the centre. All was
well, though violent storms continued to give us trouble.

Near the American coast we crossed the warm current — the
Gulf Stream. I remember how surprised and delighted we were,
when we went on deck in the morning, to see the colour of the
ocean utterly changed: from green-grey it had turned to a wonderful blue. Instead of chilly cutting air, we had 72.5°F., the sun, and
delightful weather. Exactly as if we had reached the tropics. Every
moment flying fish leaped from the water. At night the ocean glis-
tened with magnificent phosphorescence. The same on the following day: a thermometer was dipped into the water — 72.5°F. On
the morning of the third day after we had entered the Gulf Stream,
a change once more: grey skies, chilly air, the colour of the ocean
grey-green, the temperature of the water 39°–40°F., the flying fish
gone. Our clipper had entered a new cold current, running parallel
to the Gulf Stream. We bent our course to the southwest towards
New York and soon began to sight merchantmen. In October (I
don't recall the date) the American coast grew visible. We took on
a pilot and soon entered the Hudson and dropped anchor in New
York, where we found the other ships of our squadron.[8]

We remained in the United States from October 1863 until April
1864. Besides New York we visited Annapolis and Baltimore. From
Chesapeake Bay we went sightseeing in Washington. During our
stay at Annapolis it was bitterly cold, the temperature down to 2°
below zero; the river where our clipper and the corvette *Varyag* lay
froze over. The ice was so firm that we attempted to walk on it.
But the cold snap lasted only two or three days and then the river
opened.

We midshipmen and the officers got a chance to run up to Niagara from New York. The trip was made on the Hudson River by

---

[8] The above paragraph has been quoted as an example of a word-picture of the
Gulf Stream in D. O. Svyetsky and T. N. Klado: *Entertaining Meteorology* (2nd edition, 1934), pp. 258–9.

boat to Albany and from there by train. The banks of the Hudson proved very beautiful and Niagara Falls made the most marvellous impression on us. I think it was November. The leaves on the trees were many-coloured, the weather was fine. We climbed over all the rocks, went under the arch of the waterfall as far as we could on the Canadian side; we rowed in a boat as near as possible up to the falls. The impression made by the falls, viewed from various points, especially from the Terrapin Tower, is incomparable. This tower is built on rocks at the brink of the falls; it is reached over a light bridge thrown from Goat Island, which divides the falls in two: the American and the Canadian (Horseshoe Falls). The roar of the falls is indescribable and is audible for miles around. The Americans took us to Niagara Falls at their own expense, with fine hospitality to their transatlantic friends. We were shown to rooms in a magnificent hotel. All the officers and midshipmen of our squadron, divided into two parties, made the trip. Admiral Lesovsky was in our party. At the Niagara Hotel I was asked to play for the entertainment of the company. Of course I objected, went to my room, and put my boots at the door, pretending I was asleep, but at Lesovsky's order, delivered to me by someone through the door, I was obliged to dress and come to the salon. I sat down at the piano and played, I think, the Krakovyak and something else from *A Life for the Tsar*. Soon I noticed that nobody was listening to me; they were all busy talking to my accompaniment. Under cover of the conversation I ceased playing and went to bed. The next evening they did not disturb me again; nobody cared for my playing; it had been called for to satisfy the mere whim of Lesovsky, who understood absolutely nothing of music and did not like it at all. Incidentally, regarding Lesovsky, he was a well-known seaman, formerly commander of the frigate *Diana*, which had gone down near Japan during an earthquake. Lesovsky was notorious for his irascible and ungovernable temper and once, in a fit of wrath, had rushed up to a sailor guilty of some offence and bitten off his nose — for which he subsequently obtained a pension for him, according to report.

46

After two days at Niagara Falls we returned to New York by another route, through Elmira, passing within sight of Lake Erie and Lake Ontario. Our clipper again replaced spars in New York, the very spars which had just been made for it in England. Of the seven months spent by us in America, we stayed the first three or four months in New York, then made a trip to Chesapeake Bay, Annapolis, and Baltimore, as I have already mentioned. The last two months we spent again in New York. The expected war with England had not materialized, and we did not have to privateer and threaten English merchantmen in the Atlantic. While we were in Chesapeake Bay, the frigate *Aleksandr Nevsky* and the corvette *Vityaz* went down to Havana. Towards the end of our stay in North America the whole squadron assembled in New York. During the whole of our stay in the United States the Americans were engaged in their Civil War. The Northern and the Southern states fought over the question of slave-holding. We followed the course of events with deep interest, though we kept exclusively within the Northern territory, which fought under President Lincoln for the emancipation of the Negroes.

How did we pass the time while in America? We supervised our work, stood watch, read a great deal, and made rather stupid trips ashore one after another. On shore leave, arriving at a new place, we usually went to see what was worth while. We visited restaurants and lounged about, eating and occasionally drinking. There were no great revels among us, but an extra quantity of wine came somehow to be consumed rather often. On such occasions I did not lag behind the others, although I was never among the leaders in this respect. Once, I remember, our whole midshipmen's wardroom sat down to write letters. Somebody ordered a bottle of wine; it was immediately emptied " for inspiration "; then followed another, and a third; the letters were forgotten and soon the whole company went ashore, where the carousal continued. Occasionally such drinking-bouts wound up by visits to street women — how base and dirty!

In New York I heard rather poor performances of Meyerbeer's

47

Robert le Diable and Gounod's *Faust.*[9] I had entirely given up
music, save for playing the harmoniflute every now and then to
entertain the midshipmen's wardroom or duets on this instrument
with the violin played by the American pilot, Mr. Thompson. He
and I played various national American anthems and songs; to his
great amazement, I immediately played by ear the accompaniments to tunes I had heard for the first time.

By April 1864 it became known that there would be no war with
England and that our squadron would be sent on another mission.
Indeed, our clipper soon received orders to sail to the Pacific round
Cape Horn, so that a voyage round the world awaited us — two or
three more years of navigation. The corvette *Varyag* had received
similar orders; the other ships were to return to Europe. For some
reason, Captain Zelyony was most reluctant to go round the world.
But I received the news with joy rather than otherwise. By that
time I had grown almost unaccustomed to music. Letters from
Balakirev came rarely, since I, too, wrote him but rarely. Thoughts
of becoming a musician and composer gradually left me altogether;
distant lands began to allure me, somehow, although, properly
speaking, naval service never pleased me much and hardly suited
my character at all.

In April our clipper left New York to proceed to Cape Horn.
Ships sailing at this season of the year from the United States to
Cape Horn usually turn east to Europe, taking advantage of the
prevailing western winds; then, a short distance from the Azores,
they go south and, catching the favourable northeast trades, cross
the equator as far as possible from the American coast, that the

---

[9] According to George C. D. Odell's *Annals of the New York Stage*, pp. 581 ff. of
Vol. VII (1857–65), *Faust* was heard for the first time in New York at the Academy
of Music on November 25, 1863, with the great Clara Louise Kellogg as Margherita,
Mlle Sulzer as Siebel, Fanny Stockton as Martha, Mazzolein as Faust, Biachi as
Mephistopheles, Ypsolito (sic!) as Valentino, Colletti as Wagner. Though it had a
lukewarm critical reception at first, it became a popular success later on and enjoyed
its thirty-second performance on April 20, 1864, for the benefit of Bellini.
    On April 1, 1864 *Roberto il Diabolo* was first sung by Medore Laura Harris, the
famous Brignoli, Lotti, Herrmanns (basso of the German company earlier in the season), and danced by Mlle Ernestine, later in the season a highly attractive feature of
Barnum's " lecture " room.
    The above data show conclusively that Rimsky-Korsakov must have heard the
performances in question during the month of April 1864. J. A. J.

southeast trades of the Southern Hemisphere may by their direction prove the more advantageous for reaching Rio de Janeiro or Montevideo, where ships usually call before rounding Cape Horn. We, too, did this. Our voyage from New York to Rio was made under sail in sixty-five days. The length of the voyage was due, in the first place, to the fact that the clipper *Almaz* proved insufficiently fast in spite of our twice refitting its masts; secondly, because Captain Zelyony was a somewhat timid seaman and distrustful man. He had no faith at all in his officers of the watch and his first lieutenant, L. V. Mikhaylov. He obliged them to carry small sails, which were taken in at the slightest blow of wind. While merchantmen we met were under full sail, we never ventured to imitate them, but crept slowly along. During the voyage Zelyony spent all day on deck in personal command of the vessel and dozed at night in his clothes, sitting on the steps of his cabin ready to rush at the first noise and take over the command. Owing to such distrust, the officers of the watch lost their independence and referred every trifle to the commander, who used to berate them at their slightest failure and humiliate them before the crew. He was disliked by both officers and midshipmen for his habits of rudeness and distrust; he was disliked also because they felt it was impossible to gain experience under his direction. On Sundays, having first assembled the whole crew before the ikon, Zelyony usually recited prayers himself and then, on the upper deck, read the navy laws and regulations which proclaimed his unlimited power over the crew. He disliked flogging the crew, and for this one must give him credit; but he was too free with his hands and was given to coarse and indecent language.[10]

But let me leave those impressions of the voyage which concern only naval service, naval art and people, of which enough has already been said, and let me turn to my impressions of the cruise as a voyage in the narrower sense of the word. Those were impressions of an entirely different kind.

At first our cruise was of the same rough nature as our passage

---

[10] For Rimsky-Korsakov's characterization of Captain Zelyony, cf. Rimsky-Korsakov's letters to Balakirev in A. N. Rimsky-Korsakov's *N. A. Rimsky-Korsakov*, Part I, Chapter ii: " Trial by Sea."

from Russia to New York had been. Fresh and stormy winds accompanied us on our way to the coast of Europe, although this time the Atlantic was less treacherous, owing to the coming of the spring season. Soon after our southerly turn (not far from the Azores) the weather began to improve, the sky to grow more and more azure, ever more warmth was wafted through the air; finally we entered the zone of the northeastern trade winds and soon crossed the Tropic of Cancer. Wonderful weather, an even warm wind, a gently agitated sea, a dark-azure sky with white dappled clouds, did not change during our entire passage through the blessed zone of the trades. Wonderful days and wonderful nights! The marvellous dark-azure colour of the sky by day would be replaced by a fantastic phosphorescent light at night. As we went farther south the twilight grew shorter and shorter, while the southern sky with the new constellations was disclosed more and more. What radiance of the Milky Way, with the constellation of the Southern Cross, what a wonderful star Canopus (in the constellation Argo), the stars of the Centaur, the brightly blazing red Antares (in the Scorpion), visible in Russia as a pale star on bright summer nights! Sirius, known to us from winter nights, looked here twice as large and bright. Soon all the stars of both hemispheres became visible. The Great Dipper hung low just above the horizon, while the Southern Cross rose higher and higher. The light of the full moon dipping in and out among the heaping clouds was simply dazzling. Wonderful is the tropical ocean with its azure colour and phosphorescent light, wonderful are the tropical sun and clouds, but the tropical night sky over the ocean is the most wonderful thing in the world.

As we approached the equator, the difference in temperature between day and night steadily diminished; 86°F. (in the shade, of course) by day, 84°F. at night; the temperature of the water also 86°F. or 84°F. I did not feel the heat. The magnificent trade wind gives one a sensation somehow of warm coolness. To be sure, it was stifling in the cabins at night; that is why I liked night watch, when one could breathe wonderful air and admire the sky and sea. Owing to the danger from sharks, we doused one another several times a day instead of bathing in the sea. Once for a long time we watched a shark swimming behind our ship. We tried to catch it, but did not succeed, somehow. We often saw whales spouting; flying fish were visible on both sides of the ship from morning till night. One of them even flew up and tumbled on deck. We made a two- or three-day call at Porto Grande on the Cape Verde Islands. A desert and stony island with wretched, scorched vegetation, and a small town with only a coal supply, gave us nevertheless a certain degree of diversion: we had a ride on donkeys, which the Negro boys who guided them mercilessly prodded and beat with clubs. Having taken on a supply of provisions and coal, the clipper started for Rio de Janeiro. We crossed the calm zone under sail. Hot weather, a cloudy sky, frequent rain-squalls, attended our passage through this zone. Gloomy waterspouts in the shape of funnels joining clouds and sea were frequently visible on the horizon. The crossing of the equator was signalized by the usual festival of the Procession of Neptune and water-dousings — a festival described in almost every book of travels.

Having crossed the calm zone, we met with southeastern trades, and wonderful tropical weather returned. The nearer we came to the Tropic of Capricorn, the lower and lower the Great Dipper sank (the Polar star had vanished long before), and the Southern Cross shone higher and higher. About June 10 the Brazilian coast came into view; the rock called the Sugar Loaf indicated the entrance to the bay of Rio de Janeiro, and soon we anchored in the roadstead of Rio de Janeiro itself.

What a striking place! The bay, shut in on all sides, but spacious, is surrounded by green-clad mountains topped by Corcovado, at whose foot the city lies stretched. It was June — the winter month of the Southern Hemisphere. But what a wonderful winter under the Tropic of Capricorn! 77°F. or so in the shade in the daytime, 63.5°–66°F. at night; frequent thunder-storms, but generally clear and mild weather. The water in the bay was green-blue by day and phosphorescent at night, the shores and mountains a gorgeous green. The city and the docks teemed with Negroes of every possible shade, from brown to glossy black, some in shirts, some half-naked; the Brazilians dressed in black coats and top-hats. The market was filled with endless quantities of oranges, China oranges, and wonderful bananas, as well as monkeys and parrots. The New World, the Southern Hemisphere, a tropical winter in June! Everything was different, not the same as with us in Russia.

I roamed about a good deal with my comrades, especially with I. P. Andreyev, in the environs of Rio, in the woods and mountains, taking tramps of twenty to twenty-five miles a day and enjoying the beauties of nature and the magnificent sights. Several times I went to the Tijuca Waterfalls, and climbed the mountains, Corcovado and Govia. Once our party lost its way and had to stay overnight in the woods, but that was not dangerous, as there are no wild beasts in the environs of the city. I also enjoyed visiting the botanical garden, with its marvellous alley of royal palms, tall and straight as columns. I found pleasure in looking at the wonderful and varied trees of the garden. In addition to the native flora, Asiatic plants grew there too, like the clove tree, the cinnamon tree, the camphor laurel, and others. Tiny humming-birds and huge butterflies flew about by day, while in the evening gleaming insects flitted in the air.

Two or three days we spent at the Brazilian Emperor's residence, Petropolis, a small town in the mountains. There we made a splendid trip to the Imatoreti Waterfalls, in the surrounding woods of which remarkably tall tree-like ferns grew. Nor can I forget the marvellous long and sombre bamboo alley near Rio, which looked like a Gothic arch formed by the touching tops of the bamboo trees. All together we stayed in Rio de Janeiro nearly four months, for the following reason: After a two weeks' stay we had bidden farewell to Rio and had gone southward towards Cape Horn. In the latitude of St. Catherine's Island a strong pamperos blew up; that is the name of the storms which frequently burst forth near the banks of the Rio de la Plata. The wind was very strong, the sea waves rose huge — but, for some reason, this time the captain kept the clipper under steam. The screw laid bare with each rising of the stern caused a tremendous vibration; soon it turned out that the vessel had sprung a bad leak. It was impossible to proceed; we had to re-

turn to Rio de Janeiro and dock for repairs. A report was forwarded
to Russia that the clipper was unseaworthy for a long voyage round
the world. The report contained a good many exaggerations; thus,
in describing the pamperos, it said that the ship's deck had been
rippling like piano keys. One way or another, repairs were a necessity. The repairs took time, and the report had been sent. The work
of repairing kept us at Rio until October — that is, until orders came
from Russia for us to give up the idea of a voyage round the world
(to the captain's delight, be it said) and return to Europe.

Having finished the work of patching up the leak, and before the
final order to leave for Europe had been received, our clipper went
for a few days' artillery practice from Rio de Janeiro to the small
island Ilha Grande, situated not far south of Rio. At Ilha Grande
we stayed five or six days. It is a mountainous little island, covered
with a thick tropical forest. There are sugar and coffee plantations
at one end of it. We walked a great deal in its wonderful woods.
Soon after our return to Rio de Janeiro from Ilha Grande the orders
arrived. By now it was October: the summer was beginning and the
heat increasing. Somewhat regretfully, I left Rio, with its wonderful natural beauties.

Our clipper headed for Cadiz, where we were to await further
instructions. Our return voyage to the Northern Hemisphere was
made in some sixty or sixty-five days. Once more came the wonderful zones of the trade winds, but in reverse order — the appearance
of the stars of the Northern Hemisphere and the disappearance of
the Southern constellations. Somewhere this side of the equator it
was our good fortune to witness, two nights in succession, an extraordinary phosphorescence of the ocean. Probably we had got into the
so-called Sargasso Sea, a region abounding in seaweed and mol-
luscs, which lend special force to the phosphorescence of the water.
A rather powerful trade was blowing and the ocean was rough. The
whole sea surface from the ship to the horizon was flooded with
phosphorescent light, which cast its reflection on the sails. Whoever
has not seen it cannot imagine so beautiful a sight. On the third
night the phosphorescence of the water diminished and the ocean
assumed its nocturnal aspect. We reached Cadiz early in Decem-

ber, I believe. Having remained there some three days, we made, according to instructions, for the Mediterranean Sea. There we were to join, at Villafranca, Lesovsky's squadron, detailed to the now deceased Tsarevich Nikolay Aleksandrovich, who was ill and spending the winter in Nice. On our way we called at Gibraltar, where we went to see the famous rock and fortifications; we also put in at Port Mahon on the island of Minorca. To tropical warmth we had long bidden farewell; still, the weather was fine, though cool. The same weather greeted us also at Villafranca, which we reached towards the end of December.

At Villafranca we found and joined Lesovsky's squadron. Our stay at Villafranca was varied by short trips to Toulon, Genoa, and Spezia. When in Toulon, I visited Marseille, and from Genoa I went to the famous Villa Pallavicini. A pleasant walk to Nice was my usual pastime on days free from duty. I also took walks to the mountains with I. P. Andreyev. Beautiful stony mountains, olive and orange groves, and a magnificent sea made a charming impression on me. I managed also to visit the notorious Monaco, where a steamer called *Bulldog* used to run in from Villafranca; it had a reputation for its unusually disagreeable rolling, so that I, who had grown accustomed to ocean rolling, became seasick on the trip to Monaco. I tried my hand at roulette, but having lost several gold pieces, stopped, as I had not developed any taste for the game. There was an Italian opera at Nice at the time, but I did not attend it. During my trips ashore with my comrades, who were fond of music, I often played on the piano Gounod's *Faust*, which I had heard in New York. Just then *Faust* was beginning to be popular. I procured a piano score somewhere. My audience were in raptures; truth to tell, I liked it myself a good deal then.

My comrades and I were then already advanced to be midshipmen (that is, real officers) and admitted to the officers' wardroom.

In April the Tsarevich died. His body was transferred with great ceremony to the frigate *Aleksandr Nevsky,* and our entire squadron started for Russia. We called at Plymouth and Christiansand. In Norway it was warm in April and everything was in full leaf. From Christiansand I went to see a beautiful waterfall whose name I don't remember. As we were nearing the Gulf of Finland, the weather kept getting colder and colder; we even met with icebergs in the gulf. In the latter part of April we cast anchor in the Kronstadt roadstead.

My sailing in foreign lands was over.[11] Many ineffaceable memories of the wonderful beauties of nature in distant lands and the distant ocean, many mean, coarse, and repulsive impressions of naval service I brought back with me from the voyage, which had lasted two years and eight months. And what of my music? Music had been wholly forgotten, and my inclination towards artistic activity had been stifled; so stifled that, after having gone to see my mother, my brother's family, and Balakirev, all of whom soon left St. Petersburg for the summer season, I did not concern myself with music at all, though I spent the summer in Kronstadt looking after the dismantling of the clipper, and lodging with an officer friend, K. E. Zambrzhitsky, who had a piano. I cannot consider as work the playing of sonatas for the piano and violin. The latter was played by amateurs, naval friends of mine, who visited me from time to time. I myself became an officer amateur, who was not averse to playing or hearing music; but my dreams of artistic activity had entirely faded, and I felt no sorrow over the dreams that were gone.[12]

---

[11] For the comprehension of Rimsky-Korsakov's psychology during the period of his distant voyage across the high seas, the first thirty-five letters of his correspondence with Balakirev are of the greatest importance. Echoes of experiences (occasionally bitter) connected with the views that his relatives held on music and naval service may be found in Rimsky-Korsakov's still unpublished voluminous correspondence with his mother and brother. Cf. A. N. Rimsky-Korsakov's *N. A. Rimsky-Korsakov*, Part I, Chapter ii: "Trial by Sea." Rimsky-Korsakov's correspondence with his mother was utilized here in part.

[12] Written in February and March 1893.

1865-66

Return to music. Acquaintance with Borodin. My first symphony.
Balakirev and the members of his circle. The performance of the
First Symphony. The musical life of the circle. Overture on Russian
themes. My first song.

IN SEPTEMBER 1865, when the dismantling of the clipper *Almaz* was ended, I was transferred to St. Petersburg with a portion of the first naval crew, of which our clipper's company formed a part, and then began my life ashore and in St. Petersburg.

My brother with his family and my mother returned to St. Petersburg after the summer. My musical friends, Balakirev, Cui, and Moussorgsky, also arrived. I began to visit Balakirev and again commenced first to get accustomed to music and later to plunge into it. Much water had run under the bridge while I was abroad, much that was new had come into the world of music. The Free Music School [1] had been established; Balakirev and G. Y. Lomakin had become joint conductors of its concerts. On the stage of the Mariinsky Theatre *Judith* [2] had been produced,[3] and its author, Serov, had

---

[1] Opened March 18 [30], 1862.

[2] The book of this opera is founded on Giustiniani's *Giuditta*, which Serov and his librettist had seen Ristori perform. The style of the music is said to recall *Tannhäuser* and *Lohengrin*. When Wagner visited St. Petersburg in March 1863 Serov submitted the score to him, and the German composer is said to have expressed his approval of the orchestration. C. V. V.

[3] The first performance took place May 16 [28], 1863.

made a name for himself as a composer. Richard Wagner had come at the invitation of the Philharmonic Society, had made the music world of St. Petersburg acquainted with his works, and the orchestra had given model performances under his direction.[4] After Wagner's example, all conductors have since turned their backs to the audience and faced the orchestra, in order to have it under their eyes.

During my first visits to Balakirev's I heard that a new member, of great promise, had made his appearance in the circle. He was A. P. Borodin.[5] When I moved to St. Petersburg, he was not there, as he had not returned to town after the summer. Balakirev played me fragments of the first movement of his Symphony in E-flat major, which astonished rather than pleased me. Soon Borodin came; I was introduced to him, and our friendship dated from that time, although he was some ten years older than I.[6] I was introduced to his wife, Yekaterina Sergeyevna. Borodin was already professor of chemistry at the Medical Academy then, and lived near the Liteyny Bridge in the academy building. He remained until his death in the same apartment. Borodin liked my symphony, which Balakirev and Moussorgsky played four-hands. Though he had not finished the first movement of his Symphony in E-flat major, he already had material for the other movements, which he had composed abroad during the summer. I was delighted with these fragments, having now fully grasped the first movement, which had merely astonished me on first hearing. I became a frequent visitor at Borodin's, often staying overnight as well. We discussed music a great deal; he played his projected works and showed me the sketches of the symphony. He was better informed than I on the practical side of orchestration, as he played the cello, oboe, and flute. Borodin was an exceedingly cordial and cultured man, pleasant and oddly witty to talk with. On visiting him I often found him working in the laboratory which adjoined his apartment. When he sat over his retorts filled with some colourless gas and distilled it

---

[4] In February 1863.
[5] Borodin's first meeting with Balakirev occurred in the fall of 1862.
[6] A. P. Borodin was born on October 31 [November 12], 1834.

by means of a tube from one vessel into another, I used to tell him that he was "transfusing emptiness into vacancy." [7] Having finished his work, he would go with me to his apartment, where we began musical operations or conversations, in the midst of which he used to jump up, run back to the laboratory to see whether something had not burned out or boiled over; meanwhile he filled the corridor with incredible sequences from successions of ninths or sevenths. Then he would come back, and we proceeded with the music or the interrupted conversation. Yekaterina Sergeyevna was a charming, cultured woman, an excellent pianist, and she worshipped her husband's talent.

Our company, now transferred to St. Petersburg, was quartered in the Galernaya Gavan, in the so-called Dyeryabin house. I lived in a furnished room on the 15th Line of the Vasilevsky Ostrov,[8] with a printer or compositor of some sort. For dinner I used to go to my brother's at the Naval School. I could not live with my people at the time, as the Director's apartment, large though it was, had no spare room. My duties did not keep me very busy. Every morning I had to spend two or three hours at the office in the Dyeryabin house, where I had charge of correspondence, scribbled all manner of reports and statements which began: "I have the honour to report to Your Excellency" or "Enclosing herewith a copy, I beg to," and so on.

I visited Balakirev very often. Coming in the evening, I occasionally remained overnight. My visits to Borodin I have already described. I also visited Cui. Not infrequently our musical company — Balakirev, Cui, Moussorgsky, Borodin, V. V. Stassov, and others — gathered at the house of one of the above three, and a great deal of four-hand playing was done. Urged on by Balakirev, I turned once more to my own symphony; for the Scherzo I wrote the trio, which until then had been lacking; [9] again, at his sugges-

[7] The Russian expression for "chewing the rag" or the useless work of the Danaïdes. J. A. J.

[8] On the Vasilevsky Ostrov (Vasilevsky Island) every street consists of two *Lines,* the right side of the street (reckoned from the Great Neva) being denoted by even numbers (Line 2, 4, etc.), the left side by odd numbers. C. V. V.

[9] The trio was composed in October 1865.

C. A. CUI

from the drawing by I. Y. Ryepin

tion, I re-orchestrated the whole symphony and made a clean copy of it. Balakirev, then conducting with G. Y. Lomakin the concerts of the Free Music School, decided to produce it and ordered the orchestral parts to be copied. But what a terrible score it was! Of this, however, later; I shall say only that though I had picked up all sorts of smatterings, I did not know the A B C of theory at the time. Nevertheless the Symphony in E-flat minor was in existence and marked for performance. The concert was announced for December 18 in the hall of the Town Council and was preceded by two rehearsals — the usual number in those days. The conductor's art was then a mystery to me, and I looked with awe upon Balakirev, who was of the initiated. His going to the chorus rehearsals of the school and the stories about these rehearsals, about Lomakin, about various things musical and various prominent musical folk of St. Petersburg, all this was full of mysterious fascination for me. I realized that I was a mere boy who had composed something, but that I was also an insignificant ignorant naval officer who could not even play decently. And there, on the other hand, were the stories about this and that having to do with music, about these or other " real " workers, and with all this Balakirev, who knew everything and was respected by everybody as a real musician. Cui had already entered upon his activities as critic [10] on the St. Petersburg *Vyedomosti* (Korsh's) and hence, besides the love for his compositions, he, too, compelled involuntary admiration as a real worker in the field of art. As for Moussorgsky and Borodin, I regarded them as comrades rather than teachers like Balakirev and Cui. Borodin's compositions had not been performed as yet, and his first considerable work, the Symphony in E-flat major, had just been begun; in orchestration he was as inexperienced as I, although he knew the instruments better than I did, after all. As for Moussorgsky, even though a fine pianist and excellent singer (true, no longer in such good voice as formerly) and though, of his smaller pieces, a Scherzo in B-flat major and the chorus from *Œdipus* had already had public

---

[10] From the beginning he spared no effort in his endeavour to suppress the vogue of Italian opera, and to elevate Russian opera to a state of favour. C. V. V.

performances under Anton Rubinstein,[11] he yet had little knowledge of orchestration, as his compositions performed in public had gone through Balakirev's hands. On the other hand, music was not his specialty and he gave himself over to it only in his leisure hours; his real service lay in one of the ministries.[12] By the way, Borodin told me that he recalled Moussorgsky still as a very young man. Borodin was on duty as physician in a military hospital and Moussorgsky was officer on duty in the same hospital, still serving in the Guards then. There it was they had met. Soon after that, Borodin met him again at the house of friends of both, and Moussorgsky, a stripling of an officer, speaking French magnificently, was entertaining the ladies by playing something from *Il Trovatore*. What times![13] I shall observe that, in the sixties, Balakirev and Cui, though very intimate with Moussorgsky and sincerely fond of him, treated him like a lesser light, and of little promise at that, in spite of his undoubted talent. It seemed to them that there was something missing in him and, in their eyes, he was in need of advice and criticism. Balakirev often said that Moussorgsky had "no head" or that his "brains were weak."[14] Meanwhile the following relations had established themselves between Cui and Balakirev: Balakirev thought that Cui understood little in symphony and musical forms and nothing in orchestration, but was a past master in vocal and operatic music; Cui, in turn, thought Balakirev a master in symphony, form, and orchestration, but with little liking for operatic composition and vocal music in general. Thus they complemented each other, but each, in his own way, felt mature and grown up. Borodin, Moussorgsky, and I, however — we were immature and *juvenile*. Obviously, towards Balakirev and Cui we were in somewhat subordinate relations; their opinions were listened to unconditionally; we "smoked them in our pipes" and accepted them.

---

[11] The Scherzo in B-flat major under A. G. Rubinstein's direction, at the Russian Musical Society's concert of January 11 [23], 1860; the chorus from Œdipus under K. N. Lyadov's direction, at the concert of April 6 [18], 1861, at the Mariinsky Theatre.

[12] Moussorgsky served at that time in the Forestry Department.

[13] Cf. *A. P. Borodin, His Life, Correspondence, and Musical Articles* (St. Petersburg, 1889), p. 13.

[14] Cf. *Correspondence between Balakirev and Stassov*, pp. 173 and 183.

Balakirev and Cui, on the other hand, really did not need our opinions. Accordingly, the relations of Borodin, Moussorgsky, and me were those of comrades; but towards Balakirev and Cui we were in the position of pupils. Moreover, I have already mentioned how I worshipped Balakirev and considered him my alpha and omega.

After successful rehearsals, at which the musicians looked at me with curiosity, since I wore a naval coat, the concert itself took place. The program consisted of Mozart's *Requiem* and my symphony. The Myelnikov brothers were among the soloists singing in the *Requiem*. I think I. A. Myelnikov made his début then. The symphony went off well. I was called out, and surprised the audience considerably with my officer's uniform. Many people came to be introduced and congratulated me. Of course I was happy. I deem it necessary to mention that I felt almost no nervousness before the concert, and that scant disposition towards nervousness as composer has remained with me all my life. It seems to me the press spoke favourably of my work, though not over-favourably; and Cui wrote a very sympathetic article in the *Peterburgskiya Vyedomosti* (*St. Petersburg Gazette*) referring to me as the *first* to compose a Russian symphony (Rubinstein did not count!),[15] and I accepted it on faith that I was the first in the succession of Russian symphonic composers.[16]

Shortly after the performance of my symphony a dinner of the members of the Free Music School took place to which I, too, was invited. Various speeches were made and my health was drunk.

In the spring of 1866 my symphony was performed again, but this time not under Balakirev. During Lent, when there were no performances at the theatres, the Board of Directors used to give symphony concerts; originally they had been directed by Karl Schubert, as I have already mentioned, and after his death they were entrusted to the opera conductor K. N. Lyadov. The Board of Directors of the Theatres wished to perform my symphony also. How it happened I cannot explain. Probably it was not arranged without

---

[15] Cf. the St. Petersburg *Vyedomosti*, 1865, No. 340. Reprinted in C. Cui's *Musico-critical Articles* (Petrograd, 1918), Vol. I, p. 339.
[16] Written at Yalta (Crimea) on June 22 [July 4], 1893.

Balakirev's influence on Kologrivov, then supervisor of musicians at the Imperial theatres. I delivered the score to the Board, and my symphony was played under Lyadov's leadership, with some success. I was not invited to the rehearsals. Evidently both Lyadov and the Board cared little for me. I was not particularly pleased with the performance, although I recall it was not at all bad.[17] But, in the first place, I felt offended at not having been invited to the rehearsals; secondly, could I possibly be satisfied with Lyadov, when I had an only god — Balakirev? Moreover, Lyadov as conductor enjoyed scant favour in Balakirev's circle, as did all conductors save Balakirev himself. In his articles Cui often ranked Balakirev the conductor with Wagner and Berlioz. In passing, I shall say that at that time Cui had not heard Berlioz as yet. Balakirev himself doubtless believed in his own superiority and power and, to tell the truth, in those days we knew only him, Anton Rubinstein, and Lyadov among conductors. In this respect Rubinstein was in bad repute and Lyadov was on the down-path owing to loose living. Karl Schubert was remembered rather pleasantly; as to foreign conductors we did not know them except Wagner, who was considered a genius in that respect. And so Balakirev was ranked with him and Berlioz, whom only Stassov remembered. Although I had heard neither Wagner nor Berlioz, I accepted this judgment. Accordingly, I was bound to be dissatisfied with the performance of my symphony at the Board's symphony concert. Still, as I remember, there were calls for me.

How the spring of 1866 passed I cannot recall; all I know is that I composed nothing, but cannot explain why. It must have been because composition was then difficult for me through lack of technique; then, too, by nature I was not industrious. Balakirev did not rush me, did not urge me to work; his own time went senselessly, somehow. I often spent my evenings with him. As I recall, he was then harmonizing the Russian folksongs collected by him, was tinkering a great deal with them and making many changes. I

---

[17] Cf. C. Cui's review in the St. Petersburg *Vyedomosti*, 1866, No. 82: "The mutilation of the symphony was complete, its character was distorted, its delightful music was deformed. . . ."

gained a thorough knowledge of the song material collected by him and his method of harmonizing it. Balakirev had at that time a large stock of Oriental melodies and dances, memorized during his trip to the Caucasus. He often played them for me and others, in his own most delightful harmonizations and arrangements. My acquaintance with Russian and Oriental songs at the time marked the origin of my love for folk-music, to which I devoted myself subsequently. As I also recall, Balakirev had the germs of his Symphony in C major. Nearly one third of the first movement of the symphony had already been written in orchestral form. Besides, there were sketches for the Scherzo and also for the Finale on a Russian theme: *Sharlatarla from Partarla,* which I gave him as my uncle Pyotr Petrovich had sung it to me.[18] The second subject in the Finale was to be the song *A my proso syeyali* (And we were planting millet) in B minor, approximately as it appeared in his collection of forty songs.

As for the Scherzo, Balakirev once improvised its beginning in my presence:

Subsequently, however, he substituted another for it. The first movement of his Piano Concerto was ready and orchestrated; there were wonderful designs for the Adagio and the following theme for the Finale:

Then, in the middle of the Finale, there was to appear the church theme: " *Se zhenikh gryadyet* (Lo, the bridegroom cometh)," and the piano was to accompany it with an imitation of bell-ringing. In

---

18 Cf. " Correspondence between Balakirev and Rimsky-Korsakov," Letter IX.

addition he had the beginnings of an octet or nonet with piano in
F major; the first movement with the theme:

also a charming Scherzo. He was already somewhat cool towards
the opera *Zhar Ptitsa* (*Firebird*) which he had conceived; but he
played many splendid fragments, based mostly on Oriental themes.
The lions guarding the golden apples and the flight of the firebird
were magnificent. I also recall some chants and the service of the
fire-worshippers on a Persian theme:

Cui was then composing *William Ratcliff;* if I am not mistaken,
the scene at the Black Stone and Maria's aria were already in existence. Moussorgsky was busy writing an opera on a libretto taken
from *Salammbô*.[19] Occasionally he played fragments of it at Balakirev's and Cui's. These fragments called forth the highest approval
for the beauty of their themes and ideas as well as the severest
censure for disorderliness and absurdity. Mme Cui,[20] I remember,
could not stand a noisy and absurd storm in this opera. Borodin
went on with his symphony and used to bring portions of the score
to be looked over.

What I have described above constituted my staple musical food
at that time. I constantly spent my evenings at Balakirev's and
visited Cui and Borodin pretty often. But, as stated above, I com-

---

[19] Moussorgsky began this work in 1863, writing his own libretto, in which, as was
customary with him, he gave the chorus a conspicuous rôle, too conspicuous, perhaps,
considering the nature of the subject. He completed, in the course of time, one scene
of the second act and one in both the third and fourth acts, and then he put the work
aside, and did not return to it except for the purpose of drawing various numbers
from it which were transferred to his later works. C. V. V.
    The composition of the unfinished opera *Salammbô* lasted from the end of 1863
until the beginning of 1866. Cf. V. Karatygin: List of M. P. Moussorgsky's Compositions, *Musical Contemporary*, 1915–16, Nos. 5–6.
    [20] Malvina Rafayilovna Cui (née Bamberg).

posed little or nothing during the spring of 1866 and, towards summer, conceived the idea of writing an overture on Russian themes. Of course, Balakirev's overture *1000 Years* and the Overture in B minor were my ideals. I chose the themes: *Slava* (Gloria), *Oo vorot vorot* (At the gates, the gates), and *Na Ivanushkye chapan* (Ivan has a big coat on). Balakirev did not fully approve the choice of the last two, finding them somewhat similar; but, for some reason, I persisted in my view — evidently because I had succeeded in writing certain variations on both of these themes and some tricks of harmony, and I was reluctant to part with what had been begun.

I spent the summer of 1866 mostly in St. Petersburg, save one month, when I went on the yacht *Volna* for a sail in the Finnish skerries. On my return from this brief trip, I composed the projected overture, and its score was ready towards the end of the summer.[21] I cannot recall where Balakirev spent that summer — most likely at Klin, with his father. After he had come back in the autumn, he frequently played two Oriental themes, subsequently utilized by him for his piano fantasy *Islamey*. The first D-flat-major theme he had learned in the Caucasus; the other, in D major, he had possibly heard that summer in Moscow from some singer — Nikolayev, I think. Along with these he began to play more and more frequently the themes of his orchestral fantasy *Tamara*. For the first subject of the Allegro he took a melody which we had heard together while visiting the barracks of His Majesty's bodyguard in Shpalyernaya Street. I vividly recall the men, Orientals, making music on a balalaika-shaped or guitar-like instrument. Besides they sang in chorus the melody of Glinka's *Persian Chorus,* though a variation of it:

---

[21] The *Overture on Russian Themes* was composed during the interval between February and June 1866. The autograph manuscript of its orchestral score is inscribed: " Pityer [familiar for St. Petersburg, like our Frisco for San Francisco. J. A. J.], June 10 [22], 1866. But the practice sail took place during July and August 1866.

In 1866–7 a considerable part of *Tamara* was improvised by him and was often played for me and others. Soon *Islamey*, too, began to take form little by little. The Symphony in C major had not progressed, nor had any of the other beginnings.

Among the pieces of non-Russian music looked over in Balakirev's circle and played particularly for us, Liszt's compositions, principally his *Mephisto Waltz* and *Todtentanz*, figured more and more frequently after the beginning of the year. To the best of my recollection, the *Todtentanz* was played for the first time by Gerke, professor of the Conservatory, at the Russian Musical Society's concert conducted by Rubinstein in 1865 or 1866.[22] Balakirev used to relate with horror Rubinstein's opinion of this piece. Rubinstein had likened this music to a disorderly trampling of the piano keys or to something like it. Subsequently Rubinstein, though not fond of Liszt, came to have a different opinion of this work. I recall that the *Todtentanz* struck me rather unpleasantly at first, but soon I fathomed it. On the other hand, the *Mephisto Waltz* pleased me infinitely. I purchased its score and even learned to play it passably in my own arrangement. In general, I applied myself that year quite zealously to piano-playing, alone in my room. I think I lived then on 10th Line in a furnished room, at a rental of some ten rubles a month. I diligently conned Czerny's *Tägliche Studien*, played scales in thirds and octaves, studied even Chopin études. These studies were carried on without the knowledge of Balakirev, who never suggested to me work at the piano — though how necessary that was! Balakirev had long given me up as a pianist; usually he played my compositions himself. If occasionally he sat down to play four-hands with me, he would quit playing at my first embarrassment, saying he would rather play it afterwards with Moussorgsky. In general, he made me feel uncomfortable, and in his presence I usually played worse than I really knew how. I shall not thank him for that. I felt that I was making progress in my playing, after all — working rather hard at home. But I was afraid to play before Balakirev, and he was utterly unaware of my progress; moreover, I was rated " without capacity for playing " by others as well,

---

[22] At the concert of the Russian Musical Society on March 3 [18], 1866.

especially by Cui. Oh, those were wretched times! The circle often made fun of Borodin and me for our pianistic achievements, and therefore we, too, lost faith in ourselves. But in those days I had not yet become wholly disillusioned and was striving to learn things on the sly. It is singular that in my brother's house and at the houses of other people outside of Balakirev's circle, they thought me a good player, used to ask me to play for the ladies and visitors, and so on. I played. Many went into ecstasies from lack of understanding. The result was a sort of silly deception.

My service gave me little to do. I was transferred to the Eighth Naval Company, quartered in St. Petersburg. My duties consisted in attendance for the day on the company and the Naval Department's stores, called New Holland. Occasionally I was assigned to sentry duty at the prison. My musical life began to cleave: in one half, in Balakirev's circle, I was considered a man of talent for composing, a poor pianist or none at all, an amiable and short-witted stripling of an officer; in the other half, among my acquaintances and the relatives of Voyin Andreyevich, I was a naval officer, an amateur, a *splendid* pianist, a connoisseur of serious music, composing something by the way. On Sunday evenings when young folks, relatives of his wife, would gather at my brother's house, I used to play, for their dances, quadrilles of my own manufacture from *La Belle Hélène* or *Marta,* and occasionally, during the intermissions, would turn pianist, playing with excellent touch some excerpts from operas. At P. N. Novikova's house I astonished them with my skill, playing the *Mephisto Waltz.* At the house of my brother's friend, P. I. Vyelichkovsky, I played four-hands with his daughters. Vyelichkovsky played the cello, violinist friends of his also came to the house, and I arranged the *Kamarinskaya* and *A Night in Madrid* for violin, viola, cello, and piano for four hands and we played these. Balakirev and his circle had no idea of all these exploits; I carefully concealed from them these dilettante activities of mine.

Balakirev was not pleased with my overture, but, having made some corrections and suggestions, he nevertheless decided to perform it at a concert of the Free School. The concert took place on December 11 [23], 1866. Together with my overture there was also

67

performed the *Mephisto Waltz*. I remember G. Y. Lomakin, listening to the waltz at the rehearsals, half-closing his eyes as if for pleasure, and telling me: " How Mikhail Ivanovich [Glinka] loved such music! " What was meant by *such* music? Probably " sensuous, voluptuous," Lomakin meant to say. The *Mephisto Waltz* delighted the whole circle, and me, of course. Balakirev felt himself conclusively a conductor of genius; the whole circle, too, thought likewise. My overture went off well and pleased more or less. I was called out. I recall that it sounded rather colourful and the percussion instruments had been distributed by me with taste. I don't remember the press notices of this performance.[23]

In December 1866, I think, I wrote my first song: *Shchekoyu k shchekye ty moyey prilozhis'* (*Lay Thy Cheek against My Cheek*), to Heine's text.[24] Why I conceived the idea of writing it I don't remember. Most likely from a desire to imitate Balakirev, whose songs I admired. Balakirev approved it, but finding the accompaniment insufficiently pianistic (quite to be expected from me, who was no pianist), he recast it entirely and rewrote it in his own hand. With this accompaniment my song was subsequently published.

----

[23] " This Overture is a charming, well-constructed work, though it ranks somewhat below last year's Symphony as regards originality and force. . . . Its instrumentation is excellent: Mr. Korsakov's gift for instrumentation is evidently developing; there are many very important effects in his instrumentation." C. Cui: Musical Notices, in St. Petersburg *Vyedomosti*, 1866, No. 339.

[24] Inexact: the song *Lay Thy Cheek against My Cheek*, published by M. Bernard along with three others, was licensed for publication by the censor on May 13 [25], 1866 (cf. printed edition). Thus the time of composing this first song, as well as of Rimsky-Korsakov's first acquaintance with L. I. Shestakova and with S. I. Zotova (described on pp. 71 f.) and the composition of the three other songs which are part of op. 2, must be moved back approximately one year. The autograph sheet of paper containing a list of what had been composed during the years 1862, 1865, and 1866 names as the first song (which has not been preserved) the one set to the words *There Burns in My Blood* (March 1863); the song *Lay Thy Cheek* is entered under November 1865.

1866–67

Rognyeda. *The circle's attitude towards Serov. Writing the* Serbian Fantasy. *Acquaintance with L. I. Shestakova. The Slavic concert. Growing intimacy with Moussorgsky. Acquaintance with P. I. Tchaikovsky. N. N. Lodyzhensky. Balakirev's trip to Prague. Writing* Sadko *and songs. Analysis of* Sadko.

IN THE SEASON OF 1866–7 came the production of *Rognyeda*[1] at the Mariinsky Theatre. Having produced *Judith* while I was abroad, Serov delivered himself of this second opera of his, after an interval of several years.

Rognyeda created a furore. Serov grew a full foot in artistic stature. Balakirev's circle made considerable fun of *Rognyeda*, pointing out that the idol-worshippers' chorus in Act I and a few bars of the chorus in the reception hall were the only decent things in it.[2] I must confess that *Rognyeda* aroused deep interest in me, and I liked a good deal of it, especially the sorceress, the idol-worshippers' chorus, the chorus in the reception hall, the dance of the *skomorokhi* (buffoons), the hunters' prelude, the chorus in ¾,

---

[1] According to Montagu-Nathan, this opera was produced in 1865. He says that the score " is remarkable for its composer's secession from Wagnerian influences — a retrogression to the style of Halévy is notable therein." For Tchaikovsky's criticism, see Mrs. Newmarch's *The Russian Opera*, p. 155. Serov is represented in Moussorgsky's *Peep Show* by the quotation of a theme from *Rognyeda*. C. V. V.

The first performance of *Rognyeda* took place October 27 [November 8], 1865.

[2] Cf. C. Cui's review in St. Petersburg *Vyedomosti*, 1865, No. 292.

the finale, and snatches of a good deal more. I also liked its somewhat coarse but colourful and effective orchestration, whose vigour,
by the way, K. N. Lyadov considerably moderated at rehearsals.
All this I did not dare to confess in Balakirev's circle and, as one
sincerely devoted to the ideas of the circle, I even berated it before
my acquaintances, among whom my dilettante activities were going
on. I remember what a surprise it was to my brother, who liked
Rognyeda. Having heard the opera two or three times, I carried
away a good deal and played parts of it by heart, occasionally even
before the dilettante half. At that time Serov in his articles began to
inveigh mercilessly against Balakirev as a conductor, composer, and
musician in general. He also got into squabbles with Cui and an
unimaginable bickering began in the press. Serov's relations with
Balakirev, Cui, and Stassov in former days (prior to my appearance
on the musical horizon) are a puzzle to me to this day. Serov had
been intimate with them, but why the break occurred is unknown
to me. This was passed over in silence in Balakirev's circle. Snatches
of reminiscences about Serov, chiefly ironical, reached me in passing. A scandalous story, of unprintable nature, was circulated about
him, and so forth. When I came into Balakirev's circle, the relations
between Serov and that circle were most hostile. I suspect that
Serov would have been glad to make up with the circle, but Balakirev was incapable of conceding it.

In the season of 1866–7 Balakirev gave much of his time to scan-
ning folksongs, principally Slavic and Hungarian. He had a great
number of all possible collections everywhere around him. I, too,
used to peruse them with the greatest pleasure, and with pleasure,
too, I listened to Balakirev playing them in his own exquisite harmonizations. During that period he began to show great interest in
Slavic affairs. Almost at the same time the Slavic Committee came
into being. In Balakirev's apartment I often met Czechs and other
Slavic brethren who came and went.

I listened to their conversations, but I confess that I understood
them very little, taking a scant interest in the movement. In the
spring some Slavic guests were expected, and a concert, which
Balakirev was to conduct, was projected in their honour. Appar-

ently this concert stimulated the composition of the overture on Czech themes, and, contrary to his custom, this overture was written rather rapidly by Balakirev. I undertook, at Balakirev's suggestion, to write a fantasy on Serbian themes, for orchestra. In undertaking to compose the *Serbian Fantasy* I was not at all carried away by Slavism, but rather by the delightful themes Balakirev had selected for me. I wrote the *Serbian Fantasy* rapidly, and Balakirev liked it. In the introduction there is one correction of his, or rather an insert of some four bars; with this exception, everything else belongs to me. Save for the disgraceful use of the natural-scale brass instruments, the instrumentation, too, is satisfactory. Of the fact that chromatic-scale brass instruments had already been introduced everywhere, Balakirev's circle had no inkling then, but, with the benediction of its chief and conductor, it followed the instructions of Berlioz's *Traité d'Instrumentation* regarding the use of the natural-scale trumpets and French horns. We selected French horns in all possible keys in order to avoid the imaginary stopped notes; we calculated, contrived, and grew unimaginably confused. And yet all that would have been necessary was a talk and consultation with some practical musician. However, that was too humiliating for us. We followed Berlioz rather than some talentless orchestra leader. But before speaking of the Slavic concert, which did not take place till spring, I shall relate the following:

In January or February 1867 [3] Balakirev took me along one evening to see Glinka's sister, Lyudmila Ivanovna Shestakova. He had known and been friendly with her since Glinka's time, but I had not been introduced to her as yet. That evening Lyudmila Ivanovna had visitors, among them A. S. Dargomyzhsky, Cui, and Moussorgsky; also V. V. Stassov. Dargomyzhsky was reported at the time to have begun composing music to Pushkin's *The Stone Guest*.[4] I recall the

---

[3] The year given by Rimsky-Korsakov should be corrected to 1866, in accordance with the corrections made above on pp. 15 ff.

[4] Pushkin's version of the Don Juan legend, which differs considerably from the other versions. A long account of it and a discussion of other uses of the legend may be found in H. Sutherland Edwards's *The Lyrical Drama* (London: W. H. Allen; 1881). The Stone Guest, of course, is the statue of the Commander, which Don Juan invites to dine with him. Dargomyzhsky's intention was to write an opera which, in every respect, should exemplify the principles of the new Russian school. He was pre-

dispute Stassov had that evening with Dargomyzhsky over his
Rusalka. While paying due respect to many parts of the opera, particularly its recitatives, Stassov strongly reproved Dargomyzhsky for
much that was weak, in his opinion, reproaching him especially for
many ritornellos in arias. Dargomyzhsky played on the piano one of
these ritornellos disapproved by Stassov; then he closed the piano
and gave up the discussion, as if to say: " If you can't appreciate this,
there is no use discussing anything with you."

Among Shestakova's guests was one S. I. Zotova, née Belenitsyna,
a sister of L. I. Karmalina, the famous singer of Dargomyzhsky's and
Glinka's time. Amid general acclamation she sang several songs,
including Balakirev's *Goldfish*. Her singing pleased me greatly and
gave me a desire to compose songs; I had written but one thus far.
During the spring I composed three more: *The Eastern Romance,
Cradle Song*, and *Iz slyoz moyik* (*Out of My Tears*), and with my
own accompaniments, too.[5]

After that I began to visit Lyudmila Ivanovna rather frequently.
Balakirev used to be there, too. He liked to play cards on occa-
sion, and at L. I.'s house a card party would be made up for him,
of which I never was one, as I could not bear cards; I had no talent
for card-playing, even less so, perhaps, than for piano-playing.
Balakirev liked to play cards, but for no stakes or only a small one.
The card-table offered a field for his wit, for he was listened to with
profound respect. Frequently a king of clubs was likened to the
Metropolitan Isidor for I know not what reason. " Dear little Isidor,"
Balakirev would say, "he even has a nose like a potato. . . . I
should like to know what the Lord God would take this trick with! "
Balakirev would set about taking a trick with the ace of trumps, and
so on in the same manner. At times I was doomed to be an onlooker

---

occupied with the task of making the music the handmaid of the text. " With a hardi-
hood," says M. Calvocoressi, " unparalleled at that time in the annals of musical
history and which is only to be compared with that of Debussy when planning his
Pelléas et Mélisande, Dargomyzhsky chose, in place of the conventional libretto, the
actual text of Pushkin himself." The work was accepted by the group as a model and
was known as " The Gospel." C. V. V.

[5] Cf. note 24 on p. 68. On the mentioned autograph sheet of paper, the songs
referred to here are assigned: *The Eastern Romance* to February, *Cradle Song* to
March, and *Out of My Tears* to April 1866.

merely in order to see Balakirev home afterwards. In general, he never valued my time nor did he accustom me to value it. A great deal of it was wasted in those days.

In the spring our Slav brethren came together and the concert took place at the Town Council Hall on May 12 [24]. At the first rehearsal a small row occurred: the orchestral parts of the *Czech Overture* proved to contain an incredible number of errors; the musicians were disgruntled. Balakirev fumed. The concert-master, Vyelichkovsky (brother of P. I., whom I have spoken of), made some mistake, and Balakirev said to him: "You don't understand conductor's marks!" Vyelichkovsky was offended and walked out of the rehearsal. In the evening, in Balakirev's apartment, Moussorgsky and I helped correct the orchestral parts. The second rehearsal went off without a hitch. Pikkel took Vyelichkovsky's place. My *Serbian Fantasy*, too, had its première at this concert.[6]

During the season of 1866–7 I became more intimate with Moussorgsky. I used to visit him; he lived with his married brother Filaret, near the Kashin Bridge. He played me many excerpts from his opera *Salammbô*, which greatly delighted me. Then also, I think, he played me his fantasy *St. John's Eve*, for piano and orchestra, conceived under the influence of the *Todtentanz*. Subsequently the music of this fantasy, having undergone many metamorphoses, was utilized as material for *A Night on Bald Mountain*. He also played me his delightful Jewish choruses: *The Rout of Sennacherib* [7] and *Joshua*. The music of the latter was taken by him from *Salammbô*.[8] The theme of this chorus had been overheard by Moussorgsky from Jews who lived in the same house as Moussorgsky and who were celebrating the Feast of Tabernacles. Moussorgsky also played me the songs which had failed with Balakirev and Cui. Among these were *Kalistrat* and the beautiful fantasy *Night*, on a text by Pushkin.[9] The song *Kalistrat* was a forerunner of the realistic vein which Moussorgsky later made his own; the song *Night* was representa-

---

[6] Cf. V. Stassov's article "Balakirev's Slavonic Concert," in the St. Petersburg *Vyedomosti*, 1867, No. 78; or V. Stassov's *Collected Works*, Vol. III, pp. 217 ff.

[7] Composed in January 1867.

[8] Recast into the chorus *Joshua* in 1874–5.

[9] The former composed in May 1864, the latter in April of the same year.

tive of that ideal side of his talent which he himself subsequently trampled into the mire, though still drawing on its reserve stock in emergency. This reserve stock had been accumulated by him in *Salammbô* and the Jewish choruses, when he took but little thought of the coarse muzhik. Be it remarked that the greater part of his ideal style, such as the Tsar Boris's arioso, the phrases of Dmitri at the fountain, the chorus in the Boyar Duma, the death of Boris, etc., were taken by him from *Salammbô*. His ideal style lacked a suitable crystal-like finish and graceful form. This he lacked because he had no knowledge of harmony and counterpoint. At first Balakirev's circle ridiculed these needless sciences, and then declared them beyond Moussorgsky. And so he went through life without them and consoled himself by regarding his ignorance as a virtue and the technique of others as routine and conservatism. But whenever he did manage to obtain a beautiful and flowing succession of notes, how happy he was! I witnessed that more than once.

During my visits Moussorgsky and I used to talk freely, uncontrolled by Balakirev or Cui. I went into ecstasies over much that he played; he was delighted and freely communicated his plans to me. He had many more than I. *Sadko* had been one of his projects in composition, but he had long given up any thought of writing it and therefore offered it to me.[10] Balakirev approved this idea and I set out to compose.[11]

The acquaintance of our circle with Tchaikovsky belongs to the season of 1866–7.[12] After graduating from the Conservatory, Tchaikovsky went to live in Moscow, having been asked to join the staff of professors at the Moscow Conservatory. Our circle knew him only as having composed a Symphony in G minor, of which the two

---

[10] The first idea of Sadko as a subject for a musical composition originated with V. V. Stassov. Cf. his " Correspondence with Balakirev," Letter XLVI (February 13 [25], 1861). From Stassov, through Balakirev, this idea passed on to Moussorgsky, and from him to Rimsky-Korsakov. The program of *Sadko* found among Stassov's papers was written by his hand and only here and there corrected by Rimsky-Korsakov's hand. Cf. V. Karenin's Preface to the " Correspondence between Rimsky-Korsakov and Stassov " in *Russian Thought*, 1910.

[11] Written June 24 [July 6], 1893, at Yalta.

[12] The circle's acquaintance with Tchaikovsky apparently belongs to 1868 (spring). Cf. M. Tchaikovsky: *Life of P. I. Tchaikovsky*, Vol. I, pp. 288 ff., and M. A. Balakirev's *Correspondence with P. I. Tchaikovsky*, with a Preface and Notes by S. M. Lyapoonov (St. Petersburg, Moscow: J. H. Zimmermann; no date).

P. I. TCHAIKOVSKY

from a drawing by W. I. Bruckman

middle movements had been performed at the concerts of the Russian Musical Society in St. Petersburg.[13] As a product of the Conservatory, Tchaikovsky was viewed rather negligently if not haughtily by our circle, and, owing to his being away from St. Petersburg, personal acquaintanceship was impossible. I don't know how it happened, but during one of his visits to St. Petersburg, Tchaikovsky made his appearance at Balakirev's soirée, and our acquaintance began. He proved a pleasing and sympathetic man to talk with, one who knew how to be simple of manner and always speak with evident sincerity and heartiness. The evening of our first meeting he played for us, at Balakirev's request, the first movement of his Symphony in G minor; it proved quite to our liking; and our former opinion of him changed and gave way to a more sympathetic one, although Tchaikovsky's Conservatory training still constituted a considerable barrier between him and us. Tchaikovsky's stay in St. Petersburg was brief, but during the following years, when visiting St. Petersburg, he usually came to Balakirev's, and we saw him. At one of these meetings V. V. Stassov, and all of us for that matter, were captivated by the melodious theme of his overture *Romeo and Juliet,* which subsequently moved V. V. Stassov to suggest to Tchaikovsky Shakespeare's *Tempest* as a subject for a symphonic poem. Soon after our first meeting with Tchaikovsky, Balakirev induced me to go with him to Moscow for a few days. It was during the Christmas holidays. That winter the well-known Msta Bridge had burned down,[14] and, to reach Moscow, Balakirev and I had to cross the Msta River on peasant sleds to take the train waiting for us on the other bank. We spent all our time at Moscow visiting Nikolay Rubinstein (who lived with Tchaikovsky), Laroche, Dubuque, and others. What the object of Balakirev's trip was, it is hard to say. It seems to me he sought closer relations with N. G. Rubinstein. Balakirev had always shown antagonism to Anton Rubinstein's activity, denying his talent as a composer and be-

---

[13] At the concert of February 11 [23], 1867.

[14] The Msta Bridge burned down the night of October 17–18 [29–30], 1869. By February 15 [27], 1870, regular traffic was completely restored. Hence the trip to Moscow (if one is to base the fixing of its date on this event) must be moved two years forward — that is, to December 1869–January 1870.

littling as much as possible his great gifts as a pianist. As a pianist of higher standing, in contrast to him, Nikolay Grigorevich Rubinstein was usually mentioned. At the same time the latter was pardoned his artistic indolence and tempestuous life, both explained as the result of the queer Moscow life. On the other hand, the slightest thing was counted against Anton Grigorevich. As for me, Balakirev dragged me to Moscow merely that he might not be lonesome and as a sort of aide-de-camp. Otherwise it is hard to explain our trip to see people we were not intimate with.

During that season one more member, Nikolay Nikolayevich Lodyzhensky [15] joined our musical circle. Lodyzhensky, an erstwhile wealthy landowner gone to ruin, was a young man of education, queer, easily carried away, and endowed with a strong, purely lyric talent for composition, and a fairly good piano technique in the performance of his own compositions. [16] These consisted of a huge number of improvisations, mostly unrecorded. Among them were to be found separate numbers and beginnings of symphonies and even of an opera, *Dmitri Samozvanyets* (*The False Dmitri*), wedded to a non-existent and merely projected libretto; and, finally, mere musical fragments belonging nowhere in particular. All of this, however, was so graceful, beautiful, expressive, and even technically correct that it forthwith won the attention and goodwill of all of us. Among his compositions we particularly admired the wedding scene of Dmitri and Marina, and a solo with chorus for Lermontov's *Rusalka*. As a result of his Russian dilettantism, all of these remained unfinished, with the exception of a few songs which were subsequently completed and published at the solicitation of myself and others.

Among the events of 1866–7 must also be mentioned Balakirev's trip to Prague to stage *Ruslan and Lyudmila,* the première of which took place on February 5 [17], 1867, under Balakirev's leadership. [17]

---

[15] Later Russian Consul in New York City. [Author's note.]

[16] For N. N. Lodyzhensky cf. V. Karatygin: " N. N. Lodyzhensky," *Musical Contemporary*, Vol. VII (1915–16); and Chronicle of the History of Music Section of the Institute of the History of Art, *De Musica*, issue 1 (Leningrad, 1925), V. Karatygin: *N. N. Lodyzhensky's " Requiem of Love,"* pp. 91 ff. and also the Index of Names.

[17] In Appendix I the reader will find three memoranda given me by L. I. Shestakova at my request: one in her own hand and two dictated by her. These contain a

At this date I do not recall Mili Alekseyevich Balakirev's numerous stories of Prague, of rehearsals, and of the performance of *Ruslan and Lyudmila*. At all events, they centred on the intrigues with which the Russian conductor found himself surrounded among Czech musical and theatrical folk. A dark shadow hung also over the composer Smetana, who was then the opera-house conductor and was to lead the preliminary rehearsals prior to Balakirev's arrival. Often it turned out that Glinka's music had been misunderstood. Thus Lyudmila's aria in Chernomor's castle, ¾, B minor (Act IV), had been studied in an exceedingly quick tempo. Just before the first performance the orchestral score had been " mislaid " somewhere, but Balakirev came out triumphant at that critical pass: to the great surprise and bewilderment of those endeavouring to trip him up, he conducted the whole performance from memory. According to Balakirev it was an overwhelming success, and the opera went off in fine style. He had especial praise for the baritone Lev (Ruslan) and the bass Palyechek (Farlaf). Shortly afterwards the latter left the Prague opera, settled in St. Petersburg, and joined the company of the Mariinsky Theatre. Here he subsequently was made stage manager and coach, supervising the production of all operas, including mine beginning with *Mlada*. Balakirev's trip to Prague gave rise to intercourse with the above-mentioned Czechs who came to St. Petersburg.

When summer came, my friends left. Balakirev went I do not recall where, possibly to the Caucasus again. Moussorgsky left for the country, Cui went to a summer cottage somewhere, and so on. I stayed in town alone, as my brother's family lived at Tervajoki, near Viborg. During that summer and the following autumn I composed *Sadko* [18] and eight songs (Nos. 5–12); and my first four songs,

---

brief account of the production of *Ruslan and Lyudmila* at Prague and of the printing of the score of that opera. [Author's note.]

Cf. G. N. Timofeyev: *Balakirev in Prague;* also the " Correspondence between Balakirev and Rimsky-Korsakov," Letters XXXVII–XXXVIII.

[18] On July 13 [25], 1867, Rimsky-Korsakov returned from the country (Tervajoki), where he had spent three weeks with his people. A considerable part of *Sadko* was written there, but the rough draft of what had been composed was made only upon coming back to St. Petersburg. An order to sail on a cruise interrupted this work. *Sadko* was finished after returning from the cruise. In a letter of October 8 [20] to Moussorgsky, Rimsky-Korsakov writes: " *Sadko* was finished on September 30 [Octo-

to my great delight, were set up at Balakirev's solicitation and published by Bernard (who, quite as a matter of course, never paid me a cent).[19]

In September 1867 our musical circle, which had scattered for the summer, now assembled again. The orchestral score of *Sadko*, which I had begun on July 14 [26], was completed September 30. My *Sadko* won general approval, particularly its third movement (dance in ¾ time), and quite properly, too.

What musical tendencies guided my fancy when I composed this symphonic picture? The Introduction — picture of the calmly surging sea — contains the harmonic and modulatory basis of the beginning of Liszt's " *Ce qu'on entend sur la montagne* " (modulation by a minor third downward). The beginning of the Allegro ¾, depicting Sadko's fall into the sea and his being dragged to the depths by the Sea King, is, in method, reminiscent of the moment when Lyudmila is spirited away by Chernomor in Act I of *Ruslan and Lyudmila*. However, Glinka's scale, descending by whole notes, has been replaced by another descending scale of semitone, whole tone, semitone, whole tone — a scale which subsequently played an important part in many of my compositions. The D-major movement, Allegro ¾, depicting the feast in the Sea King's realm, harmonically and to a certain degree melodically as well, recalls partly Balakirev's *Song of the Goldfish,* which was then a favourite of mine, and the introduction to Rusalka's recitative in Act IV of Dargomyzhsky's opera *Rusalka.* The dance theme (D-flat major) of the

---

ber 12] and has already been sent to the binder's. I'll tell you that I am entirely pleased with it, this is decidedly my best thing. . . . To you, Modest, profound thanks are due for the idea you suggested to me as Cui's, on the eve of Malvina's [Mme Cui's] departure for Minsk. Thanks once again. Now I shall pause, for my nob has been played out a bit from the strenuous exertion. Mili is decidedly pleased with *Sadko* and did not want to make any remarks." (Cf. Rimsky-Korsakov's letters to Moussorgsky and his letter to Balakirev, No. XXXIX.)

[19] Written at Riva, June 19 [July 2], 1906.

Cf. note 24, on p. 68. The eight songs mentioned here were not composed in 1867, as is asserted here, but in 1866. On the autograph sheet of paper the following chronology of the composition of some of them (all of 1866) is given: " On a Northern Bare Cliff (The Fir Tree and the Palm) " in April; " Southern Night," " A Cloudlet slept overnight," and " On Georgia's Hills " in May; " What is there in my name to you? " in June; " Forthwith you will surely forget me " in July. The date of the censor's permission on the printed copies of these eight songs is September 16 [28], 1866.

third movement, as well as the cantabile theme following it, is entirely original. The variations on these two themes passing into a gradually swelling storm were composed partly under the influence of certain passages in the *Mephisto Waltz,* partly as representing certain echoes of Balakirev's *Tamara,* then still a long way from completion, but familiar to me from the excerpts played by its author. The closing movement of *Sadko,* as well as its introductory movement, ends with a beautiful chord passage of independent origin. The principal tonalities of *Sadko* (D-flat major, D major, D-flat major) I selected to please Balakirev, who had an exclusive predilection for them in those days. The form my fantasy assumed was due to the subject I had chosen, but the episode of the appearance of Saint Nicholas was unfortunately left out by me, and the strings of Sadko's goosli [20] had to break by themselves, without the good saint's assistance. Taken by and large, the form of *Sadko* [21] is satisfactory, but I gave too much space to its middle movement in D major, $\frac{4}{4}$ (the feast in the Sea King's realm), as compared with the picture of the calm sea and the dance to Sadko's playing; a fuller development with transition to the storm would be very desirable. I am somewhat discontented with the brevity and sparseness of this composition in general — a composition for which broader forms would be more suitable. If long-windedness and verbosity are the faults of many composers, my fault at the time was over-conciseness and laconism, and these were due to my lack of technique. Nevertheless the originality of my task; the form resulting therefrom; the freshness of the dance theme and the singing theme with its purely Russian turn, which had laid its impress also on the variations, though second hand as to their method; the orchestral colour scheme, caught as by miracle, despite my imposing ignorance in the realm of orchestration — all these made my composition attractive and worthy of attention on the part of many musicians of various tendencies, as subsequently proved. Balakirev, whose voice was predominant and decisive in our circle, paid my

---

[20] A native instrument, a kind of horizontal harp with from five to seven strings. C. V. V.

[21] *Sadko* is said to have been the first Russian symphonic poem. C. V. V.

work a certain tribute of patronizing and encouraging admiration, but characterized my compositorial nature as female and in need of impregnation by alien musical ideas. This attitude of his towards me lasted in general until I began to manifest my personal ego in the creative field. Then he began to cool little by little towards this ego, which no longer sent back so strongly the echoes of Liszt and himself.

Concerts of the Russian Musical Society. Berlioz. The circle's achievements in composition. Soirées at Dargomyzhsky's. Acquaintance with the Purgold family. Writing of Antar and first thought of Pskovityanka (The Maid of Pskov). The Popular Concert. Analysis of Antar. Trip to visit Lodyzhensky. Composing Pskovityanka.

THE SEASON OF 1867–8 at St. Petersburg was a very busy one. Through Kologrivov's representations to the Grand Duchess Yelena Pavlovna, the conductorship of the Russian Musical Society concerts was offered to Balakirev, and at Balakirev's insistence Hector Berlioz himself was invited to conduct six concerts.[1] The concerts led by Balakirev were interspersed with those of Berlioz, who led for the first time on November 16 [28].[2] At the Balakirev concerts the following numbers among others were given: Introduction to Ruslan and Lyudmila; Chorus from Le Prophète (A. K. Lyadov and G. O. Dütsch, two boys, pupils of the Conservatory and sons of well-known musicians, were in the chorus); Wagner's Faust

---

[1] On February 13 [25], 1866 Count Matvey Yurevich Vielgorsky, chairman of the board of directors of the Russian Musical Society, died. A. S. Dargomyzhsky was elected to succeed him. On January 6 [18], 1867 A. G. Rubinstein resigned from the post of Director of the Conservatory.
[2] The concerts under Balakirev's direction in 1867–8 took place on October 1 [13] and 26 [November 7], November 9 [21], December 9 [21]; under Berlioz's direction on November 16 [28] and 25 [December 7], December 2 [14], 16 [28], and 25 [December 7], December 2 [14] and 16 [28], January 13 [25] and 27 [February 8].

Overture (the only work of that composer respected in our circle); Balakirev's *Czech Overture;* my *Serbian Fantasy* (a second time); and lastly my *Sadko* at the concert of December 9. *Sadko* went off well; the orchestration satisfied everybody, and I was called out several times.[3]

Hector Berlioz came to us already an old man; though alert at rehearsal, he was bowed down by illness and therefore was utterly indifferent to Russian music and Russian musicians. Most of his leisure time he spent stretched out on his back complaining of illness and seeing only Balakirev and the Directors. Once he was entertained at a performance of *A Life for the Tsar* at the Mariinsky Theatre, but left before the end of the second act. On another occasion there was some sort of dinner of the Board of Directors with V. V. Stassov and Balakirev, which Berlioz could not escape. I imagine that it was not ill health alone, but the self-conceit of genius as well as the aloofness becoming a genius that was responsible for Berlioz's complete indifference to the musical life of Russia and St. Petersburg. Foreign notabilities used to concede and still concede with very haughty airs some musical importance to the Russians. There was no talk even of Moussorgsky, Borodin, and myself meeting Berlioz. Whether Balakirev had felt embarrassed to ask Berlioz for permission to introduce us, feeling as he did Berlioz's utter unconcern in the matter, or whether Berlioz himself had asked to be spared the necessity of meeting the young Russian composers of promise, I cannot say; all I remember is that we ourselves had not courted this meeting and had not broached the subject to Balakirev.

At his six [nine] concerts Berlioz performed *Harold en Italie; Épisode de la vie d'un artiste;* several of his overtures; excerpts from *Romeo and Juliet* and the *Damnation de Faust;* several trifles; also Beethoven's Third, Fourth, Fifth, and Sixth Symphonies, and excerpts from Gluck's operas. In a word, Beethoven, Gluck, and " I "! However, to those must be added the overtures of Weber's *Der Freischütz* and *Oberon.* Of course, Mendelssohn, Schubert, and Schumann were omitted, not to speak of Liszt or Wagner.

---

[3] Cf. A. N. Serov's extremely sympathetic reviews of the *Serbian Fantasy* (in *Critical Articles,* Vol. I, p. 1835) and of *Sadko* (ibid., pp. 1841–3 and 2026–8).

The execution was excellent; the spell of a famous personality did
it all. Berlioz's beat was simple, clear, beautiful. No vagaries at all
in shading. And yet (I repeat from Balakirev's account) at a rehearsal of his own piece Berlioz would lose himself and beat three
instead of two or vice versa. The orchestra tried not to look at him
and kept on playing, and all would go well. Berlioz, the great conductor of his time, came to us when his faculties were already on
the decline, owing to old age, illness, and fatigue. The public did
not notice it, the orchestra forgave him. Conducting is a thing
shrouded in mystery.

Having become the leader of the Russian Musical Society concerts, Balakirev became also the official conductor for the concerts
of all sorts of soloists like Auer, Leschetizky, Cross, concerts which
began in Lent according to the custom of the time. Mention must
be made of one notable rehearsal he led on behalf of the Russian
Musical Society, in the hall of the Mikhaylovsky Palace, to try out
the accumulation of new Russian compositions.[4] The principal
number at this try-out was Borodin's First Symphony in E-flat
major, then just finished by the composer. Unfortunately a wealth
of mistakes in the badly copied parts stood in the way of a fairly
decent and uninterrupted performance of this composition. The
musicians fretted at the incorrectness of the parts and continual
halts. Still it was possible to judge of the great merits of the symphony and its magnificent orchestration. In addition to Borodin's
symphony, there were performed an overture by Rubyets; an overture by Stolypin (a composer who forthwith vanished from the
musical horizon); also an overture and entr'actes to Schiller's *Wilhelm Tell*, by A. S. Famintsyn [5] (professor of musical history at the
St. Petersburg Conservatory), a rather well-read but talentless composer, and conservative and dull music-critic. Incidentally, the following funny episode occurred between him and Balakirev: When
Famintsyn had announced to Balakirev that he had written music

---

[4] This rehearsal took place on February 24 [March 7], 1868. For further details
cf. *A. P. Borodin, His Life, Correspondence, and Musical Articles* (St. Petersburg,
1889), p. 34; also " Unpublished and Forgotten Letters of A. P. Borodin " (in *Musical Annals*, 1922, No. 1, pp. 159 ff.).
[5] Moussorgsky ridiculed this pedant in *The Classicist* and *The Peepshow*. C. V. V.

to *Wilhelm Tell,* Balakirev, without a moment's thought, inquired
whether he had the following theme:

Famintsyn was exceedingly offended and never could forgive
Balakirev this sally.

Our circle's work of composition now presented this aspect:
Balakirev was finishing or had already finished his *Islamey,* a piece
considered very difficult to perform. He often played it for us, in
parts or its entirety, and gave us great delight thereby. As I have
already mentioned, the principal subject of *Islamey* had been jotted
down by him in the Caucasus; the second, subsidiary subject (like
a trio) had been given him in Moscow by some opera singer, a
Grusian or Armenian by descent, possibly Nikolayev by name.

If I am not mistaken, when Moussorgsky returned from his summer stay in the country, he brought the wonderful *Svyetik Savishna*
(*Savishna, My Darling*) and *Hopak* (to Taras Shevchenko's
words) which he had composed; and with these he began his series
of vocal compositions with the stamp of genius in their originality;
I mean *Po griby* (*Picking Mushrooms*), *Soroka* (*The Magpie*),
Kozyol (*The Billy-goat*), etc., which began to follow one another
in rapid succession.[6]

Cui was completing his wonderful *Ratcliff,* swiftly composing
one number after another.

Borodin was completing the score of his First Symphony, a trial
performance of which I mentioned earlier. Besides, the idea of an
opera on the subject of Prince Igor had been germinating since the
season before this and the first sketches and improvisations for this
work were on hand.[7] The operatic scenario had been jotted down
by V. V. Stassov, who also had been the first to conceive the idea
of this composition. Borodin, for his part, was making a conscien-

---

[6] *Svyetik Savishna* and *Hopak* bear the date of summer 1866; the other compositions mentioned here were written in 1867.

[7] The conception of the idea of *Igor* belongs to a somewhat later period — namely,
to spring 1869. Cf. *A. P. Borodin* (St. Petersburg, 1889), p. 35.

tious study of *The Story of Igor's Band* and the Hypatian Chronicle for the development and libretto of his opera. The composition of his song *Spyashchaya Knyazhna* (*The Sleeping Princess*) belongs to the same period.

Lodyzhensky was inexhaustible in improvising most interesting fragments, which usually came to nothing, though a few of them were subsequently developed into his published songs.

As for me, I was attracted by the idea of writing a second symphony in B minor,[8] again a favourite key with Balakirev. Since the preceding year there had been running through my head material for a ⁵⁄₄ scherzo (E-flat major) which was to be one of the movements of the projected symphony. The beginning of the first movement, as well as some of its mannerisms, recalled the beginning of Beethoven's Ninth Symphony.[9]

The second subject (D major) had an unwelcome resemblance to Cui's theme in the trio of the chorus *Syny svobodniye Kavkaza* (Free Sons of Caucasus), while the concluding cantabile phrase, of more independent origin, I subsequently incorporated into *Snyegoorochka* (Mizgir: "*O lyubi menya, lyubi!* Oh, love me, love me!").

I brought my symphony only as far as the "development." My form of exposition of the themes did not satisfy Balakirev, nor my other friends either. I was disappointed. Balakirev was utterly incapable of explaining to me the defects of form with any approach to clearness. As was his wont, instead of terms borrowed from syntax and logic, he used culinary terms, saying that I had sauce

---

[8] Cf. *Correspondence between Borodin and Rimsky-Korsakov*, Letters XXXVII–XL and notes thereto. From these letters it appears that the writing of the Allegro in B Minor belongs to the beginning of 1867. Hence the mention of the Allegro and its ill fate must be assigned to the preceding chapter (1866–7). In addition, Letter XXXIX, interesting as one of the earliest manifestations of Rimsky-Korsakov's growing independence towards his spiritual guardian, suggests that the Allegro existed as a finished piece. ("In my opinion this Allegro is, with all that, the best thing I have ever written. I am ready to take your word for it that it is not good, but I cannot convince myself of it, for time enough, it seems, has by now elapsed since the day of its composition.") In the list of Rimsky-Korsakov's compositions made up in 1871 for L. I. Shestakova, the following is said of this Allegro, dated 1866: "Composed and later destroyed — Allegro of the Second Symphony" (Pushkin House, Archives of the Stassovs).

[9] See cut on opposite page.

and cayenne pepper, but no roast beef, and the like. Owing to ignorance, the terms: "period," "clause" (half period), "passage," "addition," etc., did not exist then in Balakirev's vocabulary and consequently not in ours; and everything in musical forms was vague and puzzling. I repeat I was disappointed in my musical offspring and soon abandoned or postponed indefinitely the idea of writing a second symphony.

Living alone, as before, in a furnished room on the Vasilevsky Island, and taking dinner at my brother's, I spent my evenings mostly at Balakirev's, Borodin's, Lodyzhensky's, more seldom at Cui's; Moussorgsky, too, I saw frequently. I also visited the Bye-lyenitsyn sisters,[10] who lived with their mother. Moussorgsky and I had long talks on art. With Lodyzhensky we spent entire evenings on improvisations and various experiments in harmony. At Borodin's he and I used to examine the score of his symphony, talk of *Prince Igor* and *The Tsar's Bride;* to compose this opera was at one time Borodin's passing dream, as it later became mine. Borodin's day was rather queerly arranged.[11] His wife, Yekaterina Sergeyevna, who suffered with insomnia at night, had to have a nap during the day and often got up and dressed at four or five in the afternoon. Occasionally they had dinner at eleven p.m. I often stayed till three or four in the morning and, to get home, had to cross the Neva in a skiff, as the old wooden Liteyny Draw was opened for the night.

In the latter half of the season, towards the spring of 1868, most of the members of our circle met almost every week at Dargomyzhsky's; he had thrown his doors open to us. He was then composing *The Stone Guest* at white heat. Its first tableau had been completed; the second tableau was ready up to the duel scene, and the rest was being composed almost under our very eyes, to our great delight! Until then Dargomyzhsky had surrounded himself with admirers who were amateurs or musicians much inferior to him: Shchiglev, Sokolov (author of several songs and Conservatory in-

---

[10] The older sister, subsequently Princess Golitsyna, was then separated from her husband, Zotov.

[11] The order of A. P. Borodin's day, as described here, belongs to a later period — the beginning of the seventies.

spector), Demidov, and others. But now that he had devoted himself to writing *The Stone Guest,* an advanced work whose importance he clearly saw, he came to feel the need of sharing with leading musicians his newly crystallized musical ideas. Accordingly, he made a complete change in the personnel of the circle surrounding him. Now the frequenters of his soirées were Balakirev, Cui, Moussorgsky, Borodin, V. V. Stassov, and I, as well as General Velyaminov, a music-lover and devoted singer. In addition, there were among Dargomyzhsky's regular visitors the young sisters Aleksandra and Nadezhda Nikolayevna Purgold, with whose family he had long been on friendly terms.[12] Aleksandra Nikolayevna, a high mezzo-soprano, was a fine, talented singer; Nadezhda Nikolayevna, a highly talented musical temperament, was an excellent pianist, pupil of Gerke and Zaremba.[13]

Each soirée at Dargomyzhsky's showed *The Stone Guest* to have progressed markedly in regular succession, and the newly written fragment was immediately performed by the following cast: the author, in the hoarse voice of an old man, nevertheless interpreted Don Juan splendidly; Moussorgsky was Leporello and Don Carlos; Velyaminov, the Friar and the Commander; A. N. Purgold, Laura and Donna Anna; and Nadezhda Nikolayevna took the piano. Occasionally the songs of Moussorgsky were sung (by the composer and A. N. Purgold) or the songs of Balakirev, Cui, and myself. My *Sadko* and Dargomyzhsky's *Finnish Fantasy* were played in Nadezhda Nikolayevna's arrangement for four hands. These evenings were exceedingly interesting.

By the end of spring (1868) our circle had formed an acquaintance with the Purgold family. Their family consisted of the mother, Anna Antonovna; three sisters, Sofya Nikolayevna (subsequently Mme Akhsharumova), Aleksandra Nikolayevna, and Nadezhda

---

[12] Cf. Mme N. N. Rimskaya-Korsakova's reminiscences published in *Russkaya Molva,* 1913, No. 53: " My Reminiscences of A. S. Dargomyzhsky."

[13] Zaremba was satirized in Moussorgsky's *Peepshow* as that " denizen of cloudland " who addressed his pupils somewhat in the following manner:
" Mark my words: the minor key
Is the source of man's first downfall;
But the major still can give
Salvation to your erring souls." C. V. V.

Nikolayevna; and their elderly uncle Vladimir Fyodorovich, a man
of splendid spirit who was like a second father to the Purgold girls.
The other Purgold sisters were married, and the brothers lived by
themselves. The gatherings at the Purgolds' were also exclusively
musical. The playing of Balakirev and Moussorgsky, four-hand
playing, Aleksandra Nikolayevna's singing, and talks about music
made these gatherings interesting. Dargomyzhsky, Stassov, and
Velyaminov came to these evenings also. General Velyaminov was
amusing — holding on to the accompanist's chair; invariably holding a key in his right hand for some unknown reason; with one leg
flung behind the other, straining himself to sing *Svyetik Savishna*
(*Savishna, My Darling*), panting for lack of breath, and imploring
his accompanist, at nearly every bar in ⁵⁄₄ time, to give him a
chance to catch his breath. Having gasped out his plea, he resumed
singing, then immediately appealed again: " Let me catch my
breath! " and so on. Afflicted with heart disease, Dargomyzhsky did
not feel quite well at that time; yet, carried away by his work of
composing, he kept up courage, was cheerful and animated.

Having indefinitely postponed writing the Symphony in B minor,
I turned to Syenkovsky's (Baron Brambeus's) beautiful tale *Antar*,
at Balakirev's and Moussorgsky's suggestion: on this subject I had
planned to compose a symphony or symphonic poem in four movements. The desert; the disillusioned Antar; the episode with the
gazelle and the bird; the ruins of Palmyra; the vision of the Peri;
the three joys of life — revenge, power, and love — and finally Antar's death — all of this was tempting to a composer. I set to work
in midwinter. The birth of the first idea of an opera on the subject
of Mey's *Pskovityanka* [14] (*Maid of Pskov*) belongs to the same
period. This idea again was suggested to me by Balakirev and
Moussorgsky, who were better read in Russian literature than I. [15]

---

[14] This opera is now generally known as *Ivan the Terrible*. C. V. V.

[15] In Rimsky-Korsakov's archives there is a libretto of *The Maid of Pskov* written
by Vsevolod Krestovsky. Along with the rhymed lines in this libretto Rimsky-Korsakov
completely reconstructed the act in the forest where Vera Sheloga is introduced in the
guise of a hermitess. From her story Olga learns the mystery of her own birth. Matoota
kills Vera in his attack on the worshippers. In Krestovsky's treatment this scene is
incredibly long-drawn-out and grossly melodramatic. P. I. Tchaikovsky had something
to do with Krestovsky's collaborating on the libretto of *The Maid of Pskov*. In a letter

*

Repeat these four bars an
octave lower (Clar-Fag)

And so on, crescendo, with the figuration of the motive growing more and more
frequent, and finally fortissimo

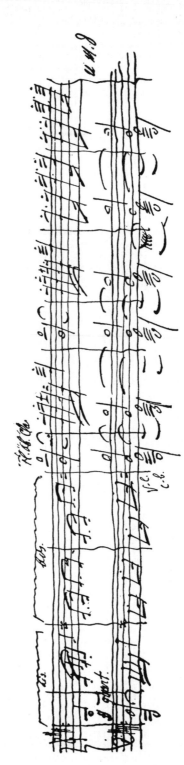

Sketches for Rimsky-Korsakov's Second Symphony

At that time Act I of the play (now the Prologue) seemed to present some difficulty. At a general conference it was decided to do away with it and begin the opera directly with the *goryelki* [16] scene; then have the drift of the Prologue conveyed in some way in the dialogue between Tsar Ivan and Tokmakov. The question of libretto had not been raised; it was assumed that I would write the libretto myself as need arose! However, for the time being, work on *Antar* came to the fore with me. Save for the principal theme of Antar himself, which I had composed under the indubitable influence of certain phrases of *William Ratcliff*, and the peri Gül Nazar's theme with its florid Oriental embellishments, all the other purely cantabile themes (the ⅚ melody in F-sharp major in the first movement, and the ¾ A-major melody — the accessory subject of the third movement) I had borrowed from a French collection of Arab melodies of Algiers, which Borodin happened to possess.[17] As for the principal subject of the fourth movement, it had been given to me, with his own harmonization, by Dargomyzhsky, who in turn had taken it from Khristianovich's collection of Arab melodies. For the beginning of the Adagio of this movement I retained Dargomyzhsky's original harmonization (English horn and two bassoons).

---

of January 29 [February 10], 1869 to Tchaikovsky, Rimsky-Korsakov writes: "Krestovsky's libretto, for which I wish to thank you again, proved very serviceable to me, though I do not altogether stick to it" (archive of the museum named after P. I. Tchaikovsky at Klin). From an unpublished letter of Rimsky-Korsakov to Moussorgsky it is evident that Rimsky-Korsakov had intended to borrow from it the text of the chorus of the maids in the woods. In reply to this letter Moussorgsky sent Rimsky-Korsakov his own text: *Ah, Thou Grove, Little Grove!* (borrowed from a Pskov song). In further work on the libretto V. V. Stassov, too, had a hand (cf. his letter to Rimsky-Korsakov of November 2 [14], 1869, in *Russkaya Mysl'*, 1910, No. 6). Moussorgsky also wrote (or discovered) a suitable text for another chorus: "From beneath the little hill, the verdant one. . . ." The texts of both choruses are extant in Rimsky-Korsakov's archives in autograph manuscripts by Moussorgsky, containing in addition a letter which reads as follows: "Friend Korsinka, here you have a text for the grannies who are honouring Vanka: according to my understanding, it is better if they begin to glorify the Tsar at the very end — for it is not in vain that he is *terrible* . . . [i.e., Ivan the Terrible — J. A. J.], (this at the end, after the text of the song). I kiss you heartily, my friend, until Wednesday. — Yours, Modest, March 27 [April 8], 1871."

Priority in selecting *Pskovityanka* for musical purposes belongs to K. Vilboa. Cf. L. Mey: *Pskovityanka*, with musical numbers composed by K. Vilboa (St. Petersburg: F. Stellovski).

[16] A Russian catching game. J. A. J.

[17] Salvador Daniel's *Collection of Algerian Melodies.* Cf. *Musical Contemporary*, 1916–17, No. 1, p. 85, note 2.

The first and the fourth movements of *Antar* were finished by me during the winter of 1867–8 and won praise from my friends, except Balakirev, who approved them with reservations.[18] The second movement, " Joy of Revenge," in B minor, which I had composed at the same time, proved a complete failure, and I left it unused. In passing, let me remark that in the spring of 1868, while I composed *Antar,* some signs of coolness sprang up between Balakirev and me for the first time. I was in my twenty-fifth year, and independence, which had been gradually awakening in me, began to assert itself by that time; Balakirev's cutting paternal despotism was growing burdensome. It is hard to state exactly what were these first signs of coolness, but soon my utter frankness towards Mili Alekseyevich began to decrease, as did later the need of frequent meetings. It was pleasant to come together and spend an evening with Balakirev, but possibly it was still more pleasant to spend the evening without him. It seems to me I was not alone in this feeling, that the other members of our circle shared it; but we never talked of it to each other nor did we criticize our older comrade. I say *older* meaning in rank and importance. Cui was a year older than Balakirev, and Borodin was a year older than Cui.

Late in the spring the writing of *Antar* was interrupted by another work; Balakirev made me orchestrate Schubert's Grand March in A minor, for Kologrivov's Popular Concert at the Manège. The orchestration of a considerable work of somebody else's, with abundant forte and tutti in addition, proved doubtless a task much harder than the orchestration of works of my own fancy, for one who knew as little as I did in this field. For such work the most important requisite was familiarity with instruments and orchestral devices, as well as experience — experience possessed by every good workmanlike leader. I possessed a certain amount of orchestral imagination, and it had served me in good stead in writing my own compositions, but of experience I had none. Nor did Balakirev possess any, and there was no one to instruct me. The instrumen-

---

[18] The first movement bears the dates January 9 [21], 1868 – January 16 [28], 1868, Pityer [St. Petersburg]; the fourth movement is dated February 20 [March 3], 1868.

tation proved lifeless, pallid, and useless for any purpose whatever. Still, the March was played, but it failed to make much impression.

V. A. Kologrivov, reputed to be a good amateur cellist, was inspector of orchestras of the theatre board of directors and one of the founders and directors of the Russian Musical Society. As inspector of theatre orchestras he was in a position to bring together all orchestral musicians and arrange monster concerts at the Mikhaylovsky Manège. The first of these concerts had taken place in the spring of 1867 under the leadership of Balakirev and K. N. Lyadov. The second concert was conducted by Balakirev alone in the spring of 1868. A vast chorus participated in addition to the orchestra. Herewith I reproduce verbatim the rather interesting program of that concert:

Sunday, May 5 [17], 1868. Concert by A. Kologrivov at the Mikhaylovsky Manège

PART I

1. Introduction to the Oratorio of *St. Paul*	*Mendelssohn*
2. *Gloria Patri* (chorus without orchestra)	*Turchaninov*
3. Prayer, *Ne perdas* (with orchestra)	*Dargomyzhsky*
4. Funeral March	*Chopin-Mauer*
5. Excerpts from *Stabat Mater*	*Lvov*
a. He who without grief and sorrow	
b. O eternal avenger of sin	
6. Symphonic work, with the national anthem	*Rubinstein*

PART II

1. Introduction to a Biblical Legend	*Mendelssohn*
2. *Gloria Domini* (chorus without orchestra)	*Bakhmetyev*
3. Introduction to *Fuite en Égypte*	*Berlioz*
4. Fragment of a Psalm	*Bortnyansky*
5. March for the Coronation of Nicholas I, orchestrated by Rimsky-Korsakov	*Schubert*
6. *Bozhe Tsarya khrani* (*God Save the Tsar!*)	

M. A. BALAKIREV, *Conductor*

All these choruses of Turchaninov, Bortnyansky, and Bakhmetyev were nothing but these authors' Orthodox canticles per-

formed in Latin, because the censor did not permit the performance of Orthodox ecclesiastical canticles at concerts together with
profane music. The chorus of Oriental hermits, to a text by Pushkin, with the words *Ne perdas* prefixed in order to mislead the
ecclesiastical censor, thus came into the class of such quasi-Catholic
prayers. Rubinstein's symphonic work with the national anthem
was but his *Festouvertüre* renamed for a similar reason. Thus, with
the help of some masquerading, the ecclesiastical censor with his
absurd regulations was duped.

When summer came, the members of our circle left for various
parts, as usual. Dargomyzhsky, Cui, and I remained in St. Petersburg. The Purgolds went to their summer home at Lyesnoy.

As in former summers, I lived at the Naval School, in the Director's apartment of my brother. It was unoccupied, as my brother
went on a practice cruise, while his family and my mother went to
pass the summer at Tervajoki, near Viborg.

During the summer of 1868 I composed the second movement
of *Antar* in C sharp (in place of the former failure in B minor) and
the third movement ("Joy of Power").[19] Thus the work on *Antar*
had been almost completed in score by the end of summer. I named
this work (rather unfortunately, too) my *Second Symphony;* many
years later I renamed it a *Symphonic Suite*. The term "suite" was
then unfamiliar to our circle in general, nor was it in vogue in the
musical literature of western Europe. Still, I was wrong in calling
Antar a symphony. My *Antar* was a poem, suite, fairy-tale, story,
or anything you like, but not a symphony. Its structure in four separate movements was all that made it approach a symphony. Berlioz's
Harold en Italie and *Épisode de la vie d'un artiste* are incontestable
symphonies, despite being program music. The symphonic development of the themes and the sonata form of the first movements of
these works remove all doubt as to incongruity between their content and the requirements of symphonic form. On the other hand,
the first movement of *Antar* is a free musical delineation of the

---

[19] The manuscript of the second movement bears the date of June 8 [20], 1868 –
June 22 [July 4], 1868; the manuscript of the third movement is dated August 4 [16],
1868 – August 24 [September 5], 1868, Pityer.

consecutive episodes of the story, save that they are musically unified by the ever recurring theme of Antar himself. It has no thematic
development whatever — only variations and paraphrases. In general the music of the introduction (the desert, Antar, and the episode of the gazelle), enfolding, as it were, the scherzo-like E-sharp-
major part in ⅚ — again, forming as it does the conclusion of the
first movement — gives the latter a rounded structure, with suggestions of an incomplete tripartite form. The second movement (" Joy
of Revenge "), in structure, brings more to mind the sonata form;
yet it is built upon a single fundamental theme of Antar himself and
upon the introductory phrase of threatening character. The first
subject is in reality a development of these motives: Antar's theme
and the introductory phrase. There is no subsidiary subject — its
place is taken by the same theme of Antar in its original complete
form (trombones in A minor). Then follows the development of the
same material, omitting only the moment of the return to the first
subject. This leads directly to Antar's complete theme (trombones
in C-sharp minor), which serves as subsidiary subject. Then follows
a coda on the introductory phrase and a soothing conclusion, again
on Antar's principal theme. The third movement (" Joy of Power ")
is a species of triumphal march (B minor — D major), with a subsidiary Oriental cantabile melody and a conclusion on Antar's
theme. Then follow a sort of middle part and light development
of the two principal subjects; return to the principal subject of the
march; transition to Antar's concluding theme, and coda built on
the subsidiary Oriental subject. The conclusion is a diverging passage of chords on an ascending eight-step scale (tone, semitone,
tone, semitone, etc.), which I had once before used in *Sadko.*

The fourth movement (" Joy of Love "), after a brief introduction borrowed from the first movement (Antar reappears amid the
ruins of Palmyra), is an Adagio. It is built in the main on the cantabile Arab subject (which Dargomyzhsky had given me) and its
development, together with the phrase of the peri Gül Nazar and
Antar's principal theme. In form it is a variety of simple rondo with
one subject and subsidiary phrases (which are episodic and enter,
now here, now there, into a passage-like working out), with a long

coda on Antar's and Gül Nazar's themes. Accordingly, in spite of its rounded forms and the constant use of symphonic development, *Antar* is, after all, no symphony; something different is associated in my mind with the conception of symphonic form. Then, also, the tonalities of the four movements of *Antar* present an unusual succession: F-sharp minor — F-sharp major; C-sharp minor — B minor — D major; and lastly D-flat major (as a dominant of F sharp).

When I examine the form of *Antar* now, after the lapse of many years, I can affirm that I did well with this form, exclusive of outside influences and hints. If the form of the first movement flows from the form of the very narrative, the tasks of depicting the joys of revenge, power, and love, on the contrary, are purely lyrical tasks, calling for no fixed form; they merely denote moods and their changes, and thus allow complete freedom of musical structure. Where I got, at the time, this coherence and logic of structure, this knack of inventing new formal devices, it is hard to explain; but now that I examine the form of *Antar* with an experienced eye, I cannot help feeling considerable satisfaction. Only a certain excessive brevity of form of movements one and two in *Antar* fails to satisfy me. The task called for broader forms, but in default of accessory subjects, the difficulty, even the impossibility, of giving the second movement a broader development is almost obvious. A certain incoherence is felt in the choice of the key of C-sharp minor for movement two in connection with the key of F sharp in movement one and B minor in movement three. But, speaking generally, the play of tonalities in the individual movements of the composition is interesting, beautiful, and legitimate. The distribution of the keys shows that there was awakening in me at the time a sense of the interplay of tonalities and their interrelation — an understanding that served me well throughout my subsequent musical activity. Oh, how many composers, including Dargomyzhsky and Wagner, too, if you like, are devoid of this understanding! To the same period also belongs the development in me of an ever keener sense of the absolute significance or shade of each key. Is this sense exclusively subjective or does it depend upon certain general laws? I think both views are true. You will not find many composers who do not consider A major the key of youth, merriment, spring, and dawn; but they are inclined to use this key to express conceptions of deep thought or a dark starry night. In spite of my inevitable blunders, due to ignorance of elementary truths and methods, *Antar,* as compared with *Sadko,* was a long step forward in the matter of harmony, figuration, contrapuntal experiments, and orchestration. The combinations of certain motives, the intertwining of one with another, were happy thoughts; for instance, the accompaniment of the singing theme of the third movement by a rhythmico-melodic dance figuration; or the appearance of Antar's theme in *flauto* during the figuration of the violas; or the sustaining of the two-note motives as against the rhythm of the cantabile theme in D-flat major in movement four. One cannot help feeling the felicity of the introductory phrase of threatening character and the harmony it forms in movement two. The chord passages bringing movement three to a close, as well as the passages which depict the bird of prey in pursuit of the gazelle, are original and logical.

In the instrumentation there were new departures, and felicitous applications of familiar devices: the low registers of flutes and clarinets, the harp, etc.; Antar's principal theme, entrusted to the violas, as I recall it, in order to please Moussorgsky, who was especially fond of violas. Familiarity with the score of *Ruslan and Lyudmila* and Liszt's *Symphonische Dichtungen* made themselves evident. The three bassoons, subsequently reduced to two, pointed to the influence of the orchestration of *Eine Faust Ouvertüre.* Nor was the writing of *Antar* uninfluenced by the orchestration of Balakirev's *Czech Overture.* Taken as a whole, the orchestration was full of colour and fancy; in the forte passages there came to my rescue my invariable instinctive striving to fill out the middle octaves — a device that even Berlioz had not always employed. The general musical influences perceptible in *Antar* emanated from Glinka's Persian Chorus (the E-major variation on the subsidiary subject in movement three) and his Chorus of Flowers, in Act IV of *Ruslan and Lyudmila* (introduction in F-sharp major in movement one and beginning of movement four); and from Liszt's *Hunnenschlacht* and Wagner's *Eine Faust Ouvertüre* (in movement two of *Antar*). Moreover, certain methods of Balakirev's *Czech Overture* and *Tamara* and the influence of random phrases from *William Ratcliff* were constantly felt in the music of *Antar*. The triplet figuration which accompanies Antar's theme in the third movement was due to a similar figuration in the finale of *Rognyeda;* only mine is better and more subtle than Serov's. The abundant use of Oriental themes lent my composition an odd turn of its own, hardly in wide use until then, and the happily chosen program gave it additional interest. It seems to me that I had properly understood the possibility of expressing the joy of revenge and of love by external means — the former as a picture of a bloody battle, the latter as the gorgeous milieu of an Eastern potentate.

In addition to this, at the request of Cui, who was in a hurry to finish the score of his *William Ratcliff*, I orchestrated during the summer of 1868 the first number of his opera, the wedding chorus in C major and the blessing of the betrothed. The orchestration of another's composition, and mainly with *tutti*, was a task beyond my powers, and it brought poor results. Nevertheless this number was performed at the Opera with my orchestration. As a rule, orchestration gave Cui trouble in those days and somehow interested him but little. In many instances he had to seek Balakirev's advice and mine. But what useful advice could I give him at that period? In passing I may mention that Maria's well-known romanza in Act III was orchestrated by Balakirev.

I visited the Purgolds at their summer home in Lyesnoy for the first time in company with Dargomyzhsky and the Cuis; we went by carriage. Afterwards I went there alone many a time. The two songs *Night* and *Secret* that I wrote that summer were dedicated to the Purgold sisters, the former to Nadezhda Nikolayevna and the latter to Aleksandra Nikolayevna. Among the events of my life during that summer must also be mentioned my trip to Ivan Nikolayevich Lodyzhensky's estate (Kashin canton of the Tver Government), where the Borodins were summering. Nikolay Nikolayevich Lodyzhensky, who early in the summer had been lodging in St. Petersburg in a tiny room near the Church of Nikola Trunila (on the St. Petersburg side), was leaving in July for his estate and asked me to come along. I remember that, sitting one day at home, in my brother's apartment, I received his note in which he had appointed the day of departure. I recall how the picture of the impending trip to the dreary interior of Russia instantly brought an access of indefinable love for Russian folk-life, for her past in general and for *Pskovityanka* in particular. How, under the pressure of these sensations, I sat down at the piano and then and there improvised the theme of the Chorus of Welcome which the Pskov people sing to Tsar Ivan (Act II, First Tableau), for I had been thinking of the opera while composing *Antar*. At Makovnitsy, the estate of the brothers Lodyzhensky, I spent pleasantly the better part of a week. I watched the *khorovods* (round dances); I rode horseback with my hosts and Borodin and exchanged all manner of musical ideas with the latter, at the piano. During my stay at Makovnitsy, Borodin composed his song *Morskaya Tsaryevna* (*The Sea Princess*), with its curious seconds in the figurations of the accompaniment. Incidentally, let me mention the song I heard in the *khorovod* at Makovnitsy, though, to my regret, for some reason or other, I could not later utilize it.

Poco allegretto

Upon returning to St. Petersburg, having completed *Antar*, I turned to some parts of *Pskovityanka*, wrote the tale " *Of Tsarevna Lada*," also made a rough draft of the chorus " *Po malinu, po smorodinu* (We're off for raspberries, for currants) " and the *goryelki* game. A. N. Purgold was a magnificent interpreter of my tale. V. V. Stassov went into raptures, he rumbled and he grumbled. However, he was not the only one to like the tale.

On their return to St. Petersburg, in the autumn, the Borodins were relating queer events which had been taking place within their sight at Makovnitsy after my departure. I heard stories of N. N. Lodyzhensky — how, under the spell of temporary asceticism, he slept on bare boards, even studded with nails, they say; how while fasting in the country, he prayed in old besmirched clothes how he went to confession mounted on an old nag, and on the next day, dressed in clothes all brand-new, driving a smart troika (three-span) on his way to confession, he turned homeward with the exclamation: " All this is nonsense! " and at home launched into dancing a polka or something of that kind. Queer, incomprehensible, eccentric! Bright, educated, and talented, and, withal, as if fit for nothing. It has been said: " Everything develops," and, indeed, much later everything " *did develop*," and N. N. evolved into a capable diplomat or, at least, a capable official of the Ministry of Foreign Affairs.[20]

[20] In the early years of the New York Russian Symphony Society (Modest Altschuler conductor), founded in 1903, Lodyzhensky was its vice-president. J. A. J.

Moussorgsky's Wedding. *Concerts of the Russian Musical Society.*
Death of Dargomyzhsky. Nizhegorodtsy *and* William Ratcliff *at the*
Mariinsky Theatre. Boris Godunov. *Concerts of the Free Music*
School. Gedeonov's Mlada. *Completing the orchestration of* The
Stone Guest. *Songs.*

THE BEGINNING OF the season of 1868–9 found me in possession of a
fully finished score of *Antar.* Moussorgsky returned to St. Petersburg with Act I of Gogol's *Wedding* [1] ready, in a draft for voice and
piano. Borodin brought new fragments for *Prince Igor*,[2] the beginning of his Second Symphony in B minor, and the song *Morskaya
Tsaryevna (The Sea Princess).* The songs *The False Note* and
Otravoy polny moyi pyesni (My songs with poison are filled) he
had composed earlier.[3] Cui had completed *William Ratcliff* and
immediately submitted it to the Board of Directors of the Theatres.
The Stone Guest was also complete, except for the finale of Tableau
I, left unfinished, for some reason — beginning with Leporello's

---

[1] Cf. Rimsky-Korsakov's letter of August 7 [19], 1868 to Moussorgsky (Archives
of N. A. Rimsky-Korsakov).

[2] In a letter of October 3 [15], 1869, to his wife, A. Borodin writes: "The musi-
cianers, too, I gratified with the *first* number of *Igor,* where Yaroslavna's Dream turned
out delightful. . . ." *A. P. Borodin* (St. Petersburg, 1889), p. 62. By mentioning
"*new fragments* for *Prince Igor* in this passage, Rimsky-Korsakov runs considerably
in advance of events.

[3] Composed in the autumn of 1868.

words: "*Vot yeshcho? Kuda kak nuzhno!* (And now comes this! And this was all we needed!)." Early in the season, Dargomyzhsky's soirées recommenced. *The Stone Guest* used to be sung in its entirety. *The Wedding* also roused considerable interest. We were all amazed at Moussorgsky's task, enthusiastic about his characterizations and many recitative phrases, but perplexed by some of his chords and harmonic progressions. Moussorgsky himself sang Podkolyosin with his native inimitable talent; Aleksandra Nikolayevna sang Fyokla; Velyaminov sang Stepan; Nadezhda Nikolayevna played the accompaniments, while Dargomyzhsky, his liveliest interest roused, copied Kochkaryov's part in his own hand and sang it with enthusiasm. Everybody was particularly amused by Fyokla and Kochkaryov — the latter expatiating about "nasty little postal clerks; nasty little rascals," and so on, with a most amusing characterization in the accompaniment. V. V. Stassov was in ecstasies. Dargomyzhsky occasionally said that the composer had gone a bit too far. Balakirev and Cui considered *The Wedding* a mere curiosity with interesting declamatory moments.

However, having composed Act I, Moussorgsky could not make up his mind to go on with *The Wedding*. His thoughts turned to Pushkin's *Boris Godunov*, and soon he set to work. Moreover, he simultaneously began to write his *Dyetskaya (Nursery)*,[4] that series of quaint compositions for voice and piano, which Aleksandra Nikolayevna Purgold interpreted so finely.

The health of Dargomyzhsky — he was suffering from heart disease — had been on the downward path since the autumn of 1868, and his soirées ceased. He used to say: "If I should die, Cui will complete *The Stone Guest* and Rimsky-Korsakov will orchestrate it." As I have already said, *The Stone Guest* was finished except for a few lines. In our circle Cui was considered a vocal and operatic composer par excellence, since *William Ratcliff* was his third opera, although *The Prisoner of the Caucasus* and *The Mandarin's Son* had not been produced as yet. As for me, I had the reputation of a talented orchestrator.

---

[4] The first number of *The Nursery*, "The Child with the Nurse," is dated April 26 [May 8], 1868; the second to the fifth belong to 1870; the rest to 1872.

I really did possess a gift for orchestral colouring, along with a liking for purity in part-writing and harmony, but I had neither experience nor fundamental knowledge. I did not know violin positions, did not know violin bowing well; confused by Berlioz's *Traité* [*d'Instrumentation*], I had a muddled idea of trumpets and French horns. The other members of our circle had not the knowledge either; Borodin, who played the flute and the cello, was somewhat better informed.

I don't remember whether Wagner's *Lohengrin* had its first performance at the Mariinsky Theatre early in the fall of 1868 or in the post-Lenten season the spring before.[5] K. N. Lyadov conducted. Balakirev, Cui, Moussorgsky, and I were in a box with Dargomyzhsky. *Lohengrin* called forth our utter scorn and an inexhaustible torrent of humour, ridicule, and venomous cavilling from Dargomyzhsky. Yet at that time Wagner had already half finished his *Der Ring des Nibelungen* and had composed *Die Meistersinger*, in which with experienced and skilful hand he had broken new paths for art, far, far in advance of us advanced Russians. I don't recall whether it was then or in regard to later performances of *Lohengrin* that Cui wrote the article: "*Lohengrin,* or Punished Curiosity." This article was dedicated to me, although the fact was not mentioned in the *St. Petersburg Gazette,* where Cui functioned as music critic.[6]

In the season of 1868–9 Balakirev conducted all of the Russian Musical Society's concerts except one which Nikolay Rubinstein had been invited to conduct.[7] Rubinstein gave the *Sakuntala* overture and Anton Rubinstein's *Ocean Symphony,* and also played con-

---

[5] The first performance occurred October 4 [16], 1868.

[6] C. Cui's review: "*Lohengrin,* Music Drama of R. Wagner," was published (signed: xxx) in the St. Petersburg *Vyedomosti* (*Gazette*) on October 11 [23], 1868 (No. 278).

[7] There were all together ten of them. Among Rimsky-Korsakov's papers there has been preserved a declaration in his own handwriting, of December 18 [30], 1868, addressed to the commander of the Eighth Naval Company, wherein he asks him to obtain permission for him to conduct the orchestra when his works are performed, "as the Russian Musical Society of St. Petersburg had expressed to him its particular desire to that effect." The decision of N. Krabbe, Secretary of the Navy, on this petition reads: "It is not agreeable to His Majesty the Tsar that officers, in general, should appear in public as participants in performances either of concerts or of theatrical representations."

certos of Liszt and Litolff. The programs of Balakirev's concerts were exceedingly interesting. There were performed: Beethoven's Ninth Symphony and *Leonore* Overture; Schumann's Second Symphony and " Overture, Scherzo, and Finale "; Berlioz's three movements of *Romeo and Juliet* and Act II of the opera *Les Troyens à Carthage* (chase; Naiads; storm in the forest); Liszt's *Les Préludes* and two episodes from Lenau's *Faust;* Glinka's *Kamarinskaya* and the chorus *Pogibnyet!* (*He shall perish!*); Dargomyzhsky's *Finnish Fantasy* (for the first time) and choruses from *Rusalka.* There is nothing surprising in the fact that excerpts from *Ruslan and Lyudmila* (Act IV) or *Rusalka* were in those days numbers of interest at symphonic concerts: *Ruslan* was given with enormous cuts, and *Rusalka* was not given at all.

Probably under pressure from the Directors of the Russian Musical Society, Balakirev also decided to add to the programs of his concerts the *Vorspiel* to Wagner's *Meistersinger,* which he hated.[8] About the performance of this number Serov wrote that any second violin of the orchestra could have conducted it as well as Balakirev.[9] Of course this was only a prejudiced thrust by the far from impartial Serov. The programs included the following works by members of our circle: Borodin's symphony, my *Antar* and the " Chorus of Welcome " from *Pskovityanka,* the theme of which I have mentioned already. The programs of Balakirev's concerts provoked all sorts of attacks on the part of Serov, Rostislav (pen-name of Fyeofil Matveyevich Tolstoy),[10] and Professor Famintsyn. They were exasperated by the lack of classical numbers on the programs and by such novelties as Borodin's symphony; by the partisanship shown in the partiality for works of the members of the circle (or " mighty

---

[8] Performed at the concert of February 22 [March 6]. Cf. A. P. Borodin's review of this work (*St. Petersburg Gazette,* 1869, No. 78; reprinted by V. Stassov in his book on Borodin, pp. 300 ff.).

[9] Serov wrote: " At one of the Society's concerts, he [Balakirev] *ruined* Wagner's standard work, the Overture of the opera *Die Meistersinger von Nürnberg* " (*Golos,* 1869, No. 119). The sentence quoted by Rimsky-Korsakov from memory did appear in the same article, but in reference to the performance of the *Eroica* and the *Requiem* under Balakirev's direction. " I am convinced that the very least musician of a vaudeville orchestra would have conducted both the *Eroica* and the *Requiem better* than Balakirev had."

[10] Caricatured in Moussorgsky's *Peepshow* as professing an undying admiration for Patti. C. V. V.

koochka" — that is, coterie — as V. V. Stassov had tactlessly called our circle),[11] and also by the absence of works of Serov, Famintsyn, etc. The frontal onslaughts were directed by the offended Famintsyn at Borodin's symphony. Its performance at the concerts had not passed off without a hint of hisses. The critics also found fault with Balakirev's interpretation. On the other hand, Cui found it beyond all praise in his articles in the *St. Petersburg Gazette.* Between Cui and the critics referred to, there was a constant wrangling, caustic remarks, bantering — in a word, party polemics in full swing. In passing, the *St. Petersburg Gazette* also dug its claws into talentless Wagner and Rubinstein, sour-sweet, bourgeois Mendelssohn, and dry, childish Mozart, and so forth and so on in the same manner. The adverse party hurled accusations of ignorance, partisanship, and *koochkism* (clannishness).

My chorus from *The Maid of Pskov* was hardly noticed.[12] *Antar,* auspiciously played for the first time on March 10 [22], 1869, found favour as a whole, and I was called out. Balakirev, who had not approved of it in general and had condemned its second movement in particular, said, nevertheless, at the first rehearsal, after he had played that movement: " Yes, it is really very fine! " I was pleased. After the performance of *Antar* F. M. Tolstoy (Rostislav) stated to me his doubts about the possibility of expressing in music the joy of power. I do not remember what Serov and Famintsyn wrote of *Antar.* After the performance of *Sadko* Famintsyn burst forth with a censorious article, in which he accused me of imitating the *Kamarinskaya* (sic!). This led Moussorgsky to create his *Classicist,*[13] which ridiculed the critic of the " rueful countenance." In its middle part, at the words: " I am foe of the newest artifices," there appeared the motive recalling the sea in *Sadko.* By singing his *Klassik*

---

[11] Cf. the last sentence of V. Stassov's article: " Mr. Balakirev's Slavonic Concert," in St. Petersburg *Vyedomosti* (*Gazette*), 1867, No. 130. Reprinted in *Collected Works of V. Stassov,* Vol. III, pp. 217–19.

[12] In a letter of January 16 [28], 1870, to his wife, when mentioning the second performance of this chorus at the Slavic Committee Concert of January 15 [27], 1870, Borodin says that this time " the effect was slighter, though Korsinka was called out twice, but less unanimously. . . ." Cf. *A. P. Borodin's Letters, with Notes by S. A. Dianin,* Part I.

[13] *The Classicist* was composed late in 1867 or at the beginning of 1868; published in 1870.

Moussorgsky gave considerable amusement to all of us, particularly V. V. Stassov.

Towards the end of 1868 Dargomyzhsky's health grew steadily worse; if I am not mistaken, volvulus had now been added to heart disease, and the news of his death came as a shock on January 5 [17], 1869. By agreement with his heirs, *The Stone Guest* was entrusted to me for orchestration, Cui being requested to finish the first scene.

At the beginning of winter Napravnik's opera *Nizhegorodtsy* (*The People of Nizhni Novgorod*) had its first performance [14] at the Mariinsky Theatre; *William Ratcliff*, too, was being prepared for production under Napravnik's leadership. K. N. Lyadov, who was killing himself with drink, was ending or had ended his career as a conductor. The date of his death I can't recall.[15]

With regard to the production of *Nizhegorodtsy*, Cui found himself in an awkward position: one had to write about *Nizhegorodtsy*, and Cui did not expect that the opera would be much good. Yet Napravnik was to begin rehearsing his *Ratcliff*. Cui found a way out by urgently pleading with me to write a review of *Nizhegorodtsy*. Being a naïve soul, I undertook the task: for a friend nothing is too steep. *Nizhegorodtsy* was given, and I wrote the desired review. I frankly disliked the opera, and my review was unfavourable, smacking of Cui himself in style and method. The characteristic expressions " Mendelssohnian leaven," " bourgeois ideas," and the like were there aplenty. The article appeared above my full signature.[16] Naturally it spoiled my relations with Napravnik for the rest of my life; soon afterwards we met and then I was in for it during my entire activity as operatic composer. Of course, Napravnik never permitted himself even a mention of my review, but I don't think he ever forgot it. The rehearsals of *William Ratcliff* began soon after. Through Cui, I became a habitual attendant at these. I liked everything in *Ratcliff*, including the orchestration.

---

[14] First performance, December 27, 1868 [January 8, 1869].

[15] K. N. Lyadov died on December 7 [19], 1868.

[16] *St. Petersburg Gazette*, January 3 [15], 1869. Reprinted in the book: N. Rimsky-Korsakov: *Musical Essays and Notes* (St. Petersburg, 1911), pp. 5 ff. The expression " bourgeois ideas " does not occur in this article.

I watched Napravnik closely and marvelled at his ear, his executive ability, his familiarity with the score. The première was in February.[17] The opera was well received by the audience. The cast (Myelnikov, Platonova, Leonova, Vasilyev I and the rest) did their best, and everything went well. Subsequent performances grew more slipshod, as the custom had long been and is to this day. Still the audiences, even though they did not quite fill the theatre, listened to the opera with attention and received it with favour. My career as a critic had not run its course with the review of *Nizhegorodtsy*: Cui asked me to review *Ratcliff* for the *St. Petersburg Gazette*. The review was written and turned out to be an unmistakable panegyric as regards both composition and author, a panegyric springing from an honest heart, but a small critical mind.[18] However, my unrestrained enthusiasm for that composition of the highest talent, at the moment of its first appearance, was natural on my part. In the article I expressed certain opinions, categorical yet undoubtedly correct. For instance, I boldly declared that the love-duet of Act III was the finest love-duet in all contemporary musical literature. V. V. Stassov highly complimented me on this opinion.[19] Strange that Cui, who naturally entertained a very high opinion of his opera, should have preferred to this duet many other passages, like the so-called scene " at the Black Stone," for instance. The composer also attached considerable importance to Lesley's comical pranks. These were the very scenes which our circle considered weaker moments.

I need not add that all the other music-critics of St. Petersburg fell upon Cui and his opera with the greatest exasperation and thereby prejudiced considerably the opinions of the public.

Having ended the series of Russian Musical Society concerts, Balakirev gave one more concert at the Free Music School, with Schumann's First Symphony and Mozart's *Requiem* on the pro-

---

[17] First performance, February 14 [26], 1869.
[18] *St. Petersburg Gazette*, 1869, No. 52. Reprinted in N. Rimsky-Korsakov: *Musical Essays and Notes*.
[19] " Concerning it [the love scene] we do not hesitate to say that there never has been in any opera a love-duet like this one." Ibid.

gram.[20] I must make a correction: Serov's saying that any second-violin player of the orchestra could have conducted as well as Balakirev referred, perhaps, to Mozart's *Requiem* and not to the *Meistersinger Vorspiel*, as I have said before.[21] But I think that really makes no difference; Serov's opinion remains partisan and is striking in its partiality and unfairness. At all events, the criticisms and intrigues of the adverse party (Serov strove with might and main to get on the Board of Directors of the Russian Musical Society) were responsible for the impaired relations between Balakirev and the Board of Directors. The latter were displeased with him. So was the Muse Euterpe (the Grand Duchess Yelena Pavlovna). Probably Balakirev, intolerant, tactless, and unrestrained, was also somewhat to blame for the dissatisfaction that had developed. There were rumours that a year earlier the Grand Duchess, who had then been well disposed towards Balakirev, had graciously offered to send him abroad, that he might get in touch with the musical world, but he scornfully refused the offer. Possibly these are mere stories, but, at any rate, Balakirev refused to conduct the concerts of the R. M. Society. This led to an unequal struggle lasting several years between him and the R. M. Society, a struggle between progress and conservatism. One day, in the spring of 1869, I called on Balakirev and found there A. M. Klimchenko, one of the Directors of the Russian Musical Society. From a few words of the conversation, which was about to close when I came in, I judged that it had been conclusive.

When *The Stone Guest* had been handed over to me, I set to orchestrating it. Tableau II was completed during the spring. Besides this, the composition of *Pskovityanka* was progressing little by little.[22]

The summer of 1869 went by quite uneventfully for me. I lived in my brother's unoccupied apartment, and went for a while to

---

[20] This concert had already taken place on March 18 [30], 1868. The last concert of Balakirev in the season of 1868–9 was given at the Russian Musical Society, on April 26 [May 8], 1869.

[21] Cf. note 9 on p. 102.

[22] Written at Riva, June 24 [July 7], 1906.

Tervajoki,[23] to see his family. I had no acquaintances in St. Petersburg. The Purgolds had a summer home in Peterhov. Work on *Pskovityanka*, in sketches, progressed, now regularly, and now at random. My official duties consisted in boresome work as officer of the day and in guard-mounting.

The season of 1869–70 was noted for Balakirev's struggle with the Directors of the R. M. Society, whose concerts had been entrusted to E. F. Napravnik. Rivalry between the concerts of the Russian Musical Society and those of the Free Music School became the main object of Balakirev's activity as conductor, from the moment of his break with the Board of Directors. The school's five concerts were announced, and with them began a war to the knife. The programs of the concerts were splendid, very interesting and advanced. I quote them in full.[24]

On the whole, the programs of the R. M. Society's concerts were also not devoid of interest, though more conservative. The concerts began, and with them began newspaper wrangling, too. The audiences of the Musical Society were not over-large, nor were those at the Free Music School. But the Musical Society had money, while the Free School had none. The result was a deficit at the concerts and the utter impossibility of undertaking concerts the following season. On the other hand, the R. M. Society was fully able to continue its concerts during the following years; accordingly, victory was theirs. I shall not describe the tension with which Balakirev's entire circle and all those close to it watched the fight between the two concert organizations, sympathizing with one and wishing all manner of obstacles to the other.[25] The R. M. Society, in the persons of its representatives, preserved the Olympic calm of officialdom, while Balakirev's excited state of mind was obvious to all.

---

[23] Concerning the stay at Tervajoki, see Rimsky-Korsakov's letter of July 27 [August 8], 1869 to Balakirev.

[24] Cf. Appendix II.

[25] Cf. A. P. Borodin's letter of November 6 [28], 1869 to his wife. Cf. also V. V. Stassov: *The Twenty-fifth Anniversary of the Free Music School* (St. Petersburg, 1887).

To this period belongs the beginning of his acquaintance with and mysterious visits to a certain female fortune-teller, who lived in Nikolaevskaya Oolitsa (Street). Occasionally, as though against his will, M. A. [Balakirev] would drop a word or two to me about these visits, but from everybody in general he concealed his mystic doings. Nor did I, for my part, betray his secret. The name of the fortune-teller is unknown to me, but, apparently, fortune-telling and soothsaying were her exclusive occupation. Through whom Balakirev had come to meet her I do not know. According to him, she was a rather young woman with large dark eyes. Her soothsaying consisted in looking into a large mirror, in which certain persons or other appeared before her; their thoughts and intentions she communicated to her clients. T. I. Filippov's wife, who in some way had known this fortune-teller, subsequently told me that she was " simply a genuine witch." Balakirev, who did not believe in God, came to be a believer in the Devil. The Devil brought it about that subsequently he came to believe in God too. . . . L. I. Shestakova told me that once this seeress had come to her house in search of Balakirev for some purpose, but he was not there. L. I. assured me that the seeress was in love with him. All of this is very odd. . . . The purpose of Balakirev's divinations was to learn the future fate of his concerts and of his struggle with the hated Russian Musical Society, and likewise to divine the thoughts and intentions of the persons who were at the helm of the Society. According to his words, the seeress described to him, by their outward characteristics, the persons seen by her in the looking-glass; among those who appeared, there were both the Grand Duchess Yelena Pavlovna and Napravnik and members of the board of directors, and others. Simultaneously their thoughts and intentions were revealed in brief; for example, this dark man is designing something evil, that blond man, on the contrary, does not wish any ill, and so forth. As a rule, Balakirev's accounts were abrupt, vague, half unuttered; the soothsaying, which took place in semi-darkness, cast a terror upon him and he related it as if unwillingly, though he always was the one to broach the subject, beginning with hints, as though he had blabbed, and then bitterly resisted any questions whatever. Conversation with me about these mysterious things sprang up rarely, but it was Balakirev himself who gave it a start, not I. One evening, while walking with me through Nikolaevskaya Street, he even pointed out to me the house where the witch lived (if I do not err, the house of Lesly).

In connection with the performance of *Sadko* [26] I made a fresh copy of the score, and some corrections and improvements. Through Balakirev's intervention,[27] *Sadko* was given to Jurgenson of Moscow to be published as an orchestral score and in an arrangement for four hands by Nadezhda Nikolayevna Purgold, who also undertook the task of making a four-hand arrangement of *Antar,* which was then on the presses of Bessel. As far as I recollect, Jurgenson as well as Bessel paid me one hundred rubles for the publishing rights of these compositions.

During this very season Moussorgsky submitted his completed *Boris Godunov* to the Board of Directors of the Imperial Theatres. It was examined by a committee consisting of Napravnik, the opera conductor, Mangeant and Betz, the orchestra conductors of

---

[26] At the concert of November 16 [28], 1869. Borodin's letter to which reference has been made in note 25 (above) was written on the day of the concert and contains a full account of it. Of *Sadko* it says: " In its new version, where many slips of orchestration have been righted and the former effects have been perfected, *Sadko* is a delight. The public greeted the piece enthusiastically and called Korsinka out three times." Serov wrote of this performance of *Sadko:* " Mr. Rimsky-Korsakov, alone of his entire faction, is gifted with enormous talent, settled, remarkable, profoundly sympathetic. In the midst of his ill-fated entourage he blazes like a diamond amid cobblestones. The very choice of the subject is in itself proof of a wealth of imagination."

In a footnote Serov observed with evident satisfaction: " When I heard Rimsky-Korsakov's composition for the first time (in 1867) it was entitled *A Musical Bylina* — which was not quite correct, because a *part* does not constitute the *whole.* After my remark to that effect (in *Music and Theatre,* No. 15), the author wrote in his program: ' Episode from the Bylina *Sadko,* Musical Tableau for Orchestra.' This caption is irreproachable, just as the composition itself is." A. N. Serov: *Critical Articles,* Vol. IV, p. 2028.

[27] From Rimsky-Korsakov's letters to P. I. Tchaikovsky it is possible to infer also a certain share of Pyotr Ilich's mediation in the matter of publishing *Sadko.* In his letter dated January 29 [February 10], 1869 Rimsky-Korsakov wrote to Tchaikovsky: ". . . for printing, it [the orchestral score of *Sadko*] must be returned to me, to be looked through and corrected; it contains a goodly number of errors, for I wrote it directly as a clean copy, even without preliminary jottings. After it has been corrected, I will forward it to you at once with a four-hand arrangement. Proofs should nevertheless continue to be sent to me; but in case of any misunderstandings in the course of printing, it would be best for Jurgenson to address himself to you . . ." (Archives of the Tchaikovsky Museum at Klin).

French and German drama respectively, and the double-bass player Giovanni Ferrero; it was rejected. The freshness and originality of the music nonplussed the honourable members of the committee, who reproved the composer, among other things, for the absence of a reasonably important female rôle. Indeed, there was no Polish act in the original score; consequently Marina's part was lacking. Much of the fault-finding was simply ridiculous. Thus the double-basses *divisi* playing chromatic thirds in the accompaniment of Varlaam's song were entirely too much for Ferrero, the double-bass player, who could not forgive the composer this device. Moussorgsky, hurt and offended, withdrew his score, but later thought the matter over and decided to make radical changes and additions. The Polish act in two tableaux and the scene "Near Kromy" were new conceptions. The scene in which the story of the False Dmitri's excommunication is told: "There came out, brethren, a deacon, burly and big, and yelled at the top of his lungs: 'Grishka Otrepyev has been damned!'" etc. was done away with and the Yurodivy (Simpleton) was transferred from this scene to that of the one "Near Kromy." This tableau had been planned as the last but one of the opera, but subsequently the composer relegated it to the end. Moussorgsky set zealously to work on the above changes, in order to resubmit his revised *Boris Godunov* to the Board of Directors of the Imperial Theatres.[28]

Within the same period falls the following work allotted to the members of our circle. Gedeonov, Director of the Imperial Theatres at the time, had conceived the idea of producing a work which should combine ballet, opera, and spectacle. For this purpose he had written the program of a stage performance in four acts on a subject borrowed from the Elba Slavs and had commissioned V. A. Krylov to work up the text. *Mlada,* with its mixture of fantasy and everyday reality, was a most grateful subject for musical treatment. Gedeonov asked Cui, Borodin, Moussorgsky, and myself to compose the music for it; moreover, Minkus,[29] the official ballet com-

[28] For this, in more particulars, see A. Rimsky-Korsakov: "M. P. Moussorgsky's *Boris Godunov,*" in *Musical Contemporary,* 1916–17, Nos. 5–6.
[29] The composer who collaborated with Léo Delibes in the ballet, *La Source,* for the Paris Opéra. C. V. V.

poser of the Imperial Theatres, was to compose the incidental ballet music. Who the initiator of this order was, I do not know. I suspect here the influence of Lukashevich, an official of the Board of Directors of the Theatres, who had begun to gain power under Gedeonov. Lukashevich was intimate with the singer Y. F. Platonova and the famous O. A. Petrov, and these two were in high favour with L. I. Shestakova. Thus some sort of working connection was springing up between our circle and the Director of Theatres. I also believe that the connection had not happened without V. V. Stassov's having something to do with it. The four of us were invited to Gedeonov's for a joint deliberation on the work. Act I, as the most dramatic, was entrusted to the most dramatic composer — Cui; Act IV, in which the dramatic moments were blended with moments of elemental force, was entrusted to Borodin; Acts II and III were distributed between Moussorgsky and myself. Some portions of Act II (folk-wise choruses) were assigned to me; the first half of Act III (flight of shadows and appearance of Mlada) was reserved for me; while Moussorgsky undertook the second half — appearance of Chernobog (Black God), for which he wanted to utilize his *Night on Bald Mountain,* heretofore unused.[30]

The thought of *Mlada* and the few sketches I made for it took me away from *Pskovityanka* and the work on *The Stone Guest.* Cui composed the whole first act of *Mlada* rather rapidly. Borodin, who had been somewhat disappointed in writing *Prince Igor,* now took much of the suitable material from it, composed some new music also, and thus wrote almost the whole draft of Act IV. Moussorgsky composed the *March of the Princes* on a Russian theme (subsequently published separately, with the *Trio alla Turca*), as well as some other portions of Act II; he also made suitable changes in his *Night on Bald Mountain* and adapted it for Chernobog's appearance in Act III of *Mlada.* On the other hand, my notes of the chorus

30 The story of the composing of *Mlada* at S. A. Gedeonov's initiative belongs to 1871–2. Thus, in mentioning this " hired-labour business," as Moussorgsky expressed it (cf. his letters to V. V. Stassov, pp. 16–17), Rimsky-Korsakov runs considerably ahead of events. For more particulars about Gedeonov's *Mlada* cf. Stassov's *A. P. Borodin,* pp. 38 ff., and also A. N. Rimsky-Korsakov's *M. P. Moussorgsky, Letters and Documents* (State Musical Publishing Bureau, 1931), where " the market scene," composed by Moussorgsky for *Mlada,* is reproduced in the Appendix.

in Act II and the flight of shadows in Act III were still uncompleted and nothing would come of them, owing to a certain haziness and indefiniteness in the task of writing music to a scenario insufficiently worked out.[31]

Gedeonov's scheme was not destined to be realized. Soon he left the post of Director of Imperial Theatres and vanished from sight. The *Mlada* affair dropped into oblivion, and all of us turned to the work we had left for it; whatever we had composed for *Mlada* found its way into other compositions later. I set to orchestrating *The Stone Guest;* in March I orchestrated Tableau I, and then the turn came for work on the composition of *Pskovityanka.* For the time being, my work was limited to pondering and writing the outline. Of the orchestral score there existed only the "Chorus of Welcome" (later rewritten, calling for an added orchestra on the stage), and Vlasyevna's fairy-tale with Styosha's preceding scene, which had been orchestrated in October 1869.

The summer of 1870 was a repetition of the preceding one: I lived in my brother's unused apartment and went to Tervajoki on a two-months leave.[32] I had no acquaintances in St. Petersburg, except one family whom I visited every now and then — the family of Blagodarev, a classmate of mine at the Naval School and a great lover of music. The Purgolds had gone abroad this time, and the Misses P. read proof on Moussorgsky's *Seminarist,*[33] which was being printed at Leipzig because conditions of censorship precluded its publication in St. Petersburg. Besides *The Maid of Pskov,* the sketch of which was growing at a snail's pace, I worked on the orchestration of Tableaux III and IV of *The Stone Guest,* and there-

---

[31] The introduction to Act III of *Mlada* has been preserved in Rimsky-Korsakov's papers, in an arrangement for the piano. As music it constitutes an anticipation of certain ideas in subsequent operas: *May Night* (Pannochka) and *Snyegoorochka* (Will-o'-the-Wisp).

[32] On Borodin's visit to Rimsky-Korsakov on May 2 [15], 1870, cf. the former's letter (number X) to his wife: "Korsinka is living alone now. He is paying 11 rubles for his tiny room. He was indescribably delighted at seeing me . . ." (*A. P. Borodin,* pp. 76 ff.). "By July the whole band of robbers had scattered little by little. The Admiral [Rimsky-Korsakov] is already in Finland, and has not managed to come back from it, even for one little minute. . . ." Cf. V. V. Stassov's letter to N. N. Purgold in *Russkaya Mysl',* 1910, Vol. VI, p. 177.

[33] This song portrays the amorous preoccupations of a theological student. C. V. V.

with all work on this offspring of Dargomyzhsky's muse was finished during my stay at Tervajoki. In addition to this, the songs *Gdye ty, tam mysl' moya lyetayet* (*Where thou art, there flies my thought*); *The Hebrew Song; V tsarstvo rozy i vina pridi* (*Come to the realm of the rose and the wine*); *Ya vyeryu, ya lyubim* (*I believe I am loved*); *K moyey pyesnye* (*To my song*) were conceived and written partly in the summer and partly in the winter of the same year.[34]

---

[34] Written at Riva sul Lago di Garda, July 14 [27], 1906.

1870–71

Orchestration of Pskovityanka. *Entering on professional duties at the St. Petersburg Conservatory.*

THE SEASON OF 1870–1 proved barren of activities for the Free Music School. The money in hand had been spent on the five concerts of the preceding season; a temporary lull in the battle with the Directors of the Russian Musical Society was unavoidable. Balakirev was forced to submit to circumstances; nevertheless the thought of resuming the rivalry the next year did not leave him. He expected to wait a year without concerts and therefore without expenses for concerts, and then, having improved the financial status of the school, resume concert activity with the season of 1871–2. With *Islamey* completed, Balakirev's activity as a composer came to a standstill: the work of writing *Tamara* stopped, and he became completely absorbed in the thought of the coming concerts. Nevertheless he showed no reluctance to playing his *Islamey* as well as music by other people at the soirées of L. I. Shestakova and the Purgolds.

In December, Anna Antonovna, the mother of the Purgolds, fell ill and died, and the gatherings at their house were broken up. In February, I began to work assiduously on the orchestration of *Pskovityanka*, which was nearly ready in the rough by then. During February, Act I as far as the beginning of the duet of Toocha with Olga was orchestrated. I cannot recall why, but the writing of my score was interrupted for three months and resumed only in June.

The summer of 1871, as in the preceding years, I lived in the apartment of my brother, Voyin Andreyevich. During that summer, Moussorgsky never left St. Petersburg at all or else only for a short time, returning very soon. I met him often; usually he came to see me. During one of his visits I introduced him to my brother, who had come to the city for a few days, from his cruise. My brother had been brought up on the music of the palmy days of Italian opera in St. Petersburg; nevertheless he listened with deep interest to excerpts of *Boris Godunov*, which Modest gladly played at his request. Moussorgsky and I frequently called on the Purgolds, who now lived in First Pargolovo, by a lake. N. N. Lodyzhensky, who spent that summer in St. Petersburg, once accompanied me when I called on them. . . .

All summer I worked hard on the score of *Pskovityanka*. Acts I and II and Tableau I of Act III were entirely ready in orchestral score between June and September.[1]

During the summer of 1871, an important event occurred in my musical life. One fine day there came to me Azanchevsky, who had just entered upon his duties as Director of the St. Petersburg Conservatory vice N. I. Zaremba, retired. To my surprise, he asked me

---

[1] Written at Riva, July 15 [28], 1906.

The orchestral score of *The Maid of Pskov*, in the Central Musical Library of the State Academic Theatres, contains the following data on the orchestration of the opera:

Overture (folios 9–22), orchestrated January 8 [20], 1872.

Act I (folios 23–100): Scene i, orchestration finished June 3 [15], 1871; Scene ii (song about raspberries), orchestration finished February 24 [March 8], 1871; Scene iii (legend of the Tsarevna Lada) orchestrated October 12 [24], 1870; Scene iv (Mikhaylo Toocha's song) orchestrated February 25 [March 9], 1871; Scene v (duet of Olga and Toocha), orchestration completed June 2 [14], 1871.

Act II (scene of the *vyeche*) (folios 101–144) was orchestrated between July 3 [15] and July 21 [August 2], 1871.

Act III, First Tableau (folios 3–34). Introduction and Scene i were orchestrated August 19 [31], 1871; Scene ii, autograph of Nadezhda Nikolayevna Rimskaya-Korsakova; Scene iii was orchestrated on August 10 [22], 1871; Second Tableau (folios 35–65) was orchestrated September 2 [14], 1871.

Act IV (folios 66–160), Introduction autograph of Rimskaya-Korsakova. The First Tableau was orchestrated September 9 [21] and 3 [15], 1871. The First Tableau was orchestrated September 3 [15], 1871. The final chorus was orchestrated October 4 [16], 1871. The title page of the orchestral score bears the inscription: " Dedicated to the musical circle dear to me." [The fifth Russian edition of *My Musical Life* teems with typographical errors. Should the dates for orchestration of the First Tableau be September 2 [14] and 3 [15], 1871? And for orchestration of the *Second* Tableau be *October* 3 [15]? J. A. J.]

to join the staff of the Conservatory as Professor of Practical Composition and Instrumentation as well as Professor (i.e., leader) of the Orchestra Class. Evidently Azanchevsky's idea was to invite new blood in my person and thus freshen up teaching in these subjects, which had grown mouldy under Zaremba. The performance of my *Sadko* at a concert of the R. M. Society during the season just ended [2] manifestly had been a preliminary step on Azanchevsky's part to get into closer relations with me and prepare public opinion for this unexpected call to me to become professor at the Conservatory.[3] Realizing that I was totally unprepared for the proposed appointment, I gave Azanchevsky no definite answer and promised to think the matter over. My friends advised me to accept the offer.[4] Balakirev, the only one to realize how unprepared I was, insisted on an answer in the affirmative, his main object being *to get one of his own men* into the hostile Conservatory. The urgings of my friends and my own delusions, perhaps, won the day, and I accepted the offer. In autumn I was to become a professor at the Conservatory, without, for the time being, giving up my naval uniform.

Had I ever studied at all, had I possessed a fraction more of knowledge than I actually did, it would have been obvious to me that I could not and should not accept the proffered appointment, that it was foolish and dishonest of me to become a professor. But I, the author of *Sadko, Antar,* and *The Maid of Pskov,* compositions that were coherent and well-sounding, compositions that the public

---

[2] At the concert of March 13 [25], 1871, under E. F. Napravnik's direction.

[3] In an unpublished letter (undated, but with a pencil record in her handwriting) to his mother, S. V. Rimskaya-Korsakova, Rimsky-Korsakov thus imparts his considerations in favour of accepting the proposal: " After a little thinking I came to the conclusion that the proposition is of advantage to me in many respects; in the first place, financially; in the second, because I shall be engaged in work which I like and for which I am best fit; in the third place, it will afford me good practice, particularly in the matter of conducting; and, finally, because an opportunity presents itself for setting myself up definitely in the musical profession and cutting loose from the service, which to continue for a long time I consider neither an altogether honourable nor seemly business. After all these considerations, I gave the Conservatory my consent. . . ."

[4] Cf. *A. P. Borodin's Letters to Rimsky-Korsakov* (Letters XII and XIII): " I am sincerely rejoicing for you; you are in the right place — could not be better, and you can be of enormous benefit to the art of music and the student youth. . . ." August 22 [September 3], 1871, at Davydkovo. [The quotation is omitted in the fifth Russian edition. J. A. J.]

and many musicians approved, I was a dilettante and knew nothing. This I frankly confess and attest before the world. I was young and self-confident; my self-confidence was encouraged by others, and I joined the Conservatory. And yet at the time I could not decently harmonize a chorale; not only had I not written a single counterpoint in my life, but I had hardly any notion of the structure of a fugue; nay, did not even know the names of augmented and diminished intervals, of chords (except the fundamental triad), of the dominant and chord of the diminished seventh, though I could sing anything at sight and distinguish chords of every sort. The terms " chord of the sixth " and chord of " six-four " were unknown to me. In my compositions I had aimed at correctness of part-writing and attained it instinctively and by ear; correctness of the grammar of music I also attained instinctively. Also, my ideas of musical forms were vague, especially of rondo forms. I, who had instrumentated my compositions with a good deal of colour, had not the requisite information as to the technique of bow instruments, of the real keys (that were used in practice) of French horns, trumpets, and trombones. As to the conductor's art, having never conducted an orchestra, nor even rehearsed a single choral piece, of course I had no conception of it. And now Azanchevsky took it into his head to offer a professorship to a musician so ill informed, and the musician accepted without blinking.

Perhaps it will be said that all the above information which I lacked was unnecessary to the composer of *Sadko* and *Antar;* and that the very fact that *Sadko* and *Antar* existed proved that that information was unnecessary. To be sure, to hear and recognize an interval or a chord is more important than to know their names, the more so as those names can be learned in a day, if need be. It is more important to orchestrate colourfully than to know the instruments, as military bandmasters know them, who orchestrate by routine. Of course, to compose *Antar* or a *Sadko* is more interesting than to know how to harmonize a Protestant chorale or write four-part counterpoint, which seems to be necessary for organists alone. But it is shameful not to know such things and to learn of their existence from one's own pupils. Moreover, soon after composing *Pskovit-*

117

yanka, the lack of contrapuntal and harmonic technique displayed itself in the abrupt cessation of my creative fancy, at the basis of which lay the selfsame devices that I had ridden to death; only the development of a technique that I bent all my efforts to acquire permitted new living currents to flow into my creative work and untied my hands for further activity as a composer. In any case, with the information I possessed, it was wrong to take up professional duties, duties that involved pupils of all possible sorts: future composers, conductors, organists, teachers, etc.

But the step had been taken. Having bound myself to guide the Conservatory pupils, I had to pretend that I knew everything and that I understood all the problems of all the pupils. I had to resort to general remarks. In this I was helped by my personal taste, my sense of form, understanding of orchestral colouring, and a certain fund of experience in the general practice of composition; but I myself had to catch information from pupils, on the fly, so to speak. In the orchestra class I had to summon all possible self-control to my assistance. I was aided in this by the fact that at first none of my pupils could imagine that I knew nothing; and by the time they had learned enough to begin to see through me, I had learned something myself! What came of all this later on? The first students who graduated from the Conservatory in my time, Haller,[5] Lujer, and Startsev, were Zaremba's pupils entirely and had learned nothing from me. Kazbiryuk (a talented individual who fell to drinking and went to the dogs subsequently), who graduated from the Conservatory two or three years after I had joined it, was also entirely Y. I. Johansen's pupil in harmony and counterpoint; if he learned anything from me at all, it lay in a certain taste in instrumentation and in the general tendency of his compositions.[6] In-

---

[5] Konstantin Petrovich Haller (1845–88), composer, teacher, and critic.

[6] Kazbiryuk was graduated from the Conservatory in 1875. Excerpts from his examination cantata were performed at the Commencement, May 26 [June 7], 1875. In *Musical Listok* (*Leaflet*), No. 25, 1874–5, June 8 [20], there appeared a very laudatory review of these excerpts. It also said of Rimsky-Korsakov: " Both compositions prove, at all events, that Rimsky-Korsakov conducts his class rationally and, as a matter of fact, has justified the hopes placed in him by introducing two such pupils [the other was Sychev], and that to call him to a professorship at the Conservatory was a happy thought on the part of Mr. Azanchevsky. . . ."

deed, Zaremba kept his pupils on Gluck, Mozart, Cherubini, and Mendelssohn, whereas I directed them to Beethoven, Schumann, and Glinka, who, indeed, were more modern and more to their liking.

Beginning with 1874, I undertook to teach harmony and counterpoint. Having thoroughly familiarized myself with orchestral instruments, I acquired a fair technique — that is, I untied my hands for my own work of composition. On the other hand, I began also to be of some use to my pupils as a practical teacher. The subsequent generations of pupils who came to me from Johansen or those who later began their studies directly under me were really my pupils and probably will not deny it. Thus having been undeservedly accepted at the Conservatory as a professor, I soon became one of its best and possibly its very best *pupil*, judging by the quantity and value of the information it gave me! Twenty-five years after, when my Conservatory friends and the Board of Directors of the R. M. Society honoured me with jubilee greetings and speeches, I expressed this very thought in reply to Cui's address. Thus matters stood in the class in theory of composition and practical composition. In the orchestra class things were somewhat different.

Having begun rather auspiciously as conductor in the orchestra class, I kept that class at a fairly high level. As early as the second year the Students' Soirées had the assistance of the orchestra under my leadership. Once I tried my complete Third Symphony in this class, but the rehearsal was a failure, as the pupils, who played from manuscript, made innumerable errors. Yet I had no heart to weed out mistakes and make the pupils learn the symphony; I did not want to exploit the student orchestra under my control nor to divert it from its regular assigned work and exercises. Generally speaking, my orchestra class got along well, if not brilliantly. Nevertheless, among some of my colleague professors the desire to conduct the accompaniments for the solo numbers of their pupils was so ardent that they frequently pushed their way into the orchestral class for that purpose; I yielded the conductor's bâton to them out of politeness — really, perhaps, out of my innate easy-going disposition. Of course, I was a very poor operatic conductor at the time; yet the task of leading the students' operatic performances should have been assigned to me. However, during the first year Azanchevsky undertook this duty himself, and then entrusted it to Ferrero. The reason he gave for doing so was that Ferrero was supposed to have operatic traditions at his fingers' ends. A brief, somewhat strained interview on this subject with Azanchevsky (I believe, in the spring of 1875) led to my resignation as the conductor of the orchestra class. The class was entrusted to K. Y. Davydov,[7] but the schedule of my theoretical courses was slightly increased, so that my salary of a thousand rubles remained as before.[8] From this period when I led the orchestra class I have retained one rather pleasant reminiscence — the arranging of a musical evening (in 1873, I think) in memory of deceased Russian composers; it was February 2, the anniversary of Glinka's death. The evening was given under my direction, though the initiative belonged to A. I. Rubyets, who had trained the chorus of Conservatory students. For the first time before an audience the student orchestra played fairly well. We gave, among other things, *A Night in Madrid;* "The Narrative of the Head" (Act II, *Ruslan and Lyudmila*); Introduction to *A Life for the Tsar*; Serov's *Hopak*; Dargomyzhsky's duet *Dyevitsy krasavitsy* (*Maids of Beauty*), sung by a chorus of women's voices. I have a recollection that Dütsch and Lyadov played instruments of percussion. Both orchestra and chorus acquitted themselves fairly well, and the impression was most favourable. After that, for several years, there was a custom of arranging public concerts of that nature every February 2; the next was again directed by me, excerpts from the older Dütsch's *Kroatka* (*The Croatian Girl*) being on the program. The subsequent annual evenings were directed by others, as I had given up the post of professor in the orchestra class. Having left that class, I found myself insufficiently prepared for the work of conducting concerts or opera. If I did, later on, achieve a certain measure of success in conducting and was able safely to lead the concerts of the Free

---

[7] Karl Davydov, cellist, composer, and teacher. Born at Goldingen, Kurland, 1838; died at Moscow, 1889. C. V. V.

[8] According to the report of the Russian Musical Society and of the Conservatory for 1875–6, the orchestra class was already in the hands of K. Y. Davydov.

Music School, the Russian Symphony concerts, and even operatic performances, it was due to my subsequent experience with the naval bands and the Student Orchestra of the Court Chapel, and again to my constant study of Napravnik's methods, when he produced my operas at the Mariinsky Theatre.

Illness and death of my brother. Living with Moussorgsky. Diffi-
culties with the censor about Pskovityanka. *N. K. Krabbe. Produc-*
tion of The Stone Guest. *Marriage and trip abroad. Production*
of Pskovityanka *and scenes from* Boris Godunov. *Symphony in C*
major. Appointment to the post of Inspector of Music Bands of the
Navy Department. Study of wind instruments.

IN THE FALL OF 1871 my brother Voyin Andreyevich's health, which
had been shattered for several years by heart disease, grew considerably worse. With his wife and his three children he left for
Pisa to spend the autumn and winter there. My mother went to
Moscow to see her niece, S. N. Bedryaga. Thus my brother's apartment was vacant all winter, and nothing attracted me to Vasilevsky
Ostrov. Moussorgsky and I agreed to live together, and we took
rooms, or rather a furnished room, in Zaremba's house on Panteleymonovskaya Street. This, I imagine, is the only case of two composers living together.[1] How could we help being in each other's
way? This is how we managed. Mornings until about noon, Mous-

---

[1] An estimate of this joint housekeeping was made by Moussorgsky in his brief
inscription on the photographic portrait which he gave Rimsky-Korsakov: " As for
our living together may it be recalled with kindness. To a Friend — Moussorgsky."
Cf. also A. P. Borodin's view of the reciprocal beneficence of the intimate relations
between Moussorgsky and Rimsky-Korsakov at that epoch, in Borodin's letter No. XIV
to his wife, p. 86.

sorgsky used the piano, and I did copying or else orchestrated something fully thought out. By noon he would go to his departmental duties, leaving the piano at my disposal. In the evening, time was allotted by mutual agreement. Moreover, twice a week I went to the Conservatory at nine a.m., while Moussorgsky frequently dined at the Opochinins'; so that things adjusted themselves in the best of fashions. That autumn and winter the two of us accomplished a good deal, with constant exchange of ideas and plans. Moussorgsky composed and orchestrated the Polish act of *Boris Godunov* and the folk-scene " Near Kromy." I orchestrated and finished my *Maid of Pskov*. Towards the beginning of October the second tableau of Act III and the whole of Act IV of *Pskovityanka* were ready; only the Overture was to be written.

Early in November the even tenor of our life was interrupted for some time as follows: From Pisa came a telegram with the news of my brother's sudden death.[2] The Navy Department dispatched me with a considerable sum of money to bring his body to St. Petersburg. Hurriedly I made ready and started for Pisa via Vienna, Semmering, and Bologna. Several days later my brother's embalmed body was sent on, and I left for St. Petersburg, escorting the family of the deceased. In Vienna we stopped to rest for some days. At the time Anton Rubinstein was in Vienna conducting a series of symphony concerts. He was preparing to give the first performance of Liszt's recently finished oratorio *Christus*. I secured Rubinstein's address and went to see him. He received me very cordially and, immediately seating himself at the piano, played me almost the whole oratorio from the advance sheets of the piano score.

[2] V. A. Rimsky-Korsakov died on November 4 [16], 1871.

Rimsky-Korsakov arrived in Pisa, November 12 [24], 1871. In his letter from Pisa, written on the day after his arrival, he wrote to Miss N. N. Purgold: " On coming home from your house that last evening, I was so unhinged that I quite forgot myself and, almost in a state of fever, wrote you, and now that letter appears in a sort of haze, but one thing I shall say, that I do not recant one single word of that letter. The following day I left St. Petersburg with an extremely morbid feeling; of course, with the sense of fatigue and the impressions of the trip that feeling has worn off to some degree. I thought of you much all through the journey . . . and whenever during the trip I happened to see something worth while, I always had a desire to gaze at it with you."

Rimsky-Korsakov departed from Pisa, on receiving from Rome leave to transport V. A.'s body by train, November 17 [29], 1871.

After I had returned to St. Petersburg and Voyin Andreyevich had been buried, my life slipped into its old groove, with Moussorgsky, in Panteleymonovskaya Street.

On Sunday afternoons one or another of our acquaintances came to visit us. In passing, let me mention the visit of N. F. Solovyov, who evidently wished to knit a closer acquaintance. But recently graduated from the Conservatory, he had been close to Serov. Upon the latter's death, Solovyov collaborated with the widow V. S. Serova to complete *Vrazhya Sila* [3] (*The Fiendish Power*) from the composer's sketches, and he also orchestrated Act V of the opera. *Vrazhya Sila* was produced at the Mariinsky Theatre [4] and scored a considerable success, though less so than *Rognyeda* in its time; but Solovyov, who had completed this composition, began to attract a measure of public attention. However, no closer relations were entered into, and he did not repeat the visit.

Let me also recall the following episode. One Sunday H. A. Laroche [5] came to see us. At first, conversation ran along safely enough, but V. V. Stassov, who dropped in by chance, was at our visitor's throat in an instant. V. V. could not stand Laroche for his ultra-conservatism in music and his views à la Katkov. Stassov had shown deep interest in Laroche's first long and splendid article on *Ruslan and Lyudmila*. But in his subsequent articles Laroche (he worked on Katkov's *Moscow Gazette*) began to express himself more and more as a convinced champion of technical perfection in art; as an apologist of the old Flemings, Palestrina, Bach, and Mozart; as an opponent of Beethoven, as a preacher of eclecticism, provided it was accompanied by perfection of technique, and as a foe of " the mighty *koochka* (band)." In view of Laroche's critical articles and their tendencies, his liking for Berlioz's music was queer and incomprehensible — music so unusual, " dishevelled," and, in any event, far from technically perfect. Stassov's squabble with Laroche was long drawn out and unpleasant. Laroche tried to be restrained and logical; while Stassov, as usual,

---

[3] Founded on a play by Ostrovsky. C. V. V.
[4] *Vrazhya Sila* was given at St. Petersburg, April 19 [May 1], 1871.
[5] Serov's successor on the *Golos*. C. V. V.

V. V. STASSOV

from the painting by I. Y. Ryepin

took the bit in his teeth and rushed into rudeness, accusations of dishonesty, and so on. One could hardly get them to stop.

In December 1871 Nadezhda Nikolayevna Purgold became my betrothed. The wedding was set for the summer, at Pargolovo. Naturally my visits to the Purgolds, rather frequent until then, grew still more frequent; I spent almost every evening with Nadya. Nevertheless my work continued. The Overture to *Pskovityanka* was being composed and was completed in orchestral score in January 1872.

I submitted the libretto to the dramatic censor. The censor Fridberg insisted that certain changes and toning down in expression should be made in the *vyeche* (free city assembly) scene. I had to submit. The words *vyeche, vol'nitsa* (volunteers), *styepyeny posadnik* (actual mayor of a free city), etc. should be replaced with the words: *skhodka* (meeting), *druzhina* (yeomanry), *pskovski namyestnik* (governor of Pskov). From Toocha's song the following lines were stricken out:

> Dented have become our swords,
> And our axes lost their edge.
> Is there nothing left on which
> We may sharpen axe and sword?

At the censor's office I was told that all changes must aim at removing from my libretto the slightest suggestion of the republican form of government in Pskov, and the *vyeche* of Act II must be transformed into an ordinary riot. In order to grasp the full bearing of the scene, Fridberg invited Moussorgsky and me to his house one evening and made us play and sing him the second act, which he enjoyed in no slight degree. But the principal obstacle was found somewhere else. In the Censorship Bureau there was a document of the forties, I believe, an order of H. I. M. Emperor Nicholas I, which stated that rulers antedating the house of the Romanovs [6] may be represented on the stage in drama and tragedy only, but not in opera. To my inquiry: why? I received the reply: "And suppose the Tsar should suddenly sing a ditty; well, it would

---

[6] 1613. J. A. J.

be unseemly." At all events, there was His Majesty's order, not to be disregarded; it was necessary to get by it in a roundabout way. In the seventies the Secretary of the Navy was N. K. Krabbe, a courtier, arrogant, a poor seaman, who had reached the post of Secretary by way of adjutant and staff service. A man fond of music and the theatre, and still more so of pretty artists, but kind-hearted at all events. My deceased brother, Voyin Andreyevich, a splendid seaman, an impartial and straightforward man, had always been at daggers drawn with the Secretary of the Navy, in all meetings, councils, and committees. They held contrary views on all questions that came up at the Ministry, and Voyin Andreyevich, who heatedly stood up for his opinions, often fought and won against the motions of Krabbe (who strove only to please august personages). Occasionally the reverse happened, and things were done that V. A. thought inadvisable. Be that as it may, official war between Krabbe and V. A. never ceased. On my brother's death, the feeling of respect for the memory of his official enemy strikingly manifested itself in N. K. Krabbe's actions. Of his own accord, he hastened to do everything possible in order to provide for the family as well as the mother of the deceased. N. K. Krabbe's feelings took me in as well, and suddenly I became a favourite with him. He sent for me unsolicited and was gracious and amiable; he proposed that I turn to him in all difficulties, and he gave me permission to visit him at any time. The censorship difficulties with *Pskovityanka* made me apply to him, and with the greatest readiness he undertook to solicit, through the Grand Duke Konstantin,[7] the abrogation of the antiquated Imperial order forbidding the representation in opera of persons reigning *before the house of Romanovs*. Grand Duke Konstantin also took up the matter with a will, and the censor shortly informed me that Tsar Ivan had been permitted to appear on the operatic boards and that the libretto had been licensed by the censor on condition of changes in the matter of the *vyeche*. At the same time my opera was accepted by the Board of Directors of the Imperial Theatres, of which the immediate management, after

---

[7] The Grand Duke Konstantin Nikolayevich, brother of Alexander II and, at this time, High Admiral of the Russian Fleet. C. V. V.

the dismissals of Gedeonov and Fyodorov, lay in the hands of Lukashevich, who was well disposed towards the members of our circle.
However, the supreme though unofficial direction of the theatres
devolved at that time upon Baron Kister, Controller of the Ministry of the Court. There was no real director. Napravnik, though
not in favour of my opera, had to bow to Lukashevich's influence,
and the work was announced for the following season. At any rate,
in the matter of its acceptance for a production at the Mariinsky
Theatre, the intercession of the Grand Duke into censorship affairs
had surely had a considerable effect. I imagine that the reasoning
of the Board of Directors of the Theatres was as follows: the Grand
Duke himself is interested in Rimsky-Korsakov's opera; consequently it is impossible not to accept it. Napravnik had become acquainted with *Pskovityanka* one evening at Lukashevich's, where
Moussorgsky and I were invited. Modest, who sang magnificently in
every voice, helped me show the opera to advantage before those
present. Of course, Napravnik did not express his opinion, but
merely praised our clean-cut execution. Generally, the performances of *The Maid of Pskov* with piano accompaniment at Krabbe's
and frequently at the Purgold house went as follows: Moussorgsky
sang Tsar Ivan Grozny, Tokmakov, and other male rôles, according
to need; a young physician Vasilyev (a tenor) sang Matoota and
Toocha; A. N. Purgold sang Olga and the nurse; my fiancée played
the accompaniment, and I, as emergency demanded, either helped
out in the other parts or played four-hands with Nadya whatever
was impracticable for two hands. She, too, made the arrangement
of *The Maid of Pskov* for voice and piano. The performances with
the above cast were excellent, clear, fiery, and full of style, and took
place every time before a considerable gathering of interested listeners.[8]

In February 1872 *The Stone Guest,* with my orchestration, was
performed at the Mariinsky Theatre.[9] I attended all rehearsals.

---

[8] Cf. the description of one of these performances in A. P. Borodin's letter to his
wife, Letter XIV, p. 85.
[9] The first performance took place on February 16 [28], 1872. The history of the

Napravnik was impassive, though his manner was irreproachable. I was content with my orchestration and quite delighted with the opera. The opera was well cast. Kommissarzhevsky, the Don Juan; Platonova, the Donna Anna; Petrov, the Leporello were all excellent; nor did the others spoil the good impression. The audiences were perplexed, but the opera had success nevertheless. I do not remember how many performances *The Stone Guest* had; but not many, at any rate. Soon the opera was off the boards, and for a long period, too.

The war between Balakirev and the Russian Musical Society was renewed: five subscription concerts of the Free Music School, with interesting programs, were announced. Balakirev worked energetically, but the attendance was insufficient; the funds gave out, and the fifth concert could not take place.[10] The war was lost; Balakirev was crestfallen. In the spring he made a trip to Nizhni Novgorod and gave a piano recital there, counting on the local interest in him as a native of Nizhni Novgorod.[11] The hall was empty. Balakirev called this concert "his Sedan"; on returning to St. Petersburg he began to avoid people, even his close friends; he drew back into his shell and for a long time gave up all activity, neither appearing in public nor doing any creative work.[12] A great moral change was going on within him: this utter unbeliever had

preliminary conversations with the Directorate of Imperial Theatres concerning this production as well as of the arrangement of the claims of A. S. Dargomyzhsky's heir has been told by V. V. Stassov in his letter of July 23 [August 4], 1870 to Rimsky-Korsakov (*Russkaya Mysl'*, 1910, Vol. VI, pp. 177 ff.).

[10] The concerts of the Free Music School were given November 20 [December 2] and December 18 [30], 1871; February 12 [24] and April 3 [15], 1872.

[11] The concert at Nizhni Novgorod, here referred to, was given in the summer of 1870. This is what A. P. Borodin wrote of it to his wife on September 22 [October 4], 1870:

" Mili was quite happy to see me. His affairs are very wretched, so wretched that perhaps he will not give a series of concerts this year, after all. In Mili's phrase, Nizhni Novgorod was his Sedan." Cf. *A. P. Borodin's Letters, with Notes by S. Dianin*.

[12] The beginning of this estrangement belongs as far back as spring 1871. Cf. V. V. Stassov's letter of April 17 [29], 1871 to Rimsky-Korsakov: " No, he is an altogether different man. Yesterday there stood before me some coffin and not the former lively, energetic M. A." (*Russkaya Mysl'*, 1910, Vol. VI, p. 184). Cf. also A. P. Borodin's letter of October 27 [November 8], 1871, to his wife. For the history of Balakirev's estrangement from the circle and from musical life, cf. A. Rimsky-Korsakov: " The Two Balakirevs " (in *Musical Annals*, 1926, No. 3) and also his book *N. A. Rimsky-Korsakov, Life and Creative Work* (State Musical Publishing Bureau, 1935), Part II, Chapter iii: " The History of a Friendship."

turned religious mystic and fanatic. During the next few years of complete estrangement from all, he held some clerical position in a freight station of the Warsaw Railroad. Rumour had it that he was mentally unbalanced; this was untrue in any case, as his spiritual reconstruction cannot be considered a derangement in the current sense of the word. It was said that his close associates were now Terti Ivanovich Filippov [13] and a certain " Old Believer " [14] priest; and that this latter had enshrouded Balakirev with the rayless gloom of ancient Russia; to that extent the rumour subsequently proved to be fairly correct. Balakirev's moral crisis and estrangement lasted for a long time, and only in the late seventies did he gradually begin to turn back to public and creative activity, but he was already a profoundly changed man.

I spent the beginning of summer at First Pargolovo, where I rented a small room in order to be near the Purgolds and my fiancée. [15] My marriage took place on June 30 [July 12]. We were married in the church of Shuvalov Park. Moussorgsky was my best man. The wedding took place in the daytime; after dinner at the summerhouse of my bride's family we went to St. Petersburg, directly to

---

[13] T. I. Filippov, Imperial Comptroller. For him cf. pp. 163 f. of this book.

[14] In *A Short History of Russian Music*, Montagu-Nathan writes concerning this sect: " During his regency, Boris Godunov made an important change in ecclesiastical administration. Hitherto the Russian Church had been governed from Constantinople in consequence of the adoption by Russia of the Byzantine form of Christianity. Godunov, desirous of obtaining the support of the Russian clergy, established a Patriarchate at Moscow. To this office Nikon was appointed in 1642. During his tenure, Nikon determined upon making what he considered a very necessary revision in the liturgical books of the Church. These had for generations past been copied by hand, and many inaccuracies had crept into their pages. On the adoption of printing, these inaccuracies were of course invested with sanction. Nikon went to the fountain-head and obtained copies of the Greek originals from Constantinople with the object of making the necessary restoration. Errors had also been made in copying the printed ikons or sacred tokens. Nikon introduced certain reforms in the ritual in reference to the manner of making the sign of the cross, of pronouncing the name of Jesus, and of alluding to the Deity in the Creed. These changes, together with those in the liturgical books, brought about the schism which divided the whole Russian Church. The adherents of the traditional and accepted form of worship called themselves Old Believers. Nothing could more plainly reveal the fanaticism which has entered into the dispute between the two bodies than the surviving rejection of all printed literature which the Old Believers still consider as more likely to contain errors than written versions. By some of the Old Believers, to cross oneself before a painted ikon is characterized as an act of blasphemy. The Orthodox Church had been doing its best for nearly three hundred years to stamp out these non-conforming sects, when, in 1906, Stolypin granted recognition to all religious sects in Russia." C. V. V.

[15] Written at Riva, July 25 [August 7], 1906.

the Warsaw Station, escorted by all of our connections, and left for abroad. Via Warsaw and Vienna we journeyed to Switzerland — to Zürich and Zug; climbed Rigi afoot, descended to Arth, and arrived in Lucerne. After a brief stay in Lucerne, we crossed on a steamboat to Flüelen, thence by horseback to the Rhine Glacier, Grimsel, Reichenbach; next, via the glacier Rosenlaui, to Grindelwald, Lauterbrunnen, and Interlaken. After a very unsuccessful visit to the Valley of Chamonix, we crossed to Italy by way of the Simplon Pass. Having spent a little time on the lakes Maggiore, Lugano, and Como, and in Milan and Venice, we turned for our homeward journey to St. Petersburg through Vienna and Warsaw.

We returned to Russia in mid-August and spent the rest of the summer at Pargolov; we paid a brief visit, however, to my mother at Tervajoki, as she still lived with my deceased brother's family. Early in the autumn my wife and I took rooms on Shpalernaya Street.

Meanwhile, at the Mariinsky Theatre, rehearsals of *Pskovityanka* began; the arrangement for voice and piano had been published by Bessel in the autumn.[16] Owing to my trip abroad, I had not read the proof of this edition, but had entrusted it to Cui. The edition came out with a multitude of mistakes in both music and text. In the text there were such errors as made it absolutely impossible to guess the sense of some of the word groups; *vanous poeks,* for instance, which actually appeared in the text, was supposed to mean: *various folks,* etc.

As customary, the rehearsals of *The Maid of Pskov* began with the choruses. I attended the choral rehearsals, accompanied the chorus, and later the soloists, myself. Petrov sang Tsar Ivan; Platonova sang Olga; Leonova sang the Nurse; Orlov sang Mikhaylo Toocha; Myelnikov, Prince Tokmakov. I. A. Pomazansky and Y. S. Azyeyev, the chorus-masters, were highly delighted with my opera; Napravnik was impassive and did not express his opinion, but his disapproval made itself felt even against his will. The singers were

---

[16] *Pskovityanka,* opera in four acts, subject taken from L. Mey's drama, composed by Nikolay Rimsky-Korsakov. Arrangement for the piano and voice by Nadezhda Purgold (censor's permission May 5 [17], 1872).

conscientious and amiable; O. A. Petrov was not quite pleased, complaining of the number of long-drawn-out passages and stage mistakes which it was difficult to overcome in the acting. He was right in many ways, but youth made me fly into a passion; I therefore yielded nothing, would not allow cuts, and naturally and obviously irritated both him and Napravnik exceedingly. After the choral and solo rehearsals, came orchestral rehearsals for weeding out mistakes. Napravnik worked magnificently, pouncing upon all errors of the copyists as well as my own slips of the pen. The recitatives he led in (normal) time, and that angered me greatly. Only later did I grasp that he had been right and that my recitatives had been written inconveniently for free and unconstrained declamation, as they were overburdened with various orchestral figures. The music of Matoota's attack on Toocha and Olga had to be lightened somewhat by changing certain orchestral figures to more practicable ones. The same thing had to be done in the scene of Matoota's visit to the Tsar. The flutist Klosé, who had struggled to blow a lengthy legato figure without rests on the piccolo, finally dropped it, as his breath had given out; I was obliged to insert rests for breathing. But save for such trifling shortcomings all went satisfactorily. The singers had considerable difficulty with the ¾ duet in Act IV; Napravnik, too, frowned, but found a way out. Finally stage rehearsals commenced; here, in putting on the *vyeche* scene the stage managers G. P. Kondratyev and A. Y. Morozov showed great zeal: they dressed in costume and took part in the mass movements, both at rehearsals and in the early performances of the opera, like any member of the cast.

The première took place January 1, 1873.[17] The performance was fine; the artists gave of their best. Orlov sang magnificently in the

---

[17] The first performance was given as Platonova's benefit performance, after several postponements (owing to Orlov's illness); the second as Myelnikov's benefit; the third was called off owing to the death of the Grand Duchess Yelena Pavlovna; the fifth took place as Petrov's benefit performance and was the occasion of particularly warm honours being paid to the beneficiary. (Cf. *Musical Leaflet*, 1872, Chronicle, in December issues.) The artists appearing in the first performance were: The Tsar, Petrov; Prince Tokmakov, Myelnikov; Matoota, Vasilyev II; Prince Vyazyesnsky, Sariotti; Mikhaylo Toocha, Orlov; Yooshko Vyelyebin, Sobolyev; Olga, Platonova; Styosha, Boolakhova; Vlasyevna, Leonova; Perfilyevna, Shreder; Watchman, Pavlov.

vyeche scene, leading off the chorus of the free city volunteers with splendid effect. Petrov, Leonova, Platonova, as well as chorus and orchestra were good. The opera met with favour, especially the second act; I was called out many times.[18] During the course of that season *Pskovityanka* was sung ten times to full houses and great applause.[19] I was pleased, though the press, with the exception of Cui, belaboured me soundly.[20] With others, Solovyov found in the piano score of *Pskovityanka* an incorrectly represented tremolo (one of the numerous misprints in that edition); evidently alluding to my professorship at the Conservatory, he venomously advised me to " go to school, and repeat and go to school." [21] Rappoport said that I " had profoundly studied the secrets of harmony " (at the time I had not studied them at all); but then followed a multitude of all sorts of " buts " proving my opera worthless. Nor did Fyeofil Tolstoy (Rostislav), Laroche, and Famintsyn pat my work on the back. Famintsyn laid especial stress on the dedication of my opera " to the music circle dear to me "; and from this he drew most extraordinary conclusions. On the other hand, the scene of the Pskov *vol'nitsa* (commonwealth volunteers) struck the fancy of the young students, who were bawling the song of the *vol'nitsa* to their hearts' content, up and down the corridors of the academy.

The Russian Opera, however, under Lukashevich's supreme direction, did not confine itself that season to the production of *The Maid of Pskov*. Towards the end of the theatre season were put on, at someone's benefit performance, two scenes of *Boris Godunov:*

---

[18] " All in all, Mr. Rimsky-Korsakov came forward in the conductor's box from ten to fifteen times." N. Solovyov, in the *Bourse Gazette*, 1873, No. 4.

[19] There were ten performances in the interval between January 1 [13] and February 15 [27].

[20] Articles about *The Maid of Pskov* appeared in 1873 as follows: in *St. Petersburg Gazette*, Cui's review in No. 9 and M.'s (from Odessa), " Three Russian Operas "; H. A. Laroche's reviews in the *Moscow Gazette* (Nos. 25 and 28) and in *Russian World;* anonymous in *St. Petersburg Leaflet*, No. 5; under the initials V. V. in *Musical Leaflet* (Nos. 16 and 17) for the years 1872–3. The articles of N. Solovyov and others point out that *Pskovityanka* had been produced in spite of an unfavourable resolution passed by the Opera Committee. We have not succeeded in checking this assertion on the basis of Archive data.

[21] This phrase does not occur in N. Solovyov's article. In mentioning the incorrect representation of a tremolo, Solovyov observes: " Such ignorance of one of the elementary rules is not a little astonishing in the edition of a work of a Conservatory professor."

the inn scene and the scene at the fountain.²² Petrov was magnificent as Varlaam; Platonova as Marina, and Kommissarzhevsky as
Dmitri, were also fine. The scenes scored a great hit. Moussorgsky
and all of us were in raptures, and it was proposed to give *Boris
Godunov* in its entirety the following season. After the above performance Moussorgsky, Stassov, Aleksandra Nikolayevna (my
wife's sister, who had married N. P. Molas ²³ in the fall of 1872),
and other people who stood close to our musical activity came together at our house. At supper, champagne was drunk, with wishes
for the early performance and success of *Boris.*

My wife and her sister, Mme A. N. Molas, two formerly active
participants in all the musical gatherings at the house of Vladimir
Fyodorovich Purgold, were already like " slices off the loaf " and
no longer in the counting. Still, the musical gatherings that had
taken place at V. F.'s house for so many years did not cease during
the autumn preceding the production of *Pskovityanka* and the
scenes from *Boris;* both *The Stone Guest* and *Boris Godunov*, in its
entirety, as well as *Pskovityanka* were sung there with the same cast.

At our house, also, Moussorgsky, Borodin, and Stassov met very
frequently. At that time Moussorgsky's thoughts had already turned
toward *Khovanshchina.*²⁴ I began writing a Symphony in C major;
for its Scherzo I took the E-flat-major Scherzo in ¾ time which I
had in my portfolio and the trio of which I had composed aboard
some steamer on one of the Italian lakes during my honeymoon
abroad. Work on the first movement of the symphony was slow,
however, and beset with difficulties; I strove to crowd in as much
counterpoint as possible; but being unskilled in it and hard put to
combine the themes and motives, I drained my immediate flow of

²² First performance – a benefit for G. P. Kondratyev – February 5 [17], 1873.
To correct Rimsky-Korsakov's inaccuracy, not two, but three scenes were put on:
the Polish two and the one at the inn. For this, in greater detail, cf. A. Rimsky-
Korsakov's article: " M. P. Moussorgsky's *Boris Godunov*," in *Musical Contemporary*,
1916–17, Nos. 5–6, pp. 120 ff.
²³ Molas was a naval officer. As Admiral of the Russian Fleet, he went down in
the flagship, *Petropavlovsk*, at the entrance of the harbour of Port Arthur during the
Russo-Japanese war. C. V. V.
²⁴ The beginning of preliminary labours belongs in the middle of 1872. *The Song
of Marfa, the Schismatic,* had already come off the press in November 1873. Cf.
Musical Leaflet, 1873–4, No. 6, Advertisements.

imagination considerably. The cause of this was, of course, my insufficient technique; yet I was irresistibly drawn to add greater interest to the structural style of my compositions. A similar fate befell the third movement of the symphony — Andante. The Finale presented somewhat less difficulty; but the combination of several subjects at its end proved another stumbling-block. Nevertheless, the sketch of the symphony was ready in the spring, and, from the rough draft, we tried it out on the piano at our gatherings.

What Borodin was composing at that time, I do not remember; most likely he recklessly divided his energies between *Prince Igor* [25] and the Second Symphony in B minor, which was still a long way from completion. Cui was once more thinking of a new opera and was composing many songs, of which *Meniscus* was dedicated to me, and *Iz vod podymaya golovku* (*Lifting the little head from the waters*) to my wife. Of those who were, so to speak, outsiders in our intimate circle, Platonova, Paskhalov, the architect Hartmann, and N. V. Galkin [26] visited us that year. I remember as if it were today that on one occasion Galkin, who had come to see us, helped us to make tea, as our only maid had suddenly left that day. With our combined efforts we tried to make the samovar work, and Galkin fanned the charcoal with a boot-leg. Paskhalov, who had come from Moscow as a newly discovered genius, played us excerpts from his opera *A Grand Rout at Satan's Court,* as well as a would-be orchestral fantasy in the nature of a dance. All this music was immature and in reality gave but slight promise. Paskhalov soon vanished from the horizon; he began to drink, composed commonplace songs to make money, and died an early death, leaving nothing remarkable in the way of compositions.[27] I also recall that one morning a friend of my wife's, one Mayev, I think, brought to

---

[25] As early as in 1876, having lost faith in *Igor* ever being composed by Borodin, V. V. Stassov offered this subject to Rimsky-Korsakov. Cf. his letter dated July 23 [August 4], 1875, to Rimsky-Korsakov (in *Russkaya Mysl'*, 1910, Vol. VI, pp. 177 ff.).

[26] Viktor Nikandrovich Paskhalov (1841–85); Viktor Aleksandrovich Hartmann (1834–73), a friend of Moussorgsky's and Stassov's; N. V. Galkin (1856–1906), violinist, professor at the St. Petersburg Conservatory, conductor.

[27] V. N. Paskhalov composed many songs, of which *Dityatko, milost' Gospodña s toboyu* (*Baby mine, the Lord's mercy be with you!*) was formerly one of the most popular songs in Russia. J. A. J.

our house a boy who had obvious musical talent and played the piano charmingly; Mayev and I were to decide together whether the boy should be sent to the Conservatory. The answer was in the affirmative. That boy was E. A. Krooshevsky, subsequently my pupil in the class of composition, later an accompanist, and finally second conductor of the Russian Opera.

During the season of 1872–3 Balakirev remained out of sight, as he had entirely withdrawn from music and from all people who had formerly been close to him. The Free Music School no longer showed many signs of life; from time to time classes of some sort as well as choir-drilling went on under Pomazansky's direction, but the Director himself was never seen, and there was no talk of concerts. The life of the school was ebbing slowly but surely.

In the spring of 1873 the Director of the Chancellery of the Navy Department, K. A. Mann, at a hint from N. K. Krabbe, summoned me and told me that there had been established a new post of Inspector of Music Bands of the Navy Department; that I had been chosen for the post; that a complement of musician pupils was being organized, as holders of Navy Department fellowships at the St. Petersburg Conservatory; and that their immediate supervision was entrusted to me.[28] My duties included the inspecting of all Navy Department Music Bands throughout Russia; thus I was to supervise the bandmasters and their appointments, the repertory, the quality of the instruments, etc.; I was also to write a program of studies for the newly appointed fellows, and to act as intermediary between the Navy Department and the Conservatory. In

---

[28] In the *Musical Leaflet* of May 25 [June 6], 1873 (No. 28), this item appeared ("News"): "The professor of the St. Petersburg Conservatory, Composer of *Pskovityanka*, Lieutenant N. A. Rimsky-Korsakov, has been appointed Inspector of Music Bands of the Navy Department, with the rank of Collegiate Assessor" [civil rank next higher to lieutenant in the Navy or captain in the Army. J. A. J.]. Rimsky-Korsakov's work as Inspector may be traced in the *Kronstadt Messenger* during the seventies and early eighties.

The order for Rimsky-Korsakov's appointment as Inspector of Music Bands of the Navy Department, with promotion to the rank of Collegiate Assessor under date May 8 [20], was published in the official section of the *Naval Magazine*, 1873, No. 6.

There, likewise, was published the Admiral-General's order and announcement for the Navy Department under date of May 12 [24] concerning the post of Inspector being instituted with the appropriation to it, as a post of the sixth class, of 1,000 rubles for salary, 1,000 rubles for board, and 800 rubles for lodging — a total of 2,800 rubles.

May the order affecting me was issued. I was appointed to the new post with civilian rank, and I parted with delight with both my military status and my officer's uniform. The post took care of me rather well financially, and I was on the roster of the Chancellery of the Naval Department. Henceforth I was a musician officially and incontestably. I was in ecstasy; so were my friends. Congratulations were showered on me. Dear V. V. Stassov delightedly prophesied that some day I would be Director of the Court Chapel, and he would on that occasion drink his beloved yellow tea in my apartment near the Chapel Bridge. Under such circumstances the summer of 1873 came, and my wife and I moved to a summer house in First Pargolovo.[29]

My appointment to the post of Inspector of Music Bands stirred up a desire of long standing in me, to familiarize myself thoroughly with the construction and technique of orchestral instruments. I obtained some of these — a trombone, a clarinet, a flute, etc. — and, with the aid of tables existing for that purpose, set out to discover their fingering. At our summer home in Pargolovo I played these instruments, so to speak, for all the neighbours to hear. I had no aptitude for brass instruments; the high notes I produced only with difficulty; to acquire a technique on the wood-winds I lacked patience; yet I became rather thoroughly acquainted with them after all. With the peculiar haste of youth and a certain rashness in the matter of self-instruction, I immediately conceived the idea of setting out to write the fullest possible textbook of instrumentation; and, with this end in view, I made various outlines, memoranda, and drawings which had reference to a detailed explanation of the technique of the instruments. I was eager to tell the world no less than *all* on this score.[30] The writing of such a manual, or rather the

---

[29] Written in Yalta, July 20 [August 1], 1893.

[30] About these studies, which apparently extended somewhat longer than Rimsky-Korsakov imagines (if one is to judge from his reminiscences), Borodin wrote to L. I. Karmalina in a letter of April 15 [27], 1875: " Korsinka is busy with the Free Music School, writes all sorts of counterpoints, is studying and teaching all manner of musical tricks. He is writing a course of instrumentation — phenomenal, the like of which does not and never did exist."

From this period of studying the wind instruments there has been preserved a bulky bound book of music of large (folio) format, with over a hundred sheets completely covered with writing in Rimsky-Korsakov's hand of the early seventies and

outlines of such sketches for it, took a great deal of my time throughout the following season of 1873–4. After having read a little in Tyndall and Helmholtz, I wrote an introduction for my book; in this I endeavoured to state the acoustical laws pertaining to the fundamentals of musical instruments. My work was to begin with exhaustive monographs of the instruments by groups, with cuts and tables, with description of all makes in use to date. I had not as yet thought of Part II of my book, which was to treat of combinations of instruments. But soon I realized that I had gone too far. The wood-winds, in particular, proved to include untold multitudes of makes; in reality each maker or each factory has an individual system. By adding an extra valve or key, the maker either adds a new trill on his instrument or makes easier some run that presents difficulties on instruments of other makes. There was absolutely no possibility of finding one's way through all this maze. In the group of brass wind instruments I found some with three, four, and five valves; the construction of these valves is not always the same on the instruments of the various firms. To describe all this was absolutely beyond my power; and of what use would it be to anyone reading my textbook? All these minute descriptions of all possible makes, of their advantages and disadvantages, would but thoroughly confuse one who wished to learn something. Naturally, the question arising in his mind would be: which instrument, then, should I write for? What is possible and what is impracticable? Again in the end he would fling my bulky textbook violently to perdition. Such reflections gradually cooled my zeal for my work, and, after struggling a year with it, I gave it up. But in return, I personally had amassed considerable information on the subject by constantly checking myself up in the music bands of the Naval Department, in a practical way, and in the work over my textbook, in a theoretical way. I had learned what every practical musician (a German military bandmaster, for example) knows, but what, unfortunately, artist-composers do not know at all. I understood the basic principle of con-

partly of a later date. Rimsky-Korsakov began writing in it from both ends: it contains a detailed exposition of the fundamentals of musical acoustics, alternating with sketches devoted to individual wood-wind and brass instruments, with painstakingly executed drawings of the instruments themselves, their descriptions and tables, etc.

venient and inconvenient passages, the difference between virtuoso difficulties and impracticability; I came to know all the uttermost tones of all instruments and the secret of producing some notes which everybody avoids through ignorance. I came to see that all I had known of wind instruments was wrong and false; and from now on I began to apply this newly acquired information in my compositions, as well as to strive to impart it to my Conservatory pupils and give them at least a clear conception, if not a full knowledge, of instruments of the orchestra. During the summer of 1873 I was occupied with practical study of wind instruments; with sketching the textbook that was never written; with polishing and orchestrating my Third Symphony, and with trips to Kronstadt and St. Petersburg for the purposes of acquainting myself with the bands prior to taking up my duties as Inspector. In the bands of musicians I was met as superiors are met: face to face! I made them play their repertory in my presence; caught the wrong notes; detected the slips (and there were very many of them) in the instrumental parts; examined the instruments and made requisitions for new or additional ones, according to what was necessary. The authorities, who had jurisdiction over the music bands, were amiable to me; but occasionally I grew rather peppery and humiliated some bandmasters undeservedly or ridiculed pieces which I did not like, though the performance of these was necessary and unavoidable in military bands. Thus matters went on until autumn.

In August we moved to the city, to a new apartment, in Kononov's house, on Furshtadtskaya Street. On August 20 [September 1] our son Misha was born.

Début as conductor. Moussorgsky. His Khovanshchina *and* Soro-chinskaya Yarmarka (The Fair at Sorochintsy). *Operatic prize con-test. Trip to Nikolayev and the Crimea. Studying harmony and counterpoint. Directorship of Free Music School.*

In the season of 1873–4 the Samara Government suffered famine owing to poor crops. I do not remember who conceived the idea of arranging a symphony concert at the Club of the Nobility for the benefit of the sufferers. I was invited to organize and conduct the musical part of the program. By agreement with A. I. Rubyets, ever responsive to any worthy undertaking, I secured the promise that he would train a large amateur choir for this concert. We began to prepare for it. In addition to my Third Symphony, which was en-tirely finished by then, the concert program included Maria's ro-manza from *Ratcliff*, Holofernes's March from Serov's *Judith*, Moussorgsky's chorus, *The Rout of Sennacherib*, A. Rubinstein's Concerto in D minor, etc.[1] Rubyets drilled the choruses; I came to purely vocal rehearsals to accompany and conduct. The thought of public appearance as conductor at a grand concert made me nerv-

---

[1] Following is a list of pieces left unnamed here: Glinka's *Jota Aragonesa*, the *Finnish Fantasy*, and three posthumous choruses from Dargomyzhsky's fairy comic opera *Rogdana*. The third of these, orchestrated by Rimsky-Korsakov, was played for the first time. In addition to these works, there were also performed songs of Dargomyzhsky, Tchaikovsky, Balakirev, Solovyov, and an aria from Dütsch's *Kroatka*.

ous in the extreme; for a whole month before the concert I could think of nothing else. I scanned the scores and went through the motions of conducting them while sitting in my study. For my début before the orchestra, I selected my new symphony, to be able to act with the greatest authority through appearing in the double capacity of conductor and composer. My nervousness before the orchestral rehearsals had reached its height, but I managed to master myself and acted like an old hand. The musicians were conscientious, and I strove not to burden them with polishing up details, especially in numbers familiar to them. In fact, advice like the following was volunteered: " Be a little stricter with us, orchestra musicians like strictness," and so forth. But how can one be strict with an orchestra imbued with *esprit de corps* and bound by no responsibility to a strange conductor, an outsider! However, all went well, we found our way through the symphony, and the ¾ Scherzo unfolded well enough. Mention must be made that I examined the orchestral parts and corrected them in good time; else, at the first misunderstanding, I should have lost my head and made a fiasco in the eyes of the musicians. After my symphony, I took up numbers by other composers: Glinka's *Jota Aragonesa* and the March from Serov's *Judith*. In the next rehearsal the choruses participated as well. The chorus *The Rout of Sennacherib* was performed partly with my orchestration. Moussorgsky had composed for it a new trio, which greatly delighted Stassov, and, owing to lack of leisure, had entrusted its instrumentation to me.

The concert for the benefit of the famine-stricken population of Samara occurred on February 18 [March 2]. M. D. Kamyenskaya and the pianist Hartvigson (who was dissatisfied with my orchestral accompaniment) were the soloists.[2] I was somewhat languid after the preceding excitement; nevertheless everything went off safely. However, we did not feed the hunger-stricken Samarans, as our audience was very small and we hardly covered the expenses of orchestra, lighting, and so on. Thus passed my début as orchestral conductor. By the way, let me mention that before the concert be-

---

[2] Rimsky-Korsakov does not mention the participation as well of Menshikova (soprano).

gan I received from Balakirev a very warm letter written in the spirit
of benediction and wishing me success.³ Personally, however, he attended neither the rehearsals nor the concert, and my symphony
remained unknown to him.

This symphony pleased my musical friends only moderately.⁴
Save for the Scherzo, it was found somewhat dry; my leaning
towards counterpoint was disapproved, and even its orchestration
appeared most ordinary to many — V. V. Stassov for instance. Apparently the symphony pleased only Borodin; yet he said that in it
I appeared to him as a professor who had put on spectacles and
composed *Eine grosse Symphonie in C,* as befitted his rank.

During the season described I often visited Borodin, and brought
along the wind instruments I owned, for us both to study and dally
with. It turned out that Borodin played the flute quite dextrously,
and, with his finger-technique on this instrument, he easily adapted
himself to playing the clarinet as well. As for the brass instruments,
their high notes he produced with extraordinary ease. We had long
talks about the orchestra and the freer use of brass instruments, as
opposed to our former practices, borrowed from Balakirev. The
result of these talks and our enthusiasm, however, was an excessive
use of the brass group in Borodin's Second Symphony in B minor,
which he was then orchestrating.

On my visits of inspection to the music bands I had charge of,
especially the band of the port of Kronstadt, that of the Company
of the Guards and of the Naval School, with full complements of
brass and wood-winds, I was led to orchestrate for military bands
and provide them from time to time with pieces of my own arrangement. During that year, and in several years following, I made arrangements of the Coronation March from *Le Prophète,* the Finale

---

³ This letter has not been preserved. The one in answer to it was published in
"Rimsky-Korsakov's Correspondence with Balakirev," in *Musical Contemporary,*
1916–17, No. 1, p. 83.

⁴ This statement does not apply to C. A. Cui. His review in the *St. Petersburg
Gazette* devotes extremely sympathetic lines to the symphony: "As a whole the
symphony is a capital work, the best of Mr. Korsakov's symphonic compositions; it
is the fruit of mature thought, felicitous inspiration, vigorous talent, in conjunction
with solid and profound knowledge of technique." Cf. *St. Petersburg Gazette,* 1874,
No. 52, "Musical Notices."

from *A Life for the Tsar;* Isabelle's aria from *Robert le Diable* (for clarinet solo); Berlioz's *Marche Marocaine;* F. Schubert's *March* in B minor; Introduction to *Lohengrin;* the grand scene of the conspiracy from *Les Huguenots;* the Nocturne and March from *A Midsummer Night's Dream,* etc. Where all these scores are now it is hard to say; but they can probably be found among the dust-covered old music of the bands of the Naval Department. In addition to my works of this nature, I asked leaders of the bands in my charge to make arrangements of pieces selected by me. Occasionally I was rather exacting towards band leaders and I even dismissed one poor old man because some musicians in his band played the bass tubas "in the wrong way" and thereby systematically introduced false notes into the pieces they played. Holders of the Navy Department fellowships who graduated from the Conservatory, I assigned to bands at my own discretion, paying no heed to requests or pressure from the naval authorities; thereby I aroused considerable dissatisfaction. I am glad, however, that while holding the post of Inspector I succeeded in placing in the Navy Department's bands two Russian bandmasters — M. Chernov and I. Koolygin — from among the Conservatory fellows, whereas before my time the leaders had been exclusively foreigners hired for the purpose.

On January 24 [February 5], 1874, *Boris Godunov* was produced with great success at the Mariinsky Theatre.[5] We all were jubilant. Moussorgsky was already at work on *Khovanshchina.* Its original plan was much broader and abounded in numerous details which never got into the final version.[6] For instance, there had been projected a whole tableau in the German suburb, where Emma and her father, the pastor, were to be the dramatis personæ. Moussorgsky even played us musical sketches of this scene in quasi-Mozartean style(!), because of the German bourgeois surroundings of that scene. Incidentally, there was most charming music in this scene. Likewise, a scene of a lottery, which is said to have been first intro-

---

[5] Cf. A. Rimsky-Korsakov: "M. P. Moussorgsky's *Boris Godunov*" (in *Musical Contemporary*, 1916–17, Nos. 5–6).
[6] Cf. V. G. Karatygin: "*Khovanshchina* and Its Authors," ibid., pp. 192–218.

duced in our country during the Khovanshchina epoch, was projected. Subsequently the music composed for this scene became the
C-major chorus at the entrance of Prince Ivan Khovansky in Act I.
The princes' quarrels in Act II were too long and too obscure in
their wording. Mother Susanna had at first played a pretty important rôle in *Khovanshchina,* taking part as she did in the religious dispute with Dosifey. In the present version she is an unnecessary character, quite forced and useless to all intents and purposes.
In Act I there had been a rather longish scene in which the people
demolished the court scrivener's booth. Subsequently, after the
composer's death, when preparing the opera for publication, I cut
out this scene, as extremely unmusical and causing the action to
drag. Of the excerpts that Moussorgsky played for our company of
friends, we all were particularly taken by the Persian girls' dance,
which he played magnificently; but in *Khovanshchina* it had been
dragged in by the hair, so to speak, as the only pretext for introducing it there was the possibility that among the old Prince Khovansky's concubines there were, or could have been, Persian slave girls.
Everybody liked, too, the court scrivener's scene in Act I. The
melody of Marfa the schismatic's song Moussorgsky had obtained,
I believe, from I. F. Gorboonov, with whom he had picked up an
acquaintance in those days. The choral song of glorification of
Prince Khovansky (G major) and Andrey's song (G-sharp minor)
in Act V are of extremely doubtful originality, with unusually queer
intervals in perfect fifths; and these also he had recorded as heard
from someone among his acquaintances. The melodies of Marfa's
songs and of the glorification (wedding song) with their original
text I incorporated, with Moussorgsky's permission, in my collection of one hundred Russian songs. Of the *Khovanshchina* excerpts
then played, mention must be made as well of the barbarous music
of empty perfect fourths, which was intended for the chorus of
schismatics and which infinitely delighted V. V. Stassov. Fortunately, Moussorgsky later somewhat changed his first idea, and the
perfect fourths remained only here and there, as odds and ends of
his former sketch in the beautiful chorus of schismatics in the Phrygian mode in D (last act of the opera).

None of us knew the real subject and plan of *Khovanshchina*, and from Moussorgsky's accounts, flowery, affected, and involved (as was his style of expression then), it was hard to grasp its subject as something whole and consecutive. In general, after the production of *Boris Godunov*, Moussorgsky appeared in our midst less frequently, and a marked change was to be observed in him: a certain mysteriousness, even haughtiness, if you like, became apparent. His self-conceit grew enormously, and his obscure, involved manner of expressing himself (which had been characteristic even before) now increased enormously. It was often impossible to understand those of his stories, discussions, and sallies which laid claim to wit. This is approximately the period when he fell to loitering at the Maly Yaroslavyets and other restaurants until early morning over cognac, alone or with companions then unknown to us. When he dined with us or with other common friends, Moussorgsky usually definitely refused wine; but hardly had night come when something at once drew him to the Maly Yaroslavyets. Subsequently, one of his boon companions of the period, a certain V-ki, whom I had known from Tervajoki, told us that in the lingo of their set there existed a special term "to trans-cognac oneself," and this they applied in practice. With the production of *Boris* the gradual decadence of its highly gifted author had begun. Flashes of powerful creativeness continued for a long time, but his mental logic was growing dim, slowly and gradually. After his retirement from service, after he had become a composer by profession, Moussorgsky composed more slowly, by fits and starts, lost the connection between separate moments, and jumped from one subject to another. Soon he conceived another opera, *Sorochinskaya Yarmarka* (*The Fair at Sorochintsy*), after Gogol. It was composed in a rather queer way. Its first act and its last act had no real scenario or text, save musical fragments and characterizations.[7] For the market scene he utilized the music from *Mlada*, which was of similar pur-

---

[7] As may be seen from what appears later on (p. 227), Rimsky-Korsakov had in mind a *detailed scenario,* and apparently did not consider as such the sketch of the scenario which has been preserved among Moussorgsky's manuscripts in the Imperial Public Library (published in V. G. Karatygin's articles on *Sorochinskaya Yarmarka,* in *Musical Contemporary,* 1916–17, Nos. 5–6, p. 68, and still earlier in 1911, in the magazine *Apollon,* No. 4: " In Memory of Moussorgsky ").

M. P. MOUSSORGSKY

from the painting by I. Y. Ryepin

port. He composed and wrote the songs of Parasya and Khivrya as well as the happily turned declamatory scene between Khivrya and Afanasi Ivanovich. But between Acts II and III there was projected (for reasons unknown) a fantastic intermezzo, "The Dream of a Peasant Lad," for which the music came from *A Night on Bald Mountain* or *St. John's Eve* (cf. the chapter, "1866–67"). With some additions and changes, this music had done duty, in its time, for the scene of Chernobog (Black God) in *Mlada.* Now, with the addition of a little picture of early dawn, it was to form the projected stage-intermezzo forcibly squeezed into *The Fair at Sorochintsy.* I vividly recall Moussorgsky playing us this music; and there was a pedal of interminable length on the note C sharp, to play which was the task of V. V. Stassov, who took great delight in its endlessness. When Moussorgsky subsequently wrote this intermezzo in the form of a sketch for piano and voices, he did away with this interminable pedal, to Stassov's profound sorrow; but it could never be restored, owing to the composer's death. The melodic phrases appearing towards the conclusion of this intermezzo — as it were, the burden of a distant song (clarinet solo on high notes in *A Night on Bald Mountain,* in my arrangement) — belonged, in Moussorgsky's first version, to the characterization of the peasant lad who sees the dream, and those phrases were to appear as "leading motives" in the opera itself. The demon language from the *Mlada* libretto was to supply the text of this intermezzo, too. An orchestral prelude, "A Sultry Day in the Ukraine," opened the opera *Sorochinskaya Yarmarka.* Moussorgsky himself composed and orchestrated this prelude, and its score is still in my possession.[8] The work of composing *Khovanshchina* and *The Fair at Sorochintsy* extended over many years; the composer's death on March 16 [28], 1881 left both operas unfinished.

What was the cause of Moussorgsky's spiritual and mental decay? To a considerable degree it was due at first to the success of *Boris* (owing to which his pride and ambition as author began to grow); later on it was due to its failure. Presently cuts were made in the

---

[8] At the present writing, arranged and orchestrated by A. K. Lyadov. (Note of N. N. Rimskaya-Korsakova.)

opera, the splendid scene " Near Kromy " was omitted. Some two years later, the Lord knows why, productions of the opera ceased altogether,[9] although it had enjoyed uninterrupted success, and the performances by Petrov and, after his death, by F. I. Stravinsky,[10] Platonova, and Kommissarzhevsky had been excellent. There were rumours afloat that the opera had displeased the Imperial family; there was gossip that its subject was unpleasant to the censors; the result was that the opera was stricken from the repertory. On the one hand, V. V. Stassov's delight in Moussorgsky's brilliant flashes of creative genius and improvisations had raised Moussorgsky's self-conceit; on the other hand, the adulation of people incomparably inferior to the author, yet his boon companions, and the approval on the part of others who admired his virtuosity, though they were unable to distinguish between its true flashes and its felicitous talent for playing pranks, still pleased and irritated his vanity. Even the barman at the restaurant knew *Boris* and *Khovanshchina* well-nigh by heart and honoured Moussorgsky's genius. Yet the Russian Musical Society denied him recognition; at the opera he had actually been betrayed, though on the surface he was still being treated with affability. His friends and companions, Borodin, Cui, and I, still loved him as before and admired whatever was good in his compositions, but we took critical measure of much else of his. The press, led by Laroche, Rostislav and the rest of them, scolded him continually. Under these circumstances, his craving for cognac and desire to lounge in taverns till the small hours grew stronger day by day. To " trans-cognac oneself " was a mere nothing to his pals; but to his morbidly nervous temperament it was downright poison. Though still keeping up friendly relations with Cui and Borodin as well as with me, Moussorgsky regarded me with a certain suspicion. My studies in harmony and counterpoint, which had begun to absorb me, did not please him at all. It looked as though he suspected

---

[9] This assertion is not quite exact: in the interval between the years 1874 and 1882 there were no performances of *Boris Godunov* only in 1881; it was taken from the repertory for good in 1882. However, the number of performances during individual years (1875, 1876, 1877, 1878, 1879) varied between one and two. Cf. the *Almanach Musorgski* (Musical Sector of the State Publishing Bureau, Moscow, 1930), Summary of Performances of M. P. Moussorgsky's Opera *Boris Godunov*.

[10] Father of Igor Stravinsky, the composer. C. V. V.

me of being the conservative professor, who might convict him of parallel fifths, and this was unbearable to him. As for the Conservatory, he could not endure it at all. His relations with Balakirev had been rather cool for some time. Balakirev, who now no longer appeared on our horizon, used to say even in the old days that Modest had great talent but "feeble brains," had suspected him of a fondness for wine, and had estranged him even then by saying so.

The year 1874 may be considered the beginning of Moussorgsky's decay, which was gradual and continued to the day of his death. I have thus far touched in general terms upon the whole last period of Moussorgsky's activity. The details and ups and downs of the subsequent period of his life, as I know it, I shall describe as I go along in the further course of my reminiscences.

During the seasons of 1872–3 and 1873–4 my wife did not give up piano-playing and took an active part at all our gatherings as both accompanist and performer. Her performances of Chopin's Scherzo in B minor, Schumann's Allegro, and many other numbers, as well as her sister's singing, gave great pleasure to all of us. N. V. Galkin, who dropped in from time to time, played violin sonatas with my wife. I have a recollection that once that year I played at Cui's the ¾ Scherzo of my Third Symphony, arranged for four hands, with Hans von Bülow (then giving concerts at the capital), and that he liked it very much.[11] That very day Cui showed him what he had composed for his *Angelo*,[12] and the two played four-hands the Introduction to the opera.

Among the episodes of 1873–4 also belongs the prize competition for an opera on the subject of Gogol's *Christmas Eve*, libretto by Polonsky.[13] The competition had been announced long before and

[11] Hans von Bülow gave piano recitals at St. Petersburg in the middle of March 1874 for the first time. Cf. A. Famintsyn's accounts of his concerts in the *Musical Leaflet* for 1873–4, No. 19.

[12] Based on Victor Hugo's play. Ponchielli used the same subject for his opera, *La Gioconda*. C. V. V.

[13] The competition was announced in 1873. The final date for submitting the orchestral scores was set for August 1 [13], 1875. The award of the prizes was made in October 1875. The history of this competition has been told circumstantially in M. Tchaikovsky's *Life of P. I. Tchaikovsky*, Vol. I, pp. 436 ff. Cf. there also Rimsky-Korsakov's letters which he exchanged with Tchaikovsky in connection with *Vakoola the Smith*.

147

now the date was approaching, set by the Board of Directors of the Russian Musical Society, for submitting the operas. I was invited to join the committee of judges, who were Nikolay G. Rubinstein, Napravnik, Azanchevsky, and others, with Grand Duke Konstantin Nikolayevich as chairman. The submitted operas were distributed to us for examination at our leisure. Two of them proved to show merit. But when the committee met at the Grand Duke's palace, it was openly said that one of the operas was Tchaikovsky's. How this became known before the seals of the envelopes had been broken I don't remember; but the prize was awarded to him unanimously. True, his opera undoubtedly was the best submitted, so that no harm came from the improper management of the competition, but still it was not in lawful order. Napravnik and N. G. Rubinstein played Tchaikovsky's opera for the Grand Duke four-hands. Everybody was enraptured with the music beforehand, knowing that it was Tchaikovsky's. At the words in the libretto: " And what sort of thing is this? " — " Go to the Devil! " (duet of Solokha with the school-teacher) Napravnik giggled in a killingly funny way.

The other opera (whether it was awarded honourable mention or the second prize [14] I don't recall) proved to be from the pen of Solovyov. That was surprising. I had actually found some of its music to my liking when I examined the piano score.

In the spring of 1874 I was commissioned to spend the summer at Nikolayev for the purpose of transforming the local port brass band into a mixed band with wood-wind instruments. I was delighted with this commission, and when the Conservatory examinations were over, my wife, little Misha, and I repaired to Nikolayev.

---

[14] According to Rosa Newmarch, both the first and second prizes were awarded to Tchaikovsky. The first title of this opera was *Vakoola the Smith*. Under this title it was produced at St. Petersburg in 1876. The revised version, known as *Cherevichki*, was produced at Moscow in 1886. This opera is known by still a third title, *Oksana's Caprice*. The Russian Opera Company which gave a brief season of Russian works at the New Amsterdam Theatre in New York in May, 1922, produced this work, under the title of *Cherevichki*, on Friday evening, May 26, and repeated it on the last night of the season, May 27. I heard one of these extremely inadequate performances, but even under the adverse conditions governing this hearing, I found the opera extremely humorous, delightful, and fantastic. *Christmas Eve* is one of the tales in Gogol's fantastic *Stories of Mirgorod*. Using Gogol's title, Rimsky-Korsakov later wrote an opera on the same subject. C. V. V.

On our arrival in Nikolayev,[15] the local authorities met us warmly and installed us in one of the wings of the so-called palace on a high bank of the Ingul River. After meeting the families of our superiors — the Nyebolsins and the Kaznakovs — we visited them frequently, occasionally making joint excursions with them to Spask, Lyesky, and other places.

Soon after my arrival I took up the task of transforming the port band. New instruments were sent for, several new musicians were engaged, while others were learning instruments anew or adjusting themselves generally to the new make-up of the band. I supervised all rehearsing personally and even conducted many selections myself. Soon the band, with its new personnel, began to appear in public, playing on the boulevard in the evening. Early in July my wife, Misha, and I went to Sevastopol by steamer. We took in the sights of the environs and Bakhchisaray, and went from there overland to the southern coast, via the Baydarsky Gate. Here we visited Aloopka, Oryeanda, and Yalta, and returned to Nikolayev by steamer. The southern coast of Crimea we liked exceedingly, even though we had but a flitting and superficial view of it. As for Bakhchisaray with its extraordinarily long street, its shops, its coffeehouses, the shouts of its venders, the chanting of the muezzins on the minarets, the services in the mosques and the Oriental music, it all made the oddest impression on us. It was while hearing the gypsy musicians of Bakhchisaray that I first became acquainted with Oriental music in its natural state, so to speak, and I believe I caught the main features of its character. By the way, I was particularly struck by the quasi-incidental beats of the big drum, in false time, which produced a marvellous effect. In those days the streets of Bakhchisaray, from morning till night, rang with music, which Oriental nations so love. In front of every coffee-house there was continual playing and singing. On our next visit (seven years later), there was no longer a trace of this left: the addle-brained authorities had decided that music meant disorder, and banished

---

[15] As to the stay in Nikolayev, cf. Rimsky-Korsakov's letter of July 26 [August 7], 1874, to V. V. Stassov, in *Russkaya Mysl'*, 1910, Vol. VII, p. 168.

the gypsy musicians from Bakhchisaray to somewhere beyond Chufut-Kale. During my first visit, Bakhchisaray had no hotels either of European or of Russian style, and we lodged at a mullah's opposite the Khan's Palace with its famous " Fountain of Tears."

On returning to Nikolayev, I continued to teach the bands for some time. In August we left Nikolayev, returned to St. Petersburg, and once more spent a few weeks at V. F. Purgold's summer home in First Pargolovo.

During the ensuing season I came to be more and more absorbed in studying harmony and counterpoint, both of which I had taken up the season before. Steeped in Cherubini and Bellermann, equipped with a few textbooks of harmony (Tchaikovsky's among them) and every imaginable sort of chorale book, I toiled assiduously, beginning with the most elementary exercises. I sat down so poorly informed that I found myself acquiring systematic knowledge even in elementary theory. I did many and various exercises in harmony, harmonizing figured bass at first, then melodies and chorales. Counterpoint I studied from Cherubini (in perfect major and minor) and from Bellermann, in ecclesiastical modes. However, I lost patience and undertook to write a string quartet in F major before I had acquired anything like the proper training. I composed it rapidly [16] and applied too much counterpoint in the form of continual fugatos (which usually begin to be wearisome in the end). But in the Finale I succeeded in creating one contrapuntal trick: the melodic pairs which form the first subject in the double canon come in subsequently in the stretto without any change whatever and form a double canon once more. One cannot always hit on such a trick, but I managed to get through fairly well.

---

[16] In Rimsky-Korsakov's letter of October 1 [13], 1873 to P. I. Tchaikovsky we read: " I returned to St. Petersburg from the summer home and, while going through a pile of music, came across the first movement of my quartet, which I had even given up as lost. A glance at it fixed in me the desire to rewrite it in its entirety, and I accomplished it in two days; and that again moved me to write a new finale — which I did — and then an Andante, which I also consummated forthwith; also a Scherzo for this quartet had been jotted down by me — that I will likewise do during the next few days, and then my quartet will be ready. The composing of this quartet constitutes a deviation from the program of activities which I have communicated to you, but I am consoling myself with the thought that the quartet per se is a splendid exercise." (Archives of the Tchaikovsky Museum at Klin. Letters of Rimsky-Korsakov to P. I. Tchaikovsky.)

As subject of the Andante I took the melody of the pagan nuptials from my music for Gedeonov's *Mlada*. My quartet was played at one of the Russian Musical Society's performances by Auer, Pikkel, Veykman, and Davydov.[17] I did not attend. I recall that I felt somewhat ashamed of my quartet. On the one hand, I had not been accustomed to the rôle of the contrapuntist who writes fugatos — a rôle considered somewhat disgraceful in our coterie; on the other hand, I could not help feeling that in that quartet I really was not myself. And this happened because the technique had not yet entered my flesh and blood, and it was still too early for me to write counterpoint and retain my own individuality without imagining myself Bach or someone else. I was told that Anton Rubinstein, who had heard my quartet performed, expressed himself to the effect that now it would seem that I might amount to something. Of course, I smiled scornfully when this was related to me.

My friends who had shown little enthusiasm for my Third Symphony were still less satisfied with my quartet. Nor did my début as conductor send anybody into ecstasies; they began, indeed, to look upon me with a certain pity as one on the downward path. Besides, my studies of harmony and counterpoint made me a suspect in the artistic sense. Nevertheless, having tried my hand at the quartet, I continued my studies. Of course, there was absolutely nothing heroic in that; it was simply that counterpoint and fugue absorbed me altogether. I played and scanned Bach a great deal and came to honour his genius very highly; yet in earlier days, without a proper acquaintance with Bach, but merely repeating Balakirev's words, I used to call him a " composing machine " and his works " maids of beauty, frozen and soulless," if I happened to be in a favourable and peaceful mood. I did not understand then that counterpoint had been the poetic language of that composer of genius; that it was just as ill-judged to reproach him with his use of counterpoint as to upbraid a poet for using verse and rhyme (which, as it were, embarrass him) instead of employing free and easy prose. I had no idea of the historical evolution of the civilized

---

[17] At the third concert of November 11 [23], 1875. Review of the quartet, by A. Famintsyn, in the *Musical Leaflet*, 1875–6, No. 11, p. 173.

world's music and had not realized that all modern music owed everything to Bach. Palestrina and the Flemings, too, began to lure me. Then it was that I saw how foolish it was of Berlioz to say that Palestrina was only a series of chords, a bit of nonsense often repeated in our coterie. How strange it is! Stassov had once been an ardent worshipper of Bach; he had even been nicknamed " Bach " owing to this worship. He had also known and admired his Palestrina and the other old Italians. Later, however, owing to the lure of iconoclasm and the quest of new shores, he had sent all that to perdition. Of Bach he now would say that " Bach is beginning *to grind flour* " whenever in his fugues the contrapuntal voices began to flow freely. With gusto it used to be related how Borozdin,[18] a friend of Balakirev's, would dance Bach's A-minor organ fugue; he would first lead off with one foot; with the entrance of the second voice he would brandish one hand, with the third voice the other foot, etc.; and he would wind up like a mill towards the end. Possibly it was even witty: for a jest one never spares one's own father. But during my study of Bach and Palestrina all this became repugnant to me; the figures of these men of genius appeared majestic, and as though staring with contempt upon our " advanced " frenzy of obscurantism.

Parallel with my study of counterpoint and my contrapuntal period, I came upon other work new to me, as follows:

In the autumn of 1874 a deputation of amateur members of the Free Music School came to ask me to become director of that institution, in place of Balakirev, who had resigned.[19] I know but little of what had led to his resignation, but I heard that it had come as the result of insistent demands on the part of some members of the school. Though retired from the world of music, Balakirev had not given up his post as Director, nor did he come to the school; and so

---

[18] Nikolay Aleksandrovich Borozdin, that friend of Borodin's who is mentioned more than once in Balakirev's correspondence with Stassov (nicknamed Petrusha, Pyotra, etc.). Cf. *Balakirev's Correspondence with V. V. Stassov* (Petrograd, 1917).

[19] The election of Rimsky-Korsakov as Director of the Free Music School had occurred somewhat earlier, in the spring and not in the fall of 1874, since the news of it had appeared already in the *Musical Leaflet* of May 12 [24], 1874.

the school was wasting away, dragging on a wretched existence. Knowing no details whatever of Balakirev's resignation, I accepted the deputation's proposal and began work at the school, which still had its quarters in the Hall of the Town Council. We announced in the papers details regarding the admission of pupils and choral rehearsals; a large chorus was the result. I divided the multitude of members into two classes: the lower class was taught elementary theory and solfeggio; the advanced class studied choral pieces and practised for the public concert. I personally conducted the rehearsals of the upper class twice a week, and accompanied them on the piano myself. The treasury had little money: its only regular income consisted of the five hundred rubles per annum granted by its Most August Patron, the Tsarevich. I began to rehearse excerpts from Bach's *St. Matthew Passion,* the vocal parts of which were in the school library. We also rehearsed a *Kyrie* of Palestrina's. The choir was large and the amateurs sang with pleasure, while I myself found the work was in full agreement with the contrapuntal mood I was then in. Our intention was to give the concert after a single orchestral rehearsal, as the funds in the treasury were low and we wanted to realize as much as possible. For the orchestral number I selected Haydn's well-known D-major Symphony. The excerpts of *Passionsmusik* were to be given in Robert Franz's [20] arrangement for a modern orchestra. The concert took place in the City Hall on March 27 [April 8], 1875, after three years of the silence of the tomb on the part of the Free School, ruined by rivalry between Balakirev's ambition and the Russian Musical Society, which was so hateful to him. The program of the concert was as follows: (I) Excerpts from the oratorio *Israel in Egypt* — Handel; (II) *Miserere* — Allegri; (III) *Symphony in D major* — Haydn; (IV) *Kyrie* — Palestrina; (V) Excerpts from the oratorio *Passionsmusik* — Bach.[21]

---

[20] For a discussion of Franz's contribution to the Bach scores, see William Foster Apthorp's *Musicians and Music-Lovers* (Charles Scribner's Sons; 1895). C. V. V.

[21] The following numbers from the *Passionsmusik* [according to St. Matthew, J. A. J.] were performed: (a) Aria, "Only bleed, thou dearest heart" (first time), sung by M. D. Kamyenskaya; (b) Aria, "Have mercy upon me, O Lord!" M. D. Kamyenskaya; (c) Aria, "From love unbounded my Saviour dieth" (first time) Kosyetskaya; (d) Final Chorus, "O Saviour blest, softly rest."

One of the music-critics (Famintsyn, I think) observed that Joseph Haydn was the *youngest* composer on the program of this concert! [22]

At the rehearsal of the concert I displayed sufficient executive ability with regard to the chorus; I was circumspect with the orchestra, and all passed off safely. At the concert the hall was full, and the box-office receipts good. The audience was pleased, and the school's financial affairs began to improve. My " classic " program astounded absolutely everybody; nobody had expected a program like that from me, and my reputation took a decided fall in the eyes of many. I had chosen such a program, first, because we had no money, and the concert had to be given with a single rehearsal, which meant the selection of numbers easy for the orchestra to perform. Secondly, and for the same reason, the orchestra had to be a modest one. Thirdly, I was then studying both counterpoint and conducting, as well as choral mass-leadership; therefore I wished to begin at the beginning and not at the end. In the fourth place, the music I gave was old, yet beautiful and most suitable and useful for an exclusively choral organization, such as the Free Music School. Nevertheless I felt somewhat disconcerted; and to me, who often had misgivings about myself, it seemed at times that I had really done something rather unseemly. I believe it was in connection with this concert (or possibly the next one in the season of 1875–6, also with an ultra-classic program, which I shall describe later) that I once received a letter from Balakirev, in which he referred to my " languidness and flabbiness of soul," or words to that effect.[23] In those days V. V. Stassov kept darkly silent, somehow, whenever conversation turned to my work; Cui on the other hand, as I recall, made rather cutting remarks about it.[24]

---

[22] Cf. A. Famintsyn's reviews in *Musical Leaflet*, 1874–5, No. 16 (Chronicle of St. Petersburg). " I am convinced that even not long ago," Famintsyn wrote, " Rimsky-Korsakov himself did not expect that he would conduct a concert of this kind; however, one must hope that he has not done it in a burst of unaccountable magnanimity, but rather as a result of having realized the truth that the horizon of every artist, and so much the more of a composer, cannot be limited only to the literature of the composers nearest to us in time. . . ."

[23] This letter has not been found in Rimsky-Korsakov's correspondence with Balakirev.

[24] To the season of 1874–5 and 1875–6 also belong the rumours and talks about

As for my work as Inspector of Naval Bands, I exploited it that season, arranging, in the autumn, a grand concert of the united bands of the Navy Department, in Kronstadt. The concert was given at the Manège; the bands of both Kronstadt and St. Petersburg participated. Among the numbers performed were several of my arrangements, including the *Egmont* Overture, the March from *Le Prophète,* and *Slavsya! (Be glorified!).* The concert went with unanimity and precision under my direction. I stayed a whole week in Kronstadt for the rehearsals. There were two and sometimes even three rehearsals a day, separately for the wood and the brass, and jointly for all. On these I spent my time from morning till night with brief respites, and, truth to tell, I was tireless. I don't know whether the naval bands will ever again play with the same finish and unanimity as they did then, but of this I am positive, that never before had they been compelled to pull themselves together to such an extent. My wife and Cui came to hear the concert.[25] The Manège was full enough. The Kronstadt audience listened with their mouths wide open in amazement at this event, so novel and unheard of; musically, however, they appreciated the concert but little. Since then, during my entire tenure of inspectorship, there was an established custom of giving annually two or three such concerts under my direction. Subsequently these concerts were

---

dissension in and the breaking up of the circle, rumours of which Borodin informs L. I. Karmalina in his letter of April 15 [27], 1875. (Cf. also another letter to her, of June 1 [13], 1876.) Borodin's view of Rimsky-Korsakov's "apostasy" is given in the same letter: "Many are grieved at present by the fact that Korsakov has turned back, has thrown himself into a study of musical antiquity. I do not bemoan it. It is understandable. . . ."

Different was Moussorgsky's attitude towards Rimsky-Korsakov and his new tendency; in his letters (to L. I. Shestakova, Letter XIII) he talks of Cui's and Korsakov's repudiation " of the legacy of art — to converse with people according to the truth." In his opinion, " the might *Koochka* had degenerated into soulless traitors " (letter of October 19 [31], 1875, to V. V. Stassov). Right upon Moussorgsky's heels, Stassov, too, intoned for Rimsky-Korsakov's benefit the prayer for the dying. In his letter of September 27 [October 9], 1875, to Golenischev-Kootoozov (*Russian Musical Gazette,* 1916, No. 42, p. 765), we read: " Nor has the Roman " [Rimsky means Roman in Russian, J. A. J.] " been sitting with folded arms; he has written sixty-one fugues (! ! !) and some ten canons. Of that I say nothing. *De mortuis. . . .*"

25 This concert was given October 27 [November 8], 1874. For C. Cui's review of it, cf. the *St. Petersburg Gazette,* 1874, No. 303; cf. also the *Musical Leaflet,* 1874–5, No. 4, where the entire program of the concert and a very sympathetic review, signed V., are given.

transferred to a theatre where seats were built on the stage as is done in St. Petersburg at the Invalid Concerts. After I had left the post of Inspector, these concerts ceased entirely.

During that same season my *Antar* was conducted by me at one of the Russian Symphony Society's concerts,[26] under the following circumstances. After Balakirev's retirement the concerts had come under Napravnik's direction. Between the time of his playing my *Sadko* in 1871 (before I became professor at the Conservatory) and the season of 1874–5, my compositions were never performed by him, for some reason. Azanchevsky told me that he had repeatedly urged Napravnik to perform one of my compositions, especially recommending *Antar* to him. " Then he might as well conduct it himself," replied Napravnik. What " then he might as well conduct it himself" meant — whether his disinclination to soil his hands with my composition or the desire to place me in a presumably diffi- cult position — I do not know. I repeat the story from hearsay. Owing to this reply, Azanchevsky proposed to me that I conduct *Antar*. I accepted without any particular fear, as I was beginning to feel a certain ease in appearing before audiences. I conducted *Antar* from memory, and it went off in an orderly fashion, and even with some success.[27] The *Antar* which was then performed had been re- orchestrated by me and harmonically somewhat purified; the score, as well as a four-hand arrangement by my wife, was soon published by Bessel. When reorchestrating it I did away with the third bas- soon and the third trumpet appearing in the original score.

In the spring of 1875 I had a number of fugues as well as rather tolerable canons written, and also tried my hand at *a capella* choruses. We rented a summer house in Ostrovky on the Neva River, near Potemkin's former estate, and soon moved there.[28]

The summer went somewhat monotonously. At Ostrovky I

---

[26] The concert of January 10 [22], 1876.

[27] In recalling this performance in his review of the Free Music School's Concert (of February 3 [15], 1876), A. Famintsyn accounts to himself for the multitudinous audience at the concert by saying that " the public was attracted by the personality of the conductor, Rimsky-Korsakov, who had before elicited such enthusiasm at the Musical Society when his *Antar* was performed " (*Musical Leaflet*, 1875–6, No. 16, p. 248).

[28] Written in Yalta, July 23 [August 4], 1893.

worked assiduously at counterpoint. From time to time I made trips to St. Petersburg and Kronstadt to review the naval bands and, aboard the steamer, wrote in my notebook,[29] without tiring, various contrapuntal exercises and fragments.[30] During that summer I composed, among other things, several successful piano fugues,[31] shortly after published by Bessel, and some *a capella* choruses, but which, precisely, I don't remember.[32] Thus the summer slipped by. We lived in solitude and had visitors on only two occasions: the pianist D. D. Klimov with his wife, and Cui. Early in [mid] September we returned to St. Petersburg.

---

[29] The blank-book, made up of 190 separate music sheets of album size, contains " counterpoint exercises " by Rimsky-Korsakov. The greater part of them were made during the spring and summer of 1875. A detailed recording of dates and places enables us to re-establish in part, almost day by day, Rimsky-Korsakov's work during the springs of 1873, 1874, and especially 1875.

[30] In regard to Rimsky-Korsakov's determination to acquire technique, Tchaikovsky, writing to Mme von Meck, says: " Rimsky-Korsakov was overcome by despair when he realized how many unprofitable years he had wasted, and that he was following a road which led nowhere. He began to study with such zeal that the theory of the schools soon became to him an indispensable atmosphere. During one summer he achieved innumerable exercises in counterpoint and sixty-four fugues, ten of which he sent me for inspection. From contempt of the schools, Rimsky-Korsakov suddenly went over to the cult of musical technique. . . . At present (1877) he appears to be passing through a crisis, and it is hard to predict how it will end." In an earlier letter (1875) to the composer of *Antar*, Tchaikovsky wrote: " You must know how I admire and bow down before your artistic modesty and your great strength of character! These innumerable counterpoints, these sixty fugues, and all the other musical intricacies which you have accomplished — all these things from a man who had already produced a *Sadko* six years previously — are the exploits of a hero. . . . How small, poor, self-satisfied and naïve I feel in comparison with you! I am a mere *artisan* in comparison, but you will be an *artist*, in the fullest sense of the word. . . . I am really convinced that with your immense gifts — and the ideal conscientiousness with which you approach your work — you will produce music that must far surpass all which so far has been composed in Russia. I await your ten fugues with keen impatience." C. V. V.

[31] *Six Fugues for the Piano*, op. 17. St. Petersburg: V. Bessel.

[32] Probably Rimsky-Korsakov speaks here of *Two Three-part Choruses for Women's Voices*, op. 13, to words by M. Lermontov, published by A. Bitner and dated 1875.

A capella *choruses. Concerts of the Free Music School. A. Lyadov and G. Dütsch. Collections of Russian songs. The pagan sun-cult. Resumption of meetings with Balakirev. The Sextet and the Quintet. Editing the scores of Glinka. Revision of* Pskovityanka.

THE SEASON OF 1875–6 was a hard one for my family. In October our daughter, Sonya, was born. My wife fell ill and did not leave her bed for several months. I was in a miserable frame of mind; still my regular work continued. The Conservatory, the Free School, the naval bands, went on as usual. As for work on counterpoint, it had now passed to the composition stage. I wrote several *a capella* choruses for mixed voices, principally of contrapuntal nature; some of them were afterwards performed at the home soirées of the Free School, and all were published.[1] Owing to the predominance of counterpoint in the work on which I was then engaged, many of the choruses are heavyish and difficult to perform; others are dry. Among the rather heavy yet successful choruses, nevertheless, I count *The Old Song* (Koltsov's [2] text), written in the variation form;

---

[1] From subsequent pages it becomes clear that Rimsky-Korsakov has in view here: (1) his collection *Six Choruses without Accompaniment,* op. 16, published by V. Bessel and permitted for publication in summer 1876, and (2) *Four Variations and Fughetta on the Theme of a Russian Song,* op. 14, with the date of 1875 (year of composition) and later published by A. Bitner.

[2] Koltsov (1808–42), a poet of the people who sang the steppes of Southern

the chorus *The Moon is Sailing* rings lighter and more transparent. The acme of difficulty, in contrapuntal invention and for purposes of execution, is to be met with in the four variations and fughetta on the Russian song *Nadoyeli nochi, nadoskoochili* (Tired am I and wearied of the nights) for four female voices. This number might serve as a thorough solfeggio for an experienced chorus, although it was written without application of enharmonization. I also published, through Bessel, three newly composed smaller pieces: *Waltz, Song,* and *Fugue* (C-sharp minor) and also handed over to him for publication the best of my piano fugues.[3] Once I showed these fugues to Y. I. Johansen, a Conservatory colleague of mine, who was considered an expert in harmony and counterpoint. He was greatly pleased with them and, I believe, was convinced henceforth that I had got somewhere and would not exactly shame my professional title. While I was studying counterpoint I occasionally asked Y. I. for advice and hints, but never showed him the exercises themselves; that was the first and the last time he saw the six fugues I had prepared for publication. The rumour that I had written some fifty fugues during the summer (the number was somewhat exaggerated; I don't remember their exact number), and that I was hard at work on counterpoint in general, also reached the Conservatory.[4] Now they began to regard me a "strict" contrapuntist and "reliable" professor, and, from the extreme left, they shifted me somewhat nearer the centre.

The Free School ran according to the system I had introduced. We gave two concerts that season. The program of the first concert [5] (February 3 [15], 1876) was classic again.[6] I gave excerpts from the Bach Mass in B minor, with which I was then enraptured. To learn

Russia, the life of the tiller of the soil, the monotonous existence of the Russian peasant woman. His poetic form has the irregularity of Russian folksong. C. V. V.

[3] *Three Pieces for the Piano,* op. 15, St. Petersburg: V. Bessel; *Six Fugues for the Piano,* St. Petersburg: V. Bessel.

[4] The "sixty fugues" written during the summer of 1875 are mentioned also by P. I. Tchaikovsky in his letter of September 10 [22], 1875, to Rimsky-Korsakov. In this letter Tchaikovsky expresses his exceptionally warm interest in Rimsky-Korsakov's studies. [See note 30, p. 157, of this book. J. A. J.] Cf. M. Tchaikovsky's *Life of P. I. Tchaikovsky,* Vol. I, p. 468.

[5] Cf. Appendix III.

[6] Cf. A. Famintsyn's review in *Musical Leaflet,* 1875–6, No. 16.

the famous and most difficult *Kyrie* was an achievement on the part of a chorus of amateurs. Excerpts from the oratorio *Samson* were given with new orchestration written partly by myself and partly by Conservatory pupils under my direction. To give *Samson* with Handel's original score, calling for a large organ, which alone could fill in all the gaps, was out of the question, and I preferred to re-orchestrate it, with the assistance of my pupils. This gave them an excellent opportunity to exercise their talents. Among the soloists taking part in this concert were Mme Shalkovskaya (Bertenson) and Kadmina. The latter subsequently committed suicide and, they say, thereby furnished Turgenev the motive for writing his *Klara Milech*. In the *Samson* recitatives I had rather a hard time as conductor, but everything went off well, including the *Coriolanus* Overture. The program of the second concert (March 23 [April 4], 1876) I made up entirely of Russian numbers.[7]

Let me remark, in passing, that Borodin's closing chorus [from *Prince Igor*] (given by us), which, in the epilogue of the opera (subsequently done away with), extolled Igor's exploits, was shifted by the author himself to the prologue of the opera, of which it now forms a part. At present this chorus extolls Igor as he starts on his expedition against the Polovtsy. The episodes of the solar eclipse, of the parting from Yaroslavna, etc., divide it into halves which fringe the entire prologue. In those days this whole middle part was non-existent, and the chorus formed one unbroken number of rather considerable dimensions.

The concert went smoothly.[8] It offered some difficulties for my conducting. Two orchestral rehearsals preceded it. At that period I was somewhat hot-headed at times, when I noted negligence. I remember that during a rehearsal of one of that season's concerts the orchestra's errand-man Yuzefovich, who had forgotten to prepare something, got such a tongue-lashing from me that the musicians actually began to hiss me. I calmed down, as I feared to irritate the orchestra. On another occasion, as I recall it, at a rehearsal of the school, I yelled at the librarian of the school, Buslayev, because he

---

[7] Cf. Appendix IV.
[8] Cf. a review, signed B., in *Musical Leaflet*, 1875–6, No. 21.

did not bring the music on time, or something of that nature. Be that as it may, I should not have raised my voice, speaking too much in the tone of a superior. The amateur librarian, of course, took offence, but the matter was arranged to our mutual satisfaction. Such fits of taking the tone of a superior occasionally seized me; with growing self-conceit, possibly the lessons of service in the Navy were resurrected in my memory.

That very season the following occurred: Those inseparable cronies A. K. Lyadov and G. O. Dütsch, my talented Conservatory pupils, quite young at the time, had grown incredibly lazy and had ceased coming to my class altogether. Azanchevsky talked the matter over with me, but, finding them unmanageable, decided to expel them.[9] Soon after their expulsion the youngsters came to my house, with the promise that they meant to work, asking me at the same time to intercede for their readmission to the Conservatory. I was immovable and refused point-blank. The question is, how had such inhuman regard for forms overmastered me? Was it the result of my contrapuntal studies, just as excesses of commandeering were the result of my military-naval school training? I do not know; but to this day bureaucratic fits of this nature occasionally overtake me. Of course, Lyadov and Dütsch should have been immediately readmitted, like the prodigal sons they were; and the fatted calf should have been killed for them. For, indeed, Dütsch was very capable and Lyadov was talented past telling. But I did not do it. The only consolation, possibly, is that everything is for the best in this world of ours — both Dütsch and Lyadov became my friends subsequently. But let me return to the Free School.

Its concert with a Russian program raised my credit anew in the eyes of my musical friends: Cui, the Stassovs, Moussorgsky, and others. In reality it proved that I was not altogether a deserter or renegade, that in my heart and soul I still clung to the Russian school. As for Balakirev, I only know that he was not entirely in sympathy with my idea of giving an exclusively Russian concert, and that the dislike of specifically Russian programs that had al-

9 Cf. A. K. Lyadov (Petrograd, 1916), pp. 7–8, where the letter of M. Azanchevsky to E. F. Napravnik concerning Lyadov's expulsion is published.

ways been with him remained with him to the end. He recognized only mixed concerts of Russian and foreign music of modern tendencies, and admitted an exclusively Russian program only as an exception, for which there was no occasion at the school. Whether he thought that by putting Russian compositions in a separate box, as it were, we showed fear of standing on a level and in company with Europe and, so to speak, chose ourselves a place at a separate table or in the kitchen out of deferential modesty; or whether he considered purely Russian concerts less varied in comparison with mixed concerts, I have been unable to make out to this day. He alleged the latter reason, but from certain signs it seemed to me that there was recognizable in him the desire to be more frequently at one and the same table with Liszt, Berlioz, and other Europeans. Liszt, Rimsky-Korsakov, Beethoven, Balakirev, Cui, Berlioz, seemed to be on an equal footing when appearing side by side. Placed apart from the foreigners, however, the Russians would not enjoy that right, as it were. I believe this was his reasoning; however, I do not set it forth as absolute truth.[10]

This year the financial affairs of the Free School grew somewhat worse. The preceding season's concert and the classic concert of this season had brought in fair receipts, though those of the second were inferior to those of the previous year; the Russian concert with its two rehearsals now brought a deficit. At that time in St. Petersburg there were already evidences of that languid attitude towards concert music which has been more and more on the increase since. The revival of the Free School and I, its new Director, had roused the public's interest at first, but even with the second season that interest began to cool, while the Russian program evidently did not strike responsive chords in the hearts of the public. It is noteworthy that the Free School's large choir, whose members, it would seem, could attract their friends to take an interest in the affairs of the school and support it, in reality did not attract the paying public.

---

[10] Edward MacDowell held a precisely similar theory in regard to American music. He stoutly maintained, and not without reason, that no great compliment was paid to American composers by giving a concert composed exclusively of American music. On the other hand, to play an American composition between an overture of Brahms and a Beethoven symphony meant something. C. V. V.

Everybody wanted to get as many free tickets as possible, and nobody was willing to pay even a moderate price. Thus matters stand in St. Petersburg today; and not only in St. Petersburg, but throughout all Russia.

According to the constitution and by-laws of the school, its financial affairs and executive powers were vested in a board of eight members, of which I was chairman. I recall being incapable of conducting the meetings. I had no idea of parliamentary rules. I was ill informed as to the method of keeping minutes, of voting, of unanimity, of minority opinion, and so on. Our conducting of business was honest beyond reproach, though negligent on occasion, and I remember that once a member of the board, P. A. Trifonov (subsequently a private pupil of mine and later one of my intimate friends), left the board owing to our slovenly methods; and he was probably right. At our general meetings for the purpose of reading annual reports and electing members of the board, I had further difficulties; administrative matters were not to my taste. In addition to the above occupations, another work, new to me, turned up in the season 1875-6. Since the previous year I had taken a strong interest in Russian folksongs; I scanned all sorts of collections, of which, up to this time, I had seen very few, with the exception of Balakirev's wonderful gathering. I conceived the idea of publishing one myself. And now T. I. Filippov, a profound lover of Russian songs, who had formerly sung them splendidly, though no musician at all, proposed to me to take down from his dictation the songs he knew, and to compile for him a collection with piano accompaniment. T. I. Filippov made this offer to me at Balakirev's suggestion.[11] During his estrangement from us all, Balakirev had grown intimate with T. I. on religious grounds, I believe. Rumours that Balakirev had become a pious man were widespread. Filippov had long been known as a man zealous in Orthodox faith and church matters. Even in the old days Balakirev used to tell as a

---

[11] In the preface to the collection, T. I. Filippov wrote: "Through the kindly mediation of M. A. Balakirev, the fate of my songs has been conveyed into the hands of an artist kindred to him in spirit, N. A. Rimsky-Korsakov, who has devoted a great deal of his valuable time and conscientious efforts to put them in order, and to whom I herewith give my profound and sincere gratitude for having turned into reality a dream of mine that had been long cherished and had never left my mind. . . ."

joke the droll story of "the passage of the holy galoshes from Bolvanovka to Zhivodyorka." The narrative was the invention of Shcherbina, I think, and related how T. I. Filippov, while in Moscow, on a visit to Pogodin's on Bolvanovka Street, had left his rubbers behind him. As a reward for his life, as it were, so filled with sanctity, the "holy galoshes" had come on by themselves to his lodging on Zhivodyorka! It was alleged that in honour of that event there was established the feast " of the passage of the holy galoshes from Bolvanovka to Zhivodyorka"! In Balakirev's actual mental state, his intimate relations with Filippov were not at all unnatural.

So then T. I. came to me with the request that I take down Russian songs as sung by him; this I did in the course of several sessions. He now possessed but the frailest remnants of a voice, reported to have been fine in former days. In those days, loving Russian songs as he did, he used to get together with the best singers from among the common folk, learning their songs from them or occasionally holding contests with them. The forty songs I recorded from his rendering were principally lyric in character (*golosoviya,* or vocal, and *protyazhniya,* or slow); some of them seemed to me to have been corrupted by the army and factory elements, while others had remained pure. Of ceremonial and game songs there were comparatively few; yet it was in those very songs that I was particularly interested, as the most ancient that have come down to us from pagan times and have therefore been preserved most nearly in the original form. The idea of making a collection of my own, comprising the greatest possible number of ceremonial and game songs, preoccupied me more and more. After making a record of Filippov's songs (and he was satisfied with their accuracy) I harmonized them twice over; I was not quite satisfied with the first harmonization, finding it was neither sufficiently simple nor even Russian. Some two years later, this collection of Filippov's songs, with a preface by the collector, was published by Jurgenson.[12]

My own collection I gathered slowly.[13] First, I incorporated into

---

[12] *Forty Folksongs,* collected by T. I. Filippov and harmonized by N. A. Rimsky-Korsakov. Moscow: P. Jurgenson; no date, censorship permission June 2 [14], 1882.

[13] Rimsky-Korsakov worked on his own collection since 1875. Its complete title is: " Chants nationaux russes recueillis par N. Rimsky-Korsakov. Dedicated to V. V.

it all the best material I had found in Prach's [14] and Stakhovich's old collections, which had become bibliographical rarities. The songs taken from these collections I set forth with a more correct division as to rhythm and bars and also added new harmonizations. Secondly, I took into my collection all the songs I had learned by heart from my uncle Pyotr Petrovich [15] and from my mother, who in their turn had heard the songs in 1810–20 in localities of the Governments of Novgorod and Oryol. Thirdly, I wrote down songs from the mouths of some of my acquaintances, such as Anna Nikolayevna Engelhardt, S. N. Krooglikov, Mme Borodina, Moussorgsky, and others in whose musical ear and memory I had sound faith. In the fourth place, I recorded songs from the mouths of such of our servant girls as had been born in districts distant from St. Petersburg. I rigidly avoided whatever seemed to me commonplace and of suspicious authenticity. Once, at Borodin's, I struggled till late at night trying to reproduce a wedding song (*Zvon Kolokol*, Ringing Bell), rhythmically it was unusually freakish, though it flowed naturally from the mouth of Borodin's maid, Doonyasha Vinogradova, a native of one of the governments along the Volga. I had all sorts of trouble with the harmonization of the songs, recasting in every way imaginable. Taken together with my other work, the making of my collection took nearly two years. I arranged the songs in departments: First, the *bylinas* (epic songs), then the *slow* and the *dance* songs. Then followed the *game* songs and *ceremonial* songs in the order of the cycle of pagan sun-worship and the festivals still surviving here and there to this day. First in this series came spring songs, then the *rusalniya* (for Whitsunday), the *troyitskiya* (for Trinity Sunday), and *syemitskiya* (for the seventh Thursday after Easter Sunday); then summer *khorovod* (round dance) songs, marriage songs, and *vyelichal'nyia* (glorification) songs. I read some descriptions and essays on this side of folk-life by Sakha-

---

Stassov. Collection of Russian Folksongs, made by N. A. Rimsky-Korsakov, op. 24 (1876). Parts I–II, at V. Bessel's, St. Petersburg; 8vo." The preface is dated November 1877. Cf. V. V. Stassov's letter of July 17 [29], 1876 to Rimsky-Korsakov and Moussorgsky's letter of May 15 [27], 1876 to Rimsky-Korsakov.

[14] It was from this collection that Beethoven culled the Russian themes he used in his Razumovsky Quartets. C. V. V.

[15] Cf. p. 7 of this book.

rov, Tereshchenko, Sheyn, and Afanasyev, for instance; was captivated by the poetic side of the cult of sun-worship, and sought its
survivals and echoes in both the tunes and the words of the songs.
The pictures of the ancient pagan period and spirit loomed before
me, as it then seemed, with great clarity, luring me on with the
charm of antiquity. These occupations subsequently had a great
influence in the direction of my own activity as composer. But of
that later.

If I am not mistaken, towards the end of the season 1875–6, after
a lapse of many years, I paid occasional visits to Balakirev, who had
begun, as it were, to thaw out of his long frozen state.[16] The immediate occasions for this renewal of visits were, in the first place, my
intercourse with Filippov for the purpose of recording songs; in the
second place, L. I. Shestakova's projected edition of the scores of
Ruslan and Lyudmila and *A Life for the Tsar,* which Balakirev had
undertaken to edit,[17] at the same time expressing a desire to have
as his collaborators myself and A. K. Lyadov (then no longer a
pupil of the Conservatory); in the third place, the lessons in musical
theory which I gave to various private individuals, recommended
by Balakirev, led to our meeting. Regarding these lessons, however,
I have something to relate.

So far, my only private pupil in harmony had been I. F. Tyumenev, afterwards author of original novels and translations, as well as
of several songs.[18] While studying harmony and counterpoint my-

---

[16] Stassov wrote Rimsky-Korsakov (July 17 [29], 1876): " The other day Balakirev told Lyudmila [L. I. Shestakova. J. A. J.] that he was working with the greatest
delight and energy on *Tamara* and hoped to play it soon for her in full. But of us he
does not want to see anyone at all, for there would be talks about music, which he
would not have under any circumstance. Nevertheless he inquires about everything
with interest. . . ."

[17] Cf. pp. 172 ff. regarding this work.

[18] As one can see from this book (cf. " 1897–99 " and " 1899–1901 "), Ilya Fyodorovich Tyumenev was not merely Rimsky-Korsakov's first private pupil, but subsequently also his close collaborator. A man of culture in various lines, even if somewhat superficially, Tyumenev was one of the first to cherish the idea of luring
Rimsky-Korsakov to collaborate on one or another operatic subject. Possessing as he
did the gift of drafting scenarios and librettos unusually rapidly and easily (his experience in translating the librettos of Wagner and others had rendered him excellent
service in this respect) Tyumenev literally besieged Rimsky-Korsakov with offers of
various subjects for operas. Of all the material proposed by him, positive collaboration
resulted in but two cases — on *The Tsar's Bride,* for which he wrote the additional
scenes at Rimsky-Korsakov's request, and on an original libretto for *Pan Voyevoda,*

self, I had found it both useful and pleasant to have a pupil in that field, to whom I imparted as systemically as possible the information and devices I had acquired through self-instruction. Now, however, when my work in harmony and counterpoint had become known in the musical world, I was gaining the reputation of a " theoretician," despite the fact that in reality I always was a " practical " man, pure and simple. At the words " theory of music," " theoretician," in the minds of people without close acquaintance with these matters, and even in the minds of those who have musical talent, yet who have been spared that cup, there forthwith arises some conception of a quite absurd nature. A similar absurd conception evidently had arisen in Balakirev's mind, too. In those days there began to spread among amateurs, particularly among piano-playing ladies, the fashion of studying the " theory of music." Balakirev, who then had again a good many piano pupils, particularly among lady amateurs, began to recommend me to them as instructor in the theory of music, and I obtained pupils one after another. My pupils, male and female (the latter outnumbered the former), did not seem to know what they wanted to learn. My instruction embraced the study of elementary theory and the beginning of practical harmony, mostly according to Tchaikovsky's textbook. Most of these women and men pupils objected to solfeggic studies and ear-training; accordingly, this vaunted study of theory was really not worth a pinch of snuff. Yet they yearned to study theory as a food without relish, and frequently passed the whole hour in talking of music in general. As they paid well for their lessons in theory, they preferred to have me teach them, coming so to speak to the fountainhead; but they did not understand that there is absolutely no need of being taught reading by a littérateur, arithmetic by an astronomer, and so forth. I complained to Balakirev that the ladies he had recommended to me often proved utterly talentless, and that I should prefer to give up certain pupils, because teaching them was labour lost. Balakirev

which the composer of the music commissioned him to write. Tyumenev left behind him the manuscript " Fragments from Reminiscences of Rimsky-Korsakov," in the text of which numerous letters of Rimsky-Korsakov are interwoven in their entirety. This manuscript and Tyumenev's voluminous diaries and projects for operas have not been published and are in the care of his son, Professor A. I. Tyumenev.

usually said that one should never give up any pupils, and should give to each even the little he is capable of grasping. This very in-artistic logic appeased me, and so I was rather busy with lessons during the next ten years. Filippov's songs, the projected publica-tion of Glinka's scores, and lessons in the homes of Balakirev's friends or acquaintances brought us close to each other once more; the more so as Balakirev was already on the mend and had come out of his seclusion. Nevertheless, I found him greatly changed, but of this later.[19]

In 1876 the Russian Musical Society announced a prize contest for a work in chamber music.[20] The desire to write something for this contest seized me, and I set to work on a string sextet in A major. I had begun it in St. Petersburg and I completed it at our summer place in Kabolovka, where we lived that summer, in the circle of relatives, together with V. F. Purgold and my wife's sisters, Mmes A. N. Molas and S. N. Akhsharumova. By then my wife had begun to recover from her illness.[21]

My sextet shaped itself into five movements. In it I now strove less for counterpoint, but the second movement (Allegretto scher-zando) I wrote in the form of a very complicated six-part fugue, and I find it very successful as to technique. It resulted in a double fugue, even with counterpoint at the tenth. In the trio of the Scherzo (third movement) I also made use of the form of a three-part fugue for the first violin, the first viola, and the first cello in tarantella time, while the other instruments play the accompani-

---

[19] Written at Yalta, July 25 [August 6], 1893.

[20] The notice of this competition, announced in the name of the Directorate-in-chief of the Russian Musical Society, was published in V. V. Bessel's *Musical Leaflet* of April 28 [May 10], 1876 (No. 22), pp. 350–1, and the final date for submitting the compositions was set for September 15 [27] of that year; the date for announcing the award, November 1 [13], 1876. For the decision of the committee on awards, cf. note 3 on p. 182.

[21] Apparently to this period also belongs Rimsky-Korsakov's intention to write a grand cantata for solo, chorus, and orchestra, under the title *Aleksandr Nevsky*, to a text derived from L. Mey's poem. The complete libretto of this projected work has been preserved among Rimsky-Korsakov's papers. Written in Rimsky-Korsakov's own hand and bearing the date of October 2 [14], 1876, Pityer, it has attached to it a care-fully worked-out plan of seventeen numbers with quartets, duets, trios, arias, and recitatives for soprano, contralto, tenor, and bass. For Rimsky-Korsakov's creative manner in the period of the middle seventies it is characteristic that numbers I and XVII of the projected cantata were indicated as choruses with double fugues.

ment to the fugue continuously in pizzicato chords. The Adagio proved melodious, with a very ingenious accompaniment. The first and fifth movements gave me less satisfaction. Taken all in all, the work proved technically good, but in it I still was not myself. After I had completed the sextet, I took it into my head to write for the same contest a quintet for the piano and wind instruments; of the latter I selected the flute, the clarinet, the French horn, and the bassoon. I composed the quintet in three movements. The first movement was in the classic style of Beethoven; the second (Andante) contained a fairly good fugato for the wind instruments, with a free-voice accompaniment in the piano. Movement three (Allegretto vivace), in rondo form, contained an interesting passage: an approach to the first subject after the middle part. The flute, the French horn, and the clarinet by turns play virtuoso cadenzas, according to the character of each instrument, and each is interrupted by the bassoon entering by octave leaps; after the piano's cadenza the first subject finally enters in similar leaps of the bassoon. Yet even this composition did not express my real individuality; but at all events, it is freer and more attractive than the sextet. The sextet and the quintet, neatly transcribed by copyists, were forwarded with mottoes to the Directorate of the R. M. Society. During the summer, I also composed several three-part choruses *a capella* for men's voices; these were later published by Bitner, and subsequently became Byelayev's property. The summer passed in work on the above compositions and my song collections; in the fall, after moving to our former rooms in St. Petersburg, our musical life resumed its usual course.

By autumn, my meetings with Balakirev became quite frequent. I have already said that I had found a striking change in him. As early as the last season, or even the season before that, V. V. Stassov, who had met him once in the street, had said: " Balakirev is not the same, not the same; even his glance is no longer what it used to be." On visiting him I observed much that was new, that had not been there. In every room, in a corner, there were icons, and icon-lamps were burning before them. His bedroom was carefully locked, and when entering it in the presence of outsiders, Balakirev would hasten to shut the door behind him, but through the door-chink one could see mysterious darkness, illumined only by the flicker of the icon-lamp. Often I heard him say that he had just returned from vespers or evening service; and whenever one happened to pass a church with him, he would remove his hat and quickly cross himself; at the rumble of thunder he would hurriedly cross himself, too, endeavouring that the others should not see it; and, if I am not mistaken, he did it also when he yawned. When anybody was called by his Christian name and that name happened to be of the less common ones, he would forthwith recall when that saint's day is to be celebrated, and would call off, without faltering, several dates in the year when the saints who bear that name are honoured. He had quit smoking and given up eating meat, and ate fish, but, for some reason, only those which had died, never the killed variety. He had no fur garments; in bitterest cold he wore some kind of autumn overcoat, with a scarf carefully wound around his neck and beard. And again the same red gloves, tea with raspberries, the same orders to the maid: " Marya, light a fire in the stove! — No, wait! First put up the samovar and go to the bakery, and after that light the fire in the stove — and also find out which *dvornik* (house porter) is on duty at the gate today." — " Marya, lock the vasistas in the kitchen! " Such orders and the like constantly distracted him from the business in hand or conversation, so that one felt distressed both for him and for oneself. Since that time he developed I know not what sort of inability or incapacity for concentration. No matter what one might talk to him about or what would be the business in hand, he would break away every minute to attend to all sorts of trivial and workaday cares. A rather large watch-dog, Druzhok (Friend), supplied him with more than a little material for these interruptions and everyday bustle. While taking a walk, the concern about the conduct of this dog and his morals, the endeavours to keep him from courting the canine fair sex, went so far that occasionally he carried this hulk in his arms. As for the *dvorniks* who would chase the dog, which stuck his snout everywhere, they usually received suitable reprimands. The love and compassion for animals reached such heights with him that whenever some kind of filthy insect — a bedbug, for instance — turned up in the room, he would catch it carefully and throw it out of the casement window, accompanying the act with the words: " Go thee, deary, in the Lord, go! " In general all this was quite odd.

However, many things did not appear absolutely new to me; I recognized some of his former traits, only they had assumed altogether fantastic forms. I scrupulously avoided touching on religion, but once I roused his irritation when I quoted the well-known saying: " Trust in God, but don't be remiss yourself " (the Lord helps those who help themselves). Still I have it on good authority that with some of his friends, like Trifonov and Lyadov, who had begun to visit him at that time, he held religious discussions; in these he usually stressed the lack of sagacity and the stupidity of those who held views differing from his. This, however, was his usual method in arguments. " Only some such little fool, or such a chicken-hearted person, could talk like that." In general, his intolerance towards people who disagreed with him in anything or acted and reasoned in any way independently, on lines different from his, was as deep-rooted as before, and the epithet " blackguard," dealt out right and left, did not leave his tongue. To this gracious epithet of his was now added a new one, " *Zhid* " ("sheeny"). Everybody for whom he felt a dislike he suspected to be of Jewish origin, and " the sheenies " he hated, because they had crucified Christ. Very frequently his religious conversations with persons whom he liked would be closed with the entreaty: " Please, just for my sake, put the sign of the cross over yourself; just once cross yourself. Now, do try! " Manifestly he believed in the miracle-working power of the sign of the cross and trusted that persons sanctified with the sign of the cross could, through its miracle-working effect, change their manner of thinking involuntarily. Usually this request to cross oneself went unheeded, as the symbol of religious convictions was respected, at any rate, and Balakirev persisted in his faith that, had his entreaty been granted, the miracle of spiritual regeneration would have been accomplished, very probably or even surely. He was fond of inviting his friends to come with him to church, and there he proved an expert as to all the minutiæ in the field of sacred objects and the

171

order of the service. He was acquainted not only with all the popes (priests) and deacons, but even with the sextons and watchmen. At parting with a visitor with whom he was on good terms he would say: "Farewell, Christ be with you!" All this medley of Christian meekness, backbiting, fondness for beasts, misanthropy, artistic interests, and a triviality worthy of an old maid from a hospice, all these struck everyone who saw him in those days. But these oddities were fated to develop subsequently into still greater incongruities, from the midst of which began to glisten many new peculiarities, no longer comical in the least, which had lain hidden in him since long before, but had emitted altogether different rays formerly.

Lyudmila Ivanovna Shestakova, who worshipped the memory of her brother's genius, had decided to publish, at her own expense, the full orchestral scores of Glinka's operas, of which Stellovsky then held the publishing rights. According to the agreement, she reserved the right to a stated number of copies of these scores, while the rest of the edition was to continue the firm's exclusive property. There existed no original full orchestral score of *Ruslan,* and we used a copy of it that Dmitri Vasilyevich Stassov had in his possession, and which, it was claimed, Glinka himself had verified. Of course, this verification by its author had been extremely superficial, and the score contained a large enough number of slips of the pen and misunderstandings, which came to light upon our perusal. The engraving was done by Röder in Leipzig, and we examined the copies made for the purpose (or copied many things ourselves) and read proof. *Ruslan* was edited first, then *A Life for the Tsar.*[22] We gave almost two years to the work; my share also included the orchestration of the stage music performed by a military band in *Ruslan and Lyudmila.* Balakirev and I proved poor proof-readers (Lyadov was the best of the lot), and we issued both scores with numerous important mistakes. For example, in the entr'acte to Act II of *Ruslan* a whole phrase for the violins was

---

[22] All in all, this work dragged out over no less than four years. The foreword to the printed orchestral score of *Ruslan* is dated 1878, and the publication of the orchestral score of *A Life for the Tsar* belongs to 1881, as is evident from the date on the title-page. In Balakirev's *Correspondence with Rimsky-Korsakov* (Letters XV–CXIX) may be found numerous echoes of this labour.

M. I. GLINKA

from the painting by I. Y. Ryepin

omitted. Some corrections made by Balakirev seem very question-able to me — like the bassoon's phrases in the romanza *Ona mnye zhizñ* (She is my life to me), or the drum introduced by him into the first *Slavsya* (Be glorified!). In Glinka's original score there had been a line with " drum " written over it, but it had no music, and the rhythmic drum figures were inserted by Balakirev on his own initiative, on the ground that Glinka had forgotten to write it in. Such corrections of quasi-misunderstandings Balakirev was very fond of making, and I trust that, at some time in the future, the scores of Glinka's operas will be republished after painstaking re-vision by a conscientious musician who knows his business.[23] Under Balakirev's influence, Lyadov and I often chimed in with him in the work on Glinka's scores. Now, however, I view the matter differ-ently and am far from being delighted with our handiwork. For my part, I was carried away by enthusiasm and did many imprac-ticable things in orchestrating for a military band the respective parts of *Ruslan*. Thus in the Introduction to Act I the stage band was to be brass, in Glinka's scheme; I followed his idea accordingly, but took a brass band with the full complement current in our Guards regiments. For Act IV, again in accordance with the com-poser's intentions, I wrote the orchestration for a mixed band of brass and wood-wind, both again with the full complement current in the Guards. Thus a performance of *Ruslan* called for two com-plete heterogeneous regimental bands. Glinka himself hardly wanted this! But that is not all. In Act V I had the imprudence to unite the two bands in full complement — the brass band and the mixed band. The result of this was sonority so deafening that no theatre orchestra could hold its own against it; and this was mani-fested once when Balakirev gave the whole *Ruslan* finale at a con-cert. The theme and all the figures for the strings were completely drowned by the military bands which performed their parts in my orchestration. To the Glinka scores were also added arrangements, for theatre orchestra alone, of the numbers whose performance,

---

[23] To mark the one hundredth anniversary of Glinka's birth, the firm M. P. Byelayev, of Leipzig, as is well known, undertook to issue new editions of Glinka's orchestral scores edited by N. A. Rimsky-Korsakov and A. K. Glazunov.

according to Glinka's score, called for a military band on the stage. These arrangements were made by Balakirev splendidly, save for the futile application of the natural-scale brass instruments; as usual, Balakirev was not strong on this, as he was guided by Berlioz's *Traité d'Instrumentation* and not by practical knowledge. However, these arrangements sound beautiful and right, and they translate Glinka's ideas correctly. The end of the Oriental dances is an exception; here Balakirev composed extra chromatic figures for the wind instruments, but they are in the spirit of Glinka. The edition of the *Ruslan* score was sumptuous; that of *A Life for the Tsar* was simpler and less fine. Of course both editions were very respectable and useful achievements, undertaken at the initiative and expense of the composer's sister, and carried out by us. But our sins were considerable, at all events, and Glinka still awaits a future definitive correction of the edition which we treated now and then in too light-minded and self-confident a spirit, even if we devoted much energy to it. No sooner had the edition come out than numerous misprints and inaccuracies were discovered. Napravnik began to conduct Glinka's operas from our scores; however, he did not correct the bassoon's phrase in Ratmir's romanza according to the new score, but had it played as of old — and he was right. Nor did he venture to introduce the drum that Balakirev had improvised in the first *Slavsya*, and that too was reasonable. As for the phrase for the violins omitted in the score (in the entr'acte to Act III), the musicians played it without further ado, as their parts had been copied from the old opera-house score. I imagine how venomously Napravnik smiled with his dappled eye (one eye of his is half brown, half grey) when he did not discover the necessary phrase in the score edited by us! When this edition came out, Balakirev detected some misprints and corrected them; soon an arrangement for a new printing of the *Ruslan* score (from the same plates) was made by Gutheil, who had just taken over the publishing rights of Glinka's compositions. But exclusive of some fifteen mistakes which Balakirev corrected, there still remained in the new edition a whole swarm of uncorrected errors. As for the score of *A Life for the*

Tsar, it retains to this day [24] all the mistakes we had overlooked.

Work on Glinka's scores was an unexpected schooling for me. Even before this I had known and worshipped his operas; but as editor of the scores in print I had to go through Glinka's style and instrumentation to their last insignificant little note. There were no bounds to my enthusiasm for and worship of this man of genius. How subtle everything is with him and yet how simple and natural at the same time! And what a knowledge of voices and instruments! With avidity I imbibed all his methods. I studied his handling of the natural-scale brass instruments, which lend his orchestration such ineffable transparency and grace; I studied his graceful and natural part-writing. And this was a beneficent discipline for me, leading me as it did to the path of modern music, after my vicissitudes with counterpoint and strict style. But my schooling, evidently, was not yet at an end. Parallel with my study of *Ruslan* and *A Life for the Tsar* I undertook a revision of *Pskovityanka.*[25]

My first thought was to compose the Prologue, which had been entirely discarded, although it plays so important a part in Mey's drama. Then followed the idea of introducing the part of Chetvyortka Tyerpigorev, friend of Mikhaylo Toocha, and simultaneously developing the part of Matoota's daughter Styosha. Thereby the opera would gain a merry, if not a comic couple. Balakirev urged me to introduce the wandering pilgrims' chorus (in the form of a song, "Aleksey, the godly man") [26] in Act IV, in the first tableau of which the action takes place in front of the Pyechorsky Monastery. The original melody of this verse in T. I. Filippov's collection was to be used for the air of the chorus. I believe that Balakirev insisted on this insert, because the tune was beautiful as well as because of his predilection for saints and for the ecclesiastical element in general. The fact that the action takes place near the monastery was the only reason advanced for this insertion; still, I yielded to the urgent admonitions of Balakirev; once an idea had

---

[24] Written in 1893.

[25] Written at Yalta, July 28 [August 9], 1893.

[26] Materials for this song in the plan of *The Maid of Pskov* have been preserved in Rimsky-Korsakov's archives. They bear the date of spring 1877.

got into his head, he usually fought stubbornly to gain his point by hook or by crook, especially if it concerned somebody else's business. With my characteristic easy-going nature, I yielded to his influence, as I had been accustomed to do in the old days. But after admitting this interpolation, I was bent on further developing it. I fell upon the following expedient: after the chorus of the wandering pilgrims who had camped out near the cave of Nikola the Simpleton, there was to appear the Tsar's hunting party, headed by Tsar Ivan, caught in the sudden rain-storm. During the storm the simpleton monk threatens the Tsar for shedding innocent blood, whereupon the superstitious Tsar Ivan, in fear, hurries away with his retainers, while the wandering pilgrims, together with Nikola, pass into the monastery. The rain-storm quiets down; along with the last distant rolls of thunder there is heard the song of girls passing through the forest in search of Olga. From here on, the action was to run as before, without any material changes. Balakirev approved my plan, as this promised the realization of his cherished idea of introducing the song about Aleksey, the godly man. Besides, he insisted upon substituting the other new music to the text of *Gospod' yediny voskryeshayet myortvykh* (The Lord alone doth resurrect the dead) for the final chorus, which he hated. He urged both the revision of *The Maid of Pskov* and the inserts. He said that since, in his opinion, I should never write another opera equal to *Pskovityanka* in merit, I ought to give myself up to it and polish it as it deserved. On what he based this assumption of his I do not know, but I suppose one ought not to suggest such a thought to a composer not yet half-way to his grave. Another in my place would have taken him in earnest. But at the time I was not inclined to meditate upon my future; I merely desired to revise my opera, the musical structure of which did not quite satisfy me. I felt its harmonic exaggerations; I was aware that the recitatives were ill made and ripping open at the seams; that there was lack of singing where singing should be; that there were both under-development and over-lengths of form, lack of the contrapuntal element, and so on. In a word, I was conscious that my former technique was unworthy of my musical ideas and my excellent subject. Nor did the instrumentation, with its absurd choice of keys of the English horns and the trumpets (two corni in F and two in C; trumpets in C), with its lack of variety in the violin bowing, with its absence of a sonorous forte, give me any rest, in spite of the fact that I had won an established reputation as an experienced orchestrator. In addition to the mentioned inserts, additions, and changes, I planned as follows: to expand the scene of the *goryelki* (catching game); to recast completely Olga's arioso in Act III, with its pungent dissonances; to insert Ivan Grozny's aria into the final tableau; to compose a short characteristic scene of the boys playing knuckle-bones and Vlasyevna's tiff with them; to introduce a conversation between the Tsar and Styosha during the women's chorus in Act III; to add voice combinations and ensembles wherever possible; to refine everything, cut down over-lengths, and recast the Overture, the closing infernal dissonances of which now gave me no rest. I set to work, and within eighteen months, approximately by January 1878, all this labour had been accomplished; [27] the Prologue had been composed; likewise the new scene at the Pyechorsky Monastery, as well as all inserts and changes had been made, and the complete score of the new *Pskovityanka* was ready. As I had now mastered my technique, it cannot be said that the work had been done rapidly. Moreover, one must take into consideration the fact that I had written my score very carefully and legibly — and that takes a good deal of time, *comparatively*. My Prologue turned out to be written in a style of composition different from the style of the opera proper. Vera's part, which included also the cradle song I had written in 1867 and published among my songs, was crowded with melody. The tempi and rhythms of the Prologue were varied; its musical fabric was well-knit and compact and did not consist of patches forcibly sewed together. For Vera's account of her visit to the Pyechorsky Monastery, I borrowed music from Act IV of the

---

[27] In a letter of April 27 [May 9], 1877 to P. I. Tchaikovsky, V. V. Stassov writes in a postscript: "According to what Balakirev and Borodin say, Rimsky-Korsakov has by now written very many *superior* compositions. The 'Roman' asked *not to insist* just now that he should show me all these things and said that very, very soon he would let you see all of them at once, that he is still fixing up some things here and there." (*Russkaya Mysl'*, 1909, Vol. III, Letter XVI.)

opera, when Olga appears in the woods near the cloister. The Boyar
Sheloga's entrance was characteristic enough, and the close was
dramatic. The Prologue was preceded by a short Overture, which
opened with a happy trumpet fanfare in Russian style; this fanfare
was subsequently intoned again and again behind the scenes, prior
to Boyar Sheloga's entrance. The real, the long Overture was to be
played after the Prologue, and just before the first act. I had made
indubitable progress in operatic composition, and this was noticeable in the Prologue, as a new composition. But in the course of the
rest of the opera considerable heaviness was apparent as a result of
the remodelling of its structure. My eagerness to make it contrapuntal, to create a wealth of independent parts, had placed a heavy
burden on the musical content. Yet there were also happy changes;
thus Olga's arioso in Act III had gained in tunefulness and sincerity
of expression. The final chorus, with wholly new music of seven-
part structure, with a crescendo of the voices on the word " Amen,"
proved greatly to Balakirev's liking; indeed, it had been written in
D-flat major to please him. The Tsar Ivan's air in the Phrygian mode
was melodious, but it led some people to remark, for some unknown
reason, that Ivan Grozny ought not to sing it. As for the new scene
near the Pyechorsky Monastery, the pilgrims' chorus written fugato
pleased Balakirev and many others; together with many others, I,
too, was pleased with the entrance of the Tsar's hunting party and
the rain-storm, written partly under the influence of the scene in the
African forest in Berlioz's *Les Troyens.* But the part of Nikola
the Simpleton was weak past question, for it had been superimposed on the orchestral background of the storm; it was an empty
rôle of dead, dry declamation.

The Prologue in its entirety was performed with piano accompaniment at my house. Mme A. N. Molas sang the part of Vera;
O. P. Vyesyelovskaya (one of the active women members of the
Free Music School) sang Nadezhda; Moussorgsky sang the part
of the Boyar Sheloga. Cui, Moussorgsky, and Stassov praised the
Prologue, though more or less guardedly. Balakirev, on the other
hand, was indifferent both to it and to the entire opera in its new
guise, excepting the pilgrims' chorus, the storm, and the final

chorus.[28] As to the other changes and inserts in *Pskovityanka,* Moussorgsky, Cui, and Stassov approved them, but their attitude towards its new form was, on the whole, cold and restrained. It looked as if even my wife regretfully looked back to its previous form and as if the changes had struck no sympathetic chord in her. Naturally all this rather hurt me; and, most important of all, I, too, felt that in its new guise my opera was long, uninteresting, and rather heavy, in spite of a better structure and notable technique.[29] It was orchestrated with natural French horns and trumpets. Now their parts were really for natural-scale instruments, and not the good-for-nothing parts that my former compositions had contained. Still, the exquisite harmony and modulations of *The Maid of Pskov* in reality called for chromatic-scale brass instruments. I adroitly got round the difficulties entailed by the natural-scale instruments. Nevertheless, I injured considerably the sonority and natural quality of the orchestration of my opera, the music of which had originally been planned without regard for natural-scale French horns and trumpets, and therefore did not rest on them in the way it should. In every other respect the instrumentation showed a step in advance: the strings played a great deal and with a variety of strokes; the forte was sonorous where the natural-scale brass did not interfere. The *tessitura* of the vocal parts was raised, and that was an improvement. After completing my work on *Pskovityanka,* in 1878, I wrote to the Directorate of the Imperial Theatres of my desire to see the opera produced in its new form.[30] Lukashevich had left the board, and Baron Kister now managed its affairs single-handed. At a rehearsal he asked Napravnik whether the latter had seen my new score; he said no. There the matter ended, and *Pskovityanka* was not revived. I confess I was pleased neither with Napravnik's attitude nor with his reply; but was Napravnik at fault in answering so curtly and indifferently? In view of my keeping aloof from Napravnik, it would have been too much to ex-

---

[28] Cf. the preceding note 27.

[29] Written at Yalta, July 30 [August 11], 1893.

[30] The rough draft of the petition addressed to Baron K. K. Kister has been preserved among Rimsky-Korsakov's papers. The principal changes and additions introduced into *Pskovityanka* are enumerated in this petition.

pect Napravnik to say anything in my favour without having seen the score. He was right a thousand times. Failures usually hurt; in this instance, however, I felt the hurt but little. I felt as though it were for the best that I bide my time with *The Maid of Pskov*. In compensation, I felt, too, that my prentice days were over, and that soon I should undertake something new and fresh.

Various compositions. The fate of the Sextet and of the Quintet. Three concerts of the Free Music School. Borodin's Second Symphony. The beginnings of May Night. *Prize contest for choral compositions. Soirées of the Free Music School. Our musical circle. Borodin's home life. Overture and entr'actes to* Pskovityanka.

DURING 1876–7 I composed — so to speak, "by the way" — variations for the oboe on a theme of Glinka's song *Chto krasotka molodaya* (Wherefore doth the beauteous maiden?) [1] and a concerto for the trombones; both of these with the accompaniment of a military (wind) band. These pieces were performed by the oboist Ranishevsky and the trombonist Leonov at the Kronstadt concerts of the United Bands of the Navy Department, under my direction. The soloists gained applause, but the pieces themselves went unnoticed, like everything performed at Kronstadt. The audiences here were still in that stage of musical development where no interest is taken in the names of composers, nor indeed in the compositions themselves; and in fact it never occurs to a good many to speculate on whether a composition has such a thing as a composer! "Music is playing," "He played that fine" — that is as far as they got in Kronstadt.[2] These compositions of mine were written

---

[1] The manuscript orchestral score (in pencil autograph) of the Variations for the Oboe is dated January 28 [February 9], 1878.

[2] A state of affairs not exclusively Kronstadtian. C. V. V.

primarily to provide the concerts with solo pieces of less hackneyed nature than the usual; secondly, that I myself might master the virtuoso style, so unfamiliar to me, with its solo and tutti, its cadences, etc. The finale of the trombone concerto was not bad, taken all in all, and was effectively orchestrated. My third and last composition of this character was a *Konzertstück* for the clarinet with the accompaniment of a military band; but this was not performed at the Kronstadt concerts, as I did not like its heavy accompaniment when I tried it at a rehearsal. During the same season (1876–7) I wrote four smaller pieces for the piano: *Impromptu, Novellette, Scherzino, Étude,* published by Bitner. The fate of my Sextet and my Quintet (sent in for the prize competition) was as follows: The jury awarded the prize to Napravnik's Trio with the motto " God loves Trinity " (All good things come in threes); it found my Sextet worthy of honourable mention, but disregarded my Quintet entirely, along with the works of the other competitors.[3] It was said that Leschetizky had played Napravnik's Trio beautifully at sight for the jury, whereas my Quintet had fallen into the hands of Cross, a mediocre sight reader, who had made such a fiasco of it that the work was not even heard to the end. Had my Quintet been fortunate in the performer, it would surely have attracted the jury's attention. Its fiasco at the competition was undeserved, nevertheless, for it pleased the audience greatly when Y. Goldstein played it subsequently at a concert of the St. Petersburg Chamber-Music Society.

As for the Sextet, the Grand Duke Konstantin Nikolayevich (who was as a rule well inclined towards me) once met me at the Conservatory and said: " What a pity that " (in awarding the prizes) " we did not know that the Sextet was thine " (he used " thou " in addressing me — a force of habit); " a great, great pity! " I bowed. One can conclude from this as to how the business of prize competitions was managed in the Russian Musical Society in those days. At the moment I recalled, too, the contest for the opera

[3] Cf. note 20 on p. 168. In the committee on awards the following acted as judges: Auer, Veykman, Davydov, Zaremba, Seyfert, Johansen, Cross, Pikkel, and Tolstoy. Together with Rimsky-Korsakov's Sextet, N. Afanasyev's Quartet in C Minor also won honourable mention.

Vakoola the Smith, when it was no secret to any of the jury that one of the operas — and such and such a one — came from Tchaikovsky's pen; the question arose in my mind whether the names of some of the composers had not been known in advance this time as well.

Balakirev was quite displeased that I had taken part in the competition; this was known to everybody, as my Sextet had received honourable mention, and the envelope containing my name had been opened. He thought that I, as well as his friends and protégés, ought to be " out of the running." But I recalled how, once upon a time, after my *Serbian Fantasy* had been written, Balakirev (then already an officer of the Russian Musical Society) had suggested sending in my *Fantasy* to a prize competition; he would take it upon himself, he said, to arrange a competition in the Society for this very purpose; but I had declined, and our conversation had never been resumed. The loser is always to blame; but the winner is always right, no matter by what means he has won. This time I was to blame; but had the competition proposed by Balakirev taken place, I should have been in the right. Nevertheless, Balakirev expressed his displeasure at my " tactlessness " — for our relations at that time were far from what they had been in the old days. Possibly my lack of piety kept him from growing intimate; however, had his attitude towards me been the old one, he would not have hesitated forthwith to begin leading me in the paths of righteousness, as he endeavoured to do with A. Lyadov, Trifonov, and others. More likely he had simply cooled towards me and tried to influence me only in so far as I was connected with affairs that interested him. As for the inner life, in which he was so fond of meddling whenever he overwhelmed me with paternal friendly cares, in that he let me severely alone. Of our talks during that period I shall cite the following two.

Once when a rumour had spread that Napravnik, who had gone to the steppes of Samara for a kumiss cure, was very ill, Balakirev summoned me and began to tell me that, in case of Napravnik's death (which Balakirev expected for a certainty) no one but I was to take his place, and that it was imperative to begin to see the proper people in advance. Purposely I replied to him, in allusion to the words of the Gospel, by saying: " Why cast lots for his garments? " Balakirev quieted down at once and made an end of the conversation. Napravnik recovered and has happily conducted opera to this day, and I am very happy that I had not rushed off to push my candidacy for his position, for which at that time I was not fit even from a technical point of view.

The other talk which I had with Balakirev I shall cite here, but just how it came about I don't remember. I told him that I considered others' advice injurious during composition, and that I preferred to have the composition come out poorer, provided it were at least original and altogether its author's. To this he replied that he viewed the matter differently; that the best method of composition would be one in which the composer, in the process of creating, had been guided by the counsels of people with fine critical abilities; that these people ought not to neglect the slightest trifle until the composition satisfied them completely; and that in this way only could a composition turn out flawless. And what did he cite in support of his views? Neither more nor less than the Jesuit Order (!), where the acts of each member are irreproachable — from the Order's point of view, to be sure — since the acts of each have been pondered and weighed by all the members; and therein lies the guarantee of the Jesuits' success. The Jesuit Order, and artistic creation! How strange a juxtaposition! No doubt, he, of all people, would never have endured collective surveillance of himself. But he would not have endured it even in the case of others whose creative gifts he had at heart; he would have done away with every vestige of collectiveness and replaced it with his own individual criticism, which he would have considered solely absolute.

The affairs of the Free School were beginning to rouse a lively interest in Balakirev, and his pressure on me was very perceptible. Balakirev insisted that we arrange several subscription concerts; deferring to him, I consented to give three. Their programs were suggested by Balakirev to a considerable extent. Nevertheless, I recall having overruled him on the point of performing Schumann's

Manfred in its entirety. For some reason Balakirev held out against it, though he had always liked *Manfred*. Or was it perhaps because *Manfred* had been suggested by me at my own initiative? [4]

The first concert, November 30 [December 12], 1876, consisted of the complete score of *Manfred,* my *Serbian Fantasy,* excerpts from Berlioz's *Lélio* ("Harp of Æolus" and fantasy on Shakespeare's *Tempest*), and Beethoven's Fifth Symphony. The concert went off splendidly; [5] only the rendering of Beethoven's symphony was somewhat ordinary. The chorus sang excellently. For the requiem in *Manfred* I placed the chorus members in the front rows of the orchestra, which had been reserved for that very purpose. The effect was excellent. This number we performed in E minor (half a tone higher than written), and the orchestra had to transpose the music. At rehearsals for this concert I had noticed that the chorus flatted irresistibly when singing this requiem in the original key. It occurred to me to raise it half a tone; and the singers kept on the given note without flatting a jot. Therefore I decided to do the same at the concert, and the chorus was sung finely; I believe it was even repeated. I had familiarized myself thoroughly with the scores of the pieces to be performed, and conducted the entire concert from memory; I remember, however, that in the transition from the Scherzo to the Finale of Beethoven's symphony my memory began to play me false, and I looked quizzically at the concert-master, Gregorovich; [6] he nodded his head at the approach of the Finale, and I was able to change the time and the tempo at the proper moment. This transition is, of course, a passage difficult to memorize, owing to the monotony of the sustained harmony and of the uniform violin figures endlessly repeated, with only the last two bars *tremolando* to warn of the approaching Finale. I could not forgive myself my absent-mindedness and my floundering, though nobody had noticed it; and since that time I decided always

[4] Cf. Balakirev's letter of October 8 [20], 1876 to Rimsky-Korsakov, from which is manifest Balakirev's close participation in making up the programs of the Free Music School during the season of 1876–7.

[5] In the Auditorium of the City Hall. There appeared a review of it (M. Ivanov's) in *Musical Leaflet,* 1876–7, No. 6, p. 88.

[6] The father and first teacher of Charles Gregorovich (1867–1921), who gave concerts in the United States in 1896–7. J. A. J.

to conduct with the score under my eyes. And really the conductor must always be in a position to come to the musician's aid during a performance and show him when to come in; yet this is utterly impossible to do in conducting a whole concert from memory. Even if it is a pleasure to the audience to watch the self-confidence of a conductor leading from memory, the opposite is always pleasanter to the orchestra. Afterwards I observed, and even had orchestra musicians tell me, that Balakirev (who up to a certain time always led from memory) never showed them when to come in, and that the musicians, unaided by him, had to be on the alert for themselves. An accident at the performance of *Sadko*, which I shall relate in its proper place, made Balakirev resort to the score ever after.

The second concert [7] of the Free School, on January 25 [February 6], 1877, consisted of Mozart's *Requiem* and Borodin's First Symphony, which latter I conducted very badly.

At the third concert (March 8 [20], 1877) I gave excerpts from Liszt's oratorio *Christus*, excerpts from Schubert's Unfinished Symphony (B minor), my own *Old Song* (chorus *a capella*) and Balakirev's *1000 Years*, not yet rechristened *Roos'* (Russia). The concert went off safely; even the *Stabat Mater Speciosa*, most difficult of performance (from Liszt's oratorio).[8] The enharmonic modulations in this latter chorus dragged the singers irresistibly to a gradual lowering of pitch, while, in the intervals between the singing of the choir, there are interludes for the organ. The organ (harmonium) was played by my conservatory pupil Bernhard (subsequently professor and inspector),[9] and, whenever the choir sang half a tone flat, he transposed his interludes also half a tone, and thus we ended safely a third below where we had started. Subsequently, when Borodin related this to Liszt, the latter said that in Germany the same thing had always happened in performances of that chorus!

---

[7] At Kononov's Hall, as also the next, third concert. For a review (M. Ivanov's) of the second concert, cf. *Musical Leaflet*, 1876–7, No. 10, p. 152.

[8] A review of the concert (by M. Ivanov) is in *Musical Leaflet*, 1876–7, No. 14, p. 217.

[9] Later Director of the Conservatory.

Having carried through three concerts with rather difficult programs, I felt, to a certain degree, accustomed to the conductor's
art; and therein lay the benefit I derived from them. As for the
money side of the business, the three subscription concerts had
quite disappointed the school, despite the fact that, thanks to Balakirev, we had several honorary members paying from fifty to a
hundred rubles. For the greater part these honorary members were
wealthy pupils of Balakirev, and he had made them see the advantage of enrolling. After all was said and done, so little money was
left in the treasury of the school that it was useless even to dream
of concerts during the ensuing year.

Among the musical events of the season of 1876–7 must be noted
Napravnik's performance of Borodin's Second Symphony in B
minor at a Russian Musical Society concert.[10] I can't recall how and
under whose influence this performance was brought about, but I
vividly remember the concert itself.

Written and revised during many years, the B-minor Symphony
was reduced to its ultimate form by the composer principally under
the influence of our talks about orchestration, talks that had begun
some three years earlier. Studying, together with me, much concerning wind and particularly brass instruments, Borodin was as
enthusiastic as I over the fluency, the ease of handling the tones,
and the fullness of the scale of chromatic brass instruments. It
turned out that these instruments were not at all those unwieldy
implements we had heretofore imagined and many composers still
imagine them to be. Military band scores and various virtuoso solos
convinced us of that. And that was perfectly true. But at this point
our enthusiasm ran away with us. The B-minor Symphony was
orchestrated too heavily, and the rôle of the brass was too prominent. How often Borodin delightedly showed me his score and how
enraptured I grew with his bold handling of the orchestra's brass!
In Napravnik's performance of the symphony the whole heaviness
of this method of instrumentation was brought out. The Scherzo
suffered most, for in this movement the rapidly changing chords

---

[10] At the fifth concert, on February 26 [March 10], 1877.

187

had been entrusted to the French horns. Napravnik found it necessary to take this Scherzo at a much slower tempo than proper —
that it might be performable and clear. And we were vexed at him
and swore at the coldness of his performance and his distortion of
the tempo; yet he was perfectly right. People liked the symphony
very moderately, and we naturally were most displeased. Some two
years later, however, the composer himself realized his mistake:
the instrumentation of the Scherzo was considerably lightened, and
at the next performance of the symphony (under my conductorship, in the season of 1878–9) it was possible to play it in the right
tempo. V. V. Stassov always called this the " Paladin Symphony,"
and this characterization is correct; the only exception is the Scherzo
(though not its trio), which is of a character alien to the rest of
the symphony. By the way, the brief modulatory transition from
B minor to F major at the beginning of the Scherzo was invented
(that is, improvised) in the old days by Balakirev; in Borodin's
scheme, the Scherzo had originally begun with the note C repeated
in the French horns.[11]

The summer of 1877 I spent at the villa in Shuvalov Park (First
Pargolovo). Here we lived with V. F. Purgold, the Akhsharumovs,
and the Molas family, as in the preceding summer. The season
slipped by uneventfully. I worked at *Pskovityanka,* devoting a good
deal of time to it; and occasionally I made brief trips to St. Petersburg and Kronstadt in connection with my official duties. That
summer, in the intervals between regular work, my thoughts turned
more and more frequently to Gogol's *May Night.* Since childhood I
had adored *Evenings at a Farmhouse;* I preferred *May Night,* perhaps, to all the other stories of that cycle.

Even during our engagement, my wife had often urged me some
day to compose an opera on this subject.[12] Together we had read

----

[11] Written at Yalta, August 1 [13], 1893.

[12] As early as December 1871 — that is, before becoming Rimsky-Korsakov's
fiancée — Nadezhda Nikolayevna wrote him: " Today I have read another of Gogol's
stories *Sorochinskaya Yarmarka* (*The Fair at Sorochintsy*). This one, too, is good,
and is even possibly suitable for an opera, but not for you, and, in general, it is not
what *Mayskaya Noch'* (*May Night*) is, for example. But what can I do? It has so
lodged in my head that nothing can drive it out. . . ." (Among Rimsky-Korsakov's
papers.)

this story on the day I proposed to her. Since then the thought of *May Night* had never left me; and that summer especially it seemed to near realization. Certain musical ideas for this opera had suggested themselves even earlier, but that summer they came with greater persistence. I had already jotted down the plan and in part the libretto; I followed Gogol exactly as to subject matter, preserving as far as possible the dialogue in which the story abounds. I recall that in the summer of 1877 I had in mind the melody of the song "about the Mayor"; the theme of the burden in the Trinity Sunday song of the girls; the beginning of Kalenik's *hopak* (Ukrainian dance), and such trifles. Still I had made no serious attempt to carry out the idea of writing *May Night;* I kept on revising *Pskovityanka.* As far as I recall, the composition, or at least the orchestration, of the *Konzertstück* for clarinet, too, belongs among my occupations of that summer. At that time I was also partly busied with preparing for the press my own as well as Filippov's folksong collection. In addition to all this, I also wrote an *a capella* chorus to the words and tune of the folksong *Pro Tatarski Polon* (*On the Tatar Captivity*). This chorus as well as another on Koltsov's text, in the form of a five-part fugue (written soon after the summer had ended), I wished to submit for the prize competition announced by the Russian Musical Society.[13] I shall relate here the history of these choruses, thus running somewhat ahead.

When the final date for submitting the choruses approached, it turned out that I had been appointed to the jury that was to judge the submitted compositions. I did not want to decline, for fear of rousing suspicion that I was one of the contestants. However, when we considered the submitted compositions, I evaded giving an opinion; and later I kept away from the final deliberations; the jury designated my two choruses among the six to which the prizes were awarded. The authors of the other prize-winning compositions were Taborovsky, Solovyov, Blaramberg, and Afanasyev, I

---

[13] This competition for choral compositions, advertised by the Directorate of the St. Petersburg branch of the Imperial Russian Musical Society, set October 1 [13], 1876 as the final date for submitting the choral compositions, and November 1 [13] of the same year as the date for awarding the prizes. The advertisement was published in V. V. Bessel's *Musical Leaflet* of May 9 [21], 1876 (No. 23), pp. 364–6.

believe.[14] The leader of the jury in awarding prizes was F. F. Czerny, professor of the choral class at the Conservatory. Solovyov, who was also on the jury, had behaved approximately as I had. At this contest there appeared for the first time on St. Petersburg's musical horizon the name of Blaramberg, who had long lived in Moscow and was instructor at P. A. Shostakovsky's Music School. P. I. Blaramberg, with whom I became intimate subsequently, was already known to me as a musician who had tried his hand in the field of composition. In years gone by I had occasionally met him in Balakirev's circle; I had known him but slightly, however, and his essays at composition had not been heard of in those days. Later on he had vanished from sight for a long time. Prior to the above contest, I had become familiar with his manuscript work; there was some sort of suite of Oriental melodies and dances, little to my liking.[15]

During the season of 1877–8 there came an involuntary lull in the activity of the Free School. There was no money; it was impossible to give concerts. Nevertheless, I strove with might and main to keep up the non-public activity of the institution. We continued rehearsing various pieces and arranged several soirées in the Town Council Hall with a low charge for admission to the public. The chorus sang either *a capella* or with piano accompaniment. Some of the amateur members of the school I instructed in Mendelssohn's quartets, which were then sung at the soirées. I also invited some Conservatory pupils for solo performances on the cello, the piano, etc. Of the vocal soloists, Mmes A. N. Molas and O. P. Vyesyelovskaya, whom I have already mentioned, sang once

---

[14] N. Afanasyev won the prize with a chorus on K. M. Golitsyn's text: " I used to believe of yore." A collection of the six choruses which had won the prizes was published by V. Bessel in the spring of 1877.

[15] To the year 1876 likewise belongs a comprehensive sketch of an eight-voice fugue on the theme of the Russian song *Slava* (*Glory*) for double chorus accompanied by orchestra. Like the earlier choruses *The Old Song, The Moon is Sailing*, and others, this chorus belongs to the pieces overloaded with counterpoint and therefore rather dry. The awareness of this defect, particularly noticeable in the utilization of the splendid Christmas folk-carol that other composers had put their hands to more than once before, probably moved Rimsky-Korsakov to drop the work at this stage in 1876. Somewhat later (in 1879–80) Rimsky-Korsakov took his chorus up anew, introduced material changes in it, and in particular flatly renounced the fugue form. See further on p. 215.

each. The sisters O. P. and Y. P. Vyesyelovskaya had been zealous amateur members of the Free Music School since the Lomakin-Balakirev days, participating at first in the chorus and later as members of the School Board. During my directorship O. P. taught singing and theory in the preparatory class, while Y. P. was treasurer of the school, accompanying the chorus at the above musical evenings " at home." Of the other active members of the school in my time let me mention the Messieurs Milanov and Tsirus. All the bustle in arranging our concerts, all sale of tickets, all billboards, sending out notices, obtaining official permits, etc., fell upon them, and I marvelled at their zeal and devotion to the cause. G. I. Tsirus, in addition, sang bass in the choir, of which he was a good and firm leader. In all " at homes " he was never averse to singing in quartet, nor would he refuse even a solo, like Glinka's *Midnight Review*. The instructor of the men's section of the preparatory class was one Mukhin, sexton and later deacon of the Church of Samson. P. A. Trifonov was no longer active at the school. S. N. Krooglikov, subsequently one of my close friends, was at that time also a member of our chorus.

Our honorary members, enrolled by Balakirev, continued to pay their dues during that slack season of the school. Our organization of honorary members was a peculiar one: one could pay fifty rubles, or a hundred rubles, but the hundred-ruble members enjoyed no spiritual or material advantages whatever over those paying fifty. Furthermore, neither the former nor the latter enjoyed any advantages over the ordinary attendant at concerts. For his fifty or hundred rubles an honorary member received a single personal ticket in the first row of the orchestra for all concerts during the year. But a first-row season ticket could be bought by a regular subscriber for fifteen or twenty rubles. This being the case, what was the object of becoming an honorary member? Well, in the Russian Musical Society such members had the privilege of attending all the concerts, regular as well as non-subscription, of the Society, all public and private soirées of the Conservatory, and all rehearsals. At the Free School there were no such privileges; the honorary members, persuaded by Balakirev, disinterestedly paid in their fifty or a hundred rubles though enjoying no special rights, not even that of sitting together with the members of their families. The latter had to buy ordinary season tickets. The dues of the honorary members supported the school; yet those members did not provide support for the school's sake or for music's sake, or for the sake of me, the School's Director, who did not know some of them from Adam. They gave solely in answer to Balakirev's pleas. In this respect, then, the school had Balakirev exclusively to thank.

Some time during these last years N. V. Shcherbachov reappeared in St. Petersburg, where he occupied a luxurious apartment at the Hotel Europe. As before, he composed a great deal. On his visits to my house, when the music circle gathered, he occasionally played his new pieces, after long coaxing. Many of his pieces we liked, though many of them seemed rather unfinished. He also played numerous fragments which never saw completion at all. To the same degree as he was at home in the purely pianistic style, he was at sea in the orchestral; accordingly, the excerpts from his *Hero and Leander, St. Cecilia,* and other symphonic and choral works are hardly destined to be heard in public. However, despite a certain lack of originality in the creative gift, there was much in his music that was beautiful and graceful. His *Zigzag, Papillons,* and much else found favour with us.

Balakirev began to visit us, even if rarely. As a rule he did not stay long, and — strange thing! — we all felt relieved when he went. In his presence we were all too shy to express an opinion, to play anything new or something recently composed, and even too shy to be unconstrained. After his departure there usually sprang up a freer conversation; and both Borodin and Moussorgsky were not at all reluctant about playing some new or fragmentary piece of theirs. Moussorgsky played excerpts from *Khovanshchina* and sang songs, of which he wrote quite a number at that time. To these days belong his *Plyaska smyerti (Dance of Death)* and *Byez solntsa (Without Sun),* written to texts by Count Golyenishchev-Kootoozov.[16] Excerpts from Borodin's *Prince Igor* and material for the

---

[16] *The Songs and Dances of Death* were composed in the spring and summer of 1875, and *Without Sun* in the summer of 1874.

A-major Quartet were played rather frequently by their composer at our house. During several preceding years Borodin had written in the rough the following parts of his opera: Konchak's aria; Yaroslavna's arioso and her lament; Vladimir Galitsky's song; Prince Igor's aria and the duet of Act IV. Konchakovna's seductive aria still remained uncompleted; it was being revised, transposed, and played in bits, and in various forms. The magnificent dance of the Polovtsy and the March were also extant in rough drafts.

V. V. Stassov was an unfailing member at all gatherings; a distinct lack was felt when he was absent. According to his invariable habit, he hardly seemed to listen to what was being played; he ceaselessly and very loudly chatted with those near him. This, however, did not prevent him from going into great raptures and exclaiming from time to time: "Splendid! Superb!" and so on. Cui's visits were comparatively rare; yet he appeared now and then with new songs, of which he composed a vast number about this time. N. N. Lodyzhensky, whose official duties kept him abroad, came on to St. Petersburg but rarely; and so his presence at our gatherings was a rarity. Having joined the service and having thus, so to speak, stricken himself from the roster of promising composers, he no longer let his ambition dwell on an opera or a symphony, nor did he play his innumerable fragments and beginnings. Notwithstanding V. V. Stassov's reminders, his *Rusalka* remained uncompleted. Every time he returned from St. Petersburg to the place of his service in the Slavic lands, he promised to send *Rusalka* and let me orchestrate it, but, to the infinite regret of all of us, his promises remained unfulfilled.[17] Approximately to the same period belongs the appearance in our circle of a young amateur singer, V. N. Ilyinsky. Having come to St. Petersburg as a medical student, Ilyinsky, who had a baritone voice, proved to be an ardent lover of the music of our circle. He amazed us all with his understanding and talented interpretation of songs, especially Moussorgsky's comic songs. Moussorgsky's *Rayok* (*Peepshow*) and *Seminarist* he

---

[17] As early as 1872, N. N. Lodyzhensky wrote N(adezhda) N(ikolayevna) Rimskaya-Korsakova: "*Rusalka* is entirely ready. I have thought out the finale and there remains now but to write it and to polish up the details, not to compose." (Among Rimsky-Korsakov's papers.)

sang superbly; the composer himself was highly pleased with the interpretations.

Of all my intimate musical friends I visited Borodin the oftenest. During these latter years his affairs and surroundings had changed as follows: Borodin, who had always given but little of his time to music and who often said (when reproached for it) that he loved chemistry and music equally well, began to devote still less time to music than before. Yet it was not science that enticed him.[18] He had become one of the prominent workers in establishing medical courses for women and had begun to participate in various societies for the aid and support of student youth, especially women. The meetings of these societies, the office of treasurer, which he filled in one of them, the bustling, the solicitations on their behalf, came to take up all of his time. Rarely did I find him in his laboratory, still more rarely at musical composition or at the piano. Usually it turned out either that he had just gone to or was just returned from a meeting; that he had spent all day driving about on those same errands, or else had been writing business letters, or working over his account-books. Add to these his lectures, the various boards and meetings of the academic conference, and it will become clear that there was no time at all left for music. It always seemed odd to me that certain ladies of Stassov's society and circle, who apparently were admirers of Borodin's talent as composer, mercilessly dragged him to all sorts of charitable committees, harnessed him to the office of treasurer, and so forth, and thereby robbed him of the time which could have been used for creating wonderful artistic musical works. Thanks to the charitable hurly-burly, his time was frittered away on trifles that could have been attended to by such as were not Borodins.[19] Moreover, knowing well his kind and easy-going nature, medical students and all sorts of student youth of the fair sex besieged him with every manner of solicitation and request, all of which he tried to fulfil with characteristic self-denial. His in-

---

[18] Cf. Borodin's self-characterization in his letter of June 1 [13], 1876 to L. I. Karmalina, and also his letter of June 18 [30], 1884 to Y. S. Borodina.

[19] " In winter," Borodin wrote to a friend, " I can only compose when I am too unwell to give my lectures. So my friends, reversing the usual custom, never say to me ' I hope you are well ' but ' I do hope you are ill.' " C. V. V.

A . P . BORODIN

from the painting by I. Y. Ryepin

convenient apartment, so like a corridor, never allowed him to lock himself in or pretend he was not at home to anybody. Anybody entered his house at any time whatsoever and took him away from his dinner or his tea. Dear old Borodin would get up with his meal or his drink half-tasted, would listen to all kinds of requests and complaints, and would promise to " look into it." People would hang on him with unintelligible explanations of their business, gabble and chatter by the hour, while he himself constantly wore a hurried look, having this or that still to do. My heart broke at seeing his life completely filled with self-denial *owing to his own inertia.* To this must be added also that Yekaterina Sergeyevna continually suffered from her asthma, passed sleepless nights, and always got up at eleven or twelve in the morning. Aleksandr Porfiryevich had a difficult time with her at night, rose early, and got along with insufficient sleep. Their whole home life was one unending disorder. Dinner-time and other meal-times were most indefinite. Once I came to their house at eleven o'clock in the evening and found them at dinner. Leaving out of account the girls, their protégées, of whom their house had never any lack, their apartment was often used as shelter or a night's lodging by various poor (or "visiting") relations, who picked that place to fall ill or even lose their minds. Borodin had his hands full of them, doctored them, took them to hospitals, and then visited them there. In the four rooms of his apartment there often slept several strange persons of this sort; sofas and floors were turned into beds. Frequently it proved impossible to play the piano because someone lay asleep in the adjoining room. At dinner and at tea, too, great disorder prevailed. Several tom-cats that found a home in Borodin's apartment paraded across the dinner-table, sticking their noses into plates, unceremoniously leaping to the diners' backs. These tom-cats basked in Yekaterina Sergeyevna's protection; various details of their biography were related. One tabby was called Rybolov (Fisherman), because in the winter he contrived to catch small fish with his paw through holes in the ice; the other was called Dlinyeñki (Longy) and he was in the habit of fetching homeless kittens by the neck to Borodin's apartment; these the Borodins would harbour, later finding homes for them. Then there were other, less remarkable specimens of the genus *Felis*. You might sit at their tea-table — and behold! Tommy marches along the board and makes for your plate; you shoo him off, but Yekaterina Sergeyevna invariably takes his part and tells some incident from his biography. Meantime, zip! another cat has bounded at Aleksandr Porfiryevich's neck and, twining himself about it, has fallen to warming that neck without pity. "Listen, dear sir, this is too much of a good thing!" says Borodin, but without stirring; and the cat lolls blissfully on.

Borodin was a man of very strong physique and health; a man of no whims and easy to get along with. He slept little, but could sleep on anything and anywhere. He could dine twice a day, or go dinnerless altogether, both of which happened frequently. Borodin would drop in on a friend during dinner; he would be invited to join the meal. "As I have already dined today, and consequently have formed the habit of dining, I might as well dine once more," Borodin would say, and seat himself at table. They would offer him wine. "As I don't drink wine as a rule, I may treat myself to it today," he would reply. Next time it might be just the contrary. Having vanished and remained lost all day, he would drop in at evening tea and calmly sit down near the samovar. His wife would ask him where he had dined and only then would he recollect that he had had no dinner at all. Dinner would be served, and he would eat it with gusto. At evening tea he would drink cup after cup without counting. His wife would ask: "Have another?" "How many have I had?" he would ask in turn. "So and so many." "Well, then I've had enough." — And it was the same in many other things.

Approximately in 1876, Tchaikovsky began to come to our house occasionally, once or twice a year.[20] He lived in Moscow at that time, but used to call on us during his flying trips to St. Petersburg. His visits often coincided with our musical gatherings. Once (I do not recall the year) he came and, in reply to the usual inquiry as to

---

[20] P. I. Tchaikovsky came to St. Petersburg during the season 1875–6 the first time late in October or early in November 1875, for the purpose of clearing up the subsequent fate of his prize-winning opera *Vakoola the Smith;* the second time en route to Moscow from abroad, in January 1876, when his Quartet in F major was performed at a quartet concert of the Imperial Russian Musical Society.

what he had composed, said he had just written his Second Quartet in F major. We begged him to let us hear it, and, without much coaxing, he played it through. All of us liked the quartet very much. A few years later Tchaikovsky ceased playing his own compositions for others. I also recall that during one of his visits at our house he stated that he was composing an orchestral fantasy on Shakespeare's *Tempest*. He added that, in depicting the sea, he intended to use as his model, within limits, Wagner's introduction to *Das Rheingold*, constructed on a single triad. Subsequently, however, when I heard the *Tempest* performed by an orchestra, I did not find any perceptible similarity between Tchaikovsky's delineation of the sea and Wagner's of the Rhine. At that time, as well as afterwards, Tchaikovsky was charming to talk to, and a man of the world in the best sense of the term, always animating the company he was in. In the course of my reminiscences I shall have numerous occasions to return to him; I shall therefore confine myself now to the above remarks.

In the autumn of 1877 I became convinced that the revision of my *Pskovityanka* had led to no satisfactory results in the artistic sense, and that it was necessary to work over the opera once more; accordingly I decided to utilize in a different way the material that came into the second version of *The Maid of Pskov* and, after suitable selection, to arrange incidental music for Mey's drama. The minor overture to the Prologue; the Introduction to the *vyeche* scene; the introduction depicting Olga (to Act IV of my first version) were exactly right for this purpose. To this I added the entr'acte to Act III of the drama; I took the music from the scene of the game of knuckle-bones and composed an additional entr'acte to the last act. In view of the reference to the Pyechorsky Monastery in this act, the theme was the melody of the verse about Aleksey, the godly man. Thus the music to Mey's drama *Pskovityanka* assumed the following form:

a) Overture to the Prologue
b) Entr'acte to Act I (Olga)
c) Entr'acte to Act II (*Vyeche*)

197

d) Entr'acte to Act III (Game of Knuckle-bones)

e) Entr'acte to Act IV (on theme of the verse)

The same orchestration was retained as in the second version of the opera (with natural-scale French horns and trumpets).[21]

---

[21] In 1882 Rimsky-Korsakov reorchestrated afresh, to a certain extent, the Overture and entr'actes to Mey's drama. On this cf. " 1881–82."

Beginning to compose May Night. *A. Lyadov. Paraphrases. Pro-posed trip to Paris. Completion of* May Night; *its characteristics. Borodin and Moussorgsky. Concerts of the Free Music School. First trip to Moscow. Compositions to commemorate the twenty-fifth an-niversary of the Tsar's reign. Beginning to write* The Fairy-tale. The Russian Quartet. *Work on* Prince Igor. *Borodin at his summer home.*

DURING THE WINTER OF 1877–8 *May Night* began to absorb me more and more, and in February I set to work in real earnest. I wrote the orchestral score directly on enormous sheets of music paper ruled lengthwise, jotting down only the roughest, most frag-mentary pencil notes. In the course of February, March, and April I had done these scenes: Lyevko; the water-nymphs and Pan-nochka (inclusive of Pannochka's disappearance); and the sunrise. The writing went easily and fast. As I recall, I worked at the end of this scene till far into the night. Besides this, I had written the *hopak* of Kalenik and the Trinity Sunday Song of Act I. I orches-trated with all manner of abbreviations (Clarinetti col Oboi, Viola col Violoncello) counting as I did on an excellent copyist, Pusto-valov (flutist in the Preobrazhensky Regiment), whom I had in view. In addition to the composed portion, there had accumulated a fair amount of material for the whole opera. The above instalment completed, I showed it only to Anatoli Lyadov. Both my wife and young Lyadov liked, without reservations, what I had composed.

That winter Anatoli and I grew more intimate; he liked to visit us — our former relations of professor and insubordinate pupil had vanished. At that time and for a long time afterwards Lyadov lived with his sister Valentina Konstantinovna (an artist of the Russian Dramatic Theatre). On his visits to our house he was usually made to play the opening of his B-flat-major Quartet, with its magnificent singing second theme. This fragment delighted us all, including Stassov, who afterwards, in his article *Twenty-five Years of Russian Art,* went so far as to proclaim that Lyadov had in his portfolio a complete, magnificent quartet. Unfortunately, that quartet has never materialized to this day, and of course never will materialize. The fact that there was no continuation of this excellent opening belongs among those incomprehensible things about Lyadov to which I shall have to refer many times. Besides this opening, Lyadov played us also other fragments of his, chiefly for the piano, his *Biryul'ki* (*Jack-straws*) for instance. At that time it was still possible to make him, a youth of twenty or twenty-one, sit down at the piano and play a composition of his own. Not so afterwards. Whether in a spirit of contrariness, or from a desire to make a show of hard-heartedness, a sort of " Let them suffer," so to speak; or whether out of sheer laziness, no amount of coaxing, in later years, could induce him to play even a fully finished composition of his own. And yet sometimes he would sit down unbidden and, for a full hour, to everybody's delight, play various fragments of compositions he had planned or actually begun. Though not a pianist, he played rather gracefully and neatly, even if somewhat sleepily, never forcing his tone beyond mezzo forte.

Anatoli Konstantinovich was the son of Konstantin Nikolayevich Lyadov, conductor of the Russian Opera, whom I have mentioned several times before this. His father, his uncle Aleksandr (conductor of the Ballet Orchestra), a second uncle (a chorister), and a third (a cellist) had received their training under the Directorate of Theatres and had each passed a lifetime as employees of the theatre, moving about in the theatrical world. I believe all of them [except the last] [1] were a little inclined to loose living.

The brilliant musical gifts of Anatoli's father were stifled in continuous revelling and carousing. He frittered away his activity as composer on mere nothings, composing dance-music and pieces to order. Of his more important works, the skilfully knit fantasy, with chorus, on the song *Vozlye ryechki, vozlye mosta* (*Near the river, near the bridge*) is still widely known.

Of Anatoli's mother I know nothing; she had long departed this world when I first came to know him. Anatoli and his sister V. K. (subsequently wife of Sariotti, a singer of the Russian Opera) had been left to grow up as best they might. Their father, deep in his carousing and his liaison with the singer L., was never at home and never laid eyes on his children for weeks at a stretch. Though he drew a good salary, he very often left his children without a copper, so that they had to borrow money occasionally from the servants, to escape starvation. Of formal education and instruction there could be no question at all. On the other hand, however, Anatoli had unrestricted access behind the scenes of the Mariinsky Theatre, where one and all, from the leading singer to the last lamplighter, spoiled him as the conductor's son. At rehearsals he larked in the wings and clambered all over the boxes. In those days — that is, before Napravnik's arrival — rehearsals were run in slipshod fashion. Not infrequently Konstantin Lyadov gathered the orchestra, in groups, of course, at his own apartment. Before much work had been accomplished, they all sat down to a bite of something. There was no such thing as a piano score for many operas. The soloists were rehearsed to the accompaniment of several desks of the quartet. The music of the missing wind instruments the conductor played on the piano or harmonium.

The social life of artists at that time was quite unlike that of the present. Wine flowed in abundance, and the treatment of the fair sex was quite free. The first week after Lent, when theatre per-

---

[1] The words set in brackets were probably added by A. K. Lyadov when reading over the proofs of *My Musical Life* or were inserted by Rimsky-Korsakov at the former's suggestion, since they are not in the original text.

formances had ceased, picnics on a large scale were the order of the day. To be sure, little Lyadov could take no active part in these, yet he could observe to his heart's content. But he, the pet of the opera troupe, the pet who frequently had nothing to eat at home, was irresistibly drawn by the operatic stage. Glinka he loved and knew by heart. *Rognyeda* and *Judith* delighted him. On the stage he appeared in processions and crowds, and later, when he had come home, he mimed a Ruslan or Farlav, before the mirror. Of singers, chorus, and orchestra he had heard enough and more than enough. Amid such surroundings his boyhood had passed, without supervision and without system. Finally he was sent to the Conservatory; he was boarded at the house of Shustov, one of the directors of the Russian Musical Society. At the Conservatory he was taught violin and piano, and indulged in numerous pranks with his cronies, G. O. Dütsch and S. A. Kazakov (subsequently a violinist in the Opera orchestra). Anatoli did not study the violin any too long; when he got as far as Kreutzer's *Études* he deserted the violin and took up theory. In Johansen's class in theory, too, he did almost no work at all, and busied himself rather with essays at composition. Music preoccupied him a great deal; in music he lived, composing in all its imaginable varieties; but he was most neglectful of class exercises. At last Johansen managed in some way to draw a tight rein on him, and Lyadov brilliantly completed his courses in harmony, counterpoint, and fugue. With all his heart he yearned to join my class, but having once entered it, he began to show less and less zeal and finally ceased coming to class altogether. At last the matter went so far that Azanchevsky was obliged to expel him and Dütsch from the Conservatory, as I have already mentioned elsewhere. The wretched surroundings of his childhood and the lack of proper rearing had made him lazy and incapable of forcing himself to do anything. When he lived at his sister's, it is said, occasionally he would ask her to give him no dinner until he completed his fugue or whatever other task had been set him at the Conservatory. He could do only what he particularly desired to do. He would receive a letter inviting him somewhere, for instance; since he had no wish to go, he made no move to — in fact, never

A. K. LYADOV

from the painting by I. Y. Ryepin

even answered the letter. But notwithstanding all this, back of Lyadov lay great natural intelligence, the kindest of hearts, and enormous musical talent.

In the spring of 1878 Anatoli made up his mind to earn a Conservatory diploma and to pass the final test, which consisted mainly in composing a cantata. In order to be able to count on a performance of this test composition at the Conservatory graduation exercises and, moreover, to avoid tests in extra obligatory courses, it was necessary to re-enter the Conservatory. With K. Y. Davydov's consent, he was enrolled in my class (to be sure, merely to comply with the above formality). That year L. A. Sakketti and A. R. Bernhard were to graduate from my class. These two Lyadov joined. The examination required the composing of music for the closing scene of Schiller's *The Bride of Messina*. That assignment, however, applied only to Bernhard and Lyadov; Sakketti composed a Symphonic Allegro and a minor psalm. All three pupils graduated brilliantly; but Lyadov gave us a really fine piece of work. How easy it all was for him! Where did he draw his experience from? Indeed, he was most talented, and so clever, too! His *scene*, performed at the graduation exercises in May 1878, caused general delight; Stassov, for his part, made a great to-do about it.

Late in the spring of that year Borodin, Cui, and I engaged on a joint composition of a peculiar nature.[2] Lyadov also joined us. Here is what it was: Some years before, Borodin, in fun, had composed a most charming and odd polka on the following motive:

Repeated over and over again, this motive was intended, so to speak, for one unable to play the piano, while the accompaniment called for a real pianist. As I recall it, I was the first to conceive the idea of writing, jointly with Borodin, a series of variations and pieces with this theme constant and unchanging. I induced Cui and Lyadov to join in the work. I recollect that at first Borodin showed hostility to this idea, preferring to publish his polka by itself, but soon he

[2] Cf. note 12 on p. 213.

joined us. In passing, I remember Cui's astonishment when I brought him the fugue on B — A — C — H (B flat — A — C — B) which I had composed with the accompaniment of the above motive. Without disclosing the secret, I played through the fugue on B — A — C — H minus the motive. Cui, naturally, did not warm to my composition. Then I asked him to play the tune; at the same time I myself struck up the fugue. Cui could not get over his amazement.

By the time we had to leave town for the summer, we had accumulated many pieces on this motive. I had even *too many* of them, and later excluded some from our collection, such as: sonatina, the chorale *Ein' feste Burg*, the recitative alla J. S. Bach, etc. A few pieces of this collection, named *Paraphrases* and christened *Táti-táti* by V. V. Stassov, were written in the summer of 1878, and some during the following season.[3] In 1880 the *Paraphrases* were given for publication to Rater (of the firm of Bitner) and he published them. The *Paraphrases* so delighted Liszt that he added a short transition of his own on the same motive and wrote us a flattering letter about them; this V. V. Stassov published in due course.[4]

Balakirev showed a violent antipathy towards the *Paraphrases;* he was indignant at us for engaging in such nonsense, printing it, and showing it off. We had asked Moussorgsky to take part in our joint composition; he had even tried his hand, composing a galop or something of the sort; he played us what he had composed. But he had swerved from our original plan and had changed the constant motive, and his result was quite different. We called his attention to it. He replied that he had no intention of fagging his brains over it; accordingly his participation in our joint writing came to nothing.

Towards the summer of 1878 the great Exposition was being pre-

[3] One of the variants of the *Paraphrases* of Rimsky-Korsakov is reproduced autographically in his " Correspondence with A. K. Lyadov " in *Musical Contemporary*, 1916–17, No. 7. The notes and materials for the *Paraphrases*, which were not included in the published edition, are kept in Rimsky-Korsakov's Archives in the Public Library.
[4] Liszt's letter concerning the *Paraphrases* was published in *Musical Review*, 1886–7, Nos. 15–17: " Seventeen Letters of Franz Liszt "; and still earlier, in 1879, in the daily *Golos*, No. 277 (cf. V. V. Stassov: *Collected Works*, Vol. III, p. 501).

pared in Paris. There were plans for concerts of Russian music at the Exposition, at the Trocadéro. The initiative in this enterprise belonged to the Russian Musical Society. K. Y. Davydov, who had taken part in the meetings held for this purpose, suggested me as conductor of the projected concerts; and this was approved by the Directorate, led by the Grand Duke Konstantin Nikolayevich. I had received no official notification; but Davydov assured me that the matter had been arranged. I was leisurely thinking out the programs of the concerts and preparing to go early in the summer. As my wife was to go with me, we did not look for a summer residence. The matter dragged along rather slowly and suspiciously. Nothing in writing and official came to me. Suddenly I learned (towards the end of May) that Nikolay Grigoryevich Rubinstein himself wished to assume the direction of these concerts, and that the Grand Duke was inclined in his favour. Probably in N. Rubinstein's mind and later in the Grand Duke's there had sprung up the thought that I was inexperienced and had, besides, exclusive and partial leanings towards our own circle, and was therefore not the person to conduct the Paris concerts; N. Rubinstein, on the other hand, was a representative musician exactly right for the occasion. Eventually it turned out that it was Rubinstein who went to Paris; I was sidetracked. Davydov felt deeply offended at this turn of affairs; he told me a rather " stormy " scene had taken place between the Grand Duke and himself. At the close of the interview with the Grand Duke, Davydov started out of the room; but the Grand Duke caught hold of his hand; he strove to free himself — in short, a semblance of a struggle took place.

Thinking over at this hour what occurred at that time, I come to the conclusion that, although it was not quite fair of Rubinstein to cut the ground from under me, nevertheless both he and the Directorate were justified in their misgivings about me.[5] I was in-

---

[5] Concerning this affair, cf. *V. V. Stassov's Correspondence with Rimsky-Korsakov*, the letters of June 20 and 28 [July 2 and 10], 1878. In her notes to this correspondence V. D. Komarova (V. Karyenin) justly observes that in 1878 Rimsky-Korsakov had viewed the mentioned incident with far from the same tranquillity with which he speaks of it in *My Musical Life*. Cf. also the letters of P. I. Tchaikovsky and V. V. Stassov in *Russkaya Mysl'*, 1909; and V. Karyenin: *V. Stassov, A Sketch of His Life and Work* (Leningrad, 1926), pp. 422 ff.

deed inexperienced; for me to go to the Paris Exposition was a trifle premature. Davydov's suggesting me had been ill-advised and the cause of Russian music had but gained by the sending of Nikolay Grigoryevich. For a year or two after, I was sulky with him, and avoided him when he visited St. Petersburg; afterwards, however, all was forgotten.

We found a summer home late at Ligovo (Mme Lapotnikova's), going there in mid-June. We rented it jointly with Vladimir Fyodorovich Purgold and the Akhsharumovs; the latter lived with us only a short while, presently going abroad.[6]

During the summer of 1878, at Ligovo, I wrote, in orchestral score, the Overture, the entire scene of Hanna with the Mayor and Lyevko, Lyevko's story, the love-duet, Lyevko's first song, and also the song about the Mayor [for *May Night*]. Besides these, in August, I composed the whole finale of Act III (after Pannochka's disappearance).[7]

Except for two or three trips to Kronstadt in connection with my official duties, I did not leave our summer home, as I recall it. In the latter part of the summer a frequent visitor was Anatoli Lyadov, who had spent the beginning of the summer in a village of the Borovichi canton. I remember that, as pastime and exercise, we each used to write a fugue a day on the same theme in D minor.

On October 5 [17], our son Andrey was born. After the usual days of bustling and uneasiness, I turned once more to my opera. In October I wrote the first tableau of Act II, except the Vinokur's (Wine-distiller's) story, as well as the *proso* (millet) chorus for Act I. Early in November, I wrote the Vinokur's story and the sec-

---

[6] Written September 5 [17], 1895.

[7] The information that the Overture (in orchestral score) was composed that summer does not tally with V. V. Stassov's statement in his letter of June 17 [29], 1879 to Borodin, in which he writes: " Rimlaynin [= Roman; i.e., *Rimsky*-Korsakov] has finished the orchestral score (except the Overture) and delivered it to the Directorate." In a letter to Borodin (undated, it is true, but beyond any doubt belonging to 1879), Rimsky-Korsakov writes: ". . . Having settled accounts with *May Night* (the Overture has been composed), I carefully examined your No. 1. . . ." The originals of both letters are in S. A. Dianin's collection. In the author's manuscript letter submitting the opera there is a notation: " The opera was begun in February 1878 and finished in October 1878." Detailed data concerning the time of composing *May Night* will be found in V. V. Yastryebtsev's *My Reminiscences of N. A. Rimsky-Korsakov*, Part II, pp. 162–5.

ond tableau for Act II. Thus the entire opera was ready in orchestral score, and I forthwith set to transcribing it for piano and voice; this I finished approximately near New Year's. The libretto was submitted to the censor and was licensed for performance; then the score, the piano score, and the libretto were forwarded, with the usual letter, to the Directorate of Theatres.

In my reminiscences of 1876–7 I spoke of my enthusiasm for the poetry of pagan worship — an enthusiasm that had originated in my work on ceremonial songs. That enthusiasm had not cooled even now; on the contrary, with *May Night* it led to a series of fantastic operas in which the worship of the sun and of sun-gods was introduced. I did this either directly, through subject-matter drawn from the ancient Russian pagan world (as in *Snyegoorochka* and *Mlada*), or indirectly, by reflection, in operas the subject-matter of which had been taken from later Christian times (as in *May Night* or in *Christmas Eve*). I say indirectly and by reflection; for though sun-worship had entirely faded before the light of Christianity, yet the whole cycle of ceremonial songs and games to this very day rests on the ancient pagan sun-worship which lives unconsciously in the people. The people, as a nation, sing their ceremonial songs by force of habit and custom, neither understanding nor suspecting what really underlies these ceremonies and games. Today, however, the last vestiges of ancient song [8] and, with

---

[8] In his preface to *Modern Russian Songs* (Oliver Ditson Co.; 1921), Ernest Newman draws an interesting distinction between the German and Russian use of folk-elements in music. "The variety of style of the Russian song is the result of the variety of influences, racial, local, and cultural, to which it has been subject. German art-song has drunk as deeply of the fountain of folksong; but German art-music and German folk-music have always been so intimately associated that it is hard to say where the one ends and the other begins. It is not so much that the folk-music has been an influence upon the composers as that it has been part of their bone and blood and being. The moods, the prosody, the structure, the cadence of the folksong run, broadly speaking, through almost all the German music, sacred and secular, vocal and instrumental, of the last three hundred years. . . . In Russia the evolution was different. Russian folk-music had existed long before Russian art-music came into being; with the result that when composers fell under its spell, it became a genuine influence of which they were more or less conscious. Art-music, as the German musician of the mid-nineteenth century knew it, could not go to the German folksong for inspiration, for it had really never quitted it. But the Russian composer who, having learned his technique and imbibed a good part of his idiom from the Western music of his day, turned then to his native folk-music, found in it an inexhaustible treasure-house of novelty. Thus we can speak of a genuine influence of Russian folksong upon Russian art-song." C. V. V.

them, all signs of ancient pantheism are evidently vanishing. All choral songs in my opera have a ceremonial colouring or a game colouring: the spring-game *proso* (millet), the Trinity Sunday song "*Zavyu vyenki*" (I shall weave garlands), the *rusalniya* songs (for Whitsunday), the slow song and the fast in the last act, and the *khorovod* itself (round dance and song) of the water-nymphs.[9] The very action of the opera I connected with Trinity or *Rusalnaya* week, called the Green Christmas; and even Gogol's drowned women I have turned into nymphs. In this way I managed to connect, with the subject I adored, that ceremonial side of folk-life which gives expression to the survivals from ancient paganism.

May Night was of great importance in my activity as composer, for reasons other than the one mentioned. Despite the abundant use of counterpoint (the fughetta *Poost' ooznayut chto znachit vlast'* — "Let them learn what power means"; the fugato on the words: "Satan, Satan! 'tis Satan himself!" the combination of the slow and the fast *rusalniya* songs; the multitude of imitations scattered everywhere), I cast off in this opera *the shackles of counterpoint* still perceptible in the revised *Maid of Pskov*. Here I introduced, for the first time, large conjoint singing numbers (ensembles). In handling the voices I adhered strictly to their real individual ranges; there is nothing of the kind in *Pskovityanka*. The numbers are always rounded off, wherever the scene permits. Singing melody and phrase replace the former inexpressive recitative superimposed on the music. Here and there a tendency is shown towards the *secco* recitative, which I employed subsequently, beginning with *Snyegoorochka*. However, in *May Night* this tendency did not bring very happy results. Its recitatives are still somewhat awkward and really unsuitable for easy execution. Beginning with *May Night*, I seemed to have mastered transparent operatic instrumentation in

---

[9] Girls, deserted by their lovers, who, according to the legend, have killed themselves and become water-nymphs. These fantastic creatures also appear in Dargomyzhsky's *Rusalka*, in Puccini's *Le Villi*, and in Adolphe Adam's ballet, *Giselle*. *May Night* was beautifully produced (though with extensive cuts) in London by Serge de Diaghileff's Russian Ballet and Opera Company in the summer of 1914. I heard one of these performances and would say that, although the opera has lovely lyric moments and some effective comic scenes, on the whole it sounds old-fashioned and is unworthy of the genius of the composer. C. V. V.

Glinka's manner, although here and there it lacks sonority. On the other hand, the strings play much and with freedom and vitality. *May Night* is orchestrated for natural-scale French horns and trumpets, in a manner to enable them really to play the opera. The scene demands three trombones without a tuba, and only in the song about the Mayor two piccolos are employed, so that, in general, the instrumental colour-scheme calls to mind that of Glinka. However, in Pannochka's singing, a distinct novelty was introduced: the accompaniment in constant glissandos of two harps.

The theme of *May Night* is bound up in my mind with memories of the time when my wife became my fiancée; and the opera is dedicated to her.

The orchestral score of my opera, submitted to the Directorate, was shortly examined by Napravnik and accepted upon his favourable verdict.[10] The Board of Directors sent it for an opinion also to K. Y. Davydov, who found it to his liking;[11] still, Napravnik's voice carried the chief and decisive weight. The parts were given to copyists; and, as early as the spring of 1879, chorus rehearsals began. The chorus-masters were I. A. Pomazansky and Y. S. Azyeyev, the same as in the days of *The Maid of Pskov*. It was scheduled for production during the following season of 1879–80.

During the season of 1878–9 the Free Music School had accumulated funds, after a year of silence and rest. Thanks to Balakirev's efforts, the honorary members had been paying their dues. Concerts could now be resumed. I announced four subscription concerts; they took place on January 16 [28] and 23 [February 4] and February 20 and 27 [March 4 and 11]. Each was a mixed program as in former years. Among others, the following numbers were performed for the first time: The *Khorovod "Proso"* (millet), the chorus of nymphs, and the song about the Mayor from *May Night;* Liszt's *Hamlet;* the chorus from Lyadov's *Bride of Messina;* Konchak's aria, the closing chorus and Polovtsian dances from Boro-

---

10 E. F. Napravnik's report is in the files of the Theatre Committee, in the Central Library of Music of the Academic Theatres in Leningrad.

11 K. Y. Davydov's report is in the same files in the form of a letter of April 5 [17], 1879, to Y. K. Albrecht. For excerpts from this letter, cf. S. Ginzberg's article " K. Y. Davydov " in *Musical Annals*, Vol. II, p. 93, Petrograd, 1923.

din's *Prince Igor;* the tableau at the Monastery of the Miracles
(Pimyen and Grigori) from Moussorgsky's *Boris Godunov;* Balakirev's *Czech Overture.* At that time *Prince Igor* moved slowly, but
progressed notwithstanding. How much pleading and importuning
I had to spend on dear old Borodin to persuade him to orchestrate
several numbers for these concerts! His swarming engagements in
connection with his professorship and medical courses for women
were always in the way. His home life I have already described.
Owing to his infinite kindliness and his entire lack of self-love, these
surroundings made it extremely inconvenient for him to work at
composition. One might come again and again and keep demanding how much he had written. Net result: a page or two of score,
or else — nothing at all. To the query: " Aleksandr Porfiryevich,
have you done the writing? " he would reply: " I have." And then
it would turn out that the writing he had done was on a batch of
letters! " Aleksandr Porfiryevich, have — you — finally — transposed
such and such a number of the opera score? " " Yes, I have," he re-
plies earnestly. " Well, thank the Lord! At last! " " I transposed it
from the piano to the table," he would continue with the same
earnestness and composure! A really definite plan and scenario
were still non-existent; at times more or less completed numbers
were composed, and again — numbers that were merely sketchy
and chaotic. Still, by this time, there had been composed: Konchak's aria, Vladimir Galitsky's song, Yaroslavna's Lament and her
arioso, the closing chorus, the Polovtsian dances and the chorus at
Vladimir Galitsky's feast. I had to beg the author for these excerpts,
for performance at the concerts of the school. Konchak's aria he had
orchestrated throughout, but there was no end to the waiting for
the orchestration of the Polovtsian dances and of the closing chorus. And yet these numbers had been announced and rehearsed by
me with the chorus. It was high time to copy out the parts. In despair I heaped reproaches on Borodin. He, too, was not over-happy.
At last, giving up all hope, I offered to help him with the orchestration. Thereupon he came to my house in the evening, bringing
with him the hardly touched score of the Polovtsian dances; and
the three of us — he, Anatoli Lyadov, and I — took it apart and be-

gan to score it in hot haste. To gain time, we wrote in pencil and
not in ink. Thus we sat at work until late at night. The finished
sheets of the score Borodin covered with liquid gelatine, to keep
our pencil marks intact; and in order to have the sheets dry the
sooner, he hung them out like wash on lines in my study. Thus the
number was ready and passed on to the copyist. The orchestration
of the closing chorus I did almost single-handed, as Lyadov was
absent, for some reason. Thus, thanks to the concerts of the Free
Music School, some numbers were finished partly by the composer
himself and partly with my help, during that year as well as during
the following season of 1879–80. At all events, had there been no
concerts of the Free Music School, the fate of the opera *Prince Igor*
would have been different.

At the rehearsal of the scene from *Boris Godunov*, Moussorgsky
behaved very queerly. Either under the influence of wine or from
mere pose (he had developed a considerable turn for posing in
those days), he often acted oddly; often he delivered himself of
obscure and involved orations. At the rehearsal in question, he
listened with a show of significant intensity to what was played
(for the most part in ecstasy at the performance of individual instruments, often during the most commonplace and indifferent
phrases), now pensively drooping his head, now haughtily lifting
it erect, shaking his mane of hair, and then again raising his hand
with the stagy gesture that had been his even before that. When,
at the end of the scene, the tomtom representing the cloister-bell
rang pianissimo, Moussorgsky made a low and deferential bow to
it, his arms crossed on his breast. That rehearsal was preceded by
a home rehearsal at the house of the singer Vasilyev I, who sang
Pimyen. I was in charge of the rehearsing and did the accompanying. Moussorgsky, too, was present. After the rehearsal, supper was
served; the host got quite drunk and talked much bosh. Moussorgsky, on the contrary, kept himself well in hand. Grishka Otrepyev's part was sung by the tenor Vasilyev II. He was the old, patient plodder of the Russian Opera, who toiled and moiled on the
stage without artistic ambition or vanity. Once upon a time he had
a very fine voice; he was a man of much routine; irreproachably

exact in all rôles; but despite all those qualities, he manifested no
talent whatsoever. But when it was necessary to learn a rôle in a
day, or to substitute owing to someone's sudden illness — for such
things, Vasilyev was the man. Goodness knows how many of the
highest and hardest parts he sang, from Sabinin in *A Life for the
Tsar* (where he took the high C with his chest) down to insignificant couriers and messengers. The artists usually took part in the
school concerts gratis. Vasilyev II, too, sang without pay, asking
only three rubles for gloves. As was his wont, he was letter-perfect
in his part; but at the end of the scene, when I suggested to him
to sing the recitative freely, ad libitum, and promised to keep
an eye on him, he refused, saying: "No! I'd rather watch
the stick (bâton)." In this respect, the singers of the Russian
Opera had been rigorously drilled by Napravnik, who allowed no
liberties.

The choruses from *May Night,* the excerpts from *Prince Igor,*
and the scenes from *Boris* went off well and met with favour. Borodin's B-minor Symphony, performed at the third concert, went well,
too. Its Scherzo was taken in the right tempo, thanks to the fact that
Borodin had made a number of corrections and had largely done
away with the piling up of brasses. Borodin and I had given a good
deal of thought to it this time; by then our craze for brass instruments had waned, and the symphony gained much from our corrections.

At the fourth concert a rather serious mishap occurred. The
pianist Klimov was to play Liszt's E-flat-major Concerto; but he
missed the rehearsal and decided to play unrehearsed; I was so
imprudent as to give my consent. At the concert Klimov grew
nervous and confused — it was impossible to follow him. During
the piano pauses, when it was easy to regain self-composure, he
would inopportunely begin to second the orchestra or nod to it, indicating wrong entrances. Thus in the opening of the Scherzo, after
the triangle solo, he played the orchestra's entrance a bar too soon,
putting everybody off; the confusion lasted to the very end of the
number. The performance was a disgrace; the orchestra was at odds
with the pianist from first to last. My mortification was unbounded,

and I literally cried for chagrin and shame on reaching home after the concert.

Throughout the winter and the spring, Cui, Borodin, Lyadov, and I went back from time to time to composing *Táti-táti*. Our collection of pieces accumulated. I believe the last numbers composed were Lyadov's galop and my tarantella. That was in June 1879, at the summer home in Ligovo, where we had gone as in the previous year.[12]

In midwinter I went to Moscow for a fortnight's stay, to conduct the orchestra in Shostakovsky's concerts. An excellent pianist, Pyotr Adamovich Shostakovsky (a pupil of the renowned Kullak) had been invited to a professorship at the Moscow Conservatory several years before, but had soon found himself at odds with its Director, N. G. Rubinstein, and had been obliged to leave. What the differences had been about I do not know exactly. According to Shostakovsky's account, the cause lay in the alleged fact that Nikolay Rubinstein could not bear near him a pianist of equal powers and would not permit him an appearance at any concert of the Russian Musical Society. How much truth there is in this it is impossible to say. But the fact is that Shostakovsky left the Conservatory and turned to giving private lessons; soon, however, he established a piano school of his own, and later even some new musical society under the name Philharmonic. During the season of 1878–9 he brought me over to conduct the orchestra, first at his own concert at the Grand Theatre, and secondly at the concert of the Philharmonic Society at the Hall of the Club of the Nobility. Besides this, he had brought over to participate in these concerts the singer D. M. Leonova, who had left the St. Petersburg Opera stage some years previously. Leonova was long past her youth, but she still had a voice.

Of my own orchestral works, I gave the Overture to *Pskovityanka* and, I believe, the *Serbian Fantasy* at Shostakovsky's concert.[13] At

---

12 Here the date must be corrected to 1878. [This apparently is my own observation. J. A. J.] From various sources it is manifest that in 1879 the *Paraphrases* already existed in printed form (first edition).

13 Shostakovsky's concert took place on April 3 [15], 1879. The *Serbian Fantasy* was really performed at that concert. The second concert was given on April 10 [22], 1879.

the concert of the Philharmonic Society I performed *Sadko*, Balakirev's Overture to *King Lear*, and other things. The concerts were
crowded, and my pieces won applause; *Sadko* was even encored.
The greatest animosity prevailed between Shostakovsky and the
Russian Musical Society, and my participation in Shostakovsky's
concerts was, evidently, a thorn in the side of the Moscow Conservatory and the Musical Society. However, friendly artistic relations grew up between Shostakovsky and me. He promised to
come to St. Petersburg to play at the Free Music School; and I
promised to come to him the following year. Thus I established,
for the first time, a musical contact with Moscow, where my name
had been all but unknown thus far; of my compositions, my Third
Symphony had been the only one given, and that in a single performance (in 1875, if I am not mistaken), N. G. Rubinstein conducting.[14] I must say, by the way, that P. I. Tchaikovsky had at that
time been music-critic on one of the Moscow dailies and had written a very sympathetic review of my symphony.[15] On my present
visit to Moscow I did not meet Pyotr Ilich, as he was not at Moscow.
At all events, by that time he had given up for good his activity
as reviewer. There was then talk aplenty about Tchaikovsky's queer
marriage. He had married a person who was ill suited to him, and
shortly (in a month or two) the couple had parted for good.[16] Pres-

---

[14] Moscow made its first acquaintance with Rimsky-Korsakov's creative work as
a symphonic composer in 1869 when his symphonic tableau *Sadko* was performed
at a concert of the Russian Musical Society. In the diary of the aged Prince V. F.
Odoyevsky (in the Manuscript Division of the Public Library) there is an interesting
account of the piece in connection with its performance: " Korsakov's *Sadko* is a
beautiful thing, full of fancy, original in orchestration. Unless Korsakov halts by the
wayside, he will be a huge talent."

[15] Rimsky-Korsakov's Third Symphony was played in Moscow at the fifth symphony concert of the Russian Musical Society in 1875. P. I. Tchaikovsky's review has
been reprinted in his *Musical Notes and Articles* (Moscow, 1898), p. 235.

[16] Tchaikovsky's marriage remains a tragic and mysterious episode in this composer's life. His biographers refer to it in veiled and suppressed whispers. Mrs. Newmarch writes that Kashkin thinks that Tchaikovsky kept his engagement secret from
his friends for some time. Kashkin met the newly married couple at a party given in
their honour at the Jurgensons'. This was the only time he ever saw them together.
Tchaikovsky continued to attend to his work at the Conservatory, but his friends observed a change in him. He had become reserved and absent-minded and seemed
anxious to avoid intimate conversation. As time went on, this marriage and its tragic
consequences were regarded as an amusing comedy by outsiders, and his intimate
friends knew few of the real facts. Kashkin was filled with the gravest apprehensions,
which proved not to be groundless. Tchaikovsky afterwards admitted that he had

ently there were rumours that he was mentally or nervously ill; immediately afterwards, however, there came complete recovery. Nevertheless, in those days he shunned friends, went nowhere, and never visited St. Petersburg except in the strictest incognito.

My trip to Moscow left a pleasant impression with me. On returning to St. Petersburg, I went back to my regular work.

In the spring of 1879 two persons — one Tatishchev and a certain Korvin-Kryukovsky — made their bow to St. Petersburg. They came to me, to Borodin, Moussorgsky, Lyadov, Napravnik, and several other composers with the following proposition: The twenty-fifth anniversary of the reign of His Imperial Majesty Aleksandr Niko-layevich (Alexander II) was to occur in 1880. For that occasion they had written a grand scenic production, consisting of a dialogue between the *Genius of Russia* and *History,* and this was to be accompanied by tableaux meant to represent various moments of that reign. For the proposed solemn performance the Messrs. Tatish-chev and Korvin-Kryukovsky had obtained permission from the proper authorities; they now turned to us with the plan that we compose orchestral music in keeping with the subject-matter of the living pictures. It must be admitted that the personalities of these gentlemen, who had lived in Paris till then, appeared somewhat odd; their mode of conversation as well as their manners recalled Bobchinsky and Dobchinsky.[17] The dialogue between the Genius of Russia and History was bombastic to a degree. Still, the moments for living pictures had been selected happily and gratefully for music; and we consented to write it. Thus were composed, partly during that season and partly during the next, my chorus *Slava* (*Glory*), on the theme of a Christmas carol;[18] Borodin's *In Central*

---

tried in many ways to end his life. Once he had gone so far as to stand in the river, with the water up to his chest, on a frosty September night, hoping to catch a fatal cold and to get rid of his troubles without scandal. A more complete account of this marriage and its consequences may be found in *Beloved Friend, the Story of Tchai-kovsky and Nadejda von Meck,* by Catherine Drinker Bowen and Barbara von Meck (Random House, 1937). C. V. V.

[17] The comic pair of cronies with one mind and two tongues, in Gogol's famous *Revizor* (*Inspector General*). J. A. J.

[18] "I have written, or, rather, renewed the chorus I had on the theme and text of *Slava*" (letter to Krooglikov of March 30 [April 11], 1880, among Rimsky-Korsakov's papers). *Slava, a Christmas Carol for Chorus and Orchestra,* op. 21

Asia (subsequently a very popular piece); Moussorgsky's march *The Capture of Kars;* [19] Napravnik's — I don't remember the name; and Zike's *The Black Sea.*[20] Moussorgsky's march was taken bodily from the music to Gedeonov's *Mlada,* where it had done duty as the March of the Princes; its trio in Oriental style (on some Kurdish theme) was newly written.[21] Subsequently this march was named simply *March, with trio, alla turca.* Our compositions, including the splendid picture *In Central Asia,* were written rapidly, but Messrs. Tatishchev and Korvin-Kryukovsky (whom Lyadov usually called Razdyeri-Rukava — that is, Rip-Sleeves — for fun) vanished no one knew where, and the question of producing the performance of their invention was dropped. Thus this scheme came to naught; only the above enumerated pieces remained, and were performed subsequently at concerts in St. Petersburg; the tableau *In Central Asia* was given rather frequently even abroad. This work took the fancy of Liszt, to whom Borodin had shown it during one of his trips abroad. Lazy and procrastinating Lyadov had not done his share.

In the summer of 1879 we lived at Ligovo at Mme Lapotnikova's summer place, just as we had done the year before. I conceived the idea of writing a large orchestral work of fantastic nature, to Pushkin's prologue to his *Ruslan and Lyudmila,* " *Oo lookomorya doob zelyony* (At the curved shore a green-clad oak)." I began, and by the end of the summer had a good part of it ready in sketch form.[22]

(St. Petersburg: A Bitner). (The date of the composition is given as 1880 on the orchestral score, 1879 on the piano arrangement.) Cf. above, p. 190.

[19] A stronghold in the Caucasus taken from the Turks in 1877 after a long siege. J. A. J.

[20] All together twelve numbers had been planned. The following were to take part in this collective task: Rubinstein, Davydov, Moussorgsky, Borodin, Cui, Tchaikovsky, Rimsky-Korsakov, Napravnik, Lyadov, Solovyov, Haller, and Ivanov. A portion of the text of the dialogue between the Genius of Russia and History has been preserved among Rimsky-Korsakov's papers.

[21] In the March of the Princes in *Mlada* there was a trio composed by Moussorgsky on a theme of Rimsky-Korsakov's (the theme of the pagan nuptials), utilized by Rimsky-Korsakov in 1875 in the Andante of his Quartet in F major; cf. above, pp. 150 f.

[22] In a letter to Krooglikov (October 6 [18], 1879), Rimsky-Korsakov wrote: " I did not produce anything during the summer. I merely commenced the musical tableau *Baba-Yaga,* but somehow it all amounts to nothing and I don't know whether I shall go on with it in the immediate future. . . ."

In addition I composed a string quartet on Russian themes; this I subsequently worked over into a Sinfonietta for the orchestra. Its separate movements bore the titles: (I) In the field; (II) At the Charivari; (III) In the *Khorovod* (round dance and song); (IV) Near the cloister. The last movement, which did not go into the Sinfonietta after all, was written on a church theme, commonly sung at Te Deums ("*Pryepodobny otche imya ryek, moli Boga za nas* — Reverend father so and so, pray God for us ") in imitational style.[23] This quartet of mine never had a public performance. Once I took it over to K. Y. Davydov and asked to have it played at a quartet rehearsal. Davydov, Auer, Pikkel, and Veykman played it for me. It did not please them much; and I found many shortcomings in it myself. The first movement was monotonous, having been written on a single theme; the Scherzo had no coda, and the Finale was dry; I did not venture to let the public hear my quartet.

Before going away for the summer, I induced Borodin to allow me to copy personally and put in some work on polishing up the chorus and the parts of the *goodochniki* (rebec-players) in the scene at Vladimir Galitsky's house in *Prince Igor*. This scene he had composed and written down rather long before, yet it was in utter disorder; some things were to be abridged, others to be transposed into other keys, here and there the choral parts were to be written, and so on. Meanwhile the work had not progressed; he was preparing, could not make up his mind, put things off from day to day — and the opera did not move. It distressed me extremely. I was yearning to aid him; I proposed myself as musical secretary to him, provided his wonderful opera derived some gain from it. After frequent refusals by him and urgings by me, Borodin consented, and I took the above-mentioned scene with me to my summer home.

---

[23] On the autograph manuscript of the last movement there is noted: " September 9 [21], 1879, Ligovo. Recast September 29 [October 11], St. Petersburg." Cf. A. Ossovsky's notice (in the magazine *Music*, 1911, No. 17). M. P. Byelayev's Archives. Among Rimsky-Korsakov's papers there has been preserved a piece arranged for four hands entitled *In the Church;* its original title, crossed out then and there, was *In the Monastery.* The motive later utilized by Rimsky-Korsakov in the opera *Sadko* for the characterization of the " oldster-mighty-paladin " is elaborated here. According to all indications, this piece, *In the Church,* is the very same fourth movement of the Quartet on Russian Themes that was not incorporated into the Sinfonietta. (See pp. 235 and 273.)

We were to correspond about the work referred to. I began my labour and really accomplished something. I wrote Borodin a letter about certain doubts that had arisen, but received no letter for a long time.[24] Finally an answer came, saying that he preferred to talk the whole matter over in the autumn. Thus the affair ended; and the scene had made only slight progress.

For several years now the Borodins had been going for the summer to central Russia, in the Toola Government principally, I believe.[25] At their summer home they lived queerly. Usually they rented it unseen. As a rule their summer home consisted of a roomy peasant *izba* (hut). They would bring but few belongings. They had no hearth-plate; cooking was done in a Russian oven. Apparently their mode of living was extremely uncomfortable, in crowded quarters, with all sorts of privations. The ever sickly Yekaterina Sergeyevna went barefoot all summer long, for some reason. But the chief discomfort of this sort of life lay in the absence of a piano. Borodin's summer leisure was in any event hardly productive, if not utterly barren. Always harassed by his official duties and all sorts of outside affairs during the winter, he could do very little work on his music; then came summer, and with it leisure, and yet work was impossible all the same, owing to the discomforts of this way of living. In this strange manner life shaped itself for Borodin, and yet what could have seemed more propitious for work than a situation like this: alone with his wife, and a wife, too, who loved him, who understood and valued his enormous talent?

[24] Cf. Borodin's letter of August 4 [16], 1879 to Rimsky-Korsakov, which begins with the words: "I do not know how to thank you for the trouble you have taken about my *Igor*. . . ." Cf. also the excerpt of Rimsky-Korsakov's letter to Borodin which Stassov published in his biographical sketch: *N. A. Rimsky-Korsakov* (St. Petersburg, 1890), p. 24. The full text of this letter of August 10 [22], 1879 was published in *Russian Musical Gazette*, 1909, Nos. 22–3. In it Rimsky-Korsakov undertakes "to arrange, copy, transpose, orchestrate" under Borodin's direction, and counsels him not to scruple, "for, believe me," he writes, "I crave, if possible more than you, that your opera should be produced on the stage. . . ." The original of the letter is in the Pushkin House (Stassov's Archives).

[25] In the Toola Government the Borodins lived but once — in the summer of 1881, on the estate of N. N. Lodyzhensky, Zhitovo.

1879-80

Production of May Night. *Opinions about it. Concerts of the Free Music School. Balakirev. Leonova and Moussorgsky. My second visit to Moscow. Beginning of* Snyegoorochka. *Krooshevsky. Sasha Glazunov.*

SOON AFTER RETURNING from the country I showed Balakirev the beginning of *Skazka* (*Fairy-tale*), which I had ready. Although he liked certain parts of it, he did not approve the work as a whole; the form conceived by me was not to his liking, nor did he like the very opening itself. All this made me cool towards *Fairy-tale;* I barely refrained from tearing up what I had composed; in any event, I abandoned the idea of continuing the composition. Soon my thoughts wandered to my *Overture on Russian Themes,* which I had written as far back as 1866. I was seized with the desire to revise it, and began gradually to ponder its revision and reorchestration. The work came to its end as late as the spring of 1880, when the thought of a new opera was already possessing me; but of this I shall speak later.

In October, rehearsals of *May Night* began at the Mariinsky Theatre. The rôles were distributed as follows: Lyevko, Kommissarzhevsky; Hanna, Slavina and Kamyenskaya; Svoyachenitsa (Sister-in-law), Bichoorina; Mayor, Koryakin and Stravinsky; Kalenik, Myelnikov and Pryanishnikov; Vinokur (Wine-distiller), Ende;

Scrivener, Sobolyev; Pannochka, Vyelinskaya. (Already in those days two performers were cast for certain rôles.) Rehearsals got along well; everybody tried his best; I invariably accompanied all rehearsals myself. Napravnik was reserved, but was attentive and accurate as usual.[1] The chorus sang well. For the ballet I had to put together the *violon répétiteur* part of the dances of the nymphs; owing to certain complexities of the music, this was rather hard to do. I went to see the ballet-master, Bogdanov, played him the dances, and told him my wishes in the matter. In due course orchestra rehearsals, too, began. As far as I recall, all was ready in December. The scenery, too, was ready. This scenery was made over from the investiture on hand for Tchaikovsky's *Kooznyets Vakoola* (*Vakoola the Smith*), which had been taken off the boards, with the sole difference that winter was turned into summer. Owing, however, to various causes and shortcomings that seemed bound to occur in our Directorate's productions of operas, *May Night* did not have its première until January 9 [21], 1880. It had considerable success. The song about the Mayor and also Lyevko's song (A major) were demanded over and over again. There were many curtain-calls for the artists and myself. Ende (Wine-distiller) and Sobolyev (Scrivener) were very comical. Bichoorina (Sister-in-law) was excellent and delivered her rapid-fire talk furiously. The others were all fair, with the exception of Kalenik's rôle, which suited Myelnikov poorly, and Vyelinskaya, who occasionally, as was her wont, sang off key. The ballet was poor. The scenery of Act III had been bungled, so the fantastic scene went badly.[2] The general verdict of the artists was as follows: the first two acts were very good; the third somewhat lacking; the Finale, they said, bad, bad altogether. Yet I was convinced that Act III contained the finest

---

[1] In his letter of December 15 [27] to S. N. Krooglikov, Rimsky-Korsakov wrote: "Today the first general orchestral rehearsal of *May Night* has taken place. In all fairness it must be said: all the artists and Napravnik exert themselves and are very courteous; what has caused it, I know not; presumably my opera has found some favour with them."

[2] In his manuscript "Fragments from Reminiscences about Rimsky-Korsakov" (see note 18 on p. 166 of this book) I. F. Tyumenev gives a detailed description of the first performance of *May Night* at the Mariinsky Theatre, which in general agrees with *My Musical Life*. Only Tyumenev speaks in very severe terms of the scenery devised for the production in general.

music and many scenic-poetic moments, the best being (1) two verses of Lyevko's song "*Oy ty myesyats yasny* (O, thou bright moon)," after which the window in the master's house opens, Pannochka's head appears, and her call is heard, accompanied by the harp glissando; (2) Pannochka's leave-taking of Lyevko and her disappearance. This latter disappearance lost in particular in the performance: Pannochka did not disappear, but simply walked off; the sunrise was gloomy and overcast, and the fantastic scene as a whole was carried through rudely and tastelessly. That season my opera was given eight times. Towards the last, Napravnik had already made cuts in Act III, the principal one being the first game of "raven"[3] (B minor). Through this omission the scene did not gain, it lost. First, Gogol was distorted; second, the sense was lost, as Lyevko was given no choice in recognizing the stepmother; third, the musical form was the loser too, and the author's intention destroyed completely, as the game, the first time, is founded on the simple theme:

while the second time, when the stepmother plays, this theme is combined with the stepmother's phrase:

which adds the ominous character so appropriate here. I felt provoked at these "*cots*" (Napravnik's pronunciation),[4] but what was to be done? The success of *May Night* at the later performances lapsed somewhat, but the house was filled nevertheless. When I recall the production of *The Maid of Pskov,* I cannot help admitting that my first opera achieved greater and more lasting success than the second. The next season *May Night* drew less well; and the next after that, still less. The receipts were fair, but hardly more

---

[3] In the game the mother covers the children, the raven seizes them. J. A. J.

[4] Napravnik, a Czech, pronounced *kupira* (with German umlaut) instead of *kupyura,* from French *coupure* (cut). J. A. J.

than that. During the subsequent seasons some of the artists were changed. Lyevko was sung by Lodi and later by Vasilyev III; after Ende died, Vinokur's part was sung by Vasilyev II. The performances grew more and more slipshod, and after eighteen representations (in three years, I believe) interest in the opera cooled, and it was stricken from the repertory.

At its première my opera pleased our circle more or less, but not much in general. Balakirev liked it but little.[5] V. V. Stassov was pleased only with the fantastic scene, and the game of "raven" above all; he made much ado about it and extolled it, giving a great deal of approval also to the *khorovod* of the nymphs, of which the principal ideas were borrowed from the *Mlada khorovod* (*kolo* [6]), which both Stassov and Moussorgsky had liked even in former years. They also liked moderately Pannochka's singing with the harps, suggestions of which, too, had existed in *Mlada* and which was therefore not unfamiliar to them. But Lyevko's songs, the nymphs' chorus, and the rest, they cared for very little. At that time Moussorgsky had grown cold to other people's music in general, and was cooler than before to the *khorovod*. He frowned a little and said of *May Night* as a whole that it had somehow missed the mark. Apparently my newly sprung tendency towards cantabile and rounded forms found little favour with them all; besides, I had so frightened all of them with my study of counterpoint that I was looked upon with some prejudice. Praise me they did, but their former " Fine! Incomparable! Capital! " were no longer heard. Cui wrote an extremely cold review, setting forth that my themes and phrases were *puny* throughout, and that the best of them were borrowed from the peasant-folk. His wife once met me at Bessel's and said with venom: " Now you have learned how to write operas,"

---

[5] With the cynical sarcasm so peculiarly his own, Balakirev characterized Lyevko's entrance serenade-song, " The sun is low, the evening draweth nigh," as " manure sprinkled with confectionery "; and about the comic trio of Act II: " Let them learn what authority means! " accompanied in the orchestra by a characteristic combination of flute and drum (Tamburino piccolo and Flauto piccolo solo), he used to say: " Nikolay Andreyevich will always find a pretext for scoffing at authority." Cf. V. V. Yastryebtsev: *My Reminiscences of Rimsky-Korsakov* (Petrograd, 1917), Part II, p. 51.

[6] *Kolo* (wheel, circle, ring-dance) is the equivalent of *khorovod* with the western and southern Slavs. J. A. J.

alluding to the decent measure of success that *May Night* then enjoyed with the public. I mention, in passing, that about that time,
Cui, in his articles, lavished praise on Napravnik as well as on
Davydov, but belittled Tchaikovsky as much as he could. Taken all
in all, the critics handled my *May Night* rather roughly, cavilling at
everything and perceiving no good points at all. Of course, all this
helped cool the public, as I have mentioned above. On the whole,
Pskovityanka had received more praise, more censure, and more
success than *May Night*.

In 1879–80 I arranged again four subscription concerts of the
Free Music School at Kononov's Hall.[7] The programs were again
miscellaneous, and were made up under strong pressure from Balakirev. Among other non-Russian numbers were given Beethoven's
Sixth Symphony and music to *Egmont;* Liszt's music to *Prometheus;*
Moszkowski's symphony *Jeanne d'Arc;* and excerpts from Berlioz's
Les Troyens. Of Russian numbers there were: Introduction to Act
III, the song of the wandering pilgrims, the entrance of the Tsar's
hunting party, the storm, and the song of the girls from my *Pskovityanka* (second version), as well as the cradle song from the Prologue and the closing chorus and Ivan Grozny's cavatina (sung by
I. P. Pryanishinkov) from the same. From *Igor* were given: Yaroslavna's Lament, Vladimir Galitsky's song, Yaroslavna's scene with
the girls — this time all orchestrated by Borodin himself. But the
excerpts from *Khovanshchina* performed at the second concert
were not all orchestrated by the composer. The chorus of *Stryeltsy*
(archers) and Marfa's song were from his pen entirely; but the
dance of the Persian girls was orchestrated by me. Though he had
promised this number for the concert, Moussorgsky dilly-dallied,
and I volunteered to orchestrate it. He assented at the first hint, and
at the performance was quite pleased with my work, although I
had made many corrections in his harmonies and part-writing. An
amusing thing occurred in connection with the program of the
fourth concert. A. Lyadov's Scherzo in D major was to have its first

---

[7] The concerts of the Free Music School were given on November 13 [25] and
27 [December 9], 1879, and January 15 [27] and February 12 [24], 1880. In the list
of compositions performed, Beethoven's Eighth Symphony should appear instead of
the Sixth.

performance, but the author, whom laziness was beginning to overcome, had had no time to finish it. Something had to take its place.
At that time I was occasionally visited by one Sandow, an English-
man by birth, still very young, who had studied in Leipzig and now
lived in St. Petersburg, where he gave music lessons. He used to
bring me his orchestral compositions — very dry and involved, most
of them. By chance he had once brought me a Scherzo and asked
me to perform it at one of the concerts. I had declined. Later I recalled his request and now proposed to him to put *his* Scherzo instead of Lyadov's on the program. And that was done. After the
performance the composer was called before the curtain, though
the Scherzo was colourless and full of petty bustle. I was assured
later that he had been called out through error, as the name Sandow
had been taken as a misprint for Lyadov, whose name was held in
high esteem.

Thus, owing to the wish to perform at the concerts of the school
a greater number of pieces from the pens of contemporary Russian
composers of talent, such as Borodin, Moussorgsky, or Lyadov, one
ran up against their insufficient activity, now orchestrating for them
and now extracting compositions from them by any and every
means, fair and foul. There was no need of applying such measures
to Cui and Balakirev; moreover, at that time, the former composed
nothing but songs, and I performed excerpts from his operas from
time to time; the latter composed nothing at all. Still, Balakirev, at
the time, was beginning more and more to resume musical activity
and to advance, though very sluggishly, his *Tamara,* which had remained at a standstill since the sixties. He had yielded to the importunate pleas of L. I. Shestakova when he turned back to it. It
was not brought about without an ecclesiastical person. This proved
to be a certain priest, of the Church of Zachary and Elizabeth, I
believe; the sensible priest, who had influence over Balakirev,
argued with him that the talent given him by God ought not to be
allowed to wither. Thus or in some other way, but about that time,
Balakirev's thoughts began to turn towards his *Tamara.* During the
year described he even made one appearance at a rehearsal of a
concert of the Free Music School (the first after a long lapse of

time), when I was preparing his Overture on Russian Themes (B minor). But he did not behave very pleasantly to me; he was irritable, now loudly scolding the violinists, who had struck a snag, now pointing out to me the true motions and methods of a conductor — an act altogether out of place at a rehearsal, in the presence of the whole orchestra.

Of soloists at the school concerts that year, in addition to some opera singers, we had also Shostakovsky, who played Liszt's E-flat major Concerto (given successfully), and D. M. Leonova, who sang excerpts from *Khovanshchina*. But if Liszt's concerto went off safely this time, the beginning of one of the excerpts from Berlioz's *Les Troyens* did not. This number was begun disgracefully owing to the orchestra's constant chattering and inattention, despite my lifted bâton. P. A. Krasnokootsky, the concert-master, was to blame more than any of them. After a bar or two had been played, we had to stop and make a fresh start. Somehow this incident remained unobserved, however, by both audience and critics; but I felt grieved and angry, of course.[8]

Leonova, who had retired from the Imperial Opera stage several years before and travelled to Japan, now lived in St. Petersburg, giving lessons in singing. She arranged these lessons in great style, establishing a sort of small music school. Leonova was a talented artist, who had once had a fine contralto voice; but in reality she had never had any training and was therefore hardly capable of teaching the technique of song. Occasionally something of the gypsy rang in her own singing. Yet in dramatic and in comic pieces she was often inimitable. And in this regard, of course, she could be of use to her pupils. For beginners, however, this was insufficient, and, accordingly, of all her many pupils, only the tenor Donskoy, subsequently an artist of the Moscow Opera, gained prominence. Thus her instruction consisted mainly in coaching in songs and excerpts

---

[8] In a letter to S. N. Krooglikov, Rimsky-Korsakov complains of the wretched financial affairs of the Free Music School. After the third concert Rimsky-Korsakov was not certain that they would manage to give a fourth one. As to his work in the school, Rimsky-Korsakov informs Krooglikov in his letter of October 2 [14], 1879: "All day long I am kept busy with the affairs of the school and the concerts and I feel a genuine hurry as if at a fire."

from operas. An accompanist and musician was needed who could supervise the correct rehearsing of the pieces, a thing that Leonova herself could not do. Moussorgsky found himself filling the post for her. At that time he had been long on the retired list, and was in need of funds. Leonova's classes furnished him some means of existence. He gave rather much of his time to instruction in these classes, teaching as he did even elementary theory and composing some trios and quartets with horrible part-writing, as exercises for Leonova's pupils.

Leonova was an artiste very fond of talking of herself, her merits and her pre-eminence. By that time her voice had grown quite worn. Still quite unaware of it, she would proudly relate how this or that artiste or famous person was constantly going into raptures over her voice, which, according to her, grew stronger and more voluminous with years. She related that a plaster cast of her throat sent to Paris had called forth universal astonishment there. According to her, the only true school of singing was to be found in her classes; she asserted that contemporary artistes did not know how to sing, that things had been better in olden days, and so on — the usual patter on the lips of aging artistes. Leonova's husband, one Gridnin, who had once written a play, managed the advertising and business end of the cantatrice's activity. Among others, concerts with Leonova's participation were arranged in the Merchants' Club; I was to conduct the orchestra. Only the first concert of the scheduled series took place. I do not remember the whole program. As I recall it, it contained *Kamarinskaya;* Laura's song (Mme Klebek); Marfa's song from *Khovanshchina* (Leonova); *Wonderful Dream* (ditto), etc. Everything ran smoothly.

Moussorgsky's association with her was an advertisement for Leonova to a certain degree. His function in her classes was, of course, unenviable; still, he was or at least tried to be unconscious of that. Work at the composition of *Khovanshchina* and *Sorochinskaya Yarmarka* flagged somewhat in those days. In order to speed the completion of *Khovanshchina* and bring some manner of satisfactory order into the ill-joined and complicated scenario, he abridged a good deal in his opera; thus, for instance, the scene in the German suburb disappeared altogether, while many details were merely basted together. In *The Fair at Sorochintsy*, too, there was something queer going on: the publisher, Bernard, undertook to issue excerpts of it for the piano, agreeing to pay Moussorgsky a small compensation for the privilege. Being in need, Moussorgsky concocted in haste for Bernard various numbers from his opera for the piano, two-hands, although he had neither a real libretto, a detailed scenario, nor rough sketches with vocal parts.[9] Moussorgsky had really finished only Khivrya's song and Parasya's song, as well as the scene of Afanasi Ivanovich and Khivrya. In those days he also wrote many songs (principally on texts by Count Golyenish-chev-Kootoozov) which remained unpublished.

I shall run somewhat ahead. Leonova undertook a concert tour to southern Russia in the summer of 1880.[10] Moussorgsky went with her in the double rôle of accompanist and participant in her concerts as pianist. Though a fine pianist in early youth, Modest Petrovich never worked on his piano technique and had no repertory whatsoever. Lately he had frequently appeared at concerts in St. Petersburg as accompanist for singers. Men and women singers were very fond of him and valued his accompaniments. He followed the voice finely, accompanying at sight, without rehearsals.

But going on tour with Leonova, he had to appear as piano soloist. This time his repertory was queer indeed; thus, at concerts in the provinces, he played the introduction to *Ruslan and Lyudmila* in an improvised arrangement, or the bell-tolling from his *Boris*.[11] With Leonova he toured many towns of southern Russia, visiting even the Crimea. Under the impression of the natural beauties of its southern coast he wrote two minor piano pieces — *Goorzoof* and *On the Southern Coast;* slightly felicitous, these pieces were published by Bernard on Moussorgsky's return. I recall, besides, that he played at our house a rather long and quite absurd fantasy that was

---

9 Cf. note 7 on p. 144.

10 Leonova's tour jointly with Moussorgsky did not take place in 1880, but in 1879. Cf. Moussorgsky's letters to V. V. Stassov and to L. I. Shestakova.

11 For Moussorgsky's repertoire during his tour with D. M. Leonova, cf. A. N. Rimsky-Korsakov's *M. P. Moussorgsky, Letters and Documents* (Moscow State Musical Publishing Bureau, 1931), pp. 389–96.

to depict a storm on the Black Sea. This fantasy, after all, remained unrecorded, and was lost forever.

In the spring of 1880 I went to Moscow for the second time, to lead the orchestra in Shostakovsky's concert. Of my compositions, I believe, I performed the *Overture on Russian Themes,* revised just then, and the Overture to *May Night.*[12] I recollect that the rehearsals were slipshod and disorderly. Towards the end of the first rehearsal I wanted to go over my Russian Overture once more, but the musicians told me very politely that it was time for them to go, that they had already sat an extra half-hour expressly for my sake and would have left much earlier had I not been I. It turned out that at Moscow rehearsals usually lasted only two hours and not three, as at St. Petersburg; yet Shostakovsky had told me that I had three hours at my disposal. All this was very little to my liking; I began to be disillusioned in Shostakovsky in general. I saw that he was not an artist, but a man striving after effect and courting self-advertisement. The date of the concert coincided with the day of Solovyov's attempt on the life of the Tsar, and I had to play *Bozhe Tsarya khrani* (*God save the Tsar*) four times in succession. Some military man demanded that the hymn be performed once more, but I did not do it. Then, with threats and demands for an explanation, he tried to get at me over the stage; to my delight, however, the theatre authorities prevented his doing so. During this trip I visited A. N. Ostrovsky in Moscow in the following connection:

In the winter I had conceived the idea of composing an opera on the subject and words of Ostrovsky's *Snyegoorochka* (*Snow-Maiden*). I had first read *Snyegoorochka* in 1874 or thereabouts, when it had just appeared in print. At that reading I had liked it but little; the kingdom of the Byeryendyeys had appeared queer to me. Why? Were the ideas of the sixties still alive in me, or did the demands, current in the seventies, that subject-matter be taken from so-called *life* hold me in their grip? Or had Moussorgsky's naturalism carried me away on its current? Probably all three together. In a word, Ostrovsky's wonderful, poetic fairy-tale had

---

[12] This concert was given April 26 [May 8], 1880, at the Grand Theatre. The above-mentioned compositions of Rimsky-Korsakov were actually performed there.

made no impression on me. During the winter of 1879–80, when I re-read *Snyegoorochka,* its wonderful, poetic beauty had become evident to me. At once I conceived a longing to write an opera on the subject; and the more I pondered my intention, the more enamoured I felt of Ostrovsky's fairy-tale.[13] My warmth towards ancient Russian custom and pagan pantheism, which had manifested itself little by little, now blazed forth in a bright flame. There was no better theme in the world for me, there were no finer poetic figures for me, than Snyegoorochka, Lyel, or Vyesna (Spring); there was no better kingdom than the kingdom of the Byeryendyeys with their wonderful ruler; there was no better view of world and religion than the worship of Yarilo-Sun. Immediately upon reading it (in February, as I recall) there began to come to my mind motives, themes, chord passages, and there began to glimmer before me, fleetingly at first, but more and more clearly later, the moods and clang tints corresponding to the various moments of the subject.[14] I got a thick book of music paper, and began to jot it all down in the form of rough notes. With these thoughts I went to Moscow to Shostakovsky and visited Ostrovsky to obtain his permission to make use of his work as a libretto, with authorization to make changes and cuts that might be necessary. A. N. Ostrovsky received me very amiably, gave me authorization to handle his drama as I saw fit, and presented me with a copy of it.[15]

---

13 On the basis of what he had heard in the mid-nineties from the mouth of Rimsky-Korsakov himself, I. F. Tyumenev (in " Fragments from Reminiscences of N. A. Rimsky-Korsakov," cf. above, note 18, p. 166) relates that many a time the theme of Rimsky-Korsakov's nightmares was the idea that the music to *Snyegoorochka* had, as it were, been composed by someone else and not by himself, and that he had let this operatic subject slip through his fingers.

14 The first sketches of *Snyegoorochka* (final chorus, Mizgir's monologue " *Natyoplom siñem morye* (On the warm blue sea, etc.) " are marked: February 27, 28, 29 [March 10, 11, 12], 1880. For the most complete dates of composing individual parts of *Snow-Maiden,* cf. V. V. Yastryebtsev's *My Reminiscences,* etc., p. 188.

15 In autumn 1880, through S. N. Krooglikov, Rimsky-Korsakov approached A. N. Ostrovsky for a second time and submitted his own libretto of the opera for an opinion. In his letter to Rimsky-Korsakov, Ostrovsky replied that " the libretto has been put together very well. I have found very few lines that require overhauling, in my opinion " (November 10 [22], 1880). Regarding these remarks of Ostrovsky, Rimsky-Korsakov wrote S. N. Krooglikov: " All corrections are so trifling that I experience great pleasure: there will be no necessity of recasting anything " (November 16 [28], 1880). On one of his subsequent trips to Moscow, Rimsky-Korsakov showed excerpts of *Snyegoorochka* to A. N. Ostrovsky. The latter's judgment of

On my return from Moscow, the whole spring was consumed in preliminary work and thinking over the opera in its individual elements; by summer I had quite a considerable number of sketches accumulated.

Among the compositions I wrote or finished during this season must be set down the chorus *Slava* (*Glory*), a Christmas carol (January), referred to earlier in my reminiscences of the past season.[16]

Of my Conservatory pupils there graduated this season E. A. Krooshevsky (subsequently active at the Imperial Russian Opera), an excellent pianist, an exceedingly capable and gifted musician as regards ear and quickness of perception, but exceedingly dry as a composer. He later wisely abandoned the field of composition in exclusive favour of the path of conducting. Disdaining neither time nor place, he sought to acquire the art of conducting, accompanied on the piano, conducted in the summer at Oranienbaum, at Dyemidov's Garden, etc. Accordingly, he developed after a time into an excellent technician, and when called to the Imperial Russian Opera, he proved at once a finished leader.

During this season Balakirev sent me several pupils in the theory of music. Usually theory proved to be only elementary theory. All these ladies and gentlemen studied scales, intervals, and so on under me at Balakirev's behest, but really took slight interest in the subject. Theory got along somehow; but in solfeggio the case was bad. My pupils belonged for the most part to the families of the Botkins and the Glazunovs. Casually Balakirev once brought me the composition of a fourteen- or fifteen-year-old high-school student, Sasha Glazunov. It was an orchestral score written in childish

---

them may be gathered from S. N. Krooglikov's letter of December 30, 1880 [January 11, 1881] to Rimsky-Korsakov: "I called on him [Ostrovsky] during the holidays, and for the entire half-hour that I stayed at his house, he talked of nothing but your opera. These are his own words: 'Korsakov's music to my *Snyegoorochka* is wonderful; I never could imagine anything more appropriate to it and so vividly expressive of all the poetry of the ancient Russian pagan cult and of this at first snow-cold, and then unrestrainably passionate heroine of the fairy-tale.'"

However, seven years previously Ostrovsky had expressed himself in similar terms concerning Tchaikovsky's music to *Snyegoorochka*: ". . . Tchaikovsky's music to *Snyegoorochka* is enchanting . . ." (Ostrovsky's letter No. CCLXI to Borodin).

[16] Cf. above, in " 1877–79."

fashion. The boy's talent was indubitably clear. Shortly afterwards (in the season of 1879–80) Balakirev introduced him, that he might take up studies under me. While giving lessons in elementary theory to his mother, Yelena Pavlovna Glazunova, I began also to teach the youthful Sasha.[17] He was a charming boy, with beautiful eyes, who played the piano very clumsily; N. N. Yelenkovsky taught him piano-playing. Elementary theory and solfeggio proved unnecessary for him, as he had a superior ear, and Yelenkovsky had covered harmony also with him to a certain extent. After a few lessons in harmony I took him directly into counterpoint, to which he applied himself zealously. Besides, he always showed me his improvisations and jotted down fragments or minor pieces. Thus work at counterpoint and composition went on simultaneously. In moments of leisure, Sasha Glazunov played a great deal and on his own initiative constantly acquainted himself with musical literature. At that time he was particularly fond of Liszt. His musical development progressed not by the day, but literally by the hour. From the very beginning of our lessons, my relations with Sasha, from mere acquaintanceship and the attitude of teacher to pupil, began to turn gradually into friendship, despite the disparity in our ages. Balakirev at that time also took considerable interest in Sasha's development, playing much to him and discussing with him, thereby doubtless attaching the responsive youth to himself. Nevertheless, a few years later their relations grew cooler, drier; frankness between them vanished, and finally a complete break came; but of this I shall speak later.

---

[17] The instruction of Glazunov commenced December 23, 1879 [January 4, 1880] and usually was given once a week on Sunday. On this point cf. V. M. Byelayev's book *Glazunov*, Vol. I (St. Petersburg, 1922), p. 30. Cf. also " Balakirev's Correspondence with Rimsky-Korsakov," Letters LXXXIII–LXXXV.

1880-81

The summer at Stelyovo. Composing Snyegoorochka. *Completion of* Skazka (*Fairy-tale*). *Analysis of* Snyegoorochka.

SPRING CAME. It was time to look for a summer home. Our nurse, Avdotya Larionovna, called our attention to the estate Stelyovo, owned by Marianov, some twenty miles beyond Looga; there she had lived before she came to care for our children. I went to look over Stelyovo. Though old, the house was comfortable; a fine, large, shady garden with fruit trees, and genuine country wilds. According to the terms of agreement, we could be complete masters of the estate during the summer. We rented the summer home and moved there on May 18 [30].

For the first time in my life I had the opportunity of spending the summer in a genuine Russian village. Here everything was to my liking, everything delighted me. A picturesque location, charming groves ("Zakaznitsa" and the Podberyezye grove), a big forest, Volchinyets, fields of rye, buckwheat, flax, and even wheat, a multitude of scattered villages, a small river, where we bathed, a large lake, Vryevo, near by, impenetrable roads, solitude, antique Russian names of villages, like Kanyezerye, Podberyezye, Kopytyets, Dremyach, Tyetyerevino, Khvoshnya, etc. — everything threw me into raptures. The excellent garden, with a multitude of cherry trees and apple trees, currants, wild and garden strawberries, gooseberries, lilacs in bloom, an infinity of field flowers and the incessant singing of birds — everything was somehow in peculiar harmony with my pantheistic frame of mind at the time and my passion for the subject of *Snyegoorochka*. A thick crooked knot or stump overgrown with moss appeared to me the wood demon or his abode; the forest Volchinyets, a forbidden forest; the bare Kopytyets hillock, Yarilo's mountain; the triple echo heard from our balcony seemed voices of wood-sprites or other supernatural beings. The summer was sultry and dense with thunder-storms. From mid-June until mid-August, thunder-storms and heat lightning occurred almost daily. On June 23 [July 5], the day of Agrafyena Koopalnitsa, lightning struck the earth near our very house, and my wife, who sat at the window, was knocked down, armchair and all, by the concussion. She was unhurt, but badly frightened, and for long afterwards under a peculiar nervous strain during thunder-storms, which she now came to dread, though formerly fond of them. She trembled and wept at the glare of the lightning and the peals of thunder. This state lasted for a month or so; only then her nerves began to calm and she again reacted to thunder-storms as before, without nervous dread. Despite this, Nadezhda Nikolayevna liked Stelyovo very much, and the children had a fine time, too. We were monarchs of all we surveyed — not a neighbour anywhere. We had at our disposal cows, horses, carriages, and the little scrawny peasant Osip with his family, who took care of the estate; all were at our service.

On the first day of settling at Stelyovo I began working on *Snyegoorochka*. I composed every day and all day; yet I managed to do much walking with my wife, helped her make preserves, gather mushrooms, and so forth. But musical thoughts and their fashioning pursued me persistently. There was a piano, old, broken, and tuned a whole tone too low. I used to call it " piano in B flat "; nevertheless I contrived to extemporize on it, and to try out what I had composed. I have said already that towards summer I had enough musical material accumulated for the opera — themes, motives, chord successions, beginnings of individual numbers; the moods and contours of separate moments of the opera were outlining themselves in my conception. All of this was partly jotted down in the thick book, partly kept in my head. I turned to the beginning of the opera and jotted it down in orchestral score approximately up to and including Vyesna's (Spring's) aria. But soon I noticed that my fancy tended to outstrip the rapidity with which I wrote the score. Moreover, from a certain insufficiency in the co-ordination of the whole, there resulted defects in the score. Accordingly I abandoned this method, formerly applied to a considerable extent in *May Night,* and began to write *Snyegoorochka* in a rough draft for voices and piano. Both composing and recording what I composed went very fast, now in the order of act and scene, and now by leaps, running ahead. Having formed the habit of superscribing the date on completing nearly each piece of the rough draft, I give them below:

June:

   1 [13]. Introduction to Prologue.
   2 [14]. Recitative and aria of Vyesna (Spring).
   3 [15]. Continuation up to the dance of the birds.
   4 [16]. Song and dance of the birds.
   17 [29]. Continuation to Snyegoorochka's aria.
   18 [30]. Snyegoorochka's aria, etc., up to Butter-week.
   20 [July 2]. Seeing out of Butter-week.
   21 [”   3]. End of Prologue.
   25 [”   7]. First song of Lyel.
   26 [”   8]. Introduction to Act I, second song of Lyel, and little chorus.
   27 [”   9]. Scene of Snyegoorochka up to Lyel's songs.
   28 [”   10]. Wedding ceremony.

July:

   2 [14]. Procession of the Tsar and hymn of the Byeryendyeys.
   3 [15]. The heralds' call.
   4 [16]. The scene of the wedding ceremony as well as the scene of the kiss from Act III.
   6 [18]. The recitative and dance of the *skomorokhs* (merry andrews).
   7 [19]. Introduction to Act III, *khorovod* and song about the beaver.

8 [20]. Continuation and the Tsar's second cavatina.[1]

9 [21]. Scene of the kiss (continuation).

10 [22]. Scene of Snyegoorochka, Koopava, and Lyel (Act III).

11 [23]. Postlude in B major and Snyegoorochka's arioso.

12 [24]. Chorus of flowers (Act IV).

13 [25]. Vyesna sinks into the lake.

15 [27]. Duet of Mizgir and Snyegoorochka (Act IV).

17 [29]. Finale of Act I.

21 [August 2]. Chorus of *gooslyars* (dulcimer-players).

22 [″ 3]. Judgment scene up to Snyegoorochka's entrance (Act II); the Tsar's first cavatina, etc., up to the final chorus.

23 [″ 4]. Snyegoorochka's entrance (Act II).

August:

2–3 [14–15]. Scene of Snyegoorochka and Mizgir.

5 [17]. Recitative in presence of the heralds (Act II).

7 [19]. Act I, after wedding ceremony to the finale.

9 [21]. Scene of Snyegoorochka and Vyesna (Act IV).

11 [23]. Chorus *Proso* (millet) and the thawing of Snyegoorochka.

12 [24]. Closing chorus.

The entire sketch of the opera was finished August 12 [24]. In the intervals where the dates are not consecutive, evidently details were thought out and the numbers missing in the above list were composed. No previous composition had ever come to me with such ease and rapidity as *Snyegoorochka.*

After completing the sketch in the latter part of August, I took up the *Skazka* (*Fairy-tale*) for orchestra, which I had begun the previous summer; I finished and instrumentated it.[2] About October 1 [13], with the entire rough draft of *Snyegoorochka* and the orchestral score of *Fairy-tale* completed, the family and I removed to St. Petersburg; after that I spent some time at Tayitsy, the summer home of Vladimir Fyodorovich Purgold. Soon, however, life at St.

---

[1] The third song of Lyel was likewise composed July 8 [20].

[2] In a letter of July 21 [August 2], 1880, to S. N. Krooglikov, Rimsky-Korsakov writes: " I have jotted down my entire *Fairy-tale* in orchestral score. There remains but to trim — that is, add here and there something in *tutti.* Have orchestrated in rough copy two movements of my Russian quartet, which I am recasting into a sinfonietta. . . ."

Petersburg began to run in its usual order — the Conservatory, Free Music School, naval bands, and all.

My principal work during the season of 1880–1 was the orchestration of *Snyegoorochka*. I began September 7 [19], and finished March 26 [April 7], 1881.³ The score contained 606 closely written pages. This time I employed an orchestra larger than the one in *May Night*. I imposed no particular limitations on myself. The four French horns were chromatic, the two trumpets likewise; a piccolo was used besides two flutes; the tuba was added to the trombones; from time to time the English horn and the bass clarinet appeared. Even here I did not dispense with the piano, as I needed an imitation of the *goosli* (dulcimer) — a method bequeathed by Glinka. My familiarity with wind instruments, acquired in the navy bands, did me good service. The *Snyegoorochka* orchestra is, as it were, the *Ruslan* orchestra perfected, in the sense of using chromatic-scale brass. I carefully strove not to drown the singers; as it turned out later, I achieved this, except in the song of Dyed Moroz (Grandfather Frost) and Mizgir's last recitative, where the orchestra had to be subdued.

In making a general review of the music of *Snyegoorochka*, I must say that in this opera I made considerable use of folk-tunes, borrowing them principally from my *Collection*. In the following moments of the opera the themes have been borrowed from folk-songs: "*Oryol voyevoda, pyerepyel podyachi* (Eagle, commander-in-chief; quail, the court clerk)," in the dance of the birds; "*Vyesel-yeñko tebya vstryechat' privyechat'* (A joy to meet thee, to greet thee)," in the seeing out of Butter-week; the initial melody (the first four bars) and the immediately following theme of the oboe in the wedding ceremony; the song "*Ay vo polye lipyeñka* (Oh, the dear little linden tree in the field)"; the theme "*Koopalsya bobyor*

---

³ From a letter to S. N. Krooglikov: "We have spent three weeks visiting with Purgold, my wife's uncle. I began to orchestrate the opera and have prepared a considerable piece each from the Prologue and Act I. Kazachevko is making the [piano] arrangement for me. The instrumentation of *Snyegoorochka* will be my exclusive occupation this coming fall; it would be fine if I succeeded in finishing everything by January" (September 23 [October 5], 1880).

(The beaver was bathing) "; and, lastly, the chorus " *Proso* (millet)." In addition to this, many minor motives or tunelets, the component parts of more or less long melodies, have undoubtedly been borrowed by me from similar little tunes in various folk-melodies that I did not introduce into the opera in their entirety. Such are certain little motives of the seeing out of Butter-week, some phrases of Bobyl and Bobylikha; Mizgir's phrase: " *Da, chto ya strashen, to pravdu ty skazala* (That I am dreadful, indeed you've told the truth)," etc. The motives of a pastoral character:

are also of folk-origin. The second motive A. K. Lyadov had communicated to me; the first I remembered from my own childhood.

The motive " *Maslyenitsa mokrokhvostka, poyezzhay doloy so dvora* (Wet-tailed Butter-week, be off the courtyard) " is a scoffingly sacrilegious reminder of the Orthodox Mass for the dead. But are not the melodies of ancient Orthodox canticles of ancient pagan origin? Are not many rites and dogmas of like origin? The holidays of Easter, Trinity Sunday, etc., are they not adaptations of Christianity from the pagan sun-cult? And the doctrine of the Trinity? For all this, cf. Afanasyev.[4]

The tune of the heralds' call I remembered from my childhood: a horseman, equipped by the monastery, would ride through the streets of Tikhvin and call in a stentorian voice: " Aunties, mothers, fair maidens, please come to rake hay for the Mother of God! " (The wonder-working icon of our Lady of Tikhvin was in the Church of the Great Friary, which owned hay meadows on the bank of the Tikhvinka River.) Some songlets of birds (cuckoo, the cry of the young merlin, etc.) were borrowed for the dance of the

---

[4] Aleksandr Nikolayevich Afanasyev (1826–71) was the first scientific collector and editor of Russian fairy-tales. His essays on the mythology of the Slavs (especially his *The Slavs' Poetic Views of Nature*) are probably what R.-K. refers to. J. A. J.

birds. In the Introduction, the cock-crow is also genuine and was given me by my wife:

One of the motives of Spring (in the Prologue and Act IV):

is the altogether accurately reproduced song of a bullfinch which had lived rather long in our cage; only that our dear little bullfinch sang it in F-sharp major, while I took it a tone lower for the convenience of the violin harmonics. Thus, in obedience to my pantheistic frame of mind, I had hearkened to the voices of folk-creation and of nature, and what they had sung and suggested I made the basis of my creative art — and for so doing I subsequently incurred not a few reproaches. The music-critics, having noticed both in *Snyegoorochka* and *May Night* two or three melodies borrowed from collections of folksongs (to notice many they were powerless, as they were ill acquainted with folk-creation), proclaimed me incapable of creating my own melodies; at every opportunity they kept stubbornly repeating this opinion of theirs, despite the fact that my operas contain far more melodies that belong to me and have never been drawn from song collections. Many melodies that I had successfully composed in folk-spirit, like all three songs of Lyel, they considered borrowed, and they used them as material evidence of my reprehensible conduct as a composer. Once I even lost my temper over a sally of this sort. Soon after the production of *Snyegoorochka* on the occasion of somebody's singing the third song of Lyel, M. M. Ivanov [5] made the remark in print, as if casually, that this piece had been written on a folk-theme. I countered with a letter to the editor requesting him to point out the folk-theme

---

[5] Music-critic (of *Novoye Vremya*), author of *A History of Russian Music* (in two volumes, 1910–12, St. Petersburg; biased), and composer (operas, symphonic works, etc.). J. A. J.

from which the melody of Lyel's third song had been borrowed. Of course no such statement was forthcoming. As for creating melodies in the folk-spirit, mine must beyond a doubt contain snatches and turns which are contained and scattered in various genuine folk-melodies. Can two things resemble each other as a whole if no component part of the one resembles any component part of the other? The question there is: if no single particle of a created melody resembles any single particle of a genuine folksong, can the whole created melody recall folk-creation?

As for making use of brief motives such as the shepherds' tunes given above, the songs of birds, and the like, does that stamp a composer as only of scanty imagination? Surely the value of the cuckoo's cry or of the three notes played by the shepherd is not the same as the value of the song and dance of the birds, of the Introduction to Act I, of the Procession of the Byeryendyeys in Act IV, is it? In the pieces mentioned, had not enough sweep and activity been left to the composer's fancy? The working up of folk-themes and motives had been bequeathed to posterity by Glinka in his *Ruslan, Kamarinskaya,* the Spanish overtures, and partly in *A Life for the Tsar* (the song of the Looga driver, the figuration accompaniment to the melody: " *Tooda zavyol ya vas* — Thither I've led you "). Or shall we accuse Glinka, too, of poverty of melodic inventiveness?

Of my former sketches for Gedeonov's *Mlada,* only two elements were taken into *Snyegoorochka:* Mizgir's soaring motive " *O, skazhi, skazhi mnye, molvi odno slovo* (Oh, tell me, tell me, say but one word) " and the harmonic base of the motive of the glow-worm. All other musical material sprang up entirely in the course of composing *Snyegoorochka.*

As in the course of composing *May Night* [the first *khorovod* " *Proso* (millet)," the songs of the approaching chorus in Act III], the ancient modes continued to interest me in *Snyegoorochka.* Lyel's first song, some parts of the seeing out of Butter-week, the call of the heralds, the hymn of the Byeryendyeys, the *khorovod* " *Ay vo polye lipyeñka* (Oh, the dear little linden tree in the field) " are written in the ancient modes or with ancient cadences, principally the degrees II, III, and V (the so-called Dorian, Phrygian, and Mixolydian modes). Certain sections, such as the song about the beaver, with Bobyl's dance, are written with transition into different keys and different modes. The striving for modes pursued me subsequently throughout my whole activity as composer, and I do not doubt that, like the other composers of the Russian school, I have achieved something new in this field; while the most recent working up of ancient modes in west-European music flashes only in individual and rare cases: Liszt's *Todtentanz* variations, Berlioz's *Nubian Dance*, etc.[6]

In comparison with *May Night* I wooed counterpoint much less in *Snyegoorochka;* yet, on the other hand, in the latter opera I felt still greater freedom than in the former, in the field of both counterpoint and figuration. I believe that the fugato of the growing forest (in Act III) with the ever varying theme:

and also the four-part fugato of the chorus " *Nye byl ni razoo porugan izmyenoyu* (Never once been defamed with betrayal)," together with Koopava's lament, furnish good examples of this.

In respect to harmony, I succeeded in inventing some new things, like the chord of six whole-tone notes of the scale, or of two augmented triads, when the wood-sprite embraces Mizgir (in theory it is hard to find a name for it) — incidentally, sufficiently expressive of the given moment — or the use of the exclusively major triads and the dominant chord of the second (also with a major triad above) almost through the whole length of the final hymn to Yarilo-Sun in $11/4$, and this lends the chorus an especially bright, sunny colouring.

I have made wide use of leading motives (*Leitmotive*) in *Snyegoorochka*. At the time I knew little of Wagner, and whatever I did know, I knew superficially. Nevertheless the employment of *Leitmotive* is present in *Pskovityanka, May Night,* and particularly

---

[6] The Russians opened this field to Debussy and the other modern Frenchmen. C. V. V.

in *Snyegoorochka*. No doubt my use of leading motives is different from Wagner's. With him they serve as the material from which the orchestral fabric is woven. In addition to this, with me the *Leitmotive* appear also in the singing voices, and often they are component parts of a more or less lengthy theme, as for example in the principal melody of Snyegoorochka herself, and likewise the theme of Tsar Byeryendyey. Sometimes the leading motives are truly rhythmic-melodic motives, but occasionally they are mere harmonic successions; in such cases they might rather be called *Leit-harmonien*. Such leading harmonies are not as easily perceptible to audiences as the Wagnerian leading motives, which recall rough military signals. And the ability to grasp harmonic successions is given only to a fine and trained musical ear — that is, a more subtle understanding. Among the leading harmonies most perceptible from the first must be numbered the characteristic augmented-fourth G-C sharp in stopped French horns *ff*, which reappears with each new miraculous apparition in the fantastic scene of Mizgir's roamings in the forbidden forest.

In *Snyegoorochka* I succeeded in giving full freedom to an easy-flowing recitative, and that, too, so accompanied that in the majority of cases the delivery of the recitative is possible *a piacere*. I remember how happy I was when I succeeded in writing the first real recitative in my life — Vyesna's (Spring's) address to the birds, before the dance. In the vocal field, too, *Snyegoorochka* represented a considerable stride forward on my part. All vocal parts proved to have been written conveniently and within the natural range of voices; some moments of the opera are even grateful and effective for performance, like the songs of Lyel and the Tsar's cavatina. Characterization of the dramatis personæ was in evidence, too; in this respect one cannot help mentioning the duet of Koopava and Tsar Byeryendyey.

In the orchestration I never manifested any tendency towards freakish effects that the musical foundation of the composition itself did not call for; I always have preferred simple means. Undoubtedly the orchestration of *Snyegoorochka* meant with me a step forward in many respects — force of sonority, for example. Until then I had

241

nowhere succeeded in reaching such tonal power and splendour as in the final chorus, or such succulence, velvetiness, and fullness as in the D-flat major melody of the scene of the kiss. I was successful in some new effects like the tremolo of three flutes in chords on the Tsar's words " *Na rozovoy zarye, v vyenkye zelyonom* (At roseate dawn, in a green wreath)." In general, I had always been inclined to more or less individualization of separate instruments. In this sense, *Snyegoorochka* abounds in all manner of instrumental solos, for both wind and string instruments, in purely orchestral moments and in accompaniment to the singing. Solos for violin, cello, flute, oboe, and clarinet occur very frequently in it, especially solos for the clarinet (then my favourite instrument in the wind group), and this gives the clarinet a very responsible part in this opera. In Act IV of the opera, in the Procession of the Byeryendyeys on the stage, I made use of a separate small orchestra of wood-winds, to represent, as it were, the shepherds' horns and reed pipes. Subsequently, however, in the new edition of the score, I did away with it, owing to the impracticability of this device.

The forms of *Snyegoorochka* partly follow the Glinka traditions — that is, they represent separate finished numbers (mainly in songs) — partly they are passagelike, fused as in Wagner (mainly in the Prologue and Act IV), but maintaining a certain architectonic plan which is manifested in consequent repetitions of certain portions and in modulatory devices.

When completing *Snyegoorochka* I felt a fully matured musician and operatic composer who had finally come to stand on his own feet.[7] Nobody knew anything of my composing *Snyegoorochka*, as

---

[7] Apace with his own maturing, which manifested itself in a particularly clear-cut manner in the course of composing *Snyegoorochka*, Rimsky-Korsakov simultaneously discerned more and more clearly the weak points of his closest musical friends' personalities *as composers*. In a letter to S. N. Krooglikov of November 9 [21], 1880, about his musical labours, he expresses, in passing, the following ideas: " Owing to inadequate technique, Balakirev writes . . . little, Borodin with difficulty, Cui in a slipshod way, Moussorgsky sloppily and often absurdly. . . . Don't imagine that my attitude towards their compositions has changed even a whit. If these people possessed a good and correct technique, what that would mean! Believe me, although, speaking perfectly frankly, I consider that they possess far more talent than I have, yet I don't envy them a penny's worth. . . . I know what Blaramberg understands by the term 'learning by oneself': it means to write and write symphonies, operas, etc., and learn by working on them; and all of it will be hazy, sloppy, impracticable

I had kept the matter a secret; when, on my arrival in St. Petersburg, I announced to my close friends that the sketch had been completed, I greatly astonished them. As far as I recall, early in the autumn I showed my opera to Balakirev, Borodin, and Stassov, playing and singing the entire *Snyegoorochka* for them, from cover to cover. All three were pleased, but each in his own way. Stassov and Balakirev were gratified chiefly with the folk-life and fantastic portions of the opera; neither of the two, however, understood the hymn to Yarilo. Borodin, on the other hand, seemed to appreciate *Snyegoorochka* in its entirety.[8] Curious that even in this case Balakirev could not curb his passion for meddling, demanding that I transpose the initial Introduction into the key of B minor, but this I refused to do. By transposing in this manner I should have deprived myself of the natural harmonics and open strings of the violins; besides, the themes of descending Spring, in that case, would be in B major (cellos and French horns) and not in A major, with which Spring was indissolubly linked in my imagination. After a

---

for performance, and bright ideas will be lost under various excrescences that will sneak in everywhere, into every line of the score. Here, what shocking things I have told you! "

[8] The opinion of Borodin and his wife was expressed in a letter of April 16 [28], 1882, to Rimsky-Korsakov (cf. Letter LXVI, p. 208); M. A. Balakirev's opinion in a letter of December 8 [20], 1880, to Rimsky-Korsakov (Letter CXVIII). In his letter of December 20, 1880 [January 11, 1881] to Rimsky-Korsakov, S. N. Krooglikov informs him: " Borodin was telling me about *Snyegoorochka*. He is greatly pleased with it and ranks it far above *May Night,* and that tells the whole story."

Here Rimsky-Korsakov confines himself to remarking on the attitute towards *Snyegoorochka* in the circle of musicians closest to himself. These data may be supplemented by a reference to Tchaikovsky's attitude towards the *Snow-Maiden.* Tchaikovsky, as is well known, was also strongly captivated by this work of Ostrovsky's as a subject for opera and had already in 1873 composed incidental music to this " spring fairy-tale " for its production on the stage of the Grand Theatre in Moscow. He felt deeply grieved by the appearance of Rimsky-Korsakov's opera. " It is disagreeable," he write to Jurgenson, " that our subject has been taken away from us, that Lyel will sing other music set to the same words, that I have been deprived, as if by force, of something mine, intimate and kindred to me, which is now being proffered to the public in a new embellished and resplendent garb. I feel offended to the point of tears."

According to Modest Tchaikovsky, Pyotr Ilich " pouted at this work [of Rimsky-Korsakov] and for a long time did not want to acquaint himself with it. Only at a much later date, in the closing eighties, he came to know the orchestral score of the opera and right there and then discerned its many beauties, reconciled himself to the accomplished fact and grew extremely fond of it." In Tchaikovsky's diary for the year 1887 there is a notation: ". . . While reading Korsakov's *Snyegoorochka* I marvelled at his masterly skill and even (shameful to say) envied him " (cf. M. I. Tchaikovsky's *Life of P. I. Tchaikovsky,* Vol. I, p. 407, and Vol. II, p. 164).

little scolding, Balakirev this time forgave me and kept praising *Snyegoorochka*, assuring me that once when he had played at home the seeing out of Butter-week, his elderly servant Marya could not resist and began to dance to it. However, this was slight consolation to me, and I should have preferred Balakirev to appreciate the poetical nature of the girl Snyegoorochka, the comic and good-natured fineness of Tsar Byeryendyey, and the rest. Anatoli was en-raptured by my opera; as for Moussorgsky, who became acquainted with excerpts of it and somehow displayed no interest in the whole, he lightly praised a few things and then remained totally indifferent to the composition as a whole. And it could not have been otherwise. On the one hand, his fatuous self-conceit and conviction that the path he had chosen in art was the only true path; on the other hand, complete decline, alcoholism, and, as a result, an ever be-fogged mind.

Skazka (Fairy-tale). *Concert of the Free Music School. Death of Moussorgsky. Resignation from directorship of the Free Music School. Trip to the south. Concerts of the Russian Musical Society. Production of* Snyegoorochka. *The critics. Balakirev's return to the Free Music School. Glazunov's First Symphony. Our circle. Work on* Khovanshchina. *Visit to Moscow. Acquaintanceship with M. P. Byelayev.* Noch' na Lysoy Gorye (A Night on Bald Mountain). *Concerto for the piano.* Tamara.

WHILE MAKING up the programs of the Russian Musical Society, Napravnik addressed an inquiry to me, as to which of my compositions I should like to hear performed at these concerts. I indicated the recently written *Skazka (Fairy-tale)* and gave the score to Napravnik. Shortly afterwards the latter proposed that I conduct the piece myself. I consented. At one of the earlier concerts of that season the *Fairy-tale* was placed on the program. I conducted.[1] The performance would have been quite successful if the concert-master, Pikkel (then growing morbidly nervous), had not jumped out, without any reason, at the entrance of the violins *divisi* towards the end of the piece and by so doing confused the other violinists. However, the violins speedily recovered, and the mistake had hardly

---

[1] In the season 1880–1, eighth concert, January 10 [22], 1881.

been noticed by the audience. Save for this episode, I was pleased
with the performance as well as with the piece itself, which sounded
colourful and brilliant. In general *Skazka* undoubtedly recalls in
style *Snyegoorochka,* as having been composed simultaneously with
it. Strange that to this day hearers grasp with difficulty the true
meaning of the *Fairy-tale's* program: they seek in it a chained-up
tom-cat walking around an oak tree, and all the fairy-tale episodes
which were jotted down by Pushkin in the prologue to his *Ruslan
and Lyudmila* and which served as the starting-point for my *Fairy-
tale.* In his brief enumeration of the elements of the Russian fairy-
tale epos that made up the stories of the miraculous tom-cat, Pushkin says:

> One fairy-tale I do recall,
> I'll tell it now to one and all,

and then narrates the fairy-tale of *Ruslan and Lyudmila.* But I
narrate my own musical fairy-tale. By my very narrating the musical
fairy-tale and quoting Pushkin's prologue I show that my fairy-tale
is, in the first place, Russian, and, secondly, magical, as if it were
one of the miraculous tom-cat's fairy-tales that I had overheard and
retained in my memory. Yet I had not at all set out to depict in it
all that Pushkin had jotted down in the prologue, any more than he
puts all of it into his fairy-tale of *Ruslan.* Let everyone seek in my
fairy-tale only the episodes that may appear before his imagination,
but let him not insist that I include everything enumerated in Pushkin's prologue. The endeavour to discern in my fairy-tale the tom-
cat that had related this same fairy-tale is groundless, to say the
least. The two above-quoted lines of Pushkin are printed in italics
in the program of my *Fairy-tale,* to distinguish them from the other
verses and direct thereby the auditor's attention to them. But this
has been understood neither by the audiences nor by critics, who
have interpreted my *Skazka* in all ways crooked and awry and who,
in my time, as usual, of course, did not approve of it. On the whole,
however, the *Fairy-tale* won sufficient success with the public.

During the season of 1880–1 I visited Moscow for the third time
for Shostakovsky, at whose concert I conducted. Four concerts of
the Free Music School were announced for that season at the Hall

of the Municipal Credit Society.² The proposed programs of these four concerts I do not recall now; of these only the first concert, of February 3 [15], 1881, took place, the assisting artists being Cross and Stravinsky. The latter sang Schumann's *Der Schlafende Ritter*, orchestrated by A. R. Bernhard (though his orchestration was considerably rewritten by me),³ and Dargomyzhsky's *Paladin* with A. K. Lyadov's instrumentation. Of orchestral pieces I gave *Antar* and Berlioz's *Carnaval Romain* — both successfully. Of choral pieces Moussorgsky's *Rout of Sennacherib* was performed. The composer was present at the concert and came out in response to calls from the audience.

This concert was the last at which a composition of Moussorgsky's was performed within his lifetime. A month or so later he was taken to the Land Hospital owing to a fit of delirium tremens. Dr. L. B. Bertenson placed him there and was attending him. On learning of the misfortune that had befallen Moussorgsky, we — Borodin, Stassov, myself, and many others — began to visit the patient. He was visited also by my wife and her sister, Mme A. N. Molas. He was frightfully feeble, had greatly changed, and had turned grey. Rejoicing at our visits, he occasionally talked with us altogether normally; yet suddenly he would pass into a mad delirium. Thus things went for some time; at last, at night, March 16 [28], he died,

---

² From Rimsky-Korsakov's letter to S. N. Krooglikov (October 9 [21], 1880): " About the Free School I don't know what to do — with not a kopeck of money, to risk giving several concerts is unthinkable, to give a single concert is not worth while; and really, for the sake of one concert, to hold rehearsals, to drill the chorus a whole year — I have not even any desire for that. In the quality of the voices the choir is poor; the ladies have all grown old, of the men there are few who are good, the tenors are hoarse, the male choir drowns out the female, the society has been taking on more and more the character of *mauvais ton*. . . . My most roseate dream is to pass the directorship on to someone; but to whom? Outside of Lyadov, I can't think of anyone. Of course all sorts of Zikkes, Solovyovs, etc., might be found, but that's taboo — well understood. A. Lyadov is somewhat unreliable, is not energetic, and is insufficiently well known as yet. But I have positively no more desire to bother. And those whose works it would give pleasure to perform — Borodin, Moussorgsky, Balakirev, for instance — write very little, and if they do, they don't orchestrate — one has to take care of them as a nurse cares for a baby, even copy their piano scores — the Lord help them! And as a conductor I do not consider myself a specialist in this line and don't see any genuine capacity for it in myself, just so so; as a person not altogether stupid and one who has seen a thing or two, I can conduct a piece; so that quitting this occupation will not sadden me. . . .”

³ Among Rimsky-Korsakov's papers has been preserved his autograph manuscript of this composition.

apparently from paralysis of the heart. His powerful organism proved to have been completely undermined by alcohol. On the day before his death we, all his closest friends, sat long at his bedside talking with him. As is well known, he was buried at the Aleksandr Nevsky Monastery.[4] V. V. Stassov and I attended to much of the dreary business in connection with his funeral.

On Moussorgsky's death all his manuscripts and sketches were brought in a mass to me that I might set them in order, complete and prepare them for publication. During Moussorgsky's last illness, at V. V. Stassov's insistence and with the composer's consent, T. I. Filippov was chosen and confirmed as his executor with the purpose that, in the event of his death, there might be no delay nor hindrance in the publishing of his works, on the part of relatives of the deceased. Moussorgsky's brother Filaret Petrovich was still living; there was sparse information about him; his attitude towards the fate of Modest Petrovich's compositions could not be known. Accordingly, the best thing to do was to choose an executor from among the disinterested admirers of the composer. T. I. Filippov was the very man. He made an agreement with Bessel's firm, to which he handed over Moussorgsky's work for publication, the firm in its turn binding itself to do it in full within the shortest time possible. The publishing house paid nothing in return.[5] For my part, I undertook to set in order and complete all of Moussorgsky's works and turn over gratis to the Bessel firm those that I should find suitable for the purpose. For the next year and a half or two years my work on my dead friend's compositions went on. The following compositions were among his remains: *Khovanshchina,* still incomplete and unorchestrated (with slight exceptions); sketches of certain parts of *Sorochinskaya Yarmarka* (*The Fair at Sorochintsy*) — the songs of Khivrya and Parasya had been published separately — a good many songs, the most recent and some of the old ones, all

---

[4] Dostoevsky, Tchaikovsky, and Rubinstein are also buried here. C. V. V.

[5] A copy of T. I. Filippov's agreement with the Bessel firm exists in V. Stassov's Archives (Pushkin House). In this agreement there is entered a manifestly fictitious figure of remuneration in the amount of six hundred rubles. The title-deed of gift from M. P. Moussorgsky assigning it to T. I. Filippov, and T. I. Filippov's covenant with V. V. Bessel, were published in full in A. N. Rimsky-Korsakov's *M. P. Moussorgsky, Letters and Documents,* pp. 525 ff.

finished; the choruses *The Rout of Sennacherib, Joshua,* the chorus from *Œdipus,* the maidens' chorus from *Salammbô; A Night on Bald Mountain* in several versions; for orchestra, Scherzo in B-flat major, Intermezzo in B minor, and the March (trio alla turca) in A-sharp major, various records of songs; juvenile sketches and the Sonata Allegro in C major of ancient days. All these were in exceedingly imperfect order; there occurred absurd, incoherent harmonies, ugly part-writing, now strikingly illogical modulation, now depressing absence of any at all, ill-chosen instrumentation of orchestrated pieces, in general a certain audacious self-conceited dilettantism, at times moments of technical dexterity and skill but more often of utter technical impotence. Withal, in the majority of cases, these compositions showed so much talent, so much originality, offered so much that was new and alive, that their publication was a positive obligation. But publication without a skilful hand to put them in order would have had no sense save a biographico-historical one. If Moussorgsky's compositions are destined to live unfaded for fifty years after their author's death (when all his works will become the property of any and every publisher), such an archæologically accurate edition will always be possible, as the manuscripts went to the Public Library on leaving me. For the present, though, there was need of an edition for performances, for practical artistic purposes, for making his colossal talent known, and not for the mere studying of his personality and artistic sins. Of my work on *Khovanshchina* and *A Night on Bald Mountain* I shall speak later, in due course; concerning the rest I consider sufficient what I have just said. I shall add only that, with the exception of sketches that proved utterly useless, all these works have been looked over, reorchestrated, arranged for the piano by me and copied in my own hand, and handed over, as soon as ready, to Bessel's, where they were printed under my editorship and with my proof-reading.

Of the Free Music School concerts, only the first, as I have said, took place; the other three had to be cancelled owing to the assassination of Tsar Aleksandr Nikolayevich (Alexander II).[6] On Tsar

---

[6] March 1 [13], 1881. J. A. J.

Alexander III's mounting the throne, new appointments came in
the administrative world. I. A. Vsyevolozhsky was appointed Director of Theatres.[7] I made it known to the Directorate that I had *Snyegoorochka* ready in my possession.[8] I made Napravnik and the
artists acquainted with my opera by playing it through for them in
the foyer of the Mariinsky Theatre.[9] All of them, in general, timidly
approved the opera. Napravnik hemmed and hawed for a long time,
but said in the end that, owing to the absence of dramatic action,
this was a " dead " opera and could not be successful; however,
he had nothing against its being produced. The opera was accepted,
for production the following season, by the Director, who manifestly aimed to make a showing with a fine production early in
his management. The publishing rights were sold to Bessel; the
piano scores were being engraved; the orchestral score was printed
lithographically, the parts were copied by the Directorate. In the
spring the chorus rehearsals began.

Balakirev's constant meddling and pressure in the affairs of the
Free Music School had become intolerable to me by that time.[10] It

---

[7] The Management of the Mariinsky Theatre was connected with that of five
other theatres: the Alexander Theatre, where Russian dramas and comedies were
given; the Mikhaylovsky Theatre, reserved for French plays; the Grand Opera House;
and two theatres in Moscow. C. V. V.

[8] I. F. Tyumenev (" Fragments from Reminiscences of N. A. Rimsky-Korsakov "; see note 18 on p. 166 of this book) relates, by quoting Rimsky-Korsakov, the
story that Vsyevolozhsky's predecessor, Baron Kister, had already asked him (R. K.)
in the spring of 1881 to come to see him, and that Rimsky-Korsakov had played
through excerpts of his opera for him, in Napravnik's presence, and that the Director
and the conductor forthwith began to discuss between them the details of the production — who was to be assigned this or that rôle, and so on. " I intend to squeeze
them a bit," said Rimsky-Korsakov; " let them first revive my *Pskovityanka*, all the
more since it has been both remade afresh and added to." The events of March 1 [13]
and the appointment of a new Director coming upon its heels put an end to these
original negotiations.

[9] K. Y. Davydov's report, incontestably favourable in tenor, was quoted (in excerpts) in S. Ginzberg's article mentioned earlier; see above, p. 209. In his letter of
January 7 [19], 1881 to S. N. Krooglikov, Rimsky-Korsakov communicates: " On Sunday (January 2 [14], 1881) I played *Snyegoorochka* at the Mariinsky Theatre before
Napravnik and Kondratyev (the opera authorities). Napravnik conducted himself
well; i.e., he treated the thing as though it had already been settled to produce the
opera."

[10] From a letter of September 17 [29], 1881 to S. N. Krooglikov: " Oh, how fed
up I feel with the Free School, simply up to here (I am pointing with my hand above
the throat)! On Monday we must begin. I think that this time I shall drop this school,
for I feel that I am ceasing to be a conscientious Director and secretly wish it all

seemed to me, and true it was, that he was eager to become its head himself. In addition to everything else, I was extremely busy with Moussorgsky's compositions, work in connection with the production of *Snyegoorochka* was looming, and I therefore decided to resign the Directorship of the Free School, of course giving lack of time as the only reason for my resignation. At first Balakirev slightly bristled up at me, saying that my action was forcing him, so to speak, to take hold of the school. I expressed the opinion that that would be a very desirable result. Immediately the Free Music School voted me an address of thanks and turned to Balakirev. He consented and thenceforth returned to the ranks of the active musical army, for some years to come.

The following summer my family went to a villa at Tayitsy, where they lived with V. F. Purgold, the Akhsharumovs, and the Molas family; while I went to Nikolaev under orders from the Navy Department.[11]

The object of my trip, according to the request of the Nikolaev port authorities, was to review the Black Sea port naval band, which I had transformed from brass into a mixed band seven years earlier. This band I found in satisfactory order; its playing was correct. At Nikolaev I met with a cordial reception on the part of the Nyebolsin family. As on the first occasion, I was again given quarters at the so-called palace on the bank of the Ingul. A concert was scheduled to be given under my direction in one of the city parks. Among other pieces, I arranged this time (for a wind band) the entire conspiracy scene from *Les Huguenots*. I also placed on the program several pieces from the repertory of my Kronstadt concerts. Zealous rehearsals began, two a day. Choristers, too, participated in the con-

---

sorts of evil as long as it is in my hands. . . ." From a letter of September 27 [October 9], 1881 to S. N. Krooglikov: "I have resigned from the Directorship and have steered the Board towards Balakirev. . . ." In a letter of October 12 [24] of the same year Rimsky-Korsakov explains in detail the motives of his resignation. He says, among other things: "Instead of this enormous talent [Balakirev], who is a thousand times more suited than I for this rôle — secretly pulling wires for the school's benefit — it is far more rational that he should become the head of the institution himself. . . ."

[11] Rimsky-Korsakov left St. Petersburg on June 1 [13] and spent almost a day and a night in Moscow with P. I. Blaramberg. He showed *Snyegoorochka* to the latter in the presence of S. N. Krooglikov. Rimsky-Korsakov arrived in Nikolaev June 5 [17].

certs, though they were not numerous enough to vie with the wind band. Finally the concert took place successfully, and then its repetition.[12] By this time Nadezhda Nikolayevna had arrived; and having finished my business with the music of the Navy Department, I left with her for Crimea via Odessa.

We put up at the Hotel Russia in Yalta,[13] and made all sorts of excursions and trips along the southern coast. Numerous acquaintances turned up at Yalta: Sofiya Vladimirovna Fortunato (V. V. Stassov's daughter) and family — she managed the Hotel Russia; P. A. Blaramberg and wife; Mme Serova, and (unexpected meeting!) P. A. Zelyony (the quondam commander of the clipper *Almaz*) and wife. Once the whole company went on a picnic to Yayla, we also being of the party. At the Fortunato house we formed an acquaintance with the family of Anastasyevs, proprietors of a small estate at Magarach; we also made them a visit and with them went to see the Nikitsky Garden. That day is memorable to me because in the evening, on our return trip from Anastasyev's, the oldest Fortunato boy entered our carriage, near Ay-Danil, with his chum, Fyeliks Mikhaylovich Blumenfeld, a youth of eighteen or so, whom he there introduced to us. Our charming new acquaintance proved to be a lively pianist of promise, a bountifully endowed musical temperament. For several days we kept meeting him constantly at the Fortunatos', in the Hotel Russia. There was a fine grand piano in the hotel drawing-room, and more than once, for my Yalta friends, I had to play excerpts from *Snyegoorochka,* which interested everybody at the time. Fyeliks seemed to listen with delight.

From Yalta we went by carriage to Simfyeropol and Sevastopol, via Alooshta and Chatyrdag. We boarded a steamer at Sevastopol and sailed to Constantinople, where we stayed three days. Our re-

---

[12] The concert was given on June 19 [July 1]; it was repeated on June 20 [July 2]. Rimsky-Korsakov wrote his wife detailed news of his stay at Nikolaev. In one of his letters he referred to his official duty as Inspector in this way: " I have just returned from the 1st and 2nd crew, where I carried out a superior authority's review of the musicians. I greeted, thanked, rewarded, in general acted like Khlyestakov in the Inspector General's rank — a rôle stupid and entirely unbecoming to me, and indeed I am incapable of filling it with befitting solemnity and gravity. . . ."

[13] The most fashionable of the Crimean bathing-resorts. C. V. V.

turn trip lay through Odessa. In crossing the Black Sea we passed
through a great storm. For old times' sake, I was not seasick at all.
On the way north we visited Kiev, and, returning to St. Petersburg,
spent the remainder of the summer at Tayitsy.

During the summer of 1881 I composed nothing. My work consisted only of some arrangements for brass bands (those I had made
at Nikolaev for the concert) and in reading proof of the orchestral
score of *Snyegoorochka,* then being lithographed. After moving to
St. Petersburg, my principal occupation during the season of 1881–2
was with Moussorgsky's compositions, on which there was work
enough.

The Free Music School was now under Balakirev's direction. At
the Russian Musical Society the following episode occurred: In one
of the newspapers (the *St. Petersburg Gazette,* I believe) there appeared an article by N. F. Solovyov (already a professor at the Conservatory) attacking the activity of Napravnik as conductor of the
symphony concerts of the Russian Musical Society. Having read
through this article, E. F. Napravnik considered it necessary flatly
to resign his conductorship of the Russian Musical Society concerts. The concerts were left conductorless. The Directors proposed
to K. Y. Davydov that he assume the vacant office. As if yielding to
entreaties, Davydov consented; as a matter of fact, of course, he
was overjoyed. Since (judging by gossip) intrigue was supposed to
have played a considerable part in the whole episode, and since the
orchestra itself apparently felt hostile, owing to the removal of the
former leader, K. Y. felt very timid about his first appearance, fearing some demonstration of protest. He therefore thought it expedient to turn to me as an outsider to the suspected intrigue; he requested me to open the concert with my *Overture on Russian
Themes;* after that, the audience, having grown a bit accustomed to
the fact that a new person had supplanted Napravnik, might be
expected to treat as calmly the appearance of Davydov himself at
the conductor's desk. This reasoning was correct; either that or else
all those " suppositions " had been figments of Davydov's imagination alone. I conducted my overture safely, and presently the entire

concert, too, went off safely.[14] K. Y. led the concerts till the end of the season.

In December, orchestral rehearsals of *Snyegoorochka* began. By then Napravnik had successfully insisted on many cuts in the opera. With difficulty I managed to maintain Butter-week and the Chorus of Flowers intact. Snyegoorochka's arietta (G minor) in Act I, Koopava's arietta, the Tsar's second cavatina "*Ookhodit dyeñ vesyoly* (The merry day is waning)," and many other bits, a bit here, a bit there, throughout the opera were remorselessly cut. The finale of Act I was also disfigured. What was to be done? One had to grin and bear it. For there was no written agreement wherein the management had pledged itself to make no cuts. The scenery was ready, the music had been copied at the management's expense; and, lastly, where else could the opera be given if not at the Imperial Theatre? For the first time in my life I had to face the question of cuts. *The Maid of Pskov* and *May Night* are short operas; there had been no talk of cuts at their production. The cuts in *May Night* were made after the first performance. *Snyegoorochka* is a long opera indeed, and intermissions, too, are long, according to the traditions of the Imperial Theatres. It was said that the profits of the refreshment-room had something to do with the length of the intermissions; on the other hand, to carry the performance beyond midnight is against custom. So it was a case of butting a stone wall! [15]

The parts in my opera were distributed as follows: Snyegoorochka, Vyelinskaya; Spring, Kamyenskaya; Koopava, Makarova; Lyel, the talented Bichoorina; Byeryendyey, Vasilyev III; Mizgir, Pryanishnikov; Moroz (Frost), Stravinsky; Bermyata, Koryakin; etc. Everybody sang with a will. Myelnikov, who also had the part of Mizgir assigned to him, declined it for some reason. At vocal rehearsals I accompanied personally; one of the rehearsals I even carried through independently, without Napravnik. The latter, as

[14] This concert of the Russian Musical Society was given on December 5 [17], 1881.

[15] Still more cuts were made in this score at the performance at the Metropolitan Opera House in New York, in 1922, under the direction of Artur Bodanzky. C. V. V.

usual, was magnificent at orchestral rehearsals in the weeding out of errors, but exacting and cold at the general rehearsals.

Nadezhda Nikolayevna was with me at rehearsals rather frequently; she was in prime health, although in the last days of pregnancy. On the night of January 13 [25], after she had attended one of the final rehearsals, our son Volodya was born.

Snyegoorochka had its première January 29 [February 10].[16] Nadezhda Nikolayevna, who had not left her bed, was in despair that she was destined not to witness the first performance of my opera. I, too, felt out of sorts over the matter; I even took too much wine at dinner, and came to the première gloomy and indifferent to all that was going on. I stayed persistently behind the scenes, trudging only, from time to time, to the stage-manager's room; I never heard my opera at all. Nor did I come out in response to calls for me. The opera was a success. I was presented with a wreath.

By the second performance, Nadezhda Nikolayevna had recovered and had left her bed. Taking all possible precautions, she came to the opera house. My spirits leaped. The opera continued to please; but still another cut was made; at the instance of Pryanishnikov, who was eager to close Act III with the scene of Mizgir, in order to make a bid for applause, the closing trio (Koopava, Snyegoorochka, and Lyel) was done away with, and the act closed with Mizgir. Yet Pryanishnikov gained no more applause than before. Best of all, the audiences liked Byeryendyey's cavatina and the third song of Lyel. They were usually encored, while Lyel's song was given even three times. Occasionally also the hymn of the Byeryendyeys, Lyel's first song, and Snyegoorochka's aria in the Prologue were demanded again. These encores and the interminable intermissions (the intermission before Act IV lasted from thirty-five to forty minutes) dragged the opera out until nearly midnight.

As had been their wont, the critics treated *Snyegoorochka* with scant sympathy. Reproaches for my lack of dramatic action, for the poverty of melodic inventiveness which manifested itself in

---

[16] A description of the première of *Snyegoorochka* is given in I. F. Tyumenev's "Fragments from Reminiscences of N. A. Rimsky-Korsakov." See note 18 on p. 166.

my partiality for borrowing folk-tunes, reproaches for insufficient originality in general, admissions that I "possessed talent" as a symphonist, but not as an operatic composer — all those showered down on me in the newspaper reviews. Nor did Cui lag behind the others, trying his best, as he did, not to praise my opera and still keep within bounds of decency. Resort was also had to the reviewers' trite trick of belittling a present work at the expense of previous ones, which, in their time, had been hounded no less. It is remarkable, however, that Cui, who treated my compositions with such discretion (as if approving with reservations), treated Napravnik's works with warmth, attention, and delight. The critics' reviews irritated me little, as in former days; perhaps I felt most provoked at Cui, and somehow ashamed of him.

After a long interval Balakirev reappeared as conductor of an orchestra at the first concert of the Free Music School, leading Beethoven's Fifth Symphony.[17] As conductor, he now appeared to me entirely different from what he had before. The former fascination had gone for ever for me. With the audience he won applause as one returned to activity.

The sixteen-year-old Sasha Glazunov, who had been developing hourly, not daily, had by then completed his First Symphony in E major (dedicated to me). On March 17 [29] it was played under Balakirev's leadership at the second concert of the Free Music School. That was truly a day of rejoicing for all of us, the St. Petersburg active workers of the young Russian school. Youthful in inspiration, but mature in technique and form, the symphony reaped great success. Stassov rumbled and grumbled full blast. The audience was astonished when the composer, in a "Gymnasium" (college) uniform, appeared in response to calls for him. I. A. Pomazansky presented him with a wreath bearing the curious inscription: "To Aleksandr Glazunov — Herman and Kazyenyov." Herman [18] and Kazyenyov were the well-known conjurors then performing in St. Petersburg.[19] On the part of the critics some fuss

---

[17] February 15 [27], 1882, at the Club of the Nobility.
[18] Herman the Great (the Elder), known in the United States. J. A. J.
[19] The presentation was made at the dress rehearsal.

A. K. GLAZUNOV

from a drawing by V. A. Serov

and froth were naturally unavoidable. There appeared also carica-
tures representing Glazunov as a suckling babe. Gossip kept busily
spinning assurances that the symphony had not been written by
him at all, but had been ordered by his wealthy parents from
" everybody knows whom," etc., etc., to the same effect. This symphony was the first of a series of original compositions by the highly
gifted artist and indefatigable worker, compositions which gradually spread also to western Europe and came to be the finest adorn-
ments of contemporary musical literature.

At the same concert my *Sadko* was played as the closing number.
This time Balakirev simply made a fiasco of it. In passing to the
second movement he indicated the change of tempo a bar too soon.
Some instruments came in, others did not. An unimaginable mess
resulted. From that time on, Balakirev abandoned his rule of conducting always from memory.

At this season's concerts of the Free Music School there appeared
the young talented pianist Lavrov, and there flitted by, too, like a
pale shadow, the Moscow pianist Myelgoonov, a dry theoretician
and compiler of a barbarous collection of Russian songs. At that
time Balakirev fussed over him like a child over a new toy.

In the autumn of the season 1881–2 our new friend F. M. Blumenfeld came to St. Petersburg and entered the Conservatory under
Professor Stein.

The personnel of the circle that visited our house was approximately as follows: Borodin, Lyadov, V. V. Stassov, Glazunov,
Blumenfeld, the talented baritone singer Ilyinsky, whom I have
referred to before, and Ilyinsky's wife. About the same time there
began to appear in our circle M. M. Ippolitov-Ivanov, who had
been graduated in the class of theory of composition, a pupil of
mine, who promised to develop into a talented composer; shortly
afterwards he married the singer V. M. Zarudnaya (an excellent
soprano). Both husband and wife became professors at the Moscow Conservatory a number of years later. Cui hardly visited our
circle at all, keeping entirely by himself. Balakirev came very
rarely. He would come in, play something, and leave at an early
hour. After his departure everybody breathed more freely; a lively

conversation began, new or recently conceived compositions were played, and so on. During the last years, besides Ippolitov-Ivanov, there graduated from my class in the Conservatory A. S. Arensky and G. A. Kazachenko — the former, subsequently our well-known talented composer; the latter, a composer and chorus-master of the Imperial Russian Opera. During my work on *Snyegoorochka* these two pupils of mine kindly aided me in making the arrangement of my opera for the piano and voices. I shall say by the way that Arensky, when still a pupil in my class, composed — partly as volunteer work and partly as class assignment — several numbers of *Voyevoda* [20] (*Son na Volgye* — Dream on the Volga) after Ostrovsky; these later formed part of his opera on this subject. I vividly recall his playing, in the classroom, of the scene at the bridge, the cradle song, etc.

In the interim between work on Moussorgsky's compositions [21] I somewhat reorchestrated the Overture and entr'actes to the drama *Pskovityanka,* changing the natural-scale to chromatic-scale French horns and trumpets. These numbers I had excluded from the second version of *The Maid of Pskov* because, on the one hand, I had no hope of having this opera produced, while, on the other hand, I had been dissatisfied with the second version. [22] In the first version I had suffered from insufficient knowledge, in the second from superabundance of knowledge and inability to direct it. I felt that the later version had to be abridged and worked over once more; that the right, desirable form of *Pskovityanka* lay somewhere midway between the first version and the second; and that, for the time being, I was incapable of striking that form. Yet, the instrumental numbers of the later version of the opera were interesting. Therefore I treated them in the above manner. The result was a composition in the style of the entr'actes to *Prince Kholmsky* or *Egmont.* [23]

---

[20] Tchaikovsky had written an opera to this libretto fourteen years previously, but subsequently destroyed the score. C. V. V.

[21] On the work on Moussorgsky's compositions, cf. a series of letters in *Rimsky-Korsakov's Correspondence with V. V. Stassov.*

[22] Cf. above, pp. 175–80.

[23] Cf. above, " 1876–77."

The summer of 1882 we spent again at dear Stelyovo. The weather was fine as a rule, but there were frequent rain-storms. Now all my time was consumed by work on *Khovanshchina*.[24] Much had to be altered, abridged, and added. In Acts I and II there turned up much that was superfluous, musically ugly, and a drag to the scene. In Act V, on the contrary, much was lacking altogether, while a good deal existed only in the roughest of rough draft records. The chorus of *raskol'niks* (schismatics), with the strokes of the bell, prior to the self-immolation, written by the composer in barbarous empty fourths and fifths, I recast entirely, as its original form was impossible. For the closing chorus there existed only the melody (recorded from the mouths of some schismatics by Karmalina and by her communicated to Moussorgsky). Availing myself of the given melody, I composed the entire chorus from beginning to end, but the orchestral figure (of the pyre blazing up) was entirely my own. For one of Dosifey's monologues in Act V, I borrowed music from Act I bodily. The variations of Marfa's song in Act III as well as the chorus " *Pryeryekokhom i pryepryekhom!* (We disputed and we argued!) " were considerably changed and worked out by me. I have said already that Moussorgsky, so often unrestrained and wanton in his modulations, occasionally ran to the other extreme: he could not struggle out of his one tonality for a long time, thus throwing the composition into utter languidness and monotony. In this case, in the latter half of Act III, from the moment of the court clerk's entrance, he clung tenaciously to the key of E-flat minor to the end of the act. That was intolerable and with no reason whatever, as the whole section undoubtedly subdivides itself into two parts — the scene of the court clerk, and the *stryel'tsy's* (Strelitz's) appeal to old Khovansky.

---

[24] In the spring of 1882 a partial performance of *Khovanshchina* was planned. In connection with this plan, Rimsky-Korsakov worked strenuously as early as in December 1881 on the materials left after Moussorgsky's death. About his labour on *Khovanshchina* and Moussorgsky's other compositions in summer of 1882, Rimsky-Korsakov wrote S. N. Krooglikov: " I am also getting ready for publication six songs of Moussorgsky to Tolstoy's texts, in general it is Moussorgsky and Moussorgsky; it seems to me that even my name is Modest Petrovich and not Nikolay Andreyevich and that I have composed *Khovanshchina* and possibly even *Boris*. And with regard to *Khovanshchina*, there is a modicum of truth in it . . ." (July 1 [13], 1882).

The first part I left in E-flat minor as in the original; the other I transposed to D minor. The result both answered the purpose better and offered greater variety. The parts of the opera that the composer had instrumentated I reorchestrated, and, I hope, for the better. All the rest was instrumented by me, too; I, again, made the arrangement (for the piano). The entire work on *Khovanshchina* could not be finished by the end of the summer and I wrote the last of it in St. Petersburg.[25]

Before removing to Pityer [St. Petersburg] I had composed music for Pushkin's *Anchar*,[26] for basso. I was not quite satisfied with the composition, and it lay in utter obscurity until 1897.[27]

In the latter part of the summer my wife and I made a trip to Moscow for a fortnight or so.[28] There was an All-Russian Exposition at that time in Moscow, at which there were planned, among other things, symphonic concerts in the name of the Moscow Directorate of the Russian Musical Society. Owing to the death of N. G. Rubinstein, N. A. Hubert filled the post of Director of the Conservatory. Having undertaken to arrange the Exposition concerts, he invited me to conduct two of them. An exclusively Russian program was desired. I assented to this plan. Thus there came about my trip to Moscow from Stelyovo. At the two concerts under my direction, there were given, among other things (I cannot recall them all), *Antar,* Glazunov's First Symphony, excerpts from *Prince Igor* (sung by Stravinsky), the aria " *I zhar i znoy* (Both heat and ardour " (Bichoorina), Tchaikovsky's piano concerto (Lavrov) and Napravnik's piano fantasy on Russian themes (Timanova). All went well and scored success. Sasha Glazunov also came expressly

---

[25] For the production of this opera in Paris and London in 1913, Maurice Ravel orchestrated the reading of the ukases, the hymn to Prince Ivan Khovansky, the duet between Emma and young Khovansky in the first act, Marfa's song, and Kooz'ka's song with chorus, after Moussorgsky's autograph sketches in the Imperial Library at St. Petersburg. C. V. V.

[26] *The Upas Tree.* C. V. V.

[27] Among Rimsky-Korsakov's papers there has been preserved the beginning of *Anchar* in orchestral score, which, to judge by the handwriting and the paper, belongs to 1882. It is of interest as evidence of an ancient intention to create a vocal piece *Anchar, with orchestral accompaniment,* which it is well known was carried out by Rimsky-Korsakov at a considerably later period.

[28] Nadezhda Andreyevna and Rimsky-Korsakov left for Moscow on August 9 [21].

for these concerts.[29] Before the rehearsal of the symphony commenced, I was approached by a tall and handsome man with whom I was not acquainted, though I had run across him in St. Petersburg. He introduced himself as Mitrofan Petrovich Byelayev and requested permission to attend all rehearsals. M. P. Byelayev was an ardent music-lover, who had been completely captivated by Glazunov's symphony at its first performance at the Free Music School and who had come now expressly for its sake to Moscow. From that moment dates my acquaintance with this remarkable man who subsequently was of such enormous consequence to Russian music.

S. N. Krooglikov (formerly active in the Free School), who had settled in Moscow some two years earlier, did not forsake Glazunov and me during our entire sojourn in Moscow. Glazunov, Krooglikov, Nadezhda Nikolayevna, and I passed our time quite pleasantly, dividing it among rehearsals, the sights of the Exposition, and walks through Moscow. Gratified with our trip, we returned to Stelyovo, where, during our absence, our children had been taken care of by my mother and my wife's brother, Nikolay Nikolayevich, the two living with us all summer.[30]

During the season of 1882–3 I continued working on *Khovanshchina* and other compositions of Moussorgsky's.[31] *A Night on Bald Mountain* was the only thing I could not find my way with. Originally composed in the sixties — under the influence of Liszt's *Todtentanz* — for the piano with accompaniment of orchestra, this piece (then called *St. John's Eve* and both severely and justly criticized by Balakirev) had long been utterly neglected by its author, gathering dust among his unfinished works. When composing Ge-

---

[29] Concerning the performance of Glazunov's First Symphony in Moscow, cf. V. M. Byelayev's book *Glazunov*, Vol. I (St. Petersburg, 1922), pp. 53 ff.

[30] Written at Vyechasha, June 14 [26], 1905.
The rest of the summer (September) Rimsky-Korsakov spent with his family at Tayitsky.

[31] Judgment on the work of orchestrating *Khovanshchina* may be formed as a whole on the basis of the following data drawn from Rimsky-Korsakov's autograph orchestral score: Act I, orchestration finished June 30 [July 12], 1882, at Stelyovo; Act II, ditto, July 14 [26], 1882, ditto; Act III, ditto, May 8 [20], 1882, St. Petersburg; Act IV, ditto, undated; Act V, ditto, December 16 [28], 1881. In addition to this, the last three pages of Act II were written October 1 [13], 1883. During the mentioned interval of time Rimsky-Korsakov was also busy with arranging *Khovanshchina* for the press.

deonov's *Mlada,* Moussorgsky had made use of the material to be found in *A Night on Bald Mountain* and, introducing singing into it, had written the scene of Chernobog on Mount Triglav (Three Peaks). That was the second form of the same piece in substance.[32] Its third form had developed in his composing of *The Fair at Sorochintsy,* when Moussorgsky conceived the queer and incoherent idea of making the peasant lad, without rhyme or reason, see the Witches' Sabbath in a dream; this was to form a sort of stage intermezzo that did not chime at all with the rest of the scenario of *Sorochinskaya Yarmarka.* This time the piece ended with the ringing of the village church bell, at the sounds of which the frightened evil spirits vanished. Tranquillity and dawn were built on the theme of the peasant lad himself, who had seen the fantastic dream. In working on Moussorgsky's piece I made use of its last version for the purpose of closing the composition. Now then, the first form of the piece was for piano solo with orchestra; the second form and the third, vocal compositions and for the stage, into the bargain (unorchestrated)! None of these forms was fit to be published and performed. With Moussorgsky's material as a basis I decided to create an instrumental piece, by retaining all of the author's best and coherent material, adding the fewest possible interpolations of my own. It was necessary to create a form in which Moussorgsky's ideas would mould in the best fashion. It was a difficult task, of which the satisfactory solution baffled me for two years, though in the other works of Moussorgsky I had got on with comparative ease. I had been unable to get at either form, modulation, or orchestration; and the piece lay inert until the following year. Work on the other compositions of my departed friend, however, was progressing. Progressing also was their publication at Bessel's under my editorial supervision.[33]

---

[32] In the library of the Leningrad Conservatory there have been preserved two of the author's versions of *A Night on Bald Mountain,* one (dated 1867) in the form of an orchestral piece, the other for two pianos with chorus. The latter bears the notation: " *The Fair at Sorochintsy,* Act I, Second Tableau " (see *Music and Revolution,* 1926, No. 5, p. ii, as well as the book *M. P. Moussorgsky, Letters and Documents,* p. 120).

[33] In November 1882 Rimsky-Korsakov went to Moscow to conduct P. A. Shostakovsky's concert (November 16 [28]), at which there were performed for the first time

Among my own works, jotted down during this season, must be set down the sketch of a Piano Concerto in C-sharp minor on a Russian theme, chosen not without Balakirev's advice. In all ways the concerto proved a chip from Liszt's concertos. It must be said that it sounded beautiful and proved entirely satisfactory in the sense of piano technique and style; this greatly astonished Balakirev, who found my concerto to his liking. He had by no means expected that I, who was not a pianist, should know how to compose anything entirely pianistic. I recollect that once a little tiff occurred between Balakirev and me regarding some detail in my concerto. Yet that disagreement did not cool him towards my composition. I cannot clearly recall exactly when I first conceived the thought of setting to work on the piano concerto, nor when the concerto was finally ready and orchestrated.[34]

During this season's concerts of the Free Music School, the famous *Tamara,* now at last completed, was performed. A fine, interesting composition, though one which seemed somewhat heavy, sewn together of patches, and not altogether devoid of dullish spots. The spell of the former improvisations of the late sixties was no longer there. And it could not be otherwise: the piece had been composing for over fifteen years (with interruptions, to be sure). In fifteen years a man's entire organism, to the very last cell, changes several times, perhaps. The Balakirev of the eighties was not the Balakirev of the sixties.

---

by him his own *Fairy-tale,* A. K. Glazunov's *First Overture* on Greek folk-themes and I. P. Blaramberg's *Scherzo* for orchestra.

[34] From a letter of January 14 [26], 1883 to S. N. Krooglikov: ". . . Have been busy during the holidays finishing my concerto and orchestrating it. . . ." There is a date, " Jan. 3 [15], 1883, N. R.-Korsakov, Pityer," at the end, on the autograph orchestral score of the concerto.

Court Chapel. The Coronation. Organizing the instrumental and the precentors' classes. Abolition of the post of Inspector of Naval Bands. Byelayev's Fridays. A. Lyadov's marriage. Textbook of harmony. Byelayev — publisher. Rehearsal at the Petropavlovsky School. Revision of Symphony in C major. Beginning of Russian Symphony Concerts. Trip to the Caucasus.

THE CHANGES occasioned by Alexander III's coming to the throne affected also the Court Chapel, of which Bakhmetyev was the director. He was dismissed. The status of the Chapel and its lists were worked out afresh. Count Sheryemetyev, who was not even a dilettante in the art of music, was made chief of the Chapel. This post was, as it were, only representative and honorary; the work in reality fell upon the shoulders of the Chapel superintendent and his assistant. Sheryemetyev chose Balakirev as superintendent, and the latter, in turn, chose me as his aid. The mysterious thread leading to this unexpected appointment was in the hands of T. I. Filippov (then Imperial Comptroller), and Procurator-General Pobyedonostsev.[1] Balakirev — Filippov — Count Sheryemetyev — the bond of these men rested on the ground of religion, Orthodox faith, and remnants of Slavophilism. Then followed Sablyer and Pobyedonostsev and Samarin, and, possibly, Katkov — those ancient bul-

---

[1] Of the Holy Synod. J. A. J.

warks of absolute monarchy and Orthodoxy. Music proper had
played only an insignificant rôle in Balakirev's appointment; still
the thread had led to him, really a remarkable musician. On the
other hand, Balakirev, who felt no firm theoretical or pedagogical
ground under his feet, took me as assistant, since I had plunged into
the theoretical and pedagogical activity of the Conservatory. My
appointment as assistant superintendent of the Court Chapel took
place in February 1883.[2]

On joining the Chapel, Balakirev and I were utterly at a loss as
to how to go about the unfamiliar undertaking. The Chapel choir
was magnificent. Its four instructors, Smirnov, Azyeyev, Syrboolov,
and Kopylov, were men of knowledge and experience. From ancient days, as far back as Bortnyansky's time, the well-arranged
matter of church singing had been running splendidly. However,
the instrumental classes for boys, their bringing up, as well as their
general instruction were beneath all criticism. The adult singers
received both salary and lodgings on a par with officials; they
throve, more or less. But the illiterate boys, beaten without mercy
as they were, uneducated, and taught the violin, the cello, or the
piano only after a fashion, they, as a rule, met with a sorry fate after
the loss of their voices. They were provided with a certain amount
of money due them and were dismissed from the Chapel to the four
quarters of the globe — ignorant and unaccustomed to work. From
their ranks came scriveners, common servants, provincial singers,
and — in the best of cases — ignorant precentors and petty officials.
Many of them took to drink and went to the devil. Our first care
was, of course, to improve their bringing up and education, to
train the most musically gifted of them as good orchestral musicians
or precentors, and to secure them bread and butter for the future.
It was unthinkable to accomplish this during the first spring of our
connection with the Chapel, and all we could do was to make observations. The instructors in musical subjects at the Chapel were:

---

[2] The appointment of M. A. Balakirev as superintendent and N. A. Rimsky-
Korsakov as assistant superintendent of the Court Chapel was made February 3 [15],
1883. Count Vorontsov's report, addressed to the Chief of the Chapel, Count Sheryemetyev, bears the date of February 23 [March 7], 1883. The salary of Rimsky-
Korsakov was fixed at 2,300 rubles.

Kremyenyetsky, violin; Markus, cello; Zhdanov, double-bass; Goldstein, piano; the ancient Joseph Hunke, theory of music. Goldstein,
a talented pianist, was not a particularly zealous instructor. Balakirev (an implacable Jew-hater) conceived a hatred for Goldstein
owing to his Jewish extraction and got rid of him that very spring.
He also dismissed the Italian Cavalli, who taught the adult voices
solo-singing. For some time at the beginning nobody was engaged
to replace these instructors.

The coronation of Tsar Alexander III was set for May 15 [27].
The entire personnel of the Chapel, Balakirev and myself included,
went to Moscow. At Moscow we had to stay some three weeks.³
First came the preparations for the solemnity, then the Emperor's
entry, the coronation proper, and, finally, the consecration of the
Temple of the Saviour. The Chapel was quartered in the Kremlin.
Balakirev and I lived in the Grand Moscow Hotel. In reality, I
personally had nothing to do. The choristers and their teachers
were busy, while all economic and administrative duties devolved
upon Balakirev. Arrayed in uniforms of the Court, we attended the
coronation at the Oospyensky Cathedral (Cathedral of the Assumption), standing in the choirs: Balakirev in the right, I in the left
one. Near me stood the artist Kramskoy, commissioned to sketch
the picture of the solemnity. He was the only man in evening dress
at the Cathedral; all the rest were in uniform. The ceremony went
off with pomp; the Emperor recited the *Credo* in a clear-cut voice;
the singing was safely over. Tears of emotion rolled in streams down
the cheeks of one of our singers, our secretary, K. A. Vargin. As a
whole, the spectacle was beautiful and gorgeous.

Also the consecration of the Temple of the Nativity of the Saviour
passed off solemnly; at the most important moment of the service
— the drawing asunder of the veil — a canticle of several bars (man-
ufactured by me), of eight- or even ten-part counterpoint was

---

³ In connection with the coronation solemnities, Rimsky-Korsakov stayed in Moscow from May 8 [20] till May 26 [June 7], 1883. In a letter written to his family,
Rimsky-Korsakov relates of his visiting the Donskoy Monastery and the Troyitsko-
Sergiyevskaya Lavra (monastery of high rank where he went to hear the monks'
chanting and to see the most magnificent library), of his meeting Razoomovsky, of
his work on the harmonization of church canticles. Blaramberg and Krooglikov were
in constant communication with Rimsky-Korsakov also during this visit.

sung.[4] After the performance in Moscow I never saw and completely forgot the score of this canticle, which Balakirev had made
me compose for the occasion. Most probably it is still lying tucked
away somewhere in the Court Chapel.

After returning to St. Petersburg with the Chapel, I moved to
Tayitsy for the summer.[5]

The summer of 1883 passed unproductively for me in regard to
composing. During the summer the Chapel was quartered at the
English Palace in Old Peterhof. Frequent trips there consumed a
good deal of my time. I gave the youngster singers whatever I
could: taught them elementary piano-playing, elementary theory,
heard their violin and cello lessons — if only to accustom them to
some slight regularity of study, to a serious attitude towards their
musical future and to kindle in them a desire and love for art. At
home, as far as I recall, I drew up plans for the future organization
of the classes, tried my hand at sketches of ecclesiastic canticles, and
partly pondered revisions of my Third Symphony in C major, with
which I was extremely dissatisfied.[6] For diversion, my wife, my son
Misha, and I made a trip to Imatra.[7] In the fall of 1883 we gave up

---

[4] This canticle was composed then and there in Moscow.

[5] To the spring of 1883 also belongs the rejection of *Khovanshchina* by the Operatic Committee of the Mariinsky Theatre. Following is a quotation on this subject
from Rimsky-Korsakov's letter of April 14 [26], 1883 to S. N. Krooglikov: " After a
hearing of *Khovanshchina,* the Committee, made up of Vsyevolozhsky, Napravnik,
Kuchera, Pomazansky, Kondratyev, Slavina, Pryanishnikov, Orlov, Albrecht, and Cui,
cast a majority of black balls (with the exception of Cui, of course, and Albrecht, who
flinched). There were no debates; Cui alone expressed himself that without doubt,
in consideration of the mere name of Moussorgsky, all would cast white balls. Nobody said anything to the contrary and the votes were cast. The devil knows what
this is! And they listened with attentive faces and expressed condolence about the
changes made by the censor. Napravnik even praised it and demanded that the Persian Women's Dance should be played without fail. . . . Plainly worthless scamps.
That is all. However, you know all this from the papers. Darling Syemyon Nikolayevich, raise a noise about it in Moscow and in the Moscow papers."

[6] From a letter of July 5 [17], 1883 to S. N. Krooglikov: " I sit composing the
Obikhod, all around me all sorts of Potoolovs, Razoomovskys, and publications of the
Holy Synod. At present the entire Vespers is ready in single-voice form and presently
it will be harmonized. The Rubric as I know it now. . . . I have turned into a sexton
altogether. Only I fear that M. A. [Balakirev] may begin to tangle matters too much,
for some snarl is already on. . . ." (For *Obikhod,* cf, note 11, p. 292. J. A. J.)

To the year 1883 also belongs the arrangement of the double-choir *Te Deum
laudamus* from a Greek cantillation of the third mode. The manuscript bears the date:
" July 18 [30], 1883. Tayitsy."

[7] A famous waterfall in Finland. J. A. J.

the apartment where we had lived for ten years.[8] With the growth of my family it had become inconvenient, and we moved to Vladi-mirskaya, corner of Kolokol'naya Street.

All my activity during this season was directed towards improv-ing the progress of the musical classes at the Court Chapel, with its former resources and instructors; the ensuing academic season, towards organizing the Chapel's instrumental class and the pre-centors' class on new principles, after having considered and worked out a clear program. I have already spoken of the instrumental class; as for the precentors' class, none such had existed at the Chapel. Young men who wished to learn a little and receive a precentor's diploma, usually came to the Chapel from the interior of Russia and were assigned to one of the four instructors in eccle-siastical singing, to learn the " deep mystery." Having studied with the teacher and having passed an examination according to some vague and indefinite program, they received the desired certifi-cate and left for the four points of the compass. The entire sys-tem of instruction, for the instrumental class as well as for those specializing as precentors — established by Lvov, the composer of *Bozhe Tsarya khrani (God save the Tsar)* — was good for nothing. Everything had to be made over, or, rather, created anew. To this end were directed all my thoughts and designs of that year.[9]

At one of the Russian Musical Society concerts, given under A. G. Rubinstein's direction, I conducted, at his invitation, the Overture and entr'actes to the drama *Pskovityanka,* as I have men-tioned earlier.[10] At the Free School concert of February 27 [March 10], 1884, my piano concerto was played by N. S. Lavrov for the first time, and excerpts from *Khovanshchina* in my arrangement and with my orchestration were performed at the same occasion.

---

[8] Furshtadtskaya Street, No. 25, Apt. 9.

[9] From a letter of September 27 [October 9], 1883 to S. N. Krooglikov: " The Chapel affords me joy: a noble spirit is breeding in it; the boys study with a will; all such things as ' putting in the corner,' ' on the knees,' etc., have almost completely vanished."

[10] During the season of 1882–3, at the seventh concert, February 5 [17]. Accord-ing to *My Musical Life*, the concert occurred in the season of 1883–4, but that is an error.

In the spring of 1884 I was relieved of my duties as Inspector of Bands of the Navy Department.[11] The new acting head of the Navy Department, Shestakov, inaugurated various reforms along with the introduction of a civil-service qualification. Among these *useful* reforms must be considered also the abolition of the post of Inspector of Bands. The corresponding post in the Guards continued to be considered indispensable, but the Navy musicians were allowed to play according to their own sweet will, as the band had been placed under the supervision of some adjutant of the Navy Staff. Accordingly, my government service was confined exclusively to the Chapel — that is, to the Court Department.[12]

M. P. Byelayev, an ardent lover of music, particularly chamber music, himself a viola-player and a zealous player of quartets, had long before then begun to gather his friends, thorough quartetists, at his house every Friday. The evenings usually opened with Haydn, then came Mozart, then Beethoven, and last some quartet of post-Beethoven music. The quartets of each composer followed one another promptly in their numerical order. If Haydn's First Quartet was played one week, the second came the following week, and so on. When the last one had been played, the first was taken up again. Towards the winter of 1883–4 Byelayev's Fridays became rather well attended. In addition to the usual quartet-players (Professor Gesechus, Dr. Gelbke, the Engineer Evald) they were attended by Glazunov, Borodin, Lyadov, Dütsch, and many others. I, too, became a regular attendant at Byelayev's Fridays. The evenings were interesting. Haydn's, Mozart's, and Beethoven's early

---

[11] Rimsky-Korsakov was relieved of his duties in the Navy Department owing to the abolition of the office of Inspector of Bands by Order of His Imperial Majesty, of March 19 [31], 1884.

[12] To characterize Rimsky-Korsakov's moods during the winter months of 1883–4, some quotations are given from his letters to S. N. Krooglikov. From a letter of November 11 [23], 1883: " Now I shall tell you that I am very preoccupied with the Chapel and do not compose anything and really there is no desire; it seems to me that I have placed a full stop after having composed *Snyegoorochka* — and some songs, concertos, and church compositions, they are merely a sort of reminiscence of affairs of long-past days. At present there is in my mind simply the Toricellian vacuum. . . ." From a letter of January 14 [26], 1884: " I am composing nothing and even the *Obikhod* I threw aside long since; even as it is, it's boresome and dry work, and with Balakirev (to boot), all ambition will disappear."

quartets were played competently; the later quartets not so well, occasionally even quite badly, although the quartet-players read the music fluently. When our circle made its appearance at the Fridays, their repertory was increased. Quartets of recent times were performed in order to instil familiarity with them. Sasha Glazunov, composing his First Quartet in D major, tried it out at the Byelayev Fridays. Subsequently all his quartets and quartet suites, even those not quite finished, were played at the house of Byelayev, who was thoroughly in love with the youthful composer's talent. In addition to his own compositions, how many different things Glazunov arranged for Byelayev's quartet! Fugues of Bach and songs of Grieg and many others, innumerable. Byelayev's Fridays grew very lively and were never permitted to lapse. If one of the quartet-players fell ill, Byelayev secured someone else in his stead. Byelayev himself was never ill. The personnel of the quartet was as follows: the cellist originally was a certain Nikolsky, whose place was taken by Evald; first violin, Gelbke; second violin, Gesechus; viola, Byelayev. Thus constituted, the quartet existed for many years, until death carried away the cordial host.

The music over with, supper was served at one in the morning. The suppers were generous, and laced with abundant libations. Occasionally, after supper Glazunov or somebody else played on the piano something new of his own, just composed or just arranged for four hands. Adjournment was late, at three a.m. Some, finding insufficient what they had imbibed at supper, would, after parting with the host, repair — to use a mild term — to a restaurant " to continue." At times after supper, during the music-making, a bottle or two of champagne appeared on the table and was opened to " baptize " the new composition.

In the course of time, during the subsequent years, the Fridays were ever more and more numerously attended. Fyeliks Blumenfeld, a graduate of the Conservatory, and his brother Sigizmund came. To quartet music were added trios, quintets, etc., with the piano. Other pianists, too, sometimes merely on a visit, appeared. Conservatory youngsters, graduated from my courses, also began to attend the Byelayev Fridays. Many violinists turned up. A. K.

Glazunov, who sometimes played the cello, also took part in the quintets, sextets, and octets. Verzhbilovich, too, made his appearance. The libations at supper also increased. But of that later.

Anatoli Lyadov, then already an instructor at the Conservatory, married during the 1883–4 season. I recall him, one morning shortly before his marriage, telling me of his intention, and the two of us leaving the Conservatory that morning and roaming about the city almost till dinner, having a heart-to-heart talk about the impending change in his life. Yet when Nadezhda Nikolayevna and I later expressed our desire to meet his wife, the queer fellow flatly refused. He said he wished his marriage to bring no change whatever in his relations with his musical friends. His home circle would be made up of the close friends and acquaintances of his wife, while towards his friends in art he wished to remain, as it were, of the bachelor estate as before. After marriage the status he had desired established itself: he introduced none of his musician intimates and friends in art to his wife, went everywhere alone, even to concerts and the theatres. Visiting him rarely, I never saw his wife, as he always received me in his study, carefully locking the doors to the other rooms. Curious by nature, Byelayev could not endure this state of affairs; knowing that Anatoli was not at home, he once rang their bell, called his wife to the door, to transmit some nonsense to her husband, and, having introduced himself, made her acquaintance. Subsequently, many years later, Lavrov, Byelayev, Glazunov, Sokolov, and Wihtol gained admittance to his family. Yet Nadezhda Nikolayevna and I never have seen his wife, despite our friendly lifelong relations with this bright, dear, and most talented man.

Upon the ancient Hunke's leaving the Chapel, I took over his class in harmony and grew exceedingly interested in teaching that subject. Tchaikovsky's system (I followed his textbook in private lessons) did not satisfy me. From constant talks with Anatoli regarding this subject, I came to know his system and methods of instruction, and conceived the idea of writing a new textbook of harmony, according to a wholly new system as regards pedagogic methods and sequence of exposition. Essentially, Lyadov's system was an outgrowth of his professor Y. I. Johansen's system, and mine of Lyadov's. Four scales were taken as the foundation of harmony: major and minor natural, and major and minor harmonic. The first exercises consisted in harmonizing the upper melodies and basses with the aid of the principal triads alone: the tonic, the dominant, and the subdominant and their inversions. With so scant a stock of chords, the rules of part-writing proved very accurate. Through exercises in harmonizing melodies, with the aid of only the principal steps, the pupil's sense of rhythmic and harmonic balance and tendency towards the tonic were developed. Later to the principal triads there were gradually added accessory ones, the dominant chord of the seventh and the other chords of the seventh. Figured bass was entirely done away with; on the other hand, to exercises in the harmonization of melodies and basses was added independent writing of half-periods from the same harmonic material. Later followed modulation, the science of which was based on the relationship of keys and the modulational plan, and not on the external connection (through common tones) of chords foreign to one another. In this way modulation proved ever natural and logical. After modulation followed suspensions, passing notes, subsidiary notes, and all other devices of figuration. Finally came the science of chromatically transformed chords and false progressions. Until the beginning of summer I only thought over, but did not write my textbook; [13] I tested my pedagogic methods on my Chapel pupils, with considerable success.

In the spring of 1884 I recast and reorchestrated my First Symphony, its principal tonality being changed from E-flat minor to E minor.[14] It seemed to me that this youthful and, for the present

---

[13] The textbook of harmony was written by Rimsky-Korsakov in the summer and autumn of 1884. From a letter of October 17 [29], 1884 to S. N. Krooglikov: " I am forwarding you . . . the first issue of the textbook of harmony, commenced together with Lyadov and finished by me." The preface to the first lithographed edition of the textbook is dated 1886.

[14] There are notations on the rough draft of the orchestral score of the first movement: " Set out to recast it on March 29 [April 10], 1884. N. R.-K." and " Finished the revision on April 5 [17], 1884. N. R-Korsakov." The second movement bears the notation: " The reorchestration was completed May 16 [28], 1884, Fayitsy. N. R.-Korsakov."

time, naïve work of mine, provided its technical side were improved, could become a repertory piece for student and amateur orchestras. Subsequently I found that I had somewhat erred in my calculations: times had changed, and student and amateur had begun to gravitate towards Tchaikovsky's and Glazunov's symphonies and my own pieces of more modern tendency than that of my first composition. Nevertheless Bessel's firm gladly undertook to publish my First Symphony in orchestral score and parts. That year there graduated from my class at the Conservatory Ryb and N. A. Sokolov — the former subsequently instructor in musical theory at Kiev, the latter a talented composer and teacher at St. Petersburg.

The summer of 1884 we spent at Tayitsy as before. On June 13 [25] our daughter Nadya was born.

As in the previous summer, twice a week or so I visited the juvenile singers at Peterhof, continuing my instruction of them and proceeding to form a pupils' or rather children's string orchestra, for which I made several easy arrangements, principally excerpts from Glinka's operas, like " *Kak mat' oobili* (When they killed mother)," " *Ty nye plach', sirotinushka* (Do not cry, thou orphan poor)," etc. While at Tayitsy, I set to writing the textbook of harmony, which was ready towards the beginning of autumn and published lithographically, with the help of my assistant at the Chapel library, the chorister G. V. Ivanitsky, who copied the textbook in lithographic ink.

Besides this I worked on my orchestral Sinfonietta in A minor, recast from the first three movements of the Quartet on Russian Themes. The fourth movement of the quartet (on the ecclesiastical theme from *Te Deum*) I did not make use of, after all.[15]

After my removal to town at the beginning of the academic year, the precentors' and the instrumental class of the Chapel were definitely organized by me. P. A. Krasnokootsky was engaged as instructor in violin; A. V. Reichard, piano; A. K. Lyadov, and later N. A. Sokolov and I. R. Shchiglev, harmony and elementary theory

---

[15] To the summer of 1884 belong the sketches of the third movement (Rondo scherzando) of Rimsky-Korsakov's Fourth Symphony, dated: " Began writing on August 15 [27] " and at the end: " August 19 [31], 1884, Fayitsy. N. R.-Korsakov."

for the precentors' class. In addition to these, the former instructors taught, as well as S. A. Smirnov, E. S. Azyeyev, A. A. Kopylov (violin, piano, church singing, and rubric). Harmony in the instrumental class was taught by me; I also taught the orchestral class (then still exclusively strings), which was already making considerable progress.

The Chapel's lists were already new ones, and its financial resources had increased.

I was invited to conduct one of the Russian Musical Society concerts. Among other numbers, there was performed for the first time the C-sharp minor Overture of the talented Lyapoonov,[16] a young composer, Balakirev's favourite, who had lately graduated from the Moscow Conservatory and recently made his bow in St. Petersburg.

My first Symphony in E minor was played that same season by the St. Petersburg University students' orchestra under Dütsch's leadership.[17]

Delighted by the brilliant beginning of Glazunov's activity as a composer, M. P. Byelayev proposed to him to publish his First Symphony (E major) in orchestral score, orchestra parts, and arrangement for four hands at his, Byelayev's, expense. Despite some objection on the part of Balakirev, who urged Sasha not to give his consent, as Byelayev had been neither music-dealer nor music-publisher, Glazunov yielded to M. P.'s pleas. Byelayev communicated with the Röder firm in Leipzig and proceeded with publication; and the young composer's symphony was the beginning of the honourable and noteworthy publishing activity of M. P., who established for ever the imperishable house of " M. P. Byelayev, Leipzig," for publishing the works of Russian composers. The symphony was followed, in progressive order, by all of Glazunov's newly appearing compositions, my piano concerto, *Skazka* (*Fairy-tale*),

---

[16] Rimsky-Korsakov conducted the concert of November 17 [29], 1884, but to judge by the *Sketch of the Activity of the St. Petersburg Branch of the Imperial Russian Musical Society*, written by N. Findeisen (St. Petersburg, 1909), Lyapoonov's Overture was not performed at the time.

[17] This concert took place December 4 [16], 1885 — that is, a year later than the one just mentioned.

the *Overture on Russian Themes*, etc.; after me followed Borodin, Lyadov, Cui; then came other young composers, and the business grew literally every hour. In accordance with Mitrofan Petrovich's fundamental rule, no composition whatever was acquired without payment therefor, as is frequently done by other publishing houses. No orchestral or chamber-music composition was published otherwise than in orchestral score, orchestral parts, and arrangement for four hands. With authors M. P. was punctual and exacting: particular as to correct proof-reading, he paid the author's fee only after the second proof had been read. In choosing works for publication M. P. was guided at first by his own taste and the greater or lesser authority of the composer's name. Later, when many young composers appeared who wished to be published by his firm, he began to consult Sasha, Anatoli, and me, constituting us into a permanent official musical committee with his firm. For the marketing of his publications M. P. made arrangements with J. I. Jurgenson's music-shop, and for the management of the publishing business in Leipzig he engaged an experienced man — G. Schäffer.

During the season of 1884–5, Byelayev, who was aflame with the desire to hear once more the First Symphony and with impatience to hear the orchestral suite Glazunov had just composed, set his mind on arranging, at the hall of the Petropavlovsky School, for an orchestral rehearsal of these compositions.[18] The opera orchestra was brought together and some people close to the matter were invited: the Glazunovs, my wife, V. V. Stassov, and others. Dütsch and the composer were to conduct. Sasha was ready to undertake it; but, seeing well that Sasha was unprepared for the conductor's task and might easily injure himself in the orchestra's eyes, I dissuaded him from appearing as conductor for the time being, convincing M. P. Byelayev, as well. This rehearsal was conducted by Dütsch and myself. Everything went off in the best of style. One of the numbers of the suite, *Oriental Dance,* very odd and savage,

---

[18] The rehearsal had occurred in the season of 1883–4, on March 27 [April 8], 1884. Its program has been reproduced in facsimile in V. M. Byelayev's book, mentioned earlier. Cf. note 17 on p. 231 above.

was left out upon my plea; everything else was given in full. The author, Byelayev, and the audience felt inordinately gratified. This rehearsal was the foundation of the Russian Symphony Concerts, inaugurated by Byelayev the following season.[19]

Absorbed by activity in the Chapel's instrumental class and pre-centors' class, I hardly turned my thoughts towards my own work as composer during this season, just as in the one preceding.[20] Yet I began to think occasionally of revising my Third Symphony in C major, the first movement of which I managed to finish during the following summer.

The summer of 1885 we spent again at Tayitsy. Trips to Peterhof to visit the Chapel, revision of the symphony, composition and harmonization of certain ecclesiastical canticles, and study of musical forms filled up my time. As far as I recall, during my visit to the Chapel I visited the Glazunovs, who had taken a house that summer in Old Peterhof. At that time Sasha began to show a very deep interest in wind instruments. He had a clarinet, a French horn, a trombone, and something more of his own. Lessons on the French horn he took from no less a player than Francke, the first French horn of the opera orchestra; on the other instruments and the cello he practised without a teacher. In order to gain closer familiarity with the wind instruments, I, too, took part in these exercises. The crowning point of my progress in clarinet-playing was reached during the following years, when I performed on that instrument the

---

[19] The Russian Symphony Concerts at popular prices began in the season of 1885–6.

[20] To spring 1885 belongs the work on Borodin's *Igor*, undertaken by Rimsky-Korsakov. In a letter to S. N. Krooglikov, Rimsky-Korsakov wrote: " I am copying the provisional piano score of *Igor* and am thus bringing it into order, and in the process I add and curtail bars here and there; I write the missing parts of the recitatives; I give the modulations their numbers; I transpose whatever is necessary; I arrange the part-writing, etc. I have finished the Prologue and First Tableau of Act I, intend to continue in the same way, and hope that by autumn *Igor* will be finished and the instrumentation may be taken up, and by springtime it may be delivered to the opera house. I imagine that Borodin will be captivated by my endeavours and will do something himself too, and in Act III his hand also is needed. A great deal is still missing there. Oh, mighty *Koochka!* Oh, Russian composérs " (Stassov's accentuation) " who are indebted to themselves for their musical education." Cf. Rimsky-Korsakov's letter of July 4 [16], 1885 to V. V. Stassov.

In the spring of 1885 P. I. Tchaikovsky offered Rimsky-Korsakov the post of director of the Moscow Conservatory. Cf. his letter to Rimsky-Korsakov under date of April 6 [18], 1885 (Letter No. VI).

part of the second violin in Glinka's Quartet,[21] Dütsch playing first violin, Glazunov cello, and Wihtol, as I recall it, viola.

Early in the season of 1885–6 the rebuilding of the Court Chapel was begun, and the Chapel itself, in its entirety, temporarily moved to a private house in Millionnaya Street. The quarters were narrow and inconvenient. The precentors' class, organized the year before, it was found necessary to install in stables in the yard, the buildings being remodelled for the purpose. The orchestra class was quartered in the dormitories of the young choristers. Nevertheless, work went on successfully. In the precentors' class there were already many non-resident pupils, principally from among the regimental singers; in the instrumental class I began, gradually, to introduce the wind instruments, for which instructors were engaged from the court orchestra and from the opera. At first the pupils in wind instruments naturally could not, as yet, take part in the orchestral class; but the players of bowed instruments had advanced considerably and were beginning to play fairly well things more or less difficult. Occasionally I invited wind instruments from the regimental band for joint playing; in that way it was possible to perform symphonies of Haydn and Beethoven in the proper manner. Once, with my orchestral class, I succeeded in giving a sufficiently neat rendering of the recently orchestrated first movement of my Symphony in C major. Borodin was present and seemed quite pleased.[22]

Hans von Bülow, who conducted the Russian Musical Society's concerts that season, was very cordial towards Glazunov, Borodin, Cui, and myself, and readily played our compositions. Of my own works he gave *Antar;* for some reason, however, he was in a capricious mood at the rehearsal, testy with the orchestra, even suggesting irritably to me that I conduct it in his stead. Of course I declined. Presently Bülow calmed down and led *Antar* in excellent fashion.[23]

---

[21] F major (1830). J. A. J.

[22] In the autumn of 1885 occurred the production of *Snyegoorochka* at the private opera house in Moscow (S. I. Mamontov's). The first performance was given October 8 [20], 1885. For a review (by S. N. Krooglikov) of this production, cf. *Musical Review*, 1885, No. 8.

[23] At the ninth concert, on March 29 [April 10], 1886.

The preceding season,[24] M. P. Byelayev had arranged a rehearsal of Glazunov's compositions before an intimate gathering; he now conceived the idea of giving this season, and at his own expense, a public concert of other works besides those of Glazunov. The concert took place at the Hall of the Club of the Nobility.[25] G. O. Dütsch was the conductor. Among other things, my concerto was played, and, of Glazunov's compositions, his very recently finished *Styeñka Razin*.[26] The audience was not particularly large, but Byelayev felt content nevertheless.

Of other musical events of this season let me note a very fair first performance of Moussorgsky's *Khovanshchina* by amateur members of the Dramatic Circle, under Goldstein's leadership.[27] The opera took the fancy of the public and had three or four performances.

My work during this season consisted in: composing a *Vespers*, in collaboration with the teachers of the Court Chapel, Smirnov, Azyeyev, Kopylov, and Syrboolov; bringing out my textbook of harmony (printed, not lithographed as in its first edition); further work on orchestrating as well as revising my Third Symphony. Of my Conservatory pupils, those graduating were Y. I. Wihtol, A. A. Petrov, and Antipov. Despite his undoubted talent, the last named, owing to insufficient activity and a very characteristic dissoluteness, would not have managed to finish the *Allegro* set for his examination task if he had not been helped on the sly by Glazunov, who orchestrated his composition for him. Glazunov dashed the thing off for his own practice exclusively; the author, meanwhile, was naïvely convinced that he himself would not have orchestrated it any worse if he had not been pressed for time. All this was kept a secret; the composition sounded well and was subsequently pub-

---

[24] In the season of 1883–4. Cf. note 18 on p. 275.

[25] November 23 [December 5], 1885.

[26] The symphonic poem, *Styeñka Razin*, writes M. Montagu-Nathan, in his *Short History of Russian Music*, is " based on a story of the Cossack raider of that name, whose revolt against the Czar Alexis (son of the first Romanov) ended in his capture and execution in 1672, the date of Peter the Great's birth. Styeñka Razin is the hero of many national ballads." C. V. V.

[27] The first performance took place on February 9 [21], 1886, at Kononov's Hall (Moyka, 63). For C. A. Cui's review, cf. *Musical Review*, 1885–6, No. 21.

lished by Byelayev, who was quite aware of the truth about it, however.[28]

Rehearsal of Glazunov's works the year before, and the concert arranged by Byelayev during this season, led me to think that several yearly concerts of Russian compositions would be most desirable; the number of Russian orchestral compositions was growing, and there were always difficulties in finding a place for them on the program of the concerts of the Russian Musical Society and other organizations. I communicated my idea to Byelayev; it struck his fancy, and with the next season he decided to inaugurate a series of annual concerts made up exclusively of Russian compositions, to be conducted by Dütsch and myself, under the name of Russian Symphony Concerts.

Having settled at Tayitsy for the summer and left our children in their grandmother's care, Nadezhda Nikolayevna and I went on a trip to the Caucasus. We travelled to Nizhnii Novgorod by rail, boarded the steamer, and went down the Volga to Tsaritsyn. Crossing to Kalach by steamer over the Don River (where we ran aground some ten times), we reached Rostov-on-Don, and thence, by rail, via the station Mineral'niya Vody (Mineral Waters), we arrived in Zhelyeznovodsk and made ourselves comfortable there for a while. No cure had been prescribed us, and we therefore spent our time in glorious tramps about the environs, to the Zhelyeznaya Gora (Iron Mountain), to Beshtau, and other places. Having also visited Pyatigorsk with Mashook and Kislovodsk and reached Vladikavkaz, we travelled by carriage over the Military Gruzian (Georgian) Road as far as Tiflis. We stayed a few days at Tiflis, took in Borzhom, then boarded the steamer at Batum,[29] started for the Crimea to Yalta and, via Simfyeropol, journeyed to Lozovaya; from here, after a visit to the estate of M. M. Ippolitov-Ivanov, who lived there, we returned to St. Petersburg and Tayitsy. In all, this trip consumed nearly two months and was exceedingly pleas-

---

[28] To the autumn of 1885 belong the eminent successes of Russian music in Belgium, where *Antar* and the *Serbian Fantasy*, among other compositions, were performed in a series of concerts. Notes on these concerts appeared in *Musical Review*, 1885–6, No. 15, pp. 118 ff.

[29] Centre of the famous Russian oil-fields. J. A. J.

ant and interesting. The Volga, the Caucasus, the Black Sea, the Crimea, and many other things worthy of note had left the best impression with us.

During our stay at Zhelyeznovodsk, I did some work on the revision of my Third Symphony; I finished it, however, only partly at Tayitsy; the rest I did after our removal thence to St. Petersburg, the following season.[30]

---

[30] The following dates are on the autograph orchestral score of the Third Symphony: on the first movement, "April 20 [May 2]," on the second movement, "September 28 [October 10], 1886, St. Petersburg. N. R.-Korsakov," on the third movement, "Composed anew at Zhelyeznovodsk and Kislovodsk in June and July 1886. Written and orchestrated in Fayitsy, August 31 [September 12], 1886," on the fourth movement, "August 30 [September 11], 1886, Fayitsy."

Russian Symphony Concerts. Fantasy for the violin. Death of Boro-din. Balakirev's circle and Byelayev's compared. Orchestrating Prince Igor. *Composition of* Capriccio *and its performance.* Sche-herazada. Easter Overture.

THE PLAN OF Russian Symphony Concerts was carried out during the season of 1886–7. Four concerts were given by M. P. Byelayev at Kononov's Hall on October 15, 22, and 29 and November 5.[1] The first and the third of these were conducted by me, the second and the fourth were led by G. O. Dütsch. The attendance, though not over-large, was fair, and the concerts were a success morally if not materially. Among other numbers I did particularly well with Borodin's Symphony in E-flat major, with which I took especial pains on this occasion, having first noted down numerous fine nuances in the orchestral parts. The composer, as I remember, was delighted.

The orchestration of *A Night on Bald Mountain,* which had baf-fled me so long, was finished for the concerts of this season, and the piece, given by me at the first concert in a manner that could not be improved upon, was demanded again and again with una-nimity. Only a tomtom had to be substituted for the bell; the one

---

[1] For the programs of these and subsequent seasons, cf. *Programs of the Russian Symphony Concerts for Fifteen Years* (*1885–1900*) (St. Petersburg, 1900).

I selected at the bell-store proved to be off pitch in the hall, owing to a change in temperature.

Having finished the revision of my Third Symphony and having grown interested in violin technique (I had gained a rather thorough familiarity with it in the instrumental class), I conceived the idea of composing some virtuoso piece for the violin with orchestra. Taking two Russian themes as a basis, I composed a Fantasy on these and dedicated it to P. A. Krasnokootsky, violin instructor at the Chapel, to whom I was indebted for many explanations in the field of violin technique. This Fantasy I tried out with my orchestra of Chapel pupils, who had made considerable progress by that time. I was pleased with the piece, and took it into my head to write another virtuoso piece for violin and orchestra on Spanish themes. However, having made a sketch of it, I gave up the idea, preferring as I did to compose, subsequently, an orchestral piece with virtuoso instrumentation, on the same themes. Mention must also be made of the joint composition of a quartet on the theme of B — la — f (B-A-F)[2] for M. P. Byelayev's birthday, which was celebrated at a gathering of numerous friends, and accompanied with gigantic dining and wining on an equally heroic scale. As is well known, the first movement of this quartet belongs to my pen, the Serenade to Borodin, the Scherzo to Lyadov, and the Finale to Glazunov. The quartet was performed before the dinner, and the hero of the occasion was thoroughly delighted with the surprise we had given him.

Early in the morning, at an unaccustomed hour, on February 16 [28], 1887, I was astonished by a visit from V. V. Stassov at our house. V. V. was beside himself. "Do you know," he said with agitation, "Borodin is dead." Borodin had died late the evening before, suddenly, instantaneously. Gay and animated, among guests gathered at his house, he had fallen dead instantly, in the very act of talking to someone. Yekaterina Sergeyevna was at Moscow that winter. I shall not say what a blow this death was to me and all his other intimates. Immediately the question came up:

---

[2] Be-la-ef = Byelayev. J. A. J.

what was to be done with the unfinished opera *Prince Igor* and his other unpublished and unfinished compositions? Together with Stassov I forthwith went to his apartment and carried all his musical manuscripts to my house.

After Aleksandr Porfiryevich had been buried at the cemetery of the Nevski Monastery, Glazunov and I together sorted all the manuscripts. We decided to finish, orchestrate and set in order all that had been left behind by A. P., as well as prepare it for publication, on which M. P. Byelayev had resolved. In the first place there was the unfinished *Prince Igor*. Certain numbers of the opera, such as the first chorus, the dance of the Polovtsy, Yaroslavna's Lament, the recitative and song of Vladimir Galitsky, Konchak's aria, the arias of Konchakovna and Prince Vladimir Igorevich, as well as the closing chorus, had been finished and orchestrated by the composer. Much else existed in the form of finished piano sketches; all the rest was in fragmentary rough draft only, while a good deal simply did not exist. For Acts II and III (in the camp of the Polovtsy) there was no adequate libretto — no scenario, even — there were only scattered verses and musical sketches, or finished numbers that showed no connection between them. The synopsis of these acts I knew full well from talks and discussions with Borodin, although in his projects he had been changing a great deal, striking things out and putting them back again. The smallest bulk of composed music proved to be in Act III. Glazunov and I settled the matter as follows between us: he was to fill in all the gaps in Act III and write down from memory the Overture played so often by the composer, while I was to orchestrate, finish composing, and systematize all the rest that had been left unfinished and unorchestrated by Borodin. Communicating to each other our intentions and taking counsel together about all details, Glazunov and I went at our task at the beginning of spring. Among Borodin's other works, the two movements of the unfinished symphony held the place of honour. For the first movement there existed an unrecorded exposition of the themes, which Glazunov remembered by heart. For the second movement there had been projected a recorded ¾ Scherzo for the string quartet, without trio; for this latter the composer had intended to use material that had not gone into the opera — the narrative of the merchants.

Of the concerts of the season of 1886–7 let me mention one given under Balakirev's direction, by the Free Music School, in memory of Franz Liszt, who had died in the summer of 1886.[3] As I have already said, Balakirev's conducting fell far short of weaving about us that potent spell which we had felt in old days. Who had changed, who had advanced — Balakirev or we? We, I suppose. We had grown, had learned, had been educated, had seen, and had heard; Balakirev, on the other hand, had stood stock-still, if, indeed, he had not slid back a trifle.

But who were we in the eighties? In the sixties and the seventies we were Balakirev's circle, at first under his absolute leadership, later little by little casting off the yoke of his absolutism and gaining greater independence in the persons of our individual members. This circle, which had been ironically nicknamed the "mighty *koochka* (coterie)," had consisted of Balakirev, Cui, Borodin, Moussorgsky, myself, and later Anatoli Lyadov and, to a certain extent, Lodyzhensky. The circle's member in perpetuity, V. V. Stassov, as one who was not a musician by specialty, I place in a class by himself. *Our* circle of the eighties, especially beginning with the latter half of that decade, was no longer Balakirev's circle, but Byelayev's. The former had centred in Balakirev as its senior member and their teacher; the latter grouped around Byelayev as its Mæcenas, publisher, impresario, and host. Moussorgsky was no longer among the living, and in 1887 Borodin, too, followed him. Having received an appointment to Slavic lands, in the service of the Department of Foreign Affairs, Lodyzhensky had vanished, completely forsaking all musical study. Cui, though keeping up cordial relations with Byelayev's circle, held aloof, nevertheless, and by himself, gravitating more towards foreign (Parisian and Belgian) music folk, with the aid of the Countess Mercy d'Argenteau.[4] But Balakirev, as the former head of his scattered circle, ad-

---

[3] This concert was given on November 22 [December 4] at the Hall of the Club of the Nobility.

[4] In 1882 the Countess Mercy d'Argenteau, a music-lover living in Belgium, re-

mitted no intercourse whatever with Byelayev's circle, which he apparently held in scorn. As for his relations with Byelayev personally, they were more than cool, owing to the latter's unwillingness to subsidize the concerts of the Free Music School, as well as owing to certain misunderstandings in the publishing field. Balakirev's attitude towards Byelayev soon began to turn to open enmity towards Byelayev himself, to the whole circle, and to all its affairs; beginning with the nineties, all intercourse between Byelayev's circle and Balakirev was broken off. Balakirev was joined for good and all by S. M. Lyapoonov who had fallen completely under his sway. The relations between Balakirev and Cui also became rather strained, but with me Balakirev was somewhat more intimate, owing to our joint duties in the Chapel. So then the " mighty *koochka* " had gone to pieces irrevocably. The connecting links between the former circle of Balakirev and the newly formed circle of Byelayev were Borodin, Lyadov, and I; and, after Borodin's death, Lyadov and I alone. Glazunov cannot be counted a connecting link, since his appearance in the field coincides with the time of the mighty coterie's dissolution.

Beginning with the latter half of the eighties, *we,* or Byelayev's circle, consisted of Glazunov, Lyadov, Dütsch, Fyeliks Blumenfeld, his brother Sigizmund (a talented singer, accompanist, and composer of songs), and myself. Later, as they graduated from the Conservatory, there appeared N. A. Sokolov, Antipov, Wihtol, and others, of whom I shall speak in due course. The venerable V. V. Stassov always preserved the same cordial and close relations with

---

ceived from a friend a copy of some dances by Napravnik. She was interested enough to ask her friend to write Napravnik for more information in regard to his own music, and the music of the important modern Russian composers. Napravnik, entirely academic in his tastes, sent her the required particulars in regard to himself, and added that, outside of Tchaikovsky, he knew of no other Russian composers of outstanding merit. The Countess, after examining the works received, decided that Napravnik's works were " conductor's music " and that the music of Tchaikovsky left her " cold." The following year her friend sent her compositions by Borodin and Cui. Especially liking Cui's piece, she wrote to the composer and received in return his pamphlet, *Music in Russia.* This pamphlet gave a full chronicle of the work of the Five, and the Countess lost no time in procuring all the available compositions of the Band. The early knowledge of the Modern Russian school in Belgium was due to her enthusiasm. Through her intervention, *The Prisoner of the Caucasus* was produced at Liége in 1886, and Cui was invited to superintend the production. C. V. V.

the new circle as well, but his influence in it was no longer the same as in Balakirev's.

Can Byelayev's circle be looked upon as a continuation of Balakirev's? Was there a certain modicum of similarity between one and the other and what constituted the difference, apart from the change in personnel in the course of time? The similarity, indicating that Byelayev's circle was a continuation of Balakirev's circle (in addition to the connecting links), consisted in the advanced ideas, the progressivism, common to the two of them. But Balakirev's circle corresponded to the period of storm and stress in the evolution of Russian music; Byelayev's circle represented the period of calm, onward march. Balakirev's circle was revolutionary, Byelayev's, on the other hand, was progressive. If we leave out of account Lodyzhensky, who had accomplished nothing, and Lyadov, who had appeared later, Balakirev's circle consisted of Balakirev, Cui, Moussorgsky, Borodin, and me (the French have retained the denomination of "*les cinq*" for us to this day). Byelayev's circle was numerous and grew more so in the course of time. All the five members of Balakirev's circle were subsequently recognized as prominent representatives of Russian musical creative art. The other circle was variegated in make-up: it contained prominent composers of talent, and men of lesser gifts, and men who were not composers at all, but conductors, like Dütsch, for instance, or solo performers, like N. S. Lavrov. Balakirev's circle consisted of musicians of feeble technique, amateurs almost, who were pioneering by sheer force of their creative talents, force that occasionally served them in lieu of technique and occasionally (as frequently with Moussorgsky) was insufficient to conceal its shortcomings. Byelayev's circle, on the contrary, consisted of composers and musicians technically trained and educated. The origin of music that interested it was traced by Balakirev's circle no further back than to Beethoven; Byelayev's circle respected not only its musical fathers, but its grandfathers and great-grandfathers as well, going back as far as Palestrina. Balakirev's circle recognized well-nigh exclusively the orchestra, the piano, the chorus, and vocal solos with orchestra, ignoring chamber music, vocal ensembles (excepting the

M. P. BYELAYEV

from the painting by I. Y. Ryepin

operatic duet), the chorus *a capella,* and the solo for bowed instruments; Byelayev's circle had a broader outlook on these forms. Balakirev's circle was exclusive and intolerant; Byelayev's was more indulgent and eclectic. Balakirev's circle did not want to study, but broke paths forward, relying upon its powers, succeeding therein and learning; Byelayev's circle studied, attaching as it did great importance to technical perfection, but it also broke new paths, though more securely, even if less speedily. Balakirev's circle hated Wagner and strained to take no notice of him; those in Byelayev's circle had their eyes and ears open with eagerness to learn and respect. The relations of the one circle to its head were those of pupils to a teacher and elder brother, relations that had grown weaker as each of the lesser ones grew older, as I have pointed out more than once. Byelayev, on the other hand, was not the head, but rather the centre of his circle. How could Byelayev become such a centre and wherein lay his force of attraction? Byelayev was a wealthy man of commerce, with a number of personal crotchets, but withal an honest, kind man, frank to the point of brusqueness, occasionally straightforward to the verge of rudeness, yet with a heart that possessed tender strings undoubtedly; a cordial host and hospitable man. But his force of attraction did not lie in his broad cordiality nor the opportunities of feeding at his table. It lay (aside from the sympathetic spiritual qualities of his nature) in his unlimited love for music and his devotion to it. Having conceived an interest in the Russian school through his acquaintance with Glazunov's gifts, he gave himself up completely to the fostering and advancement of that school. He was a Mæcenas; but he was no gentleman-Mæcenas to squander money on art to suit his whims while really advancing it nowhere. To be sure, had he not been wealthy, he would have been unable to do for art what he did do; but in this regard he planted himself on noble, firm soil. He became a concert impresario and publisher of Russian music without counting on any personal benefit; on the contrary, he gave to the cause enormous sums of money, concealing his name moreover to the utmost of his ability. The Russian Symphony Concerts he founded proved subsequently an institution with a life assured for ever, while the publishing house *Belaieff, Leipzig* became one of the honoured and best-known European firms, likewise secured for all time.

Accordingly, Byelayev drew people to him by his personality, his devotion to art, and his wealth, not *per se,* but as a means he applied towards a sublime and disinterested object; and this made him the centre of attraction of the new circle of musicians, who had only a certain hereditary connection with the quondam " mighty *koochka.*"

By force of matters purely musical I turned out to be head of the Byelayev circle. As the head Byelayev, too, considered me, consulting me about everything and referring everybody to me as chief. I was considerably older than the other members of the circle (but some eight years younger than Byelayev); I was the general teacher of the members of the circle, the majority of whom had graduated from the Conservatory under my guidance or had at least received some measure of instruction from me. Glazunov had not studied much under me and soon came into the relation of younger friend. Lyadov, Dütsch, Sokolov, Wihtol, and others became my pupils in instrumentation and free composition, after having been pupils of Y. I. Johansen up to fugue inclusive. Somewhat later I began to guide my pupils from harmony on; accordingly, men like Cherepnin, Zolotaryov, and others were my pupils entirely. In the early days after the formation of Byelayev's circle and at the beginning of his activity as a free lance, every young composer of the circle usually first showed me his new composition and availed himself of my criticism and my advice. Being devoid of Balakirev's exclusiveness and despotism, or perhaps being merely more " omnivorous," I strove to make my influence on them felt less and less as they gained more and more independence in creative work, and I rejoiced at all self-reliance developing in my former pupils. In the nineties Glazunov and Lyadov began to share the leadership with me; upon M. P.'s death, in accordance with his last will and testament, they formed with me a board of trustees to manage the publishing business, the concerts, etc. But I shall speak of that in the proper place when I relate (in the orderly course of connected reminiscence) the details of the mutual relations of the circle's members to each other and to Byelayev.

For several years the Russian Musical Society's concerts had been passing from Rubinstein's hands to visiting conductors (Hans von Bülow, for one) and then back to Rubinstein. A certain shakiness and instability made themselves felt. Once, at the end of the season, Rubinstein called me to his office and proposed that I conduct the concerts of the Russian Musical Society the following season. I meant to think the proposal over, and even jotted down a program in the rough; but there the matter rested. Somehow, Rubinstein suppressed this question, nor did he raise it the next season; probably he did not like my program or else was in general reluctant to rely on my powers. Of course, I never mentioned it to him again.

For the summer of 1887 we rented a villa on the bank of Lake Nyelay, at the Nikol'skoye estate, in the Looga canton. Throughout the summer I worked assiduously on the orchestration of *Prince Igor* and managed to accomplish a great deal. In the middle of the summer this work was interrupted: I composed the *Spanish Capriccio* from the sketches of my projected virtuoso violin fantasy on Spanish themes.[5] According to my plans the *Capriccio* was to glitter with dazzling orchestra colour and, manifestly, I had not been wrong. The work of orchestrating *Prince Igor* also came easily, without strain, and was evidently a success.

That summer there was a total eclipse of the sun, as if purposely coincident with my work on *Igor*, wherein the Prologue depicts a solar eclipse as an evil omen to Prince Igor, who is starting out on an expedition against the Polovtsy. At Nikol'skoye the eclipse did not produce the right impression, as the sky was overcast, and the eclipse occurred early in the morning (soon after sunrise). Our nurse, Avdotya, even went so far as to deny the very fact of eclipse, considering it a gloom due to the frowning cloudy sky.[6]

---

[5] At the end of the autograph orchestral score there is a date: "July 23 [August 4], 1887, Nikol'skoye."

[6] To the first half of the year 1887 belongs the idea of a *Ukranian Fantasy* on folk-themes. The pencil recording of various materials which has been preserved in sketch form bears the date: "January 29 [February 10]," and the fragment of the orchestral score (fourteen pages): "July 28 [August 9], 1887."

Visiting Peterhof from time to time in connection with my official duties and usually staying overnight at the Glazunovs', who had a summer home there, I had talks with Aleksandr Konstantinovich, and the two of us together pondered and discussed our work on *Prince Igor*. During the season of 1887–8 this work continued. To the task of orchestration was now added the need of a vocal score exactly agreeing with the orchestral score. This work was undertaken by Glazunov, Dütsch, my wife, the two Blumenfelds, and myself. The orchestral score and the piano score were being prepared for publication, which M. P. Byelayev had undertaken. Soon printing began, and proof-reading became the order of the day.

The new quarters of the Court Chapel were now ready, and, quitting its temporary abode in Millionnaya Street, the Chapel had a house-warming.

This time, for M. P.'s birthday, Glazunov, Lyadov, and I composed a quartet suite, *Imyeniny* (*Birthday*), in three movements, of which the third, *Khorovod*, was from my pen.

The Russian Symphony Concerts (five in number) of this season were given at the Small Theatre.[7] Owing to G. O. Dütsch's illness, I conducted all of them. The first concert was given in memoriam of Borodin and consisted of his compositions; among these there was performed for the first time the March of the Polovtsy from *Prince Igor;* I had orchestrated it in the summer, and it proved effective in the extreme. [After the performance of this number I was presented with a large laurel wreath bearing the inscription: " In the name of Borodin." This same concert also saw the premières of the Overture to *Prince Igor* and of the two movements of the unfinished Symphony in A minor.] [8]

At one of the subsequent concerts my *Spanish Capriccio* was played.[9] At the first rehearsal the first movement (A major, in ¾)

---

[7] On Saturdays, October 24 and 31, November 7 and 21, and December 5 [November 5, 12, 19, and December 3 and 17], 1887.

[8] The words enclosed in brackets are not in the manuscript. Instead, in the margin there is a note in Rimsky-Korsakov's handwriting: ". . . to add details," and several blank lines are left.

[9] At the fifth concert.

had hardly been finished when the whole orchestra began to applaud. Similar applause followed all the other parts wherever the pauses permitted. I asked the orchestra for the privilege of dedicating the composition to them. General delight was the answer. The *Capriccio* went without difficulties and sounded brilliant. At the concert itself it was played with a perfection and enthusiasm the like of which it never possessed subsequently, even when led by Nikisch himself. Despite its length the composition called forth an insistent encore. The opinion formed by both critics and the public, that the *Capriccio* is a *magnificently orchestrated piece,* is wrong. The *Capriccio* is a brilliant *composition for the orchestra.* The change of timbres, the felicitous choice of melodic designs and figuration patterns, exactly suiting each kind of instrument, brief virtuoso cadenzas for instruments solo, the rhythm of the percussion instruments, and so on, constitute here the very *essence* of the composition and not its garb or orchestration. The Spanish themes, of dance character, furnished me with rich material for putting in use multiform orchestral effects. All in all, the *Capriccio* is undoubtedly a purely external piece, but vividly brilliant for all that. I was a little less successful in its third section (Alborada, in B-flat major), where the brasses somewhat drown the melodic designs of the wood-winds; but this is very easy to remedy, if the conductor will pay attention to it and moderate the indications of the shades of force in the brass instruments by replacing the fortissimo with a simple forte.

In the Russian Symphony Concerts of this season, besides my *Capriccio* there was also played my Fantasy for violin (Krasnokootsky) and the Andante from Borodin's Quartet, which I arranged for violin solo with orchestral accompaniment.[10] The Andante attracted no attention on the part of either audience or violinists, and quite undeservedly, in my opinion.

In the middle of the winter, engrossed as I was in my work on *Prince Igor* and other things, I conceived the idea of writing an orchestral composition on the subject of certain episodes from *Scheherazada,* as well as an overture on the themes of the *obi-*

---

[10] Together with the *Spanish Capriccio* at the fifth concert.

khod.[11] With these intentions and suitable music sketches I moved with my entire family, early in the summer, to the estate of Glinki-Mavriny, Nyezhgovitsy, some twelve miles beyond Looga, on the Cheryemenyetskoye Lake. In January a daughter, Masha, was born to us.[12]

During the summer of 1888, at Nyezhgovitsy, I finished *Scheherazada* (in four movements) and *The Bright Holiday*,[13] an *Easter Overture* on themes of the *obikhod*.[14] In addition, I wrote for violin and a small orchestra a mazurka on the Polish themes sung by my mother and heard in the thirties and remembered by her from the time when her father was Governor of Volhynia. These themes were familiar to me from infancy, and the idea of basing some composition on them had long interested me.[15]

The program I had been guided by in composing *Scheherazada* consisted of separate, unconnected episodes and pictures from *The Arabian Nights*, scattered through all four movements of my suite: the sea and Sindbad's ship, the fantastic narrative of the Prince Kalender, the Prince and the Princess, the Bagdad festival, and the ship dashing against the rock with the bronze rider upon it. The unifying thread consisted of the brief introductions to the first, second, and fourth movements and the intermezzo in movement three, written for violin solo and delineating Scheherazada herself as telling her wondrous tales to the stern Sultan. The final conclusion of movement four serves the same artistic purpose. In vain do people seek in my suite leading motives linked unbrokenly with

---

[11] *Obikhod* of church singing is a collection of the most important and most frequently used canticles of the Orthodox Church. The *obikhod* was the first printed music in Russia (Moscow, 1772). J. A. J.

[12] Written in Riva, June 30 [July 13], 1906.

[13] The popular Russian name for Easter. J. A. J.

[14] On the autograph orchestral score of *Scheherazada* there are the following dates at the ends of movements: on Movement I: "July 4 [16], 1888, Nyezhgovitsy"; on Movement II: "July 11 [23], 1888, Nyezhgovitsy"; on Movement III: "July 16 [28], 1888, Nyezhgovitsy"; on Movement IV: "July 26 [August 7], 1888, Nyezhgovitsy."

The *chronométrage* (playing-time) of the movements was computed by the composer as follows: $8 + (1) + 10 + (1) + 8 + (1) + 10 = 39$ minutes.

On the *Easter Overture* there is the date: "Commenced July 25 [August 6], completed March 20 [April 1], 1888."

[15] This piece remained unpublished and the musical material it contained was subsequently used for the opera *Pan Voyevoda*. Cf. "1899–1901."

ever the same poetic ideas and conceptions. On the contrary, in the majority of cases, all these seeming *Leitmotive* are nothing but purely musical material or the given motives for symphonic development. These given motives thread and spread over all the movements of the suite, alternating and intertwining each with the others. Appearing as they do each time under different illumination, depicting each time different traits, and expressing different moods, the same given motives and themes correspond each time to different images, actions, and pictures. Thus, for instance, the sharply outlined fanfare motive of the muted trombone and trumpet, which first appears in the Kalender's Narrative (second movement), appears afresh in Movement IV in the delineation of the wrecking ship, though this episode has no connection with the Kalender's Narrative. The principal theme of the Kalender's Narrative (B-minor, ¾) and the theme of the Princess in the third movement (B-flat major, ⅝, clarinetto) in altered guise and quick tempo appear as the secondary themes of the Bagdad festival; yet nothing is said in *The Arabian Nights* about these persons taking part in the festivities. The unison phrase, as though depicting Scheherazada's stern spouse, at the beginning of the suite appears as a datum, in the Kalender's Narrative, where there cannot, however, be any mention of Sultan Shakhriar. In this manner, developing quite freely the musical data taken as a basis of the composition, I had in view the creation of an orchestral suite in four movements, closely knit by the community of its themes and motives, yet presenting, as it were, a kaleidoscope of fairy-tale images and designs of Oriental character — a method that I had to a certain degree made use of in my *Skazka* (*Fairy-tale*), the musical data of which are as little distinguishable from the poetic as they are in *Scheherazada*. Originally I had even intended to label Movement I of *Scheherazada* Prelude; II, Ballade; III, Adagio; and IV, Finale; but on the advice of Lyadov and others I had not done so. My aversion for seeking too definite a program in my composition led me subsequently (in the new edition) to do away with even those hints of it which had lain in the headings of each movement, like The Sea; Sindbad's Ship; The Kalender's Narrative; and so forth.

In composing *Scheherazada* I meant these hints to direct but slightly the hearer's fancy on the path which my own fancy had travelled, and to leave more minute and particular conceptions to the will and mood of each.[16] All I had desired was that the hearer, if he liked my piece as *symphonic music,* should carry away the impression that it is beyond doubt an Oriental narrative of some numerous and varied fairy-tale wonders and not merely four pieces played one after the other and composed on the basis of themes common to all the four movements. Why then, if that be so, does my suite bear the name, precisely, of *Scheherazada?* Because this name and the title *The Arabian Nights* connote in everybody's mind the East and fairy-tale wonders; besides, certain details of the musical exposition hint at the fact that all of these are various tales of some one person (who happens to be Scheherazada) entertaining therewith her stern husband.

The rather lengthy, slow introduction of the *Easter Sunday Overture* on the theme of " Let God Arise! " alternating with the ecclesiastical theme " An angel wailed," appeared to me, in its beginning, as it were, the ancient Isaiah's prophecy concerning the resurrection of Christ. The gloomy colours of the *Andante lugubre* seemed to depict the holy sepulchre that had shone with ineffable light at the moment of the resurrection — in the transition to the Allegro of the Overture. The beginning of the Allegro, " Let them also that hate Him flee before Him," led to the holiday mood of the Greek Orthodox Church service on Christ's matins; the solemn trumpet voice of the Archangel was replaced by a tonal reproduction of the joyous, almost dance-like bell-tolling, alternating now with the sexton's rapid reading and now with the conventional chant of the priest's reading the glad tidings of the Evangel. The *obikhod* theme, " Christ is arisen," which forms a sort of subsidiary part of the Overture, appeared amid the trumpet-blasts and the bell-tolling, constituting also a triumphant coda. In this Overture were thus

---

[16] On the autograph orchestral score, immediately after the brief program, there was planned the following note, which, however, did not appear in the published copy: " The composer did not cling to an interlineary reproduction of any single fairy-tale, leaving it to the listener to find out by himself the images at which the program hints."

294

combined reminiscences of the ancient prophecy, of the Gospel
narrative, and also a general picture of the Easter service with its
" pagan merry-making." The capering and leaping of the Biblical
King David before the ark, do they not give expression to a mood
of the same order as the mood of the idol-worshippers' dance?
Surely the Russian Orthodox chime is instrumental dance-music of
the church, is it not? And do not the waving beards of the priests
and sextons clad in white vestments and surplices, and intoning
" Beautiful Easter " in the tempo of *Allegro vivo,* etc., transport the
imagination to pagan times? And all these Easter loaves and twists
and the glowing tapers — how far a cry from the philosophic and
socialistic teaching of Christ! [17] This legendary and heathen side of
the holiday, this transition from the gloomy and mysterious evening
of Passion Saturday to the unbridled pagan-religious merry-making
on the morn of Easter Sunday, is what I was eager to reproduce in
my Overture. Accordingly, I requested Count Golyenishchev-Kootoozov to write a program in verse, which he did for me. But I was
not satisfied with his poem, and wrote in prose my own program,
which is appended to the published score. Of course in that program I did not explain my views and my conception of the " Bright
Holiday," leaving it to tones to speak for me. Evidently these tones
do, within certain limits, speak of my feelings and thoughts, for
my Overture raises doubts in the minds of some hearers, despite the
considerable clarity of the music. In any event, in order to appreciate my Overture even ever so slightly, it is necessary that the hearer
should have attended Easter morning service at least once and, at
that, not in a domestic chapel, but in a cathedral thronged with
people from every walk of life, with several priests conducting the

[17] N. A. Sokolov, a fine and gifted story-teller, once described to me afterwards
the following little scene: during Holy Week, on Vladimirskaya Place, a half-drunken
snip of a peasant stopped in front of the bell-tower, where all the bells were rung full
tilt; at first he kept crossing himself, then became pensive, and at last broke out into
dancing to the sound and rhythm of the tolling. Truly a spiritual merriment!

[Although the censor in tsarist Russia allowed Christ's teachings to be labelled
socialistic, the censors of " free Russia " under the Communists have expunged in
the fourth and fifth Russian editions the words: " philosophic and socialistic " in the
text, as well as N. A. Rimsky-Korsakov's footnote (17) in the fifth edition, and the
conclusion of the paragraph, beginning with: " In any event . . ." and ending with
. . . " the Tikhvin Monastery itself." J. A. J.]

cathedral service — something that many intellectual Russian hearers, let alone hearers of other confessions, quite lack nowadays. As for myself, I had gained my impressions in my childhood, passed near the Tikhvin Monastery itself.

The *Capriccio, Scheherazada,* and the *Easter Overture* close this period of my activity, at the end of which my orchestration had reached a considerable degree of virtuosity and bright sonority without Wagner's influence, within the limits of the usual make-up of Glinka's orchestra. These three compositions also show a considerable falling off in the use of contrapuntal devices, which is noticeable after *Snyegoorochka.* The place of the disappearing counterpoint is taken by a strong and virtuoso development of every kind of figuration which sustains the technical interest of my compositions. This trend lasted with me for several years longer; but in the orchestration, after the works referred to, there is noticeable a change which I shall speak of in my further narrative.

Production of Der Ring des Nibelungen. *The* Polonaise *from* Boris Godunov *with new orchestration. Russian Symphony Concerts. Beginning of* Mlada. *Trip to Paris. Completion of the sketch of* Mlada *and its orchestration. Trip to Brussels. Domestic misfortunes. Quarter-of-a-century jubilee. New tendencies in Byelayev's circle. Production of* Prince Igor. *Production of* Mlada *does not take place. Revision of* Maid of Pskov. *Reorchestrating* Sadko. *Acquaintanceship with Yastryebtsev.*

DURING THE SEASON OF 1888–9 the Directorate of Imperial Theatres began to lead us a fine dance with the production of *Prince Igor,* which had been finished, published, and forwarded to the proper authorities. We were led by the nose the following season as well, with constant postponements of production for some reason or other.

In the middle of the season of St. Petersburg's operatic life there occurred a very important event: Neumann, the impresario from Prague, turned up at the Mariinsky Theatre with a German opera company to produce Wagner's *Ring des Nibelungen* under Muck as conductor. All musical St. Peterburg was interested. Glazunov

and I attended the rehearsals, following them score in hand.[1] Muck
— an excellent conductor — rehearsed Wagner's works with great
care. Our orchestra strove with all their hearts and surprised Muck
with their ability in quickly grasping and mastering whatever he
demanded. Wagner's method of orchestration struck Glazunov and
me, and thenceforth Wagner's devices gradually began to form a
part of our orchestral tricks of the trade. The first application of
Wagner's orchestral methods and of an increased orchestra (in the
wind choir) was made in my orchestration of the Polish dance from
Boris Godunov for concert performance. As regards orchestration,
this *Polonaise* was one of the less successful portions of Moussorgsky's opera. The composer had first orchestrated it, for the performance of the Polish scene in 1873, almost exclusively for bowed
instruments. Moussorgsky conceived the unfortunate and wholly
indefensible idea of imitating the " *vingt-quatre violons du roi* " —
that is, the orchestra of the time of the composer Lully (Louis
XIV). What connection there was between this orchestra and the
time of the False Dmitri,[2] as well as the life of Poland of that period,
is incomprehensible. This was one of Moussorgsky's crotchets. The
Polonaise, performed in *Boris Godunov* " *à la vingt-quatre violons
du roi*," produced no effect, and for the following year — that is, for
the performance of the opera in its entirety — the composer recast
the orchestration. Nevertheless, nothing of consequence resulted
from it. Yet in its music the *Polonaise* was characteristic and beautiful; for this reason I undertook to turn it into a concert piece, the
more so as *Boris Godunov* was no longer on the boards. I linger on
this intrinsically lesser opus of mine because I attach importance
to it, as being my first essay in the new field of orchestration that I
entered therewith.

Der Ring des Nibelungen was given in several subscription cycles, but Wagnerism had not yet taken hold with the St. Petersburg
audiences, as it did later, beginning with the close of the nineties.

During the season of 1888–9 the Russian Symphony Concerts,

---

[1] The guest performances by the German company at the Mariinsky Theatre took
place during the period between February 27 [March 11] and March 21 [April 2]
(four cycles of four evenings each).

[2] 1605–6. J. A. J.

under my direction, were transferred to the Club of Nobility; they were six in number.[3] *Scheherazada* and the *Easter Overture* were played with success at the concerts of this season.[4] Glazunov, too, made his bow as conductor of his own compositions. His first essays in this field were by no means brilliant. Slow by nature, maladroit and clumsy of movement, the maestro, speaking slowly and in a low voice, manifestly displayed little ability either for conducting rehearsals or for swaying the orchestra during a concert perform-ance. Nevertheless, the consciousness of the great merits of his compositions induced the orchestra to aid rather than obstruct him. With each fresh appearance, moreover, he made progress and lost constraint at both rehearsals and concerts. Practice and his own great, incomparable musicianship did their part, and in a few years he had developed into an excellent performer of his own as well as of other people's compositions; in this he was helped by the ever growing authority of his name. When making his first appearance as a conductor he was more fortunate than I in this respect. He knew the orchestra and orchestration better than I had known either at the time of my first appearance; besides, I could guide him and give him advice. As long as I had found it inadvisable to allow him to appear as conductor, he made no appearance, Byela-yev's pleas to the contrary notwithstanding. As for myself, nobody had helped or advised me in my time.

The conducting of concerts and the study of *Der Ring des Nibe-lungen* did not allow me to concentrate on composition. In addition to orchestrating the *Polonaise,* I also reorchestrated my *Serbian Fantasy* for the new edition undertaken by Byelayev, who had brought it back from the Yohanson firm.[5] Not contenting himself with newly appearing works, Byelayev bought from the publishers, in addition, as far as possible, the publishing rights to some Russian compositions. Bitner's firm readily surrendered to him my *May Night;* Yohanson, the *Serbian Fantasy* and Moussorgsky's songs.

---

[3] On Saturdays, October 22 [November 3], November 19 [December 1], Decem-ber 3 [15], 17 [29], 1888; January 21 [February 2] and February 4 [16], 1889.

[4] *Scheherazada* in the first, the *Easter Overture* in the third concert.

[5] On January 10 [22], 1889 Rimsky-Korsakov set to work anew on *The Maid of Pskov* (introduction to Act III and Olga's recitative).

Evidently these firms did not charge him much and were glad to get rid of publications that brought them no profits. But with Bessel's firm the case proved different. The author of *Prince Igor* had incautiously given to Bessel's firm two or three numbers from his opera with the French translations by the Countess Mercy d'Argenteau. After the composer's death, when Byelayev had acquired the right to publish the opera and it turned out that the above-mentioned numbers had been published by Bessel's already, Byelayev had to pay Bessel's exactly three thousand rubles in order to buy back these numbers from him, while Bessel's had got them from Borodin possibly for nothing.

On the second anniversary of Borodin's death,[6] V. V. Stassov, Glazunov, Lyadov, Byelayev, my wife, and I gathered in Borodin's former apartment (now occupied by his successor Dianin[7]) in order to spend a few hours together in memory of the dear man and to play various sketches for *Mlada* as well as others that had not found their way into *Prince Igor*, and had not been published or brought into any sort of order. Among these was the finale of *Mlada*, which depicted Morena's exorcism, the inundation, the destruction of the temple, and the apotheosis. I must say in passing that the music of the inundation, composed by Borodin for *Mlada*, had at one time been planned for transfer to the third act of *Prince Igor*. The author had read somewhere that during Igor's flight with Ovloor from the camp of the Polovtsy the Don overflowed its banks and hindered the Polovtsy from pursuing the fugitives. Nevertheless, Borodin gave up this idea, as too minute a detail. On this ground Glazunov and I had made no use of this material in working over the third act. While glancing over the sketch of this finale I decided to orchestrate it, and subsequently did. In the midst of talk and reminiscence of Borodin, Lyadov was suddenly struck with the thought that the subject-matter of *Mlada* was exactly suitable for me. He expressed himself to that effect, and, without much reflection, I replied decisively: " Yes, you are right; I shall set out forthwith to work on this opera-ballet." From that moment my

---

[6] February 15 [27], 1889.
[7] In the chair of chemistry at the Academy of Medicine and Surgery.

thoughts began to dwell on the proposed subject. Gradually, musical ideas came also, and a few days later there was no doubt that I was composing *Mlada*. I made up my mind not to restrict myself in means, but to have in view an increased orchestra like Wagner's in the *Ring*. V. V. Stassov was delighted with my decision and made quite a to-do about it. During the spring the composition began to progress. The missing text was made by myself.

In the summer of 1889 the Paris Universal Exposition took place. Byelayev decided to give there two symphonic concerts of Russian music at the Trocadéro, under my direction. Having got in touch with the proper authorities, he arranged the matter and invited Glazunov, the pianist Lavrov, and me to go with him. Our children were again placed at our summer home in Nyezhgovitsy, under my mother's care, while my wife and I, with Byelayev, Glazunov, and Lavrov, left for Paris, expecting to rejoin our families after the concerts were over and to spend the rest of the summer at Nyezhgovitsy.

The concerts [8] were set for Saturdays, June 22 and 29, new style. Upon our arrival in Paris, rehearsals commenced. The orchestra, which proved to be excellent, the men being amiable and painstaking, had been borrowed from Colonne. Their playing in the concerts was fine; among the chance shortcomings I recall the oboe-player's mistake in the fourth movement of *Antar*. The success was considerable,[9] with plenty of applause, but the attendance was not

---

[8] Cf. Appendix V.

[9] In Alfred Bruneau's *Musiques de Russie* (Bibliothèque-Charpentier, 1903; p. 20) that French composer-critic writes: "I made the acquaintance of Rimsky-Korsakov during the Exposition of 1889, at the Trocadéro, where he gave the first Paris audition of his *Antar*. At this epoch, already distant, the French were only slightly familiar with modern Russian music. *In the Steppes of Central Asia* by Borodin and some other short pieces by Slavic composers had been performed here and there, to be sure, but we were ignorant of the longer works that we are applauding now. M. Rimsky-Korsakov was our initiator. . . . I came away from the concert full of enthusiasm and, as I was just beginning my career as critic, I wrote the following concerning *Antar:* 'It is necessary to place Rimsky-Korsakov's *Antar* outside the rank of symphony. It is an instrumental tale in four parts strongly bound together by themes which combine and interlace with extraordinary ease. The composer, here, possesses not only a brilliant palette to which we owe his melancholy ruins, his leaping gazelle, and his heavy black bird. He also paints, in a searching study, the three great human passions: Vengeance, Power, and Love. All that with an incomparable vigour and originality. It is there that the superiority of music shows itself. These

large, in spite of the Exposition and the enormous throng of visitors. The immediate cause of this is to be sought in our inadequate advertising. Europe is fond of advertising and needs it, whereas Byelayev was an enemy of all publicity-seeking. While advertisements of every kind of institution were being displayed at every street-corner, shouted everywhere, carried on people's backs, printed in newspapers in large type, Byelayev confined himself to modest announcements. His reasoning was as follows: whoever is interested will find out and come, and he who does not find out is *ipso facto* not interested; while those who come because they have nothing else to do are not wanted at all! With such ideas no large attendance was to be expected. Byelayev lost a large sum of money — had expected to do so — but Russian symphonic music was not any the more known, nor had it attracted sufficient attention on the part of Europe and Paris; Byelayev could not have desired it. Back of this immediate cause of the incomplete success of the concerts, due to lack of advertising, there lay another radical reason: the insufficient importance of Russian music in the eyes of foreigners. Audiences are incapable of becoming acquainted with the unfamiliar; they welcome only what is known, familiar, and fashionable — that is, again, what is known. Art is released from this magic circle by two things: tempting advertisements and popular artists. Neither of these two things was on hand this time. The only practical result of the Russian Symphony Concerts at the Exposition was an invitation to me to come to Brussels the following year, although this was rather the outcropping of the seeds sown there by Countess Mercy d'Argenteau.

In the midst of rehearsals we visited the Exposition. There were also dinners in honour of the Russian musicians at Colonne's house and in the editorial offices of some paper where, after dinner, a loathsome, old, stout operetta diva sang, and my *Capriccio* and Glazunov's *Styeñka Razin* were played four-hands on a grand piano

---

three sentiments, each flowing through measures, tonalities, and various rhythms over which hovers the leading phrase of Antar, are faithful reflections of our tormented, indecisive, and mysterious souls. Sounds alone can render the infinite mobility of thought. M. Rimsky-Korsakov has expressed all these profound nuances of the heart in a language which is eloquent, solid, new, and hardy.' " C. V. V.

by Pugno and Messager. We were also invited for a soirée to the Ministre des Beaux-Arts, where we met, among other guests, Massenet with the singer Sanderson and the ancient Ambroise Thomas. Of the musical acquaintances made in Paris I shall also mention Delibes, Mme Holmès, Bourgault-Ducoudray, Pugno, and Messager. We also made the acquaintance of Michel Delines, subsequently translator of *Onyegin* and of my *Sadko*. With the exception of Delines, all these acquaintanceships proved most superficial. Delibes gave one the impression of a merely amiable gentleman,[10] Massenet of a crafty fox; the composer Mme Holmès was a very décolletée person; Pugno proved an excellent pianist and reader of music; Bourgault-Ducoudray, a serious musician and bright man; Messager was rather colourless. Saint-Saëns was not in Paris. Delines was a kind man, danced attendance upon us, aided us in many things. All the other transient acquaintances — editors, critics, etc. — seemed to me fairly empty babblers. At the Grand Opéra we saw Shakespeare's *Tempest* in Ambroise Thomas's musical setting, and at the Opéra-Comique Massenet's *Esclarmonde* with Miss Sanderson in the title-rôle. The performance was excellent. In the orchestra of the Opéra-Comique we recognized musicians from Colonne's orchestra, who had played in the Russian Symphony Concerts. The building of the Paris Conservatoire and its library we also went to see.

Of my musical impressions of Paris I shall mention the music in the Hungarian and Algerian cafés at the Exposition. The virtuoso-playing on the *tsevnitsa* (Pan's pipe) gave me the idea of introducing this ancient instrument in *Mlada* during the scene of the dance before the Queen Cleopatra. At the Algerian café, in the dance of a little girl with a dagger, I was captivated by the sudden blows struck by a Negro on the large drum at the dancer's approach. This effect, too, I borrowed for the Cleopatra scene.[11]

Having done with the concerts, my wife and I parted with our

---

[10] This is an allusion to the two characters in Gogol's *Revizor;* under the dramatis personæ they are denoted as: " A lady pleasant in every respect " and " a merely pleasant lady." J. A. J.

[11] This music was employed for the entrance and unveiling of the Queen in the Russian Ballet, *Cléopâtre.* C. V. V.

friends (who stayed on in Paris) and left for Russia via Vienna, making brief visits at Lucerne and Zürich and going to see Salzburg with Mozart's house, and the salt mines at Salzkammergut and Königsee. Early in July we were already back at Nyezhgovitsy. I immediately set to work on *Mlada*. The final impulse was given by the idea of introducing on the stage, in the scene of Cleopatra's dances, an orchestra consisting of Pan's pipes, lyres glissando, a large drum, small clarinets, etc. The outline of *Mlada* grew by the hour, not by the day, and was finished by September.[12] To be sure, the musical material had been maturing in my head since spring, yet the recording of it all in proper sequence and the working out of details and of the scheme of modulations were done this time particularly fast. The contributing factors were, in the first place, too great laconism of the text (in contrast with Wagner), which I had been unable to develop, so that its dramatic part proved rather weak; in the second place, the Wagnerian system of leading motives had considerably accelerated composing; in the third place, notable absence of contrapuntal writing also helped to speed the work. But to make up for it, my orchestral intentions were novel and ambitious à la Wagner; there was in store for me enormous labour on the orchestral score and it consumed a whole year of my time.

In September we moved to governmental quarters at the Court Chapel.[13] At the house-warming I had to treat V. V. Stassov to *yellow tea*, as many years before that he had predicted that he would drink yellow tea in my home at the Court Chapel. On what he had based his prediction I don't know, but here I really found myself at the Chapel, and yellow tea had to be brewed.[14]

---

[12] From a letter of August 31 [September 12], 1889 to S. N. Krooglikov: " On February 15 [27] Lyadov suggested to me the idea of composing *Mlada*, and on August 15 [27], I wrote the last little note of the rough draft; i.e., it all took exactly six months, and from this must be excluded the month and a half of examination time, one month for the trip abroad, and the two weeks of arranging *Scheherazada* for four hands." For detailed data on the composing of *Mlada* in the order of individual numbers and their chronological sequence, cf. V. V. *Yastryebtsev's Reminiscences*, Part II, pp. 222 ff.

[13] Bol'shaya Konyushennaya St., II, Apt. 66. At present the numbers of the apartments in this house have been changed.

[14] Between October 17 [29] and 22 [November 3], 1889 Rimsky-Korsakov was

The Russian Symphony Concerts of this season were given again at the Hall of the Club of the Nobility,[15] under my direction, Glazunov conducting his own compositions. It had been and became thereafter a custom to give invariably at least one composition by Glazunov at each Russian Symphony concert. The productive author gave no occasion for breaking this rule, and the public began to grow more and more accustomed to his name and appreciative of his talent. Yet his name did not draw audiences, just as the Russian Symphony Concerts' reputation, which began to gain a solid footing, did not add to the number of followers of the " young Russian school," as the circle of composers centring in Byelayev began to be called at that time.

I began the orchestration of *Mlada* with Act III of the opera. When this act was finished, I placed it on the program of the Russian Symphony Concerts and it was performed with Lodi as Yaromir and the opera chorus taking part in the performance.[16] The Pan's pipes were played by the musicians of the Finnish Regiment, the small clarinets by Afanasyev and Novikov, pupils of the Court Chapel and, later, artists of the Court Orchestra. The pipes of Pan had been made to my order; their glissando caused no slight wonder among the auditors. All in all, my orchestral contrivances hit the mark, and the successions of the fantastic colouring of the afterworld, of the flight of shadows and of Mlada's appearance, of the hellishly ominous appearance of Chernobog, of Cleopatra's Oriental bacchanal, and of day awakening with the birds produced

---

in Moscow, where he conducted a symphony concert of the Russian Musical Society on October 21 [November 2] at the Club of the Nobility.

[15] On Saturdays, October 22 [November 3], November 11 [23] and 25 [December 7], December 10 [22], 1889; January 20 [February 1] and February 18 [March 2], 1890.

[This list is a jumble: November 3, December 22, and March 2 were Sundays; November 23, December 7, and February 1 were Saturdays. J. A. J.]

[16] On the autograph orchestral score of *Mlada* there are the following dates: Introduction, " October 10 [22], 1889." Act I, " Commenced *cherveñ* = July 28 [August 9]; completed *syerpeñ* = August 9 [21], 1890, Nyezhgovitsy." Act II, " Finished June 24 [July 6], 1890, Nyezhgovitsy." Act III, " Nyezhgovitsy, July 20 [August 1], 1890." Act IV, " Opera completed *syerpeñ* = August 31 [September 12], 1890."

The third act of *Mlada* was performed for the first time on February 16 [28], 1891, at the sixth Russian Symphony concert.

a deep impression. I was pleased with the new current that had flowed into my orchestration. As for performance, my contrivances offered no difficulties. Work on the orchestral score of *Mlada* ran smoothly, though the Conservatory, the Court Chapel and the Russian Symphony Concerts took up rather a large amount of my time.

During Lent I received an invitation to come to Brussels to conduct two concerts of Russian music. I accepted the offer and left at the end of Lent. It turned out that my invitation to Brussels had been occasioned by the refusal on the part of Joseph Dupont, the permanent conductor of the symphony concerts at Brussels, to lead during that season, owing to some unpleasantness with the directors. It had been decided to invite foreigners. Besides me, the invitation had been extended also to Edvard Grieg, Hans Richter, I believe, and someone else. I met with a kindly reception in Brussels. Joseph Dupont, who had not completely withdrawn·from the concerts, but had merely refused to direct them, gave me every possible assistance. I met all the prominent musicians of Belgium: Gevaert, Edgar Tinel, Huberti, Radoux, and others. They invited me everywhere, they dined and they wined me in cabarets. There were two concerts [17] with six rehearsals apiece, including the general rehearsal to which the public was admitted. Among other pieces the following were performed: Borodin's First Symphony; *Antar; Capriccio Espagnol;* Introduction and Entr'actes from Cui's *Le Flibustier;* Glazunov's *Poème Lyrique;* the Overture to *Ruslan and Lyudmila;* Balakirev's *Russian Overture; A Night on Bald Mountain.* The rehearsals took place at the hall, the concerts at the Théâtre de la Monnaie. The houses were full, and the success was pronounced. I was presented with a wreath. The concerts attracted Belgian musicians from other cities — Liége, Malignes, etc. In Brussels I had the good fortune to hear *Der fliegende Holländer,*

---

[17] There were not two concerts, but only one — on Sunday, April 13 [25], 1890. At this concert all the Russian works enumerated later, except *Antar* and the Overture to *Ruslan and Lyudmila,* were played, and, furthermore, Rimsky-Korsakov's *Easter Overture.* Rimsky-Korsakov speaks of two concerts, because in addition to the concert proper (Sunday matinee, April 13 [25]) there was a dress rehearsal attended by the public on the day before, Saturday, April 12 [24]. The extraordinary number of rehearsals (six) was in keeping with the vast scale of the program.

to see the Conservatoire museum, to hear Gevaert play the spinets and clavecins, and also to become acquainted with the oboe d'amore. The Belgians parted friends with me.

On returning to St. Petersburg I found my wife ill with a dangerous inflammation of the throat. Soon my son Andrey also fell ill. Spring passed in worry and dread.[18] For the summer we moved to Nyezhgovitsy again. In the winter our family gained one more member: in December 1889 a son, Slavchik, was born to us. My mother (eighty-seven years old) felt exceedingly feeble, yet expressed a desire to live with us, and I brought her to the summer home.

Incidentally, before the summer I had managed to orchestrate the finale of Borodin's *Mlada* for publication, and during the entire summer I was engaged in orchestrating my own *Mlada,* which I intended to finish in the fall.[19] Work on it progressed.

In August my mother had to be removed to St. Petersburg, that we might call in medical aid for her. However, in spite of all measures we could take, she rapidly sank and soon died, because of mere old age.[20] After burying her at the Smolyenskoye cemetery, we spent the remaining days at Nyezhgovitsy and then removed to St. Petersburg. Bad luck pursued the family: in December [1890] little Slavchik fell ill and died, and later Masha, too, was taken ill.

December 19 [31],[21] 1890, marked twenty-five years of my activity as composer (since the production of my First Symphony). My friends decided to celebrate my jubilee. Byelayev got up a con-

---

[18] The moods of this period may be judged from a letter of May 9–10 [21–2], 1890, to S. N. Krooglikov: "In the apartment everything is topsyturvy, the children scattered in various homes; everything must be collected and made ready in order that as soon as possible — nay, these very days — they may be shipped to the country, while they are still whole and well. . . . This year has been extremely unfortunate for me: I am never out of dangers and squabbles, and all this toppled on my unfortunate *Mlada,* which probably will be my last composition . . . (at least of consequence). . . ."

[19] From a letter of September 3 [15], 1890 to S. N. Krooglikov: "The other day I completely finished the orchestral score of *Mlada.* Tomorrow or the day after tomorrow the fourth act shall leave for Röder's in Leipzig. . . ."

[20] Sofya Vasilyevna Rimskaya-Korsakova died August 31 [September 12], 1890, at the age of eighty-eight.

[21] In the manuscript, December 20, 1890 [January 1, 1891].

cert of my works at the Hall of the Club of the Nobility, under the direction of Dütsch and Glazunov.[22] The numbers performed were: the First Symphony, *Antar*,[23] the Concerto for the piano (Lavrov), the *Easter Overture*. Songs had also been scheduled (Fride); of them, the song *The Fir Tree and the Palm*, orchestrated by me shortly before that, was published in orchestral score as a surprise to me.[24] Unfortunately, owing to Fride's sudden illness, the songs could not be given. There were also played *Glorifications*, composed by Glazunov and Lyadov for this occasion. One had been written by Glazunov on the Russian theme " *Slava*." The audience was rather large; there were numerous calls for me, presentations, speeches, wreaths, and so forth. They came to my house with congratulations and addresses. I was greeted by the Conservatory with Rubinstein at the head, Balakirev with the Chapel, etc. In answer to all these honours, we gave a dinner at home to our more intimate friends. The guests were many and the dinner was lively and without constraint. The only one who failed to accept our invitation was Balakirev, with whom I had had a falling out over some trifling matter shortly after the jubilee festivities. When I went to invite M. A. to my house, he replied in a hard, cold voice: " No! I won't come to dinner at *your* house." Relations between us grew worse ever after and finally came to a complete break.[25]

In the winter or spring of 1891 Tchaikovsky came to St. Petersburg on quite a long visit, and from then dated his closer intimacy with Byelayev's circle, particularly with Glazunov, Lyadov, and me. In the years following, Tchaikovsky's visits became quite frequent. Sitting around in restaurants till three in the morning with Lyadov, Glazunov, and others usually put a finishing touch to the time spent together. Tchaikovsky could drink a great deal of wine and yet keep his full powers, both physical and mental; but few

[22] Extra concert, December 22, 1890 [January 3, 1891].
[23] By the way, A. G. Rubinstein, on hearing *Antar*, expressed himself: " It is *ballet* music." [Author's note.]
[24] The date on the author's manuscript orchestral score is September 25 [October 7], 1888.
[25] Cf. A. N. Rimsky-Korsakov's book *N. A. Rimsky-Korsakov, Life and Creative Work*, Part II, Chapter iii, pp. 54–6.

could keep up with him in this respect. In their company Laroche began to appear more and more frequently. I avoided Laroche to the best of my ability and as a rule dawdled very little in restaurants, leaving long before the rest. At this time there begins to be noticeable a considerable cooling off and even somewhat inimical attitude towards the memory of the "mighty *koochka*" of Balakirev's period. On the contrary a worship of Tchaikovsky and a tendency towards eclecticism grow ever stronger. Nor could one help noticing the predilection (that sprang up then in our circle) for Italian-French music of the time of wig and farthingale, music introduced by Tchaikovsky in his *Pikovaya Dama* (*Queen of Spades*) and *Yolanta*. By this time quite an accretion of new elements and young blood had accumulated in Byelayev's circle. New times, new birds; new birds, new songs.[26]

During his visit in 1891 Tchaikovsky came once to our house; Byelayev, Glazunov, and others were also there. Unbidden, Laroche dropped in and stayed through the whole evening. However, Nadezhda Nikolayevna treated him so stiffly that he never came again.

On October 23 [November 4], 1890 *Prince Igor* was produced at last, rehearsed fairly well by K. A. Kuchera, as Napravnik had declined the honour of conducting Borodin's opera. Both Glazunov and I were pleased with our orchestration and additions. The cuts later introduced by the Directorate in Act III of the opera did it considerable harm. The unscrupulousness of the Mariinsky Theatre subsequently went to the length of omitting Act III altogether. Taken all in all, the opera was a success and attracted ardent admirers, particularly among the younger generation.

At one of the six Russian Symphony Concerts, the third act of my *Mlada* was performed anew. After its publication by Byelayev, *Mlada* was submitted by me to the Director of Theatres, Vsyevolozhsky. Becoming interested in its scenery, he immediately agreed to produce it and faithfully promised to carry out all my conditions to make no cuts, to procure all necessary instruments, and, in general, scrupulously to follow out my directions as author.

---

[26] Apparently this paragraph should be dated 1890.

In the spring of 1891 I turned my hand to *Pskovityanka*.[27] Its first version was unsatisfactory to me, the second still more so. I made up my mind to revise my opera; I meant to keep closely to its first version in general, without increasing its bulk, and yet replace parts that did not satisfy me, with corresponding portions borrowed from the second version. The place of honour among these borrowings belonged to the scene of Olga with Vlasyevna prior to Tsar Ivan's entry. Chetvyortka Tyerpigorev of the second version was to be done away with, Nikola Salos likewise, and so were the wandering pilgrims. The thunder-storm and the Tsar's hunting party I intended to retain, but only as a stage tableau before the G-major chorus of the girls. The Tsar's talk with Styosha during the entertainment I planned to introduce into my new revision, but the final chorus I left in its original form, save that I meant to develop it somewhat. The entire orchestration with its natural-scale brass was good for nothing, and the opera was to be orchestrated on a new principle, partly with Glinka's orchestra, partly with Wagner's.

During my entire activity as composer, now one and now another subject attracted my attention from time to time, without, however, actually coming to realization. Thus the subjects of *Tsarskaya Nyevyesta* (*The Tsar's Bride*), *Servilia*, and *Sadko* had flitted before me more than once, tempting me to turn my hand to them. Before the summer of 1891 the subject of *Zoryushka* (*Daybreak* or *A Night at the Cross-roads*) had preoccupied me, but not for long; yet some musical ideas, which proved of use subsequently, had begun to germinate in connection with the subject.

The summer of 1891 we spent abroad, as Masha's illness made it necessary. We lived in Switzerland, on the Sonnenberg near Lucerne, in Engelberg, at Lugano, and again on the Sonnenberg. I did no work at all during the whole summer, unless it be an attempt to orchestrate some songs — quite unsuccessfully, however. Our trip abroad brought no relief to our poor dear little girl.[28]

---

[27] The orchestral score of the first tableau of Act I is marked April 22 [May 4], 1891; the Intermezzo between the first tableau and the second tableau, April 17 [29].

[28] Rimsky-Korsakov returned alone, August 6 [18], 1891, in order to relieve Bala-

The production of *Mlada* did not take place during the season of 1891–2. The choral portions were being rehearsed, but for the rest we were being deceived. Moreover, Napravnik fell ill. In order not to delay the matter, I proposed to him to conduct in person the "weeding out" rehearsals of the orchestra, and two of these took place. The scenic artists maintained that between the scenes of Chernobog and the Cleopatra scene no dextrous scene-shifting was possible if directions were followed as indicated in the score. Feeling tired and incapable of further work on the composition of *Mlada,* I requested Glazunov to write an intermezzo on my themes, so as not to interrupt the music during the change of scenery. Glazunov consented and skilfully composed an intermezzo by cleverly adapting himself to my style. Subsequently, however, this intermezzo was not used, as it was found possible to shift the scenery in a moment, and my original plan was adhered to. Napravnik recovered, but the production of *Mlada* was postponed until the ensuing season. To make up for it, during Lent, at the concert of the Directorate of Imperial Theatres, the entire third act was given under Napravnik's leadership; its success, however, was not overwhelming.[29] Along with it was given Napravnik's *Don Juan* [30] — a tedious, uninteresting, and interminable composition.

The Russian Symphony Concerts ran their course.[31] I was engaged on *The Maid of Pskov* [32] and, in addition, orchestrated anew

kirev at the Chapel, and at first had to travel repeatedly to what he called the "Peterhof Prison" or "barracks," where the Chapel was, as usual. By that time, Rimsky-Korsakov's longing to have done with the Chapel had grown considerably stronger.

[29] The third act of *Mlada* was played three times, at the concerts of March 2, 4, and 5 [14, 16, and 17], 1892 (Mariinsky Theatre).

[30] Incidental music to Aleksey Tolstoy's drama *Don Juan,* op. 54, 1891 (solo, chorus, orchestra, declamation). Of Tolstoy's trilogy, one, *Tsar Ivan the Terrible,* was played in New York (March 1, 1904) by Richard Mansfield, and *Tsar Fyodor* by Orlenev and Nazimova, in Russian (1905), and by the Moscow Art Theatre (1922–3). J. A. J.

[31] There were two of them in the season of 1891–2: November 30 [December 12], 1891, and January 25 [February 6], 1892 (without counting the chamber concerts).

[32] From a letter of April 22 [May 4], 1892 to S. N. Krooglikov: "I have worked rather much on *Pskovityanka,* of which I have nearly finished the orchestral score; there remain to be done the Overture, the final chorus, and trifles." On the autograph orchestral score of the second tableau of Act I there is the date: "April 11 [23], 1892 "; on the second tableau of Act II: "December 26, 1891 [January 7, 1892] "; on the first tableau of Act III: "December 26 to January 26, 1892 [January 7 to Febru-

the entire second scene of *Boris Godunov* (the coronation scene), which was the cornerstone in my further revision of Moussorgsky's work — undertaken later. At the end of the season I did one more piece of work: I rewrote the orchestration of my *Sadko* (tone-poem). With this revision I settled accounts with the past. In this way, not a single larger work of mine *of the period antedating May Night* remained unrevised.[33]

My acquaintance with V. V. Yastryebtsev, an ardent admirer of mine, dates approximately from this time. Introduced to me at a concert, he gradually visited me more and more frequently, recording (as proved afterwards) his talks with me, the ideas expressed by me, and so on, in the form of memoirs.[34] In his library he had all my compositions in full scores; he collected my autographs, and knew by heart well-nigh every little note in them — at all events, every interesting harmony. The time of the beginning and completion of each of my compositions was recorded by him with the greatest care. In the company of acquaintances, constant and passing, he was a fervent partisan of my compositions and my defender against every variety of critical onslaught. During the first years of our intimacy he was also a violent admirer of Berlioz. Subsequently this passion of his died down considerably and gave way to a worship of Wagner.[35]

---

ary 7, 1892] ”; on the second tableau of the same act up to the final chorus: " April 7 [19], 1892 ”; final chorus: " April 2 [14], 1894.”

From the same letter, after enumerating all these labours: " In one word, I have done and shall do a great deal of what is new (! ! !). Then I teach, learn, give instruction, and study, am sore at many a thing, am establishing an objective attitude. Am training and nurturing within me a feeling of supreme aversion towards Balakirev (and successfully, too).” Cf. A. N. Rimsky-Korsakov's *N. A. Rimsky-Korsakov, Life and Creative Work,* Part II, Chapter iii, p. 57.

[33] To judge from notes jotted down, belonging to the winter of 1891, Rimsky-Korsakov also busied himself with the *Textbook of Instrumentation* during this period.

[34] A portion of these reminiscences was published as a supplement to the *Russian Musical Gazette* for 1916 and 1917 and constitutes two parts (approximately one eighth of the entire extant material) of V. V. Yastryebtsev's *My Reminiscences of N. A. Rimsky-Korsakov* (St. Petersburg, 1917), Parts I and II.

[35] Written in Florence, August 8 [20], 1906.

Studying æsthetics and philosophy. Production of Mlada. Yolanta. *" Friendly " dinner. Weariness and ill health. Production of* Snyegoorochka *in Moscow.* Altani. May Night *on a private stage. Leoncavallo. Safonov. Impressions of visit to Moscow. Russian Symphony Concerts. Krooshevsky.* Ruslan and Lyudmila *anniversary.*

THE SUMMER OF 1892 I spent with my whole family at Nyezhgovitsy without leaving it once. Of my task with *Pskovityanka* there remained to revise the Overture and the closing chorus, and that I did in the course of three or four weeks of stay in the country. This work I did very unwillingly, feeling a sort of weariness and aversion for it. Nevertheless, thanks to my being an experienced hand, the revised Overture was rather successful, and the thought of adding " Olga's chords " at the end of the closing chorus can only be called felicitous. As before, I left the chorus in E-flat major; I transposed the Overture to the key of C minor; I completely reorchestrated and changed the end, substituting more decent music for the barbarous dissonances of the first version. I was also in a hurry to finish the work on *The Maid of Pskov* for the reason that I was more and more absorbed in the thought of writing a comprehensive article or even a book about Russian music and about Borodin's, Moussorgsky's and my own compositions.[1] Strange as it may seem, the

---

[1] The mighty crisis, the doubts and disillusionments in himself and in Russian music, which Rimsky-Korsakov had gone through at this time are testified to by a

thought of writing a critical estimate of myself pursued me persistently. I began. But my work was to be preceded by a lengthy introduction embracing general æsthetic theses to which I should be able to make reference. I jotted it down rather rapidly, but immediately and of my own accord perceived great shortcomings and gaps and tore it up. Then I set out to read: I read Hanslick's *Vom Musikalisch-Schönen*, Ambros's *Die Grenzen der Poesie und Musik*, and La Mara's biographies of great composers. Reading Hanslick, I was nettled at that writer of slight wit and exceeding paradox. This reading aroused in me once more the desire to proceed with my article. I began, but the thing grew more and more bulky than before. I fell to delving into general æsthetics and the treatment of all the arts in general. From all the arts I was to pass to music, and from this latter to the music of the young Russian school in particular. While working on this, the feeling grew on me that I lacked not only philosophic and æsthetic training, but even familiarity with the most necessary terms of the subject. Once more I threw up my work and turned to reading Lewes's *History of Philosophy*. In intervals between reading I jotted down brief articles on Glinka and Mozart, on conductors and musical education, etc. All of this proved clumsy and immature.[2] Reading Lewes, I made transcripts from the book and from the philosophic doctrines he quoted and also recorded my own ideas. For days at a stretch I pondered these matters, turning my fragmentary thoughts this way and that. But lo and behold! one fine morning, at the end of August or the beginning of September I was overtaken by an extreme lassitude accompanied by a sort of rush to my head and utter confusion of thinking. I was frightened in real earnest, and the first few days even lost my appetite completely. When I told my wife of it, she, of course, urged me to give up all work. I did so and, until we left for St. Petersburg, read nothing whatever, but walked all day long, taking care

---

series of Rimsky-Korsakov's letters to Mme Rimsky-Korsakov and S. N. Krooglikov during the period of 1891 and the years immediately following. Cf. A. N. Rimsky-Korsakov's *N. A. Rimsky-Korsakov, Life and Creative Work*, Part III.

    [2] These articles were included in the posthumous collection of *Articles and Notes on Music* (*1869–1907*) which were published in 1911 under N. N. Rimskaya-Korsakova's editorial supervision, with an introductory chapter by F. M. Gnyesin.

not to remain alone. Whenever I did remain alone, unpleasant ob-
trusive, fixed ideas persistently crept into my head. I thought of
religion and of humble reconciliation with Balakirev. However, the
walks and the rest helped, and I moved to St. Petersburg quite
myself again. But I had grown altogether cold to music, and the
thought of occupying myself with philosophic education pursued
me unremittingly. Against Dr. T. I. Bogomolov's advice, I began to
read a great deal. I had a textbook of logic, and Herbert Spencer's
philosophy, Spinoza, the æsthetic works of Guyot and Hennequin,
various histories of philosophy, etc.[3] Nearly every day I bought
books and read them, jumped from one to the other, scribbled
notes in their margins, meanwhile unceasingly pondering, pondering, making memoranda and writing notes. I conceived a desire to
write a magnum opus on the æsthetics of musical art. For the time
being, the Russian school was shouldered aside. But instead of
æsthetics I was straying into general metaphysics, for fear lest I
begin too near and too superficially. And more and more frequently
very unpleasant sensations began to recur in my head: something
like fluxes, or possibly refluxes, perhaps dizziness, but most likely
a weight and pressure. These sensations, which went hand in hand
with various fixed ideas, greatly oppressed and frightened me.

I found some diversion, however, in the production of *Mlada* at
the Mariinsky Theatre. Quite energetic rehearsals of my opera commenced at the beginning of the theatrical season, and I was invited
to the rehearsals, choral and orchestral. Even as early as September
the choruses sang well; the only thing that offered difficulties in
the way of commitment to memory was the idol-worshippers'
chorus of Act IV, owing to its constant change of measures ($\frac{3}{4}$, $\frac{1}{4}$,
$\frac{5}{4}$, etc.). Napravnik kept me uneasy with fear that, with all its
willingness, the chorus would be unable to memorize that number.

[3] Some of the philosophical works enumerated here have been preserved in
Rimsky-Korsakov's library, with numerous pencil notations on the margins, made by
Rimsky-Korsakov's hand: H. Spencer: *First Principles,* translated by L. Alekseyev
(Kiev: F. Yohanson; 1886); Spencer: *Principles of Psychology,* translated from the
second English edition, Vols. I–IV (St. Petersburg: N. I. Bilibin; 1876); B. Spinoza:
Ethics, translated by V. I. Modestov (second edition, St. Petersburg: L. A. Pantyele-
yev; 1892); George H. Lewes: *History of Philosophy,* translated from the English
(second edition, St. Petersburg, 1892); A. W. Ambros: *Boundaries of Music and
Poetry,* translated by I. T. (V. Bessel, 1889); and others.

At one of the choral drills, when an attempt had been made to sing it by heart, one of the best choristers — Myelnichenko (tenor) — lost his way and dragged others with him. Napravnik laid great stress on this occurrence. Pomazansky and Kazachenko, the chorus-masters, assured me that Napravnik exaggerated and that the chorus could be memorized — which presently proved the fact; I myself had never had any misgivings on that score. In the opera lobby, where the united choral rehearsals were held, the voices rang beautifully, the closing chorus of bright angels being given particularly well and with great zeal. At one of the rehearsals an incipient scandal occurred: instead of the words: " *chookh, chookh!* (hear, hear!) " the choristers began to sing: " *choosh, choosh!* (nonsense, nonsense!)." I remarked to them that I did not doubt at all that it really was great nonsense, but nevertheless I should ask them to sing what was written. As if to apologize for the men's lack of tact, the women of the chorus began to applaud me after the rehearsal was over. Still I was told that the next day the chorus had received a good wigging from the stage-manager.

As Mme Litvin [4] had left, the solo parts were distributed as follows: Voyslava, Sonki; Loomir, Dolina; Yaromir, Mikhaylov; Mstivoy, Stravinsky and Koryakin. Mme Sonki asserted that in her part in Act IV there were some awkward moments, and that it was an achievement for a songstress to take the high C sharp in Act II. With a voice like hers it was, of course, shameful to talk like that, and yet I had to make a slight, imperceptible change for her benefit. I stated to G. P. Kondratyev, head stage-manager, that no substitutes had been assigned for the parts of Voyslava and Yaromir and that the opera might be the sufferer on that account. However, none could be found for the tenor part: for Figner the rôle was considered unsuitable for some reason, and why Myedvyedyev [5] had not

---

[4] Felia Litvinne (1863–1936), sister-in-law of Édouard de Reszke, sang in New York in 1885–6 (as Litvinoff), making her début November 4, 1885 as Leonora (*Il Trovatore*) in Colonel Mapleson's company at the Academy of Music; and in 1896–7 at the Metropolitan Opera House. For a considerable period she was the principal dramatic soprano at the Paris Opéra. J. A. J.

[5] A dramatic tenor who (with voice half gone) visited New York in 1898 and gave (on the East Side) performances of *La Juive, Otello, Carmen,* and *Samson et Dalila* that were among the most memorable I have seen. J. A. J.

been assigned the part I don't know; but, at my suggestion, a sub-stitute for Voyslava's part was found in Mme Olgina, and this rôle, fateful C sharp and all, proved easy for her. At rehearsals Krooshev-sky accompanied on the piano, while Napravnik followed, orches-tral score in hand. This time I declined to play the accompaniments (not as I had done at the productions of *May Night* and *Snye-goorochka*) as I felt that latterly I had grown altogether unaccus-tomed to the piano. Soon the orchestral rehearsals, too, began. Napravnik called two preliminary rehearsals: one for the strings, the other for the wind-instruments alone; then followed three gen-eral rehearsals of the whole orchestra, and later the singers also were added. All together there were not more than five or six re-hearsals for the orchestra with the singers. As a detector of false notes, Napravnik was inimitable as usual, but he laid insufficient stress on shading and detailed polish, alleging lack of time. On this occasion, however, I had no quarrel with him as regards tempi; whether I had pleased with my tempi, or whether he was willing to carry out my directions exactly, I do not know, but he was ami-able and charming to me in general, evincing if anything a certain liking for my composition. And things at the Russian Opera really did everlastingly shape themselves in such a manner that time was indeed lacking. Singers constantly falling ill and, consequently, changes of repertory necessitated thereby demanded innumerable extra rehearsals of old operas. Eternal haste, five performances a week, a stage that is not always free for rehearsals, being often occupied by the ballet — all these take time from quiet and sedulous rehearsals, such as are required for proper artistic execution. More-over, above all this there often reigns at the Mariinsky Theatre a spirit of presumptuousness, routine, and weariness, in conjunction with fine technique and experience. Singers, chorus, and orchestra all consider themselves first *hors concours*, and, secondly, experi-enced artists who have seen enough in their lives, whom nothing can take aback, and who are weary of everything, nevertheless feel they will manage quite well, even though it is not worth while to tire oneself too much for it. This spirit often crops out through all outward courtesy and even cordiality, when theatrical impresarios, warmly pressing the composer's hand, tell him how much pains they have taken on his behalf. I suppose that at Bayreuth, and Bayreuth only, matters stand differently, thanks to the Wagner cult that has developed. Be that as it may, nobody can so quickly grow tired, fall into routine, and think he has fathomed all mysteries as do the native Russians and with them those foreigners who have grown up with us in Russia. Imagine how astonished Conductor Muck was when, having produced in St. Petersburg *Der Ring des Nibelungen* with only six orchestral rehearsals for each of the four lyric dramas (abroad they have from twenty to thirty of them), he saw that in the first cycle of Wagner's work everything went perfectly, in the second cycle worse, in the third downright slovenly, and so on, instead of improving as the composition became more familiar. The cause of this lay in the fact that in the early days the orchestra had striven to show off before a conductor from abroad and really had shown off; while during the subsequent cycles self-confidence, routine, and weariness got the upper hand even of the spell of Wagner's name. The orchestral and general rehearsals of *Mlada* went safely; the orchestra did not drown the voices, the orchestration proved full of colour, varied, and individual — I was pleased with it. Only the Pan-pipes were not up to the mark in sound, and that, too, I imagine, was due to the exasperating acoustics of the Mariinsky Theatre. Soon the scenery was being added; to my mind it appeared handsome, but the effects of various lightings and tableaux could not be called altogether successful. The stage rehearsals in conjunction with the scenic effects proved very complicated and required many repetitions. In the midst of this I had two surprises: one a pleasant one, the other quite the reverse. The pleasant one was that the shifting of the first scene in Act III (mountain pass) to Cleopatra's hall was made instantaneously, as I had planned while composing; hence it was found possible to omit the intermezzo that had been written by Glazunov to gain time for the slow change of scenery, and the soft chord of D-flat major (⅜), with which Cleopatra's scene begins, came in immediately after Chernobog's exorcism ("Appear, O Cleopatra!") and the crash of the tomtom. This sudden change of mood and colouring

318

— after the spirits' wild shouts and Chernobog's conjuration in utter darkness, a soft purple light illuminating the Egyptian hall which gradually emerges from obscurity — has always seemed to me one of the most poetic moments of *Mlada*. The unpleasant surprise was as follows: the scenery of the final apotheosis was so arranged that it was impossible to start the procession of the bright gods and spirits of light through the clouds, and it was necessary to be content with a motionless tableau. As a result, the closing chorus proved too long, as the scene was tedious and annoyingly monotonous. It was impossible to remodel the scenery, and I was obliged to make a considerable cut in the closing chorus; this grieved me in the extreme. And all of it occurred because at the Russian Imperial Opera the scene-painter's department, the costumes, the machinery, and the stage-management, and the music run each for itself, and in the Directorate there is no person to unify them all. Each of these departments knows only itself and is ready to play a trick on the others rather than attune itself to them. When the time comes to produce an opera and to "reduce everything to a common denominator," it turns out that many things don't dovetail; and still everyone considers himself free from responsibility for the actions of others. This even though the production of *Mlada* had been preceded as early as the year before by a meeting of the heads of the various departments; but at one sitting it is impossible to clear up everything, and, besides, many things were forgotten.

Thus, in spite of my stern warnings in the preface of *Mlada,* where I requested that no cuts be made or that my opera be postponed altogether,[6] a cut had to be made after all. The only conclusion to be drawn from that is that no words and no prohibitions whatever will avail if it is impossible to hail one into a court of justice for violating the conditions. Now, the Directorate of the Imperial Theatres cannot be hailed into a court, and therefore it be-

---

[6] As a preface to *Mlada*, where music and dance alternate in the most remarkable manner, Rimsky-Korsakov placed a list of directions which are worthy of a place side by side with the famous notes that Berlioz made for his *Les Troyens:* "Should the firemen be afraid of fire, the machinists of water, the theatre-managers of everything together, this symphonic intermezzo should be stricken out"; or: "I indicate here this cut, being fully aware of the feeling of happiness that inspires managers, singers and conductors, firemen, machinists and illuminators, whenever they can insult an

hooves a composer to be gentle and meek. Richard Wagner would
have given it to them one and all in Germany if a trick like this had
been played on him!

The productions of operas at the Mariinsky Theatre lack a sufficient number of complete rehearsals. Now the orchestra men are
all on hand, but the singers sing half-voice; now orchestra and
singers function properly, but the scenery is lacking, because there
is to be a performance in the evening, and there is no time to make
the change; again, the scenery is in place, but the lighting is out of
order, or the rehearsal is held to the accompaniment of a piano, and
so on. And yet it is necessary that an opera, and particularly one so
fantastic and complicated as *Mlada,* be rehearsed many times with
full stage settings. Only then can all stage-scenes and changes be
fitted to the corresponding bars of music and, moreover, the groupings of singers be properly arranged so that the voices produce the
desired effect in accordance with the acoustic properties of the
theatre and, if necessary, the change made in certain dynamic
nuances in the singing of the chorus, in accordance with those same
acoustic conditions. Such joint rehearsing is not at all in vogue at
the Mariinsky Theatre. Thanks to it, many things in *Mlada* turned
out differently from what I had intended. For instance, in Act I the
chorus accompanying the appearance of the goddess Lada and
placed, according to my intentions, on high, among the rafters, was
hardly audible; the orchestration, transparent as it was in this passage, had to be hastily abated. The chorus behind the scenes, which

author and down his work; I should feel unhappy, if I did not, to the utmost of my
powers, contribute to the gratification of such noble instincts." Along with the painful
irony of the Frenchman one may appreciate the imperious masterfulness of the Slav:
"The opera must be given without cuts or abbreviations: (1) because it will not
fatigue anyone, thanks to its brevity (two and one quarter hours of music); (2) because the author has thoroughly weighed his intentions. The composer permits no
change in individual parts; the orchestral, choral, and solo parts have been written in
a form that is fully practicable. He wishes that every species of various noises on the
stage (such as thunder, wind, etc.) be avoided, as only the orchestra and it alone
has to imitate those sounds. He attaches great importance to the descriptive portions
of his music; hence he does not permit the slightest deviation from his ideas in this
regard. . . ."

Cuts, it may be stated, pursued Rimsky-Korsakov throughout his career, in spite
of his horror of them. Since his death his widow has protested against the performance of *Scheherazada* and *Le Coq d'Or* as ballets. Recently the *Chant Hindou* from
the opera *Sadko* has been made into a fox-trot and used for dancing. C. V. V.

accompanies the appearance of the shades in Act IV, missed fire completely, because the very appearance of the shades had not been tried out until the dress rehearsal proper, and the choir had been placed too deep in the wings. The closing chorus lost much because the choristers could not be placed near the proscenium and they, too, had to be shoved into the wings. In general, among the short-comings in the productions at the Mariinsky Theatre must be counted the fact that the chorus people who sing with finesse and shading at the rehearsals in the lobby forget the shading and begin to sing roughly on emerging upon the stage, and yet no proper attention is paid to it. During the scenic rehearsals, O. O. Palyechek, the chorus-master, showed special zeal, incessantly leaping on a chair and indicating the proper moments to the choristers. Thanks to his efforts, many choral scenes went off vividly and naturally, especially the market scene in Act II. The handling of the dances and of the mimetic movements was poor as a whole. The ballet-masters Ivanov and Ceccheti usually do not know the music to which they fit the dances they put on, and if the music is not of the routine ballet type, they don't understand it at all. Despite the de-tailed directions given by me in the piano score, they looked into it too late, it seems to me. As in ancient days, the ballet rehearsals are usually conducted to the playing of two violins which are to translate the entire orchestra. The music becomes almost unrecog-nizable, not to the ballet-master alone, but even to the musicians themselves; hence the character of the movements invented by the ballet-masters is invariably ill suited to the character of the music. To the accompaniment of a heavy forte, graceful movements are put on; to a light pianissimo, ponderous leaps; the short notes of melodic runs are thumped out with the feet with a zeal worthy of a better fate. Of all the dances, only the Hindu dance, thanks to the dancer Skorsyuk, a lively, vigorous artist of the gypsy type, as well as the groups of shades, elegantly arranged by the ballet-master Ceccheti, met with success. But, on the other hand, Ceccheti failed utterly with the dances and groupings in the scene in Cleopatra's chamber. The combination of two simultaneous dances, one slow and passionate, the other rapid and frenzied, missed fire com-

pletely, since Ceccheti had not grasped at all the combination of
two contrasting rhythms in the music. Nor were happier results
attained with the *khorovod* (*kolo* of Act II), which proved monotonous and boring in the production. Ceccheti was amusing at the ten-
tative ballet rehearsals. He ran about, capered, made faces to represent the devil, his head bound with a handkerchief which soaked
up the sweat that ran like beads of hail down his face. I doubt that
Mme M. M. Petipa, who played the shade of Mlada, knew and
understood her rôle or was letter-perfect in the verses that explained
the purport of her performance. Her appearance at the beginning
of Act III had not been settled finally even as late as the dress
rehearsal. She made her entry now at the right, now at the left;
now on the rock and now below it. The difficulty was how to place
Yaromir (who followed her) in such a manner that he might be
heard distinctly. Instead of rehearsing this scene separately several
times, Mlada's entry was changed at every rehearsal, and each time
the result was precipitate and incoherent. The persistent thought
of "not delaying rehearsals" is uppermost in everyone's mind, and
hence the lack of finish in the production.

At one of the last rehearsals Mikhaylov, who had caught cold,
grew hoarse and began to sing half-voice. At the dress rehearsal
(to which the public was admitted) the same thing happened. In
the matter of mise-en-scène the dress rehearsal was very shaky. In
Act IV the shades, instead of vanishing, fairly ran off, as the stage
was not sufficiently dark. The musical part went off without a hitch.
The theatre was crowded, but the success was slight and approval
inaudible. After the dress rehearsal there was to be another, at
which the Tsar and the Imperial family were expected. But the
Tsar did not come, for some reason, and the rehearsal was the
usual one, with interruptions. The first performance took place on
October 20 [November 1], a non-subscription night. The house was
full. My family and I sat in a first-tier box on the left side. As usual,
the whole musical world was present in the theatre. After the introduction (played fairly well) meagre applause was heard. The first
act met with a rather chilly reception. Sonki sang Voyslava. Mikhaylov, a sick man, had to force himself to sing in order not to have

the performance cancelled. After the second act loud clamours broke out: " The composer! " I came before the footlights several times and was presented with a huge wreath which V. V. Stassov had, of course, arranged for. After the third act, as well as at the end of the opera, there were numerous curtain calls for me. I came out alone, then with the artists, and presently with Napravnik. Behind the scenes the usual handshakings, expressions of gratitude, and wishes for success bubbled forth. I have spoken of the short-comings in the producing and rehearsing; the performance as a whole was rather smooth. The opera ended early. After it was over, V. V. Stassov, Byelayev, Lyadov, Trifonov, Glazunov, and other close friends gathered at my house.

The second performance of *Mlada* was called off because Mi-khaylov had grown very ill. Then, after a lengthy interval, it was given in turn to all the three sets of subscribers without any success. There were no curtain calls for me, and very few for the artists. Then, after a long lapse, it was given once or twice with consider-able success to non-subscribers. At one of the performances Kroo-shevsky conducted, and quite correctly, though without prepara-tion, in place of Napravnik, who had fallen ill. The majority of the newspaper reviews of *Mlada* were unfavourable, while many re-views were downright hostile. In passing, Solovyov, as had been his wont, inflicted a very ill-disposed critical article upon me. I be-lieve for the most sympathetic review I was indebted to young Gaydeboorov (once a pupil of Moussorgsky's), the music-critic of the *Nyedyelya* (*The Week*). Many (like the *Novoye Vremya*, for instance) imputed Mikhaylov's illness to the difficulties and clumsi-ness in the rôle of Yaromir; in one humorous magazine I was rather amusingly represented as driving a carriage drawn by devils.[7]

The season subscription audiences, indifferent to art, sleepy, stolid, and haunting the theatre only because of besetting habit, that they might be seen and chatter of everything but music — they were all bored to the very death by my opera. As for the non-subscribers, it was given for them only twice, and why the Lord alone knows! Perhaps because the artists had scant success

---

[7] Written at Yalta, June 10 [22], 1893.

in it, as well as because His Majesty's Court had shown no interest whatever: the expected visit of the Emperor at the final perform-ance had not materialized; only the Tsarina and her children came. Nor had the Tsar attended any rehearsal, despite his habit of com-ing with the entire court to dress rehearsals. As I had been told, the Minister of His Majesty's Court had not found my opera to his liking, and that is of supreme importance in the eyes of the Direc-torate. The newspaper reviews had belittled *Mlada* to the best of their abilities in the eyes of the public, whose musical brain-centres are saturated and supersaturated with the " Figner cult." Evidently, on the basis of all this, an impression was created that *Mlada* was not much of a composition, and this opinion of the majority has probably been established for a long time to come; hence I don't by any means expect success for my opera in the nearest future, nor indeed at any time at all, for that matter. There is also this opinion current: " What under the sun have we to do with all these gods, spirits, devils? Let us have drama and drama, let us have living human beings! " In other words: " Let us have mellifluous singing with high notes and gasping parlandos in between."

Be that as it may, it turned out that my opera was given an un-precedentedly small number of times for a first season, although all performances brought good houses. At the end of the season it might have been given several times, but Tchaikovsky's *Yolanta* and Mascagni's *Cavalleria Rusticana* interfered. The rehearsals of these operas were attended by the Imperial family, and both Figner and Medea ⁸ sang in them — so everything was fine. *Cavalleria Rusticana* I did not hear, but *Yolanta* I heard at a rehearsal and found it one of Tchaikovsky's feeblest compositions. To my mind, everything in it is unsuccessful — beginning with impudent bor-rowings like Rubinstein's melody " *Otvoritye mnye tyemnitsu* (Open wide my dungeon cell) " and ending with orchestration which in this particular case Tchaikovsky somehow had written

---

⁸ Nikolay Figner, with a rather dry tenor voice of mezzo quality, but of unusual finesse and interpretative abilities, and his wife, Medea Mey (an Italian by birth), a soprano of extraordinary quality, a strikingly beautiful woman of burning tempera-ment and supreme dramatic gifts, were the reigning favourites of the Imperial Opera House (1887–1903). Medea Mey sang in Buenos Aires in 1903. J. A. J.

topsyturvy: music suitable for strings had been allotted to wind instruments and vice versa, and hence it occasionally sounds even fantastic in the most unsuitable passages (the introduction, for instance, scored, for some unknown reason, for the wind instruments alone).

During this season I rarely took a peep behind the wings of the Mariinsky Theatre after the production of *Mlada;* I had no desire to keep my memory green, though the artists were amiable and kind to me in the same old way. Apparently, after the production of *Mlada* the artists gave me a place in the ranks of " real honest-to-goodness " composers; that was evident at least from the fact that soon after the first performance of *Mlada* the artists invited my wife and me to a " friendly " dinner at the Myedvyed' restaurant. Pogozhev himself also attended the dinner. Napravnik, being ill, did not come. The dinner went off in a somewhat formal fashion: the first toast, drunk to the health of His Majesty the Emperor, was accompanied with the singing of the national anthem *Bozhe Tsarya khrani* (*God save the Tsar*), Koryakin's voice dwarfing all others. Then followed all sorts of toasts — to the success of the opera, to the performers, and so forth. By the way, in his speech, Pogozhev called *Mlada* an archæological opera, for reasons best known to himself, while Figner and Medea asked me to write an opera " for them." In this connection I must mention that at one of the rehearsals of *Mlada,* Figner had taken me aside and told me that nothing would please him better than to sing in my *May Night* and that he had spoken to Kondratyev and Napravnik, but they had said that *May Night* could be produced only provided I rewrote the third act. I told Figner that I should be pleased to have him sing in *May Night,* but I did not see any need of rewriting Act III; and that I was surprised at Kondratyev and Napravnik — and what they wanted with it. That ended the conversation.

The production of *Mlada* did not by any means spur me to further composing, and I kept reading and jotting down various notes. Fatigue and unpleasant headaches came more frequently. Yielding to the pleas of my wife and Aleksandr Pavlovich Dianin, I consulted Dr. Erlitsky, who ordered complete rest and physical exer-

cise as well as certain medicines.[9] I gave up reading; but, possessing
no inclination for manual labour, contented myself with long walks,
meanwhile regularly taking the medicines. I confess that my condition depressed me. By fits and starts I would do a little reading,
but it tired me and caused pressure in my head; thereupon, sinking
into despondency, I dropped my reading again. However, the ab-
stinence from reading, as well as the walks, was of benefit to me,
and a trip to Moscow to see the production of *Snyegoorochka* diverted me particularly. Having heard from Moscow that nothing
was known there concerning the production of the opera, I believed
that it had been called off altogether. Yet in January I received an
invitation from Altani to come to the two final rehearsals and the
first performance, announced for January 26 [February 7]. After
brief reflection I left, and went directly from the train to the theatre. The rehearsal had already started. Altani halted it, and, after
presenting me to the artists, recommenced from the very beginning. *Snyegoorochka* was given in its entirety, without cuts. The
impression of the rehearsal was most pleasant to me. Snyegoorochka
(Mme Eichenwald) and Koopava (Mme Sionitskaya) were very
fine; all the others were quite fair; the orchestra had been drilled
with great care, the tempi, in the majority of cases, were correct,
and not those of St. Petersburg; the chorus did some acting while
singing on the stage, with close attention to nuances that one
looked for in vain in St. Petersburg; the acoustics were splendid.
Two days later the dress rehearsal took place. The performance
was fine, the scenery sufficiently handsome, but the metamorphoses
and entries in Act III were nothing to brag about. The costumes
were middling fair. Evidently in the decorative domain Moscow is
weaker and more primitive than St. Petersburg. Among the inter-
preters some were excellent and some good; but the opera had been
studied finely. The orchestra, which is probably inferior to that of

---

[9] The medical certificate signed by Privatdocent Erlitsky and dated November
1 [13], 1893, reads: " N. A. Rimsky-Korsakov is suffering from general neurasthenia
(*Neurasthenia cerebrospinalis*), which is combined with a slight degeneration of
brain vessels and expresses itself in intensified tendency to fatigue, depressed frame
of mind, the feeling of heaviness in the head, occasional numbness of the extremities,
agitation in the region of the heart, etc. . . . ."

St. Petersburg in some wind instruments, proved able to play with finesse; of the qualities of the chorus, headed by Chorus-master Avranek, I have spoken already. I observed that the performers had treated my opera lovingly; the absence of cuts proved it. I heard my opera in its entirety for the first time, and how much it gained thereby!

I had met Ippolit Karlovich Altani during one of my visits to Moscow to conduct at Shostakovsky's concerts. This acquaintance-ship was of the most transient, and since then I had not seen him. On renewing acquaintance, during the production of *Snyegoo-rochka*, he left with me the impression that he was an experienced technician-conductor, but not an artist of the first rank; I was the more pleasantly surprised and gained the conviction that, given the usual technique of an operatic conductor plus a love for the work performed, it is possible to accomplish a great deal; that is, to put on an opera in the way the composer wants it. It was said that Altani had held some incredibly large number of rehearsals for *Snyegoorochka;* Napravnik, on the other hand, contrives it all with a smaller expenditure of the labour of others and himself. But the result is what counts. In Moscow, *Snyegoorochka* went off finely, with less choice orchestral forces and with a conductor who does not enjoy any especial musical authority in anybody's eyes. On the other hand, in St. Petersburg, with an experienced and ex-cellent orchestra, with a conductor who possessed the highest au-thority both with the public and with musicians, it had been played in a cold, dead manner, at tempi scurrying officially fast, and with most disgusting cuts. I actually conceived a hatred for St. Peters-burg and its " great artisan," as V. V. Stassov nicknames Napravnik. His inestimable virtue is his ear, sensitive to the point of morbidity; his knack of pouncing on mistakes and correcting them on the spot at " weeding-out " rehearsals is truly astounding. " Second French horn — C sharp! " " First bassoon, what have you, E flat or E? " " One must not play piano when mezzo forte is indicated! " etc., keep flying about at his weeding-out rehearsals. A firm character, preciseness, a beautiful beat, and clear-cut syncopations are also among his attributes. But what further? Then — often impossibly

rapid tempi, metronomic evenness, total lack of softness and round-
ness in the change of tempi, and, in the last analysis, lack of artistic
interpretation. But I have strayed from the Moscow affairs.

The dress rehearsal went finely, except the scenic part, and the
performance had been set for the following day (January 26
[February 7]). My wife surprised me by coming to Moscow on the
day of the performance. I had a first-tier box on the right; it accom-
modated my wife, S. N. Krooglikov, myself, and N. M. Shtroopp,
who had come on from St. Petersburg especially for the performance of *Snyegoorochka*. The performance began at 7.30 sharp and
ended at 12.45. This was owing to the unusually long intermissions.
The success of the opera was considerable. The songs of Lyel, Snyegoorochka's arietta, the duet of Koopava and the Tsar, the hymn
of the Byeryendyeys, the song about the beaver, and the dance of
the *skomorokhs* (merry andrews) were encored. I was presented
with several wreaths: from the professors of the Conservatory,
from the Moscow Philharmonic Society, from the orchestra, and
so on. Mme Eichenwald (Snyegoorochka) also received a wreath.
Eichenwald (whose mother played the harp in the orchestra) was
very fine and graceful. Her polished silvery soprano voice fitted
the part of Snyegoorochka to perfection. Sionitskaya (Koopava)
played and sang magnificently. Zvyagina (Lyel) was off pitch
somewhat, but on the whole sang rather well; good also was Klem-
entyev (Bobyl), who danced the *tryepak* splendidly. Bartsal was
a good Byeryendyey in spite of a voice long past its prime. Krooti-
kova (Spring) was correct, but Korsov (Mizgir) fell somewhat
short of his part. Taken as a whole, the performance was good, and
showed united efforts. The artists, Altani, Avranek, and I were
called to the footlights over and over again. After the opera was
over, I went with my wife and N. M. Shtroopp to the Moscow
Hotel, where we had taken rooms, and there drank tea in a modest
way. The following day we left for St. Petersburg, by the fast train.
Before we departed, the artists of the opera gave a luncheon for us,
with the toasts and good wishes usual on such occasions. Stage-
manager-in-chief Bartsal and Altani saw us off to the depot.

This time in Moscow I also had an opportunity to hear my *May*

Night given by Pryanishnikov's private opera company in Shela-
pootin's Theatre. The performance was very painstaking — even
exaggeratedly so. The funny pranks were stressed, the *hopak* was
danced in some incredible fashion. The small orchestra played
rather accurately under Pribik's leadership, but, for some unknown
reason, without any piano; this was of considerable injury to the
orchestration of Act III, and even produced occasionally a very
undesirable emptiness. The tiny chorus sang quite correctly, yet
the scene of the nymphs was a total failure. *May Night* was being
given, I believe, for the fourteenth time (it had not been produced
previous to this season); the house was full and the opera enjoyed
success. On learning that I was present, the audience began to call
for me; the artists gathered on the stage and applauded me with
the curtain up. Pryanishnikov told me that *May Night* kept up his
receipts tremendously and that only about that time Leoncavallo's
opera *Pagliacci* began to supplant it in this respect. That opera, as
well as Cui's *The Mandarin's Son*, I also heard in Pryanishnikov's
performances. I did not like Leoncavallo's opera. A cleverly handled subject of the realistically dramatic style and genuine swin-
dler's music, created by that contemporary musical career-chaser,
precisely similar to Mascagni, the author of *Cavalleria Rusticana,*
caused a furore. These gentlemen are as remote from old man
Verdi as they are from a star in the heavens. *The Mandarin's Son*
appeared to me a talented composition with music unsuited for the
subject, which in itself needs no music at all and is so poor that it is
nauseating to hear and see it.

During my stay in Moscow I also had an opportunity to attend
a concert of the Russian Musical Society under V. I. Safonov, with
d'Albert as assisting artist. Excerpts from Saint-Saëns's *Le Déluge,*
the Overture to Gluck's *Iphigenia,* and Liszt's E-flat major Concerto were performed. Safonov led the orchestra excellently. I also
had a chance to be present at a rehearsal of the Conservatory pupils'
concert. Beethoven's Mass in C major was sung; here, too, Safonov
seemed to me a musician who knew his business. Until then I had
formed no impression of him as a conductor.

I left Moscow generally pleased and rested; yes, even filled with a desire to remove to Moscow, where life seemed to me somehow more youthful and fresher than in St. Petersburg, where everybody is weary of everything, everything is familiar to everybody, and nothing can surprise or rejoice anybody! [10] I also had become convinced not only that *Snyegoorochka* was my best opera, but taken all in all — as to its idea and its execution — possibly the best of contemporary operas. It is long, but it has no long-drawn-out passages and should be given in its entirety or else with most trifling cuts. When I called Altani's attention to the fact that the performance was dragging too much and that perhaps some slight cuts would be insisted upon, I was therefore pleased to hear from him that first of all he would endeavour to reduce the duration of the intermissions, and, secondly, that he would try to avoid encores desired by the audience; that only then would he see whether cuts could or could not be dispensed with.

On returning to St. Petersburg, I began again to read little by little, as I felt rested; but the unpleasant sensations in my head had not left me entirely. I was also engaged in reading proof of the new orchestral score of *Pskovityanka* (then in the process of engraving), as well as in reading proof of the orchestral score of *May Night*, engraved by Byelayev, who had bought this edition from the Bitner firm. This latter had passed from the deceased Rater into the hands of the adventurer Müller.

Of the musical events of this year I shall note the following: After my refusal to conduct them, the Russian Symphony Concerts were placed in the hands of Glazunov.[11] But he fell ill before the open-

---

[10] Of this intention Rimsky-Korsakov writes at length to S. N. Krooglikov in a letter which bears no date, but evidently belongs to a time later than his return from Moscow: ". . . I feel the need of renovation, of other air, of less foggy and gloomy winter days; it seems to me that in a different environment I should recover my spirits, perhaps should once more set myself to composing, etc." Towards the beginning of 1893 the idea of moving to Moscow lost its practicability and was cast into limbo by Rimsky-Korsakov. In his letter of February 9 [21], 1893, Rimsky-Korsakov wrote to S. N. Krooglikov: "I needs must cease acting like an old woman, ailing, fretting at Balakirev — and rather get down to business — that is all. It does not take long to take a stupid and rash step and then things can't be mended."

[11] Rimsky-Korsakov had long since begun to feel the burden of his conducting, and particularly of the Russian Symphony Concerts. As far back as 1891 (September), he added, when briefly telling S. N. Krooglikov the program of the forthcoming concerts: "How uninteresting all this is! I have a feeling that the concerts have

ing concert and A. K. Lyadov took his place at Byelayev's and my own urgent request. He conducted finely the first concert, which he had at first done his best to escape. Among other numbers there were given Glazunov's Third Symphony in D major (first time) and the Overture to *May Night*, which Lyadov conducted delightfully, quite unlike Napravnik's fashion in days gone by, at the Mariinsky Theatre. I felt well pleased with my " classic " instrumentation of the Overture, with its natural-scale trumpets and French horns. The second Russian Symphony concert went well, under the direction of Glazunov, who continued making progress in conducting. Though there were some faults in the performance of *Sadko* given at the concerts from the new score, everything else went splendidly. As in the years previous, the chorus of the Russian Opera took part also. Among other numbers, there was given the coronation scene from *Boris Godunov* in my revision. The effect achieved was magnificent; and of this, it would seem, even those of Moussorgsky's admirers were convinced who had been ready to accuse me of spoiling his works, because of the alleged Conservatory learning I had acquired — learning that ran counter to the freedom of creative art — for example, Moussorgsky's harmonic incoherence. By the way, in this scene I was particularly successful with the bell-tolling, which sounded so beautiful under Moussorgsky's fingers on the piano and failed so utterly in the orchestra. Once again the tolling of bells! How many times and in what different forms had I reproduced in the orchestration this invariable feature of ancient Russian life, which is still preserved in our own days! [12]

---

run their life-span. And still I am the one conducting them." In a letter of November 16 [28], 1891 to the same person and on the same subject (regarding the invitation to conduct a concert in Moscow), Rimsky-Korsakov wrote: ". . . Being tied with a rope to the Russian Symphony Concerts, I cannot get away from them, but outside of these, I have no desire to appear as conductor for I do not feel in the slightest that I have a special vocation for it. Every musician must be able to lead through a composition, but he is not obliged to be among the Berliozes, the Bülows, the Napravniks, etc. . . ." To this time (August 1892) belongs Rimsky-Korsakov's short article: " The Epidemic of Conductorship," included in the collection of his *Articles and Notes on Music.*

[12] The Russian composers are fond of reproducing the effect of bells in their music. Other examples may be found in the orchestral prelude to *Khovanshchina*, the prelude to the coronation scene in *Boris*, in *Pskovityanka*, and in Tchaikovsky's Over-

The concerts of the Russian Musical Society were under Krooshevsky's direction this season.[13] However, for one concert there
came from Paris Lamoureux,[14] who was little to my liking. Among
other things, Krooshevsky produced Liszt's *Legende von der heiligen Elisabeth* and, it was said, rather unsuccessfully, thanks to an
utter lack of understanding of Liszt's tempi. Borodin's Second Symphony and my *Scheherazada* were performed by him beautifully.
The last named I did not hear myself, however, as I had to stay at
home owing to my son Andrey's dangerous illness. I also did not
hear Balakirev's *Tamara* in his interpretation; very poor, it was
said. Krooshevsky, a former Conservatory pupil of mine, is a fine
musician, a dextrous pianist who accompanies from piano scores
the most difficult passages at sight and in proper tempo, without
omitting a single note for glibness. His fine ear, splendid beat, organizing ability, and sang-froid make him a living replica of Napravnik. He is no artist at all, and once he has gained a footing at
the Opera as accompanist and coach of solo singers, he does not
bother about anything apart from his official duties. Napravnik is
a composer himself; he has his likes and dislikes in music; to Krooshevsky, however, music means a series of sounds forming melodies
and chords in various measures and tempi, with various shades of
force, etc. — a trade for which one is paid, but not a poetic art. It
seems to me he is a born *assistant* conductor, and not a conductor,
exactly as there are associate ministers, who are very useful but can
never become ministers, or deacons who are never promoted to be
priests, and so forth. Napravnik is very fond of him, and already
he is known as second conductor of the Opera; in time to come he
will be principal conductor. But he is under no circumstances the
conductor for a prominent concert organization like the Russian
Musical Society. He has no tendencies, no ideals. Apparently he has
never attended any other concerts than those at which he has ac-

ture, *1812.* The effect is also to be noted in Rachmaninoff's choral setting of Poe's
The Bells and in Stravinsky's song, *The Cloister.* C. V. V.

[13] E. A. Krooshevsky conducted the concerts of the Russian Musical Society during the season of 1892–3.

[14] The concert (the sixth) under Lamoureux's direction took place December
6 [18], 1892.

companied, either because concerts have not interested him, or because he has been busy giving lessons. He is not conversant with either Russian or foreign music literature, and hence does not know the traditions. I imagine that if he had done well with Borodin's Symphony and *Scheherazada*, it was because, this time, he submitted to the orchestra, who knew these works. But *Tamara* the orchestra hardly knew, and hence it fared badly at his hands. However, Krooshevsky had wanted to see me about the tempi of *Tamara*, and that was conscientious on his part; but, owing to the composer's being within reach, I advised him to apply to the author. When I mentioned it to Balakirev, he said to me with his characteristic misanthropy: " Oh, please deliver me from that! Show him the tempi yourself, if you wish." Nevertheless Krooshevsky, whom I had already given the address, reached Balakirev. What their talk was like I don't know. Krooshevsky reported that Balakirev had shown him whatever was necessary. Of course, Balakirev did not come to rehearsal.

In addition to the production of *Mlada, Yolanta, Shchelkoonchik* (*Nutcracker*),[15] and *Cavalleria Rusticana*, there was also revived *Ruslan and Lyudmila* for the fiftieth anniversary since its production.[16] Especially for this Myelnikov sang, who had then not a shred of voice left. Lyudmila Ivanovna Shestakova sat in a first-tier box and was presented with a wreath (of course V. V. Stassov's hand was behind it). My wife and I were among those in the procession presenting the wreath. To mark this solemnity, the Head's narrative and the finale of the third act were restored in their entirety. Napravnik's tempi were shocking, as usual. The Overture, the entr'actes to Acts II and IV were played with the speed of an electric current, if not with the speed of light. The famous finale of the Oriental dances was not restored after all, and the usual ugly coda was performed. With *Mlada's* happy omen the Opera House now possessed a double-bassoon; still Napravnik had not thought of introducing it into *Ruslan*, even for this festive occasion, and yet it is named in Glinka's orchestral score of *Ruslan and Lyudmila*.

---

[15] Tchaikovsky's ballet given with *Yolanta*, 1892. J. A. J.
[16] November 27 [December 9], 1892.

Quartet prize competition. Decision to leave the Chapel. Summer at Yalta. Tchaikovsky's death and the Sixth Symphony. Trip to Odessa. My return to composing. Beginning of Christmas Eve. *Summer. Vyechasha. Continuation of* Christmas Eve *and beginning of* Sadko. *Death of Rubinstein. Trip to Kiev.* Pskovityanka *at the Society of Musical Gatherings. Censorship difficulties with* Christmas Eve. *Composing the opera* Sadko. *Byelsky.*

THE EXAMINATION of the quartets sent in for the prize competition of the St. Petersburg Quartet Society took place in March. This time the competition was open to none but Russian subjects, and the money was given by M. P. Byelayev. With Tchaikovsky and Laroche I was of the committee of judges. Few quartets were submitted. We awarded two prizes of third rank. One went to my former pupil Aleksey Avgustovich Davidov (a brother of Ivan A. Davidov, also a pupil of mine, whom I have mentioned before); the other went to Evald, the cellist of Byelayev's Quartet. Thus two more were added to the rather long list of names of composers of Byelayev's circle. Both quartets were written in a well-ordered manner, but nothing beyond that. During the season described, I seldom attended Byelayev's evenings, as they had deteriorated considerably in musical interest. Well-known works of Russian composers were played invariably. Among the slighter novelties, two pretty pieces for the cello, Sokolov's *Elegy* and *Barcarole*, stood out in a refreshing manner. My son Andrey, who had by that time shown some signs of progress in cello-playing, was studying them under P. A. Ronginsky. Occasionally, V. V. Stassov put in an appearance at Byelayev's evenings, as in former days, and demanded that one of Beethoven's last quartets be played. The evenings were also attended by Vyerzhbilovich and Hildebrand, who occasionally took a hand in the music. Once Lyadov delivered himself of a small composition for quartet. But somehow the society at the Byelayev evenings did not pull together; all in all, too many new elements began to intrude into it, and a sort of tedium and routine made themselves felt.

In February the ten-year period of my service at the Court Chapel was to terminate; I was entitled to a pension under the regulations of the Ministry of the Court, as more than thirty years of my services had accumulated in all. I got it into my head to carry out the idea that had long pursued me — to retire. The relations between Balakirev and me had become so strained, affairs at the Chapel were managed so stupidly, the entire personnel at the Chapel — except the music-instructors — was so distasteful to me, the whole atmosphere of the Chapel was so permeated with gossip and partiality, that it was quite natural on my part to be eager to get out; to all of this was added my fatigue at the time. I had a private talk with Balakirev about resigning "because of illness." But owing to the fact that just at that time he was ridding the Chapel of the inspector of classes in general subjects, Nazimov, with whom he was dissatisfied, Balakirev suggested to me that I delay my resignation until autumn. My leaving he treated in a very fine and conscientious spirit, promising to do his very best in regard to arranging the pension. Complying with his wishes, I decided to wait until autumn, but obtained from him a leave of absence for the summer. Yet the following circumstances soon made me forgo temporarily the thought of resigning.

Masha's sickness still persisted and dragged on, depressing our spirits throughout the winter of 1892–3. This state of affairs had been going on for two and a half years. In the spring my wife left for Yalta with Masha and Nadya, at the advice of physicians. They planned to live there all of the spring, summer, and autumn, owing to the beneficial effect on Masha of the local climate. But what was to be done the coming winter? It was quite likely that my wife might have to stay in the Crimea for the winter as well, or go abroad. Under these circumstances, retirement from service began to look to me inopportune, owing to the decrease of income it would entail. I made up my mind to defer my resignation until February 1895, the more so as this retirement had been put off until the fall to meet Balakirev's wishes. In February 1895 I was to round out thirty-five years of service and would get an increase in pension. I had another talk with Balakirev and obtained his consent to my waiting till the time mentioned.

Having banished Nazimov from the Chapel, Balakirev managed to have B—ov appointed in his place. Once he had got a foothold in the Chapel as steward, this favourite of Balakirev's was becoming his right hand. In all likelihood he had been the one who had ousted Nazimov. Whence he came and what his virtues were that had so endeared him to Balakirev is a mystery. Thanks to the fact that B—ov had been confirmed as inspector of the Chapel classes in general subjects, Balakirev ventured to give me (privately) leave of absence for all of three months, as, in the event of his usual departure in August, he would be able to hand over the management of the Chapel to B—ov and not to me as on former occasions.

Before leaving for Yalta to join my wife and daughters I had a talk with Krasnokootsky about my desire to resume, in the fall, the orchestra class of the Chapel, which I had handed on to him for one year only. Krasnokootsky had no objections. But, on learning of my intention, Balakirev wrote me a letter in which he persuaded me — nay, almost insisted — not to take upon myself the orchestra class. The reason he gave was my irritability, which he asserted had developed owing to illness and might recur, despite my coming summer's rest, if I began to teach the orchestra class. Such solicitude on Balakirev's part concerning my health and tranquillity clearly showed me that he was highly pleased with the fact that I had not led the orchestra class for a year and that there could have been no

N. A. RIMSKY-KORSAKOV

from the painting by V. A. Serov

disputes or discontent between us in the matter. In brief, he was evidently pleased to get rid of me; hence I thought his wish equivalent to a command, and abandoned for good and all the thought of taking back into my hands my own creation — the orchestra class of the Chapel.

After the examinations at the Conservatory and at the Chapel had ended, I left, on May 13 [25], for Yalta, whence disquieting news had been reaching me of Masha's condition. For two or three weeks before leaving I paid several visits a week to the studio (near the Kamyenny (Stone) Bridge) of I. Y. Ryepin, who was painting my portrait on an order from Byelayev.[1] Prior to my departure, on my saint's day, in the evening, Tchaikovsky, Byelayev, Glazunov, Lyadov, Yastryebtsev, Sokolov, and Trifonov came to my house. We sat and talked. Among other things Tchaikovsky and I discussed the meeting which had taken place a few days before of the Board of Directors of the St. Petersburg branch of the Russian Musical Society; to this meeting there had been invited also Auer, Solovyov, Laroche, and I, although we were not on the Board. The discussion had centred on electing a conductor for the concerts of the Russian Musical Society for the ensuing season; I had mentioned Tchaikovsky. My suggestion had been accepted, and the Board had already approached Tchaikovsky with the request, but he was still undecided. A. S. Taneiev, one of the members of the Board, happened to be on the train by which I travelled. He told me that Tchaikovsky had consented to take charge of four or five concerts, while for the others various other conductors would be invited, and among these, Lyadov (for two concerts), a fact which I was exceedingly glad to hear.

On reaching Yalta I found my poor little girl feeling worse than when she had left St. Petersburg. The latter half of May and June went monotonously with us. I read much, was busy writing the piano score of *Pskovityanka*, began taking sea-baths, but walked little. We did not know how long we would stay at Weber's villa (near Yalta), where we had put up, and so I did not venture to

---

[1] The famous portrait, which has been at the Russian Museum in Leningrad since M. P. Byelayev's death.

rent a piano. Towards the end of June I did rent one after all, but improvised ever so little; I jotted down a small piece for the cello and recorded some few other things. But, Masha's health taking a turn for the worse, we decided to take her back to St. Petersburg and I gave up the piano. Our departure was postponed, however, as at first Masha was too weak to travel; then she felt a little better and, on her physician's advice, we resolved to wait. For nearly a year I had not played the piano, and whenever I did come near it, it was to accompany the playing of my children: Volodya on the violin, and Andrey on the cello. When engrossed in reading I felt in no musical mood. Here at Yalta this mood came over me for two or three days in succession. Masha's illness and our apprehension for her produced a depressing effect on my wife and me. Delightful Yalta, with its wonderful views, flora, and blue sea grew downright unbearable to us this time. At the beginning of my sojourn in Yalta I had made some progress on the instrumentation of *Pskovityanka* and had even turned to writing a textbook of musical forms and a textbook of the theory of harmony; but instead of simple and sensible textbooks, some sort of philosophic dreams came into being. I attempted to go on with my interrupted work on the æsthetics of musical art, work to which I had returned several times in St. Petersburg during the spring, but even in Yalta I was dissatisfied with my sketches.[2] I gave up this work and turned to writing my reminiscences; but as I had not at hand certain materials for describing that long-bygone time, I recorded everything that I remembered concerning the just-ended season of 1892–3, and, accordingly I can resume writing my diary, which I have long intended to turn to and now proceed to do.[3]

By August Masha's condition grew worse. Some time after the 20th of that month [September 1] I was to return to St. Petersburg, as my leave of absence was then to end. We wrote to Misha and

---

[2] All these sketches I burned (January 21 [February 2], 1894), as being good for nothing. [The author's own note.]

[3] Written at Yalta, July 13 [25], 1893.

In a footnote to this passage Rimsky-Korsakov says: " The writing of the diary did not materialize and the reminiscences of the end of the summer, though written ten years later, are added here."

Sonya that they were to come on to Yalta so that my wife might not remain alone in attendance on the sick little girl. Soon after Misha and Sonya arrived, I left for St. Petersburg alone, but en route, in Kharkov, a telegram from Yalta overtook me, announcing the death of Masha on August 22 [September 3]. I returned to Yalta immediately. We buried our poor little girl at the Yalta cemetery and started for St. Petersburg all together.

In view of my expected retirement from the Chapel, we immediately began to look for an apartment, all the more so as the apartment at the Chapel brought back sad memories of Masha's illness and of the death of Slavchik. My wife conceived a positive horror of this apartment. By September 20 [October 2], new rooms (on Zagorodny Prospekt, 28) were found, and we moved into them.[4]

While serving my last months in the Court Chapel, I took a somewhat languid attitude towards my duties; yet I attended very regularly. My own work oscillated between compiling textbooks of counterpoint and instrumentation and writing æsthetic philosophical articles. Mid-season I threw up these fruitless and absurdly misdirected beginnings (I destroyed them completely later on), and my thoughts took a different turn. I once more expressed a desire to take up the directing of the Russian Symphony Concerts, and Byelayev received this suggestion with joy.

During this autumn Tchaikovsky died,[5] after having conducted his own Sixth Symphony only a few days before his death. I recall having asked him, during the intermission, after the performance

---

[4] Written at St. Petersburg, January 22 [February 3], 1904.

Originally this apartment was designated as 24; later on it was renumbered as 39. Rimsky-Korsakov lived there until his death. In the course of the years that followed the main body of the house at No. 28 in which Rimsky-Korsakov had lived became a rear-yard house, since the former squat wooden wing, its windows facing the Zagorodny Prospekt, was replaced by a new stone extension of the same property. After Rimsky-Korsakov's death, Mme M. A. Lavrova, proprietress of No. 28, acting on her own initiative, put up a marble memorial tablet on the street-facing building. Thanks to the efforts of the *Zhakt* (Dwelling-Lease Co-operative Society) in collaboration with the Society "Ancient St. Petersburg–New Leningrad" this tablet was restored in 1934 and unveiled anew at a public meeting of the Society.

At present the same Society in conjunction with the *Zhakt* is organizing a children's park in the court of No. 28 and is planning to put up marble memorial tablets directly on the wing building where Rimsky-Korsakov used to live. The artist-architect F. G. Bernshtam has charge of the artistic form of this project.

[5] P. I. Tchaikovsky died on October 25 [November 6], 1893.

of the symphony, whether he had a program for this composition. He replied that there was one, of course, but that he did not wish to announce it. During that last visit of his to St. Petersburg I saw him only at the concert.[6] A few days later the news of his grave illness was in everybody's mouth. The whole world filed to his apartment several times a day to inquire about his health. How strange that, although death had resulted from cholera, still admission to the Mass for the dead was free to all! I remember how Vyerzhbilovich, totally drunk . . . kept kissing the deceased man's head and face. His sudden death was a blow to one and all. Soon after the funeral the Sixth Symphony was repeated at a concert with Napravnik as conductor. This time the public greeted it rapturously, and since that moment the fame of the symphony has kept growing and growing, spreading gradually over Russia and Europe. It was said that the symphony had been made understandable to the public of St. Petersburg by Napravnik's interpretation, something that Tchaikovsky, who was not a gifted conductor, had been unable to accomplish. Hence, they said, at the first performance under its author's direction the public had greeted it with considerable restraint. I think this is not true. The symphony was played finely by Napravnik, but it had gone very well at its author's hands, too. The public had simply not fathomed it the first time, and had not paid enough attention to it; precisely as several years earlier it had failed to give due attention to Tchaikovsky's Fifth Symphony. I imagine that the composer's sudden death (which had given rise to all sorts of rumours), as well as stories of his presentiment of approaching death (to which mankind is so prone), and, further, the propensity towards discovering a connection between the gloomy mood of the symphony's last movement and such a presentiment — all these now focused the public's attention and sympathies on this work, and the splendid composition soon became famed and even fashionable.

Upon the organization behind the Russian Symphony Concerts devolved the moral obligation of devoting its first concert to the memory of Tchaikovsky. As far as I recollect, that, to a considerable

---

[6] At the concert of October 16 [28], 1893.

degree, was precisely what had induced me to undertake the concerts once more. The concert of Tchaikovsky's compositions was given November 30 [December 12], under my direction, with the assistance of F. M. Blumenfeld (the Fourth Symphony, *Francesca da Rimini, Marche slave,* pianoforte pieces, etc.).

The conducting of the Russian Symphony Concerts (that season there were three in all; [7] at the final concert, my *Verse about Aleksey, the Godly Man,* had its first performance), and the invitation D. D. Klimov had sent me to come to Odessa to conduct two concerts, gradually diverted me from my fruitless work on the textbook of æsthetics. On the other hand, I made a final decision to retire from the Chapel, as the pension I was entitled to appeared sufficient, while service in the Chapel had grown unbearable, and the relations between Balakirev and me were manifestly impaired for all time. In January 1894 I tendered my resignation [8] and went off to Odessa. I had been asked to conduct, in the Municipal Theatre, one concert in memory of Tchaikovsky and one with a program of my own compositions. In Odessa they paid me no end of attention and granted me many rehearsals. I practised the program numbers with the strings alone, and the brass instruments alone in various pieces, drilling a fair but provincial orchestra as if they were pupils; and I got out an excellent performance. The assisting artists in the concerts were the singer Mme Zherebtsova and the pianiste Dronseyko (a pupil of Klimov). The program in memory

---

[7] November 30 [December 12] and December 18 [30], 1893, and January 22 [February 3], 1894.

[8] The application for retirement was tendered November 3 [15], 1893. In his letter of December 16 [28], 1893 to S. N. Krooglikov, Rimsky-Korsakov wrote: " Of talk concerning my retiring, there is no end. Balakirev is being accused, a quarrel is suspected, etc. The reasons for my retiring are the following for everybody: I feel unwell and overtired; I have worked thirty-three years, and retiring as I do through illness, it makes the full thirty-five years of service behind me to entitle me to a considerable pension and an additional maintenance granted me by the sovereign for twenty-five years of useful musical activity; I wish to free myself of superfluous occupations in order to have leisure time for composing. . . . Don't these seem to be sufficient reasons? Now for you I shall add that all this veritable truth must be supplemented with the statement that serving with Balakirev in the pious and sanctimonious Chapel (which some very suspicious persons have entered lately) is unbearable to me. My relations with Balakirev are good for nothing, as you well know; consequently it is also natural that I am constantly in a state of irritation, which is both unpleasant and harmful to me. . . ."

of Tchaikovsky (February 5 [17]) was as follows: Third Symphony
in D major; aria from *Orlyeanskaya Dyeva* (*The Maid of Orleans*);
the First Concerto for the piano; songs; and the Overture *Romeo
and Juliet*. The concert suffered somewhat through Dronseyko,
who played in ragged rhythm in the second movement and thereby
kept both orchestra and me at a loss. The program of the other
concert (February 12 [24]) included the First Symphony in E
minor; the song of Lyel; *Sadko;* songs; and the *Spanish Capriccio*.
The success of both concerts was quite considerable. I was induced
to conduct one more concert (for the benefit of the orchestra); the
Capriccio was repeated, and also the *Shchelkoonchik* (*Nutcracker*)
Suite. My wife came on to attend these concerts. We had to spend
our time in social calls and at the musical soirées of the Odessa
Music School. The Governor of the city of Odessa at the time was
P. A. Zelyony, my quondam chief, once commander of the clipper
Almaz. A meeting with him would have afforded me no pleasure;
but, as luck would have it, he was out of town just then. However,
we had many occasions to meet his wife; once she even invited us
to dine with her, but we slipped out of that. In Odessa we made the
acquaintance of the painter N. D. Kooznyetsov and his wife (she is
a genuine Ukrainian).

Walks along the sea gave me my first thoughts of taking up, some
day, a Homeric theme such as the episode of Nausicaä; but the intention was only a passing one.

On my return to St. Petersburg I felt refreshed by the trip. To
our joy, my resignation had been accepted. I had been granted a
satisfactory pension.[9]

To this period belongs the printing of the new orchestral score
of *The Maid of Pskov*, undertaken by Bessel's. I was deluged with
proof-reading. The concerts, the trip to Odessa, my retirement from
the Chapel, my work on *Pskovityanka,* all these together distracted

---

[9] On February 19 [March 3] [1894. J. A. J.], Rimsky-Korsakov paid a " diplo-
matic " visit to I. A. Vsyevolozhsky for the purpose of clearing up the question why
none of his operas was given on the Imperial stage. Vsyevolozhsky promised that
" he would keep in mind Rimsky-Korsakov's operas when framing the coming repertoire." Cf. V. V. Yastryebtsev: *My Reminiscences of Rimsky-Korsakov* (Petrograd,
1917), Part II, pp. 40–1.

attention from those barren, dry, and nerve-racking occupations as well as from my thought-wanderings in philosophical and æsthetic jungles. The desire seized me to write an opera. With the death of Tchaikovsky, the subject of *Christmas Eve,* so attractive also to me, had been released, as it were. Despite many of its musical pages, I had always considered Tchaikovsky's opera weak, and Polonsky's libretto good for nothing. During Tchaikovsky's lifetime I should have been unable to take up this subject without causing the man himself a heartache. Now I was free in that respect, too, in addition to having always been entitled to it morally.

Towards the spring of 1894 I finally made up my mind to compose *Christmas Eve* and began to write the libretto myself, closely following Gogol. But my predilection for Slavic " goddom " and devildom and sun-myths had not left me since the days of *May Night* and especially *Snyegoorochka;* it had not run its course in me even with the writing of *Mlada.* I clung to fragmentary motives occurring in Gogol's works like *Christmas carolling, the stars playing at blind man's buff,* the flight of *oven-forks* and *hearth-broom,* the encounter with a *witch,* etc. Having read and re-read in Afanasyev (*The Slavs' Poetic Views of Nature*) about the connection between the Christian celebration of Christmas and the birth of the sun after the winter solstice, with vague myths of Ovsyeñ, Kolyada,[10] etc., I conceived the idea of introducing these extinct beliefs into the Ukrainian life described by Gogol in his story. In this way my libretto, while clinging on the one hand faithfully to Gogol (not even barring his language and expressions), contained, on the other hand, in its fantastic portions, much extraneous matter dragged in by me. To me and those who desired to delve into it and understand me, this connection was clear; but to audiences, subsequently, it proved utterly incomprehensible and even disturbing. My enthusiasm for myths, and my combining them with Gogol's story, were of course a mistake on my part, but a mistake

---

[10] Ovsyeñ or Avsyeñ, originally the first day of spring, March 1 (March was then the first month of the year); now transferred to New Year or New Year's Eve. Kolyada (from Latin *calendæ,* the first of a month), the carolling and glorification by youngsters under people's windows in order to get a few pennies during Christmas week and New Year, until Epiphany. J. A. J.

which offered the opportunity of writing a wealth of interesting music.

Soon a respectable amount of musical material had accumulated, and the First Tableau had been written in rough draft. I remember that shortly before our going to the country, Shtroopp, Trifonov, Yastryebtsev, and some other people gathered at our house. Without telling them precisely what I was composing, I played them the introduction to the opera and asked them to guess what it was about. To be sure, it was hard to guess, but most conjectures revolved about what was approximately correct; therefore I told them of my work and set forth the plan of the opera.

Christmas Eve was the beginning of my uninterrupted operatic activity that followed.

In May we moved for the summer to the estate of Vyechasha, in the Looga canton (Plyoossa Station).[11] Vyechasha is a charming spot: a wonderful large lake, Pyesno, and a vast ancient orchard with century-old lindens, elms, and so forth. The house was a heavy and clumsy structure, yet spacious and comfortable. The proprietress — an old woman — with her daughter, an overripe maiden, lived close by, in a tiny house, but did not interfere with us. The bathing was fine. At night the moon and the stars cast wonderful reflections on the lake. There was a multitude of birds. I had stumbled upon this estate, and it took my fancy at once. Near by were the villages Zapyesenye and Polosy; not far away was the Lubensk manor, owned by Mme Bookharova. The woods were somewhat far, but fine. We were all in love with Vyechasha.

The Second Tableau of my opera had been begun by me when I was still in St. Petersburg; here the composition advanced rapidly. I composed almost without a break, devoting but a little time to bathing and walking; by the end of the summer the entire opera, except the last tableau, had been written in rough draft,[12] while Act I had even been orchestrated to a considerable extent. The thought of introducing Tableau VIII (the last but one) with Va-

---

[11] Written May 22 [June 4], 1904.

[12] The first idea of *Christmas Eve* came on April 10 [22], and by August 16 [28] the opera was already finished, in rough draft, of course. (Letter of September 8 [20], 1894 to S. N. Krooglikov.)

koola's return flight and the procession of Ovsyeñ and Kolyada, came to me during the summer and was carried out forthwith.

At the end of the summer, Trifonov, Yastryebtsev, and Byelayev each spent two or three days with me, and I played them passages from the opera I was writing.

Shortly before my coming to Vyechasha, I had received a letter from N. F. Findeisen [13] in which he urged me to set to work on an opera on the subject of *Sadko* and proposed a certain plan for the libretto. As an operatic subject, *Sadko* had interested me from time to time, as early as the eighties.[14] Findeisen's idea brought it to my mind once more. In the very midst of other work — that is, while composing *Christmas Eve* — my thought frequently turned also to *Sadko*. My project differed somewhat from Findeisen's. I wrote Stassov of my idea; in reply, he, too, suggested several things; thus he gave me the idea of the first scene of the opera, which I had not had in view originally. During the summer the plan of the " opera *bylina* " (epic song, legend) *Sadko*, as I re-

[13] Nikolay Fyodorovich Findeisen (1868–1928), noted student of Russian musicology and editor of the *Russian Musical Gazette,* the first serious musical magazine in Russia (monthly 1894–9; weekly thereafter until 1918). J. A. J.

[14] Among Rimsky-Korsakov's papers has been preserved a manuscript libretto of *Sadko,* written by V. Sidorov and dedicated to Rimsky-Korsakov, but judging from the date on the title-page, it must belong to 1883. In its general conception V. Sidorov's poem has little resemblance to the " opera *bylina* " composed later by Rimsky-Korsakov to a text of his own. In his letter on the last page of this manuscript V. Sidorov dedicates his work to Rimsky-Korsakov and cites his enthusiasm for the music of the symphonic poem *Sadko* as his motive. The letter is dated March 25 [April 6], 1883. Cf. also the substantial corrections introduced into the history of the libretto of *Sadko* by the publication of the " Correspondence between Rimsky-Korsakov and V. V. Stassov " and noted by V. D. Komarova in her preface to this correspondence (cf. *Russkaya Mysl'*, 1910, VI–IX). Stassov's immediate part in *Sadko's* assuming literary form is made clear in these letters. It is curious that the historian and publicist N. I. Kostomarov had already written to Countess Bloodova in a letter dated April 12 [24], 1861: " When one examines attentively and delves into the treasures of Russian folk-poetry, one unceasingly regrets not having been born a poet, a painter, a composer. Take for instance the songs about Sadko, the wealthy merchant of Novgorod: new variants of this [epic. J. A. J.] song have now been published by Rybnikov. My Lord! What a marvellous subject for an opera! One cannot imagine a broader and more fertile field in which music would be able to unite its powers with the full artistry of the *mise en scène*. It strikes me that with us music will attain a high point. For in spite of so slight a fund of familiarity with folk-poetry as we possessed in the thirties, Glinka was nevertheless able to divine the folk-tone and create amidst that darkness of night. And how that same talent would manifest itself at a period when the mystery of the folk-soul ceases being a hieroglyphic for our educated society." Cf. also note 10 on p. 74.

call it, took final shape in my mind, though subsequently there crept into it certain important additions, of which I shall speak in due course. I had in view to utilize for this opera the material of my symphonic poem, and, in any event, to make use of its motives as leading motives for the opera. To be sure, the writing of *Christmas Eve* held first place with me; yet even at that very time there came into my head some new musical ideas for *Sadko* also, like the melody of *Sadko's* aria, the theme of Nyezhata's *bylina;* something for the finale of the opera. I remember that often the place where I composed such material was on the long plank foot-bridges running from the shore to the bathing-pavilion on the lake. The bridges ran down among bulrushes; on one side were visible the tall bending willows of the garden, on the other side lay the wide expanse of Lake Pyesno. The whole environment, somehow, disposed me to thoughts of *Sadko.* Yet the true, real writing of *Sadko* had not commenced and was postponed until the completion of *Christmas Eve.*

On my return from Vyechasha to St. Petersburg I soon finished writing the entire rough draft of *Christmas Eve* and set out to orchestrate the opera as well as to put the finishing touches to it. Byelayev agreed to publish my opera; and, as the orchestral score grew ready under my hands, it was sent on piecemeal for engraving by Röder in Leipzig. I can't recall the exact month when I had the entire orchestral score finished and had made the arrangement (of the piano score); I believe it was towards the end of the winter of 1894–5. All in all, it took a little less than a year to do the entire composition with its instrumentation.[15]

On September 28 [October 10] my *May Night* was revived at the Mikhaylovsky Theatre with Chooprynnikov as Lyevko, and Slavina in the rôle of Hanna.[16] The performance of the opera was not bad. Napravnik conducted, and apparently with a will. It was given several times at the Mikhaylovsky Theatre, with middling success.

---

[15] On the autograph orchestral score of *Christmas Eve* there are the following dates: Act I, First Tableau, "February 6 [18], 1895"; Act I, Second Tableau, "February 22 [March 6], 1895"; Act II, Third Tableau, "January 6 [18], 1895." (The remaining tableaux are not among Rimsky-Korsakov's papers.)

[16] The first performance took place September 28 [October 10], 1894.

In the autumn A. G. Rubinstein died.[17] The funeral surroundings
were solemn. The coffin was set in the Izmaylovsky Cathedral; musicians kept vigil at the coffin day and night. Lyadov and I were
on duty between two and three in the morning. I recall how amid
the church obscurity there entered the sable mourning figure of
Malozyomova,[18] who came to kneel before the ashes of her Rubinstein, whom she had worshipped. There was even something of the
fantastic about it.

The Russian Symphony Concerts of this season (they were four
in number) were under my direction.[19] The first concert was devoted to the memory of Rubinstein. The program consisted of: the
Third Symphony in A major; aria from *Moses; Don Quixote;* the
Fourth Piano Concerto in D minor (Lavrov); songs; and dances
from the ballet *Vinogradnaya Loza (The Grapevine).* At the succeeding Russian Symphony Concerts the following numbers were
given for the first time: Glazunov's *Ballet Suite* and *Fantasy;* [20] also
(at the fourth concert, with the assistance of Mravina): Introduction; Oksana's aria; *Kolyadka* and *Polonaise* from *Christmas Eve.*
Everything sounded excellent.

Among the events of my musical life of this season belongs the
delightful performance of *Snyegoorochka,* at my house, by artists
of the Imperial Theatres. Mravina, Dolina, Kamyenskaya, Runge;
Yakovlev, Vasilyev III, Chooprynnikov, and Koryakin kindly consented to sing the opera to the accompaniment of a piano. Fyeliks
Blumenfeld played the accompaniments; Vyerzhbilovich played
the cello solo in Byeryendyey's cavatina. We even had a miniature

---

17 November 8 [20], 1894.
18 Of this lady Mrs. Newmarch writes as follows: " Mme. Malozyomova, whom I
met in St. Petersburg, was for many years *dame de compagnie,* or chaperon, at Rubinstein's classes at the Conservatoire. She was a devoted friend of the master's, and
few people knew more of his fascinating personality or spoke more eloquently of
his teaching." According to Riemann, Sofiya Aleksandrovna Malozyomova was a little
more than a *dame de compagnie.* Born in 1845 in St. Petersburg, she was educated
at the Smolny Institute; in 1863 she entered the St. Petersburg Conservatory, from
which she was graduated in 1866. She was a pupil of Leschetizky and Rubinstein.
Later she devoted her life to piano instruction at the Conservatory. C. V. V.
19 On Saturdays, December 3 [15] and 17 [29], 1894, January 14 [26] and February 4 [16], 1895.
20 Op. 52 and op. 53. J. A. J.

347

female chorus of opera choristers, who gave their services gratis. The guests were numerous; everything was charming.[21]

In January I made a trip to Kiev, at the invitation of the directors of the local opera, to witness the production of *Snyegoorochka* there.[22] I attended the dress rehearsal and the first two performances. The part of Byeryendyey was sung by Morskoy (then still a private opera artist), Snyegoorochka by Karatayeva, Lyel by Koryetskaya, Vyesna (Spring) by Azyerskaya, etc. The conductor, Pagani, was baffled by the ¼ time of the final chorus, after all. In general, a composer's coming directly to the dress rehearsal has little sense: it is too late then to make corrections or changes, while to insist upon postponement of the performance is both inconvenient and unpleasant. On the whole, all went off in a fair, though provincial, way; the orchestra was sufficiently spirited during the entire Butter-week chorus. There was dancing till their feet refused to bear them; especially did Dooma, the stage-manager, exert himself above all others. As prescribed by provincial taste, Bobyl cut capers, while at the performance proper, during Byeryendyey's cavatina, he played the mountebank, and clambered on the throne behind the Tsar's back, thereby drawing loud bursts of laughter from the audience. Morskoy, who had no suspicion of this, felt embarrassed and apprehensive lest this laughter of the onlookers was the result of some disorder in his own costume. At the dress rehearsal a very funny thing happened: I was standing on the stage; while the chorus at the beginning of Act III was being sung, I noticed that the motive:

which was played by the first violins, was at the same time being played three octaves below that, by one of the double-basses.

[21] This soirée occurred on December 26, 1894 [January 7, 1895]. It is circumstantially described in V. V. Yastryebtsev's *Reminiscences*, Part II, pp. 190 ff.

[22] The first performance took place on January 23 [February 4], 1895. [The fourth and fifth Russian editions of *My Musical Life* erroneously state *December* 23, 1895. J. A. J.] The billboard read: "The opera has been produced in the presence of the composer."

Pagani, who was not particularly keen of ear in harmony, did not perceive it and kept on conducting. I went over to the double-bass player and satisfied myself that he was really reading the motive from his music. I stopped the orchestra and asked the double-bass player to show me his part. It turned out that, instead of the violin cue, the copyist had actually foisted this motive upon him, and in the bass clef at that. I forbade the musician to play this motive and struck the motive from his part. Then the double-bass player, who evidently seemed to have taken a fancy to that motive, said to me in an imploring voice: " Mr. Rimsky-Korsakov, please let this motive stay in and permit me to play it! It sounds so well this way." Of course, I could not allow it, and thereby brought sorrow upon the unfortunate player. After the second performance my wife and I returned to St. Petersburg. In Kiev they quite took to my opera, where it later had a long run.

In Kiev I had a chance to meet my former pupils Ryb and the composer Lysenko.[23] At the latter's house I ate *varyeniki*[24] and listened to excerpts from his opera *Taras Bulba*.[25] Did not like it — I mean *Taras Bulba*, not the *varyeniki*.

The Society of Musical Gatherings,[26] which had sprung up several years before this in St. Petersburg and had shown few signs of life heretofore, suddenly came to life this season, under the chair-

---

[23] Lysenko also wrote an opera on the subject of Gogol's *Christmas Eve*. Solovyov and Shchoorovsky were others who set this theme. C. V. V.

[24] Dumplings filled with curds, or berries, or cabbage, etc. This national dish of the Ukrainians is considered a great delicacy. J. A. J.

[25] Based on Gogol's famous story by that name. J. A. J.

[26] Already during the first year of its renewed existence (1894–5) the Society of Musical Gatherings presented itself as follows: I. N. Davidov, Chairman; A. K. Glazunov, Associate Chairman; G. A. Blokh, A. A. Davidov, N. M. Shtroopp, Members of the Board. Among the Founder-Members were listed: G. A. Blokh, V. G. Valter, Baron V. G. Vrangel, A. I. Vyshñegradsky, A. K. Glazunov, I. A. and A. A. Davidov, and others. Among the Honorary Members: Balakirev, Byelayev, Cui, Laroche, Napravnik, Rimsky-Korsakov, Stassov, and A. D. Sheryemetyev. Among the Active Members: V. I. and R. I. Byelsky, L. G. Kantser-Chegodar, I. I. Lapshin, A. V. Ossovsky, V. P. Semyonov-Tyanshañsky, V. L. Tookholka, N. F. Findeisen, N. M. Shtroopp, V. V. Yastryebtsev.

The Maid of Pskov was given four times in 1895: April 6, 7, 13, and 16 [18, 19, 25, and 28]. The business arrangements were in the hands of the secretary of the society, N. M. Shtroopp, assisted by N. V. Solovov and R. I. Byelsky. On I. A. Davidov's resignation in September 1895, his brother A. A. Davidov was elected chairman.

manship of my former pupil Ivan Avgustovich Davidov. They planned to produce my *Pskovityanka* at the Panayevsky Theatre, under Davidov's direction, after its new score as recently published by Bessel's. Choral and orchestral rehearsals were begun, and, as author, I was called in for guidance. My Sonya sang in the chorus. Owing to Davidov's illness, the orchestral rehearsals for weeding out errors fell to my lot; later the recuperated Davidov came into his own. *The Maid of Pskov* was given on Thursday, April 6 [18], and had three more performances. Ivan Grozny was sung by Koryakin, Toocha by Vasilyev III, Vlasyevna by Mme Dore, Tokmakov by Lunacharsky,[27] Olga by Mme Vyelinskaya (no longer of the Mariinsky Theatre at that time). At the second performance Sokolovskaya sang Olga; at the third performance the part was to be sung again by Vyelinskaya, but owing to some caprice she refused and the part was sung by L. D. Ilyina (a mezzo-soprano), who transposed her aria in Act II a third lower. At the first performance a scandalous scene occurred. The orchestra came to a stop, and it was necessary to begin afresh from section number so-and-so. In general, however, the opera was given fairly well, considering its amateur chorus, its amateur conductor, and its amateur rehearsing.

During the season of 1894–5 the instrumentation and printing of *Christmas Eve* were making forced headway, and I apprised Director of the Theatres Vsyevolozhsky of the existence of my new opera. He demanded that I submit the libretto to the dramatic censor, at the same time expressing serious doubt about its being approved by the censor, owing to the presence of the Empress Catherine II (the Great) among the dramatis personæ. As I was somewhat familiar with censorship requirements, I had not introduced that name into the opera from the very outset, having called the character merely *Tsaritsa,* and invariably calling St. Petersburg merely *grad-stolitsa* (capital city). It would seem that the censor might be satisfied: how many are the varieties of tsaritsas that appear in operas? On the whole, *Christmas Eve* is a fairy-tale, and the Tsaritsa merely a fairy-tale personage. I submitted the libretto

---

[27] M. V. Lunacharsky, brother of the future prominent figure in the October revolution.

in this form to the dramatic censor, being positive it would be approved and fearing for my scrivener rather than for my Queen. But nothing of that sort! At the censorship bureau I was flatly refused permission to put on Tableau VIII of the opera (scene before the Queen's palace), as, under an Imperial Order of 1837 to the censorship bureau, under no circumstances might Russian monarchs be introduced in operas. I argued that there was no personage of the Romanov house in my opera, that only some fantastic Queen appears in it, that the theme of *Christmas Eve* deals with a mere fairy-tale, an invention of Gogol's, in which I have a right to change any one of the dramatis personæ, that even the name " St. Petersburg" is mentioned nowhere, that consequently all allusions to actual history have been steered clear of, and so forth. At the censor's I was told that Gogol's story was familiar to everybody and that nobody could have any doubts about my Queen being none other than the Empress Catherine, and that the censorship bureau had no right to sanction the opera! I made up my mind, if possible, to petition in the higher spheres for permission to produce the opera. In this I was aided by the following circumstances.

In the autumn of 1894 Balakirev left the Court Chapel; a new director had to be appointed. One fine day the Minister of the Imperial Court, Count Vorontsov-Dashkov, summoned me. I had to go to see him at the appointed hour, leaving the rehearsal of the Russian Symphony Society concert and delegating its continuation to Glazunov, who conducted his ballet suite. The Count suggested that I assume Balakirev's functions in his stead, hinting that Balakirev's nature was hard to get along with and that he, Vorontsov, fully realized that I had left the Chapel because joint service with Balakirev had been burdensome to me. Though there was a great deal of truth in this, still my free position, outside all government service, seemed so attractive to me at the time that I did not feel the slightest inclination to join the Chapel again, even in the independent position of Director. I declined Count Vorontsov's offer, assuring him that even though Balakirev's character was hard to get along with, still no one would be able to get along with him as well as I, who had been on terms of friendship with him since the

years of my youth, and that the cause of my refusal lay solely in my
desire for rest and for the free time which I so needed for composition. The Count was exceedingly amiable with me and talked of
many things concerning the Chapel. Seeing that he was in good
spirits and an amiable mood, I took it into my head to pray his
intercession with the Emperor to permit the use of the *Christmas
Eve* libretto on the stage. Vorontsov heard all my arguments and
promised to do everything in his power. In accordance with his
recommendation I drew up a petition concerning the matter and
submitted it to him. During the Christmas holidays a courier came
to me and brought from the director of the administrative section
of the Ministry of the Court an announcement to this effect: " In
accordance with the most devoted report on the petition submitted
by you to the Minister of the Imperial Court, His Majesty the
Emperor's permission has been granted for admitting the opera
Christmas Eve composed by you to be produced on the Imperial
stage without change in the libretto " (December 31, 1894 [Janu-
ary 12, 1895]).[28] I was in a transport of joy and told Vsyevolozhsky
of the matter. Once the libretto had been sanctioned by His Majesty, and the censor had received a slap in the face, a certain stir
had been created in the higher spheres; the case, consequently, had
assumed a different aspect. Vsyevolozhsky delightedly seized upon
the idea of giving *Christmas Eve* an especially magnificent production with which he might even please the Court. He had a magnificent portrait of Catherine II and he would exert himself to have
my Queen made up to resemble as closely as possible that Empress, and in the *mise en scène* he would endeavour to reproduce
with accuracy the gorgeous surroundings of Catherine's Court.
With all that he would manifestly do something pleasing to the
Court, and that is the main thing among the duties of a Director of
Theatres. I attempted somewhat to cool this ardour of Vsyevolozhsky's and suggested to him not to stress particularly my Tsaritsa's
resemblance to Catherine II, saying that it was not necessary. But
Vsyevolozhsky would have his own way. Immediately arrangements were made to accept my opera for production the ensuing

---

[28] I have this document in my possession. [The author's own note.]

season, in 1895–6. During Lent a beginning was made with drilling the choruses, parts were distributed to the artists, the scene-painting was begun, and the enterprise was in full swing.

Towards the spring of 1895 much musical material for the opera *Sadko* had matured in my mind; the libretto was almost ready and definitely worked out in part; for this I had scanned and used as a basis many *bylinas*, songs, etc. In the spring I began and finished in sketch the first tableau (the feast at Novgorod), which gave me satisfaction. In May we moved once more to dear Vyechasha for a summer's stay.[29]

This time my summer's sojourn at Vyechasha was exactly like the previous one. The work of composing *Sadko* ran on uninterruptedly.[30] Tableaux I, II, IV, V, VI, and VII were ready one after the other, and towards the end of summer the whole opera (according to its original plan) was finished in rough draft and partly (Tableaux I and II) also in orchestral score. Whenever I felt slightly tired, I stopped work for a day or two at the utmost, and then with as great a will once more picked it up where I had dropped it. I have said that the work of composing went on according to the original plan; Sadko's wife, Lyubava Booslayevna, had not been included in this plan, and, therefore, the present Tableau III of the opera did not exist as such. Nor, of course, did the scenes dealing with Lyubava Booslayevna in Tableaux IV and VII exist either. Moreover, the scene in the public square was incomparably less developed than subsequently: the wandering pilgrims and Nyezhata did not appear in it, and, besides, Sadko's recital of his adventures in Tableau VII did not include the participation of the chorus.

In the middle of the summer I was visited at Vyechasha by Vladimir Ivanovich Byelsky, who had been introduced to me and had become intimate with me the previous year at St. Petersburg. He was spending this summer at the Ryeteñ estate, some six or

---

[29] Written January 24 [February 5], 1904.

[30] On the work of composing *Sadko*, cf. *Correspondence between A. K. Lyadov and N. A. Rimsky-Korsakov* (Petrograd, 1916), reprinted from *Musical Contemporary*, 1915–16, No. 7.

seven miles away from Vyechasha. A keen, educated, scholarly man, graduated from two faculties — law and natural sciences — and an excellent mathematician to boot, Vladimir Ivanovich was a great connoisseur and lover of Russian antiquity and ancient Russian literature — *bylinas* (epic songs), songs, etc. To judge by appearances, this modest, bashful, and most upright man could not even be suspected of possessing the knowledge and intellect which came to the fore on closer acquaintance. A passionate lover of music, he was one of the warm partisans of modern Russian music in general and of my works in particular.

During his stay at Vyechasha I played him some of the music I had composed for *Sadko*. He was in utter rapture. As a result, there cropped up endless talks about the subject and its details. The idea occurred of introducing Sadko's wife and making certain additions in the folk-like scenes of the opera, but for the time being, all remained mere talk and I could not bring myself to make any changes, for the scenario was engrossing and well-knit even without them. In August, when the rough draft of the whole opera had been finished according to the original plan, my thoughts began to turn to Sadko's wife. It is laughable, but at that time I developed an indefinable longing for the F-minor tonality, in which I had composed nothing for a long time and which thus far I had made no use of in *Sadko*. This unaccountable yearning for the key of F minor drew me irresistibly to compose Lyubava's aria, for which I jotted down the verses on the spot. The aria was composed; it was to my liking and led to the origin of the third tableau of the opera, for which I asked Byelsky to write the rest of the text.[31] Thus at the

---

[31] As far as one can judge from the variant versions of the scenario and libretto of *Sadko* which are among Rimsky-Korsakov's papers and also from Rimsky-Korsakov's correspondence with V. V. Stassov and N. M. Shtroopp, both V. V. Stassov and N. M. Shtroopp (stepson of V. I. Lamansky) had had a consultative participation in working out the scenario of the opera-*bylina*.

In 1895 the collaboration of the libretto of *Sadko* passed into the hands of V. I. Byelsky. The immediate occasion for this was the concept of Sadko's wife, Lyubava, whose introduction into the libretto necessitated new scenes and text, all of which was entrusted to V. I. Byelsky. However, Byelsky's rôle was not confined to this. At Rimsky-Korsakov's request he also touched up sundry passages in the former text. Thus, for instance, *the songs of all the three foreign merchants*, which had crystallized in Rimsky-Korsakov's imagination in their basic textual and musical contents prior to Byelsky's coming upon the scene, eventually underwent an editorial trim-

end of the summer it became definite that there was to be an additional tableau in my opera and that, in conformity with it, much
must be added in Tableaux IV and VII — the additions occasioned
by the introduction of the figure of the beautiful, loving, and faithful Lyubava. Thus finished late in the summer — that is, finished in
accordance with the original plan — the opera turned out to be
unfinished after all, as that plan was now growing more comprehensive, the more so as greater development of the folk-scene at
the beginning of Tableau IV was also proving advisable.[32]

---

ming by Byelsky on the basis of music already composed. After a fresh partial re-
adaptation by Rimsky-Korsakov's hands, they present in their definitive form (as
adopted in the published text) in an exact sense the fruit of conjoint creative work
of the composer and the librettist. In the author's *rough draft* of the opera-*bylina* the
music of the foreign merchants is set to a text which, even if similar, is in spots different formally. Thus the song of the Hindu guest, with the same music, resounded
in Rimsky-Korsakov's work to the following text:

Sans count the pearls are in depths of ocean —
The wonders of the sacred Ind!
Lost in blazing heaven
Peaks are Himalayas. —
Sempiternal sentries
Of the sacred Indies,
O'er the river Ganges
Palm groves blue are looming.
O'er it there tower
Shrines of God — the Brahma —
Where the rigid Brahman
Reads his book of Vedas. . . .

In its present guise the first and the third stanzas of the song of the Varangian
(Viking) merchant stem from Rimsky-Korsakov; the middle one is Byelsky's. The
slow introductory part of the Venetian merchant's song (andante in ¾ time) is
closer to Byelsky; the allegretto, in ⅝ time, runs nearer to Rimsky-Korsakov.

[32] In his letter of September 22 [October 4], 1895 to S. N. Krooglikov, Rimsky-
Korsakov wrote, speaking of his work during the preceding summer: " I am not in-
tending to write the opera *Sadko*, but have already written it while living in the Looga
canton; that is, I sketched it in the rough, and now I have two acts already orchestrated. . . ." Then follows an account of the scenario which was subsequently supplemented.

Orchestrating Sadko. *Production and adventures of* Christmas Eve. *Work on* Boris *and completing* Sadko. Boris *at the Society of Musical Gatherings. Russian Symphony Concerts and Glazunov. The operas* Mlada, Christmas Eve, *and* Sadko *compared. Writing songs. Beginning of* Mozart and Salieri.

ON MOVING BACK to St. Petersburg, I did not undertake to carry out all my new intentions, particularly as I had entrusted Byelsky with writing for me the new portions of the libretto, and he was faced with a huge and difficult task. In the meantime I set out to orchestrate the parts of the opera that were not to undergo any changes, such as Tableaux V and VI, as well as considerable portions of Tableaux IV and VII.[1] I recall that the first half-year I was completely occupied with pondering and writing a rather complicated orchestral score, and that towards the end of winter I had

[1] On the autograph copy of the orchestral score of the opera *Sadko* (St. Petersburg) there are the following basic dates:

End of Tableau I, " Vyechasha, June 23 [July 5], 1895." Last folio of Tableau II, missing in the manuscript. End of Tableau III, " Smyerdovitsy, July 21 [August 2], 1896." End of Tableau IV, " August 9 [21], Vyechasha; October 29 [November 10], 1895, St. Petersburg; July 15 [27], Smyerdovitsy." End of Tableau V, " Vyechasha, July 8 [20], 1895; St. Petersburg, September 22 [October 4], 1895." End of Tableau VI, " August 14 [26], 1896, Smyerdovitsy." End of Tableau VII, " July 31 [August 12], 1895, Vyechasha; August 3 [15], 1896, Smyerdovitsy; September 3 [15], Smyerdovitsy."

developed a feeling of fatigue, I may say even of indifference and almost aversion towards this work. This frame of mind manifested itself for the first time then, but subsequently it would recur invariably towards the end of all my major works. It always made its appearance suddenly somehow: the work of composition would run on as it should, with complete enthusiasm and concentration; then, suddenly, weariness and indifference would creep on from apparently nowhere. After a lapse of time this sickening mood would pass of its own accord and I would again resume work with all my former zeal. This mood had no resemblance whatever to the one I had experienced during the years 1891–3. There was no terrifying thought-rambling through philosophic and æsthetic jungles. On the contrary, from then on I was ever ready, perfectly calmly, without fear and without pain, to play at home-spun philosophizing, as nearly everybody does, to discuss matters weighty, " to ponder universes " [2] as a pastime, to turn upside-down the beginnings of all beginnings and the ends of all ends.

The première of *Christmas Eve* was set for November 21 [December 3], as a benefit performance to commemorate O. O. Palyechek's twenty-five years of service as a teacher of stage deportment. The following circumstances had preceded the performance: As usual there were rehearsals, orchestral and choral. The rôles had been distributed as follows: Vakoola, Yershov; Oksana, Mme Mravina; Solokha, Mme Kamyenskaya; the Devil, Chooprynnikov; the Dyak (Sexton), Oogrinovich; Choob, Koryakin; the Mayor, Mayboroda; the Tsaritsa (Empress), Pilts. Vsyevolozhsky kept amusing himself with the schemes for the *mise en scène,* and hence everybody worked hard — the scenery and costumes were on a lavish scale, the rehearsing was fine. Finally the dress rehearsal was announced, with the public admitted by tickets. Simultaneously a placard appeared with a complete and accurate designation of the dramatis personæ, as per the libretto. The Grand Dukes Vladimir Aleksandrovich and Mikhayil Nikolayevich came to the dress rehearsal and both of them showed indignation at the presence (on the stage) of the Queen, in whom they insisted on recognizing the

---

[2] Serov's phrase about Wagner. (Author's note.)

Empress Catherine II. Vladimir Aleksandrovich was roused to particular exasperation by it.

After the end of the dress rehearsal all the performers, the stage-managers, and the theatre administration lost heart and changed their tune, saying that the Grand Duke had gone from the opera directly to the Emperor to ask that my opera be forbidden a public performance. For his part, the Grand Duke Mikhayil Nikolayevich ordered the Cathedral to be daubed over on the drop representing St. Petersburg and the Petropavlovskaya Kryepost (Fortress of St. Peter and St. Paul), visible in the distance; in this fortress, he cried, his ancestors lay buried, and he could not permit it to be represented on the stage of a theatre. Vsyevolozhsky felt utterly taken aback. Palyechek's benefit performance had been announced, the tickets were on sale; everybody was nonplussed and quite at a loss what to do. I considered my case lost, as, according to report, the Emperor had fully sided with Grand Duke Vladimir Aleksandrovich and had withdrawn his sanction for producing my opera. Vsyevolozhsky, who was eager to save Palyechek's benefit performance and his own production, suggested that I substitute a Most Serene Highness (baritone) for the Tsaritsa (mezzo-soprano). From a musical point of view this change presented no difficulties: a baritone could easily sing the part of mezzo-soprano an octave lower, the part consisting of recitatives throughout, without a single ensemble. To be sure, the result was not what I had had in mind, the result was foolish, it amounted to an absurdity, as the master of the Queen's wardrobe turned out to be a Most Serene. Further explanations on the subject are superfluous on my part. True, it caused me both sorrow and amusement, but a human head is of no avail against a stone wall, after all — so I consented. Vsyevolozhsky began to pull wires — through whom, I don't know — but he did obtain from the Emperor permission to produce *Christmas Eve* with a Most Serene Highness instead of the Tsaritsa. Soon a poster with this change was placarded, and the opera was produced as a benefit performance for Palyechek.

I did not attend the first performance, my wife and I staying at home.[3] I wished at least thereby to show my displeasure at everything that had happened. My children were at the theatre. The opera won a decent success. Yastryebtsev brought a wreath to my house. After Palyechek's benefit *Christmas Eve* was given once to all subscribers and three more times on non-subscription evenings. Of course, not one member of the Imperial family attended any of the performances, and after that Vsyevolozhsky's attitude towards me and my compositions underwent a profound change.

During the season of 1895–6 the Russian Symphony Concerts (four in number) [4] were given under the direction of A. K. Glazunov and myself, the two of us sharing the program of each concert almost equally.

My rapprochement with the leaders of the Society of Musical Gatherings, the brothers Davidov, Goldenblum, and others, a rapprochement that had taken place the previous season, beginning with the production of *Pskovityanka,* was progressing. This time the leaders in some way got together with Count A. D. Sheryemetyev, who had a full concert orchestra of his own, led by the conductor of the Court Orchestra, G. I. Varlikh. Count Sheryemetyev's orchestra was permanently quartered at his estate, Oolyanovka, not far from the Ligovo station. Davidov, Goldenblum, and I with them visited the Count several times at Oolyanovka; the Count used to take us there by special train and then by horses. After dinner we heard his orchestra, which performed program numbers fairly well. Once I tried out even the coronation scene from *Boris Godunov;* I was busy on it just about that time, writing the orchestral score and making a fresh arrangement for piano and voices.[5] By the way, at first the work of orchestrating *Sadko* and then work on *Boris Godunov* had so worn me out by springtime

---

[3] From a letter to S. N. Krooglikov at the end of November [early in December] 1895: " I did not attend the first performance, because there was no desire — since my opera has been disfigured by the remodelling of which you are aware; the third performance and the fourth I went to see. A baiting of my opera is on in the papers."

[4] On Saturdays, January 20 [February 1], February 17 [29] and 24 [March 7], and March 9 [21], 1896.

[5] Work on *Boris Godunov* belongs to the period between December 1895 and May 1896.

that I recall the following: On one occasion, I believe while finishing the piano-score arrangement of the next to the last tableau, I kept thinking with repugnance that I still had the arrangement of the last tableau to do, and had a feeling of horror at the prospect of such a task. After I had ransacked my writings, I suddenly convinced myself that I had made the arrangement of the last tableau, and quite recently, too. Of course, I felt very happy at having escaped so unpleasant a task for the future, but at the same time I was in a fright about myself and my memory. How in the world could I have forgotten that so sizable a work had been done by me! That was bad; and, in any event, it showed deep fatigue.

The Society of Musical Gatherings, which planned to produce Schumann's *Genoveva* in the spring, had asked Count Sheryemetyev to lend them his orchestra for the purpose. The Count consented, and *Genoveva* was given on April 8 [20], with the assistance of his orchestra under Goldenblum's direction, at the Mikhaylovsky Theatre, the use of which the Society had obtained from Vsyevolozhsky.

For the summer of 1896 we did not intend to go to Vyechasha, where certain disorders had developed of late in the management; and we rented a summer home at Smyerdovitsy, on the estate of Baron Tiesenhausen, on the Baltic Railroad. In May we moved there. By then I felt rested again and could once more resume work on *Sadko* as well as the additions to it.

The manor at Smyerdovitsy proved very roomy, even too much so for my family. Near the house there was a magnificent park; the rest of the locality had nothing attractive to offer: scrubby, ill-kempt woods, with stumps and hillocks everywhere; a miniature lake with low banks and chilly water that permitted little indulgence in bathing. Not far from the house (approximately 1,700–1,800 feet away) ran the railroad roadbed; there the whistling of the train echoed and re-echoed. That summer Volodya and Nadya had the measles, which caused my wife and me some anxiety. Nevertheless I worked on *Sadko* assiduously and to good purpose, as well as composing whatever had been lacking in accordance with my new plan; I also orchestrated much of it — namely, Tableaux IV and VII. In Tableau IV, I developed the big folk-scene in the public square according to Byelsky's text (with the wandering pilgrims and merry andrews inserted) and also the scene between Lyubava and Sadko. In Tableau VII, Lyubava's Lament and her duet with Sadko were composed, Sadko's narrative was rewritten afresh, and the finale of the opera developed. A few things I had to finish in the autumn, on returning to St. Petersburg.[6] By arrangement with M. P. Byelayev, the printing of my opera was undertaken.

V. I. Byelsky visited me at Smyerdovitsy, and we had long talks with him and discussed the libretto of the opera *Sadko.*

As early as the spring of 1896, after the production of *Genoveva,* the Society of Musical Gatherings, which I. A. Davidov had given up for reasons unknown to me, had asked me to accept the chairmanship of the Society. I consented. At the same time there sprang up in the Society the idea of a stage production of *Boris Godunov* in my revision. Choral rehearsals had begun in the spring under my guidance. In the fall of 1896 they commenced once more and went on with the greatest zeal. Goldenblum and Aleksey Avgustovich Davidov assisted me with ardour. Soloists were engaged, and they studied their parts. With the Court Orchestra a rehearsal was conducted once by Goldenblum, both to test the orchestration and to weed out copyists' mistakes in the parts. For the performances a composite orchestra was planned, as Count Sheryemetyev had suddenly disbanded his orchestra that summer, and it was no longer in existence. The performances were announced for the large hall of the Conservatory. I do not remember who painted the scenery, but for the production of *Boris Godunov* a rather considerable collection of money was made among certain lovers of music (among others, T. I. Filippov, too, contributed). I conducted the orchestral rehearsals; Aleksey Avgustovich Davidov and Goldenblum led and assisted in the wings. The opera was given under my direction on

---

[6] A part of the ideas jotted down for the *Textbook of Instrumentation* also belong to the summer spent in Smyerdovitsy. These random jottings Rimsky-Korsakov continued setting down even after returning to the city, as is evidenced by these very recordings.

Thursday, November 28 [December 10]. Boris was sung by Lunacharsky; Shooysky by Safonov (subsequently prompter of the Imperial Russian Opera); Pimyen by Zhdanov; the False Dmitri by
Morskoy; Varlaam by Stravinsky; Marina by Mme Ilyina; Rangoni [7] by Kyedrov. The opera went well and gained success. A
slight, insignificant misunderstanding occurred only in the chorus
of the wandering pilgrims, though it was remarked by none. I conducted correctly and attentively.

The second performance of *Boris Godunov* and the third took
place on November 29 [December 11] and December 3 [15] under
Goldenblum's direction, and the fourth, on December 4 [16], was
to be given again under mine; but suddenly I succumbed to an
unaccountable timidity and handed the directing over to Goldenblum again. At one of the performances the part of the Nurse [8] was
sung by my daughter Sonya. In general, the cast varied slightly at
each performance. After the production of *Boris Godunov* the
activity of the Society of Musical Gatherings diminished somewhat,
and the winter in general passed in the usual way.[9]

At the Russian Symphony Concerts of this season [10] there were
played Glazunov's wonderful Sixth Symphony in C minor (first
time); the Overture to Taneiev's *Oresteia;* Tchaikovsky's *Fatum;* [11]
Rachmaninoff's Symphony in D minor, etc. These concerts were

---

[7] The scene of the plotting Jesuit Rangoni (in the Polish tableau), always cut in
the performances at the Metropolitan Opera House, was restored on March 7, 1939,
when Ezio Pinza appeared as Boris for the first time. J. A. J.

[8] The manuscript erroneously states: " the rôle of Tsarevich Fyodor."

[9] The first performance of *Snyegoorochka* in Kharkov took place on October
11 [23], 1896.

[10] In the season of 1896–7 there were four Russian Symphony Concerts — on
Saturdays, February 8 [20] and 15 [27], March 15 [27], and 22 [April 3], 1897.

[11] The following quotation from the poet Batyushkov, suggested to Tchaikovsky
after he had completed the score, served as a motto to *Fatum* (Destiny):

> Thou knowest what the white-haired Melchisedek
> Said when he left this life: Man is born a slave;
> A slave he dies; will even Death reveal to him
> Why thus he laboured in this vale of tears,
> Why thus he suffered, wept, endured — then vanished?

Mrs. Newmarch asserts that Tchaikovsky destroyed the score of this work, " but
as he was fully aware of the existence of all the orchestral parts, it may be presumed
that a restoration of this work would not be altogether disrespectful to the wishes of
the composer." She gives the date of the first performance as March 15 [27], 1869. The
score was published, as a matter of fact, by Byelayev in 1896. There is a copy in the
Library of Congress at Washington. C. V. V.

given under the direction of Glazunov and myself; F. M. Blumenfeld played the accompaniments of the solo numbers at some of
the concerts. The program of the concert of February 15 [27] was
devoted to Borodin's compositions, to commemorate the tenth anniversary of his death. Among these, his *Spyashchaya Knyazhna*
(*Sleeping Princess*) was sung (by Mme Markovich) with my instrumentation; to the latter nobody paid any attention, as nobody
heard in the orchestra the familiar tapping out of seconds [12] (in
days gone by, that had been considered a great harmonic discovery,
but to my mind it was merely an auditory delusion alone).

The author of *Raymonda* and of the Sixth Symphony had by this
time reached the gorgeous flowering of his enormous talent, leaving far behind him the deeps of *The Sea*, the jungles of *The Forest*,
the walls of *The Kremlin*, and those other compositions of his transition period. His imagination as well as his astounding technique
had attained at this time the highest point of their development.
By then he had become as a conductor an excellent interpreter of
his own compositions; but neither the public nor the critics would
or could understand that; his authority in music grew, not by the
year, but by the day. His astounding ear for harmony and his
memory for detail in the compositions of other people staggered all
of us musicians.

In manner and methods of composition, *Christmas Eve* and
Sadko undoubtedly belong with *Mlada*. The insufficiency of purely
contrapuntal work in *Christmas Eve*, the high development of interesting figurations, the proneness to sustain chords (Act III of
Mlada, the nocturnal sky in *Christmas Eve*, the sea deeps at the
beginning of Tableau VI of *Sadko*), the glowing, rich orchestral
colours — all are the same as in *Mlada*.

Though they have a splendid ring in singing, the majority of the
melodies are nevertheless of instrumental origin. In all three operas
the fantastic element is broadly developed. In each of these operas
there is a skilfully wrought, complex folk-scene (the market in
Mlada; the great *kolyadka*, Christmas carolling, in *Christmas Eve*;

---

[12] The accompaniment of the entire song is written in sustained seconds. J. A. J.

the scene in the town square at the beginning of Tableau IV in
Sadko). If *Mlada* suffers from meagre development of the dramatic
element, which inadequately supplements its folk-wise and fantastic sides, in *Christmas Eve* the fantastic and mythological elements, well developed and even somewhat foisted upon it, weigh
down the light drollness and humour of Gogol's theme much more
than they do in *May Night*. The *bylina* (heroic) opera *Sadko* is
more fortunate than its two immediate predecessors in this regard.
The folk-life and the fantastic elements in *Sadko* do not, by their
nature, offer purely dramatic claims; they are seven tableaux of
fabulous, epic content. The real and the fantastic, the dramatic
(as far as denoted by the *bylina*) and the folk-wise, are here in
complete harmony one with the other. The contrapuntal web,
which had worn thin in the two previous operas and the orchestral
compositions that had preceded them, begins to be restored again.
Mlada's orchestral exaggerations had begun to disappear even in
Christmas Eve, though the orchestra does not lose its picturesque-
ness; while in the matter of splendour, the orchestra of *Mlada*
hardly anywhere surpasses the scene " Gold! Gold! " in Tableau IV
of *Sadko*. The system of leading motives has been applied to a considerable extent and successfully in all three operas. The comparative simplicity, harmonic and modulatory, in the realistic portions
of the opera, and the over-refinements of harmony and modulation
in the fantastic portions, are a procedure common to all three of
the operas. But the feature that does single out my *Sadko* from the
whole series of all my operas, and possibly not my operas alone,
but operas in general, is the *bylina*, epic-legendary, recitative.
Whereas in *Mlada* and *Christmas Eve* the recitative (with few exceptions, such as the scene of the Sexton with Solokha, or the scene
of the two peasant women in *Christmas Eve*), though correct in
most cases, had been undeveloped and not characteristic, the
recitative of the *bylina*-opera, and especially that of Sadko himself, is characteristic to an unheard-of degree despite a certain in-
ternal uniformity of structure. This recitative is not conversational
language, but a sort of conventionally regulated narration of par-
lando singing, of which the prototype may be found in the declama-

tion of Ryabinin's [13] *bylinas*. Running through the entire opera as a red thread, this recitative invests the whole composition with the national historical character that can be fully appreciated only by a Russian. The chorus in 11/4, Nyezhata's *bylina*, the choruses on the ship, the melody of the verse about the *Golubinaya Kniga* (Dove Book),[14] are other details which help, for their part, to lend the opera its historical and national character. I imagine that of the three above-named folk-scenes in the last three operas, the scene in the public square (prior to Sadko's entrance) is the most elaborate and complex. The stage animation, the change of dramatis personæ and groups, such as wandering pilgrims, merry andrews, soothsayers, gay women, and so on, and the bringing them together, in conjunction with a clear and broad symphonic form (somewhat recalling a rondo), cannot but be called successful and new. The fantastic scenes — the tableau on the bank at the Ilmen Lake with the Sea Princess's narrative, the catching of the goldfishes, the intermezzo preceding the scene in the submarine realm, the dancing of little rivers and little fishes, the procession of water-monsters, the wedding around the cytisus bush, the introduction to the last tableau — are no whit inferior in their fairy-tale colouring to the corresponding scenes and moments of *Mlada* and *Christmas Eve*.

First hinted at in Pannochka and Synegoorochka, the fantastic maidenly image, thawing and vanishing, makes a fresh appearance in the form of the shade of Princess Mlada and of the Sea Princess who turns into the Volkhova River. The variations of her cradle song, her farewell to Sadko, and her disappearance I consider among the best pages of my music of a fantastic nature. In this way *Mlada* and *Christmas Eve* have been for me, as it were, two major studies that preceded *Sadko;* while the last, representing as it does the most faultless harmonic combination of an original subject and

---

[13] Trofim Grigoryevich Ryabinin, a native of the bleak north (village of Syeryodki, Olonyetsk Government, on the White Sea), a maker of fishermen's nets by trade, was a true rhapsode of *bylinas*, which he recited, cantillated by heart. His son, Ivan (1844), had a still larger repertory than his father, of 6000 verses, considerably differing. The son *recited* in St. Petersburg (1892) and R.-K. probably refers to him. J. A. J.

[14] Probably a misapplied reference to the symbol of the Holy Ghost. The book is full of Apocryphal mysticism. J. A. J.

expressive music, brings to a proper close the middle period of my activity in the field of opera. I have purposely lingered in greater detail on the characterization of these three operas in order to pass to the ideas that allured me in the latter half of the season of 1897.

I had composed no songs for a long time. Turning to Aleksey Tolstoy's poems, I wrote four songs, and the feeling came over me that I was not composing in the same way as I used to. The melody of these songs, following though it did the sinuosities of the text, turned out purely vocal with me; that is, it became such at its very birth, with but mere hints of harmony and modulation accompanying in its train. The accompaniment formed and developed after the melody had been composed, whereas formerly, with few exceptions, either the melody was created as if instrumentally (that is, apart from the text, though in harmony with its general purport) or it was stimulated by the harmonic foundation which occasionally preceded the melody. Feeling that my new method of composition was the true vocal music, and feeling satisfied, too, with my first essays in this direction, I composed song after song to words by A. Tolstoy, Maykov, Pushkin, and others. By the time we removed to the country, I had well-nigh a score of songs ready. Besides this, I once sketched in a minor scene from Pushkin's *Mozart and Salieri* (Mozart's entrance and part of his talk with Salieri), my recitative flowing freely, ahead of everything else, precisely like the melodies of my latest songs. I had a feeling that I was entering upon some new period and that I was gaining mastery of the method which heretofore had been quasi-accidental or exceptional with me.

With these thoughts, though without having outlined any definite plan for myself, I moved to our summer home at Smychkovo, four miles from Looga.[15]

---

[15] *My Musical Life* contains no mention of the reinstrumentation and partial remodelling of *Antar* in 1897. The dates on the manuscript are: at the end of the first movement, " March 2 [14], 1897 "; at the end of the second movement, " March 12 [24], 1897 "; at the end of the third movement, " April 9 [21], 1897 "; and at the end of the fourth movement, " April 17, 18, and 19 [29, 30, and May 1], 1897." Nor is the writing of two ariosos for basso voice: *Anchar* and *The Prophet*, to words by Pushkin, mentioned in the book. The first arioso, begun as early as in 1882 in Stelyovo, was completed at Smychkovo on June 23 [July 5], 1897; the second, June 22 [July 4], at the same place.

In the summer of 1897, at Smychkovo, I composed much and ceaselessly. My first composition was *Svityezyanka,* a cantata for soprano, tenor, chorus, and orchestra, with music borrowed from an old song of mine. However, the new method of vocal composition was not utilized in it. Then followed a series of numerous songs, after which I turned to Pushkin's *Mozart and Salieri,* in the form of two operatic scenes in recitative-arioso style. This composition was purely vocal, indeed: the melodic web, following the sinuosities of the text, was composed ahead of all else; the accompaniment, fairly complicated, shaped itself later, and its first outline differed greatly from the final form of its orchestral accompaniment. I felt content: the result was something that was new for me, and it approached most closely the manner of Dargomyzhsky in his *Stone Guest,* but without the form and modulatory scheme of *Mozart and Salieri* being quite so much an accident as in Dargomyzhsky's opera. For my accompaniment I took a reduced orchestra. The two tableaux were connected by a fugue-like intermezzo, which I subsequently destroyed.[16] In addition to this I composed a Quartet in G major for bowed instruments and a Trio for violin, cello, and piano in C minor. The latter composition remained unfinished, and both of these chamber-music compositions proved to me that chamber music was not my field; I therefore resolved not to publish them.[17]

In the middle of the summer I wrote two duets for voices: *Pan* and *The Song of Songs;* and towards the end of the summer a vocal

---

[16] This Intermezzo has been preserved among N. A.'s papers in the form of an orchestral score as well as of an arrangement for four hands. (Note by Mme R.-K.)

There is a date: "August 5 [17], 1897, Smychkovo," at the end of the autograph orchestral score of *Mozart and Salieri.*

[17] On the manuscript of the String Quartet there are the following dates: On the *clean copy:* first movement, "September 22 [October 4], 1897"; second movement, "September 23 [October 5], 1897"; third movement, "September 26 [October 8], 1897"; fourth movement, "September 1897." On the *rough manuscript:* first movement, no date; second movement, "September 8 [20], 1897"; third movement, "September 16 [28], 1897"; fourth movement, "September 18 [30], 1897."

On the *rough sketch* of the entire Trio there are the following dates: At the end of the first movement, "August 9 [21], 1897"; second movement, "August 31 [September 12], 1897"; third movement, "September 2 [14], 1897"; fourth movement, "August 22 [September 3], 1897." On the *clean manuscript* copy of the two middle movements: at the end of the second movement, "August 31 [September 12], 1897"; third movement, September 2 [14], 1897."

trio, *Harvest-fly,* with a chorus of women's voices and orchestral accompaniment, on a text by A. Tolstoy.[18]

On June 30 [July 12] we celebrated the twenty-fifth anniversary of our marriage, and I dedicated to my wife a song set to words by Pushkin — *Nyenastny dyeñ potookh* (*The rainy day has died away*), as well as four songs on texts by A. Tolstoy.[19]

---

[18] The duets *Pan* and *The Song of Songs* were composed: the former May 9 [21], St. Petersburg, July 5 [17], 1897, Smychkovo; the latter, June 23 [July 5], 1897, likewise at Smychkovo. In the author's manuscript the trio *Harvest-fly* bears no date either in the rough draft or in the clean copies.

[19] From Rimsky-Korsakov's letter of September 28 [October 10], 1897, to S. N. Krooglikov: " The news that I have composed thirty-nine songs and an opera, *Mozart and Salieri,* is really false, for I have written forty songs, two duets, *Mozart and Salieri,* a cantata, *Svityezyanka,* for soprano, tenor, and chorus with orchestra, and moreover a trio for the piano, violin, and cello, but in rough draft only, which I shall now begin to polish up (particularly the piano part); everything else — i.e., *Mozart* and *Svityezyanka* — has been fully orchestrated. After I had moved to St. Petersburg in September I composed some other things — shall tell you later. You probably feel surprised? But there is nothing surprising in this, it is as it should be. Thirty years have already gone by since the time when V. V. Stassov wrote that in the year eighteen hundred and sixty-something the Russian school manifested a lively activity: Lodyzhensky has composed one song, Borodin has planned something, Balakirev is preparing to rewrite something, etc. It is high time to have done with this and enter upon the normal artistic path. . . ."

A music-paper notebook preserved among Rimsky-Korsakov's papers bears testimony that he systematically practised writing fugues and preludes and made analyses of Mozart's and Bach's fugues and preludes during July and August 1897, in addition to all the above compositions.

Sadko *at S. I. Mamontov's private opera.* Vera Sheloga. The Tsar's Bride. *Russian Symphony Concert.* Snyegoorochka *at the Mariinsky Theatre. The young composers of Moscow.* Tsar Saltan. Lay of Olyeg the Prophetic. *S. I. Taneiev.*

DURING THE FIRST HALF of the season of 1897–8 I was engaged in preparing for publication my newly accumulated songs. The songs were published by Byelayev in two keys — for high voice and low voice. They had to be transposed, proofs had to be read, and so forth.

Mozart and Salieri, performed at home to the accompaniment of a piano, pleased everybody. V. V. Stassov made a great to-do about it. The Mozartean improvisation I had composed hit the mark and proved of sustained style. G. A. Morskoy and M. V. Lunacharsky were the singers. F. Blumenfeld was the accompanist.

That very autumn [1] I submitted my *Sadko* to the Directorate of Theatres. For the purpose of becoming familiar with this work, a hearing was arranged. In the presence of Director Vsyevolozhsky, Napravnik, Kondratyev, Palyechek, and others, as well as of several artists, the opera was performed to the accompaniment of a piano. F. Blumenfeld played the piano; I sang along and ex-

---

[1] To October 1897 belongs the continuation of jottings for the *Textbook of Instrumentation.* About the same time Charles Lamoureux was inviting Rimsky-Korsakov to come to Paris to conduct two concerts, but Rimsky-Korsakov declined.

plained as much as I could. I must confess that Fyeliks was not in the vein for some reason, and played reluctantly and somewhat carelessly; I was nervous and soon grew hoarse. Apparently the listeners had understood nothing and not a soul seemed to like the opera. Napravnik was surly and sour. The opera was not played to the end "owing to the lateness of the hour." Evidently my composition had failed in Vsyevolozhsky's eyes, and, having now become acquainted with it, he assumed an entirely different tone in his negotiations with me. He said that the confirmation of the repertory for the coming year did not depend on him, but, as ever, on the Emperor, who always scrutinized it personally; that there were other works which the Directorate was bound to produce at the desire of members of the Imperial family; but that notwithstanding and nevertheless he did not finally refuse to produce *Sadko.* But it was clear to me that this was untrue, and I made up my mind to leave the Directorate in peace, never again to trouble it with offers of my operas.

In December there came from Moscow, to visit me, Savva Ivanovich Mamontov, who had that year become head of a private opera company in Solodovnikov's Theatre. He informed me that he intended within a short time to produce *Sadko;* and this idea he actually carried out during the Christmas holidays.[2]

Nadezhda Nikolayevna and I went to Moscow for the second performance. The scenery proved fairly good, although between

---

[2] The preliminary correspondence (about producing *Sadko* in Moscow) between Rimsky-Korsakov and S. N. Krooglikov, who had meanwhile come into a close relationship with the Moscow Private Opera, had been carried on already in the summer of 1897. In answer to Krooglikov's invitation to come to see the production of *Sadko* in Moscow, Rimsky-Korsakov wrote (December 15 [27], 1897): " I cannot come to the rehearsals and the performance, as on December 27 [January 8] I conduct the second Russian Symphony concert, which it is impossible to shift to another day. . . ." " As to S. I. Mamontov," Rimsky-Korsakov wrote to Krooglikov, " I know him personally and respect him highly. Should he find it possible to put on *Sadko* and thereby rub it into whoever deserves it, I shall be very happy. But the one desirable thing is to have a full orchestra . . . and a sufficient number of orchestral rehearsals, with a good drill-study in general. . . ." (Cf. Rimsky-Korsakov's Archives in the Manuscript Division of the State Public Library.)

The four Russian Symphony Concerts of the season 1897–8 took place on Saturdays, November 15 [27], December 27, 1897 [January 8, 1898], January 10 [22], and March 21 [April 2], 1898. *Sadko* was given for the first time at the Private Opera in Moscow on December 26, 1897 [January 7, 1898].

Tableaux V and VI there was an interruption in the music for change in scenery. Some of the artists were good, but as a whole the opera had been poorly rehearsed. Esposito, an Italian, conducted. In the orchestra there rang many false notes; moreover, it lacked several instruments; in Tableau I the chorus sang from the music they held in their hands as though it were a menu; in Tableau VI the chorus did not sing at all, the orchestra alone playing. Everything was explained away by *the hurry of production*. Yet with the public the opera was an enormous success, and that is what was wanted. I was exasperated; but there were curtain calls and wreaths for me; the singers and S. I. gave me every mark of honour; the only thing that was left was to bow and thank them. Among the singers Syekar-Rozhansky as Sadko, and Zabyela (wife of the painter Vrubel) as the Sea Princess, distinguished themselves. Both were known to me, having been former pupils of the St. Petersburg Conservatory.[3]

By Lent,[4] Mamontov's opera, in its entirety, turned up at St. Petersburg, with the theatre hall of the Conservatory as its home. The performances were to open with *Sadko*. Assiduous rehearsals of the opera under my direction were begun. I drilled the orches-

---

[3] An energetic interchange of views between Rimsky-Korsakov and N. A. Krooglikov took place early in January 1898 in connection with the concert of Russian music which Mamontov intended to give with the assistance of the vocalists of his opera company. This correspondence broke off with the news of the fire at Solodovnikov's Theatre the night of January 19–20 [31–February 1]. Regarding this fire Rimsky-Korsakov wrote to Krooglikov: " I was stunned by your telegram. What a pity, and what mortification! However, the end of the telegram, saying that the opera is moving to another(?) theatre, cheered me up, and the newspaper item, that the artists were left without jobs, therefore did not make much impression on me. Nevertheless, all this is quite sad: the undertaking was just beginning to run well, and now — confusion at all events! I imagine what a peck of troubles S. I. [Mamontov] and the administration now have. I suppose there is no use even thinking of the concert for the time being; however, I am looking forward to your letter, which will clear up everything. Yours, N. A. Rimsky-Korsakov, January 21 [February 2], 1898, St. Petersburg."

At the same time Rimsky-Korsakov wrote to S. I. Mamontov: " You can imagine how stunned and saddened I was by the news of the fire at the theatre. Even though the Private Russian Opera will pull through this unexpected misfortune — thanks to your energy and love for the cause of opera — and will move to another theatre, nevertheless the detriment to the enterprise is indubitable." (Cf. Archives of the New Museum of Russian Literature, Letters of Rimsky-Korsakov to S. I. Mamontov.)

[4] Already before that time — namely, on January 23 [February 4], 1898 — Rimsky-Korsakov had composed Two Duets, op. 52: *The Mountain Spring* and *The Angel and the Demon.*

tra with great care, together with Esposito, who proved a very fair musician. Errors were corrected, difficult passages that had been performed in a slovenly manner were studied painstakingly; nuancing was strictly demanded. The chorus learned the passages in which they were weak, the soloists, too, received certain suggestions, and *Sadko* was produced in quite a decent manner. The solo singers, except possibly Byedlyevich (the Sea King), whom I could not endure, were good. Zabyela sang magnificently and made a most poetic figure of the Princess; Syekar-Rozhansky, too, was in the right place. The opera pleased the public greatly and was given several times. In addition to *Sadko*, there were performed *Khovanshchina*, Gluck's *Orfeo ed Euridice*, Tchaikovsky's *Maid of Orleans*, as well as *May Night* and *Snyegoorochka*. I conducted the first performances of the last two operas myself quite accurately. But the cast of artists in *May Night* was unsatisfactory, particularly Inozyemtsev, the Lyevko. As for Snyegoorochka, Mamontov selected the young singer Paskhalova, a protégée of his. With a beautiful though at the same time small voice, she was utterly inexperienced and could do nothing with her part. To my regret, the rôle of Snyegoorochka was entrusted to Zabyela only at the final performance.[5]

The Mamontov opera company's visit at St. Petersburg lasted till the first week after Easter or possibly later, and enjoyed considerable success with the audiences; it did not draw full houses, however, and occasionally, as in Gluck's *Orfeo*, played to almost empty houses. During the company's stay in St. Petersburg we became well acquainted with N. I. Zabyela and her husband, the painter M. A. Vrubel.[6]

---

[5] Owing to disagreements on questions of filling individual rôles and his general attitude towards the musical side of the enterprise, there sprang up between Rimsky-Korsakov and Mamontov a certain temporary coolness, the echoes of which have been handed down to posterity in Rimsky-Korsakov's correspondence with S. N. Kdrooglikov. Unfortunately the considerable bulk of these letters does not permit of quoting them here. In the course of the summer and fall of 1898 the former relations between S. I. Mamontov and Rimsky-Korsakov were completely restored. To this period belongs the idea of an opera from the epoch of the War of 1812 [against Napoleon. J. A. J.], both the subject and the libretto belonging to Mamontov — an idea which, for various reasons, was never turned into reality.

[6] The beginning of a brisk correspondence between Rimsky-Korsakov and Nadezhda Ivanovna Zabyela dates from spring 1898.

In the spring of 1898 I composed several more songs and turned my hand to the Prologue to Mey's *Pskovityanka*, "*Boyaryña Vera Sheloga*," treating it from two points of view: as a separate one-act opera, so to speak, and as the Prologue to my opera. Vera's narrative I restored, with trifling modification, borrowing its content from the second and unrealized *Pskovityanka* version of the seventies; thus, too, the end of the act; on the other hand, the entire beginning as far as the cradle song and after it to Vera's narrative I composed anew, applying the newly mastered methods of vocal music. I retained the former cradle song, but gave it a new revision. The composition of *Vera Sheloga* went rapidly and soon was finished, together with its orchestration. Thereupon I set out to realize my ambition of long standing — the composing of an opera on the subject of Mey's *Tsarskaya Nyevyesta* (*The Tsar's Bride*).[7] The style of this opera was to be cantilena par excellence; the arias and soliloquies were planned for development within the limits of the dramatic situations; I had in mind vocal ensembles, genuine, finished, and not at all in the form of any casual and fleeting linking of voices with others, as dictated by the present-day requirements of quasi-dramatic truth, according to which two or more persons are not supposed to talk simultaneously. For this reason there were to be certain additions and modifications in Mey's text, in order to create lyric moments of greater or lesser length for arias and ensembles. These additions and modifications were undertaken at my request by I. F. Tyumenev, well versed in literature and antiquities, and a former pupil of mine, with whom I had lately grown intimate again. Even before moving to Vyechasha, which we had rented again for the summer, I had already set to work on Act I.

The summer of 1898 in dear Vyechasha passed quickly in composing *The Tsar's Bride*, and the work went rapidly and easily.[8]

---

[7] The first jottings for *The Tsar's Bride* in Rimsky-Korsakov's notebook are marked with the date " February 1898."

[8] In rough draft *The Tsar's Bride* was composed in full during the interval between April 15 [27] and July 24 [August 5], 1898.

In a letter of May 20 [June 1], 1899 to Zabyela, Rimsky-Korsakov quotes parts of his letter to S. I. Mamontov: " In accordance with your promise, I count on Marfa's rôle as belonging to N. I. Zabyela. This rôle, the special object of my affection and polishing, was written with her voice and skill in my mind. . . ."

During the summer the entire opera was composed, and an act and a half were orchestrated. In the midst of this work the song *A Midsummer Night's Dream,*[9] on a text by Maykov, was also composed. This latter and the song *The Nymph,*[10] written in the spring, were subsequently dedicated to the Vrubel pair.

The work of composing the ensembles — the quartet of Act II and the sextet of Act III — aroused in me the particular interest of methods new to me; and I suppose that in the matter of cantilena and grace of independent part-writing there had been no such operatic ensembles since Glinka's time. Taken in general, Act I of *The Tsar's Bride* presents possibly one or two somewhat dry moments; but after the folk-wise scene (in Act II), written by a hand that had already become expert, the interest begins to grow, and the touching lyric drama reaches powerful intensity in the course of the entire Act IV. *Tsarskaya Nyevyesta* proved to have been written for strictly defined voices, and most gratefully for the singers, in addition. Despite the fact that the voices had been invariably held to the fore by me and the orchestra had been taken in its usual complement, the orchestration and the handling of the accompaniment proved effective and interesting everywhere. It is sufficient to point out the orchestral intermezzo, the scene of Lyubasha with Bomelio, the entry of Tsar Ivan, the sextet, etc. I decided to leave Lyubasha's song in Act I entirely without accompaniment, with the exception of the intermediate chords between the stanzas, and this greatly frightened the singers, who feared they might get off key. But their fear proved groundless; the range of the melody in the Æolian mode in G minor proved to have been chosen so conveniently that all the singers, to my surprise, always kept up to pitch; I told them that my song was a magic one.

Contrary to my custom, in composing *The Tsar's Bride* I did not utilize a single folk-theme, except the melody of *Slava,* demanded by the subject itself. In the scene in which Malyuta Skooratov proclaims the will of Tsar Ivan, who had chosen Marfa to be a wife to

---

[9] On the manuscript there is the date: " May 31 [June 12], 1898."
[10] The date on the manuscript is " September 7 [19], 1898."

him, I introduced the theme of Ivan Grozny (the Terrible) from *Pskovityanka* and combined it contrapuntally with the *Slava* theme.[11]

At the beginning of the summer my son Andrey, who had completed his first year's examinations at the University, went for rest to the estate of the Dobrovolskys, Latovka (Government of Kherson), where my older son Misha was then on a mission from the University, for zoological studies. Soon Nadezhda Nikolayevna, too, went to south Russia and, meeting Andrey, as had been agreed, the two together made a trip to the Crimea to visit Masha's grave in Yalta. Thus our family found itself somewhat reduced in numbers in the early part of the summer in Vyechasha. The faithful Yastryebtsev spent a few days with us. Also Byelsky dropped in on us; we had endless discussions with him on various opera subjects suitable for me. Upon the return of Nadezhda Nikolayevna and Andrey, we resumed our usual mode of living — all together. Almost every evening various chamber-music trios were played at our house, as my sons had then made considerable progress (Andrey on the violin, and Volodya on the piano), and with Nadezhda Nikolayevna's assistance chamber music began to flourish among us.

In the autumn of 1898 I was occupied exclusively with the orchestration of *The Tsar's Bride*.[12] This work was interrupted only for a brief while, owing to my trip to Moscow to attend the production of *Boyaryña Vera Sheloga* and *Pskovityanka* at Mamontov's.[13] The Prologue received scant attention, despite its excellent interpretation by Mme Tsvyetkova. On the other hand, *The Maid of*

---

[11] Montagu-Nathan notes a decided Western influence in the music of this opera. " The subject, of course, is purely national, but the treatment in general is of a kind which savours of Mozart and the Italian opera." This dictum will appear to be absolute nonsense to anyone who has heard *The Tsar's Bride*, one of the most characteristically Russian of the composer's works. Before the Revolution it was more popular in Russia than any of the other Rimsky-Korsakov operas. It was produced in New York, in a vile manner, by the Russian Grand Opera Company at the New Amsterdam Theatre, May 17, 1922. C. V. V.

[12] *The Tsar's Bride* was completed on November 24 [December 6], 1898.

[13] Even before this trip, Rimsky-Korsakov had journeyed to Moscow to conduct the Russian Symphony concert of October 17 [29], 1898, in which S. I. Taneiev took part.

Pskov enjoyed success, thanks to the highly talented Chaliapin, whose Tsar Ivan was a creation beyond compare. *Sadko* was also performed.[14] Dinners, mild drinking-bouts, arranged by S. I. Mamontov, calls at the Vrubels' home, on Krooglikov and others filled all my " free " time.[15]

I invited N. I. Zabyela to sing my Prologue in concert form at one of the Russian Symphony Concerts of this season, and she willingly gave her consent.[16] The monetary remuneration was not mentioned. Yet there was in store an unpleasant situation out of which a way had to be found. Byelayev, who did not like soloists in general and singers, male and female, in particular, had established once for all a compensation of fifty rubles to a soloist per concert. To certain artists who were in straitened circumstances, so slight a compensation could still be offered, as, after all, it meant just that much help to them; but to artists who did not feel the pinch of necessity, it was unthinkable to offer such beggarly compensation, and in their time I had asked Mme Mravina and others to take part without any pay whatever, merely out of their interest in art. Nevertheless, an artist from Moscow could not be expected to travel to St. Petersburg and spend her own money on fare and other expenses for the sake of a Russian Symphony concert; while to offer her a compensation of fifty rubles was absurd. Despite all my talks with Byelayev, time and again, to the effect that in certain cases the remuneration must be increased, he would not listen. I offered Zabyela one hundred and fifty rubles and, without telling her, added one hundred of my own to Byelayev's fifty. This remained a secret to both Zabyela and Byelayev; but in order to make up the loss, I expressed to Byelayev the desire to draw again the fee he had established for conducting the concerts, a fee I had waived

---

[14] *Sadko* had its première in Kharkov on December 17 [29], 1898 (management of Prince Tseretelli).

[15] The second trip to Moscow, referred to in the text, was made late in December. Rimsky-Korsakov witnessed the performance of *Pskovityanka* at Solodovnikov's Theatre on December 31, 1898 [January 12, 1899]. In addition to the operas here enumerated, Rimsky-Korsakov heard, during this visit, for the first time his *Mozart and Salieri*, produced by the Moscow Private Opera on November 6 [18], 1898.

[16] In the season of 1898–9 the Russian Symphony Concerts were given on Saturdays, December 5 [17] and 19 [31], 1898, February 13 [25] and March 20 [April 1], 1899. The second concert, of December 19 [31], is here referred to.

FYODOR CHALIAPIN

as Ivan the Terrible in Rimsky-Korsakov's Pskovityanka, Act III

several years before. To this M. P. gave his consent immediately.

In order to perform Vera Sheloga's narrative, the participation of a second woman singer was necessary for the rôle of Nadezhda. I secured one from among Mme Iryetskaya's Conservatory pupils, at a fee of fifty rubles, in accordance with Byelayev's rule. The narrative was performed splendidly, although Zabyela's lyric soprano did not entirely suit the rôle of Vera,, which demands a more dramatic voice. The audience treated the music with comparative indifference. The cause of this attitude lay in the very character of the composition, which needs a theatre and not a concert stage. Marfa's aria from *The Tsar's Bride,* sung by Zabyela, was liked, though receiving scant notice; but the Act IV aria given as an encore, to the accompaniment of the piano, was not noticed at all. The singer won a few plaudits, but nobody even attempted to find out what she had sung, while the critics expressed surmise that it was one of my new songs.

Evidently the Board of Directors of the Imperial Theatres felt somewhat ashamed that *Sadko*, which had met with success both in Moscow and St. Petersburg in private opera houses, had avoided the state theatres, which had not noticed it. On the other hand, after my uncomfortable experience with *Christmas Eve* in 1895, not a single opera of mine had been given on the Mariinsky stage. One way or another, Vsyevolozhsky suddenly conceived the desire of producing my *Snyegoorochka* with a magnificence befitting the Imperial Theatres. New scenery and new costumes were ordered, and the opera was produced on December 15 [27]. The settings and costumes were really costly, dainty but utterly unfitted for a Russian fairy-tale. Moroz (Frost) proved something like Neptune; Lyel resembled a Paris; Snyegoorochka, Koopava, Byeryendyey, and others were decked out in like fashion. The architecture of Byeryendyey's palace and the little hut of Byeryendyeyevka village, the sun, painted in the cheapest woodcut style, at the end of the opera, were badly suited, to the verge of the ludicrous, to the subject-matter of the spring fairy-tale. In all this there were apparent both the inability to grasp the problem and the French mythological tastes of Vsyevolozhsky. The opera was given with success. Mravina, the Snyegoorochka, was fine, but the omissions had not been restored, and the opera dragged till late, thanks to the interminable intermissions.[17]

Towards Lent [1899] Mamontov's opera company, this time with Truffi as conductor, paid its second visit to St. Petersburg. *Pskovit-yanka,* with *Sheloga; Sadko; Boris Godunov* with Chaliapin, were the operas. *Mozart and Salieri* was also produced. Chaliapin won enormous success, and from this time dates his fame and the growth of his popularity. But taken all in all, Mamontov's opera was not warmly enough attended; they made ends meet only thanks to S. I. Mamontov's playing the Mæcenas.

We formed friendships with some of the opera singers. On one of my visits to M. A. Vrubel, he showed me his painting *The Sea Princess.*[18] On the canvas, among other things, there was pictured dawn and the crescent in the shape of a sickle, the latter with its concave facing towards the dawn. I called the artist's attention to this error, explaining to him that in the morning, at dawn, only the waning moon can be seen, but never the new moon, and that, moreover, the convex side is always towards the sun. M. A. was convinced of his mistake, but would not consent to do his painting over again. I do not know whether the painting retained that astronomic absurdity or whether he changed it subsequently, after all.

Byelayev's circle was growing perceptibly. It was increased by those of my pupils graduating from the Conservatory, Zolotaryov, Akimyenko, Amani, Kryzhanovsky, and Cherepnin,[19] as well as by

---

[17] Rimsky-Korsakov wrote Zabyela (January 19 [31], 1899): "About myself I shall say that I am occupied and at the same time unoccupied. I am busy with proof-reading, the Conservatory, and the committees on arranging the Pushkin celebration [one-hundredth anniversary of his birth — May 26 [June 7], 1899. J. A. J.] — but I am not occupied with compositions: I have no time, and I am tired."

In February 1899 Édouard Colonne invited Rimsky-Korsakov to come to Paris for two concerts. In the end Rimsky-Korsakov refused to make the journey, in spite of the correspondence that had sprung up in connection with it.

[18] This painting is now in the Russian Museum in Leningrad. Cf. S. P. Yaryomich: *M. A. Vrubel* (Kiev, 1913), p. 114.

[19] Nikolay Cherepnin, born in 1873, abandoned his studies in the legal profession to become a pupil of Rimsky-Korsakov. Probably his best-known works, both produced by the Russian Ballet, are *Le Pavillon d'Armide* and *Narcisse.* Fyodor Akimyenko, born in 1876, studied piano under Balakirev, harmony with Lyadov, and

that star of first magnitude, newly risen in Moscow, the somewhat warped, posing, and self-opinionated A. N. Scriabin.[20] The other Moscow star, S. V. Rachmaninoff, though his compositions had been performed in the Russian Symphony Concerts, kept apart, his works being published by Gutheil. In general, Moscow of late had become rich in young composer blood, such as Grechaninov, Koryeshchenko, Vasilyenko,[21] and others; Grechaninov, however, was partly a denizen of St. Petersburg, as being a former pupil of mine. Together with these, there began to appear also signs of decadence wafted from western Europe. Of Scriabin I shall speak later on.

During the winter [1898–9] I often saw V. I. Byelsky, and, together with him, worked up Pushkin's *Fairy-tale of Tsar Saltan* as a subject for an opera. Our interest was also attracted by the legend of the *Invisible City of Kityezh* in connection with the legend of St. Fyevroniya of Moorom; we were drawn also to Byron's *Heaven and Earth,* as well as to *Odysseus at the Palace of King Alcinoüs* and other things, but all of it was put off for some future occasion, our attention focusing on *Saltan,* for which we discussed the scenario together. With the coming of spring V. I. began to write his splendid libretto, making use of Pushkin as much as was possible, and artistically as well as skilfully imitating his style. He would hand me the scenes one by one as they were finished, and I set to work on the opera. By summer (which we had made up our minds

---

composition with Rimsky-Korsakov. Nevertheless, even in his early works, there is little trace of nationalistic influence, and after he had visited Paris, he fell distinctly under the influence of the modern impressionists and composed pieces entitled, *In the Luxembourg Gardens* and *Under the Arches of Notre Dame.* Kryzhanovsky, born in 1867, is also an eclectic. His compositions are mostly for piano. C. V. V.

[20] The rapprochement between A. N. Scriabin and M. P. Byelayev began, as is well known, in 1894. Cf. their *Correspondence,* with introduction and notes by V. Byelayev, published in book form by the State Philharmonic Academy (Leningrad, 1922).

[21] Sergey N. Vasilyenko, born in Moscow in 1872, won a gold medal for his cantata, *The Invisible City of Kityezh,* afterwards produced as an opera. His other works include a symphony in G minor, and a symphonic poem, *The Garden of Death.* A. T. Grechaninov, born in Moscow in 1864, has written operas, symphonies, cantatas, and works in several other forms. His works show German influence. He wrote the first Russian revolutionary anthem. A. N. Koryeshchenko, born 1870, pupil of Taneiev and Arensky at the Moscow Conservatory, has written three operas, a ballet, and a large number of instrumental works. His style is said to be based on the music of Tchaikovsky and Arensky. C. V. V.

to spend at Vyechasha as before) the Prologue (Introduction) was
ready in sketch.[22]

Exactly as the case had been with *Tsarskaya Nyevyesta* (*The
Tsar's Bride*) the previous summer, the entire *Saltan* was composed, and its Prologue, Act I, and part of Act II were orchestrated
during the summer of 1899. The libretto came to me piecemeal,
continuously from Byelsky. *Saltan* was composed in a mixed manner which I shall call instrumental-vocal. Its entire fantastic part
belonged rather to the first manner, the realistic part to the second
manner. As far as the application of purely vocal creative art is
concerned, I was particularly pleased with the Prologue. The entire
dialogue, of the two sisters with Babarikha, after the ditty for two
voices; the younger sister's phrase; Saltan's entrance, and the closing conversation flow freely with strictly musical sequence. And
yet the really melodic element lies invariably in the voices, which
do not cling to fragments of melodic phrases in the orchestra. A
structure of similar nature is to be found in the comic trio at the
beginning of Act II of *May Night,* but there the musical edifice is
far more symmetrical; it is subdivided into manifest units and it is
less compact than here. The intention there, too, was excellent; but
for execution the pre-eminence must be awarded to *Saltan.* Symmetry again, in the boasts of the older sister and the middle one,
invests the piece with an intentionally fairy-tale character. Act I,
entirely bound with folk-life in its first half, grows dramatic in its
second. The fantastic singing of the Swan in Act II is in a way instrumental; but its harmonies are novel. The dawn and the city's
rise into view recall *Mlada* and *Christmas Eve* in the method employed; but the solemn chorus greeting Gvidon, written partly on
an ecclesiastical theme of the third mode ("the churchly choir
doth praise the Lord," as Pushkin's poem reads), stands alone. The
marvels in the tales of the shipmasters are made real in the last
tableau of the opera by a suitable development of that very music.
The transformation of the Swan into the Princess Swan is based

---

[22] In April, at S. I. Mamontov's request, Rimsky-Korsakov orchestrated his
Prophet, which was scheduled to be performed at the Pushkin Evening in Moscow.
On the autograph copy of this orchestration there is a date: "April 20 [May 2],
1899."

again on a similar development of previous leading motives and harmonies. In general, I have made wide use of the system of *Leitmotive* in this opera, while the recitatives have been invested with a special character of fairy-tale naïveté. In memory of our nurse Avdotya Larionovna, who had died a year before, I took the melody of the lullaby she had sung to my children for the nurses rocking little Gvidon to sleep.

The same summer, as a rest and a pastime, I wrote also *The Lay of Olyeg the Prophetic* for solo and chorus; however, I had conceived it the preceding winter. Yastryebtsev and Byelsky, as usual, visited us at Vyechasha this summer also, and I let them see such new things as I had composed. As always, Yastryebtsev was somewhat hesitant at first hearings, but later went *into wild raptures* (his own pet expression). On the other hand, Byelsky usually seized and mastered from the first the very " littlest " shreds of detail, thereby astonishing me not a little.

The first half of the season [23] of 1899–1900 I spent on orchestrating *Skazka o Tsarye Saltanye*.[24] This time there was to be no overture or prelude to my opera: the prelude was supplied by the Introduction itself; that is, by the scenic prologue. Each *act*, on the contrary, was preceded by a long orchestral prelude with a program of definite content. But to make up for that, both the prologue and each of the acts or tableaux began with the same brief trumpet fanfare, which had the meaning of a call or invitation to hear and see the act which began immediately after it. This is a device quite original and suitable for a fairy-tale. Out of the rather longish orchestral preludes to Acts I, II, and IV, I resolved to put together a suite under the title: *Little Pictures for the Fairy-tale of Tsar Saltan.*

As early as the spring, when I set out to compose *Saltan*, I had spoken to Byelayev of it and inquired whether he would undertake to publish it. Byelayev replied more or less dryly and in the negative, stating that the ever growing number of my operas was be-

[23] On November 2 [14], 1899 the first performance of *Sadko* was given in Odessa (management of Prince Tseretelli). The composer did not attend it.

[24] The manuscript orchestral score of the final tableau of the *Skazka* (*Fairy-tale*) bears the date of January 19 [31], 1900.

ginning to be a burden to his publishing business. Accordingly I
offered *Saltan* to Bessel, who gladly consented to bring it out,
though at an honorarium of two thousand rubles only — considerably less than the remuneration established by Byelayev. We had
come to an agreement with Bessel, and he was now waiting only
for me to finish the score. At this juncture Byelayev, who had developed an interest in the *Little Pictures*, made me an offer to publish
them. I replied that I had already come to terms with Bessel. Evidently this refusal of mine, as well as my agreement with Bessel, offended Byelayev in a measure. But what was to be done? The fault
lay with him, not with me. Nevertheless this did not affect our relations, which remained as cordial as ever; but after that M. P. made
up his mind not to publish any opera scores in general, ostensibly
because of the accumulation of orchestral and chamber music that
begged publication so much more pressingly than operatic music,
for which publishers would always be found. However, he swerved
from his own resolve when he undertook the publication of Taneiev's *Oresteia*. It will be apropos to tell here that for some years
past there had been appearing on the horizon a wonderful musician
and highly trained teacher, Sergei Ivanovich Taneiev. Once a pupil
of Tchaikovsky and N. G. Rubinstein at the Moscow Conservatory,
an excellent pianist, Taneiev had been Professor of Counterpoint
at that Conservatory for many years. Absorbed as he was for many
long years in research in the field of so-called double counterpoints
and canons, as well as in preparing materials for a comprehensive
textbook, he had rarely lent himself to composition; and, indeed,
his compositions had been most dry and laboured in character. I recall him, then still a very young man, but recently graduated from
the Conservatory, coming to St. Petersburg to show his piano concerto.[25] I remember also a later visit of his, with his cantata *Johannes*

---

[25] S. I. Taneiev (1856–1915) composed the first movement (Allegro. [E-flat
major, ¾] Poco piu mosso. — Piu mosso) and the second movement (Andante
funèbre [E-flat minor, ¾]) of his Concerto for the pianoforte with orchestra in
1876. The third movement (Finale — Allegro) was planned, as evidenced by his
correspondence. In a letter of March 24 [April 5], 1877, to Tchaikovsky, from Paris,
Taneiev expressed his intention to complete the work during the summer, but never
wrote a single line for the Finale. Various remarks in Tchaikovsky's hand are found
on the autograph copy of the first movement. The Concerto is listed under No. 19 of

Damascenus. I remember also his *Solemn Overture* in C minor, with its extraordinary contrapuntal subtleties, which was performed at a concert of the Russian Musical Society in the eighties.

Taneiev of the eighties had been a man of glaringly conservative opinions in musical art. Towards Glazunov's early appearances he had shown deep distrust; Borodin he had considered a clever dilettante and no more; and Moussorgsky had merely made him laugh.[26] Probably he had placed no high estimate on Cui, either, or on me. But my study of counterpoint (about which he had learned from Tchaikovsky) had unbent him towards me in some measure. He worshipped Tchaikovsky; and Tchaikovsky had singled me out from the rest of the St. Petersburgers surrounding me. His opinion concerning Balakirev is unknown to me; but I do know of his clash with Balakirev at a rehearsal of the concert during the festivities in connection with the unveiling of a monument to Glinka at Smolensk [27] (where Mili Alekseyevich conducted a concert of works by Russian composers).[28] At the rehearsal of the concert he publicly declared to Balakirev: " Mili Alekseyevich! We are dissatisfied with you." I picture to myself Balakirev constrained to swallow a rebuke of this sort. Honest, upright, and straightforward, Taneiev always spoke sharply and frankly. On the other hand, Balakirev, of course, could never forgive Taneiev his harshness and frankness with regard to his own person.

In the nineties Taneiev's opinions of St. Petersburg composers underwent a marked change: he came to appreciate Glazunov's activity and treated Borodin's compositions with respect, regarding only Moussorgsky with dislike and ridicule. This change in attitude coincided somehow with the beginning of the new period in his activity as composer, after he had thrown himself more freely into creative work and was guiding himself by the ideals of contemporary music, though still preserving his astounding contrapuntal

the complete register of Taneiev's works in the volume *Sergei Ivanovich Taneiev, His Personality and Creative Work* (Moscow: State Publishing Bureau, Music Sector; 1925), pp. 120–3.

[26] Cf. Taneiev's opinions of St. Petersburg musicians in *Correspondence of P. I. Tchaikovsky with S. I. Taneiev* (Moscow: Jurgenson; 1916).

[27] May 20 [June 1], 1885. J. A. J.

[28] The words in parentheses were added by N. N. Rimskaya-Korsakova.

technique. He arrived in St. Petersburg with his recently finished opera *Oresteia,* played it at our house, and astonished us all with pages of extraordinary beauty and expressiveness.[29] He had been at the composition of his opera for a long time, possibly ten years. Before setting out for the real expounding of a composition, Taneiev used to precede it with a multitude of sketches and studies: he used to write fugues, canons, and various contrapuntal interlacings on the individual themes, phrases, and motives of the coming composition; and only after gaining thorough experience in its component parts did he take up the general plan of the composition and the carrying out of this plan, knowing by that time, as he did, and perfectly, the nature of the material he had at his disposal and the possibilities of building with that material. The same method had been applied by him in composing *Oresteia.* It would seem that this method ought to result in a dry and academic composition, devoid of the shadow of an inspiration; in reality, however, *Oresteia* proved quite the reverse — for all its strict premeditation, the opera was striking in its wealth of beauty and expressiveness.

The opera was submitted to the Directorate, and was produced at the Mariinsky Theatre. Napravnik dodged conducting *Oresteia* and let Krooshevsky do it. The opera met with instant public favour. Yet after the first two or three performances the Directorate (I imagine with Napravnik's connivance) introduced many cuts. The composer was exasperated, refused to sign a contract with the Directorate; and the opera was stricken from the repertory. Byelayev, who liked the opera, quite sympathized with Taneiev; and indignant at the Directorate's conduct, he immediately proposed to Taneiev to publish his opera for him. The publication was begun forthwith. Taneiev revised and signally improved the orchestration, which had not been uniformly satisfactory. It is worthy of note that thereafter Taneiev began to avail himself of Glazunov's advice in orchestration; of course he now made rapid strides in that field.

Now then, the business of publishing my operas beginning with

---

[29] During the season of 1896–7, at one of the Russian Symphony Concerts (the first, on February 8 [20], 1896), S. I. Taneiev was the assisting artist (Andante and Finale for the piano, op. 79, by P. I. Tchaikovsky); there, too, the Overture to the *Oresteia* trilogy was performed for the first time.

Saltan had passed into the hands of Bessel, who also took over my *Olyeg*. Nevertheless the *Little Pictures for the Fairy-tale of Tsar Saltan* were announced for performance at the Russian Symphony Concerts; [30] but the *Lay of Olyeg the Prophetic* I promised for the concerts of the Russian Musical Society, at the request of its Directorate.[31]

In the autumn Mamontov's opera company in Moscow studied *The Tsar's Bride*, and I made a trip to that city to attend rehearsals and the first performance.[32] The opera was a success.[33] Once more curtain calls, wreaths, suppers, and so forth. Zabyela, in the rôle of Marfa, sang excellently; the high notes in her arias rang out wonderfully, but, as a whole, this rôle suited her less well than that of the Sea Princess, and her costume, made, as ever, according to her husband's sketch, could hardly be called felicitous this time. Syekar-Rozhansky, who sang the part of Lykov, requested me to write an aria for him, pointing out a suitable moment for it in Act III. I had never composed special arias for anybody; but this time I could not help agreeing with him, as his remark about the more than inopportune brevity and incompleteness of Lykov's part was quite correct. On my return to St. Petersburg I asked Tyumenev to write suitable words, and on Christmas I composed the aria in Act III; I sent it on to Syekar-Rozhansky and decided to interpolate it permanently in my opera.[34]

---

[30] During the season 1899–1900 the Russian Symphony Concerts were given on Saturdays, November 20 [December 2], December 4 [16], 1899, February 18 [March 3] and March 18 [31], 1900, at the Grand Hall of the Conservatory. The *Little Pictures for the Fairy-tale* were performed at the third concert.

[31] Performed at the symphony concert of the Russian Musical Society on December 18 [30], 1899.

[32] By this time (fall of 1899) Mamontov had been declared insolvent, and the Opera was no longer called Mamontov's Private Russian Opera, but *Association* of Russian Private Opera.

[33] The première was given on October 22 [November 3], 1899. The cast of artists was as follows: Sobakin, Mootin; Marfa, Zabyela; Gryaznoy, Shevyelyev; Malyuta, Tarasov; Lykov, Syekar-Rozhansky; Lyubasha, Rostovtseva; Bomeli, Shkaffee; Saboorova, Gladkaya; Doonyasha, Strakhova; Pyetrovna, Kharitonova. Conductor, M. M. Ippolitov-Ivanov. The scenery was executed from sketches made by M. A. Vrubel.

[34] This aria was sung by Syekar-Rozhansky for the first time at the performance of January 3 [16], 1900. Rimsky-Korsakov went to Moscow to hear this performance. In the address presented on that occasion by the directors of the Private Opera, the hope was expressed that the first performance of *Tsar Saltan* as well would be entrusted to its care.

Olyeg I led personally at the concert of the Russian Musical Society. The soloists were Sharonov and Morskoy, the choir was very mediocre. Its success was slight. The composition won scant notice. The same thing had happened the previous year with *Svityezyanka.* I think that this is the fate of all cantatas, ballads, etc., for soloists and chorus with us; [35] our audiences do not like them and don't know how to listen to them. Nor do those performing at concerts like this form of composition: rehearsals have to be held, the choruses have to be drilled. The soloists like a plain solo, the choirs like merely separate choruses. The publishers, too, don't like these compositions, as nobody buys them. Very sad. . . .

The Russian Symphony Concerts of this season were, contrary to custom, given in the Grand Conservatory Hall, owing to repairs being made at the Hall of the Club of the Nobility. The *Little Pictures for the Fairy-tale of Tsar Saltan* sounded brilliant in the orchestra and were much liked.

---

[35] This distaste is not peculiar to Russian audiences. C. V. V.

Beginning of Servilia. May Night *at the Frankfurt am Main Opera House. Trip to Brussels.* The Tsar's Bride *on a private stage in St. Petersburg. Composing and orchestrating* Servilia. Sadko *at the Imperial Opera.* Tsar Saltan *on a private stage in Moscow. Resignation from conductorship of Russian Symphony Concerts. Thirty-fifth anniversary. Various operatic plans.*

HAVING DONE with the orchestral score of *Saltan* [1] and having laid aside for the time being the subjects jointly worked out by Byelsky and myself, I began to give more and more thought to Mey's *Servilia.* [2] The plan of turning it into an operatic subject had come to me often even in former years. This time my attention was attracted to it in earnest. A subject dealing with ancient Rome gave one free rein in the matter of unhampered style. Anything was appropriate here, except what was *manifestly contradictory*, like the obviously German, the evidently French, the undoubtedly Russian, etc. Of antique music not even a trace has been preserved; nobody

---

[1] From a letter of January 18 [31], 1900 to his son Andrey Nikolayevich: " This day I have at last finished the orchestral score and [piano] arrangement of *Saltan.* I rejoice at this, as at achieving every desired end, and, besides, I feel fatigued and hence rejoice doubly at having finished. All that remains to be done is to set a few things to rights and to fill in here and there the instruments that have not been written down. . . ."

[2] From a letter of April 8 [21], 1900 to N. I. Zabyela: " Oh, how I crave to write an opera! "

has heard it, nobody has a right to reproach the composer because his music is not Roman, provided the condition of avoiding what is *manifestly contradictory* has been observed by him. Consequently there was almost entire and complete freedom. But music outside of nationality does not exist, and, in its essence, all music which it is customary to consider universal, is national after all. Beethoven's music is German music; Wagner's, indubitably German; Berlioz's, French; Meyerbeer's also; possibly only the contrapuntal music of the old Flemings and Italians, music rooted in calculation rather than in direct feeling, is devoid of any national tinge. Accordingly, for *Servilia,* too, it was necessary to select in general some one most appropriate national colouring. Partly the Italian, partly the Greek colouring seemed to me the most suitable. As for the moments depicting the folk-life, for dances with music, and the like, according to my understanding, the Byzantine and Oriental tinge was highly appropriate there. For, indeed, the Romans possessed no art of their own; there was only what they had borrowed from Greece. On the one hand I am convinced of the close kinship of ancient Greek music to the Oriental, while on the other hand I believe that the remains of ancient Greek music are to be sought in Byzantine art, of which the echoes are heard in the ancient Orthodox church singing. These are the considerations that guided me when the general style of *Servilia* began to grow clear in my mind. I spoke to no one of my decision to compose *Servilia;* and, taking Mey's drama, I began to work out the libretto of my opera. There was little to recast and add; beginning with the latter half of the season of 1899–1900, musical ideas, too, began to crowd into my mind.

The disturbances which commenced at the University [3] in the academic year 1898–9 caused my wife and me to prefer sending our son Andrey to one of the foreign universities. The University of Strassburg was our choice. In the autumn of 1899 Andrey left for Strassburg. In the meantime the management of the Opera at Frankfurt am Main desired to produce my *May Night* and wrote

---

[3] The famous massacre of student youth of both sexes by Cossacks on Vasilevsky Ostrov (Island) occurred on February 8 [20], 1899. These disturbances and slaughters of students were a chronic disease in Russia, the massacre of March 4 [17], 1901 being especially notorious. J. A. J.

to me for suggestive information. Whatever I could I suggested by letter, but that was manifestly insufficient, yet I saw no possibility of going there myself. Just before production time it turned out that Vyerzhbilovich [4] was going to Frankfurt, where he had been engaged to appear in concerts. I asked him to call at the opera house upon his arrival in Frankfurt, and in my name to give them certain directions that had to do chiefly with the *mise en scène,* the folk-life side of the opera, and the acting, lest there creep in some too palpable absurdities in interpreting Ukrainian life, with which the Germans were entirely unfamiliar. However, Vyerzhbilovich, who had amiably and obligingly undertaken this errand, did absolutely nothing, and never even showed up at the Frankfurt Opera House. Of course I should not have charged Vyerzhbilovich with any such errand. . . .

The performance was finally announced, and our Andrey, learning of it, slipped over to Frankfurt and was present at the first performance.[5] The musical part, especially the orchestra, went not at all badly; but all the doings on the stage proved a shocking caricature. Thus, for example, the Mayor, the Scrivener, and the Distiller, in the second tableau of Act II, knelt down and kept shouting: " Satan! Satan! " and so on. The opera was given three times and then taken off the boards and immediately forgotten by everybody. As for the critics, they treated it condescendingly, and that is all. The relations that sprang up with the Prague Opera were more successful: at Prague, in the course of several succeeding years, were produced *May Night, The Tsar's Bride,* and *Snyegoorochka,* all with considerable success.

Having received an invitation to come to Brussels to conduct a concert of Russian music at the Théâtre de la Monnaie, I went there in March.[6] This time a certain d'Aoust, a wealthy and well-trained music-lover, was at the head of affairs. Joseph Dupont was no

---

[4] The great Russian cellist (1849–1911), pupil and successor of the famous Davydov. J. A. J.

[5] The première was given on May 3, 1900, at Frankfurt am Main, under the direction of Kapellmeister Dr. Rottenberg.

[6] Rimsky-Korsakov left St. Petersburg at the end of February and returned March 7 [20] or 8 [21]. The concert took place on March 18, 1900.

longer among the living. I had a cordial reception. D'Aoust and his
family were most attentive and amiable; there were rehearsals
aplenty, exactly as on my former visit, and the performance itself
was excellent. I put on *Sadko, Scheherazada,* a suite from Glazunov's *Raymonda,* etc. *Sadko* pleased moderately, *Scheherazada*
very much. The concert was attended by Vincent d'Indy, but he
did not come to see me in the green room. I met many of my
former Brussels acquaintances, but did not get to see Gevaert, as he
was ill. All in all, my trip was a success. On returning home, I set
to work assiduously on *Servilia.*

During the Easter season [1900] the Kharkov private opera company under the management of Prince Tseretelli began a season
of performances at Panayev's Theatre in St. Petersburg. Among
others they gave also *Tsarskaya Nyevyesta.* The talented M. N. Insarova made a beautiful figure as Marfa. But I was extremely exasperated by the cuts: the sextet in Act III and the ensemble during
Marfa's fainting-spell had been omitted. I asked the conductor,
Suk (a thorough musician), for an explanation; he told me that
they had been in a hurry with the production of *The Tsar's Bride*
in Kharkov and had made cuts to speed matters. Again haste was
the cause! But in reality it was laziness and a slipshod attitude towards music. Nobody even thinks of the impression of the whole.
Why rehearse some sextet or other when it is possible to do without
it? The opera can be studied more rapidly and the money diddled
out of the public. Indeed, the public pays the same money for the
opera *with* the sextet and *without* the sextet. The friendly critics
are not familiar with the opera and consequently will praise in
equal measure a production with the sextet and one without the
sextet; while unfriendly critics will abuse in equal measure anyway.
How disgusting! And yet there is no redress for a situation which
could be alleviated only by sound criticism and sound audiences.
The author's rights can be of but slight help in such cases. How,
indeed, can an author residing in St. Petersburg keep track of what
is going on in Kharkov or Kiev? But a good musician like Suk ought
to feel ashamed to make such cuts, since they clearly reduce his
own worth as a musician. In addressing these words to Suk, I ad-

dress them to all other opera conductors. I insisted that the sextet be restored, and this was done after a few performances. And how much the opera gained thereby, and how pleased the artists themselves felt! As for the ensemble of Act IV, I did not succeed in having that restored, owing to lack of time, after all.

Late in the autumn V. A. Tyelyakovsky, Director of the Moscow State Theatres, came to see me quite unexpectedly. The purpose of his visit was to ask me to let him have my *Skazka o Tsarye Saltanye* (*Fairy-tale of Tsar Saltan*) for production at the Grand Moscow Theatre the following season. I had to refuse him, as I had already promised that opera to the company of Solodovnikov's Theatre. Of course I felt regret that the management had come to this notion a bit too late; but it could not be helped, and I had to refuse. I suggested to Tyelyakovsky that he put on some other of my compositions, *Pskovityanka* for example, the more so as Chaliapin [7] — the inimitable Tsar Ivan — was at his disposal, since joining the Imperial Opera. Tyelyakovsky gladly accepted my suggestion, but the production of *The Maid of Pskov*, as it turned out afterwards, did not take place until a year later.

We decided to spend the summer *en famille* abroad near my son Andrey, who was studying at the University of Strassburg. Via Berlin and Cologne we followed the Rhine as far as Mainz and, after a brief stop in Strassburg, settled for a fairly long stay at Peterstal, in the mountains of the Schwarzwald. Andrey usually came to spend the week-ends with us. When the University vacations arrived, he and the rest of us went to Switzerland, where we lived chiefly at Vitznau by the Lake of the Four (Forest) Cantons,[8] on the slope of the Rigi. After visiting Lausanne and Geneva we made a very successful trip to Chamonix, with full opportunity to gaze to our hearts' content at Mont Blanc and walk among its foothills (Mer de Glace, Mauvais Pas, etc.). Our return journey lay again via Berlin. We returned to St. Petersburg by September.

---

[7] Fyodor Ivanovich Chaliapin (1873–1938) was then barely twenty-seven and had been famous for four years. J. A. J.

[8] Lac des Quatre-Cantons (German, *Vierwaldstättersee*), also known as the Lake of Lucerne. J. A. J.

I had no piano either at Peterstal or at Vitznau, where we made long stays. Nevertheless the work of composing *Servilia* got along without the aid of a grand piano. Acts III and IV were jotted down in their entirety, and Acts I and V, in part.[9] The only opportunity I had to play these on the piano was at Lucerne, where there was an excellent concert grand at the Catholic Society's Hotel. True, music written without the aid of a piano is distinctly "heard" by the composer; nevertheless, when chance offers one an opportunity to play (on the piano) for the first time a considerable quantity of music composed without a piano, there is a peculiar impression, unexpected in its way, and one to which the composer has to grow accustomed. The cause of this probably lies in being weaned from the sound of the piano. During the process of composing an opera the tones imagined mentally belong to voices and the orchestra, and when performed for the first time on the piano they sound somewhat strange.

Accordingly, on my return to St. Petersburg I brought with me (including what I had composed in the spring) Acts I, III, and IV complete, a few things for Act II, and the half-composed Act V, which I finished in a short time; only the work of composing Act II dragged somewhat. I immediately turned to the orchestration. I took the usual make-up of orchestra, exactly as in *The Tsar's Bride*, with the bass clarinet added here and there. The prevailing dramatic theme of *Servilia*, like the theme of *The Tsar's Bride*, demanded a purely vocal manner of composing; in this field I felt quite free now, and my vocal phrases as well as melodies proved tuneful and full of substance. As for the orchestration, my task this time seemed to me to demand that I not merely refrain from drowning the voices but rather give them good support and help them, and this I achieved, as was proved subsequently in the performance. I imagine that Servilia's aria in Act III, and her death scene in particular, hit the mark in this respect. The subject-matter of *Servilia* presented but a single opportunity for resorting to a broad

---

[9] On the autograph orchestral score of Acts III and IV of *Servilia* there are the following dates: " June 19 [July 2], Villa Victoria, 1900 "; " January 22 [February 4], St. Petersburg, 1901 "; and " July 26 [August 8], Villa Victoria; April 6 [19], 1901. St. Petersburg. N. R.-K."

vocal ensemble. This moment proved to be the quintet at the end of Act III. I believe that this quintet, with its beginning enunciated in canon form, is not inferior to the similar forms of *The Tsar's Bride* in its sonorousness and its delicacy of part-writing; yet, being interrupted by the messenger's entrance, it does not produce the full impression on the hearers, as they love emphasized and definite endings and are not sufficiently developed as yet to grasp ensembles interrupted for dramatic purposes. The material for the closing multi-voiced *Credo* had been borrowed by me from the closing *Amen* of the second version of *Pskovityanka*, where it was out of place. I cannot help feeling pleased with the transition from the voices of the soloists to the voices of the chorus growing crescendo in this *Credo*. As in my preceding operas, the system of leading motives was applied on a wide scale in *Servilia*. Thus the work of orchestrating *Servilia* preoccupied me during the first half of the season; after that I finished composing and brought into order the missing Act II. Here the ensemble of the banqueting Romans, Montanus's declamation, and the dance of the Mænads, as folk-life elements, were rigorously sustained by me in Greek modes. Towards spring the entire work was finished, and its printing undertaken by Bessel's.

I. V. Vsyevolozhsky was replaced by S. M. Volkonsky.[10] The new Director immediately proceeded to produce *Sadko* at the Mariinsky Theatre. The scenery was painted from the sketches of A. Vasnyetsov; the costumes also were made after his drawings. The best artists from among the company were pressed into service. The Princess was sung by Bolska, Sadko by Yershov, who for some reason, however (intrigue or caprice), did not sing at the first performance, being replaced by Davydov. Napravnik did the rehearsing and con-

---

[10] Prince Sergei M. Volkonsky lectured at the University of Chicago, the lectures being printed in *Progress* (Chicago), February 1897, pp. 355–84, and as *Pictures of Russian History and Russian Literature* (Boston: Lowell Lectures; 1897). J. A. J.

Prince S. M. Volkonsky was appointed Director of the Imperial Theatres in 1899 and retained that post only until 1901, when V. A. Tyelyakovsky succeeded him. The negotiations concerning the production of *Sadko* had commenced already in the fall of 1899. Then, likewise, Volkonsky had proposed to Rimsky-Korsakov to write a small fantastic ballet, though he did not tie Rimsky-Korsakov down to any subject whatever. This plan was never carried out.

ducting without a frown; nevertheless he subsequently yielded my opera to Fyeliks Blumenfeld, who had by that time been placed on an equal footing with Krooshevsky. Thus *Sadko* was finally produced at the Imperial Theatre (high time long ago!), but for this a new broom in the person of Prince Volkonsky proved necessary. The opera went excellently.[11] It was a pleasure at last to hear my music with a large orchestra and after proper rehearsing. The so-so performances of private opera houses were beginning to oppress me. After the first three or four performances Yershov, too, made his appearance and gave prominence to the rôle of Sadko. *Sadko* was given with some cuts that I had marked myself, as, in my opinion, things dragged. Subsequently, however, I came to the conclusion that, with slight exceptions, even those cuts were undesirable. Nyezhata's *bylina* is indeed a bit too long and monotonous, but with the cut a fine orchestral variation is lost. The scene on the ship, even though longish in itself, hardly gains by cutting. Here a cut is more in place at the departure of the ship, when Sadko has descended on a plank, with his *goosli* (dulcimer). An omission of the repeats of certain parts in the dances of little rivers and goldfishes is perhaps desirable. But a sizable cut in the finale of the opera spoils things after all. If *Sadko* lives some fifteen or twenty years longer on the stage, it is likely these cuts will be done away with, as in Wagner's operas, which were formerly given abroad with cuts and are now performed uncut.[12]

Prior to the production of *Sadko,* I made a trip to Moscow in October to attend the production of *Tsar Saltan* by the company of Solodovnikov's Theatre.[13] The so-called Mamontov Opera had lost its patron this year. S. I. Mamontov was jailed for debts incurred as a result of some commercial mishap in building the

---

[11] From a letter of February 5 [18], 1901, to N. I. Zabyela: " About *Sadko* I shall tell you that it has been put on well . . . but the impress of officialdom and lack of love [for the opera] are felt in everything. Even though the audiences call me before the curtain, they do so rather coldly. . . . I have made the same cuts as at the Moscow Opera and after the second performance a few more have been made. . . ."

The première of *Sadko* at the Mariinsky Theatre took place on January 26 [February 8], 1901.

[12] This is an error. Wagner's music dramas are seldom performed without cuts save at festival performances. C. V. V.

[13] Rimsky-Korsakov left for Moscow on October 11 [24].

Arkhangelsk Railroad.[14] His opera company organized into an association and began to perform independently, with almost the same personnel as at Solodovnikov's Theatre. *Saltan* was produced as well as could be expected of a private company. The scenery had been painted by Vrubel; the costumes were also made after his drawings. Mootin as Saltan, Syekar-Rozhansky as Gvidon, Tsvyetkova as Militrisa, Zabyela as the Swan, and all the others were fine. Even the Courier was sung by the prominent baritone Shevelyev. As before, M. M. Ippolitov-Ivanov was the conductor. The opera[15] had its première on October 21, with much success. I received several gifts.

Beginning with this season [1900–1], I resigned from the conductorship of the Russian Symphony Concerts, though remaining their director-in-chief. Conducting had ceased to have attractions for me; I could not make any advance in this field — I was too old for that. In the sense of conducting, the Russian Symphony Concerts offered no complete satisfaction; the orchestra was not sufficiently large in the personnel of its strings; and then it was high time to yield to younger blood. I decided to conduct only occasionally, when circumstances should make it necessary for some reason or other. The R. S. Concerts passed on to Lyadov and Glazunov, and subsequently to F. Blumenfeld and Cherepnin. However, this very season I had to conduct one concert of the Russian Musical Society of Moscow, whither I was called by V. I. Safonov,[16] who had fallen dangerously ill.

This concert had been set for December 23 [January 5, 1901],[17] while on December 19, 1900 [January 1, 1901] occurred the thirty-fifth anniversary of my activity as composer. The Moscow Private

---

[14] By the time of the production of *Saltan*, S. I. Mamontov was already free and lived in Paris.

[15] For an enumeration of the folksongs used in *Tsar Saltan*, see a footnote on page 317 of Rosa Newmarch's *The Russian Opera*. C. V. V.

[16] Vasili Ilyich Safonov (1852–1918), Director of the Moscow Conservatory, a prominent pianist and world-known conductor, was conductor of the New York Philharmonic Society in 1903–6 as guest conductor and in 1906–9 as its permanent and sole leader. J. A. J.

[17] This refers to the symphony concert of the Imperial Russian Musical Society, at which A. K. Glazunov's First Symphony, Rimsky-Korsakov's *Fairy-tale*, Haydn's Concerto for the cello (Jacobs), aria from Borodin's *Igor*, and Liszt's *Mephisto* were performed.

Opera Company, availing itself of my presence in Moscow, announced a performance of my *Sadko* for December 19 [January 1, 1901], sent me an invitation, and arranged a celebration of my jubilee. On the same evening, owing to my anniversary, the Grand Theatre produced my *Snyegoorochka;* having been invited by the Private Opera Company, however, I could not simultaneously attend the performance of *Snyegoorochka,* and this had a somewhat disadvantageous effect on my relations with the Moscow Directorate of Imperial Theatres. I regret it.

I was also honoured at the concert of the Russian Musical Society. Worn out by all these ovations, I returned to St. Petersburg. But here a sort of continuous round of honours during a whole month was in store for me.[18] Now this and now that musical society arranged a concert of my compositions, invited me to dinner or supper, showered me with addresses and wreaths. There were so many of these greetings and festivities that I cannot begin to enumerate them — everything has grown confused in my head. V. V. Yastryebtsev probably knows the particulars. I am grateful for all of it, but it was all unbearably boring and tiresome. I called my jubilee " chronic," like a lingering disease. Indeed, to hear day after day: " Deeply honoured Nikolay Andreyevich! During thirty-five years . . ." or " It is thirty-five years since . . ." is unbearable. And I don't believe, in fact, in the sincerity of it all. It seems to me that my jubilee in some cases did service merely as an advertisement, as an opportunity to nudge the world concerning the advertisers themselves. Only the Directorate of the Imperial Theatres took no part; and for this I give it my profound thanks. Of course, had I at all been able to foresee what a protracted form my jubilee would take, I should have fled in good season and as far as I could; but of that I had not even a suspicion, and having accepted greetings from one, it was unbecoming to refuse another. I wish no one a jubilee of like nature! . . .

During the season I continued pondering various subjects for operas. At my request, I. F. Tyumenev wrote an original libretto,

---

[18] From a letter of January 20 [February 2], 1901, to N. I. Zabyela: " So then, still the jubilee, behind and ahead — one interminable jubilee."

Pan Voyevoda, being guided by my specifications. I gave him an order for a play from Polish life of the sixteenth and seventeenth centuries, of dramatic content, but without political colouring. The fantastic element was to be present in a limited degree, in the form, perhaps, of fortune-telling or witchcraft. Polish dances, too, were a desirable consideration.

The thought of writing an opera on a Polish subject had long engrossed me. On the one hand, several Polish melodies, sung to me by my mother in my childhood, still haunted me, though I had already made use of them in composing a mazurka for the violin. On the other hand, Chopin's influence on me was indubitable, in the melodic turns of my music as well as in many of my harmonic devices; but this fact the gimlet-eyed critics had never observed, to be sure. The Polish national element in Chopin's compositions (which I worshipped) always aroused my delight. In an opera on a Polish subject I wished to pay homage to my rapture for this side of Chopin's music, and it seemed to me that I was capable of writing something Polish, national. The libretto of *Pan Voyevoda* suited me perfectly; in it Tyumenev had cleverly touched upon the folk-life element; the drama itself had nothing new to offer, but it presented grateful moments for music. Nevertheless the composing of *Pan Voyevoda* was put off for the time being. With V. I. Byelsky I had discussed and worked out the subjects of *Nausicaä* and *The Tale of the Invisible City of Kityezh;* fragments of the libretto of the first had even been written by V. I.[19] However, a different subject had riveted my attention.

One fine day there came to see me Y. M. Petrovsky, an assistant of N. F. Findeisen in the publishing of the *Russian Musical Gazette,* a man of education, a good musician, a fine and witty music-critic, and a passionate, irrevocable Wagnerite. He offered me a fanciful libretto in four short tableaux which he had written, under the title *Kashchey the Deathless.* This libretto gripped my interest. But I found it too long-drawn-out in its last two tableaux, nor did I like

---

[19] There is a sketch for the libretto of *Nausicaä* in the Manuscript Division of the State Public Library. In one of Rimsky-Korsakov's notebooks one can also find musical jottings for the proposed opera under that title. See also the beginning of the next chapter.

the versification. I stated my doubts to Petrovsky, and shortly afterwards he submitted to me a different and more comprehensive version of the same subject; this, however, I did not like at all. Preferring it in its first garb, I resolved to puzzle out the necessary changes myself. Thus the matter rested without any definite settlement, and I left town for my summer stay without knowing what to take up first.

Composing the prelude-cantata From Homer *and* Kashchey the Deathless. Vera Sheloga *and* The Maid of Pskov *at the Grand Theatre in Moscow. Composing* Pan Voyevoda. *New orchestration of* The Stone Guest. Servilia *at the Mariinsky Theatre.* Kashchey *on a private stage in Moscow. Composing* The Tale of Kityezh. Sheloga *and* Pskovityanka *at the Mariinsky Theatre.* Tsar Saltan *on a private stage. Byelayev's death and his last will.* Pan Voyevoda *and* Servilia *on private stages.* Boris Godunov *at the Mariinsky Theatre. Death of Laroche.*

THE SUMMER OF 1901 we spent at the estate Krapachookha, near the Okoolovka station. Early in the summer I was still engaged in orchestrating Act II of *Servilia,* which was then on the press. Having done with *Servilia,*[1] I composed a prelude-cantata, as if to serve as proem to *Nausicaä.* The orchestral prelude depicted the stormy sea and Odysseus tossed thereon, while the cantata was, as it were, the singing of dryads meeting the sun's emergence and welcoming the rosy-fingered Dawn. As I had not definitively settled the fate of *Nausicaä,* I named my prelude-cantata *From Homer.*[2]

---

[1] From a letter of May 31 [June 13], 1901 to N. I. Zabyela: "Yesterday I finished it [*Servilia*] at last entirely."

[2] The manuscript orchestral score of *From Homer* bears the dates: at the beginning, "July 28 [August 10], 1901," and at the end, "Krapachookha, August 8 [21],

Thinking over *Kashchey* [3] in the meantime, I arrived at the conclusion that the contents of the last two tableaux could be easily combined into one. I decided to write this short opera in three tableaux without a break in the music, and I turned to the libretto, with my daughter Sonya, the two of us together writing new lines. The music of *Kashchey* began rapidly to take form in my head, and towards the end of the summer the first tableau was ready in orchestral score, the second in rough draft. The composition was acquiring a stamp of individuality, thanks to some new harmonic devices that had heretofore not existed in my repertory as composer. These were the false relations formed by the progression of major thirds, the inner sustained tones, and various interrupted and false cadences with turns toward dissonant chords, and also a multitude of passing chords. The rather lengthy scene of the snowstorm I succeeded in plotting almost entirely on the sustained diminished chord of the seventh. The form evolved was connected, continuous, but the play of tonalities and the modulatory scheme, as always with me, were not due to chance. The system of leading motives was in full swing. Here and there, in lyric moments, the form assumed stable character and periodic structure, without, however, possessing full cadences. The vocal parts proved melodious, but the recitatives shaped themselves mostly on an instrumental foundation, in contrast to *Mozart and Salieri*. The orchestra was taken in its usual make-up; the chorus — only behind the scenes. All in all, the mood arrived at was gloomy and bleak, with rare flashes of light and occasionally with ill-boding gleams. Only the Prince's arioso in the second tableau, his duet with the Princess in Tableau III, and the finale on the words:

1901." It contains a written-in program in the form of a rhapsodist's words. Originally these words should have played the part of an *introductory recitative* for the entire composition.

[3] " Kashchey," writes W. R. S. Ralston in his *Russian Folk-Tales*, " is merely one of the many incarnations of the dark spirit . . . sometimes he is described as altogether serpent-like in form; sometimes he seems to be of a mixed nature, partly human and partly ophidian, but in some stories he is apparently framed after the fashion of a man . . . he is called ' immortal ' or ' deathless ' because of his superiority to the ordinary laws of existence . . . sometimes his ' death ' — that is, the object with which his life is indissolubly connected — does not exist within his body." An example of this latter instance occurs in Stravinsky's ballet, *The Firebird*, in which Kashchey's " death " is concealed in an egg. C. V. V.

FYODOR CHALIAPIN

in Rimsky-Korsakov's Mozart and Salieri

> O reddening sun!
> Freedom, Spring, and Love!

were to possess a bright character and thus stand out against the general background of gloom.

With the beginning of autumn I continued working on *Kashchey,* instrumentated its second tableau, and, after some intermission, jotted down and instrumentated the third. Publishing rights for *Kashchey* were granted to Bessel, who immediately proceeded in the matter.[4]

Prince Volkonsky, who had produced my *Sadko* on the Mariinsky stage the preceding season, put on also *The Tsar's Bride* during the season of 1901–2.[5] The opera went off with considerable success. Napravnik conducted willingly, but afterwards surrendered the opera to Fyeliks Blumenfeld. Bolska as Marfa; Fride and Markovich as Lyubasha; Morskoy as Lykov; Syeryebryakov as Malyuta; Kastorsky and Sibiryakov as Sobakin, were fine. But Yakovlev as Gryaznoy spoiled it all. This singer, with his voice gone and his tastelessly exaggerated expression, was simply unbearable to me. Yet, whether owing to his still handsome appearance or to his former successes, he contrived to win plaudits from the audience after all. The opera was given without cuts.

During the same season the Moscow Imperial Opera produced my *Maid of Pskov* together with *Vera Sheloga* at the Grand Theatre. I attended the dress rehearsal as well as the first performance.[6] Judged as a whole, the performance was good, while Chaliapin was inimitable. *Pskovityanka* was given in its entirety, with the scene in the woods, and then and there I was convinced that this scene is superfluous. The Prologue received scant attention, although Mme Salina as Vera Sheloga was very good.[7]

---

[4] From the jottings of *Kashchey* it is possible to establish the following original chronology of its composition: Tableaux I and II were finished in rough sketch September 1 [14], 1901; Tableau III was dated February–March 1902 in the original sketch.

[5] The first performance was given on October 30 [November 12], 1901.

[6] The première of *Pskovityanka* occurred on October 10 [23], 1901.

[7] In December 1901 Rimsky-Korsakov made a trip to Moscow, where he conducted the third act of his *Mlada,* in concert arrangement (*Night on Mount Triglav*) at an extra concert of the Russian Musical Society for the benefit of the fund for assisting the widows and orphans of artists and musicians in Moscow.

In the spring I made a definitive start on *Pan Voyevoda*.

The summer of 1902 we decided to spend abroad. My son Andrey matriculated at the University of Heidelberg for the summer semester, in order to attend old Kuno Fischer's lectures; for this reason Heidelberg was selected as our principal place of residence. There we found a villa; we rented a piano, and I resumed work on *Pan Voyevoda*.[8] In addition to this I had another task. Long since beset by the thought that the orchestration of *The Stone Guest*, done as it had been by me in my youth, in the period preceding *May Night*, was inadequate, I resolved to orchestrate afresh Dargomyzhsky's great work. As I had orchestrated Tableau I some two or three years before in spare moments between other work, I now took up the rest, softening here and there the extreme harshness and harmonic follies of the original. Work went well. *Pan Voyevoda* moved, the orchestration of *The Stone Guest* moved,[9] and, in addition, I read proofs of *Kashchey*, published by Bessel.

After a two months' stay in delightful Heidelberg, we left with the advent of the University vacations. We made a trip through Switzerland, visiting this time the Horner-Grath, and via Munich, Dresden, and Berlin returned home towards September. In Dres-

---

[8] From a letter of Rimsky-Korsakov to V. V. Bessel, dated July 8 [21], 1902, Heidelberg: "We are living here very quietly and propitiously. We have rented the villa Orotava and are its full masters. We have a fine large garden. Back of the garden starts the uphill approach to Mount Heiligenberg, which offers splendid walks through vineyards, chestnut and beech woods, with magnificent views of the Neckar plain. On the horizon the Rhine, the Vosges Mountains, the Harz Mountains, etc., are visible. We have acquired household articles of our own. The womenfolk are even cooking jams. We wear our old clothes — in a word, just as in Russia at a summer place. Before going back to Russia, we shall most likely make a trip somewhere: to Munich, Dresden, or the like. . . ."

At Heidelberg, Rimsky-Korsakov made his first acquaintance with the youthful endeavours at composing of Igor Fyodorovich Stravinsky, then still a student at the University of St. Petersburg. Rimsky-Korsakov recognized the composer's talent in these attempts, but simultaneously found that Stravinsky's ear for harmony was too undeveloped and his preparation in general for work as a composer altogether inadequate. Accordingly he recommended that, before applying to him, Stravinsky should engage some one of his (Rimsky-Korsakov's) experienced pupils, like V. P. Kalfati for instance, for the study of harmony. This counsel was punctually carried out by Stravinsky during the immediately following years.

[9] In the manuscript (which lacks Tableau I) preserved among Rimsky-Korsakov's papers, there are the following dates: at the end of Tableau II, " July 18–21 [July 31–August 3], 1902, Villa Orotava "; at the end of Tableau III, " August 4–17 [17–30], 1902, Heidelberg, Villa Orotava. N. R.-K."; and at the end of Tableau IV, " September 19 [October 2], 1902, St. Petersburg."

den we were fortunate enough to hear an unabridged performance of Wagner's *Götterdämmerung*, conducted by Schuch. The performance was excellent.

I came back to St. Petersburg with a considerable mass of rough drafts for *Pan Voyevoda* and immediately set out to continue the opera as well as to orchestrate what I had composed.

The post of Director of Imperial Theatres was held by Tyelyakovsky,[10] in place of Prince Volkonsky, who had left it. As early as the spring, as is usually done, the repertory for the season of 1902–3 was decided upon, and *Servilia* was included in it. Early in the autumn choral rehearsals were begun under F. Blumenfeld's direction, as Napravnik had fallen ill. Blumenfeld got things as far as orchestral rehearsals. As I appreciated his labours and realized his desire to conduct my *Servilia* independently and not merely as Napravnik's substitute, I addressed the latter, then already on the mend, with a request that he relinquish my opera in favour of Fyeliks. Napravnik consented with no suggestion that his feelings were offended in any way. In October *Servilia* was given an excellent performance.[11] Mme V. I. Kooza in the title-rôle of Servilia was very fine; Yershov as Valerius, Syeryebryakov as Soranus, and all the others were fine. The opera had been rehearsed excellently, and the artists, apparently, sang gladly and diligently. Yakovlev alone, as Ægnatius, was impossible, try as he might. Since the production of *The Tsar's Bride* I had conceived a sort of fear of baritone parts, as there rose before me visions of their being inevitably filled in the future by Yakovlev at the Mariinsky Theatre. Both in *Pan Voyevoda* and in *The Tale of the Invisible City of Kityezh*, which followed it, I began to avoid important baritone rôles, replacing them with high basso parts, for which Yakovlev was altogether unfit.

Servilia won a *succès d'estime* at the first performance, and none at all (as usual) in the subscription performances. Given once more to non-subscribers, it did not fill the theatre by half and was taken off the boards undeservedly. The next season the Directorate

---

[10] Previously Director of the Moscow State Theatres. Cf. p. 391. He succeeded Volkonsky in 1901.

[11] The first performance took place on Tuesday, October 1 [14], 1902.

projected it for production in Moscow with the St. Petersburg scenery and all the rest of the local *mise en scène*. During the same winter the Mariinsky Theatre produced *Die Götterdämmerung*. Thus the entire cycle of *Der Ring des Nibelungen* was in full swing. Also Napravnik's new opera *Francesca da Rimini* [12] was given. In Moscow meanwhile *Kashchey* was produced; [13] for this production I was indebted again to the " Association." It was sung together with *Yolanta,* and, for a private opera company, the performance was not bad. I was pleased with the sustained mood of my opera, and the rôles of the soloists proved quite singable; but the hearers hardly found their bearings among their impressions. Wreaths and calls for the author (and there was no lack of them) do not prove anything in themselves, especially in Moscow, where they are fond of me for some reason.

In the midst of work on *Pan Voyevoda* Byelsky and I pondered intensively the subject of *The Tale of the Invisible City of Kityezh and of the Maiden Fyevroniya*. When the outline had been definitively drawn, V. I. set hand to the libretto and finished it by summer. It was still spring when I composed Act I in rough draft.[14]

For the summer [1903], after the wedding of my daughter Sonya, who had married V. P. Troyitsky, we moved to Krapachookha for the second time. After settling in our summer home, I finished the orchestration of *Pan Voyevoda* (Act II) first of all, and then turned to sketch *Kityezh*. Towards the end of the summer Act I and both tableaux of Act IV were ready in detailed rough draft, and much else was sketched in fragments. On returning to St. Petersburg, I jotted down the first tableau of Act III; then Act II. I took up orchestrating.[15]

---

[12] With libretto based on Stephen Phillips's tragedy *Paolo and Francesca.* J. A. J.

[13] The first performance of *Kashchey* at Solodovnikov's Theatre took place on December 12 [25], 1902. The opera was given on the same evening with Tchaikovsky's opera *Yolanta*. The artists in the cast were: Kashchey, Oshoostovich; the Princess, Zabyela; Ivan Korolyevich, Bocharov; Kashchey's Daughter, Petrova; Boorya-Bogatyr' (Storm the Paladin), Osipov. Conductor, M. M. Ippolitov-Ivanov. The scenery was executed from sketches by the painter S. V. Malyutin.

[14] The end of this rough draft of Act I is dated May 28 [June 10], 1903. At the beginning of this rough draft Fyevroniya is still called Alyonooshka or Olyenooshka.

[15] The orchestration of *Kityezh* was completed by November 1904.

On September 18 [October 1], 1903, the piece *Sérénade pour violoncelle,* dedicated " To my son Andrey," was composed.

The season of 1903–4 was signalized to me by the production of *Pskovityanka* with *Sheloga* at the Mariinsky Theatre.[16] Chaliapin was magnificent. Napravnik conducted. The opera was given with the cut indicated by me: the scene in the forest was not performed, whereas the music of the forest, of the Tsar's hunting party, and of the rain-storm was played as a symphonic tableau before Act III and concluded with the girls' ditty (G major) behind the lowered curtain. Given thus, the result was good.

Chaliapin won success past all belief; the opera so-so, not what it had had in its first days.

At the Conservatory Theatre *Saltan* was performed by a private Russian opera company under the direction of the impresario Guidi.[17] However, since the music-critic of one of the dailies of St. Petersburg (a person with whom it was undesirable to have any dealings) was its principal, though unofficial, director of repertory, I attended neither rehearsals nor performances of *Saltan*. I was told they were quite poor.

The Christmas holidays came. M. P. Byelayev, who had not been feeling well for a long time, made up his mind to undergo a serious operation. The operation was performed successfully, but two days later his heart gave way, and he died in his sixty-eighth year.[18] One can easily imagine what a blow this was for the whole circle whose centre had gone with him. In his detailed last will and testament, after providing for his family, Byelayev bequeathed all his wealth to the cause of music; he divided it into funds for the Russian Symphony Concerts; the publishing business and composers' fees; prizes in memory of Glinka; prize competitions in chamber music; and relief of needy composers. There were some other, minor bequests besides. As the heads of the directorate of all these funds and his entire music business he had designated three persons: Glazunov, Lyadov, and myself, who were duty-bound to select our successors. These funds were so large that only the interest from them, and

---

[16] The first performance of the revival of *Pskovityanka* at the Mariinsky Theatre was given on October 28 [November 10], 1903.

[17] Guidi's management of the Conservatory Theatre belongs to the season of 1902–3.

[18] M. P. Byelayev died on December 28, 1903 [January 10, 1904].

even then in part only, was to be expended on the concerts, publishing business, etc.; the principal itself was to remain untouched, growing larger and larger in the course of time.

Thus, thanks to Mitrofan Petrovich's unselfish love for music, an institution until then unparalleled and unheard-of was founded, which for ever assured Russian music of publishers, concerts and prizes; and at the head of it, for the first time, stood our triumvirate. Still, there is no perfection in this world, and this institution, in the very testament of the deceased, already contained certain momentous shortcomings, of which I shall speak some time in the future.

Under M. P.'s will, at first the Russian Symphony Concerts were to be limited to three each year. During Lent we announced three concerts. For the opening concert I composed a short orchestral prelude, *Nad Mogiloyu* (*At the Grave*), on obitual themes from the *obikhod* (round of church canticles), with an imitation of the monastic funeral knell which had remained in my memory since my childhood at Tikhvin. This prelude was dedicated to Byelayev's memory. The concert [19] opened with it, and I conducted it myself. The prelude was hardly noticed. The other numbers of the concert were conducted by Lyadov and Glazunov. At the end my *Easter Overture* was excellently played under Sasha's bâton. Thus we honoured Byelayev's memory. The other two concerts were given under the direction of F. Blumenfeld and Cherepnin.

For the summer [of 1904] we moved to our dear familiar Vyechasha. During the summer I composed the unfinished second tableau of Act III of *The Tale of Kityezh* and completed the orchestration of the opera.[20] In addition to this I was engaged in reading proof on *Pan Voyevoda*, which was in print at Bessel's and was to appear in orchestral score and other guises towards autumn. On the other hand it was intended to have *Kityezh* done by the Byelayev firm, so as not to burden the Bessel house too much.

Prince Tseretelli, who had supplanted Guidi as impresario of the Conservatory Opera Theatre, expressed a desire to open his season

---

[19] Russian Symphony concert of February 19 [March 3], 1904.
[20] As is apparent from the notations on the autograph orchestral score of *Kityezh*, it was finished on September 27 [October 10], 1906.

with *Pan Voyevoda*, which had been accepted by the Directorate of Imperial Theatres for Moscow this time and not for St. Petersburg. At Tseretelli's *Pan Voyevoda* had been properly rehearsed by Suk, without cuts, and was given with Insarova as Maria.[21] This opera had a *succès d'estime* at the first performance, and audiences small in numbers at the other performances.

In October or November *Boris Godunov*, in my revision, with Chaliapin in the title-rôle, was produced at the Mariinsky Theatre. F. Blumenfeld conducted.[22] The opera was given without cuts. After several performances, however, the scene " Near Kromy "[23] was omitted, probably owing to political disturbances which began to break out, now here, now there.

I remained inexpressibly pleased with my revision and orchestration of *Boris Godunov*, heard by me for the first time with a large orchestra. Moussorgsky's violent admirers frowned a bit, regretting something. . . . But having arranged the new revision of *Boris Godunov*, I had not destroyed its original form, had not painted out the old frescoes for ever. If ever the conclusion is arrived at that the original is better, worthier than my revision, mine will be discarded, and *Boris Godunov* will be performed according to the original score.[24]

---

[21] The first performance was given on October 3 [16], 1904.
The sketches for the *Textbook of Instrumentation* belong to October 1904.
[22] The first performance was given on November 9 [22], 1904, for the benefit of the artists of the orchestra.
[23] This is the scene in the last act, depicting the advance of the Pretender, and concluding with the wails of the village idiot. C. V. V.
[24] Rimsky-Korsakov's emendations of *Boris Godunov* have offered opportunity for a great deal of discussion. Montagu-Nathan admits that Rimsky seems to have " toned down a good many musical features which would have won acceptance today as having been extraordinarily prophetic." Stassov was opposed to the alterations. " While admitting Moussorgsky's technical limitations," writes Rosa Newmarch, " and his tendency to be slovenly in workmanship, he thought it might be better for the world to see this original and inspired composer with all his faults ruthlessly exposed to view than clothed in his right mind with the assistance of Rimsky-Korsakov. . . . We who loved Moussorgsky's music in spite of its apparent dishevelment may not unnaturally resent Rimsky-Korsakov's conscientious grooming of it. But when it actually came to the question of producing the operas, even Stassov, I am sure, realized the need for practical revisions, without which Moussorgsky's original scores, with all their potential greatness, ran considerable risk of becoming mere archæological curiosities." Arthur Pougin (*Essai historique sur la musique en Russie*) falls in with this theory: " In reality the music of Moussorgsky only became possible when a friendly, experienced hand had taken the trouble to look it over and carefully cor-

The opera stock company of Solodovnikov's Theatre in Moscow
(that is, the former Mamontov opera company) had moved the
previous season to the Aquarium Theatre; at Solodovnikov's Theatre a new association had installed itself under the direction of
Kozhevnikov, Lapitsky, and others. This association had decided to
produce my *Servilia,* and I gave them permission to do so, as the
Moscow Imperial Theatre did not intend to put it on. Its conductors were the composer Kochetov and an Italian, Barbini. Although
N. R. Kochetov had not the reputation of being a good or experienced conductor, I selected him in preference to the Italian, when
the choice was left to me, because a composer's musicianship was

---

rect it." James Huneker writes: " Moussorgsky would not study the elements of orchestration and one of the penalties he paid was that his friend, Rimsky-Korsakov,
' edited ' *Boris Godunov* (in 1896, a new edition appeared with changes, purely practical, as Calvocoressi notes, but the orchestration, clumsy as it is, largely remains the
work of the composer) and *Khovanshchina* was scored by Rimsky-Korsakov, and no
doubt ' edited,' that is revised, what picture experts call ' restored.' " In his life of
Moussorgsky, Calvocoressi contents himself with this laconic statement: " In 1896 a
new edition of *Boris Godunov* appeared, revised by M. Rimsky-Korsakov. Certain of
the changes that one marks in this have a purely practical end, which is to facilitate
the execution; others are only motivated by the desire to take away from the isolated
aspect of the work, to render it less disconcerting to the public." But Jean Marnold
(in *Musique d'autrefois et d'aujourd'hui*) screams with rage: " He [Rimsky-Korsakov]
changes the order of the last two tableaux, thus denaturing, at its conclusion, the
expressly popular essence and the psychology of the drama. The scene of Boris with
his children is especially mutilated. Rimsky-Korsakov cuts, at his happiness, one, two,
or three measures, as serenely as he cuts fifteen or twenty. At will, he transposes a
tone, or a half-tone, makes sharps or flats natural, alters modulations. He even cor-
rects the harmony. During the tableau in the cell of Pimyen, the liturgical Dorian
mode is adulterated by a banal D minor. The interval of the augmented fifth (a
favourite device of Moussorgsky) is frequently the object of his equilateral ostracism.
He has no more respect for traditional harmony. Nearly every instant Rimsky-Korsakov changes something for the unique reason that it is his pleasure to do so. From
one end of the work to the other he planes, files, polishes, pulls together, retouches,
embellishes, makes insipid, or corrupts. Harmony, melody, modulation, tonality, all
inspire him to make changes. In comparing the two scores one can hardly believe
one's eyes. In the 258 pages of that of Rimsky-Korsakov there are perhaps not
twenty which conform to the original text."
   Moussorgsky's orchestral score of *Boris* long lay buried in the Imperial Library at
St. Petersberg. In 1874 Saint-Saëns brought a piano and vocal score from Russia and
yet another example of this score seems to have found its way to Paris. Also for some
time there has been a copy of this original vocal score in the Library of Congress at
Washington. These have been semi-available for examination, but it was not until
April 1922 that Robert Godet published his study, *Les deux Boris,* in *La Revue Musi-
cale,* giving comparative examples from the two scores. The evidence is deadly. " The
difference in the two versions does not lie," Godet points out, " in slight transposi-
tions and casual retouching: they attest, on the contrary, to the flagrant and persistent

more valuable in my eyes than a fine Italian hand. And I had made no mistake. When I came by invitation to Moscow to the dress rehearsal I found that the orchestra had been drilled conscientiously, that the tempi were correct, and that my music had been properly grasped by the conductor. The soloists and the chorus were not sufficiently good, but that was not the conductor's fault. As for the opera, it was given fairly decently and again with a *succès d'estime*.[25] Generally speaking, I had long felt disappointed in the Russian private opera impresarios and made up my mind under no circumstances to give my *Kityezh* to a private theatre.

Laroche, once famous among us as a music-critic, but in reality a copy of Eduard Hanslick, died after having dragged out a pitiful existence.[26] Grown lazy and slovenly during his last years, he now lived even without a roof over his head, finding shelter now at Byelayev's, now at Lyadov's, and now with others who harboured him out of friendship. Though living among strangers, he nevertheless contrived to annoy them with his caprices and demands to have his whims complied with. In his very last days he received some support from his children and lived in a furnished room. The sympathy shown him by the members of Byelayev's circle is in-

---

antagonism of the two mentalities. It appears difficult, indeed, after a first inspection of the documents, not to become indignant over the sacrilege, to cry, one is never betrayed save by one's friends! The more one examines the two versions, however, the more one is inclined to modify this excessive impression. Translated into the language of good sense one finishes by summing the situation up in this wise: let us not speak of betrayal, rather let us call it simply incompatibility of character." In a number of *The Sackbut*, published almost simultaneously in London, Edwin Evans discusses the question, suggesting that if a revision seems necessary it should be made in an advanced manner, by some one like Stravinsky, rather than in a conservative or traditional manner. He points out that because Moussorgsky wrote a good many pages which the musicians of his time did not understand, it has always been held that he did this through lack of knowledge, rather than intentionally. He modulated abruptly without a formal reason. He interrupted himself. He contradicted himself. Moved by compulsion, he passed rapidly, without transitional passages, from one idea to another. It is these possibly intentional manifestations of original genius that Rimsky-Korsakov has taken it upon himself to correct. In 1928 the original orchestral score, edited by Professor Paul Lamm, was published by the Music Section of the Russian State Publishing Department at Moscow and by the Oxford Press in England and America. This has been performed in Russia, in Philadelphia, under the direction of Stokowski, in Berlin, I think, and possibly elsewhere. It is much too soon to be certain which version, the original or that of Rimsky-Korsakov, will hold the stage. C. V. V.

25 The first performance took place on November 2 [15], 1904.

26 H. A. Laroche died on October 18 [31], 1904, in St. Petersburg.

comprehensible to me. Many said "thou" to him, forgetting the past. Fortunate that his verdicts had not been enforced and his prophecies never came true. His activity was mere grimace and gesticulation, lies and paradoxes, exactly like the activity of his Viennese prototype.

Disturbances among student youth. Performance of Kashchey in St. Petersburg. Textbook of Instrumentation. Pan Voyevoda in Moscow. Arensky's death. Affairs at the Conservatory. Revival of Snyegoorochka. Concerts: Ziloti, Russian Symphony, and Russian Musical Society. Additions to the score of Boris Godunov. Moussorgsky's Wedding. Summer of 1906.

THE COURSES at the Conservatory went on more or less successfully until the Christmas holidays. Before the beginning of the Christmas recess, however, a certain state of excitement began to be noticeable among the pupils who reacted towards the disturbances going on in the University. Then came January 9 [21], and political ferment seized all St. Petersburg. The Conservatory, too, was affected; its students were in turmoil. Meetings were called. The cowardly and tactless Bernhard began to interfere. The Directorate of the Russian Musical Society also began to meddle. Special meetings of the Art Council and of the Directorate became the order of the day. I was chosen a member of the committee for adjusting differences with agitated pupils. All sorts of measures were recommended: to expel the ringleaders, to quarter the police in the Conservatory, to close the Conservatory entirely. The rights of the pupils had to be championed. Disputes and wrangling grew more and more violent. If one were to believe the conservatives among

411

the professors and the Directorate of the St. Petersburg Branch, I myself was possibly the very head of the revolutionary movement among the student youth. Bernhard behaved in the most tactless fashion imaginable. In the daily *Roos'* (*Russia*) I made public a letter[1] in which I took the Directorate to task for not understanding the pupils, and argued that the existence of the Directorate of the St. Petersburg Branch was unnecessary, as well as that self-government was desirable. At a meeting of the Art Council, Bernhard devoted himself to examining and condemning my letter. Counter-arguments were uttered, and he broke up the meeting. Then a considerable group of professors, together with me, suggested in a letter that he leave the Conservatory. The result of it all was that the Conservatory was closed, more than a hundred pupils were expelled, Bernhard left, and I was dismissed from the ranks of professors of the Conservatory by the chief Directorate, without previous consultation with the Art Council. On receiving notice of this dismissal[2] I wrote a letter[3] about it to the newspaper *Roos'* and simultaneously resigned my honorary membership in the St. Petersburg Branch of the Musical Society. Then something incredible occurred. From St. Petersburg, Moscow, and every corner of Russia, there came flying to me from every variety of institution and all sorts of people, both connected with music and having no connection with music, addresses and letters bearing expressions of sympathy for me and indignation at the Directorate of the Russian Musical Society. Deputations from societies and corporations, as well as private individuals, kept coming to me with declarations to the same effect. Articles discussing my case began to appear in all the papers; the Directorate was trampled in the mud and had a very difficult time of it. Some of its members left it, men like

---

[1] Cf. Appendix VI.

[2] For certain details, cf. Y. Veysberg's reminiscences, "The Conservatory in 1905," in *Russkaya Molva*, December 18 [31], 1912, and the *Red Evening Gazette*, 1925, Nos. 307 and 309. The notice of this dismissal, written on a letter-head of the I[mperial] R[ussian] M[usical] S[ociety], St. Petersburg Branch, file number 651, is signed: "For N. Klimchenko, Chairman — G. Toor, Secretary," and bears the date of March 21 [April 3], 1905. Attached to it is a transcript from the minutes; a quotation from this transcript, in its turn, is given in Rimsky-Korsakov's letter to the newspaper *Roos'* (cf. Appendices VI and VII).

[3] Cf. Appendix VII.

412

Persiani and Aleksandr Sergeyevich Taneiev.[4] To cap it all, the students set their minds on giving, at Mme Kommissarzhevskaya's Theatre, an operatic performance consisting of my *Kashchey* and concert numbers.[5] *Kashchey* had been rehearsed very finely under Glazunov's direction. At the conclusion of *Kashchey* something unprecedented took place: I was called before the curtain, addresses from various societies and unions were read to me, and inflammatory speeches were delivered. It is said that someone in the uppermost tier shouted: " Down with autocracy! " The din and hubbub after each address and each speech were indescribable. The police ordered the iron curtain to be lowered and thereby stopped further excitement. The concert portion did not materialize.

Such exaggeration of my services and my quasi-extraordinary courage may be explained only by the excitement of Russian society as a whole, which desired to express, in the form of an address to me, the pent-up indignation against the governmental régime. Realizing this as I did, I had not the emotion that satisfies ambition. I waited only to see how soon it would end. But it did not end soon, it dragged on for two whole months. My position was unbearable and absurd. The police issued orders forbidding the performance of my compositions in St. Petersburg. Some of the crotchety provincial governors also issued similar orders in their domains. On this basis there was also forbidden the third Russian Symphony concert, the program of which included the Overture to my *Pskovityanka.* Towards summer the force of this absurd prohibition began

---

[4] (1850–1917), an uncle of the more famous Taneiev. J. A. J.

[5] This performance occurred on March 27 [April 9], 1905. The artists who took part in the opera were: Kashchey, A. I. Gurovich; the Princess, K. Y. Mayzels; Ivan Korolyevich, F. V. Povlovsky; Kashchey's Daughter, N. F. Lezhen, Boorya-Bogatyr', I. I. Pavlov. In the concert portion which did not materialize there were planned appearances by the artists E. Zimbalist, L. Kreytser, and several others.

Among Rimsky-Korsakov's papers has been preserved a *copy* of a memorandum; it was made in Rimsky-Korsakov's hand and signed " Military Melomaniac." It contains the following announcement: " The last obstruction which Count Bobrinsky witnessed and the character of the ovations on March 27 [April 9] called forth grave keenness of observation on the part of the police, the result of which is the sudden prohibition of the concert of March 31 [April 13]. Considerable annoyance may be expected for some who have signed their names in the papers, and particular harm may come to Nikolay Andreyevich [Rimsky-Korsakov], Aleksandr Konstantinovich [Glazunov], and Jewish students. . . ."

to weaken little by little, and, owing to my being in fashion, my compositions came to figure with considerable frequency on the summer programs of out-of-town orchestras. Only in the provinces the zealous martinets persisted in considering them revolutionary for some time longer.

The classes did not resume at the Conservatory. Glazunov and Lyadov sent in their resignations. My other colleagues, however, after talking and making some little noise, remained, every one except (for reasons unknown) Vyerzhbilovich, Mme Esipova (who went abroad), and F. Blumenfeld, who grasped this favourable moment to quit the Conservatory, a step he had been aching to take in any event. On the other hand, at the private meetings, held at Sasha Glazunov's home during these troublous days, it was decided, by an imposing number of the instructors, to elect Glazunov director of a self-governing conservatory. But there the matter rested.

The events of the spring of 1905 at the Conservatory and my own story have been described very briefly; but the materials — articles, letters to editors, the official message to me containing my dismissal — I have in complete order. Whoever wishes may avail himself of that material; as for me, I have no desire to enter upon a detailed description of this long pause in my musical life.[6]

For the summer of 1905 we moved again to Vyechasha. My son Andrey, suffering from rheumatism, had gone abroad with his mother and was taking the cure at Nauheim, whence they returned to Vyechasha only at the end of the summer. Fortunately, the cure brought the desired benefit, but another visit to Nauheim the following year was planned in order to have Andrey's health completely restored.

Quite upset by the incident at the Conservatory, I could not turn to anything for a long time. After trying my hand at an article containing an analysis of my *Snyegoorochka*,[7] I finally turned to carry-

---

[6] The materials of which Rimsky-Korsakov speaks have been preserved in their entirety in his archives.

[7] The author's own analysis of *Snyegoorochka* was published in the posthumous collection: N. A. Rimsky-Korsakov: *Articles and Notes on Music* (St. Petersburg, 1911). It first had appeared in the *Russian Musical Gazette*, 1908, Nos. 39–40. Though planned as an all-inclusive analysis of *Snyegoorochka*, this essay was left far from finished — more correctly, just begun. The published portion, devoted to the

ing out a thought of long standing — to write a textbook of orchestration with illustrations culled exclusively from my own compositions.[8] This labour consumed the entire summer. In addition to this, the orchestral score of *The Tale of Kityezh* was prepared for printing, and much had to be copied clean and polished a bit. This time publication had been undertaken by Byelayev's firm. I shall also mention rewriting the duet *Gorny Klyooch* (*The Mountain Spring*) as a vocal trio, as well as orchestrating it, together with two duets and the song *The Nymph*.[9]

After my return to St. Petersburg, all my time was spent in hunting up illustrations for my manual of orchestration and in evolving the form of the manual itself. The Conservatory was closed. My pupils studied under me at my house.

Early in the autumn I was called to Moscow to attend the production of *Pan Voyevoda* at the Grand Theatre. The talented Rachmaninoff conducted. The opera proved to have been well rehearsed, but some of the artists were rather weak, for instance Mme Polozova, the Maria, and Petrov, the Voyevoda. Orchestra and choruses went splendidly. I was pleased with the sound of the opera in both voices and orchestra. What had sounded fair at the private opera house gained manifoldly with a large orchestra. The whole orchestration had hit the mark squarely, and the voices sounded beautiful. The beginning of the opera, the Nocturne, the scene of fortune-telling, the Mazurka, the Krakovyak, the Polonaise pianissimo during the scene of Yadviga with Pan Dzuba, left nothing to be desired.

---

thematic material of *Snyegoorochka*, was completed only as far as the first category of themes was concerned. This part constitutes pages 3–18 of the autograph manuscript. The subsequent pages (18–39) present the beginning of a detailed act-by-act analysis of the opera, which breaks off on Snyegoorochka's A-flat-major aria in the Prologue. The lack of finish in the matter of style does not prevent these pages from possessing considerable interest as a sample by which a judgment may be formed concerning the scope of the work as planned and its character as a whole. To judge by the dates, the entire episode of writing the analysis falls approximately in the space of one week (June 27 to July 3 [July 10–16], 1905).

[8] On the manuscript of the jottings for the *Textbook of Orchestration* which belong to this period there is the date: "Commenced July 4 [17], 1905."

[9] In addition to these, the recording of a part of these reminiscences belongs to the summer of 1905. To the summer of 1905 as well belongs Rimsky-Korsakov's correspondence with A. I. Ziloti concerning the proposed inauguration of "higher musical courses." For echoes of this correspondence, cf. "Correspondence of A. K. Lyadov and N. A. Rimsky-Korsakov" (in *Musical Contemporary*, 1915–16, No. 7).

The song of the dying swan, which had taken very well at St. Petersburg, came out more pallid here at Polozova's hands, while Petrov's execution of the Pan's aria was colourless.

The time of the production of *Pan Voyevoda* at Moscow was riotous. A few days before the first performance a strike of printing shops broke out. Except for the theatre billboards, no advertisements whatever could appear, and the first performance did not draw a full house by half.[10] There was nevertheless a *succès d'estime;* but the ever growing frequency of the strikes, the political disturbances, and finally the December uprising in Moscow led to the disappearance of my opera from the repertory after several performances. Tyelyakovsky was present at the first performance. On learning from Rachmaninoff that I had *The Tale of Kityezh* completed, he expressed a desire to produce it in St. Petersburg the following season. I told him that henceforth I did not intend to submit my operas to the Directorate; let the Directorate itself select whichever it wished of my published operas. Still, owing to the fact that Tyelyakovsky took an interest in my *Tale of Kityezh,* I should present him with an autographed copy of it upon its publication; but whether my opera were produced or not, that would rest with him: if he wished to put it on, I should be pleased; if he decided not to do so, I should take no steps to remind him.

After listening to my *Sadko* at Solodovnikov's Theatre in a wretched performance under Pagani's direction, I returned to St. Petersburg.[11]

---

[10] The first performance was given on September 27 [October 10], 1915. The artists who appeared in the première were: Pan Voyevoda, Petrov; Yadviga, Yoozhina; Dzuba, Tyntyunnik; Olyesnitsky, Sinitsina; Chaplinsky, Barsookov; Poslavsky, Borisoglyebsky; Oskol'skaya, Polozova; Marshalok (Elder " in-law "), Uspensky; Dorosh, Tolkachov.

[11] Soon after his return from Moscow, Rimsky-Korsakov narrowly escaped falling a victim of a hoax which might have brought extremely unpleasant consequences to him in the conditions of the political régime and the aggravated revolutionary ferment of the time. In No. 23 of the daily *Russkiya Vyedomosti* of January 24 [February 6], 1906, under the caption: " *Attention of Artists!* " there was published a letter to the editor, over the signature of Prof. N. A. Rimsky-Korsakov, which read as follows:

" On January 22 [February 4] in a first-class compartment of a Warsaw-Vienna train approaching the St. Petersburg depot, I found a water-colour of symbolistic-sectarian character of the following contents in Old-Church Slavic interlaced lettering:

" ' Brethren! Behold the tears of hell and the path of salvation . . . walk straight

In the autumn, death carried off A. S. Arensky.[12] A former pupil of mine, upon being graduated from the St. Petersburg Conservatory he had become professor at the Moscow Conservatory and had lived in Moscow a number of years. According to all testimony, his life had run a dissipated course between wine and card-playing, yet his activity as composer was most fertile. At one time he had been the victim of a nervous ailment, which had, however, evidently left no lasting effect. Having left the staff of professors of the Moscow Conservatory in the nineties, he removed to St. Petersburg and for some time was director of the Court Chapel, succeeding Balakirev. At this post, too, the same mode of life continued, though on a reduced scale. On leaving the Chapel, after Count A. D. Sheryemetyev had been appointed head of the Chapel, Arensky found himself in an enviable position: listed as some privy-commission functionary in the Ministry of the Court, he drew a pension of some six thousand rubles, and was absolutely free to work at his composing. He did work much at composition, but that is just where he began to burn the candle at both ends. Revels, card-playing, health undermined by this mode of living, galloping consumption as the final result, dying at Nice, and death at last in Finland. Upon settling in St. Petersburg, Arensky had always been on friendly

---

and woe betide ye if ye stop and retreat *when* (kol') *whither* (kooda) *onto* (na) *the track* (slyed) *nowise* (nikak) *to the devil* (chortoo). God be with us!'

"The artist's name is illegible, the envelope stamp-dated 'Moscow, December 1905.' Please call between the hours of 3 and 5 on January 23 and 24 [February 5 and 6] at the Hotel Metropole. Prof. N. A. Rimsky-Korsakov."

The text italicized by me forms words that were insolent according to those times. "To the devil with Nickie (Tsar Nicholas II) and the heir to the throne! [When differently allotted the italicized meaningless *kol'* (when) *kooda* (whither) *na* (onto) *slyed* (the track) *nikak* (nowise) *chortoo* (to the devil) read: *Kol'koo* (Nickie) *da* (and) *Naslyednika* (the heir to the throne) *k* (to) *chortoo* (the devil). J. A. J.]

S. P. Byelanovsky, who forthwith got in touch with Rimsky-Korsakov about this matter and took all possible steps to forestall any unpleasant consequences whatsoever for R.-K., states, in a memorandum relating the case, that according to the police inspector of the precinct the letter in the *Russkiya Vyedomosti* was the pre-arranged advertisement of the meeting of the socialist revolutionaries. Governor-General Doobasov raged and fumed regarding the letter itself and its repudiation. The editorial offices of the *Russkiya Vyedomosti* were raided by the police and the threat of a raid hung for a time also over Rimsky-Korsakov. As for S. P. Byelanovsky, the police inspector advised him to break off all correspondence with Rimsky-Korsakov for some time, "as all letters would be examined and, possibly, would even be withheld."

[12] A. S. Arensky died on February 25 [March 10], 1906, and not in the autumn

terms with Byelayev's circle, but had kept aloof, all by himself, as a composer, recalling Tchaikovsky in this respect. By the nature of his talent and his tastes as composer he was the closest approximation to A. G. Rubinstein, but he was inferior in the force of talent for composition, though in instrumentation, as the child of more modern times, he outdistanced A. G. In his youth Arensky had not escaped entirely my own influence; later he fell under that of Tchaikovsky. He will be soon forgotten.

The all-Russian strike broke out. October 17 [30] came with the street demonstration of the 18th [31st] and the carnage started by General Min. A temporary unlimited freedom of the press came, then the withdrawal of liberties, repressions, the Moscow uprising, again repressions, and so on.[13] Work on my manual, too, flagged for some reason or other.[14] Nevertheless, in the midst of all these disturbances, provisional rules for the Conservatory of a somewhat self-governing character were promulgated. The Art Council was granted the right to engage professors independently of the St. Petersburg Directorate and to elect from their own ranks a director for a definite term of years. On the basis of these new principles, the Council immediately invited me, and all the other professors who had left the Conservatory because of me, to come back into their midst. At our first general meeting Glazunov was unanimously elected Director. The expelled students were reinstated. But there was no way of resuming studies, as the students' meeting that had been called had passed a resolution forbidding it, owing to the non-resumption of studies in other higher educational institutions. It was decided to permit only graduation examinations in May. My instruction of the pupils continued at my house. The meetings of

---

[13] On December 4 [17], 1905, at Tyenishov's Hall, there was a concert, " arranged by N. A. Rimsky-Korsakov," with the assistance of artists of the Imperial Theatres (all the best talent). The program read: " The entire proceeds of the concert will be given to the families of destitute workingmen." The program of the concert was printed on brilliant red paper.

On December 21, 1905 [January 3, 1906] the opera *Mozart and Salieri,* with Chaliapin in the cast, was performed for the first time at the Mariinsky Theatre as a benefit for the chorus. Leoncavallo's opera *Pagliacci* was the second part of the bill.

[14] The *Textbook of Instrumentation* is meant here.

the Art Council were stormy to the point of indecency. Some advocated the opening of classes, slandering the student body in every possible way, and quarrelling with Glazunov, who clung to the resolution passed at the meeting; others of his former partisans turned their backs on him under the influence of the reaction which had overwhelmed a part of society. The position of Glazunov, who was worshipped by the students, was a difficult one. The conservative group of instructors snarled at him like dogs, at every meeting. At one of these I lost my temper and left the meeting, saying that I could stay at the Conservatory no longer. Some of them ran after me, begged me, tried to calm me. I wrote a letter of explanation to the Art Council,[15] confessing that I should not have flown into a passion, but stating the motives that had incensed me. Having made up my mind to remain with the Conservatory until summer, I had in view to leave it by the following autumn, the more so as the St. Petersburg Directorate, which had at first shrunk to zero, began to show signs of life by putting all manner of financial obstacles in the way of Glazunov's endeavours. I spoke to Glazunov of my intention to leave, urging him, too, to leave the Conservatory, which had become unbearable. He was in despair, saw in my departure seeds of further disorders, and would not consent to go himself, expecting still to be of use to the institution. The month of May came and with it the time of examinations. Glazunov conducted the examinations zealously and energetically. The minds of the students, too, had calmed somewhat with the beginning of the examinations, and the academic year came to a safe close. Out of pity for beloved Sasha as well as for my numerous pupils, I decided to delay my leaving until autumn, because Glazunov's intentions were of the best, and it came hard to frustrate his plans.

During the latter half of the season [spring, 1906] at the Mariinsky Theatre, *Snyegoorochka* was revived and given eleven times under the direction of F. Blumenfeld. Notwithstanding the disturbed times, the performances drew good houses. *Sadko* had also been projected, but it did not materialize and was postponed till

---

[15] This letter of explanation has been given as Appendix VIII in this edition.

the next season. *The Tsar's Bride,* produced early in the spring, apparently had been stricken from the repertory, and, in the spring, rehearsals of *The Tale of the City of Kityezh* began at the instance of Tyelyakovsky, who had received from me a copy of the opera as a present.

At the Ziloti Concerts my Symphony in C major was given [16] — its first performance not under my direction. Heretofore conductors apparently had been afraid of it, probably because of its Scherzo in ⅘. In reality the symphony did not prove too difficult, and Ziloti conducted it successfully. Glazunov's *Ey ookhñem* (*Heave-ho*) and my *Doobinooshka* (*The Little Cudgel*),[17] composed under the influence or rather on the occasion of the revolutionary disturbances, were played at another concert. Exactly as much as Glazunov's piece proved magnificent, just so much did my *Doobinooshka* prove short and insignificant, even though sufficiently noisy.

The prohibition of its third concert in the spring of the previous year affected the pecuniary affairs of the Russian Symphony Concerts, and this season it was found necessary to limit the concerts to two only, under the direction of Blumenfeld and Cherepnin.[18] In memory of Moussorgsky, on the twenty-fifth anniversary of his death, several of his pieces were performed (and all in my orchestration!).

The concerts of the Russian Musical Society dragged on their sad existence. The shadow that had fallen on this organization as a result of the previous spring obfuscated these concerts, particularly at the beginning of the season. Foreign conductors refused to come, our own also fought shy. The young conductor Volchok did not attract any audiences. The concerts were saved by Auer and the German Beidler, who came to conduct two of them.

---

[16] The Third Symphony, in C major, was performed at the concert of October 30 [November 12], 1904 (i.e., during the second season of the Ziloti Concerts); *Doobinooshka* and *Ey ookhñem* at the concert of November 5 [18], 1905 (i.e., in the third season).

[17] This folksong, possibly even better known than *Ey ookhñem,* has always been *the* revolutionary song of Russia, and its singing was forbidden for years. J. A. J.

[18] The Russian Symphony Concerts of the season 1905–6 took place on February 23 [March 8] and March 2 [15], 1906.

My own musical life ran somehow barrenly, owing to my feeling
out of sorts and fatigued. Byelsky and I turned over certain operatic
subjects in our minds, namely *Styeñka Razin* (a highwayman's
song) and *Heaven and Earth.*[19] V. I. Byelsky even jotted down the
libretto, but the musical ideas which infrequently came into my
head were short and fragmentary. The manual of orchestration, too,
had come to a standstill. On the one hand its form would not take
shape, while on the other hand I wished to wait for the production
of *Kityezh,* in order to draw some of my illustrations from that
source.[20]

Nevertheless, in the spring I took up and finished another piece
of work on Moussorgsky's compositions. The reproaches which I
had had occasion to hear more than once for having omitted some
pages of *Boris Godunov* when revising it spurred me to turn once
more to that composition and, after subjecting the omitted portions
to revision and orchestration, to prepare them for publication as a
supplement to the orchestral score. In this wise I orchestrated
Pimyen's story of the Tsars Ivan and Fyodor, the story about
"*popiñka*" (parrot), "the chiming clock," the scene of the False
Dmitri with Rangoni at the fountain, and False Dmitri's soliloquy
after the Polonaise.[21]

The turn had come even of the famous *Zhenit'ba* (*Wedding*).
By agreement with Stassov, who had until then concealed this
manuscript from curious eyes, within the walls of the Imperial
Public Library, *The Wedding* was performed one fine evening at
my house by Sigizmund Blumenfeld, my daughter Sonya, the tenor
Sandoolyenko and the young Goori Stravinsky. Nadezhda Nikolayevna was at the piano. Dragged into the light of day, this composition struck us all by its wit, combined with a certain preconceived unmusicalness. Having thought over and deliberated a

---

[19] Rimsky-Korsakov's notebooks contain sundry ideas and notes for *Heaven and Earth.*

[20] In January 1906 Rimsky-Korsakov completed the instrumentation of Borodin's *The Sea,* which for some unaccountable reason had baffled him at first, when commenced as early as March 1905.

[21] Rimsky-Korsakov makes no mention here of the sixth minor scene, "Over the Map of Muscovite Land," which constitutes No. 2 in the series of additional scenes that had not been included in the edition of 1896.

course of action, I decided (to V. V. Stassov's profound delight) to hand this composition over to Bessel for publication, after having first looked it over and made the necessary corrections and simplifications, with a view to orchestrating [22] it at some time in the future for a stage production.

In addition to the above-mentioned occasion of the performance of *The Wedding* at our house, close friends gathered there on every other Wednesday, and we had music, principally vocal. New compositions were looked over and sung. The gatherings were often rather numerous. Once Glazunov played his Eighth Symphony. Quite frequently F. Blumenfeld came and Mme N. I. Zabyela, who was then already an artist of the Mariinsky Theatre. Her husband, the painter Vrubel, for more than two years a victim of a mental disease, had in addition completely lost his eyesight; he was then in a hospital, without any hope of recovery. Until then his mental malady had run a course with intervals of lucidity, when he would take up work again. With the loss of eyesight, work became impossible even in moments of mental tranquillity. A terrible situation!

I have already said that it was necessary for my son Andrey to make another trip to Nauheim for the complete recovery of his health. Accordingly, at the beginning of May he went abroad with his mother. After passing his final examinations, our son Volodya became free, having graduated from the University that year. We decided to spend the whole summer abroad. The three of us, Volodya, Nadya, and I left early in June, via Vienna,[23] for Riva, on Lago di Garda, whither also Nadezhda Nikolayevna was to come with Andrey as soon as his cure had been completed. After their arrival we spent some five weeks at delightful Riva. I was busy orchestrating my songs *Son v lyetñuyu noch'* (*A Midsummer Night's Dream*) and *Anchar;* I also orchestrated three songs of

---

[22] The first 12 pages of the orchestral score, in clean copy, have been preserved among N. A.'s papers. (Mme R.-K.'s note.)

[23] In Vienna, Rimsky-Korsakov heard performances of *Rheingold* and *Die Meistersinger*. The profound impression left upon him by the performance and especially the music of *Die Meistersinger* (which he heard here for the first time in its entirety and in a stage production) was vividly expressed in a letter to his son Andrey Nikolayevich. Excerpts from this letter were published in *Russkaya Molva,* 1912.

Moussorgsky; [24] composed a development and continuation with coda for my too brief *Doobinooshka;* and developed somewhat the conclusion of *Kashchey* (which had not satisfied me) by adding a chorus behind the scenes.[25]

But the ideas of the mystery *Heaven and Earth* did not pull together; nor did *Styeñka Razin* get anywhere. . . . Besides, the thought whether it was not high time to write finis to my career as composer [26] (a thought that had haunted me since I had finished *The Tale of Kityezh*) did not leave me. The news from Russia nursed my restless frame of mind,[27] but I decided not to leave the Conservatory, unless circumstances impelled me to take that step, the more so as the letters of Glazunov, who had taken up the orchestration of his Eighth Symphony, gave me consolation. I resolved not to part with him and Anatoli [Lyadov]; as for composing, let come what might. In any event I had no desire to get into the stupid position of a " singer who has lost his voice." *Qui vivra verra.*

After we had lived quietly at Riva nearly five weeks, we made a trip to Italy and, having visited Milan, Genoa, Pisa, Florence, Bologna, and Venice, returned to dear Riva for two more weeks.

---

[24] The songs were *Hopak, Picking Mushrooms,* and *Kolybyel'naya* (*Cradle Song*).

[25] At Riva, in addition to the works enumerated, Rimsky-Korsakov was writing the closing chapters of his *Musical Life.*

[26] Rimsky-Korsakov was yet to write *Le Coq d'Or!* C. V. V.

[27] Numerous reactions to the political events appear in Rimsky-Korsakov's letters of this period. Three excerpts follow, as especially characteristic of his frame of mind at the time. From a letter of July 16 [29] to M. O. Steinberg, from Riva: " I can't seem to believe in any measurably speedy dénouement, and it seems to me that the interminable affair will drag on for a long time to come. Rather let a long crescendo lead to a good *ff*, and not, as is often the case with Wagner, go on crescendo, crescendo, and lo! go sour, and then a crescendo starts once more from a *pp*."

From a letter of July 27 [August 9] to S. N. Krooglikov, from Riva: " With the Duma dispersed I can't foresee anything for the immediate future but repression, and afterwards, of course, something will come, though the chronic form of that something is utterly killing. The feeling of egoism says let it rather be some time later, when we are dead; we had rather live awhile longer amid tranquillity and culture, but immediately one feels conscience-smitten. Of course, in the midst of the present turmoil and that looming ahead, one endeavours to do one's work as far as possible, but the possibility grows less and less, for the strength gradually grows old."

From a letter of August 7 [20] to M. O. Steinberg, from Florence: " I am a great sceptic, and hence things in Russia look quite rotten to me. We have no harmony, no unity, everything goes its own way, hence we have no success. We know how to reproach and blame one another, but we can't manage to do anything sensibly. All these Sveaborg and Kronstadt affairs seem to me premature, not unified by a general plan, without taking account of one's forces. How much blood has been shed! . . ."

Tomorrow we leave Riva and go to Russia via Munich and Vienna.

The Chronicle of My Musical Life has been brought to its close. It is without order, is unequally detailed throughout, it is written in wretched style, often even extremely dry; but, in compensation, it contains *nothing but the truth*, and this will lend it interest.

On my arrival in St. Petersburg, perhaps, my long yearned-for idea — of writing a diary — will be realized. Whether the idea will last long — who knows? . . .

N. Rimsky-Korsakov

Riva sul Lago di Garda
August 22, Old Style [September 4], 1906

CHRONICLE

OF N. A. RIMSKY-KORSAKOV'S LIFE

during the period not included in

My Musical Life (*September 1906–June 1908*)

COMPILED BY A. RIMSKY-KORSAKOV

1906

Return from abroad. *Sadko* in Moscow. Death of V. V. Stassov. Beginnings of *Le Coq d'Or*.

September 1906

After returning from abroad, on *Saturday, September 2* [*15*], Rimsky-Korsakov at once plunged into his usual current affairs (Conservatory, the Byelayev Board of Trustees, etc.).

On the day after his return, Rimsky-Korsakov went to V. V. Stassov's soirée, at which F. I. Chaliapin sang.

On Monday, the 4th [*17th*], the Byelayev Board had its meeting, Rimsky-Korsakov taking part in it.

On September 16 [*29*] the first performance of *Sadko* at the People's House (Kirikov and Zimmerman, managers; conductor, Zelyony).

Excerpt from [Petrovsky's] review in the *Russian Musical Gazette:* "The great success of *Sadko*, so marked at the first two performances (September 16 [29] and 18 [October 1]), which was given before houses crowded with people who had paid for their tickets as well as those who had free passes, has clearly shown what should be the aims of the impresarios to whom a subsidized government institution has been granted on lease."

On September 22 [*October 5*] the following note appeared in the section of " Theatre and Music " of the Moscow daily *Noviy Poot'* (*New Path*): " A few days ago the following incident occurred at the Grand Theatre. *Sadko* is being prepared for production. With N. A. Rimsky-Korsakov's consent the administration appointed the young conductor N. A. Fyodorov to direct the opera. Much labour has been put in by Mr. Fyodorov in the course of several months. . . . But Mr. Suk, the conductor-in-chief of the Imperial Theatres, conceived a desire to get the opera into his own hands and turned to the administration with such a request. . . . The administration did not take Mr. Suk's plea into consideration. Thereupon Mr. Suk addressed his plea to the composer. . . . The administration refused the composer as well. In fine, Mr. Fyodorov himself declined to conduct the opera. . . ."

From a letter of the singer S. Sinitsyna to Rimsky-Korsakov, *some time after* September 20 [October 3]: " This announcement [of Fyodorov's declination subsequent to Rimsky-Korsakov's letter] was communicated to us at the beginning of the orchestral rehearsal. Everybody was so stunned and offended in behalf of a comrade that it was unanimously resolved to express to Fyodorov (through the inspector of music) the most heartfelt sorrow on the change made and regret about the unpleasantness that had befallen him. The rehearsal was ended, to everybody's great sorrow, and the première was postponed until October 24 [November 6]. All the artists are aroused and are waiting for something to happen."

September 23 [*October 6*] in a letter to S. P. Byelanovsky, Rimsky-Korsakov writes: " What is published in the newspaper-notice *is false;* the administration appointed Fyodorov *without any consent and knowledge on my part.*"

September 24 [*October 7*] S. N. Krooglikov writes: " At the Grand Theatre there is a regular mutiny. For some unknown reasons that fool, the Bureau, as befits a fool, committed a tactless act, and now it is shuffling, eager at all costs to shake the guilt off itself and unload its full weight upon someone else, even upon you — perhaps. . . ."

" For the orchestra, the chorus, and the soloists engaged in *Sadko* the situation is so pictured that you are responsible for the fact that *Sadko,* entrusted to Fyodorov by yourself, was again taken away by you and handed to Suk, after Fyodorov had gone through ten rehearsals."

September 25 [*October 8*] Rimsky-Korsakov stated in his reply to S. N. Krooglikov: " When I had learned of Suk's engagement, I at once told V. A. Tyelyakovsky that I wished my opera to be given under Suk's direction. But after I had received a letter from Fyodorov saying that he was rehearsing *Sadko,* I immediately wrote to von Boöl [Superintendent of the Moscow office of the Imperial Theatres] that he should give my opera to Suk, whom I knew as an excellent conductor, and that, though I had nothing against Fyodorov, I could not find anything in his favour either, as I knew nothing about his former activities as conductor. . . ."

On the same subject in a letter of Rimsky-Korsakov to S. P. Byelanovsky under date of October 1 [14]: "I suppose that by the time of the first performance of *Sadko*, all disturbances will have been settled and forgotten and in the long run Fyodorov himself will have no ill feeling against me, the more so as Suk will certainly have won the merited respect of the artists. As for getting anything of this affair into the papers, I had no such intentions. Suk came to me with the score and consulted me about all the details. Accordingly I assume that *Sadko* will be put on in accordance with my intentions."

September 27 [*October 10*], at 28 Zagorodny Prospekt, the usual musical Wednesdays began. The regular habitués during this and the following season were: V. V. Yastryebtsev, N. I. Rikhter, the Stravinskys — Igor Fyodorovich and his brother Goori Fyodorovich the singer, N. I. Zabyela, M. O. Steinberg, I. I. Lapshin, the Byelskys, the Mitoosovs, the Blumenfelds, A. P. Sandoolyenko, and others. *Frequent* visitors: the Ossovskys, the Stassovs, the Komarovs, the Cherepnins, Lyadov, Glazunov, N. A. Sokolov, N. D. Kooznyetsov, and others; *more rarely* A. Ziloti, S. I. Taneiev, A. N. Scriabin, and others.

September 30 [*October 13*], from a letter of V. V. Stassov to Rimsky-Korsakov: "You astounded — yes, but by what? By that joy, that gush of happiness which the other day I beheld in you when you had learned that your son had been exempted from the military vileness! — Ah what happiness it was, what jubilation, what instantaneous tempestuous upsweep, over a hundred and fifty steps to the peak of a mountain, as if you had stepped on the summit of some Dhaulagiri with a single stride! And shall I conceivably forget your downright "St. Vitus dance," your jumping and tearing about the room, your impetuous whirling, as if in those seconds you had become the mad fakir from *The Ruins of Athens* — and then . . . and then, how you rode across the room mounted on the back of your exempted Son!

"Shall I conceivably ever be able to forget all that?

"Is it likely that some time there will part from me the sensation I experienced at the time when I murmured gently: 'Ah, how marvellous, oh, how incomparable, that I have been brought here in these *great* moments!!!'"

October 1906

October 4 [*17*], the orchestration of the new, more fully developed finale of *Kashchey*, which had been composed in the summer at Riva.

Beginning with *October 8* [*21*], Rimsky-Korsakov participates with Lyadov, Ziloti, Ryepin, Tyelyakovsky, Ossovsky, and others in the sessions of the jubilee committee to organize the festivities in honour of A. K. Glazunov on the occasion of the twenty-fifth anniversary of his musical activities. During these days Rimsky-Korsakov also visited V. V. Stassov, who had fallen gravely ill.

October 10 [*23*]: death of V. V. Stassov; 11–13 [24–6], requiem masses for Stassov, and his funeral. From the Rimsky-Korsakovs a wreath came with the inscription: " To our best friend."

On *October 11* [*24*], the orchestral score of *Doobinooshka* (cf. *My Musical Life*, p. 423) in a new version.

October 15 [*28*]: in the notebook there is dated the first sketch of the *Golden Cockerel's* theme: " Kiri-koo-koo! Reign lying on your side."

October 24 [*November 6*]: first performance of *Sadko* at the Grand Theatre in Moscow. The performance lasted from 8.10 p.m. till 12.35 p.m. After the " Undersea Kingdom " the audience began to thin out.

November 1906

November 2 [*15*]: first performance of *Tsar Saltan* at Zimin's Theatre in Moscow (during the season of 1906–7 there were twenty-four performances of this opera).

November 6 [*19*]: from Rimsky-Korsakov's letter to S. P. Byelanovsky: " The opera [*Kityezh*] will not be given before December, as the production of *Nero* had lagged very much and delayed everything else. Owing to Napravnik's illness, *Cherevichki* will be given somewhat later and *Kityezh* will probably come earlier, as it will be produced under Blumenfeld's direction. Nevertheless, one cannot expect its production before December, because rehearsals in earnest have commenced only now."

November 8 [*21*]: from S. N. Krooglikov's letter to Rimsky-Korsakov: " The Grand Theatre is giving wearisome performances of *Sadko*. . . . But at Zimin's *Saltan* is given quite charmingly."

November 15 [*28*]: at the " regular Wednesday " at the Rimsky-Korsakovs', the composition of *Le Coq d'Or* is spoken of as a thing not only settled, but even being put into execution. In the diary of V. V. Yastryebtsev under this date, there is an entry: " Apparently Rimsky-Korsakov is terribly pleased that he is composing once again, although many things prevent his concentrating in a proper way."

November 25 [*December 8*]: the first Russian Symphony Concert under the direction of F. M. Blumenfeld, in memory of V. V. Stassov (made up of compositions dedicated to him). Of Rimsky-Korsakov's works *Scheherazada* was played. According to V. V. Yastryebtsev's reminiscences, Rimsky-Korsakov felt hurt at the slovenly treatment his suite had received at the hands of the orchestral musicians.

November 26 [*December 9*]: at a soirée in Rimsky-Korsakov's house, Chaliapin recited and sang *Mozart and Salieri* (both rôles).

December 1906

December 8 [*21*]: Second Russian Symphony Concert (first time of A. Glazunov's Eighth Symphony).

December 13 [*26*]: S. I. Taneiev was present at the "regular Wednesday" at the Rimsky-Korsakovs' and played a great deal (piano pieces of A. S. Arensky). Debate between Rimsky-Korsakov and Taneiev over Arensky, whose musical individuality Taneiev esteemed highly.

Rehearsal of *Kityezh* at the Mariinsky Theatre. In the second act, at Rimsky-Korsakov's request, the balalaikas introduced by him were left out owing to their unsatisfactory effect.[1] The bells do not ring entirely true to pitch. Composition of *Le Coq d'Or* goes on apace.

December 14 [*27*]: The first act has been composed as far as the King's reply in the Duma: "Honour to Gvidon's brain!"

December 25 [*January 7, 1907*]: Ditto, up to the Astrologer's appearance.

---

[1] That Rimsky-Korsakov's disappointment in the effect of balalaikas in the score of his *Kityezh* did not doom them may be gathered from the following passage:
"Next after these songs [written some time after July 1925. J. A. J.] I composed a fantasia on Russian themes entitled *At the Villagers' Spinning-Bee* for the balalaika as an independent virtuoso instrument accompanied by a full symphony orchestra. For this fantasia I utilized two folksongs. . . . As an experiment I decided to overlook the power of the balalaika's sonority, leaving it to cope with the symphonic orchestra and merely taking into consideration the colourfulness of its share in various orchestral combinations.
"I wrote this composition at the request and instance of the exceptional balalaika-virtuoso N. P. Osipov, to whom I dedicated it as a token of my amazement at his skill. By his exceptional virtuoso gifts, he, along with B. S. Troyanovsky, has advanced the balalaika into the ranks of virtuoso instruments on a par with the violin, the piano, and the cello. To be sure, one does not elicit great tonal volume out of the balalaika, but that is the fault of the instrument and its limited resources; but the virtuosity and novelty of the various combinations with diverse orchestral groups are past all doubting.
"This achievement of the balalaika must be welcomed, just like the admittedly slow but sure promotion of the balalaika into the ranks of orchestral instruments. On V. V. Andreyev's auspicious initiative balalaikas, orchestras made up of balalaikas and domras (round-bodied balalaikas) have won the right of citizenship, and complete development, prodigious perfection, and general recognition in our days." M. M. Ippolitov-Ivanov: *Fifty Years of Russian Music in My Recollections* (Moscow: State Musical Publishing Bureau; 1934), p. 119. [Cf. also footnote to January 15 [28], 1907. J. A. J.]

1907

Composition of *Le Coq d'Or*. A. K. Glazunov's jubilee. First performance of *The Tale of the Invisible City of Kityezh*. Trip to Paris. Correspondence concerning *Snyegoorochka* at the Opéra Comique and *Sadko* at the Grand Opéra. Completion of *Le Coq d'Or* and its printing.

January 1907

During the year 1907–8 regular work of Rimsky-Korsakov with I. F. Stravinsky (instrumentation, in conjunction with advice on composition), usually once a week, on Wednesday, 4–6 p.m.

January 1 [14]: The Astrologer's entrance composed

January 13 [26]: Third Russian Symphony concert. Among other pieces on the program, Rimsky-Korsakov's songs: *The Nymph* and *Midsummer Night's Dream*, with orchestral accompaniment, for the first time (N. I. Zabyela).

January 14 [27]: Composition of Act I as far as the words: " And for ever shall forget that there's misery in the world."

January 14 [27]: In Paris, under [Eugène] G[eorges] Marty's direction, at the ninth concert of the Conservatoire National de Musique, the second tableau of the opera *Sadko* was performed in its entirety in French and by French artists. The program book contained explanatory notes by M. Emmanuel.

January 15 [28]: Rimsky-Korsakov received a letter from V. V. Andreyev: [2] " I have heard that you have left the balalaikas out of *Kityezh*," he wrote, " and thereby put back, by five or six years, my labours for according certain rights to Russian folk-instruments. . . . In itself this really minor fact is historical, but for my cause it is truly deadly. . . . Thanks to L. Kuchera's courtesy, I familiarized myself with the orchestral scoring of the balalaikas in *Kityezh* and performed its music with my orchestra. The sonority obtained was such that hardly any symphonic orchestra, even *tutti*, will drown it, and my orchestra consists of thirty-two musicians."

From a letter of Michel Delines of *January 17 [30]* from Nice: " Prob-

---

[2] Vasili Vasilyevich Andreyev (1862–1918), conductor of an incomparable balalaika orchestra. He gave a series of concerts with his band of twenty-five players throughout the United States during the season of 1910–11, winning extraordinary success alike with the audiences and critics. The orchestra made its début at Carnegie Hall on November 28, 1910. J. A. J.

ably you know already from the papers how great a success the second tableau of *Sadko* met with at the concert of the Paris Conservatoire on January 27 [N.S.]. *Sadko* will be repeated on Sunday next."

In January *Zdravitsa* (*A Toast*) for A. Glazunov's jubilee festivities was composed.

According to Yastryebtsev's reminiscences, quoting the words of Rimsky-Korsakov: " *Le Coq d'Or* somehow is getting nowhere, thanks to all these concerts, jubilees, rehearsals " (rehearsals of *Kityezh* at the Mariinsky Theatre).

January 27 [February 9]: Twenty-fifth anniversary of A. K. Glazunov's activity as composer. Concert, with Rimsky-Korsakov taking part in it.

January 30 [February 12]: from a letter of Rimsky-Korsakov to S. N. Krooglikov: " The jubilee concert went off splendidly before a filled auditorium. The program was as follows: (I) the First Symphony (conductor — I), then (II) *Welcome* by Lyadov, amid the sounds of which the fêted composer appeared on the stage. The addresses began. There were more than forty delegations which presented greetings, wreaths, etc.; the greetings were not read; finally the long list of telegrams from Russia and foreign countries was read. . . . Glazunov left the stage amid the sounds of (III) my *Zdravitsa* (*Toast*), which was repeated by request. Then (IV) came the Eighth Symphony under Ziloti's direction, and in conclusion Chaliapin, to the accompaniment of the orchestra, sang [A. K. Glazunov's] *The Bacchic Song* as a sort of greeting."

From a review in the *Russian Musical Gazette* (Nos. 5–6, 1907): " N. A. Rimsky-Korsakov appears on the stage. He attempts to conduct the First Symphony but that is not so easy a thing to do at first. With its prolonged, warm, and joyous plaudits, the audience demonstrates how infinitely it loves and cherishes this tall, spare old man, so austere and grave." After the symphony: " The procession is led by N. A. Rimsky-Korsakov. Changing his usual way of walking into an unnaturally slowed gait that is meant to be solemn, he slowly advances towards the fêted man at the head of the committee group. A few brief words: ' It has been resolved to establish a fellowship in your name,' a copy of the address is handed over, and then — the most magnificent and significant moment of the jubilee celebration — a long, prolonged, repeated kiss, with which Rimsky-Korsakov ended his greeting."

February 1907

February 3 [16]: during the day, dress rehearsal of *Kityezh* at the Mariinsky Theatre.

February 7 [20] (the day of elections for the First Imperial Duma):

the first performance of *The Tale of the Invisible City of Kityezh;* the performance began at 8.05 p.m. and ended at 12.20 a.m. Conductor, F. M. Blumenfeld; *mise en scène* by V. P. Shkafer. Scenery for Act I and the first tableau of Act IV, from sketches by the painter K. A. Korovin; Acts II and III and the second tableau of Act IV, from sketches by the academician A. M. Vasnyetsov. Principal artists: Kooznyetsova, Yershov, Filippov, Labinsky. Beginning with the first act, curtain calls and ovations. Jointly proffered wreath from friends; a special one from I. F. and Y. G. Stravinsky.

February 8 [*21*]: Congratulations from C. A. Cui upon *Kityezh:* " Yesterday I found my way to a considerable degree and, of course, to my greater pleasure. An original and strikingly homogeneous work. Praise unto you! Yours, C. Cui."

During the days immediately following the first performance of *Kityezh,* reviews in the daily press: in the paper *Roos'*, enjoying a wide circulation at the time, the critic recommends leaving out Act II as least in keeping with the general character of the work, and combining Act III with Act IV (retaining of the latter only the scene of Fyevronia's death and the appearance of the ghost) and turning the final tableau into a brief apotheosis (V. Kolomiytsev, *Roos'*, 1907, No. 44).

Review by V. G. Karatygin in the March issue of the *Golden Fleece:* " On the whole, in spite of an abundance of ' lengths ' and episodes in general, Russian style, *The Tale of Kityezh* is a precious and original contribution to the treasure-store of Russian opera literature."

February 19 [*March 4*]: Death of V. V. Bessel, head of the publishing firm, at Zürich.

March 1907

March 6 [*19*]: Rimsky-Korsakov sixty-three years old.

March 8 [*21*]: From a letter to S. N. Krooglikov: " I am keeping on with *Le Coq d'Or*, although I have little time for it. Nadezhda Nikolayevna's sister, M. N. Sokolova, died; the day previous, Professor Tolstov [3] was buried; the next day, V. V. Bessel; today — M. N."

March 15 [*28*]: Death (at Nice) of the composer P. I. Blaramberg, an old friend of Rimsky-Korsakov.

March 17 [*30*]: Jubilee festivities at the St. Petersburg Conservatoire in honour of A. K. Glazunov.

March 21 [*April 3*]: Act I of *Le Coq d'Or* (orchestral score) finished.

March–April: correspondence and personal conferences of Rimsky-

---

[3] V. P. Tolstov (1843–1907), professor of piano-playing.

Korsakov with S. P. Diaghileff concerning a trip to Paris for Russian concerts and the proposed operatic productions on the stage of the Grand Opéra.

From an undated letter of Diaghileff: " I am not giving up the hope of your collaboration in Paris. With all the infinite difficulties which this enterprise presents, I cannot work without thinking of support on the part of my beloved and dear teacher. Just think of how sad you will make us by a refusal and, more still, what injury you will do to the cause for which you had expressed your sympathy. In the name of the Lord, say yes to our plea. This journey will not be fatiguing for you; we shall surround you with every possible care. We shall be completely at your service, and you will do us the greatest favour and will help us as *no one else* can help."

In answer to the insistent coaxings of S. P. Diaghileff, Rimsky-Korsakov ended by sending his consent, couched in a humorous form of the well-known saying: "'I go if I have to go,' said the parrot as the cat was dragging him from the cage."

April 1907

April 2 [15]: The piano score of Act I of *Le Coq d'Or* was finished.

In March–April, at the Conservatoire, the production of *Kashchey the Deathless* and Act II of *The Tsar's Bride* were in preparation.

April 9 [22]: Dress rehearsal of *Kashchey* and of Act II of *The Tsar's Bride.*

April 10 [23]: Performance of the above. Conductor, M. G. Klimov.

April 18 [May 1]: In the presence of V. I. Byelsky, M. O. Steinberg, I. F. Stravinsky, V. V. Yastryebtsev, and the household, the first act of *Le Coq d'Or* was performed. M. O. Steinberg played from the manuscript.

April 20 [May 3]: From a letter of Rimsky-Korsakov to S. N. Krooglikov: " I have finished Act I of *Le Coq d'Or* in orchestral score and have advanced considerably Act II in rough draft; at present (owing to my departure for Paris) I shall have to call a halt. . . ."

End of April: A conference at V. A. Tyelyakovsky's with Rimsky-Korsakov taking part, regarding the new production of *A Life for the Tsar*. It was decided to perform the opera according to the new edition of M. P. Byelayev, published under the editorial supervision of Rimsky-Korsakov and A. K. Glazunov (in 1907).

April 28 [May 11]: From a letter of Rimsky-Korsakov to S. N. Krooglikov: " Today I am leaving for Paris; all of mine, likewise."

May 1907

In Paris, during the month of May, five Russian concerts were given (N.S., *May 16, 19, 23, 26, and 30*): "Cinq Concerts Historiques Russes donnés sous le patronage de la Société des grandes auditions musicales de France." At four of these, compositions of Rimsky-Korsakov were performed. Following is the list:

1. *Christmas Eve*, moving musical tableaux;
2. Introduction to Act I and two songs of Lyel from *Snyegoorochka;*
3. *Night on Mount Triglav;*
4. Suite from *Tsar Saltan;* and
5. Introduction and scene of the Undersea Kingdom from *Sadko.*

The first three numbers were conducted by Rimsky-Korsakov himself, the other two by Arthur Nikisch.

In numberless articles and notices devoted to Diaghileff's brilliant scheme, the French newspapers welcomed Rimsky-Korsakov's new appearance before the public of Paris.

May 14 [*27*]: On C. Saint-Saëns's initiative, a reception in the Salle Pleyel. After a brief concert of the Société des Instruments Anciens, a luncheon in honour of the visitors.

At the Théâtre Châtelet, performances of *Salomé* were given, under Richard Strauss's direction, with the Colonne orchestra. Rimsky-Korsakov attended one of them.

At the soirée at Colonne's house, Rimsky-Korsakov met Richard Strauss. Beyond the exchange of a few words of no consequence, the acquaintance did not progress. Rimsky-Korsakov had heard of the remark uttered by Strauss concerning Russian music: "We are children no longer."

In the presence of Rimsky-Korsakov and a number of other musicians (Rachmaninoff, Glazunov, Blumenfeld, [Josef] Hofmann, and others), A. N. Scriabin showed his *Poème d'Extase*. Scriabin's dreams of his *Mystery* and the music of *Poème d'Extase* gave Rimsky-Korsakov the impression of morbid eroticism. "Isn't he getting out of his mind, perhaps?" Rimsky-Korsakov said half-jokingly.

The attempt of prominent representatives of Russian society to draw Rimsky-Korsakov within the orbit of the "august" patrons of Russian music who were in Paris at that time — the Grand Duchess Maria Pavlovna and the Grand Duke Pavel Aleksandrovich — ended in failure. Rimsky-Korsakov was unwilling to go either to the reception at the Grand Duke's or to the Grand Duchess's box at the Théâtre de l'Opéra, in spite of the gracious solicitations.

Beginning with *May 1* [*14*] Rimsky-Korsakov retired as member of

A. N. SCRIABIN

from the drawing by E. Zak

the Board of Trustees for Russian Composers. Rimsky-Korsakov was moved to this decision when he had realized the importance of having a man of business-experience among the Board's members. Rimsky-Korsakov named N. V. Artsybushev as his successor. Rimsky-Korsakov's business connection with the Board of Trustees was kept up only through N. V. Artsybushev, who consulted Rimsky-Korsakov on sundry questions (as, for example, concerning concert programs).

May 24 [June 6]: Rimsky-Korsakov returned from Paris.

May 30 [June 12]: From a letter of Rimsky-Korsakov to A. K. Glazunov: "Altschuler [conductor of the Russian Symphony Concerts in New York. A. R.-K.] arrived and came to see me. . . . Your *Middle Ages* he performs in this order of movements: IV, II, III, I, finding that for Americans it is better so. Your Third Symphony is played with cuts (!) for the American citizens. All this hardly commends him. In general, 'there is no truth on earth,' although this, too, is untrue, for the truth does exist on earth, but only in Art and Science. Science is not for you and me, but Art is in our line. My dear, return to pure art; in it alone will you discover the truth and yourself act in accordance with truth — that is, without errors and misunderstandings."

June 1907

Early in June, Rimsky-Korsakov went for the summer to the Lyubensk estate, situated along the Warsaw railroad line, ten miles from the Plyussa station.

June 13 [26]: From Rimsky-Korsakov's letter to his son Mikhayil Nikolayevich: "We are all enraptured with Lyubensk and talk all the time about what we are going to do and how, when it is ours, because its purchase by us has been practically settled. . . . I even feel some anxiety because no deposit has been paid. The children and Mamma are making all kinds of household projects and I sit and listen in rapture. . . ."

On the same date, from a letter to Yastryebtsev: "I have been thinking all these days of *Le Coq d'Or;* I am orchestrating Act II (the end of which is still uncomposed) while I devote a little thought to Act III."

June 14 [27]: From A. K. Glazunov's letter to Rimsky-Korsakov, from Folkestone (England): "I have been commissioned to inquire of you in private as to how you would look upon accepting the doctor's degree at Oxford or Cambridge, for which you would have to come over in person. For myself I shall add that the ceremony is not at all fatiguing and no speech-making is required."

June 20 [July 3]: From Rimsky-Korsakov's letter to A. K. Glazunov: "Your letter from Folkestone has been received. This is my prayer to you: the title of Doctor of the University of Oxford or Cambridge I wish decidedly to decline; in the first place, because I don't consider any honorary titles as becoming to composers in general and me in particular (perhaps this is my queerness, but let that be); in the second place, because I have no intention of journeying to England. Pleading of course only the latter reason, ward off from me the proposal I am threatened with, and, in my name, thank the persons who have given you this errand for their (according to their conviction) flattering and honorary intention."

In June–July, correspondence with I. F. Stravinsky about his fantastic scherzo (*Bees*), which took final form later, during Stravinsky's study under Rimsky-Korsakov in the winter of 1907–8; also about the performance of the suite *The Faun and the Shepherdess* at the Russian Symphony Concerts.

Beginning with early July, correspondence with Albert Carré, Director of the Opéra Comique, about the proposed production of *Snyegoorochka* in Paris. A. Carré sends word of his intention to come to St. Petersburg or Moscow during the coming season to see the production of *Snyegoorochka* on the Russian stage. In subsequent letters he complains of the excessive demands made by Bessel, of his unwillingness to sell music material to the theatre; he even indicates a possible refusal to produce the opera, if Bessel stubbornly persists in his demands. These misunderstandings had not as yet been settled in October, as may be seen from a letter from Carré of October 15, 1907.

From April till the end of August goes on the correspondence of Rimsky-Korsakov with S. P. Diaghileff concerning the plan to produce *Sadko* and *Boris Godunov* on the stage of the Grand Opéra in Paris and about *the cuts* to be made in them. As early as in his letter of *April 19* [*May 2*] Diaghileff wrote to Rimsky-Korsakov: "Don't forget that I have to convince the Grand Duke Vladimir that our undertaking is useful from the national point of view; the Minister of Finance — that it is profitable from the economic point of view; and even the Director of Theatres that it will be of benefit for the Imperial Theatres. And how many others! And how difficult this is!"

From a letter of S. P. Diaghileff of *June 5* [*18*], 1907: "Withal I venture to undertake May next the production of *Sadko* and *Boris Godunov* in Paris, at the Grand Opéra. *Sadko* we propose to put on with French artists and in French (Sadko — Alvarez); *Boris Godunov* for the present in Russian, with Chaliapin and Sobinov." [4]

---

[4] Lyeonid Vitaliyevich Sobinov (1872–1934), the only singer who could share equal admiration of the public in performances with the dazzling Chaliapin. His lyric tenor of crystalline transparency and extraordinary flexibility possessed that unique

From a letter of S. P. Diaghileff, of *June 11* [*24*]: " The Russians in this production [*Sadko*] must be — the conductor, the stage-manager, scene-painter, and costumer. This is no trifle — the entire organization is in our hands."

From a letter of *July 17* [*30*]: " Once the question has come up about this most complex and most difficult affair, if you will, I even prefer to lay before you in writing my view of it, for at an interview your charm, your authority, finally your ' divine ' side so eclipse your ' human ' side, that I know I shall be quailing and shall not say half of what I think. . . . To turn to *Sadko* — Lord, how hard it is! — I shall be again stoically sincere and shall mention the portions which I take the liberty to like less in this, on a par with *Ruslan and Lyudmila,* best Russian fairy-tale opera." Then follows information of curtailments in *Sadko* which are possible in Diaghileff's opinion. " You see," adds Diaghileff, " the question is not of cuts, but rather of remodelling. . . . *Frenchmen are absolutely incapable* of listening to an opera from 8 till 12. Even their own *Pelléas* they cannot forgive its length and soon after 11 they frankly flee from the theatre, and that produces a deadly impression."

From a letter of *August 11* [*24*]: " How much I need, how much I crave to see you! How many tears and supplications I have prepared, how many bright and irrefutable arguments! You just imagine how I shall hypnotize you with arguments that really ' the most rational thing ' (these are your words) is to leave Lyubava in Russia, that the tableau in her room does not enhance the interest of the action; that in the market scene, her two phrases which interrupt the chorus on the ship might be sung by the women's section of the chorus; and that the finale of the entr'acte, after the Undersea Kingdom, concludes as though purposely in A-flat major, in order to make a perfectly natural transition to the D-flat major closing hymn, against a background of a stylized, beautiful bright landscape with the blazing cupolas of glorious Novgorod and the broad overflow of the river Volkhova. . . ."

From a letter of Rimsky-Korsakov to S. P. Diaghileff (in Rimsky-

---

quality of eternal youth so characteristic of Melba's voice prior to 1910. But, in addition, Sobinov had an aristocratic stage presence and powers of dramatic characterization which in their way were as remarkable as Chaliapin's.

The great Nikisch thus retailed his impressions after conducting *Lohengrin* (with Sobinov) for the benefit of the opera orchestra in Moscow, November 3 [16], 1909: " The famous A-major *alla breve* fortissimo of general ecstasy passes into a melting pianissimo, a holy stillness and reverential silence — the knight steps down, turns to the swan, and bids him farewell. . . . What a heavenly vision! What a heavenly voice! I conduct and feel that an involuntary tear is rolling down my cheek. . . . How many Lohengrins have I seen and listened to in my lifetime, but never have I experienced anything like this deeply poetic overpowering moment." J. A. J.

Korsakov's files there has been preserved a rough draft, without date):
"Obviously my moving letters cannot move you from your theatrico-political point of view. The firmness with which you hold on to it deserves a better fate. You said that without my advice you would not venture to undertake *Sadko,* but my advice has nothing whatever to do with it, as you have formed a firm plan of action prior to any advice from me, and, at that, a plan from which you do not intend to swerve. I assure you that I, too, have a theatrico-artistic point of view from which it is impossible to dislodge me. Once there are mixed up in this business the nationalism of the Grand Duke Vladimir Aleksandrovich and the calculations of the Minister of Finance, success becomes imperative at all costs. But for me there exists only the artistic interest, and to the taste of the French I remain utterly indifferent, and even, on the contrary, want them to esteem me such as I am, and not adapted to their customs and tastes, which are by no means law. I have had an orchestral score of *Sadko* sent to me, and, having examined it, have come to the conclusion that in this work everything is legitimate, and that only those cuts which are current at the Mariinsky Theatre can be sanctioned by me. Not only the suppression of the last tableau, or of its major part, is inadmissible, but even the elimination of Lyubava's person is equally not to be thought of. If to the weakling French public (in dress coats, who ' drop in ' to the theatre for a while, who give ear to the voice of the venal press and hired clappers) *Sadko* is heavy in its present form, then it ought not to be given. . . ."

August 26 [*September 8*] from a letter of S. P. Diaghileff: "The idea of producing *Sadko* did not originate with me, the directors asked me about it. There is left the last combination — to give several tableaux from *Sadko,* without cuts or any changes whatever (save those indicated by you for the Paris theatre) and that it should be so stated; e.g., Tableaux I, II, IV, and VI from the opera-*bylina Sadko. . . .* This latter combination, since it does not inflict injury upon anybody's interests, and does not change anything in the opera, I shall propose to Messager and Broussan, whose spokesman I have been so far before you."

End of June [*early July*]: A letter from the Paris publisher Leduc, with an inquiry about publishing the *Textbook of Harmony* in French. The correspondence on this subject lasted from June till December, and concluded with the *Textbook* being published in a translation by P. Dorfman. The title of the French edition was as follows: *Traité d'harmonie théorique et pratique de N. Rimsky-Korsakoff. Alph. Leduc, Paris, s.a.* (no date).

June 30 [*July 13*]: Albert Carré asks for permission to entrust the rôle of Lyel to a tenor, owing to the dislike for *travesti* on the part of the

French. Rimsky-Korsakov sent a categorical refusal in answer to this request.

July 1907

July 2 [15]: From a letter of Rimsky-Korsakov to V. V. Yastryebtsev: "*Le Coq d'Or* I am composing assiduously and have finished the rough draft of Act II today. . . . In a few days I shall set to writing the orchestral score of Act II — that is the most pleasant part of creative work. The very writing of the rough draft somehow oppresses, disturbs one, one feels dissatisfied and hurries somewhere, which in the end wearies one beyond endurance. On the other hand, in putting in the finishing touches and orchestrating, one has the feeling of satisfaction that the composition is assuming its final form, which is the goal of the very composition. And what can be better than the orchestral score? And when one writes the orchestral score, both the harmony and the rhythm and the melodic movement of a third-rank voice — in a word, everything — must be clear and finished. . . . Meanwhile one's soul is calm in the thought that the thread of the composition has been spun and that in one way or another the composition is already in existence. . . ."

July 3 [16]: The beginning of Act II of *Le Coq d'Or* was orchestrated.

July 6 [19]: Act II up to the words: "Answer me, bright orb of day!"

July 10 [23]: Ditto, up to the words: "What a song, you just pay heed."

July 10 [23]: From a letter of I. F. Stravinsky to Rimsky-Korsakov from Oostiloog: "Was awfully glad to get your letter and was glad once more to convince myself of your attitude towards me and my compositions. This consciousness that you are constantly interested in my compositions has a marvellously beneficial effect on me, and I long to work much and zealously. . . ."

July 16 [29]: The second act has been orchestrated up to the words: "First kisses of passion, where are you, where?"

July 17 [30]: Same act, up to the words: "Cheer flows forth from the Queen's mouth. . . ."

July 18 [31]: From a letter of Rimsky-Korsakov to M. O. Steinberg: "I have finished the sketch of Act II, and am at present writing the orchestral score of it, but quite slowly, with considerable labour and preliminary rough drafts. Altogether, so far 60 pages are ready. . . ."

From a letter of I. F. Stravinsky from Oostiloog of *mid-July* [*end of July*]: "Yesterday I received a letter from you with the most flattering and most joyous news for me.[5] I am exulting! Mentally I am making a

---

[5] The reference is to the inclusion of Stravinsky's suite *The Faun and the Shepherdess* in the prospectus of the Russian Symphony Concerts of the season 1907–8.

low bow to my benefactors and to you, dear Nikolay Andreyevich, *twice.*
. . . You tell me how much you have composed of *Le Coq d'Or.* ' Owing
to old age, it progresses quite slowly.' Oh, if in my young age I could
work as fast as you – it would not be so bad! "

July 19 [*August 1*]: Act II has been orchestrated up to the words:
" Pale, ethereal, transparent."

July 21 [*August 3*]: From a letter to M. O. Steinberg: " My summer
place I am particularly pleased with: the house stands on a comparatively elevated spot, a beautiful view of the lake, an immense orchard,
lilacs in profusion, and at this moment gorgeously blooming jasmines
and fragrant peonies. . . . After my arrival from town, I could not, for
a long time, pull myself together to compose, and orchestrated for the
time being, even though in rough draft, a certain part of Act II; but, at
this moment even composition – i.e., completing Acts II and III in hints
and fragments – began to progress.

" As for Dodon, I hope to disgrace him for good. However, I shall
hardly manage to bring the opera to the end in orchestral garb this
summer – of work there is plenty, and the summer is nearly one third
gone. . . . Many newspaper clippings, sent from Paris, have reached
me here; by and large, they are all favourable. I am provoked at R–,
who in his talk with Kashkin, which was published in a Moscow newspaper, spoke disapprovingly of Lamoureux's orchestra, of Nikisch, etc.
In my opinion, it is both untrue and tactless. . . ."

On the same date: Act II of *Le Coq d'Or* has been orchestrated up to
the words: " A swarm is flying."

July 22 [*August 4*]: Ditto, up to the words: " When you have come to
the East. . . ."

End of July–early August [*early August–middle August*]: Correspondence with Byelsky concerning the idea suggested by A. N. Rimsky-
Korsakov of concluding the opera with the Astrologer's epilogue (see
below).

August 1907

August 2 [*15*]: 10.45 in the evening, the rough draft of Act III was
completed.

August 6 [*19*]: Act II of *Le Coq d'Or* was orchestrated up to the words:
" Ah, what boots it to recall this . . . ? "

August 8 [*21*]: Ditto, up to the words: " As Dodon will start to
dance. . . ."

August 9 [*22*]: Dance in G Major.

August 9 [*22*]: From a letter to his son Mikhayil Nikolayevich: " You
cannot imagine in what constant agitation I have been all summer: the

question of the apartment, the purchase of Lyubensk, and the military service looming before Volodya make me unspeakably nervous. . . . All these unsettled questions give me no rest, the more so as in old age one becomes imaginative and timorous more than of yore.

" In this way the intensive and accelerated composition of *Le Coq d'Or* becomes the means of having one's thoughts elsewhere and forgetting the disturbing questions."

August 10 [*23*]: Act II of *Le Coq d'Or* has been orchestrated up to the words of the Queen of Shemakha: " And meanwhile I shall seat me down here."

August 11 [*24*]: ditto, up to the words: " Sing and glorify the groom."

From a letter of A. K. Glazunov to Rimsky-Korsakov: " Thanks that you do not forsake the Conservatory, on the one hand, and do not deprive us of your support, on the other."

On the same day, a letter came from V. I. Byelsky with a reply concerning the idea of the Epilogue in *Le Coq d'Or*: " I always was against an Epilogue in *Le Coq d'Or* and for the very purpose of avoiding it I have managed to fit in the words: ' The fairy-tale is a lie, but it has a hint . . .' at the beginning of the opera. I counted on a serious (possibly even a painful) impression from the final scene and chorus; I feared that every apostrophe to the audience would destroy the reality of the events just lived through and would turn them into a jest. And meanwhile there is a poor jest here. But, manifestly, this idea is not in full keeping with your nature, which profoundly fathoms even the most gloomy, but ever prefers the bright to it; in this question there is in you positively a necessity for soothing the gloomy impression and ending the opera with a jocose chord. Well, have your way! "

August 13 [*26*]: Act II of *Le Coq d'Or* orchestrated to the end.

August 14 [*27*]: Instrumentation of Act III begun.

August 15 [*28*]: Ditto up to the words: " If we get a drubbing, we must be deserving it."

August 18 [*31*]: Ditto to the words: " 'Tis for you that we were born and have provided ourselves with families."

August 19 [*September 1*]: Ditto, the appearance of the Astrologer, up to Dodon's words: " Step up nearer, and what wish you? "

August 20 [*September 2*]: Ditto to the words: " Cease thou! Knowest who I am? "

August 20 [*September 2*]: From a letter of Rimsky-Korsakov to A. K. Glazunov: " I am assiduously writing the orchestral score of *Le Coq d'Or* and am now in the middle of Act III, although I am composing this act somewhat sketchily; i.e., without writing the doubling in forte passages; nor do I always write out the percussion instruments. I have grown lazy and am shoving it off until after my return to the city. While here I want to work up the orchestral score in this guise to its very end."

August 21 [*September 3*]: Ditto, up to Dodon's words: "Know, then, how with me to quarrel."

August 22 [*September 4*]: Ditto, as far as the "Pecking."

August 23 [*September 5*]: Ditto, up to the words of the people: "If all this is not a dream!"

August 24 [*September 6*]: Ditto, up to the words: "What are we without a Tsar?"

The end of *Le Coq d'Or* has several notations: August 25 [September 7] at 1.45; August 26 [September 8] at 11.45. On the Epilogue there is a notation of August 28 [September 10] and finally August 29 [September 11]: "When everything was finished."

On the title-page of the orchestral score there is a note (later, during plate-making, carefully stricken out): "A fine song, good man! A pity that the Mayor is mentioned in it in terms that are not altogether decent" (quotation of the Wine-distiller's words from *May Night.* — A. R.-K.).

The absence of V. P. Shkafer, who had fallen ill, moved Rimsky-Korsakov to ask V. A. Tyelyakovsky to delay the autumn performances of *Kityezh* until October. But Tyelyakovsky replied with a refusal, citing the necessity of giving *Kityezh* to the subscribers before shipping it to Moscow.

September 1907

September 2–6 [*15–19*]: Rimsky-Korsakov was in town; on *September 4* [*17*] he was at the performance of *Kityezh*, back-stage.

September 10 [*23*]: The piano score of Act II of *Le Coq d'Or* was finished.

September 19 [*October 2*]: Rimsky-Korsakov returned to town for good.

September 20 [*October 3*]: From a letter to S. N. Krooglikov: "About *Le Coq d'Or*, you may announce in your paper: 'Opera, fable-story in three acts, libretto by V. I. Byelsky (after Pushkin). The orchestral score has been finished. There still remains editorial work aplenty. Publisher, Jurgenson.'"

September 23 [*October 6*]: From V. V. Yastryebtsev's Diary: "The piano score of *Le Coq d'Or* has been completed already. The last act was arranged in three days."

October 1907

From October on till the day of Rimsky-Korsakov's death, a lively business correspondence with B. P. Jurgenson.

October 6 [19]: From a letter of Rimsky-Korsakov to S. N. Krooglikov: "Diaghileff is still in Paris, hence the question of producing Russian operas in Paris has not as yet assumed its final shape. They have in view *Boris Godunov* in Russian with Chaliapin, with ' Marina's Boudoir ' and ' Near Kromy ' omitted, and four tableaux of *Sadko* (I, II, IV, and VI, or II, IV, V, and VI) in French, as I refuse to sanction cuts, and for the French, it is alleged, short performances are necessary."

August–September–October: Kityezh is performed at the Mariinsky Theatre.

October 6 [19]: From a letter of Rimsky-Korsakov to S. N. Krooglikov: "What nonsense they have published about me in connection with *Kityezh!* I never had in mind anything like preference of Moscow to St. Petersburg. I gave *Kityezh* to the Board of Directors with the right of producing it in St. Petersburg and Moscow; hence there could have been no question of my consent to the transfer of the opera *mise en scène* to Moscow from St. Petersburg, and if the Board of Directors does it, it by no means affords me joy, as the production of *Kityezh* in Moscow under such circumstances shuts it out of the St. Petersburg repertory."

Subsequently the shifting of *Kityezh* to the Grand Theatre in Moscow was decided upon by the Board of Directors.

Beginning with the *middle of October,* correspondence with V. I. Suk as to the forthcoming production of *Kityezh* at the Grand Theatre.

October 7 [20]: From a letter of S. I. Mamontov to Rimsky-Korsakov: "I have received a letter from Carré, Director of the Opéra-Comique, with regard to the sketches for the production [*Snyegoorochka*]. I shall gather together what I can and send it on. . . . If help is needed in putting it on, I am ready to make a trip myself. It is imperative that it should be very fine, that it should be a genuine conquest."

October 8 [21]: From a letter to V. V. Yastryebtsev: "All this week I have been working without unbending my back; by the way, I happened to have bronchitis, which forced me to stay at home for a few days. Now I go out again. Today, at the *Kityezh* performance, the motive of the bells was as follows [musical illustration from which it appears that the upper A and C dropped out of the motive. — A. R.-K.], because one of the bells had grown hoarse, and the other — had lost its voice."

October 11 [24]: From a letter of Rimsky-Korsakov to S. P. Byelanovsky: "This season I have refused to conduct, in the first place, in the Moscow Russian Musical Society, and, secondly, in the Kyerzin [6] con-

---

[6] A. M. Kyerzin, an attorney-at-law, and his wife (a talented and keenly sensitive musician) inaugurated the concerts (to cultivate the Russian art-song), at the house of their friend Sergeyev, before an audience of twenty to thirty. The concerts grew so successful, that after several years sold-out houses of three thousand became the rule. J. A. J.

certs; consequently I must likewise forgo the concert proposed by you; I do so because I have abandoned the conductor's labours for good and all, in general, and have grown unused to it by now. If the Paris concerts in the spring constituted an exception for me in this regard, it was so because of their special exclusiveness. But at the Paris concerts I conducted only two of my own orchestral pieces, and not a whole program, which I would not have undertaken to do. Accordingly, do not feel peeved with me for my refusal."

Mid-October [*end of October*]: The transfer agreement for *Le Coq d'Or* was signed with the firm of P. Jurgenson.

In *October* the Moscow artiste Salina sent Nikolay Andreyevich a request to come to Moscow and conduct the first performance of *Kityezh* at the Grand Theatre — for her farewell benefit performance. Rimsky-Korsakov sent a refusal.

In October, Rimsky-Korsakov read the proofs of Moussorgsky's *Kolybel'naya* (*Cradle-song*), which he had orchestrated at Riva in the summer of 1906.

October 19 [*November 1*]: Rimsky-Korsakov finished *A Neapolitan Ditty* for orchestra (Funiculi-Funicula).

After the *end of October* [*early November*]: Engraving of the orchestral score of *Le Coq d'Or.*

October 30 [*November 12*]: Solodovnikov's Theatre in Moscow burned down.

October 31 [*November 13*]: At 28 Zagorodny Prospekt, the regular " Odd Wednesdays " began.

November 1907

November 2 [*15*]: From a letter signed by the members of the Quartette des Instruments Anciens (A. Casella, H. Casadesus, M. Devilliers, and E. Sully): " Je profite de cette occasion pour vous exprimer en mon nom et en celui de mes camarades, qui tiennent et signent cette lettre avec moi, toute l'admiration qu'a fait naître en nous l'audition de l'œuvre merveilleuse qu'est ' Sadko.' Nous avons assisté avant-hier à l'opéra de Moscou à la représentation de cette œuvre géniale qui nous a très enthousiasmés! "

November 7 [*20*]: Instrumentation made of both inserts in the scene of Boris's coronation (composed at S. Diaghileff's request for the Paris production).

November 9 [*22*]: From a letter of S. P. Byelanovsky to Rimsky-Korsakov: " At the last performance [*Sadko*] there were present the French visitors from the Grand Opéra; the opera went off finely and with a full house."

Lapitsky is working on the production of *Kityezh* in Moscow.

It has been settled that the translation of *Le Coq d'Or* will be made by M. D. Calvocoressi.

November 11 [*24*]: In No. 45 of the *Russian Musical Gazette*, Rimsky-Korsakov's opinion of the " simplified orchestral score " (reply to a questionnaire) was published.

Mid-November [*end of November*]: Rimsky-Korsakov was elected corresponding member of the Académie des Beaux Arts to fill the place made vacant through the death of Edvard Grieg (died September 4 at Bergen).

November 11 [*24*]: From a letter of C. A. Cui: " Of all scientific-artistic institutions this *undoubtedly* is the most *honorary*. In the section of Music, there are but six corresponding members. Of Russians there were Rubinstein, Tchaikovsky, and I — as if in consolation for the catastrophe with *Flibustier*. You are the fourth. This election does not bind you to anything. . . ."

November 25 [*December 8*]: In No. 47 of the *Russian Musical Gazette* there appeared " A Plan for Reorganizing the Program of the Theory of Music and Practical Composition in Conservatoires " (a memorandum submitted by Rimsky-Korsakov to the St. Petersburg Conservatory as early as 1901, but published here for the first time).

November 27 [*December 10*]: At the rehearsal of A. Ziloti's concert the *Neapolitan Ditty* was tried out. Rimsky-Korsakov took it off the program, finding that it had missed the mark.

November 27 [*December 10*]: The Board of Trustees (Byelayev's) awarded to N. A. Rimsky-Korsakov a prize for *Mozart and Salieri* (700 rubles) and for *Kashchey* (1,000 rubles). Along with Rimsky-Korsakov, Y. I. Wihtol, S. I. Taneiev, and N. N. Cherepnin were the recipients of prizes this time.

Replying to an ironic congratulation from A. T. Grechaninov, Rimsky-Korsakov wrote: " Regarding your twofold congratulation ' on the wonderful discovery of a talent that needs encouragement' which you have addressed to the Board that awards prizes in Glinka's name, I hasten to explain to you that the Board, on which I sat until May 1 [14], 1907 myself, did not and does not find it possible to award prizes to its own members, which fact the Board announced at the time of entering upon its duties. Therefore, at all events, of some sort of discovery — there must be no talk."

December 3 [*16*]: From his second letter on the same subject: " Responsibility for the distribution of this year's prizes falls entirely on the Board, of which I am no longer a member; but, considering myself at this time cut off *from the family of my musical friends which is so dear to me,* I cannot enter into an appraisal of its actions. I shall only say that I am grateful to it for the awards and that its selection of two of my works is a pleasure to me."

November 30 [*December 13*]: The last performance of *Kityezh* in St. Petersburg prior to its transfer to Moscow.

December 1907

December 12 [*25*]: The representative of Zimin's Private Moscow Opera inquires of Rimsky-Korsakov, through B. P. Jurgenson, as to the chance of securing the right to the first performance of *Le Coq d'Or* in case of refusal by the Directorate of the Imperial Theatres.

December: Strenuous proof-reading on *Le Coq d'Or* and various business correspondence.

During the last ten days of December [early January 1908], Rimsky-Korsakov was ill with bronchitis.

December 27 [*January 9, 1908*]: *Snyegoorochka* was revived at the Moscow Grand Theatre. The first performance was given for the benefit of Vasilevsky. According to the communication sent by S. P. Byelanovsky, Rimsky-Korsakov's regular news-purveyor, the performance was extremely slow and boring: " Owing to the celebration after Act III . . . the performance dragged till very late. (Your telegram was read first, of course, and provoked long ovations.) For this reason a whole tableau (the scene of Mizgir with Snyegoorochka in the forest) was omitted."

1908

Kityezh in Moscow. Censorship difficulties with *Le Coq d'Or. Snyegoorochka* at the Opéra Comique in Paris. Illness. Death.

January 1908

Early in January [*mid-January*] Rimsky-Korsakov, together with Balakirev, Glazunov, and C. Cui, was elected honorary member of the Moscow Branch of the Imperial Russian Musical Society.

January 8 [*21*]: From a letter of Rimsky-Korsakov to S. P. Byelanovsky: " Concerning Duncan, I shall tell you that I have never seen her. Presumably she is very graceful, a splendid mime, etc.; but what repels me in her is that she foists her art upon and tacks it onto musical compositions which are dear to my heart and do not at all need her company, and whose authors had not counted upon it. How chagrined I should be if I learned that Miss Duncan dances and mimically explains, for in-

stance, my *Scheherazada, Antar,* or *Easter Overture!* Musical works intended for dancing and miming must really be accompanied by the
latter, and, moreover, in certain decorative surroundings, but works not
intended for it do not require any mimic interpretation, and, in truth,
it is powerless to interpret them. All in all, miming is not an independent
kind of art and can merely accompany words or singing, but when it
foists itself unbidden upon music, it only harms the latter by diverting
attention from it."

January 12 [*25*]: The seventh subscription concert of A. Ziloti at the
Mariinsky Theatre, at which the *Overture on Russian Themes* and
Antar in its third version (in manuscript) were played under Ziloti's
direction.

In the *middle* [*end*] *of January* Moussorgsky's song *Night* was orchestrated.

January 19 [*February 1*]: From a letter of Rimsky-Korsakov to B. P.
Jurgenson: "Two copies of the libretto [of *Le Coq d'Or*] I have forwarded today to Tyelyakovsky for submission to the dramatic censor."

January 26 [*February 8*] at Ziloti's eighth subscription concert Borodin's *The Sea* and Moussorgsky's *Commander-in-Chief* (sung by I. V.
Yershov) with Rimsky-Korsakov's orchestration were performed.

January 29 [*February 11*]: From a letter of Rimsky-Korsakov to V. I.
Suk: "I cannot consent to the omission of the scene of the letter to
Kooter'ma in the last tableau. There was talk about this even in St.
Petersburg. Fyevroniya's letter is the culminating moment of her whole
personality. Having attained beatitude, Fyevroniya recalls and is solicit-
ous about her implacable foe and destroyer of Kityezh the Great. Let
the auditors ponder on this and not treat the final tableau of the opera
as if it were an apotheosis. . . . I cannot come to witness the production
and the first performance of *Kityezh,* owing to my duties and concerts
in St. Petersburg of great interest to me, at which my compositions will
be played for the first time. And the first performance, to my regret, will
be spoiled by Mme Salina's jubilee: first, the jubilee will bring together
an altogether special audience; and, second, the festivities in her honour,
the ovations and the reciting of: 'Profoundly honoured Nadezhda Vasilyevna,' etc., will completely throw the hearers out of mood and drag
out the performance till one in the morning."

End of February [*January*]: In a letter (dated February 11, New
Style) written under Albert Carré's instructions, M. Doré asks a Russian
conductor to be named who would be able to direct *Snyegoorochka* in
Paris in accordance with the composer's intentions and demands. In his
reply Rimsky-Korsakov suggested N. N. Cherepnin.

January 29 [*February 11*]: From a letter of Rimsky-Korsakov to B. P.

Jurgenson: " As a whole, both Byelsky and I are pleased with the translation [*Le Coq d'Or*]; Calvocoressi has struck the right path."

January 31 [February 13]: At the Kiev Municipal Theatre, the first performance of *The Fairy-tale of Tsar Saltan* took place for the benefit of the chorus and orchestra. E. D. Esposito conducted; *mise en scène*, Bogolyubov's.

End of January–beginning of February: intensive rehearsals of *Kityezh* at the Grand Theatre.

Artists and friends are awaiting Rimsky-Korsakov's arrival for the first performance.

February 1908

February 2 [15]: From a letter of Rimsky-Korsakov to S. P. Byelanovsky: " The other day I received from von Bool a letter inviting me to come to the dress rehearsal of *Kityezh* which is to take place on Saturday, February 9 [22], as the first performance has been scheduled for Tuesday, February 12 [25]. I replied that, viewing my presence at the dress rehearsal of slight use, I preferred to come to one or two orchestra rehearsals (prior to the dress rehearsal), at which I might, in case of need, make some suggestions."

February 3 [16]: At a Sheremetyev concert, there were played: *Svityezyanka; The Lay of Olyeg the Prophetic;* an excerpt from *Pskovityanka;* the " Berceuse " from *Vera Sheloga;* and the *Spanish Capriccio.*

February 9 [22]: First Russian Symphony Concert.

Early in [middle of] February: Rimsky-Korsakov received from B. P. Jurgenson the advance copies of separate numbers (of *Le Coq d'Or*), " Introduction " and " Wedding March," and the libretto.

February 12 [25]: From a letter to V. I. Suk: " Circumstances do not permit me to come for the première of *Kityezh*. With full tranquillity and assurance I entrust it to your talent and experience. I will endeavour to come for one of the subsequent performances, if there are any during Lent."

February 15 [28]: First performance of *Kityezh* in Moscow, on the stage of the Grand Theatre. The performance ended at 12.45 a.m. Between Act I and Act II, celebration in N. V. Salina's honour. During the days immediately following, eulogistic reviews by N. D. Kashkin and Y. D. Engel.

February 16 [29]: At the Russian Symphony Concert, under F. M. Blumenfeld's direction, the " Introduction " and " March " from *Le Coq d'Or* were played with enormous success; in addition, the program contained Borodin's Second Symphony, A. Glazunov's *The Sea*, I. Stravinsky's *The Faun and the Shepherdess*, and three songs of Moussorgsky's

(*Cradle Song, Picking Mushrooms*, and *Hopak*) with Rimsky-Korsakov's orchestration.

February 18 [*March 2*]: From a letter of Rimsky-Korsakov to V. I. Suk: " I do not doubt even for one minute that the musical part of the production of *Kityezh* which was in your hands was excellent. I know it likewise from many reports and I sincerely thank you for it. But as to the scenic production — that is another matter; stylization in the second act is not only a thing undesirable, but even inadmissible, and I shall ask for a complete revision of this production for next season. . . . My *Kityezh has not at all been taken off the boards* of the Mariinsky Theatre owing to boredom, excessively long passages, etc. On the contrary, it was impossible to procure seats for the last performance. And the opera was transferred to Moscow in accordance with Tyelyakovsky's original plan, formed by him prior to the production at St. Petersburg."

February 20 [*March 4*]: From a letter to B. P. Jurgenson: " Tomorrow I shall forward you my foreword to the piano score and the orchestral score. From Tyelyakovsky I have received word that *Le Coq d'Or* will pass the dramatic censorship without changes. On Saturday the playing of the ' Introduction ' and ' March ' created the greatest furore at the Russian Symphony Concert."

February 25 [*March 9*]: From a letter of A. Krupyensky: " The dramatic censorship has permitted performances of the opera *Le Coq d'Or* composed by you, but with the omission of a few passages in the text (the entire Introduction, the Epilogue and 45 lines of the text)."

Under the same date, from a letter to B. P. Jurgenson: " So then, *Le Coq d'Or* cannot be given in Russia. Of changing anything I have no intention. Perhaps it will come in handy for Paris. However, that depends on the success of *Snyegoorochka* and *Sadko* there.

February 26 [*March 10*] from a letter to B. P. Jurgenson: " I am sending you herewith . . . the copy of the libretto mutilated to the limit by the censor. You will convince yourself that all the erasures have been made at random, without any logic. This is what happened. The dramatic censorship returned the libretto to the Directorate as permitted for performances without any erasures, and the following day demanded the return of the libretto and sent it back with erasures. Someone has played us dirt. What a s . . . . . .[7] [skunk]: ' the cap fits.' "

February 27 [*March 11*]: From a letter to B. P. Jurgenson: " V. I. Byelsky insists that I go together with him to see Belgard (Director of Press Affairs) and talk over the censorship instructions with him. He thinks that we ought to bargain and yield something, first having made clear the madness of the censors who forbid at random and, full-shoulder,

---

[7] The six dots in Russian would make it *svoloch'* — riff-raff, dregs. J. A. J.

strike out lines of Pushkin's. I shall do so, but will not stand for too much bullying, and at worst shall consent to an alteration here and there. But I imagine the libretto ought to be placed on sale without changes, while on the stage they will sing, according to the censor, to the glory of the powers that be (to say the least)."

February 29 [*March 13*]: From a letter to B. P. Jurgenson: " Evidently Tyelyakovsky himself is the cause of the censor's captiousness, having called the latter's attention to Moscow and the ruthlessness of your Gershelman. Still, according to Tyelyakovsky, the censor has over-reached himself, forbidding as he did even verses of Pushkin's. On this score he has already had a talk with Belgard, who turned out to be willing to meet us half-way in the sense of easing the censorship's demands. With Tyelyakovsky the three of us read over everything that the censor had stricken out. Right there and then Byelsky improvised certain changes, in case Belgard should prove obstinate on some points. All of Pushkin's lines Tyelyakovsky took upon himself to save, likewise the Introduction in its entirety and the Epilogue with a substitution of the word *unexpected* for *bloody* dénouement. Instead of a *new* dawn there will be a *white* dawn; a few verses have been softened; ' reign lying on your side ' is left in. Tomorrow Tyelyakovsky will have an interview with Belgard, and the form in which the piece will be sanctioned for performance will become definitely clear. Tyelyakovsky is resolved to produce it without delay in Moscow and desires right now to proceed to rehearsals, and the preparation of the scenery with the aid of Korovin."

March 1908

March 3 [*16*]: From a letter of S. N. Krooglikov to Rimsky-Korsakov: " After the first Moscow performance of *Kityezh* I began to love it, if possible, still more than after having made its acquaintance at the Mariinsky Theatre. On its musical side here it stood out both more delicate and clearer, and in greater relief. . . . In a word, I enjoyed myself to the full, having taken a copious dose of beauty and incomparable poetry. The final tableau of Paradise moved me deeply and literally chained me to my seat. . . . Don't feel cross, my dear friend, at the stage-manager Mikhaylov's stylizing. Granted that in doing so he has somewhat exaggerated in general and made use of it to no good purpose in the second act; but the music has not suffered from it, it has come into its own, and the best of the Moscow folk bowed to it. I am saying this sincerely, without the least cunning. And how happy I should be if I could smooth out the wrinkles in your countenance with my tidings! "

March 5 [18]: A letter from S. I. Mamontov in which he apprises Rimsky-Korsakov of costumes for *Snyegoorochka* having been ordered in the Government of Toola and of his desire to journey over to Paris "*donner un coup de main.*"

March 6 [19]: Rimsky-Korsakov turned sixty-four.

In conversation, Rimsky-Korsakov complains that his heart has been growing weak (asthma, inability to breathe full-chest, etc.).

March 8 [21]: After the third Russian Symphony concert, at which, among other numbers, M. O. Steinberg's First Symphony had been played, at supper in 28 Zagorodny Prospekt, in the presence of friends, a toast was drunk to the health of the bride and the bridegroom (Nadezhda Nikolayevna Rimskaya-Korsakova and M. O. Steinberg).

From a letter of Rimsky-Korsakov to B. P. Jurgenson on the same date: "With the dramatic censorship things are as follows: Tyelyakovsky is parleying with Belgard, and certain verses for which Byelsky and I had stood out — e.g., Pushkin's line: ' reign, reposing on your side ' — are not permitted, after all. The *Introduction* has been allowed absolutely, the Epilogue absolutely forbidden (?!!?). At the Censorship Bureau they can even read awry: they read that the Epilogue is spoken by Dodon and not by the Astrologer. The deuce take them — what sort of idiots! Owing to all this, Tyelyakovsky (another fine fellow!) sent for Byelsky, and the latter introduced new changes of certain elements of the text and, among their number, an entirely new text for the Epilogue. In this way Tyelyakovsky had a new talk with Belgard, and one may hope they will come to an agreement on something or other, and the piece will be permitted for performance. However, if the censor does not consent even to the new, utterly inoffensive Epilogue, then I will not consent either and shall take back my libretto, and the censorship I shall hold up to shame in the paper; there is a limit to everything. I hope that it won't happen. As to developments I shall immediately inform you. . . .

" To come back to the question of censorship, I consider that neither in the piano score nor in the libretto should any changes be made. The piano score and the orchestral score must remain in their original form for all time, and the libretto, too, must be preserved. In an old novel of Paul de Kock's ' Mumsey ' enjoins upon her ' daughter dear ' instead of the word *amour* always to use the word *topinambour* [Jerusalem artichoke]; well, then, let it be that way also on our stage."

March 10 [23]: From B. P. Jurgenson's letter: " I sincerely sympathize with your indignation at the censors and their hysterical demands, but hope that they will succeed in finding some sort of compromise. . . ."

In March, at two sittings on the same day, V. A. Serov made for S. P.

Diaghileff the famous crayon portrait of Rimsky-Korsakov. When some one of his close friends made the remark that the portrait has the character of an iconographic image, V. A. Serov came back with: " That is just what is needed; let the Frenchmen pray to it."

In March, intensive proof-reading of *Le Coq d'Or*.

March 14 [*27*]: From a letter to B. P. Jurgenson: " The last changes made by Byelsky have been approved by the censor, and the libretto will be returned to the Directorate with the licence. . . ."

March 19 [*April 1*]: N. N. Cherepnin dropped in to say good-bye to Rimsky-Korsakov before leaving for Paris for the production of *Snyegoorochka*.

March 25 [*April 7*]: From a letter of Rimsky-Korsakov to B. P. Jurgenson: " Has the Directorate of Imperial Theatres sent in a demand for piano scores and chorus parts for the Moscow Grand Theatre?

" In the libretto all the requisite alterations have been made and signed by Byelsky. Definitively Tyelyakovsky has taken this whole business into his hands, but nevertheless nothing has been heard of him up to this time. Is the libretto on sale and, if so, has it been forwarded to St. Petersburg? . . ."

March 27 [*April 9*], N. I. Zabyela's concert; on the program, along with other numbers, there are vocal pieces of Rimsky-Korsakov's (among these " Hymn to the Sun " from *Le Coq d'Or*).

March 28 [*April 10*]: From a letter of Rimsky-Korsakov to B. P. Jurgenson: " Today I received the orchestra-score proofs of half of the second act and one copy of the piano score, for which latter I thank you very much, as I find the printing splendid. I am surprised that the Directorate of Imperial Theatres has not, until now, requisitioned piano scores for the Moscow Opera. If they really wish to produce *Le Coq d'Or* next season at the Grand Theatre, it is time to proceed to it; for the training of the chorus ought to be commenced, and they should begin to think of selecting their soloists, for they had never laid their eyes on the music. However, nowadays in the Directorate they think only about the scenery and the painters Korovin and Golovin. . . ."

On the same date, from a letter of Rimsky-Korsakov to B. P. Jurgenson: " Yesterday, at her concert, Zabyela sang, with great success, the aria of the Queen of Shemakha (from Act II) from manuscript. This song ought to be kept in view for publication as a separate number; but its beginning and end have only now taken on a definitive form in my imagination, and therefore it will be necessary to make special plates for the separate edition. . . .

" I ask you also to say to the highly esteemed proof-reader that he should not put in so many question-marks on the proof-sheets, where the need of corrections is manifest, but should simply correct them; for I am not a Richard Strauss and do not compose notoriously false harmonies and I think that my compositions cannot be charged with being illogical. Let him, then, put in question-marks only when something is really obscure or unintelligible or requires an explanation on my part. . . ."

April 1908

April 8 [*21*]: An official letter from the Grand Duke Vladimir Aleksandrovich (as patron of the Diaghileff Committee) containing an invitation to attend the performances of *Boris Godunov* in Paris.

April 14 [*27*]: From a letter of Rimsky-Korsakov to B. P. Jurgenson: " I have received the parcel from you today. The edition of the piano score is splendid; I thank you for it and for the ' author's copies.' "

In *April,* several letters from Cherepnin, from Paris, dealing with the rehearsing and staging of *Snyegoorochka* at the Opéra-Comique.[8]

From a letter of Cherepnin of *April 9* (New Style): " First of all I shall tell you that the general attitude of everybody to *Snyegoorochka* is exceedingly businesslike and quite earnest, and that I shall hardly err when I say that until now I have never witnessed such a careful, detailed, and substantial preparation of an opera.

" But when the first performance will take place — that is utterly uncertain, for, even though all artists sing everything by heart, and have partly rehearsed it also with stage-settings, even though the orchestra plays already now with great finesse (by the way, the orchestra is really of the first rank and is a delight to work with), *il y a un grand but* — to this day I have not heard the choruses, for they are not ready as yet."

From a letter of N. N. Cherepnin of *April 12* (New Style): " Ruhlmann deemed himself exceedingly mistreated, because Carré had turned over to me the direction of the rehearsals and he had been successful so far in that he will himself conduct all of them, as well as the performances, of course, and thus my rôle is confined to supervising the exactness and correctness of his execution, and all my suggestions, considered as if the author's own, are carried out religiously and with the greatest willingness.

---

[8] Rather extensive quotations from N. N. Cherepnin's interesting and vivid letters are given, not alone in view of their objective historical interest, but first of all because they had doubtless entered, as one of the essential and determining elements, into Rimsky-Korsakov's psychic make-up *during the last month of his life,* partly diverting his conscious ego from the grave presentiment of the looming end, and partly stirring his consciousness as an author in a manner easy to understand, thereby pouring oil, as it were, upon the fire which day after day was bringing him nearer to the fatal outcome.

" Now as to the production: upon closer investigation, it turned out that the scenery for *Snyegoorochka* has been done by a French painter — Juissac or something like that,[9] but not by Roerich; as for Savva Mamontov, there is not so much as a trace of him, as the saying goes, and the opera is produced by Carré himself. Of the drops I have seen but the Prologue, in which there was one extraordinarily idiotic thing, but after long conversations I managed to have that done away with. As a matter of fact, after the scene between Spring and Frost — during the singing of the chorus behind the scenes, the seeing-out of Butter-week, before the entrance of the chorus on the stage — the winter-scape, I may say in passing, very charmingly painted — suddenly changes into *plein été* with a backdrop in the form of blooming valleys of Hungary from the last act of *Raymonda,* with curly-lock shrubbery on the slope of sky-high mountains veiled in bluish crape. And into this [piece of] loveliness the Byeryendyeys tumble with their sleighs. Don't you think that would not be so very bad after all!

" Now, thank the Lord, it will not happen, and the entire Prologue will be done in a winter landscape.

" Next I must tell you that Carré's closest adviser and, *ma foi,* the evil genius of the production is a certain old woman with an enormous hat, the maîtresse de ballet by profession.[10]

" For this reason, at the first stage rehearsals there was dancing every-where. I began even to have my doubts whether *Snyegoorochka* was not a ballet, by some chance, and only by means of the greatest efforts, I think, shall we succeed in getting rid of this abomination.

" The chorus, the seeing-out of Butter-week, regardless of your cate-goric direction, was put on as a ballet number: to the playing of music in A-flat major, twelve couples of the ballet corps would dart forth, and ' this lady ' would indicate to the piano-player the speed of motion, and, consequently, also the tempos of the choruses, and the ballet kept danc-ing all the time. After long discussions I managed to suppress all this nightmare of nonsense and to restore the correct tempos.

" As long as I stay here, I will, like a watch-dog, guard over *Snyegoo-rochka,* but who can tell whether they will not think up something when I am gone, for it seems I shall not see the performance take place. . . . In my opinion, it will not be ready before the middle of May.

" Speaking in general, the musical side will undoubtedly be at the proper high level, and the stage side, too, if we discard these idiotic dances, which I hope to exterminate completely, is not devoid of taste. . . . "

[9] Jusseaume. J. A. J.
[10] Mme Mariquita. J. A. J.

From a letter of N. N. Cherepnin of *April 16* (New Style): "On each successive occasion I like Ruhlmann more and more. He already feels quite at home in the opera now, knows the orchestral score splendidly, has completely mastered the rhythms, and succeeds in getting very refined nuances from the orchestra, which is truly incomparable. Moreover, he keeps in constant touch with me and carries out all my intentions exactly and immediately, and our team-work is exceedingly harmonious.

"I repeat once more, dear Nikolay Andreyevich, that *Snyegoorochka* is in very reliable hands, and that, probably, the best part, as far as execution goes — will be the orchestra. . . .

"What casts a bit of melancholy over me is — the choruses, although they are being drilled strenuously and every day: there are both too few of them and they sing below pitch, while Carré is stressing the acting all the time, and thereby creates superfluous difficulties — at a time when it is hard enough as it is."

From N. N. Cherepnin's letter of *April 20* (New Style): "Yesterday we had again a grand rehearsal of the orchestra (in their seats) for *Snyegoorochka,* and, from the musical point of view, it may be said that the opera is beginning to run smoothly. The portion which was worst is the finale of the opera — it has been studied both less and probably also not with such attention to details.

"The day before yesterday I saw Acts III and IV with the stage-settings for the first time, and felt worried first of all about the *Khorovod* (choral dance). When I had shown them how *Khorovods* are done (I had to clamber on the stage for that), I came back to the auditorium in order to regale myself with the effect — and, oh horror! my ladies began to move with such speed and bustle that the result was indeed some sort of a *grand rond* of a quadrille, and besides, taking advantage of the pauses in the singing, they squealed. What ever will come of this! Then '*la dame Blanche*' from the avenue Boieldieu put on the dance of the jesters with tambourines, with a scorching gypsy beauty at their head (the same also a human snake, for, in bending over in the course of the dance, she can easily nibble at her heels), and yet, in spite of the fact that the music is attacked directly vivace, at its first sounds the procession of jesters emerges slowly and gravely and bows to the King — and only later, when a goodly third of the dance has been played, does it set about its task. But what kind of task!!! All this would be laughable if it were not so offensive and stupid. Why is it that when we produce *Manon* or, in general, anything that demands a certain amount of previous training in the line of style, preliminary schooling is always there, or at least we seek it. But these gentlemen consider it possible to arrive at our Russian private life by the same means as Tyapkin-Lyapkin [11] arrived at the creation of the world.

"There will be three more rehearsals of *Snyegoorochka* while I am here, and one of them on Thursday — the entire opera with orchestra and stage-settings.

"After that I intend to leave Paris and personally convey to you my impressions more circumstantially, and here I repeat that whatever depends on me, I will endeavour to do and retain, but I consider that as far as the musical side is concerned the main points have already been achieved and the opera is more or less on the right track, but as regards the stage — I am not too much at home in that myself. . . ."

April 10 [*23*]: (On the eve of the first attack), in the morning, at breakfast, A. K. Lyadov came to see Rimsky-Korsakov. During the day Rimsky-Korsakov called on Glazunov. In the evening, till late in the night, he had a conference with M. O. Steinberg about the *Textbook of Instrumentation*.

During the night of *April 10–11* [*23–4*] (the night before Great Friday [Good Friday]), the first severe attack of asthma (angina pectoris).

April 14 [*27*]: The piano score of *Le Coq d'Or* arrived from Jurgenson, from Moscow.

During the night of *April 15–16* [*28–9*]: The second attack of asthma (oxygen, morphine administered). The physician prescribed complete rest and a rigid diet-regimen. Visitors were not permitted to see Rimsky-Korsakov.

April 18 [*May 1*]: Medical consultation, in which Professor Sirotinin took part.

April 21 [*May 4*]: From a letter of Nadezhda Nikolayevna (Mme Rimsky-Korsakov) to S. N. Krooglikov: "Unfortunately the paper did not tell a story: Nikolay Andreyevich has really fallen ill with asthma of the chest. He has had two severe and very painful attacks of asthma. The first happened during Holy Week. If he had taken care of himself after it and had allowed himself complete rest, it is very probable that the second attack would not have occurred, or at least it would not have followed so soon. But Nikolay Andreyevich is accustomed to being on the move, to activity, so that in spite of all efforts it was impossible to make him lie still for a while and receive no one. And so during Holy Week, in the night of Tuesday–Wednesday, the second attack occurred, after which he grew very weak. At this point the physicians (there was a consultation of three of them) absolutely forbade any movements, work, seeing visitors; and he obeyed. This is the sixth day that he has not left his bedroom; he is in bed or sits in the armchair and does not

---

[11] A character in Gogol's comedy *Revizor* (*The Government Inspector*). J. A. J.

busy himself with anything; he has given up smoking altogether, does
not drink coffee, and eats no meat. . . . The whole family is around
him, and everyone, by various attentions, tries to do whatever is within
his powers. Today we recovered our spirits, because he feels better. But
there is dread for the future. How can all harmful influences be removed,
how can all causes of agitation and excitement, which may bring on a
recurrence of the attacks, be avoided? "

April 24 [*May 7*]: Rimsky-Korsakov gradually begins to scan the
proofs of *Le Coq d'Or*.

April 25 [*May 8*]: The physician allowed one visitor a day. A. K.
Glazunov was the first to be admitted.

A telegram from S. P. Diaghileff and F. M. Blumenfeld from Paris to
the effect that the insertions made by Rimsky-Korsakov for *Boris* " sound
ideal."

April 27 [*May 10*]: From a letter of Rimsky-Korsakov to B. P. Jurgenson: " I really was ill; at the present moment I feel considerably better,
but perfect rest has been prescribed to me for a complete recovery. I
am awaiting the proof-sheets of the orchestral score and shall correct
them as far as my strength and opportunity will allow, with the collaboration of a person close to me and a magnificent musician, M. O. Steinberg.

" The copy-book with the French text I shall procure from Byelsky.

" Prior to my illness I had had an interview with Tyelyakovsky. He
told me that the censored copy of the libretto of *Le Coq d'Or* was in
Moscow in the hands of von Bool, who was going to show it to Gershelman. If the latter knits his brow or gets it into his head to abridge or
change anything, Tyelyakovsky will not produce *Le Coq d'Or* in Moscow, but will put it on in St. Petersburg a season later. All this will be
cleared up about May 1 [14]. How tedious and stupid all this is! "

At the *end of April* [*early in May*]: Rimsky-Korsakov is repeatedly
visited by Lyadov, Glazunov, Cui, Byelsky, Yastryebtsev, and others.

May 1908

Early in May [*middle of May*]: Reading the proofs of *Le Coq d'Or*.
Work on the *Textbook (Principles) of Instrumentation*.

May 2 [*15*]: From a letter of Nadezhda Nikolayevna Rimskaya-Korsakova to S. N. Krooglikov: " Nikolay Andreyevich has grown quite strong,
walks about all the rooms, even though with slow steps, attends to his
affairs, has taken up again the *Textbook of Instrumentation*. The cough-
ing has completely left him, his heart functions better, the swelling in
the soles of his feet is almost gone. The apprehensions of the physicians
concerning the kidneys have proved groundless. . . ."

In a letter from Paris, Alfredo Casella communicates the brilliant success of the " Introduction " and " March " from *Le Coq d'Or,* which had been played under his direction by Colonne's Orchestra.

May 7 [20]: First performance of *Snyegoorochka* at the Opéra-Comique.

May 6 [19]: From a letter of von Bool's: " As to your latest opera, it has not been included in the repertory of the coming season. It seems to me that Vladimir Arkadyevich [12] wishes to produce it at the Mariinsky Theatre in St. Petersburg."

May 8 [21]: A telegram from Paris: "Suis heureux vous annoncer grand succès *Snégourotschka.* Albert Carré." Likewise a telegram from F. Blumenfeld from Paris about the brilliant success of *Boris.*

May 9 [22]: Commencement Day at the Conservatory (Day of St. Nicholas [13]). Rimsky-Korsakov has a multitude of callers, the majority of whom were denied admission, owing to his feeling tired.

May 10 [23]: From a family letter of Rimsky-Korsakov's: " All is well with me. . . . I feel fairly well, only in the morning it is a bit harder to breathe."

The removal to Lyubensk is delayed owing to repairs on the house.

May 13 [26] and the following days: " Reading the proofs of *Boris* for the Breitkopf and Härtel edition; work on the *Textbook.*"

May 8 (New Style): From a letter of F. M. Blumenfeld from Paris: " Why, this is history, what we are living through! (1) Sunday, the 17th, rehearsal of *Boris.* (2) Tuesday, the 19th, first performance of *Boris.* (3) Wednesday, the 20th, dress rehearsal of *Snyegoorochka.* (4) Thursday, the 21st, second performance of *Boris.* (5) Friday, the 22nd, first performance of *Snyegoorochka,* etc. . . . At two theatres in Paris two Russian operas in one week!!! A pity Stassov is gone! There is the one who would keenly feel all this!!! The old man did not live to see this day, but indeed he had laid many a stone at the foundation of this monument to Russian Music."

In the *middle [end] of May:* Echoes of the Paris production in the Russian papers.

May 16 [23]: From a letter of Rimsky-Korsakov to B. P. Jurgenson: " What will you say to the following idea of mine? I have in mind to make a small orchestral suite from *Le Coq d'Or,* similar to what I have in my *Christmas Eve.*

" This suite should also include the ' Introduction ' and ' March,' which have already been published by you, and several excerpts in addition:

---

[12] V. A. Tyelyakovsky. J. A. J.
[13] Rimsky-Korsakov's Saint's Day.

the beginning of Act II, the Dance, the Finale of Act II, the beginning of Act III, etc. The suite will be in the form of a single rather long piece without break. . . .

"When the printing of the orchestral score of my opera has been finished, what will be the fate of the copy of the final (third) proof, which has been accumulating in your possession? If it then proves utterly unnecessary to you, won't you send it to me for my perpetual hereditary possession? I have always been in the habit of presenting the proofs of my orchestral scores to my pupils (even single acts). No misuse can come from this; on the other hand the pupils are for the most part people without means and will never pay 150 rubles for a score. I am writing you about this in order that you may give me your opinion on this matter perfectly frankly. . . ."

May 17 [*30*]: From B. P. Jurgenson's letter: "Your idea of making a suite from *Le Coq d'Or* I like very much, and we shall publish it with pleasure."

May 20 [*June 2*]: From a letter of Rimsky-Korsakov to B. P. Jurgenson: "Yesterday I talked by telephone to Tyelyakovsky, who had just returned from abroad. *Le Coq d'Or* will indeed not be produced in Moscow; but he has the intention of giving it in St. Petersburg possibly during the coming season of 1908–9, together with *The Fairy-tale of Tsar Saltan* or in lieu of the latter, or he will produce *Le Coq d'Or* during the season of 1909–10 and *Skazka o Tsarye Saltanye* during the coming season. All this, according to what he said, depends on the scene-painters Korovin and Golovin,[14] and will be settled in a very short time; of that he will immediately inform me and I shall inform you. But to me it looks as if *Tsar Saltan* and *Le Coq d'Or* may, both of them, not be given the coming season. No doubt Tyelyakovsky wishes to produce both, but he is enmeshed in the cobweb spun by the scene-painters and the officials. At all events *Le Coq d'Or* is at Zimin's disposal in Moscow, in case he should want to produce it. Cannot you, Boris Petrovich, propose it to Zimin in your name? The trouble is that last year Zimin asked what I wished him to put on; as *Le Coq d'Or* had been pledged by me to the Imperial Theatres, I asked him to produce my *Christmas Eve*. Zimin gave his promise and never did it. Moreover I asked him to entrust my *Saltan* to the conductor Kuper — I was refused that. For all these reasons I should not like to ask him, or to offer him *Le Coq d'Or*, which has now been released. When proposing *Le Coq d'Or* to Zimin in your name, you are at liberty to refer to me.

"I have just received your letter of May 17 [30]. Thank you for your readiness to place at my disposal the *Coq d'Or* proof we are done with,

---

[14] Oh, these painters, they will be the death of me! (Author's note.)

as well as for your willingness to publish my suite, which I shall turn over in my mind in the summer. . . ."

May 21 [*June 3*]: Removal to Lyubensk.

May 30 [*June 12*]: From V. A. Tyelyakovsky's letter: " As regards *Le Coq d'Or,* there is trouble in store. The Governor-General of Moscow is opposed to the production of this opera and has informed the censorship to that effect, and hence I think that in St. Petersburg, too, they will be against it."

June 2 [*15*]: From a letter of Rimsky-Korsakov to S. N. Krooglikov: " First of all, thank you, dear fellow, for the felicitations and the interest you have shown with regard to my illness. From Nadezhda Nikolayevna's letter you know that in St. Petersburg I had apparently completely recovered; i.e., went about from room to room, I drank, I ate as befits a decent human being, and busied myself as much as was possible; all of this, of course, with a goodly amount of caution. The journey to the country was accomplished safely and I did not even feel tired, but the first night I again had an attack of choking, though not so violent as the preceding; but after it I had to lie still once more and sit in an armchair for more than a week and, in general, to be treated as a sick or feeble man. At the present moment I have recuperated once more. I go out not only on the balcony, but even into the gardens, but I walk slowly and for only short periods. The third attack brought on mournful thoughts that, in spite of the doctoring and precautions, I find myself far from being ensured against the hateful attacks. Well, what can one do?

" I began to work; shall endeavour to forge ahead with my *Textbook* or Notes on Orchestration, conceived long ago.

" I rejoice that you like *Le Coq d'Or.* I am sorry you did not begin with the first act, for indeed a few things are to be found there: the Astrologer, the Dreams of Dodon, the Alarms, the scene with the Parrot, etc. The day after tomorrow is Nadya's wedding, without ceremony, country-fashion. The season is good; lilacs, acacia, apple trees are in bloom; only the weather is fickle.

June 4 [*17*]: The wedding of M. O. Steinberg and N. N. Rimskaya-Korsakova in the village church at the estate Kritsy. Rimsky-Korsakov was not present at the church.

June 5 [*18*]: An attack, not particularly severe.

June 6 [*19*] (two days before his death): From a letter of Rimsky-Korsakov to B. P. Jurgenson: " I am indignant at V. A. Tyelyakovsky's communication, which I quote verbatim in the excerpt from his letter to me:

" '. . . But as regards *Le Coq d'Or,* there is trouble in store. The Governor-General of Moscow is opposed to the production of this opera and has informed the censorship to that effect, and hence I think that in St. Petersburg, too, they will be against it.'

" How do you like this? This is what has been done by Tyelyakovsky and his adviser, the painter Korovin, who frightened him with the Moscow bugbear. There is no use even to think of talking to Zimin after all this. Perhaps even with Kiev it may come to naught. Would you not try to take your chance in Paris through Calvocoressi's mediation? "

June 7 [*20*]: Last date of jottings for *Textbook of Instrumentation.*

On the night of June 7–8 [*20–1*] after a brief but violent storm and downpour — the last attack of suffocation and death.

June 10 [*23*]: Funeral services in the church of the St. Petersburg Conservatory and burial at the cemetery of the Novodyevichi Monastery. Subsequently, on Rimsky-Korsakov's grave his family erected a monument (after a sketch by N. K. Roerich) representing the top of a mound with an ancient Novgorod Cross and, around the grave, a ring of archaic flagstones with an inscription in ancient script of interlaced letters: " Nikolay Andreyevich Rimsky-Korsakov. March 6, 1844–June 8, 1908."

APPENDICES

APPENDIX I

Dear Nikolay Andreyevich:

I had not intended writing, but was so overjoyed on finding all you want that I was seized with the desire to let you know it; besides, while rummaging in the papers I found sketches which may perhaps be of use to you — hence it would not be a bad idea for you, when you have a free moment, about 10 or 11 in the morning, to drop in on me.

Yours,

L. *Shestakova*

September 8 [20], 1895

M. A. Balakirev made his first trip to Prague in 1866, in the month of June, on my requesting him to make a stage production of *Ruslan* there. However, he returned towards the end of July without having accomplished this errand. In September of the same year, having obtained a letter of introduction from V. I. Lamansky [1] to Rüger, in Prague, I went there on the 16th [28th], and, with the latter's assistance, the question of producing *Ruslan* was settled in a few hours. Taking with him all the sketches of scenery, costumes, and accessories, made by Gornostayev at my request, M. A. Balakirev went to Prague a second time on December 21 of that year [January 2, 1867], and there applied himself to the production of *Ruslan* and *A Life for the Tsar*. It was our desire that *Ruslan* should be given on the stage for the first time on February 3 [15], the anniversary of my brother's death; but for some reason that could not be done, and the première of *Ruslan* in Prague took place on February 4 [16], 1867, with M. A. Balakirev conducting.

THIRD NOTE OF L. SHESTAKOVA

Stellovsky did not allow me to publish the orchestral score of *Ruslan and Lyudmila*. After Stellovsky's death I arranged with his heirs the matter of publishing *Ruslan*, and entrusted to V. N. Engelhardt all negotiations with Röder in Leipzig concerning the publication of that score. The negotiations began in the summer of 1876, and in November of the

---

[1] Famous scholar (Slavic philology) and prominent leader of Slavophils. J. A. J.

same year Balakirev, Rimsky-Korsakov, and Lyadov engaged in preparing them for print and usually brought me whatever they had got ready. What they had set right I used to send to Leipzig, and I handed them the proofs received from Leipzig. I got the first published copy of the orchestral score of *Ruslan* from Leipzig on November 10 [22], 1878, and the very next day, November 11 [23], I invited the co-workers and " Bach "[2] for the evening. All of us together made a joyous time of it, drank at supper a glass to my brother's memory, and I thanked them all, heartily congratulating them upon bringing the cherished task to completion. In 1880, by agreement with G. Hake, Stellovsky published the orchestral score of A *Life for the Tsar* in St. Petersburg.

---

[2] V. V. Stassov.

APPENDIX II

FIVE SUBSCRIPTION CONCERTS OF THE FREE MUSIC SCHOOL

I

October 26 [November 7], 1869, at 1.30 p.m., in the Hall of the Club of the Nobility

I · *Eine Faust Ouvertüre.*   Richard Wagner

II · Scene at the Church, excerpt from the music to *Faust,* for solo, chorus, and orchestra (first time).   Schumann
     The part of Gretchen will be sung by Mme Y. F. Platonova. The part of the Evil Spirit by G. I. Kondratyev.

III · Fantasy for the pianoforte with orchestra on themes from *Ruines d'Athènes* of Beethoven (first time).   Liszt

IV · *1000 Years,* a musical tableau for orchestra.   Balakirev

V · Excerpts from the opera *Oberon;* (a) Chorus of Elves; (b) Chorus of the Khalif's courtiers.   Weber

VI · Fifth Symphony in C minor, for orchestra.   Beethoven

II

November 2 [14], 1869, at 1.30 p.m., in the Hall of the Club of the Nobility

I · Overture to the opera *Iphigenia in Aulis* with concert ending by Richard Wagner.   Gluck

467

ɪɪ · Concerto for the cello with orchestra, in A
minor (first time).   Schumann
    The cello part will be played by K. Y. Davy-
    dov.

ɪɪɪ · *Ivan Grozny,* a musico-characteristic picture
for orchestra (first time).   Anton Rubinstein

ɪᴠ · Songs with piano accompaniment, sung by
Mme A. A. Khvostova.
    (a) *Lied der Braut.*   Schumann
    (b) *Hebrew Song: I sleep, but my watchful
        heart is not asleep.*   Rimsky-Korsakov
    (c) Laura's song from the opera *The Stone
        Guest.*   Dargomyzhsky

ᴠ · Excerpts from the monodrama (drama for one
personage) *Lélio:*
    (a) The Harp of Æolus (orchestra); (b)
        Fantasy on Shakespeare's *Tempest*
        (chorus and orchestra).   Berlioz

ᴠɪ · Overture to Shakespeare's drama *A Midsum-
mer Night's Dream.*   Mendelssohn

III

November 16 [28], 1869, at 1.30 p.m., in the Hall of the Club

of the Nobility

ɪ · Excerpts from the oratorio *Legende von der
heiligen Elisabeth* (first time).
    (a) Introduction (orchestra); (b) March
        and chorus of Crusaders (orchestra and
        chorus); (c) Death of St. Elizabeth
        (solo and chorus). Solo part will be
        sung by Mme Y. F. Platonova.   Liszt

ɪɪ · Episode from the *bylina Sadko,* musical tableau for orchestra.   Rimsky-Korsakov

ɪɪɪ · Third Concerto (on Danish themes) in E-flat
major, for piano and orchestra. The piano part
played by F. O. Leschetizky.   Litolff

ɪᴠ · First Symphony in B-flat major, for orchestra.   Schumann

IV

November 30 [December 12], 1869, at 1.30 p.m., in the Hall of the

Club of the Nobility

i . Overture to the tragedy *Coriolanus*.   Beethoven

ii . First Concerto (E-flat major) for piano and
orchestra.   Liszt
    The piano part will be played by N. G. Ru-
binstein.

iii . Excerpts from the unfinished fairy comic opera
Rogdana.
    (a) Chorus of Dervishes; (b) Chorus of
      Rogdana's fairy maidens.   Dargomyzhsky

iv . Piano pieces.
    (a) Berceuse   Laskovsky
    (b) Romance   Tchaikovsky
    (c) Oriental fantasy *Islamey*   Balakirev
      Played by N. G. Rubinstein.

v . Symphony in C major, for orchestra.   Franz Schubert

V

March 2 [14], 1870, at 1.30 p.m., in the Hall of the Club

of the Nobility

i . Two episodes from the music to Lenau's *Faust*
for orchestra.
    (a) Nocturnal procession; (b) Waltz of
      Mephistopheles.   Liszt

ii . Introduction to the opera *Ruslan and Lyud-
mila* (without cuts).   Glinka
    The part of Bayan will be sung by V. M.
Vasilyev.

iii . Ninth Symphony, for orchestra, chorus, and
solos.   Beethoven
    The solo parts will be sung by: Mmes Y. F.
Platonova, Y. A. Lavrovskaya; Messrs. V. M.
Vasilyev, I. A. Myelnikov.

APPENDIX III

February 3 [15], 1876, at 8 p.m., in the Hall of the Town Council

I · Overture to the tragedy *Coriolanus.*   Beethoven

II · Excerpts from the Mass in B minor.
    (a) Kyrie eleison (first time); (b) Aria *Qui
    sedes,* sung by Mme Kadmina; (c)
    Chorus *Crucifixus;* (d) Chorus *Dona
    nobis* (first time).   Bach

III · Excerpts from the oratorio *Samson:* (a) Chorus
of Israelites: "Then round about the starry
throne"; (b) Air of Dalila with chorus of Vir-
gins: "With plaintive notes and am'rous moan,"
sung by Mme O. A. Skalkovskaya; (c) Chorus
of Israelites: "Hear, Jacob's God, Jehovah,
hear!"; (d) Air and chorus of Philistines:
"Great Dagon has subdued our foe," solo sung
by O. A. Skalkovskaya; (e) Air and chorus of
Israelites: "Weep, Israel," solo sung by Mme
Kadmina; (f) Recitative and chorus of Israelites: "Glorious hero"; (g) Closing chorus:
"Let their celestial concerts all unite."   Handel

APPENDIX IV

March 23 [April 4], 1876, at 8 p.m., in the Hall of the Town Council

    i · Overture to the tragedy *King Lear*.   Balakirev

   ii · Chorus from the last act of the opera *Prince Igor* (first time).   Borodin

  iii · Romanza from Act III of the opera *William Ratcliff*, will be sung by Mme A. N. Molas.   Cui

  iv · Piano solo, will be played by   D. D. Klimov

   v · Two choruses from the unfinished fairy comic opera *Rogdana:* (a) Oriental chorus of hermits; (b) chorus of Princess Rogdana's maidens. (Orchestrated by Rimsky-Korsakov.)   Dargomyzhsky

  vi · Narrative from Act IV of the opera *Boris Godunov*, will be sung by V. I. Vasilyev.   Moussorgsky

 vii · Songs: (a) On the Hills of Gruzia.   Rimsky-Korsakov
               (b) The Orphan.   Moussorgsky
               (c) Come to Me.   Balakirev
        Sung by Mme A. N. Molas.

viii · Chorus: " Tatar Song."   Cui

  ix · *Kamarinskaya,* fantasy for orchestra.   Glinka

APPENDIX V

EXPOSITION UNIVERSELLE DE 1889
AUDITIONS MUSICALES
PALAIS DU TROCADERO

Le Samedi 22 Juin à 2 Heures Précises

PREMIER CONCERT RUSSE

Cent Musiciens sous la Direction de

RIMSKY–KORSAKOW

PROGRAMME

Première Partie

I · Ouverture de Rousslan et Ludmilla.	Glinka
II · Dans les steppes de l'Asie centrale, tableau musical.	Borodine
III · Allegro du 1-er concerto de piano avec orchestre.	Tschaikowsky
Exécuté par M. Lavrow.	
IV · Antar, 2-e symphonie, d'après un conte arabe.	Rimsky-Korsakow

Deuxième Partie

V · Ouverture sur des thêmes russes.	Balakirew
VI · Marche solennelle.	Cui
VII · (a) Impromptu.	Cui
(b) Intermezzo en si b. majeur.	Liadow
(c) Prélude en si mineur.	"
(d) Novellette en ut majeur.	"
Exécutés par M. Lavrow.	
VIII · Fantaisie sur des airs Finnois.	Dargomijsky
IX · Stenka Razine, poème symphonique, exécuté sous la direction de l'auteur.	Glazounow

472

Two Concerts at the Trocadéro

PALAIS DU TROCADERO
AUDITIONS MUSICALES
Le Samedi 29 Juin à 2 Heures Précises

DEUXIEME CONCERT RUSSE

Cent Musiciens sous la Direction de

RIMSKY–KORSAKOW

Première Partie

I . 2-e symphonie en fa dièse mineur sous la di-
rection de l'auteur.   Glazounow
    I . Andante maestoso. Allegro.
    II . Andante.
    III . Allegro vivace.
    IV . Intrada. Andantino sostenuto. Finale-
    Allegro.
II . Concerto pour piano et orchestre.   Rimsky-Korsakow
    Exécuté par M. Lavrow.
III . Kamarinskaya, Fantaisie sur les thêmes russes.   Glinka

Deuxième Partie

IV . (a) Marche Polovtsienne.
    (b) Danses Polovtsiennes.
        (de l'opéra le Prince Igor.)   Borodine
(Les Polovtsi étaient une peuplade sauvage de race Turque en Russie
au XII-e siècle.)
V . Une nuit sur le Mont-Chauve, tableau musi-
cal.   Moussorgsky
VI . (a) Mazurka en sol bémol majeur.   Balakirew
    (b) Barcarolle.   Tschaikowsky
    (c) Etude en la majeur.   Blumenfeld
    Exécutés par M. Lavrow.
VII . 1-er Scherzo pour orchestre.   Liadow
VIII . Capriccio Espagnol.   Rimsky-Korsakow

473

APPENDIX VI

1. OPEN LETTER TO THE EDITOR
OF THE DAILY *ROOS'*

Dear Sir:

In No. 52 of your esteemed daily there appeared a brief statement of the thoughts expressed by me at the meeting of the Art Council of the Conservatory on February 24 [March 9] — thoughts concerning the desirability of broader powers for the Art Council. Finding that this news item is not sufficiently complete, I hasten to state it in greater detail. Briefly speaking, I had expressed myself: (1) that the local Directorate of the Imperial Russian Musical Society, which had given life to the Conservatory in the sixties, had given it its material support during many years, and had obtained its constitution and by-laws for it, had, in subsequent years, and because of that very constitution, proved (in its personnel) to be a casual element and only indirectly in touch with musical art; (2) that for the Conservatory, which at this moment appears to me a grown-up and mature institution, there has grown ripe the need of changes in the constitution, with a view to giving the Conservatory full autonomy (under which the local Directorate will become a superfluous bureaucratic court of resort between the Conservatory and the Directorate-in-chief of the Imperial Russian Musical Society) as well as with a view to establishing correct relations between the Director of the Conservatory and the Art Council by granting this latter greater independence and broader powers of action. I suggest that the Conservatory insist upon this, in the hope that the Directorate of the local branch will lend it assistance instead of resistance. In conclusion I expressed the idea that the Art Council would hardly refuse greater autonomy and broader powers of action, and the Directorate shrink from the more frequent cooperation of such an institution as the Art Council. May the two jointly, in the nearest future, work out a suitable statement which they will submit to the Directorate of the local branch and the Directorate-in-chief of the Imperial Russian Musical Society.

N. Rimsky-Korsakov

2. AN OPEN LETTER TO THE DIRECTOR OF THE ST. PETERSBURG CONSERVATORY

My dear Avgust Rudol'fovich:

The movement which assumed the form of a strike of the students of the Higher Educational Institutions has affected also the St. Petersburg Conservatory, which undoubtedly belongs with them in its problem of musical education. From the very outset of this agitation, together with several other of my colleagues, I made efforts by word and deed to pacify this movement and calm the participants' minds. When, in spite of this, the movement had spread, the Conservatory was temporarily closed, till February 28 [March 13]. At the Art Council meeting of February 24 [March 9], I was one of the twenty-seven instructors who cast their votes in favour of closing the Conservatory until September 1 [14]. Nevertheless, by order of the Directorate of the St. Petersburg Branch of the Imperial Musical Society, the Conservatory proved only temporarily closed, until March 15 [28]. Because of anticipated disorders that might break out with the reopening of the Conservatory, disorders amid which the normal course is unthinkable, I insisted once more that the period in which the Conservatory remain closed be prolonged until September 1 [14], as had been decided by the majority of votes in the Art Council. Now that the strike of Higher Educational Institutions is a reality which the professors and the Government have to face, the Conservatory, guided by the Directorate of the Musical Society, has taken a stand apart from all other educational institutions and, contrary to the example of all the others (in spite of the resolution of the Art Council), has decided to reopen its classes beginning March 16 [29]. The consequences foreseen have become a reality: today after 11 a.m. the Conservatory found itself surrounded by a cordon of mounted and foot police who scattered those pupils vainly desiring to enter the building. Admission into the Conservatory was by tickets distributed beforehand to pupils who wished to go on with studies; in this category of pupils only an insignificant number put in an appearance (some ten in all). Thus it has been today, so it will be tomorrow, the day after tomorrow, etc. The striking pupils have been left to the tender mercies of the police; while those who have not gone on strike are guarded by the same police. Is a regular course of instruction possible under such conditions? I find it impossible; many other instructors find it so likewise. The Conservatory authorities — the Director, the Inspectors, the Directorate of the Musical Society — view it differently, without being disconcerted by things that make the Government itself stop to think. Is any progress in the cause of artistic music possible at an institution where the resolutions of the Art Council have no value; at an institution where, under its constitution, the musical artists are subordinated to the Directorate — that is, to a circle of amateur dilettantes — at an institution where, under the same constitution, the Director is not elected for a term, but represents an irremovable element; at an institution, finally, that is utterly indifferent to the fate of its pupils in questions of education? All the above regulations of the constitution as well as the acts of the Conservatory administration I find inopportune, anti-artistic and harsh from the moral point of view, and I deem it my duty to express my moral protest.

N. Rimsky-Korsakov

St. Petersburg, March 16 [29]

APPENDIX VII

In accordance with the Directorate's resolution adopted at a meeting on March 19 [April 1], 1905, and officially communicated to me, I have been, under Art. 5, § 14 of the Constitution of the Conservatory and § 55 of the Constitution of the Russian Imperial Musical Society, dismissed from the duties of professor at the Conservatory, because I had

" publicly, in sharp manner, and with perversion of facts expressed a protest against the Directorate's actions aiming at restoring the interrupted studies at the Conservatory; and this manifestly hinders the Directorate's efforts to bring tranquillity and the even tenor of educational life into the Conservatory ";

and hence the Directorate

" considers impossible my further activity as professor."

If in my letter to the Director of the Conservatory reference has been made to the twenty-seven votes cast in favour of closing the Conservatory until that length of time, while the majority favoured closing the Conservatory " until passions shall have calmed " — an inexactness of that nature on my part cannot manifestly alter the sense of my letter, while the phrase " passions shall have calmed " points to a space of time possibly still more remote than September 1 [14]. For it cannot be asserted that on March 15 [28] the calming of passions occurred. Wherefore I request the Directorate to state what facts have suffered perversion on my part. Without that, the hint (undeserved by me) of my alleged bad faith will prove a not altogether honourable procedure on the Directorate's part. As for the act of dismissing me over the heads of the Art Council, this but proves once more that I am right in thinking that it is from the Constitution that the abnormality in the relations between the Art Council, the Director of the Conservatory, and the Directorate arises. I herewith beg to renounce my honorary membership in the St. Petersburg Branch.

N. Rimsky-Korsakov

March 24 [April 6]

PS. Several hours before the Directorate meeting of March 19 [April 1], at which my dismissal was decided upon, I had received, from one of the members of the Directorate, a letter containing the following lines: "Would it not be more advisable, if, instead of protesting, you agreed, for the sake of calming the passions of youth, to take up the reins of administration, instead of A. R. Bernhard?" — Probably the member of the Directorate held a minority opinion, but signed the resolution, nevertheless. I sent a negative reply.

APPENDIX VIII

TO THE ART COUNCIL OF THE ST. PETERSBURG CONSERVATORY

Realizing as I do that in a free interchange of opinions every contrary opinion or conviction requires objections made with coolness and restraint, I deem it my duty to express to the Art Council that I regret in the extreme my momentary outburst of temper at the meeting of January 26 [February 8].

But when I analyse in my memory the feeling which provoked that involuntary outburst, I do not feel ashamed of it and find justification for it.

During the meeting of January 26 [February 8] there were too many speeches, conversations, sundry exclamations and remarks, in which there was expressed with regard to the student youth (which so warmly reacts on present-day events) a hostile sentiment, beginning with formal fault-findings at the insufficient correctness of managing the affair and ending with demands for eradicating "revolution" from the Conservatory's walls. Too much trust was expressed in all manner of gossip and calumnies of the young people, not even excepting the unworthy provocateur's message, in which possibly its anonymity was the only thing that was not approved unanimously. Such speeches and conversations were kept up during the entire meeting by persons hostile from time immemorial, as well as by persons who have but lately assumed an attitude hostile to the liberal movement and the self-government of the Conservatory. On the other hand, only the Director and very few of the staff of instructors spoke in defence of the student youth, whereas to my respected and beloved A. K. Glazunov there were addressed so many reproaches and so much distrust, which took the final form of a demand that he give his word of honour to support his views, that all of it taken together caused my sudden outburst.

The arguments and pleas of some of my colleagues have moved me to retract the words about my leaving the Conservatory, since, in their opinion, this leaving might result in things unfavourable to the very students on whose behalf I had spoken.

Now that I have decided to stay at the Conservatory, I cannot help saying that in acting contrary to the resolution of the students' meeting, or ignoring the Students' Committee, the Art Council *eo ipso* violates the principles of self-government, which were not at all granted to the Conservatory by the provisional rules but had in fact been won by it.

By appealing, in the name of lawfulness, justice, and liberty, that a fight be waged against the despotism of the students in the person of their committee, we thereby are preparing a state of undesirable stagnation for the Conservatory, while our hostile attitude towards the representatives and rights of the students even pushes our institution back into the depths of bygone time.

To all the above I add that in case of voting — I cast my ballot for non-resumption, in the matter of resuming or not resuming the art classes; [1] on the question of calling a meeting for reconsidering, I vote against calling one; and as to the question of ignoring the Students' Committee as constituted at present, I cannot consent to it. In case the voting results are contrary to the opinions I have expressed, I request that these latter be incorporated in the minutes, to which I beg to add also this present letter.

January 30 [February 12], 1906

N. Rimsky-Korsakov

---

[1] At the Russian Conservatories there were two kinds of classes: (1) art classes in which the regular music instruction was given to all students; (2) classes in general academic subjects for those who had not the academic education required for graduation from a Conservatory. J. A. J.

INDEX

i

Index

Index

v

Index

Index

Index

Index